COMMUNICATION AND COMPUTING SYSTEMS

PROCEEDINGS OF THE 2ND INTERNATIONAL CONFERENCE ON COMMUNICATION AND COMPUTING SYSTEMS (ICCCS 2018), 1-2 DECEMBER 2018, GURGAON, INDIA

Communication and Computing Systems

Editors

B.M.K. Prasad, Karan Singh, Shyam S. Pandey & Richard O'Kennedy

CRC Press
Taylor & Francis Group
Boca Raton London New York

CRC Press is an imprint of the
Taylor & Francis Group, an **informa** business

A BALKEMA BOOK

Published by:
CRC Press/Balkema
P.O. Box 447, 2300 AK Leiden, The Netherlands
e-mail: Pub.NL@taylorandfrancis.com
www.crcpress.com – www.taylorandfrancis.com

First issued in paperback 2021

ISBN 13: 978-1-03-223934-7 (pbk)
ISBN 13: 978-0-367-00147-6 (hbk)

DOI: 10.1201/9780429444272

Typeset by Integra Software Services Pvt. Ltd., Pondicherry, India

Library of Congress Cataloging-in-Publication Data

Communication and Computing Systems – Prasad et al. (eds)
© *2019 Taylor & Francis Group, London, ISBN 978-0-367-00147-6*

Table of Contents

Secure computing

Soft computing, intelligent system, machine vision and artificial neural network

Software engineering & emerging technologies

VLSI & embedded systems

Communication and Computing Systems – Prasad et al. (eds)
© 2019 Taylor & Francis Group, London, ISBN 978-0-367-00147-6

Preface/Forward

2nd International Conference on Communication and Computing Systems (ICCCS-2018) took place at Dronacharya College of Engineering, Gurgaon on December 01–02, 2018. The purpose of the conference was to establish a platform for interaction among the knowledge holders belonging to industry, academia and various areas of society to discuss the current scenario of the advancements in the field of communication and computing systems. The Conference theme was chosen to facilitate discussions and personal interaction between academics involved in engineering and technology from different cultural backgrounds. The theme allowed the participants to identify and present best collaborative research and innovative ideas, as well as examples relevant to the main theme.

This book is a collection of accepted papers. The papers presented in the proceedings were peer- reviewed by 2–3 expert referees. This volume contains 5 main subject areas: 1. Signal and Image Processing, 2. Communication & Computer Networks, 3. Soft Computing, Intelligent System, Machine Vision and Artificial Neural Network, 4. VLSI & Embedded System, 5. Software Engineering and Emerging Technologies. The committee of ICCCS-2018 would like to express their sincere thanks to all authors for their high quality research papers and presentations. Also, we would like to thank the reviewers for their valuable comments and advises. Finally, thanks are expressed to CRC Press/Balkema as well for producing this book.

Organizing Committee of ICCCS-2018
Conference Chair
Prof. Chandra Shekhar Singh & Prof. Yashwardhan Soni
Dronacharya College of Engineering, Gurgaon

Acknowledgement

The organizing committee of ICCCS-2018 would like to thank the Senior Editors, Associate Editors as well as Taylor & Francis / CRC Press and the following reviewers who have generously given up their valuable time for making 2ⁿᵈ International Conference on Communication and Computing Systems a success. The accomplishment of ICCCS-2018 is purely fruit of their care and competence. Their conscientiousness is much appreciated.

Dr. Kamna Solanki
HOD, CSE Department
UIET, Maharshi Dayanand University, Rohtak

Mrs. Amita Dhankhar
Assistant Professor, CSE Department
UIET,M.D.University, Rohtak

Dr. Nahld Fatlma
Assistant Professor in School of Applied Sciences at Amity University Haryana.

Dr. Rekha Vig
Associate Professor, EECE Department
THE NORTHCAP University, Gurgaon

Dr. Neeta Singh
Gautam Buddha University, Greater Noida

Dr.Vidushi Sharma,
Gautam Buddha University, Greater Noida

Dr. Karan Singh, JNU, New delhi

Dr. B.B Sagar, BIT, Noida

Dr. Sandeep Sharma, GBP, Greater Noida

Mr. R P Ojha, GU, Greater Noida

Dr. K.V.S.S.S.S.Sairam
Professor, Dept of ECE NMAM Institute of Technology Karkala, India

Communication and Computing Systems – Prasad et al. (eds)
© 2019 Taylor & Francis Group, London, ISBN 978-0-367-00147-6

Committees

SCIENTIFIC COMMITTEE

Prof. Goutam Sanyal
NIT Durgapur

Prof. Pramod Kumar Srivastava
GCET, Greater Noida

Prof. Rudra Pratap Ojha
GCET, Greater Noida

Prof. Annappa
National Institute of Technology, Karnataka

Prof. Alexander Gelbukh
Center for Computing Research (CIC) of the National Polytechnic Institute, Mexico

Prof. Tapodhir Acharjee
School of Technology, Assam University

Prof. Sunanda
Shri Mata Vaishno Devi University, J&K

Prof. Brahmjit Singh
National Institute of Technology, Kurukshetra

Prof. B. Sathish Babu
SIT Tumkur

Prof. Paresh V. Virparia
Sardar Patel University, Gujarat

Prof. P. Kalavathi
Gandhigram Rural Institute, Tamil Nadu

Prof. Dimitrios Koukopoulos
University of Patras, Greece

Prof. G. Sahoo
Birla Institute of Technology, Mesra

Prof. Arnab Paul
Assam University, Silchar

Prof. Dimitrios A. Karras
Sterea Hellas Institute of Technology, Hellas

Prof. Namita Gupta
Maharaja Agrasen Institute of Technology, Delhi

Prof. Manoj Kumar Panda
G.B. Pant Engineering College, Garhwal

Prof. Ram Shringar Rao
Ambedkar Institute of Advanced Communication Technologies and Research, Delhi

Prof. Sajai Vir Singh
Jaypee Institute of Information Technology, Noida

Prof. Noor Elaiza Binti Abdul Khalid
Faculty of Computing and Quantitative Sciences University Technology, Mara Shah Alam

Prof. Sushil Kumar
Jawaharlal Nehru University, New Delhi, India

Prof. Chitreshh Banerjee
Amity University, Rajasthan

Prof. Narendra Kohli
Harcourt Butler Technological Institute (H.B.T.I.), Kanpur

Prof. Amit Prakash Singh
Guru Gobind Singh Indraprastha University, New Delhi

Prof. M.S. Bhatti
Guru Nanak Dev University, Punjab

Prof. Debashis De
Maulana Abul Kalam Azad University of Technology, West Bengal

Prof. Neelesh Kumar Jain
JUET, Guna

Prof. Dushyant K. Singh
MNNIT, Allahabad

Prof. Arun Sharma
Indira Gandhi Delhi Technical University for Women (IGDTUW), Delhi

Prof. Pratiksha Saxena
Gautam Buddha University, Greater Noida

Prof. V. Bhuvaneswari
School of Computer Science and Engineering, Bharathiar University, Coimbatore

Prof. Manoj Kumar
Ambedkar Institute of Advanced Communication Technologies & Research, Delhi

Prof. Vinay Rishiwal
SMIEEE, MJP Rohilkhand University, Bareilly, UP

Prof. Arup Kumar Pal
IIT(ISM), Dhanbad

Prof. P.C. Jain
Shiv Nadar Univesity, Greater Noida

Prof. I. Joe Louis Paul
SSN College of Engineering, Kalavakkam

Prof. Anurag Singh Baghel
School of Information and Communication Technology, Gautam Buddha University, Greater Noida

Prof. Buddha Singh
Jawaharlal Nehru University, New Delhi, India

Prof. Amit Kumar Manocha
Director, Punjab Institute of Technology, GTB Garh, Moga

ORGANIZING COMMITTEE

Chief Patron

Dr. Satish Yadav
Dronacharya College of Engineering, Gurgaon

Patron

Prof. (Dr.) B.M.K. Prasad
Dronacharya College of Engineering, Gurgaon

General Chair

Prof. (Dr.) Sri Krishan Yadav
Dronacharya College of Engineering, Gurgaon

Conference Chair

Prof. Chandra Shekhar Singh
Dronacharya College of Engineering, Gurgaon

Prof. Yashwardhan Soni
Dronacharya College of Engineering, Gurgaon

Editorial Committee

Prof. (Dr.) B.M.K. Prasad
Dronacharya College of Engineering, Gurgaon

Dr. Karan Singh
Jawaharlal Nehru University, New Delhi

Prof. (Dr.) Shyam S. Pandey
Kysu Institute of Technology, Japan

Prof. Richard O'Kennedy
Dublin City University. Ireland

Registration Chair

Mr. Krishanu Kundu
Dronacharya College of Engineering, Gurgaon

Sponsorship Chair

Prof. Vineet Mishra
Dronacharya College of Engineering, Gurgaon

Ms. Dupinder Kaur
Dronacharya College of Engineering, Gurgaon

Ms. Neha Verma
Dronacharya College of Engineering, Gurgaon

Industry Track Chair

Dr. Yogita Shukla
Dronacharya College of Engineering, Gurgaon

Mr. Ashish Gambhir
Dronacharya College of Engineering, Gurgaon

Mr. Hansraj
Dronacharya College of Engineering, Gurgaon

Posters Chair

Prof. Sanghamitra V. Arora
Dronacharya College of Engineering, Gurgaon

Dr. Sangeeta Singla
Dronacharya College of Engineering, Gurgaon

Workshop Chair

Ms. Parul Bansal
Dronacharya College of Engineering, Gurgaon

Ms. Pooja Jain
Dronacharya College of Engineering, Gurgaon

Dr. Jyoti Anand
Dronacharya College of Engineering, Gurgaon

Publicity Chair

Prof. Ashima Mehta
Dronacharya College of Engineering, Gurgaon

Ms. Parul Bansal
Dronacharya College of Engineering, Gurgaon

Ms. Megha Goel
Dronacharya College of Engineering, Gurgaon

Cultural Chair

Prof. Dimple Saproo
Dronacharya College of Engineering, Gurgaon

Mrs. Ashu Khurana
Dronacharya College of Engineering, Gurgaon

Hospitality Chair

Mr. Ashok Kumar
Dronacharya College of Engineering, Gurgaon

Mr. Chain Singh
Dronacharya College of Engineering, Gurgaon

Finance Chair

Brigd. (Retd.) R.S Kochar
Dronacharya College of Engineering, Gurgaon

Mr. Rajesh Mattoo
Dronacharya College of Engineering, Gurgaon

Communication and Computing Systems – Prasad et al. (eds)
© 2019 Taylor & Francis Group, London, ISBN 978-0-367-00147-6

Features

- The conference aimed at providing a platform for researchers to exchange their ideas in the field of communication and computing systems.
- Development of collaboration between Researchers, Academicians and Industry experts from around the world.
- Supporting exchange of ideas and promising future association between members of these groups.

With the advancement of communication and computing systems a lot of research in this area is undergoing. Thus, to cater to the needs of technologists, academicians, researchers, students, this book provides both theoretical and practical applications in the field of Signal and Image Processing, Communication & Computer Networks, Soft Computing, Intelligent System, Machine Vision and Artificial Neural Network, VLSI & Embedded System, Software Engineering and Emerging Technologies. Engineers and researchers may refer and understand the upcoming trends in these fields and it will be a valuable tool for everyone involved in engineering and related applications.

Image processing and its applications

Communication and Computing Systems – Prasad et al. (eds)
© 2019 Taylor & Francis Group, London, ISBN 978-0-367-00147-6

3D Tumor segmentation using surface rendering technique

K. Sudha Rani
Associate Professor, Department of EIE, VNR VJIET, Bachupally, Hyderabad, India

K. Mani Kumari
Assistant Professor, Department of Mechanical Engineering, Vardaman College of Engineering, India

K. Aruna Kumari
Assistant Professor, Department of ECE, VNR VJIET, Bachupally, Hyderabad, India

T. Gnana Prakash
Assistant Professor, Department of CSE, VNR VJIET, Bachupally, Hyderabad, India

ABSTRACT: In Biomedical image processing region/image segmentation is very important in detecting the tumor. Brain tumor inside the skull limits the functioning of the brain and its activities. Unwanted cells are increasing in the brain. Image processing techniques for identifying tumor plays a vital role in better visualization, shape and area where it located. Image processing techniques include morphological techniques, thresholding, classifiers, surface rendering, interactive, wireframe modelling etc. In this work, Initially Two dimensional MR images are taken converted into a three-dimensional image using the connected component method, that three-dimensional image is projected in the two-dimensional form using surface rendering techniques. Interactive segmentation enables us to differentiate background and foreground which helps us to select particular region. Wireframe modeling enables to see through the smooth surface rendered the three-dimension image. Automated thresholding technique has applied to detect the volume of the tumor.

1 INTRODUCTION

MRI technology performs very important role in image segmentation for an analysis of brain tumor and helps in better visualization of tumor. In order to create a three dimensional image from a collection of two dimensional MR images we use different techniques like connected component, surface rendering, interactive segmentation and wire frame modeling. Connected component collects all the two dimensional images using a particular algorithm and forms a three dimensional image out of it. Interactive segmentation separates the background and foreground so that a particular region can be selected on which surface rendering can be applied. Surface rendering projects the three dimensional image in two dimensional form, it uses voxel to pixel conversion algorithms to perform this action. Wire frame modeling enables the better visualization of the tumor. Thresholding is applied to calculate the area and volume of tumor.

The objective is to create a three dimensional view of tumor which is presented inside rain and calculate its area and volume. Also calculate the growth or shrinkage of tumor considering two different MR images of same patient taken at two different times.

2 METHODOLOGY

The research work has been characterized into two ways, as shown in the Figure 1.

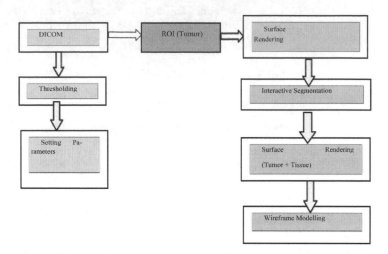

Figure 1. Block diagram development of 3D tumor.

1. Development of 3D tumor
2. Detection of area and volume of the Tumor.

2.1 *Development of 3D tumor*

Initially, 2D DICOM data set has taken and then manually highlighted the interested region i.e. tumor presented in the brain. Figure 1 Block Diagram Development of 3D tumor, after identifying the tumor area then Simple surface rendering method has been applied on the tumor. Surface rendering algorithm is as shown in the Figure 2.

Rendering is the final process of creating the actual 2D image or animation from the prepared scene. Narkbuakaew. W (2010) explained the 3D reconstruction of the human body parts. Sub sampling method has been used in huge volumetric data, and created contours. Anne Talkingtom (2014) in the paper entitled "Estimating Tumor Growth Rates In vivo "developed methods for inferring tumor growth rates from observation of tumor volumes at two time points.

The DICOM images are first loaded and checked for the presence of tumor. If the tumor is present then the region of interest is selected manually. After selecting the region of interest the region is then surface rendered. The surface rendered image is a three dimensional image of the selected region. Feng Zhao (2013) introduced the interactive image segmentation techniques in many medical applications. Rukhsar Firdous (2014) compared different methods of thresholding. Sreeparna Roy (2017) developed a new algorithm for 3D surface construction and complements 2D CT, MR, and SPECT data by giving physicians 3D views of the anatomy. Pratik Chavada (2014) discussed about the region of interest in the medical images, the region of interest should not be distorted after compression. Castorina, P (2007) discussed the growth laws for cancer. Comen et al. (2012) derived the mathematical modelling for growth rates. Megha & Arakeri (2013) explained the 3D reconstruction and estimated the volume data. N. Dyn (2003) developed a 3D triangulation method. Humphreys & Greg (2004) explained the mathematical theory behind the physical rendering.Arai K (2006), Graham (2010) & M. Sezgin (2002) have discussed the 3D reconstruction techniques.

2.1.1 *Surface rendering*

The technique Surface rendering which projects the three dimensional image formed from two dimensional MR images into two dimensional plane. The region of interest and surface rendering has shown in the Figure 3 and Figure 4. It uses certain types of illuminations to project the data.

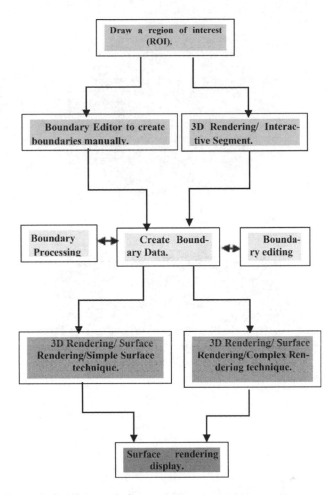

Figure 2. Block diagram of surface rendering.

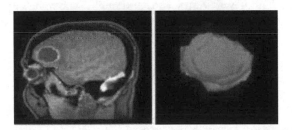

Figure 3. Region of interest selection Figure 4: Surface rendering of tumor.

2.1.2 *Interactive segmentation*

Interactive segmentation of the current 3D image is used to extract object boundaries automatically, where it divides an image into foreground and background using weighted geodestic distance. A pixel's distance from both foreground and background scribbles are calculated and set as foreground or background accordingly.

Figure 4.   Simple surface rendering for the skull.

Figure 5.   Wire frame modelling.

Once the thresholding is done surface rendering is applied to both tissue and tumor. Once it is done a surface rendered human skull is visible through which the tumor we selected is visible. For better visualization wire frame modeling of the tissue is done.

2.1.3   *Wire frame modeling*

Wire frame modeling uses marching cube algorithm. This algorithm includes two steps initial step is to develop the surface of the skull. For this, user specified value is identified for the surface and then triangles have developed. Second step is, to develop the normals for the surface of the skull at each and every vertex of each triangle. Marching cubes algorithm depends on the divide-and-conquer method. The wireframe model applied to the skull is shown in the Figure 5.

3   RESULTS

3.1   *Result of volume calculation*

Area and volume are calculated with the help of thresholding. Automatic thresholding has been applied for the calculation of area and volume. Initially, load the data set, identify the tumor and select the part of tumor using automatic segmentation method. Calculated Tumor area and volume is as shown in the Figure 6.

3.2   *Result for surface rendering*

This algorithm has been verified with different patient data and applied techniques like region of interest, surface rendering of the tumor, interactive segmentation, surface rendering of tumor and skull and wire frame model, result is as shown in the Table 1.

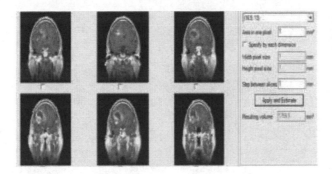

Figure 6.   Volume calculation.

Table 1.   Surface rendering algorithm for different data sets.

Input MR image	Selected region of interest	Surface Rendering of tumor	Interactive segmentation	Surface rendered (tumor+ tissue)	Wire Frame model

4 CONCLUSION

3D brain tumor segmentation and detection has been developed with the connected component method, surface rendering, interactive segmentation, thresholding, wire frame modelling. Total 40 real time data has been tested, segmented tumor and then finally computed the volume of the tumor. Excellent results of 3D segmented tumor have been developed.

REFERENCES

Anne Talkingtom. 2014. Estimating Tumour Growth Rates In vivo: Dept. of Math, Duke University, Durham, NC.

Arai K.2006. MR signal of the solid portion of pilocytic astrocytoma on T2 weighted imaging: is it useful for differentiation from medulloblastoma? Neuroradiology 48(4):233–237.

Castorina, P. 2007. Growth laws in cancer: Implications for radiotherapy. Radiation Research. 168,349-356.

Comen, E., Morris, P.G., and Norton, L. 2012. Translating mathematical modeling of tumor growth patterns into novel therapeutic approaches to breast cancer. J. Mammay Gland Biol. Noeplasia. 17, 241–249

Dyn N. 2003. Optimizing 3D triangulations using discrete curvature analysis, Mathematical Methods for Curves and Surfaces.

Feng Zhao. 2013. Interactive Segmentation of Medical Images: A Survey: Department of Computer Science, Swansea University, Swansea SA2 8PP, UK.

Graham Leedham. 2010. Comparison of Some Thresholding Algorithms for Text/Background Segmentation in Difficult Document Images, Proceedings of the Seventh International Conference on Document Analysis and Recognition

Humphreys, Greg. 2004. Physically based rendering from theory to implementation. Amsterdam: Elsevier/Morgan Kaufmann. ISBN0-12-553180-X.

M. Sezgin. 2002. Quantitative evaluation of image thresholding methods and application to nondestructive testing, PhD Thesis, Istanbul Technical University,Turkey

Megha P, Arakeri. 2013. An Effective and Efficient Approach to 3D Reconstruction and Quantification of Brain Tumor on Magnetic Resonance Images: National Institute of Technology Karnataka (NITK), Surathkal,India.

Narkbuakaew. W. 2010. 3D Surface Reconstruction of large Medical Data Using Marching Cubes In vtk: Nationl Electronics and Computer Technology Center, Phahon Yothin Rd, Klong Luang, Pathumthani,Thailand.

Pratik, Chavada.2014. Region of Interest Based Image Compression: International Journal of Innovative Research in Computer and Communication Engineering.

Priyanka. 2015. A Review of Image Thresholding Techniques, International Journal of Advanced Research in Computer Science and Software Engineering, Volume 5, Issue 6.

Rukhsar Firdousi. 2014. Local Thresholding Techniques in Image Binarization: GD Rungta College of Engineering and Technology,Bhilai.

Sreeparna, Roy. 2017. Comparative Study of Marching Cubes Algorithms for the Conversion of 2D image to 3D: International Journal of Computational Intelligence Research ISSN 0973-1873 Volume 13, Number 3 (2017), pp.327-337.

T Romen Singh. 2011. A New Local Adaptive Thresholding Technique in Binarization IJCSI International Journal of Computer Science Issues, Vol. 8, Issue 6, No 2, November.

Communication and Computing Systems – Prasad et al. (eds)
© 2019 Taylor & Francis Group, London, ISBN 978-0-367-00147-6

Integration of big data and cloud computing for future Internet of Things

Saksham Mittal, Shreejay Mall & Shivam Juyal
Computer Science and Engineering Department, Graphic Era Hill University, Dehradun, India

Rahul Chauhan
Electronics and Communication Engineering Department, Graphic Era Hill University, Dehradun, India

ABSTRACT: Cloud Computing and the Internet of Things (IoT) are the two most popular terms, nowadays. IoT is defined as the global network of physical devices or objects which are embedded with various IoT elements, so they are able to share and exchange data. And cloud computing is defined as that instead of the hard drive of your computer, the Internet is used to store data and programs and accessed from the Internet as well.

In this paper, the integration of IoT, big data and cloud computing is presented in a simpler manner. As IoT is getting popularized very quickly in the world, nowadays, a lot of data, i.e., big data is generated at a very fast rate, so the best way is to store and manage the data on clouds and this method is known as cloud computing which is explained in the detail further. Paper discussed the various issues of IoT followed by its architecture, its various elements like sensors, WSN, RFID, etc. Further, the big data concept is being discussed and how much amount of big data can be generated per day. Various issues of cloud computing and IoT are discussed. And at last, benefits & services of cloud computing and its integration with IoT are discussed.

KEYWORDS: Cloud computing, IoT, Big data, WSN, RFID, ZigBee

1 INTRODUCTION

IoT stands for Internet of Things. As the name suggests, it shows that the computer's next generation will be based on the network or the invisible environment with which we are going to interact and all the things will be connected through the internet. Hence, a huge amount of data will be generated every second. All the data which we generate will be stored in the cloud and as our normal hard disks wouldn't be able to store and it is possible to access the data from anywhere. The most important essence to IoT is how we connect the context-aware network using existing networks. The booming 4G and Wi-Fi connections have already shown us that how important is IoT in our day to day life. One of the misconceptions which most of the people have is that they think IoT is only related to mobile computing and all the portable wearables which are doing quite well in today's market like Samsung gear but IoT is not restricted to this only, instead it combines all the components or devices which are connected through wireless network connection to interact with the environment surrounding us. Everything which is connected to or will be connected to the internet comes under the hood of IoT.

The term Internet of things first came into play when (Ashton 2009) gave its definition in 1999. Though in the past it had a wide scope but the main aim of IoT still remains the same that is how to use automata through which the efforts of humans will be less, like if for doing a work ten people are required, the same work could be done by five machines or devices which will not only act as a dummy but will also have artificial intelligence to do the work more efficiently and effectively without our input, such as satellites sent on space possess artificial intelligence to do their work. It is the interconnection of objects through the internet and it should be like a machine which will not only physically interact with the environment but at the same time will share information, analyze and will help in communication using the current internet protocols.

Services like Facebook, WhatsApp and many more have led to Internet revolution by interconnecting people to a large extent and the next wave that is going to emerge is the interconnection between objects for smarter generation of machines, that it is already said, will basically interact with the environment. As of present scenario, about 9 billion devices are interconnected and it is predicted that by 2020, this will be at a humongous amount of about having approximately 24 billion. An estimation given by GSMA tells that this interconnection of devices wave will give the mobile network a revenue of about $1.3 trillion.

1.1 *Flourishment of computation in the next decade*

In the late 1980s, researchers tried to make an interface of human to human through the technology which was present at that time, this, in turn, resulted in a computer discipline so that it could do every work we want it to. In the present era, the portable devices like smartphones are not only the source to get information but it has been greatly interactive to the environment. One of the pioneer scientist, Mark Weiser gave us a definition of what exactly is called smart environment "the physical world that is richly and invisibly interwoven with sensors, actuators, displays, and computational elements, embedded seamlessly in the everyday objects of our lives, and connected through a continuous network" (Weiser 1999).

Another scientist named Rogers proposed a different theory which is to have an unambiguous computer which uses human's brain to discover more and more new things to exploit and make full use of it, and this concept is completely contradictory to what Weiser gave (Rogers 2006). He said, "In terms of who should benefit, it is useful to think of how ubicomp technologies can be developed not for the sales of the world, but for particular domains that can be set up and customized by an individual firm or organization, such as for agriculture production, environmental restoration or retailing."

After 20 years of unambiguous computing in the play, the progress and the challenges were discussed by Caceres and Friday (Caceres 2012). They talked about the basic things of ubicomp and how will the present systems will cope with the present world and from where they discovered the two of the most important technologies in today's world, that is first the Internet of Things and other was the Cloud Computing.

With the development and help of micro-electro-mechanical system and digital electronics, we have now been able to make miniature devices which are capable to compute as well as communicate wirelessly. Miniature devices are also referred to as noted which interconnect and form wireless sensors and are widely used in retail, infrastructure monitoring etc. (Su W. 2002). To make the words of Weiser right, we use miniature devices having sensing capability which is ambiguous, the most important aspect for ubicomp (Weiser 1999). To make IoT what it is, security, storage and market need are the essential points to be kept in mind. A recent example of this is the cloud computing in which all the data is stored in the invisible cloud technology (Caceres 2012).

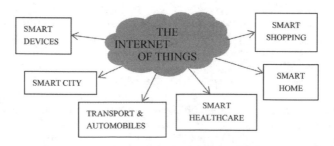

Figure 1. IoT and its applications.

2 THE ARCHITECTURE OF IOT

There is no particular architecture for IoT, but we have designed its worldwide accepted architecture basically divided into three layers (Tsai 2014), namely perception layer, network layer and at the topmost layer that is application layer.

Perception layer:-It is the layer which perceives or we can say senses the environment, that is, it basically interacts with the environment. As the network finds digital information more convenient to transmit, so this layer is responsible to change the given information which it has collected into digital form. In order to increase the processing and sensing capabilities, it is recommended to append microchips with the given object as the perseverance of some object is not direct. Hence in this layer, embedded intelligence and also the Nanotechnology have an important role in it as with the help of nanotechnology we will make smallest chips to plant it in any given object in our environment and with the embedded intelligence it will be possible to further enhance the processing capabilities so that it could deal with the requirements of application which will be developed in the future (Kashyap S.2015).

Network Layer:-It is the middle layer and processes the data that it has received from the perception layer and transmits the data to the layer above it, i.e. the application layer, with the help of different technologies of the network like Local Area network (wired/wireless). Some of the foremost or main media used for the transmission of data are Wi-Fi, ZigBee, infrared, UMB, Bluetooth, 3G/4G and the list goes on (Kashyap S. 2015). A sound middleware will be provided, so as to process and store the huge amount of data which is carried by the network. This can only be achieved with the help of cloud computing.

Application layer:-This is the uppermost layer and the main frontend of IoT architecture which exploits the full potential of IoT. Moreover, this layer gives the developers the tools, for example, actuating devices, so that they can realize the real vision of IoT which includes intelligent transportation, safety, identity authentication, logistics management, location-based service, etc.

3 IOT ELEMENTS

We have a taxonomy that defines the required components for the Internet of Things. Basically, there are three components: a) Hardware- which includes sensors, embedded hardware for communication and actuators b) Tools- Data Analytical tools for computation and c) Presentation – understanding, interpretation and visualization tools depending on different applications and can be accessed on various platforms. There are some technologies which make the above components.

3.1 *Sensors*

In a general way, a sensor is said to be a device which produces an optical output signal in accordance to the changes detected in the inputs. A sensor is one of the key components in building up of IoT. Different sensors are available according to their need, like for detecting temperature thermocouple sensor is used. In our day to day life we come across different types of sensors, mainly:

1. Temperature sensor
2. Touch Sensor
3. IR sensor, etc.

Temperature sensor: In a layman's term, the temperature is defined as the degree of hotness or coldness of a body. Therefore, to sense the temperature in different applications, different temperature sensors are used like a semiconductor temperature sensor, thermistor, thermocouple, resistance temperature detector, etc. (Agarwal T)

Touch Sensor: These sensors are more like a switch which when touched gets activated. According to their touch, there are basically three types of sensors namely resistance touch switch, capacitive touch, piezo touch.

Capacitive Touch:-In order to function, it has a single electrode fitted behind a panel which is non-conductive. It detects the capacitance that is the electrical charge produced by the human body and works according to it by increasing the capacitance when we touch interface and then it engages the switch.

Resistive Touch:-Unlike capacitive which only require only one electrode, it requires two electrodes which are in contact with each other through a conductive material like a finger. In this, the resistance between two metal pieces is decreased in order to make resistive switch operational. Just by placing and removing your finger in it, it gets ON and OFF respectively.

Piezo Touch:-This as the name suggest it works on the properties of piezo-ceramic which are installed behind the surface and this allows the integration of switch with any material.

Infrared Sensor: It can be defined as an electronic device which in order to sense the surroundings, it emits rays. IR sensors which detect the motion and heat of object are called passive IR sensors as rather throwing IR rays they only measure up the quantity. Generally, all body in IR spectrum emits invisible thermal radiation and can only be detected by an infra-red sensor. In a simple term, a detector is an IR photodiode and emitter is IR LED the detector is sensitive to IR light which is of wavelength equal to the wavelength of the emitter. When the detector receives a beam of IR light, the output voltage as well as resistance changes in accordance to IR light received.

3.2 *Radio Frequency Identification (RFID)*

RFID is one of the main technologies in the hardware system which is used for communicating and wireless communication of data for microchips is designed through it. It acts as an electronic barcode and helps in automatic identification of anything they are attached with. The Passive RFID tags use the interrogation signals of the reader for communicating the unique ID with RFID. It has an application in the Transportation sector in replacement of tickets and also in bank cards.

3.3 *Wireless Sensor Network (WSN)*

Availability of efficient, cheap, less power consuming devices which are used in remote sensing application are due to the technological advances in wireless communication. This leads to the utilization of a sensor network which enables the valuable data analysis and processing, collected in a different kind of environments (Cayirci F 2002). Lower end WSN is similar to active RFID with limited storage and processing capability. For the realization of the potentials of WSNs, some scientific challenges must be overcome that is multidisciplinary as well as substantial in nature (Cayirci F 2002).

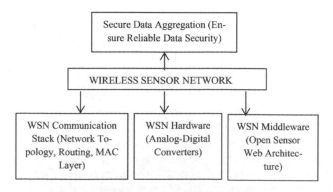

Figure 2.   WSN Building Block (Juels A 2002).

4 VARIOUS APPLICATIONS OF IOT

Smart Homes:-Smart home is a concept which is in great demand for a futuristic technology. In a smart home, all the devices such as air conditioning, TVs, lighting and heating devices, security systems, etc. are able to communicate with each other as well as with us and can be accessed remotely with the help of the Internet.

Transportation:-An intelligent and smart transport system includes that vehicles on the road are able to communicate with each other in a network and with the driver also. This can be made possible with the help of IoT. This also ensures better safety and more coordinated transport system.

Agriculture:-Smart agriculture is a way by which the farmers can enhance the productivity of their crops by consistently monitoring it with the help of IoT. They can check the soil moisture and nutrients with the help of sensors and can also control the usage of water for the optimal growth of plants.

Healthcare:-IoT plays a major role in healthcare. With the help of various sensors, the health of patients can be constantly monitored and the appropriate care and treatment can be delivered to the patient from the remote location.

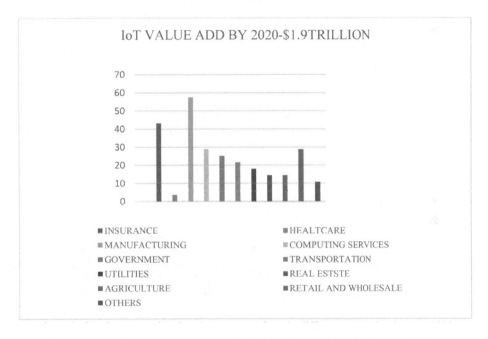

Figure 3.   Graph representing the advancement of IoT in different sectors by the year 2020.

5 BIG DATA AND MANAGEMENT

The result of this evolving field leads to the generation of a large amount of data. Big Data is dealing with this large and complex dataset which can be structured or unstructured (includes documents, customer service records, pictures and videos etc.) and will not store into memory to be processed (Nugent 2013). Some data generated from website interactions and social media sites are known as human-generated data. It has to be processed, so computation is to be performed where data stores for processing.

Although each data sources can independently manage, the today's challenge is how the designer can interact with all these different kinds of data. When we have a lot of information for many tasks, it becomes impossible to manage it in traditional ways (Nugent 2013). Therefore, we have to perform calculations about management. It is the big data opportunity and challenge. Today, cloud-based storage is the better solution for this challenge.

Let's take the example of Facebook:

1. 2500 million status updates, photos, wall posts, videos are shared every day.
2. 2700 million Likes each day
3. 0.3 billion photos are uploaded each day
4. 100 PB disk space in FB's Hadoop
5. 105 TB data is scanned in every 30 minutes
6. 500 TB or more new data is added in databases per day

Imagine this amount of data is generated through a single application and we have thousands of application running around the world. So data management is an important issue.

5.1 Evolution of data management

Data management has a holistic perspective and viewed through a software lens (Prajapati 2013). Technology advancement in hardware, networking, storage and computations like virtualization and cloud computing. The change in evolving technologies and reduction in cost has changed the new era of data management and create new opportunities. Big data is one of the latest emerging technologies due to these factors.

6 CLOUD COMPUTING

The process of delivery of computing services like servers, databases, storage, software, networking, analytics and more-over the Internet (known as the "cloud") is called cloud computing. In the simple words, it can also be said that instead of your computer's hard drive, the Internet is used to store data and programs and accessed from the Internet as well (Griffith)

The companies that provide this type of services are termed as cloud providers and according to the usage of such services, the client has to pay to cloud providers.

6.1 Uses of cloud computing

Even if you don't realize, but cloud computing is being used right now. If you send email, watch movies or TV, edit documents, play games or store pictures and other files or listen to music online, it is all likely possible because of cloud computing. The first cloud computing services are approximately 10 years old, but already most of the organizations, such as from government agencies to non-profits, from tiny start-ups to global corporations, all are including the technology for various purposes . The fewer things that can be done with the cloud are as follows:

1. Create new apps and services
2. Host websites and blogs
3. Stream audio and video
4. Store, back up and recover data
5. Deliver software on demand

6.2 Top benefits of cloud computing

The few questions that arise about cloud computing are: What is it about cloud computing that produces a great change from the traditional businesses thinking about IT resources? Why has cloud computed so much popularity in the present world (Pearson)? The most possible reasons are as follows:

1. Expenses

   Expenses of purchasing hardware and software, managing a large number of servers, setting up, the requirement of the IT experts for management of infrastructure-all are reduced or eliminated by the use of cloud computing.

2. Availableness

   The services provided by most cloud providers are extremely reliable. The availability of Internet connection is always there and till workers have the connection, the needed applications can be accessed by them from anywhere. Some applications even work off-line (Coles).

3. Improved mobility

   The employees have always the availability of data and applications. Workers can do their work anywhere through smartphones, tablets or any other devices.

4. Better performance

   The popular and large cloud computing services running on a global network of secure data centers that are regularly updated to the latest computing hardware and this helps in enhancing the performance of the system. This offers several benefits such as reduced network latency for applications and greater economies of scale over a single corporate data centre.

5. Reliable and Trustworthy

   Services provided by various cloud providers like data backup, disaster recovery, etc. make cloud computing reliable. The users' data is copied at multiple redundant sites on the cloud provider's network.

6.3 Types of cloud services

The three categories of cloud computing services are as follows:

1. Infrastructure as a service (IaaS)
2. Platform as a service (PaaS),
3. Software as a service (SaaS).

To achieve business goals, it is very important to know what these services are and how are they different from each other.

6.3.1 Infrastructure-as-a-service (IaaS)

It is the primary category of cloud computing services. With this type of services, cloud providers provide the infrastructure of IT, such as servers and virtual machines (VMs), storage, networks and operating system to us and we have to pay according to the usage of the infrastructure.

6.3.2 Platform-as-a-service (PaaS)

Platform-as-a-service (PaaS) is the cloud computing service in which the cloud providers provide developing, testing and delivering environment and manage software applications whenever needed. PaaS is different from IaaS because, in PaaS, the developers can quickly create or design their web or mobile applications without worrying about setting up or managing the underlying infrastructure of servers, network, storage and databases needed for development (Weiser 1999).

6.3.3 Software-as-a-service (SaaS)

Software-as-a-service (SaaS) is a cloud computing service in which cloud providers provide their many software applications over the internet and we can select from that applications as per our requirement. The cloud providers host and manage the software application and underlying infrastructure on their own. Users, usually with a web browser on their mobiles or PC, connect to the application over the Internet.

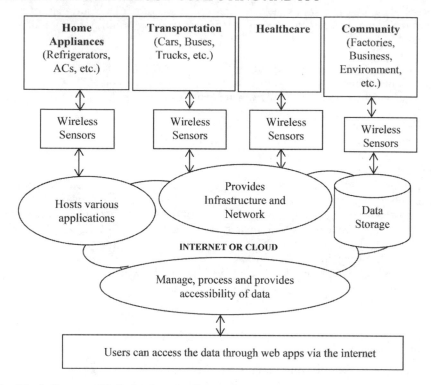

Figure 4. Block diagram of IoT-cloud computing.

Cloud Computing and the Internet of Things (IoT) are the two most popular terms, nowadays. Cloud Computing and the IoT, both have a complementary relationship with each other. They both help in increasing the efficiency of our everyday works.

A large amount of data i.e., big data is generated by the IoT and cloud computing provides a way to store, process, manage and access that data.

REFERENCES

Ashton K 2009, et al., Internet of Things‖ Thing, RFID Journal.

Agarwal Tarun, Know all Types of Sensors with their Circuit Diagrams.

Cayirci, E, Sankarasubramaniam Y. 2002, I.F. Akyildiz, W. Su, Wireless Sensor Networks: a Survey, Computer Networks 38 393–422.

Cameron Coles, https://www.skyhighnetworks.com/cloud-security-blog/11-advantages-of-cloud-computing-and-how-your-business-can-benefit-from-them/

CW. TSAI, Lai, CF. & Vasilakos, A.V. Wireless Network (2014) 20: 2201.

Das S.K, A. Ghosh 2008, Coverage and connectivity issues in wireless sensor networks: a survey, Pervasive and Mobile Computing. 4 303–334.

eN-touch Team, Capacitance vs Resistive vs Piezo Touch Switches

Friday A, Caceres R 2012, Ubicomp Systems at 20: Progress, Opportunities, and Challenges, IEEE Pervasive Computing 11

Finn Pearson, https://channels.theinnovationenterprise.com/articles/why-cloud-computing-is-so-popular-and-how-it-transforms-business

Juels A 2006, RFID security and privacy: A research survey, IEEE Journal of Selected Areas in Communication 24.

Griffith E, http://in.pcmag.com/networking-communications-software/38970/feature/what-is-cloud-computing.

Kashyap S, 10 Real World Applications of Internet of Things (IoT) - Explained in Videos.

Ling, Lu, Wu, F., Du, M., Sun, T., H.J 2010., Research on the architecture of internet of things. In: 3rd International Conference on Advanced Computer Theory and Engineering (ICACTE), IEEE.

Nugent A, Kaufman M, Hurwitz J, Fern Halper 2013 Book named 'Big Data for Dummies', Wiley Publications.

Prajapati V 2013 Book named 'Big Data Analytics with R and Hadoop', 2013 Ltd., by Vig.

Rogers Y 2006, moving on from Weiser's vision of calm computing: Engaging ubicomp experiences, Ubi-Comp Ubiquitous Computing.

SuW., Akyildiz. F, Cayirci E, Sankarasubramaniam Y 2002, Wireless Sensor Networks: A Survey, Computer Networks 38 393–422.

Welbourne E, Raymer S.,Rector K, Cole G., Battle L, Gould K 2009, et al., Building the Internet of Things Using RFID The RFID Ecosystem Experience, IEEE Internet Computing 13 48–55.

Tandjaoui D, Imed Romdhani, Mohammed Riyadh Abdmeziem, 2015 Architecting the Internet of Things: State of the Art.

https://azure.microsoft.com/en-in/overview/what-is-cloud-computing/.

https://doi.org/10.1007/s11276-014-0731-0.

https://www.gartner.com/newsroom/id/2636073.

Communication and Computing Systems – Prasad et al. (eds)
© 2019 Taylor & Francis Group, London, ISBN 978-0-367-00147-6

Five-grade cancer classification of colon histology images via deep learning

Manju Dabass, Rekha Vig & Sharda Vashisth

The NorthCap University, Gurugram, India

ABSTRACT: Colorectal Adenocarcinoma is the most primarily universal category of Colon Cancer. It basically originates in the intestinal glandular structures. Thus, in clinical practices, to forecast and map its course of cure, the intestinal glands' morphology along with architectural structure and glandular development information is used by the pathologists. A lot of digital automated techniques are proposed on regular basis for removing the need for manual grading and providing better accuracy. However, achieving accurate cancer grading still remains a big challenge for modern pathology. In order to curb this challenge, an automated supervised technique using deep learning keeping original image size is proposed in this paper for doing five-grade cancer classification via 31 layers deep CNN. The proposed model results classification accuracy of 96.97% for two-class grading and 93.24% for five-class cancer grading.

1 INTRODUCTION

For determining the malignancy extent, cancer grading is the most common process used. This is one of the preliminary stage criterion performed in clinical practice for deciding projection as well as the treatment course planning for individual patients. Although a lot of scrutinies are performed during the manual grading, still achieving accurate reproducibility is one of the main challenges that exist in pathology practice (Shen, D., Wu, G. and Suk, H.I., 2017). Various techniques have been introduced till now for getting the accurate classification of malignancy in cancerous images. However, with the increased availability of digitized histology slides, a viable solution can be offered in form of digital pathology (Madabhushi, A, Lee, G., 2016)

Demir et al. proposed a technique using pixel-level information where every tissue components were represented in the form of a disk. This technique first performs glandular segmentation using region growing technique for which initial seed points were identified using graph connectivity and then performs the classification according to the segmentation result. The main limitation of this method was that its validation was limited to a dataset comprising of healthy as well as benign cases only. Fu et al. proposed a technique using polar coordinate based segmentation. This proposed algorithm was giving better performance for both benign as well as malignant cases which were tainted mainly by Hematoxylin and DAB. But its validation was restricted only to healthy cases of regular H&E stained images.

Sirinukunwattana et al. proposed a technique for five class cancer grading using segmentation based on Bayesian Inference. This approach showed the high-performance result on all histological cancer grades except the undifferentiated colorectal cancer grade in H&E stained image. Also, this method was very slow.

Along with these conventional methods, a lot of work is also done using deep learning techniques. Xu.. Y proposed a technique in which classification was done by combining 11 Layer CNN inspired by alexnet with Support Vector Machine (SVM). For this, each pathological image was first divided into sets of overlapping square patches of 336×336 size whose numbers were reduced by rectangular grid formation followed by discarding white background patches.

Then by using feature extraction and feature selection, a total of 100 feature components were selected and inputted to the SVM Classifier. The overall resulted accuracy was 97.5% for two-class classification.

Kainz et al. proposed a classification technique based on the combination of sampling strategy along with 7 Layer CNN model inspired by LeNet-5 architecture in the same way as done in (Xu, Y et al 2017). For doing classification, each Histo-pathological was sampled into 101×101 pixel size patches. Also, data augmentation was done by exploiting rotation-invariance and additional nine rotated versions of patches were introduced for every 36o. The overall accuracy achieved was 95% for two-class classification.

Thus in this paper, to follow the footsteps of (Xu, Y., Jia, Z., Kainz, P et al 2017)

an algorithm using 31 layers deep CNN is proposed in order to achieve an accurate and fast classification of all the five cancer grades specially benign i.e. healthy and adenomatous along with malignant i.e. moderately differentiated, moderately-to-poorly differentiated and poorly differentiated where each patch of whole slide histological image is labeled according to the extent of malignancy. Here, each whole patch i.e. 775×522 is given as input and the predicted label comes as output. Unlike the previous techniques where due to patch sampling, problems like sample overlapping, over-fitting, etc. occurs, the proposed model was free from these problems as these were curbed by using original image patch size.

1.1 *Dataset used*

The dataset used here is taken from GlaS Challenge .(Sirinukunwattana, K 2017). It is basically having 165 images which are resultant from 16 patients whose H&E stained histological sections mainly of T3 or T4 stage colorectal Adenocarcinoma are taken during biopsy and here, T represents the spread of the primary tumor. All the images are in BMP format and are of 775×522 size. These are taken at 20X resolution (0.62005μm/pixel) by Zeiss Mirax MIDI Scanner. The whole database consists of 165 images and these images are labeled as benign i.e. healthy and adenomatous along with malignant i.e. moderately differentiated, moderately-to-poorly differentiated and poorly differentiated. The description of this dataset is given in Table 1. For our classification model, this dataset is divided into 80% and 20% ratio for training and testing part respectively. Figure 1 shows some of the images present in the GlaS Challenge database.

Table 1. GlaS challenge dataset for 2-class classification.

S. No.	Histologic Grade	Number of Images
1	Benign	74
2	Malignant	91

Table 2. GlaS challenge dataset for 5-class classification.

S. No.	Histologic Grade	No. of Images
1	Adenomatous	31
2	Healthy	43
3	Moderately differentiated	45
4	Moderately-to-Poorly differentiated	20
5	Poorly differentiated	26

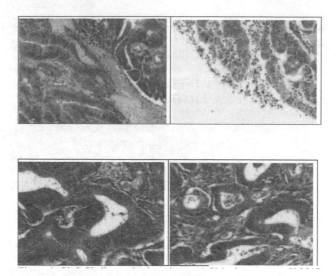

Figure 1.   GlaS challenge database images (Sirinukunwattana, K 2017).

2   PROPOSED CNN ARCHITECTURE

In the current scenario, CNN has become one of the largest well-known techniques used for deep learning of image data. In comparison to conventional machine learning where significant features are extracted manually, the deep learning techniques take raw images as their input for learning certain features. CNNs basically consists of an input layer and an output layer and in between them, present several hidden layers mainly in form of convolutional layers, pooling layers, ReLU layers, optimization layers, dropout layer and fully connected layers. The various CNN architectures differ mainly in quantity or type of implemented layer for their specific application. They comprise of various degree of hidden layers where activation volumes are modified with the help of differentiable functions. The four standard types of hidden layers which are used to build CNN are:

- Convolutional Layer (Convn): Here, convolutional filters of different sizes are used for derivation of activation map from the input data.
- Rectified Linear Unit Layer (RELU): It blocks all the negative values and thus provides only the resulting positive values in order to fasten the training time.
- Pooling Layer (POOL): It performs the non-linear down-sampling in order to cut down the number of parameters for giving simpler output.
- Fully Connected Layer (FU): It calculates the probability percentage of each class and gives an output vector of C dimension where C represents the number of Classes. All the neurons are connected to this layer.

By using the combination of these basic layers along with other layers, various CNN is proposed for various specific applications. In our work, the proposed CNN architecture is built by taking inspiration from the Alexnet (Krizhevsky, A et al 2012) . The various parameters used for parameter evaluation are accuracy, precision, and recall (.Dabass, M 2017). The various preprocessing techniques can be applied to further enhance the classification accuracy (Dabass, J. 2017). The whole architecture of the anticipated model is revealed in Figure 2 and is explained in Table 3. The whole sculpt is simulated via the use of a single GPU and optimized using ADAM optimization. The proposed model contains six convolutional and pooling layers along with two dropout layers and one fully connected layer.

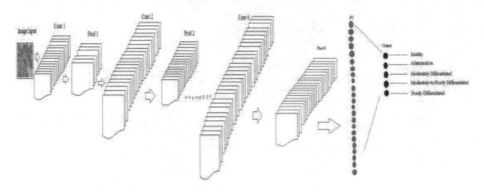

Figure 2.   Proposed CNN architecture.

Table 3.   Proposed layer wise CNN architecture.

S. No.	Layer Name	Layer	Layer Description
1	Input-I	Image Input	522x775x3 input image having 'zero center' normalization
2	Convn-1	Convolution	24 5x5 convolutions having stride [1 1] along with padding [1 1 1 1]
3	Norm-1	Batch Normalization	Batch Normalization
4	ReLU1	ReLU	ReLU
5	Pooling 1	Max Pooling	2x2 max pooling having stride [2 2] along with padding [0 0 0 0]
6	Convn-2	Convolution	8 3x3 convolutions having stride [1 1] along with padding [1 1 1 1]
7	Norm-2	Batch Normalization	Batch Normalization
8	ReLU2	ReLU	ReLU
9	Pooling 2	Max Pooling	2x2 max pooling having stride [2 2] along with padding [0 0 0 0]
10	Convn-3	Convolution	16 3x3 convolutions having stride [1 1] along with padding [1 1 1 1]
11	Norm3	Batch Normalization	Batch Normalization
12	ReLU3	ReLU	ReLU
13	Pooling 3	Max Pooling	2x2 max pooling having stride [2 2] along with padding [0 0 0 0]
14	Convn-4	Convolution	16 7x7 convolutions having stride [1 1] along with padding [1 1 1 1]
15	Norm4	Batch Normalization	Batch Normalization
16	ReLU4	ReLU	ReLU
17	Pooling 4	Max Pooling	2x2 max pooling having stride [2 2] along with padding [0 0 0 0]
18	Convn-5	Convolution	16 9x9 convolutions having stride [1 1] along with padding [1 1 1 1]
19	Norm5	Batch Normalization	Batch Normalization
20	ReLU5	ReLU	ReLU
21	Pooling 5	Max Pooling	2x2 max pooling having stride [2 2] along with padding [0 0 0 0]

(Continued)

Table 3. (*Continued*)

S. No.	Layer Name	Layer	Layer Description
22	Convn-6	Convolution	16 9x9 convolutions having stride [1 1] along with padding [1 1 1 1]
23	Norm6	Batch Normalization	Batch Normalization
24	ReLU6	ReLU	ReLU
25	Pooling 6	Max Pooling	3x3 max pooling having stride[1 1] along with padding [0 0 0 0]
26	Drop1	Dropout	50% dropout
27	ReLU7	ReLU	ReLU
28	Drop2	Dropout	50% dropout
29	FC	Fully Connected	5 fully connected layer
30	Softmax	Softmax	Softmax Layer
31	Classification	Classification Output	Crossentropyex

3 RESULTS

The proposed CNN model is compared with the model given in (Xu, Y., Jia, Z et al., 2017) and (Kainz, P, Pfeiffer, M. et al, 2017) terms of accuracy and input size. This experiment is performed on NVIDIA GPU enabled Laptop having of core i5 generation using MATLAB version 2017b. The training time taken to train 132 images is 23 minutes 28 seconds and classification time for a test image is 3 seconds. The results are shown in Table 4. The various hyper-parameters used for the model optimization are given in Table 4. The training and validation results for 2-class and 5-class classification are shown in Figure 3 and Figure 4 respectively.

Table 4. Results comparison for 2-class classification.

Model	Input Size	Accuracy
Xu et al.	336×336×3	97.5 %
Kainz et al.	101×101×3	95 %
Proposed	**522×775×3**	**96.97%**

Table 5. Training-relevant hyper-parameters obtained.

Hyper-parameter	Initial learning rate	Epoch Size	Dropout ratio	Mini-batch size	L2 Regularization	Validation Frequency	Validation Patience
Value	0.001	15	50%	10	0.0001	2	80

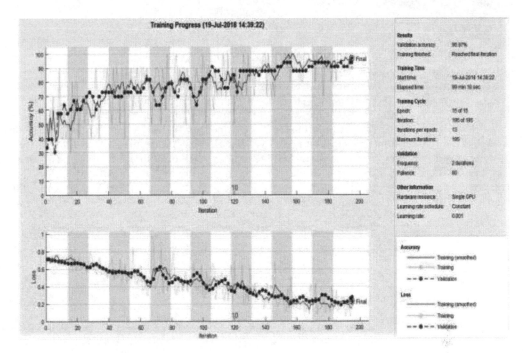

Figure 3. Training and validation result for 2-class cancer classification.

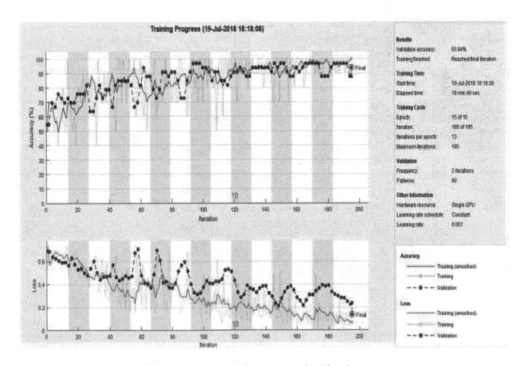

Figure 4. Training and validation result for 5-class cancer classification.

4 CONCLUSION AND FUTURE SCOPE

Earlier for doing classification, images were needed to be first divided into small patches. But with the proposed CNN classifier, there is no need to change the input image size. Due to this, this classifier takes less execution and training time. With 2-Classes, this CNN classifier is giving an accuracy of 96.97 % which is higher as compared to(Kainz, P, Pfeiffer, M. et al, 2017)]on the same dataset. Also, this same CNN model is applied for 5-class classification where it achieves 93.94%. The simulations are performed on NVIDIA GPU enabled Laptop having of core i5 generation using MATLAB version 2017b. The training time taken to train 132 images is 23 minutes 28 seconds and classification time for a test image is 3 seconds. Future work can be focused on increasing accuracy while reducing training and classification time. The accuracy can be increased by many factors like decreasing the mini batch size, use of other optimization techniques and increasing the size of the training dataset. On the other hand, the training time can be decreased by using parallel GPUs based or cloud-based GPU computation. Thus, in brief it can be infer that deep learning is the present flavor of the season not just because of the current research trend but owing to its various advantages and features that it offers.

REFERENCES

Dabass, J. and Vig, R., 2017, October. Biomedical Image Enhancement Using Different Techniques-A Comparative Study. In International Conference on Recent Developments in Science, Engineering and Technology (pp. 260-286). Springer, Singapore.

Dabass, M., Vashisth, S. and Vig, R., 2017, October. Effectiveness of Region Growing Based Segmentation Technique for Various Medical Images-A Study. In International Conference on Recent Developments in Science, Engineering and Technology (pp. 234-259). Springer, Singapore.

Fu, H., Qiu, G., Shu, J. and Ilyas, M., 2014. A novel polar space random field model for the detection of glandular structures. IEEE transactions on medical imaging, 33(3), pp.764-776.

Gunduz-Demir, C., Kandemir, M., Tosun, A.B. and Sokmensuer, C., 2010. Automatic segmentation of colon glands using object-graphs. Medical image analysis, 14(1), pp.1-12.4.

Kainz, P., Pfeiffer, M. and Urschler, M., 2017. Segmentation and classification of colon glands with deep convolutional neural networks and total variation regularization. PeerJ, 5, p.e3874.

Krizhevsky, A., Sutskever, I. and Hinton, G.E., 2012. Imagenet classification with deep convolutional neural networks. In Advances in neural information processing systems (pp. 1097-1105).

Madabhushi, A. and Lee, G., 2016. Image analysis and machine learning in digital pathology: Challenges and opportunities. Medical Image Analsis, 33, 170-175.

Shen, D., Wu, G. and Suk, H.I., 2017. Deep learning in medical image analysis. Annual review of biomedical engineering, 19, pp.221-248.

Sirinukunwattana, K., Snead, D.R. and Rajpoot, N.M., 2015. A stochastic polygons model for glandular structures in colon histology images. IEEE transactions on medical imaging, 34(11), pp.2366-2378.

Sirinukunwattana, K., Pluim, J.P., Chen, H., Qi, X., Heng, P.A., Guo, Y.B., Wang, L.Y., Matuszewski, B.J., Bruni, E., Sanchez, U. and Böhm, A., 2017. Gland segmentation in colon histology images: The glas challenge contest. Medical image analysis, 35, pp.489-502

Xu, Y., Jia, Z., Wang, L.B., Ai, Y., Zhang, F., Lai, M., Eric, I. and Chang, C., 2017. Large scale tissue histopathology image classification, segmentation, and visualization via deep convolutional activation features. BMC bioinformatics, 18(1), p.281.

Communication and Computing Systems – Prasad et al. (eds)
© *2019 Taylor & Francis Group, London, ISBN 978-0-367-00147-6*

An RGB image steganography algorithm with dual layer security

Kusan Biswas & Satish Chand
School of Computer & Systems Sciences, JNU, New Delhi, India

ABSTRACT: In this chapter we propose a *secure* spatial domain data hiding algorithm for embedding secret data in RGB image cover files. In our proposed approach, chaotic redistribution of the secret data and chaotic selection of embedding destination leave no trace of the original pattern of the data in the final stego-image. Experimental results show that, if intercepted, the stego image passes all the tests in NIST, DIEHARD and ENT test suites, thus making it extremely difficult to make sense without the keys. Further, it is shown that the proposed algorithm has very good visual quality as measured in Peak Signal to Noise Ration (PSNR) and Structural Similarity (SSIM).

1 INTRODUCTION

Steganography is the science and art of concealing a secret message inside a public medium such that the presence of the secret message is not suspected and undetectable. Digital steganography is largely divided in two major domains: A) Spatial Domain and B) Transform Domain. In spatial domain approach, message bits are directly embedded in the cover image pixels. Transform Domain techniques use mathematical transforms such as DCT and DST and therefore are computationally complex. Spatial Domain techniques on the other hand, are simple and fast. However, spatial domain techniques are vulnerable to statistical steganalysis attacks (Dumitrescu et al. 2003; Fridrich 2004; Xia et al. 2014). In literature, many data hiding techniques have been discussed. In LSB methods, some LSBs are modified according to the secret message bits. There have been different approaches in LSB based methods: Local pixel adjustment proccss(LPAP) (Wang et al.2000), optimal Pixel Adjustment Procedure(OPAP) (Chan and Cheng 2004) and pixel indicator technique (PIT) (Gutub 2010). Wang et al. (2000) discussed an LPAP based method to minimise quality degradation of the stego-image. The usage of LPAP resulted in better distortion characteristics than the simple LSB substitution approach. Chan et al. (2004) further improved upon (Wang et al. 2000) by introducing an optimal Pixel Adjustment Procedure(OPAP) Chan. According to them, this improved method results in 50% reduction of worst mean square error(WMSE) between the cover image and stego-image. Gutub et al. gutub2010pixel discussed pixel indicator technique (PIT) that uses all three channels in RGB image. Da-chunWu et al. (2003) proposed a new method based on pixel value differences(PVD). In parallel to the research for better spatial domain steganography, many statistical steganalysis methods have been proposed (Dumitrescu et al. 2003; Fridrich 2004; Fridrich et al. 2001; Ker 2004; Zhang and Ping 2003). These steganalysis attacks can, to a varying degree of success, reveal the insecurity of spatial domain algorithms. These developments were motivations for research in *secure* steganography algorithms. In this paper we propose a *secure* spatial domain steganography algorithm. It uses a 2D Arnold's Cat Map (Weisstein) and a set of three Logistics Maps for chaotic redistribution of secret data and selection of embedding destination. The non-linear behaviour of the chaotic map ensures chaos and randomness of the embedded data and makes it extremely difficult to recover the embedded data without the knowledge of the key.

2 BACKGROUND: CHAOS THEORY AND CHAOTIC MAPS

Chaos Theory is the study of the behaviour of dynamical systems that are extremely sensitive to the initial condition. It is observed that some simple rules, when iterated many times, may give rise to complex behaviour. This highly sensitive dependence of a system's dynamics on its initial state is known as the *Butterfly Effect* (Lorenz 1963). The butterfly effect occurs even though these systems are deterministic. This behaviour is known as deterministic chaos, or simply chaos (Werndl 2009). Cat Map (Arnol'd & Avez 1968) is a chaotic map, discovered by Vladimir Arnold. He demonstrated the effect of it on an image of a cat, hence the name. The generalised iterative form of Arnold cat map (Chen et al. 2004) symmetric for an image $I(x_i, y_i)$ of dimension $N \times N$ is given by:

$$\begin{bmatrix} x_{i+1} \\ y_{i+1} \end{bmatrix} = \begin{bmatrix} 1 & a \\ b & ab+1 \end{bmatrix} \begin{bmatrix} x_i \\ y_i \end{bmatrix} \bmod N \tag{1}$$

where a and b are two control parameters.

A property of the discrete Arnold's cat map is that, when applied on an image, the image perfectly reappears after applying it a certain number of times. This is called the property of *periodicity*. The period depends on the image dimension. Let period be C. After any iteration i such that $1 < i < C$, the pixel positions of the resulting image are chaotically redistributed. This phenomena is demonstrated in Figure 1. The Logistic Map is a polynomial mapping of degree two given by Equation (2)

$$x_{i+1} = rx_i(1 - x_i) \tag{2}$$

Here, r is the population parameter and $x_i \in (0, 1)$. Logistic map shows extreme sensitivity to the initial condition (i.e., x_0) for $r \in [3.57, 4]$. This phenomenon is demonstrated by the time series plot of x_i in Figure 2.

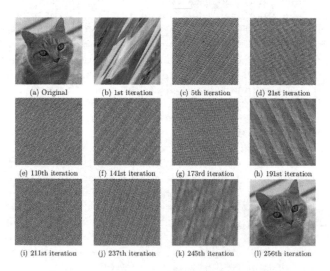

(a) Original	(b) 1st iteration	(c) 5th iteration	(d) 21st iteration
(e) 110th iteration	(f) 141st iteration	(g) 173rd iteration	(h) 191st iteration
(i) 211st iteration	(j) 237th iteration	(k) 245th iteration	(l) 256th iteration

Figure 1. Demonstration of Arnold's Cat Map operation on an image. The original image is shown in (a). In (b), (c) to (k), resulting chaotically redistributed images are shown. It can be seen that in the iteration no. 256, the original image reappears perfectly.

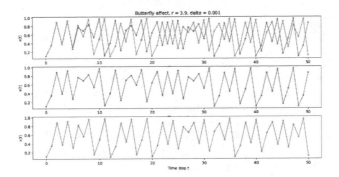

Figure 2. Time series plot of the logistic map with $r = 3.9$ and two different initial conditions $x_0 = 0.12$ and $x_0 + 10^{-3}$.

3 PROPOSED WORK

In the proposed framework, text data is embedded in RGB cover images. The stego-image is then transmitted to the recipient. If an eavesdropper somehow manages to get hold of the image while it is being transmitted over the network, he may try to detect embedded data using statistical steganalysis methods (Dumitrescu, Wu, & Wang 2003; Fridrich 2004; Fridrich, Goljan, & Du 2001; Ker 2004; Zhang & Ping 2003) and then possibly extract it. Chaotic reshuffling of secret data before embedding and chaotic selection of embedding venues and extreme sensitivity to the initial conditions ensure that recovery of the embedded data is difficult without the security key.

3.1 Embedding process

Let us assume that the RGB cover image is of dimension $M \times N \times 3$. The input secret data is first converted to binary. Next, the binary data is reshaped to a 2D square matrix of dimension $D \times D$. If total number of bits in the binary data is K, D is the smallest integer such that $D^2 \geq K$. If K is not a perfect square, $D^2 - K$ number of bits are padded to form a square matrix of dimension $D \times D$. This padding is done with 0s. Next, the generalized 2D cat map of Equation (1) is applied on the data matrix and its period(i.e., the number of iterations after which the original matrix reappears) is determined. Let the period be P. The values of parameters a and b are arbitrarily selected. Next, an integer Q is randomly selected such that $Q \in [\frac{P}{5}, \frac{4P}{5}]$. The 2D cat map is then applied on the data matrix Q times. The value of Q is selected randomly in the above range to prevent it from being too close to 0 or P to ensure better shuffling of data bits of the data matrix. Next, three logistic maps $x_{i+1} = r_1 x_i (1 - x_i) \, mod \, 1$, $y_{i+1} = r_2 y_i (1 - y_i) \, mod \, 1$ and $z_{i+1} = r_3 z_i (1 - z_i) \, mod \, 1$ are taken where r_1, r_2 and r_3 are three parameters in the range (3.57, 4]. The values of the parameters are taken from (3.57, 4] because in this range the logistic map exhibits chaotic behaviour. The initial values of these maps are arbitrary real numbers $x_0, y_0, z_0 \in (0, 1)$. With these parameters r_1, r_2, r_3 and initial conditions x_0, y_0, z_0 we iterate the logistics maps. At each iteration i, these maps output a three tuple $x_i, y_i, z_i \in (0, 1)$. These values are mapped to the range of the dimension of our cover image. x_i is mapped to $(0, M]$, y_i is mapped to $(0, N]$ and z_i is mapped to $(0, 2]$ as follows:

$$x_i' = \lfloor x_i \times M \rfloor, y_i' = \lfloor y_i \times N \rfloor, z_i' = \lfloor z_i \times 2 \rfloor \qquad (3)$$

These tuple (x_i', y_i', z_i') thus generated at each iteration i is used as index to the embedding destination. At every iteration i, a bit from the shuffled data matrix is copied and embedded in the least significant bit of the pixel addressed by the i th tuple (x_i', y_i', z_i'). A flag matrix of dimension $M \times N \times 3$ is used to prevent the data from being embedded more than once in each pixel. The flag matrix is initialised with zeros. Once a bit is embedded in a coordinate (x'_i, y'_i, z'_i) of the cover image, the 0 bit at the same coordinate in the flag matrix is flipped to 1 to indicate that the pixel at this position have been embedded with data bit and no more data can be embedded here in the next iterations. In the next iteration $i + 1$, the next bit from the data matrix is copied and embedded in the pixel at the location $(x'_{i+1}, y'_{i+1}, z'_{i+1})$ of the cover image. At any iteration, if it is found that a location has already been used, that location is skipped. This process continues until all the data bits are embedded. The embedding is done according to $F' = 2\lfloor\frac{F}{2}\rfloor + d$, where F is the original pixel value, d is the data bit, which can either be 0 or 1 and F' is the modified pixel value. The parameters and initial conditions of the three logistic maps, the random number Q, the period C and the parameters a and b of the 2D cat map and the data matrix dimension D form the Key. Therefore the key is the 11-tuple: $\{r_1, x_0, r_2, y_0, r_3, z_0, Q, C, a, b, D\}$

3.2 Extraction process

The extraction process is the reverse of the embedding process. The inputs to the extraction algorithm are the stego-image and the 11-tuple key that contains: $\{r_1, x_0, r_2, y_0, r_3, z_0, Q, C, a, b, D\}$. First, a square data matrix of dimension $D \times D$ is initialized. Next, three logistic maps $x_{i+1} = r_1 x_i (1 - x_i) \, mod \, 1$, $y_{i+1} = r_2 y_i (1 - y_i) \, mod \, 1$ and $z_{i+1} = r_3 z_i (1 - z_i) \, mod \, 1$ are initialized with parameters r_1, r_2, r_3 and initial values x_0, y_0, z_0 as given in the secret key. Now, these maps are iterated and at each iteration i, a 3D coordinate (x'_i, y'_i, z'_i) is generated exactly as given in the Section. 3.1. This coordinate is used to index to a pixel in the stego-image and its least significant bit is copied. This bit is placed at location $(0, 0)$ of the 2D data matrix. In the next iteration $i + 1$ the logistic maps generate the address $(x'_{i+1}, y'_{i+1}, z'_{i+1})$. The LSB of the pixel at this position is then copied and placed to the next position of the data matrix. similar to the embedding process, a flag matrix is used to prevent multiple extraction from the same location. This process continues until the data matrix is full. The data matrix thus formed is the shuffled data matrix that was formed by applying the 2D cat map Q times in the embedding process. Since we applied the 2D cat map on the original data matrix Q times before embedding and since the period of the 2D cat map is $C(>Q)$, applying the cat map $C - Q$ times is effectively equivalent to applying the cat map $Q + C - Q = C$ times. Since C is the period, it gives us the original data matrix. Therefore, we initialize a 2D cat map (Equation (1)) with control parameters a and b and iterate it on the data matrix $C - Q$ times. The output of this is our original data matrix. Since we use the same parameters and initial conditions as we used in the embedding process, the same sequence of coordinates are generated and the data is recovered in the correct sequence. The butterfly effect of chaos ensures that even the slightest difference of the initial values will generate completely different sequence and the data can not be correctly recovered. This ensures the security of our proposed method.

4 EXPERIMENTAL RESULTS

For experiments, we have considered eight JPEG RGB standard images namely Lena, Peppers, Baboon, Fruits, Airplane, Boats, Lion and Orion as our cover images. As secret message, we have used plain text version of wikipedia articles.

4.1 Imperceptibility tests

Tests for imperceptibility of the embedded information in the stego-image is carried out in terms of two measures: peak signal to noise ratio(PSNR) and structural similarity(SSIM) wang2004image. From Table 1, it can be seen that, when 1 bit of data is embedded in each pixel of each of the R, G and B channels, the PSNR values are above 50. When 2 data bits are embedded in each pixel of each channel, the PSNR value is above 45 for all the eight cover images. It is also seen that, in both cases (1 and 2 bit embedding) the SSIM values are above 0.99, which indicates high similarity among cover and stego-images.

Table 1. PSNR and SSIM values achieved when 1 bit and 2 bits of data are embedded in each channel per pixel.

Test image	PSNR(1 bit)	SSIM(1 bit)	PSNR(2 bits)	SSIM(2 bits)
Lena	50.99	0.9993	45.32	0.9987
Peppers	51.42	0.9992	46.07	0.9988
Baboon	51.97	0.9993	45.74	0.9987
Airplane	50.97	0.9991	46.19	0.9983
Fruits	52.13	0.9993	46.35	0.9986
Boats	51.02	0.9992	45.83	0.9985
Lion	50.89	0.9991	45.99	0.9987
Orion	52.00	0.9992	46.05	0.9985

4.2 *Security analysis*

In security analysis, extract LSB bits from stego-images and combine them to form a binary bit stream and save in text files. In one experiment, 1 bit of data is embedded in 1 LSB of the cover image, in other experiment, 2 bits of data is embedded in a pixel per channel. Correspondingly, in two experiments 1 and 2 LSBs are copied from stego-image pixels. The randomness of extracted data is then evaluated by the three test suites: NIST (Rukhin, Soto, Nechvatal, Smid, & Barker 2001), DIEHARD (Brown) and ENT (Fourmilab) and the results are shown in Tables 2 and Table 3 and Table 4 respectively. It can be seen that the data passes all tests of randomness. These results demonstrate that our proposed steganography scheme places the message bits in the stego-image very chaotically. Therefore, without the Key, it is

Table 2. Results from the NIST test suite. Second and third column is the result of 1 bit embedding and fourth and fifth column is of 2 bit embedding.

Tests	p-value	Result	p-value	Result
Frequency	0.778282	SUCCESS	0.768282	SUCCESS
Block frequency	0.690189	SUCCESS	0.680199	SUCCESS
Cusum forward	0.855892	SUCCESS	0.849280	SUCCESS
cusum reverse	0.764975	SUCCESS	0.732081	SUCCESS
Runs	0.738102	SUCCESS	0.724149	SUCCESS
Long runs of 1s	0.619306	SUCCESS	0.609336	SUCCESS
Rank	0.752001	SUCCESS	0.714447	SUCCESS
FFT	0.683027	SUCCESS	0.650127	SUCCESS
Universal	0.577351	SUCCESS	0.580416	SUCCESS
Approx. entropy	0.946754	SUCCESS	0.920973	SUCCESS

Table 3. Results from the DIEHARD test suite. Second and third column is the result of 1 bit embedding and fourth and fifth column is of 2 bit embedding.

Tests	p-value	Result	p-value	Result
Birthday spacing	0.713968	PASSED	0.720124	PASSED
Overlapping perm.	0.626027	PASSED	0.627170	PASSED
Binary rank 31x31	0.685347	PASSED	0.683354	PASSED
Binary rank 32x32	0.684321	PASSED	0.684349	PASSED
Binary rank 6x8	0.628190	PASSED	0.619970	PASSED
Bitstream	0.700099	PASSED	0.710618	PASSED
OPSO	0.551921	PASSED	0.561167	PASSED
OQSO	0.561916	PASSED	0.568078	PASSED
DNA	0.619101	PASSED	0.620853	PASSED

Table 4. Results from the ENT test suite. Second and third column is the result of 1 bit embedding and fourth and fifth column is of 2 bit embedding.

Tests	p-value	Result	p-value	Result
Entropy	7.8893	PASSED	7.8905	PASSED
Arithmetic mean	127.8147	PASSED	127.81344	PASSED
Monte Carlo	3.141379	PASSED	3.141191	PASSED
χ-square	265.51	PASSED	266.51	PASSED
SCC	0.0002004	PASSED	0.0002201	PASSED

extremely difficult for any adversary to extract meaningful information from the stego-image. To an adversary, the data will look like a random bit stream.

5 CONCLUSION

In this paper we have proposed a new *secure* steganography scheme that is suitable for RGB cover images. The security is achieved with the use of two chaos maps: Arnold's cat map and the logistic map. Experimental results show that the proposed method is highly resistant of statistical attacks which makes it extremely difficult for an attacker to extract embedded data from the cover image without the key. It is also shown that the stego images have excellent imperceptibility characteristics as measured in PSNR and SSIM values.

ACKNOWLEDGEMENT

This research is partially funded by Council of Scientific and Industrial Research, India, vide grant id. 09/263(1045)/2015-EMR-I.

REFERENCES

Arnol'd, V. I. & A. Avez (1968). Ergodic problems of classical mechanics.

Brown, R. G. Robert g. brown's general tools page.

Chan, C.-K. & L. Cheng (2004). Hiding data in images by simple {LSB} substitution. Pattern Recognition 37(3), 469–474.

Chen, G., Y. Mao, & C. K. Chui (2004). A symmetric image encryption scheme based on 3d chaotic cat maps. Chaos, Solitons & Fractals 21(3), 749–761.

Dumitrescu, S., X. Wu, & Z. Wang (2003). Detection of lsb steganography via sample pair analysis. IEEE transactions on Signal Processing 51(7), 1995–2007.

Fourmilab. Ent test suite.

Fridrich, J. (2004). Feature-based steganalysis for jpeg images and its implications for future design of steganographic schemes. In *International Workshop on Information Hiding*, pp. 67–81. Springer.

Fridrich, J., M. Goljan, & R. Du (2001). Detecting lsb steganography in color, and gray-scale images. IEEE multimedia 8(4), 22–28.

Gutub, A. A.-A. (2010). Pixel indicator technique for rgb image steganography. Journal of Emerging Technologies in Web Intelligence 2(1), 56–64.

Ker, A. D. (2004). Quantitative evaluation of pairs and rs steganalysis. In *Security, Steganography, and Watermarking of Multimedia Contents VI*, Volume 5306, pp. 83–98. International Society for Optics and Photonics.

Lorenz, E. N. (1963). Deterministic nonperiodic flow. Journal of the atmospheric sciences 20(2), 130–141.

Rukhin, A., J. Soto, J. Nechvatal, M. Smid, & E. Barker (2001). A statistical test suite for random and pseudorandom number generators for cryptographic applications. Technical report, Booz-Allen and Hamilton Inc, Mclean Va.

Wang, R.-Z., C.-F. Lin, J.-C. Lin, et al.(2000). Hiding data in images by optimal moderately-significant-bit replacement. Electronics Letters 36(25), 2069–2070.

Wang, Z., A. C. Bovik, H. R. Sheikh, & E. P. Simoncelli (2004). Image quality assessment: from error visibility to structural similarity. IEEE transactions on image processing 13(4), 600–612.

Weisstein, E. W. Arnold's cat map.

Werndl, C. (2009). What are the new implications of chaos for unpredictability? The British Journal for the Philosophy of Science 60(1), 195–220.

Wu, D.-C. & W.-H. Tsai (2003). A steganographic method for images by pixel-value differencing. Pattern Recognition Letters 24(9), 1613–1626.

Xia, Z., X. Wang, X. Sun, & B. Wang (2014). Steganalysis of least significant bit matching using multi-order differences. Security and Communication Networks 7(8), 1283–1291.

Zhang, T. & X. Ping (2003). A new approach to reliable detection of lsb steganography in natural images. Signal processing 83(10), 2085–2093.

Communication and Computing Systems – Prasad et al. (eds)
© 2019 Taylor & Francis Group, London, ISBN 978-0-367-00147-6

Software requirements selection using different patterns of pairwise comparison matrices of analytic hierarchy process

C.W. Mohammad & S. Khan
Computer Science and Technology Research Group, Department of Applied Sciences and Humanities, Faculty of Engineering and Technology, Jamia Millia Islamia (A Central University), New Delhi, India

M. Sadiq
Software Engineering Research Group, UPFET, Jamia Millia Islamia (A Central University), New Delhi, India

ABSTRACT: Analytic hierarchy process (AHP) is an important multi-criteria decision making algorithm which is employed to select the alternatives or software requirements (SR) based on distinct criteria like cost, usability, security, performance, etc. In industrial applications, AHP has been considered as useful and trustworthy method for the SR selection. In AHP, pairwise comparison matrices (PCM) are used to specify the preferences of the alternatives or SR on the basis of different criteria. In literature, we identify that during the SR selection process less attention is given to check whether the PCM of AHP is consistent or not. Therefore, to address this issue we proposed a method for the selection of SR. In our work, we use the goal oriented method for the elicitation of the SR of the Institute Examination System.

KEYWORDS: Software requirements selection, AHP, Pairwise comparison matrices, Types of requirements

1 INTRODUCTION

Software requirements selection (SRS) is a *"multi-criteria decision making"* (MCDM) problem; and its aim is to choose *"those requirements that would be implemented during different releases of the software"* (Sadiq, 2017). In software engineering, *"non-functional requirements"* (NFR) are employed as criteria to choose the *"functional requirements"* (FR) from the list of the FRs (Sadiq and Jain 2014). Research in the area of SRS are divided into two parts, i.e., (i) SRS *"methods based on MCDM algorithms"* (ii) SRS methods in *"search based software engineering"* (SBSE) domain. Different types of the MCDM techniques have been used in SRS like *"analytic hierarchy process"* (AHP) (Mu and Pereyra-Rojas, 2017), *"techniques for order preference by similarity to ideal solutions"* (TOPSIS), etc. (Behzadian *et al.*, 2012). There are various methods for the solution of SRS like *"ant colony optimization"*, *"teaching learning based algorithm"*, *"genetic algorithms"*, etc. (Zhang *et al.*, 2007; Bagnall *et al.*, 2001). In SBSE, SRS is also known as *"Next Release Problem"* (NRP). NRP was formulated by Bagnall et al. (2001). Karlsson *et al.* (1998) investigated the following methods for the prioritization of SR, i.e., *"AHP"*, *"hierarchy AHP"*, *"spanning tree"*, *"bubble sort"*, *"binary search tree"* and *"priority groups"*. As a result they identify that AHP is one of the useful and trustworthy methods for the software requirements (SR) prioritization in industrial application. Therefore, it motivates us to apply the AHP for the selection of SR.

In AHP, *"pairwise comparison matrices"* (PCM) are employed to compare different alternatives based on different criteria. In other words, you can say that PCM stores the results of the alternatives after evaluation on the basis of different criteria by different decision makers.

In literature, we identify that AHP has been applied for SRS but checking the consistency of the PCM has received less attention by the researchers and academicians. There are some studies, which have focused on the generation of the consistent results on the basis of the consistent PCM. Sadiq and Afrin (2017) generated the different patterns and sub-patterns for the PCM of size 3X3, by considering three requirements. In their study, they have generated 8 patterns and for one pattern they have generated 48 sub-patterns. After generating the 48 different patterns, a database was maintained in which the values of the entire consistent ratio were stored. Whenever the decision maker will generate any PCM, the pattern of that PCM will be compared with the results of the database. If the database suggests that PCM is valid then only the PCM would be used during the SRS process, otherwise, the database will suggest you for other PCM. In our work, we extend the work of (Sadiq and Afrin, 2017) and generated the 64 patterns for 8 patterns; as a result we have generated 512 patterns for the PCM of size 3X3; and proposed a method for SRS. Therefore, the contributions of this paper are given as below: (1) To elicit the FR and NFR using goal oriented method, (2) To generate the consistent PCM for ten FR and three NFR, and (3) To select the FR from the set of ten FR on the basis of three NFR only when the PCM are consistent

The remaining part of this paper is structured as follows: Related work is given in section 2. An insight into AHP is given in section 3. Proposed method is explained in section 4. In section 5, we present a case study based on Institute Examination System. Section 6 contains the conclusion and future work.

2 RELATED WORK

In this section we present the related work in the area of SRS. Lai *et al.* (2002) conducted a case study based on one of the popular MCDM algorithm, i.e., AHP; and developed a "*group decision making*" (GDM) system for the selection of multi-media authorizing system. As a result authors find out that AHP is an effective method to develop the consensus among the stakeholders in GDM system. Wei *et al.* (2005) proposed an essential structure for the selection of ERP to support the following: "*business goal and strategies of an enterprise*", "*identify the appropriate attributes*", etc. Min (1992) proposed a method for selecting a proper logistics software using AHP to deal with "*qualitative and quantitative factors in MCDM environments*". Schniederjans and Wilson (1991) proposed an information system selection method using AHP with goal programming model framework. Karsak and Ozogul (2009) proposed a "*framework for ERP software selection*".

Apart from the above studies, we have identified some other studies in which SRS/goal selection have been used as one of the important steps of the different methodologies used in goal oriented requirements engineering (Sadiq and Jain, 2015), stakeholder identification methods (Sadiq, 2017), etc. For example, Sadiq *et al.* (2017) apply the AHP in "*goal oriented requirements elicitation method for the prioritization of the software requirements*" to develop the AHP-GORE_PSR methodology. This methodology was extended by Sadiq and Afrin (2017) in which they have generated the "*different patterns of PCM to check whether the PCM are consistent or not*". In recent studies, Sadiq and Nazneen (2018) proposed a method for the "*elicitation of software testing requirements from the selected set of software's functional requirements in goal oriented requirements elicitation process*". In another study, a method for stakeholder identification was proposed by Sadiq (2017) on the basis of the importance of SR. Importance of the SR was determined by the "*selected set of the software requirements*". On the basis of our literature review, we find out that in the above studies AHP has been widely used in SRS but without considering whether the PCM is consistent or not. Therefore, in our study we mainly focus on the consistency of the PCM during SRS.

NRP is classified into two parts, i.e., (i) single objective NRP and (ii) multi-objective NRP. Single objective NRP was formulated by "*Bagnall et al. (2001)*"; and its objective was "*to find the ideal set of requirements that balance the customer requests within resource constraints*". NRP is a classical instance of "*0/1 knapsack problem*". It is an NP hard problem because it involves several contrary objectives that have to be addressed by the engineers. SBSE methods have proven to be essential in requirements optimization. Sagrado and Aguila (2009) proposed a method to show that "*ant colony optimization*" (ACO) algorithm can be used to solve the SRS problem. They suggest that ACO system should be compared with Greedy and Simulated Annealing algorithms. Sagrado *et al.* (2010) used ACO algorithm for SRS problem. They have evaluated the proposed method with other algorithms, i.e., "*Simulated Annealing*" (SA) and "*Genetic Algorithm*" (GA). A case study was used to compare the ACO, SA, and GA. In our work, we mainly focus on the SRS method based AHP. An insight into AHP is given in next section, i.e., section 3.

3   AN INSIGHT INTO AHP

AHP is a popular MCDM algorithm which was developed by the "*Thomas L. Saaty in 1980*" for the selection as well as prioritization of the alternatives on the basis of the different criteria (Saaty, 1990). AHP has been widely used in software engineering. For example, Khan *et al.* (2014) apply the AHP for the "*selection of software development life cycle models*". For the evaluation of the alternatives on the basis of different criteria's, Saaty (1990) proposed a scale to specify the preferences of one alternative over another. One common scale, adopted by the Saaty is shown in Table 1.

Table 1.   Saaty rating scale.

Intensity of importance	Definition	Intensity of importance	Definition
1	"Equal Importance"	7	"Very much more important"
3	"Somewhat more important"	9	"Absolutely more important"
5	"Much more important"	2,4,6,8	"Intermediate values"

In AHP, PCM are used to specify the preferences of the stakeholders. Different algorithms have been developed to compute the priority values of the PCM. In our work, following algorithm is used to compute the "*ranking values*" (RV) of the PCM (Saaty, 1990):

Algorithm A:

Step 1: Add the column of the PCM and store the result in Column$_{PCM}$
Step 2: Normalized the Column$_{PCM}$ and store the results in Normalized_ Column$_{PCM}$
Step 3: Take the average of the row from Normalized_ Column$_{PCM}$. As a result the we will get the priorities of the alternatives and store the results in P_1, P_2, ...P_N. Where N is the total number of requirements
Step 4: Multiply the first column with P_1, second column with P_2, and Nth column with P_N; and store the results in Weighted_Column
Step 5: Calculate the sum of each row from Weighted_Column; and store the results in Weighted_Sum (WS) as WS_1, WS_2, ...WS_N
Step 6: Divide the elements of the WS_1, WS_2, ...WS_N by the P_1, P_2, ...P_N as:
Lambda-1: WS_1/P_1;
Lambda-2: WS_2/P_2 ...
Lambda-N: WS_N/P_N
Step 7: Compute the average of the Lambda-1, Lambda-2 and Lambda-N; and store the results in Lambda-Max (λ_{max})
Step 8: Calculate the "*consistency ratio*" (CR) by using the following equation,

$$CR = ((\lambda_{max}-N)/N-1)/RI$$

Here, RI is the "*consistency index of a randomly generated*" PCM. The value of the RI for 3, 4, 5, 6 requirements would be 0.58, 0.9, 1.12, and 1.24, respectively.

4 PROPOSED METHOD

The steps of the "*SRS using different patterns of PCM of AHP*" are given below:

Step 1:Identify the different types of the SR using goal oriented method
Step 2:Generate different patterns and sub-patterns of PCM
Step 3: Compute the CR of each PCM
Step 4: Identify those patterns which do not produce the consistent results
Step 5:Select the CR on the basis of the consistent PCM

Explanations of the above steps are given in next section, i.e., Case Study.

5 CASE STUDY

In our work, we apply the proposed method to select the SR of "*Institute Examination System*" (IES). The explanation of the proposed method in the context of IES is given below:

5.1: Step 1: Identify the different types of the SR using goal oriented method

Goal oriented method (GOM) are the popular methods to visualize the different types of the SR like FR and NFR using AND/OR graph. In GOM, "*high level objective of an organization are refined and decomposed until the responsibility of the goals/sub-goals are assigned to some agents and systems*". Traditional methods (Sadiq, 2017) play an important role to get the background of the software project. On the basis of the results of the traditional method, we apply the GOM to get the complete set of software's FR and NFRs. After applying the traditional methods and the GOM, we have identified the following FR and NFR of IES:

List of FRs: FR1: Login module of IES for different types of the users, i.e., students, teacher, and the administration, **FR2**: To send the SMS/email on the mobile of the students or parents to submit the examination fee before appearing in the examination, **FR3**: To display the results of the students of different courses, **FR4**: System should generate the seating arrangement and the same should be forwarded on the mobile/email of the students, **FR5**: To generate the date sheet of the theory and practical courses, **FR6**: To generate the hall ticket of the eligible students, **FR7**: Filling of semester/annual examination form, **FR8**: Approve examination form, **FR9**: Online conduct of examination for those courses which requires multiple objective based question papers, **FR10**: To enter the internal assessment marks and the end semester marks of the theory and the practical courses. **List of NFRs: NFR1**: Security; **NFR2**: Performance; **NFR3**: Usability

Step 2: Generate different patterns and sub-patterns of pairwise comparison matrix (PCM)

After identifying the FR and NFR, the PCM are generated for FR and NFR. In our study, we have ten FR and three NFR. For ten FR there would be 1024 patterns and in the case of 3 NFR, there would be eight different patterns. Because of the limitations of the pages, we mainly focus on the generation of the patterns and sub-patterns on NFRs because for three NFRs, we have eight patterns and each pattern we have 64 sub-patterns. Therefore, finally, we have 8X64 s=512 sub-patterns. In our case study, for three NFRs following patterns have been generated: **Pattern 1**: When NFR1 is favourable over NFR2, when NFR1 is favourable over NFR3, and when NFR2 is favourable over NFR3; **Pattern 2**: When NFR1 is favourable over NFR2, when NFR1 is favourable over NFR3, and when NFR3 is favourable over NFR2; **Pattern 3**: When NFR1 is favourable over NFR2, when NFR3 is favourable over NFR1, and when NFR2 is favourable over NFR3; **Pattern 4**: When NFR1 is favourable over NFR2, when NFR3 is favourable over NFR1, and when NFR3 is favourable over NFR2; **Pattern 5**: When NFR2 is favourable over NFR1, when NFR1 is favourable over NFR3, and when NFR2 is favourable over NFR3; **Pattern 6**: When NFR2 is favourable over NFR1, when NFR1 is favourable over NFR3, and when NFR3 is favourable over NFR2; **Pattern 7**: When NFR2 is favourable over NFR1, when NFR3 is favourable over NFR1, and when NFR2 is favourable over NFR3; **Pattern 8**: When NFR2 is favourable over NFR1, when NFR3 is favourable over NFR1, and when NFR3 is favourable over NFR2.

NFRs	NFR1	NFR2	NFR3
NFR1	1	3	3
NFR2	1/3	1	3
NFR3	1/3	1/3	1

Figure 1. First sub-pattern for pattern 1, i.e., when NFR1 is favourable over NFR2, when NFR1 is favourable over NFR3, and when NFR2 is favourable over NFR3.

For the explanation point of view, we generate the first sub-pattern for pattern 1 in Figure 1.

Algorithm A is employed to calculate the "ranking values" (RV) of NFRs, and for the sub-patterns 1, as shown in Figure 1, we find out that the value of the CR is 0.1524. Similarly, we compute the consistency ratio of all the sub-patterns. The next four PCMs are exhibited from Figure 2 to Figure 5.

NFRs	NFR1	NFR2	NFR3
NFR1	1	3	3
NFR2	1/3	1	5
NFR3	1/3	1/5	1

Figure 2. Sub-pattern 1.2.

NFRs	NFR1	NFR2	NFR3
NFR1	1	3	3
NFR2	1/3	1	9
NFR3	1/3	1/9	1

Figure 4. Sub-pattern 1.4.

NFRs	NFR1	NFR2	NFR3
NFR1	1	3	3
NFR2	1/3	1	7
NFR3	1/3	1/7	1

Figure 3. Sub-pattern 1.3.

NFRs	NFR1	NFR2	NFR3
NFR1	1	3	5
NFR2	1/3	1	3
NFR3	1/5	1/3	1

Figure 5. Sub-pattern 1.5.

Step 3: Compute the consistency ratio of each PCM

In this step, we compute the "*consistency ratio*" (CR) of all the sub-patterns of pattern 1 to pattern 8. In the case of the first pattern, we observe that the value of CR is less that 10% for the following sub-patterns of pattern 1, i.e., sub-pattern 1.5, 1.9, 1.10, 1.13, 1.14, 1.25, and 1.29. Similarly, we identify the sub-patterns of all the patterns in which the value of the CR is less than 10%.

Step 4: Identify those patterns which does not produce the consistent results.

In our study, we observe that pattern 3 and pattern 6 are not useful during decision making process because in these two patterns the value of the CR is greater than 10%.

Step 5: Select the software requirements on the basis of the consistent PCM.

In this step, we select the FR from the set of ten FR on the basis of three NFR only when the PCM is/are consistent. Now the decision makers will generate the PCM for the NFRs. Suppose the decision makers generate the following PCM for the NFRs.

Now the pattern of the NFR, as shown in Figure 6, will be compared with the patterns and sub-patterns for three NFRs. As a result, we identify that the above PCM matches with the first pattern; and within the first pattern given PCM matches with the pattern 1.5, as shown in

NFRs	NFR1	NFR2	NFR3
NFR1	1	3	5
NFR2	1/3	1	3
NFR3	1/5	1/3	1

Figure 6. PCM generated by the decision maker.

Figure 5. As we know that, the CR of pattern 1.5 is less than 10%. Therefore, the above PCM would be used in the selection of FR. After applying the Algorithm A, the ranking values of the NFRs are computed; and the final results of the NFR value are given below: NFR1 = 0.636986, NFR2 = 0.258285 and NFR3 =0.104729. On the basis of our analysis, we find out that NFR1, i.e., Security, has the highest priority; therefore, it would be used during the selection of the software requirements process. Now, the FR would be evaluated on the basis of the Security requirements. For the ten FR, we first construct the consistent PCM of FR. The contents of the PCM for ten FR are given in Table II. The CR of the above PCM is consistent; and the value of the CR is 0.0139, which is less that 10%. The PCM as shown in Table II would be used in our study. After applying the Algorithm A we get the following "ranking values" (RV) of the FRs: *"FR1= 0.135, FR2, 0.223, FR3=0.223, FR4=0.135, FR5=0.079, FR6= 0.028, FR7=0.053, FR8=0.018, FR9=0.028, FR10=0.079"*. Above RV would be used by the decision makers to select those SR that would be developed during different release of the software. If the decision makers decide that only the top three requirements would be implemented. Then FR2 and FR3 have the first priority; FR1 and FR4 have the second priority, FR5 and FR10 have the third priority. In the first release of the software following set of the requirements would be designed and developed: FR2, FR3, FR1, FR4, FR5, and FR10.

Table II. Evaluation of FR on the basis of security requirements.

FR	FR1	FR2	FR3	FR4	FR5	FR6	FR7	FR8	FR9	FR10
FR1	1	1/2	1/2	1	2	5	3	7	5	2
FR2	2	1	1	2	3	7	5	9	7	3
FR3	2	1	1	2	3	7	5	9	7	3
FR4	1	1/2	1/2	1	2	5	3	7	5	2
FR5	1/2	1/3	1/3	1/2	1	3	2	5	3	1
FR6	1/5	1/7	1/7	1/5	1/3	1	1/3	2	1	1/3
FR7	1/3	1/5	1/5	1/3	1/2	3	1	3	3	1/2
FR8	1/7	1/9	1/9	1/7	1/5	1/2	1/3	1	1/2	1/5
FR9	1/5	1/7	1/7	1/5	1/3	1	1/3	2	1	1/3
FR10	1/2	1/3	1/3	1/2	1	3	2	5	3	1

6   CONCLUSIONS AND FUTURE WORK

In AHP, PCMs are used to specify the preferences of the decision makers/stakeholders. Keeping in view the importance of the PCM, we developed an algorithm for SRS; and it includes the following steps: *"(i) identify the different types of the SR using goal oriented method, (ii) generate different patterns and sub-patterns of PCM, (iii) compute the consistency ratio of each PCM, (iv) identify those patterns which do not produce the consistent results, (v) select the SR on the basis of the consistent PCM"*. Proposed method has been applied to select the SR of IES. In future, we will extend our work by evaluating the set of FR on the basis of the other two NFRs, i.e., performance and usability..

REFERENCES

Sadiq, M. 2017. A Fuzzy-Set Based Approach for the Prioritization of Stakeholders on the basis of the Importance of Software Requirements. IETE Journal of Research, Vol. 63. Taylor and Francis 616-629

Sadiq, M., Jain, S.K. 2014. Applying Fuzzy Preference Relation for Requirements Prioritization in Goal Oriented Requirements Elicitation Process. International Journal of Systems Assurance Engineering and Management, Springer, Vol. 5. Springer, 711-723

Mu, E., Pereyra.-Rojas., M. 2017. Understanding the Analytic Hierarchy Process. Practical Decision Making, Springer, 7-22

Behzadian, M., Otaghsara, S.K., Yazdani, M., Ignatius, J. 2012. A State-of the –art Survey of TOPSIS Applications, Expert Systems with Applications, Vol. 39. Elsevier,13051-13069

Zhang, Y., Harman, M., Mansouri, S.A. 2007. The Multi-Objective Next Release Problem, in Proceedings of the ACM 9th Annual Conference on Genetic and Evolutionary Computation, New York.

Bagnall, A. J., Rayward–Smith, V. J., Whittley, I. M. 2001. The Next Release Problem, Information and Software Technology, 43(14), 883-890.

Sagrado, J., Aguila, I. M. 2009. Ant Colony Optimization for Requirements Selection in Incremental Software Development, in Proceedings of the 1st IEEE International Symposium on Search Based Software Engineering. Cumberland Lodge, Windsor, UK, (2009)

Sagrado, J., Aguila, I.M., F. J. Orellana, F.J. 2010. Ant Colony Optimization for the Next Release Problem: A comparative Study, in Proceedings of the 2nd IEEE International Symposium on Search Based Software Engineering, Benevento Italy.

Karlsson J., Wohlin C., and Regnell B. 1998. An Evaluation of Methods for Prioritizing Software Requirements. Information and Software Technology, 39, 939-947.

Sadiq, M., Afrin, A. 2017. Extending AHP-GORE-PSR by Generating Different Patterns of Pairwise Comparison Matrix. International Conference on Information, Communication and Computing Technology, CCIS, Springer-Verlag, Singapore.

Lai V. S., Wong Bo K., Cheung W. 2002. Group Decision Making in a Multi-criteria Environment: A Case using the AHP in Software Selection. European Journal of Operational Research, 137 (1), 134-144.

Wei C. C., Chien C-F., Wang M. J. 2005. An AHP-based Approach to ERP System Selection. International Journal of Production Economics, 96(1), 47-62.

Min H. 1992. Selection of Software: The Analytic Hierarchy Process. International Journal of Physical Distribution and Logistics Management, 22(1), 42-52.

Schniederjans M. J. and Wilson R. K. 1991. Using the Analytic Hierarchy Process and Goal Programming for Information System Project Selection. Information and Management, 20(5),333-342.

Karsak E. E. and Ozogul C. O. 2009. An Integrated Decision Making Approach for ERP System Selection. Expert Systems with Applications, 36(1), 660-667.

Sadiq, M., Jain, S.K. 2015. A Fuzzy Based Approach for the Selection of Goals in Goal Oriented Requirements Elicitation Process. International Journal of Systems Assurance Engineering and Management, Vol. 6. Springer, 157-164.

Sadiq, M., Hassan, T., Nazneen, S. 2017. AHP_GORE_PSR: Applying Analytic Hierarchy Process in Goal Oriented Requirements Elicitation Method for the Prioritization of Software Requirements. 3rd IEEE International Conference on Computational Intelligence and Communication Technology, 10-11.

Sadiq, M., Nazneen, S. 2018. Elicitation of Software Testing Requirements from the Selected Set of Software's Requirements in GOREP. International Journal of Computational Systems Engineering, Inderscience.

Saaty T. L. 1990. How to Make a Decision: The Analytic Hierarchy Process. European Journal of Operational Research, 48 (1), 9-26.

Khan M. A., Parveen A, and Sadiq M. 2014. A Method for the Selection of Software Development Life Cycle Models Using Analytic Hierarchy Process. IEEE International Conference on Issues and Challenges in Intelligent Computing Techniques (ICICT), pp. 539-545

Communication and Computing Systems – Prasad et al. (eds)
© 2019 Taylor & Francis Group, London, ISBN 978-0-367-00147-6

Identification of the forged images using image forensic tools

A. Parveen & Z.H. Khan

Department of Applied Sciences and Humanities, Jamia Millia Islamia (A Central University), New Delhi, India

S.N. Ahmad

Department of Electronics and Communication Engineering, Jamia Millia Islamia (A Central University), New Delhi, India

ABSTRACT: The contents of the digital images can be easily manipulated with image editing software like Adobe Photoshop, Pixelmator, Inkscape, Fireworks, etc. In real life applications, it is indispensable to check the authenticity of the digital images because forged images could deliver misleading information and messages to our community. Different tools have been developed to detect the forged images. In literature, there is no study which presents an insight into image forensic tools and their evaluation on the basis of different criteria. Therefore, to address this issue, we present an insight into digital image forensic tools; and evaluate it on the basis of 15 different parameters like *"error level analysis"*, *"metadata analysis"*, *"JPEG luminance and chrominance data"*, etc. For our experimental work, we choose *"FotoForensics"* tool to show the forged region in digital images; and JPEGsnoop tool has been used to extract the metadata of the images.

1 INTRODUCTION

In today's digital era, *"Seeing Is No Longer Believing"* because it is easier to tamper digital images due to the image editing software like Adobe Photoshop, Pixelmator, Inkscape, Fireworks, etc. (Farid, 2009). Fake or forged images could spark flare-up of violence. Therefore, it is important for those people who are addicted to the social media to check the authenticity of digital pictures or news before sharing it on their wall or friend lists. In literature, different tools have been developed to detect the forged images like *"FotoForensics"*, *"JPEGsnoop"*, *"Ghiro"*, and *"Forensically"*, etc. Apart from these tools, different algorithms have also been developed to check the authenticity of the digital images based on active and passive methods (Parveen et al, 2018). Active methods include *"digital signature"* and *"digital watermarking"* in which prior information about the signature or watermark is necessary to detect the forged images. Most of the images captured today do not contain any signature and watermark. Therefore, researchers started to work in the area of passive methods where prior information about the images is not necessary to check the authenticity of the digital images (Mahdian et al. 2010; Fridrich et al. 2003; Christlein et al.2012; Hu et al. 2011).

On social media, people are posting images of their *"functions"*, *"vacations"*, *"social events"*, and *"graduation ceremonies"*; and from those photographs it is difficult to spot altered photos from the real photos. Image forensics expert have tools to identify the fake or hoax images. Hany Farid, *"a mathematician and digital forensics experts"* suggested different ways to check the authenticity of the images when it pops up on Twitter or Facebook. If an image has been re circulated from another website then it can be discovered by *"Reverse Image Search"* (RIS), using Google Images or TinEye. In real life, we have seen that *"whenever there is a natural disaster, people circulate the same silly images of sharks swimming down the street"*. This type of images can be checked from RIS process. Burrowing into image data can be used to detect the forged image quickly. There are different websites where you can upload your photos and it will strip out the metadata of your images. This metadata includes the *"make of the camera"*, *"time of the day the photo was snapped"* and *"GPS coordinates, if it was enabled"*. Keeping in view the user's privacy, anything uploaded on the Twitter or Facebook will have its metadata automatically stripped.

Parveen et al. (2018). performed a *"systematic literature review (SLR) in the area of digital image forensic"*. In their study, the focus was on the different methods which are used to detect the forged part in digital images rather than on the tools which are also used to get the quick information about the forged images. Therefore, it motivates us to work in the area of digital image forensic tools. Kaur *et al.*(2012) presented a method based on the photo forensic tool to detect the fake or hoax images using *"HxD"* hex editor. This editor generates the following information about the image: *"JPEG file interchange format"* (JFIF), camera specifications including make and model, quantization table values, and Huffman values. Carner (2011) discussed the different tools which are used to check the authenticity of the audio, video and images. Based on our review (Parveen et al, 2018), we identify that in literature there is no study which presents an insight into different photo forensic tools and evaluates these tools on the basis of different criteria. Therefore, in this paper, we focus on different photo forensic tools; and evaluate these tools based on 15 different criteria. For our experimental work, we choose *"FotoForensics"* tool to show the forged region in digital images because it is freely available online tool to perform the *"error level analysis"* (ELA); and *"JPEGsnoop"* tool has been used to extract the metadata of the images.

The remaining part of this paper is organized as follows: Section 2 presents an insight into different photo forensic tools. An evaluation of four different image forensic tools, i.e., *"FotoForensics"*, *"JPEGsnoop"*, *"Forensically"*, and *"Ghiro"*, is given in section 3. The experimental work is carried out in section 4. Finally, section 5 presents the conclusion and suggest for future research work.

2 AN INSIGHT INTO IMAGE FORENSIC TOOLS

In literature, we have identified different tools to detect the forged images; and a brief description about some of the popular forensic tools is given below:

2.1 *FotoForensics*

This tool is used to decode any type of forged pictures and manipulations. In this tool, error level analysis is used to identify the different compression levels in the image. Practically, JPEG images have same error level. If the image contains different error levels then it simply shows the digital modification in the image. FotoForensics works like a microscope which highlights those details of the image that the human eye may not be able to identify. Following features are used for the analysis of the digital images like error level analysis, metadata analysis, last save quality, and color adjustment, etc.

2.2 *JPEGsnoop*

To examine and decode the inner details of the images, JPEGsnoop tool is the best choice because it is free windows application. The JPEGsnoop tool was designed to expose those details from the images to decide whether the image has been forged or not. Using JPEGsnoop tool we can extract the following information of an image, i.e., quantization table matrix (chrominance and luminance), Chroma subsampling, estimates JPEG quality setting, JPEG resolution settings, Huffman tables, EXIF metadata, RGB histograms. In this paper, we have used JPEGsnoop tool for our experimental work because it is easy to understand and download it on our system.

2.3 Forensically

It is a free digital forensic tool which includes "*clone detection*", ELA, "*meta-data extraction*", etc. In this tool, the objective of the clone detection is to highlights the copied regions within an image. This feature is used as an indicator that the picture has been manipulated. Error level analysis compares original image to recompressed version. ELA is a forensic method which is used to determine whether the picture has been digitally modified or not. With ELA, we identify the portion of digital images with different level of compressions. ELA identifies the areas in an image which are at different compression levels. JPEG images have the same compression levels. If any portion of an image has different error level then it likely indicates that the image has been modified. ELA highlights differences in the JPEG compression rate. The noise analysis feature of this tool is used to identify manipulations in the image like airbrushing, deformations, etc. This tool works well on high quality images. In this tool, principal component analysis is used to identify certain manipulations and details in the images.

2.4 Ghiro

Ghiro is open source software for the digital image forensics. It has the following features that are used to show the authenticity of digital images, i.e., metadata extraction, GPS localization, MIME information, error level analysis, thumbnail extraction, signature engine, and hash matching. In Ghiro, content of a file is described by the "*multipurpose internet mail extensions*" (MIME). MIME is detected using magic number inside the image. Metadata is a special feature of the Ghiro which identify the following: name of the owner, copyright and contact information, what camera created the file, etc. This tool mainly extracts the EXIF metadata, "*International Press Telecommunication Council*" (IPTC) metadata, and "*Extensible Metadata Platform*" (XMP) metadata of an image. "*Exchangeable Image File Format*" (EXIF) metadata includes the standard EXIF tags, Canon MakerNote tags, Fujifilm MakerNote tags, Minolta MakerNote tags, Nikon MakerNote tags, Olympus MakerNote tags, Panasonic MakerNote tags, Pentax MakerNote tags, Samsung MakerNote tags, Sigma/Foveon MakerNote tags, and Sony MakerNote tags.

3 AN EVALUATON OF IMAGE FORENSIC TOOLS

In this section, we evaluate the four image forensic tools on the basis of the following criteria: (i) "*error level analysis*" (ELA), (ii) "*metadata analysis*" (MA), (iii) "*last save quality*" (LSQ), (iv) "*JPEG luminance and chrominance*" (JLC), (v) digest, (vi)"*file type extension*" (FTE), (vii) MIME type, (viii) "*image width and height*" (IWH), (ix) "*bits per sample*" (BPS), (x) "*color components*" (CC), (xi) "*cryptographic hash function*" (CHF), (xii) "*clone detection*" (CD), (xiii) "*principal component analysis*" (PCA), (xiv) "*noise analysis*" (NA), and (xv) GPS-Localization (GPS-L). Table 1 exhibits the results after evaluation of the four image forensic tools based on the above 15 criteria.

The objective of the evaluation of the image forensic tools is to find out that which criteria is mostly adopted by the tools in order to show the forged portion in the image. Based on our results, we find out that ELA is the key feature of the three image forensic tools, i.e., FotoForensics, Forensically, and Ghiro. MA is also the mostly supported feature in the FotoForensics, JPEGsnoop, and Ghiro tools, which includes the following: resolution of the image, camera make and model, etc. JLC is also the common criterion which captures the quantized luminance and chrominance data in the following tools: FotoForensics, JPEGsnoop, and Forensically. This data helps to find out the quality of the last save image. GPS-localization (GPS-L) is only supported by the Ghiro tool, see Table-1. GPS-L is "*embedded in the image metadata sometimes there is a geotag, a bit of GPS data providing the longitude and latitude of where the photo was taken, it is read and the position is displayed on a map*".

4 EXPERIMENTAL WORK

In this section, we check the authenticity of digital images using the following image forensics tools i.e., *"JPEGsnoop"* and *"FotoForensics"* tools.

4.1 *Results generated through JPEGsnoop tool*

JPEGsnoop tool is very useful for the metadata analysis as well as to generate the luminance and chrominance data of the quantization tables, see Table 1. We import the one of the testing images in JPEGsnoop tool to extract the EXIF data and the luminance and chrominance data of the quantization tables. The JPEG luminance and chrominance data are exhibited in Table 2 and Table 3, respectively. The snapshot of JPEGsnoop tool is exhibited in Figure 1.

Table 1. An evaluation of different image forensic tools.

Selected features	Tools			
	FotoForensics	JPEGsnoop	Forensically	Ghiro
ELA	√		√	√
MA	√	√		√
LSQ	√			
JLC	√	√	√	
Digest	√			
FTE/MIME type	√			√
IWH	√	√		
BPS	√	√		
CC	√	√		
CHF	√			√
CD			√	
PCA			√	
NA			√	
GPS-L				√

Table 2. $JPEG Q_0$: Luminance.

6	4	4	6	9	11	12	16
4	5	5	6	8	10	12	12
4	5	5	6	10	12	12	12
6	6	6	11	12	12	12	12
9	8	10	12	12	12	12	12
11	10	12	12	12	12	12	12
12	12	12	12	12	12	12	12
16	12	12	12	12	12	12	12

Table 3. $JPEG Q_1$: Chrominance.

7	7	13	24	20	20	17	17
7	12	16	14	14	12	12	12
13	16	14	14	12	12	12	12
24	14	14	12	12	12	12	12
20	14	12	12	12	12	12	12
20	12	12	12	12	12	12	12
17	12	12	12	12	12	12	12
17	12	12	12	12	12	12	12

4.2 *Results generated through FotoForensics tool*

In this section, we check the authenticity of six images that we have created for our experimental work. The FotoForensics tool shows the forged part in digital images by using ELA. Initially, we consider the Image-1, as shown in Figure 2, for our experimental work. When the Image-1 was loaded into the tool then as a result we identify that in some places the compression level of the objects were different, which clearly indicates that someone has tried to forge some part of the image, as shown in Figure 3. Similarly, we test the remaining images, i.e.,

Image-2, Image-3, Image-4, Image-5, and Image-6, as shown in Figure 4, Figure 6, Figure 8, Figure 10, and Figure 12, respectively. We call these images as the testing images. The results of Image-2 to Image-6 are given in Figure 5, Figure 7, Figure 9, Figure 11, and Figure 13, respectively. In this section, we also analyse the test images using JPEG %, which is an important feature of the *FotoForensics* tool. This feature shows the quality of the last saved images. After testing all the images using JPEG% feature of FotoForensics tool, we identify that all the images have the same quality value, i.e., *"JPEG last saved at 86% quality"*. This quality is determined from the quantization tables, as shown in Table 2 and Table 3. In our study, we find out that the results of Table 2 and Table 3 are same as the results produced by the *JPEGsnoop* Tool.

Figure 1.   A snapshot of JPEGsnoop tool.

Figure 2.   Image-1 for Testing.

Figure 4.   Image-2 for Testing.

Figure 3.   Output of Image-1.

Figure 5.   Output of Image-2.

Figure 6.   Image-3 for Testing.

Figure 10.   Image-5 for Testing.

Figure 7.   Output of Image-3.

Figure 11.   Output of Image-5.

Figure 8.   Image -4 for Testing.

Figure 12.   Image-6 for Testing.

Figure 9.   Output of Image-4.

Figure 13.   Output of Image-6.

5 CONCLUSIONS

This paper presents an insight into different image forensic tools to check the authenticity of the digital images. In our work, we select the four image forensic tools like (a) FotoForensics, (b) JPEGsnoop, (c) Forensically, and (d) Ghiro. We evaluate these tools on the basis of following fifteen different criteria: (i) *"error level analysis"* (ELA), (ii) *"metadata analysis"* (MA), (iii) *"last save quality"* (LSQ), (iv) *"JPEG luminance and chrominance"* (JLC), (v) digest, (vi)*"file type extension"* (FTE), (vii) MIME type, (viii) *"image width and height"* (IWH), (ix) *"bits per sample"* (BPS), (x) *"color components"* (CC), (xi) *"cryptographic hash function"* (CHF), (xii) *"clone detection"* (CD), (xiii) *"principal component analysis"* (PCA), (xiv) *"noise analysis"* (NA), and (xv) GPS-Localization (GPS-L), etc. Among these criteria, we identify that ELA, MA, and JLC are the common features which are present in the image forensic tools. On the basis of our analysis we identify that FotoForensics tool detect the forged part in digital images using ELA; and it also generates the quantized tables that were employed to change the images. In future, we shall extend the systematic literature review (SLR) of digital image forgery methods by considering the digital image forensic tools. We shall also propose some algorithms to detect the forged images based on the knowledge of the quantization tables.

REFERENCES

Carner, D. 2011. Detect and Prevent File Tampering in Multimedia Files. Weblink: *http://forensicprotection. com/Detecting_and_preventing_file_tampering.pdf*.

Christlein, V., Riess, C. Jordan, J., Riess, C., & Angelopoulou, E. 2012. An evaluation of popular copy-move forgery detection approaches. IEEE Transactions on Information Forensics and Security, 7 (6), 1841-1854.

Farid, H. 2009. Seeing is not believing. IEEE Spectrum, 44-51

Fridrich, J., Soukal, D. & Lukas, J. 2003. Detection of copy-move forgery in digital images. Digital Image Forensic Workshop, 1-10.

Hu, J., Zhang, H., Gao, Q. & Huang, H. 2011. An improved lexicographical sort algorithm of copy-move forgery detection. IEEE 2nd International Conference on Networking and Distributed Computing, 23-27.

Kaur, B., Blow, M. & Zhan. J. 2012. Authenticity of Digital Images in Social Media. Cyber Security Research and Education Institute, The University of Texas at Dallas, USA. Web link: *csi.utdallas.edu/ events/NSF/papers/paper03.pdf*

Mahdian, B. & Saic, S. 2010. A bibliography on blind methods for identifying image forgery. Signal Processing: Image Communication, 25(6), 389-399.

Parveen, A., Khan, Z. H. & Ahmad. S. N. 2018. Pixel Based Copy-Move Image Forgery Detection Techniques: A Systematic Literature Review. In 5th IEEE International Conference on Computing for Sustainable Global Development, 663-668.

KNN classification using multi-core architecture for intrusion detection system

B.S. Sharmila & Rohini Nagapadma
The National Institute of Engineering, Mysuru, Karnataka, India

ABSTRACT: Network security is important aspect in today's world, as number for internet users are increasing rapidly. Security for these devices could be provided by software tool Intrusion Detection System (IDS) which monitors and analyze the network traffic. There are different machine learning approaches to design IDS which varies with accuracy, execution time and false alarm rate. This paper presents multi-core architecture on K-Nearest Neighbor (KNN) algorithms using python language. The experiments of the IDS are performed with KDD99 dataset. Evaluation results show that computational time decreased with exploitation of multicore architecture. So, this approach can be implemented for resource constrained Internet of Things.

1 INTRODUCTION

A large number of devices connecting to the internet increasing significantly, makes hackers to exploit the computer resources. The exploitation occurs in various forms like privacy violation, altering, attempt for unauthorized access, destroying target devices etc., which can be further utilized as a resource or platform for attacks (Aggarwal, Preeti et al.,2015). To monitor and detect vulnerabilities or malicious activities in the network, IDS implemented. This IDS works on the basis of pattern recognition by comparing the network traffic with known attack patterns.

In order to create a pattern of attacks for IDS, it is necessary to have a dataset having signatures of attacks and normal network traffic. Most of the researchers use Knowledge Discovery and Data Mining - KDD99 dataset, for signature based IDS (KDD99CUP Dataset). There are different machine learning approaches for analyzing the huge network traffic, a simple and efficient algorithms is KNN classification. But KNN is lazy learner technique, as it consumes more computational time (Chaurasia S et al.2014) . So, our paper focuses on implementing a fast and efficient IDS using multi-core architecture for KNN classification algorithm to reduce computational time.

2 KDDCUP'99

The KDD99 dataset is most widely used dataset for Intrusion Detection System (KDD99CUP Dataset). This huge dataset is collected using tcpdump packet analyzer capable of capturing TCP/IP and other packets transmitted over a network. This data was built by stolfo et al. (Kumar Vipin et al.2013) in 1998 DARPA for Intrusion Detection System. The simulation was conducted for about five million connection records. This Dataset is comprised of 4 gigabytes of binary tcpdump data of seven week network traffic having 41 features and is labeled as either normal or specific attack name System (KDD99CUP Dataset). These attacks mentioned in dataset falls under following four categories:

1) Denial of service Attack (DoS): is an attack in which attackers flood the target with traffic which leads to consumption of huge system resources and finally may end up with crash. The victims of these types of attack are mainly high-profile organization such as banking, commerce and media.

2) User to Root Attack (U2R): is an attack in which attacker's first request for normal user account and later acquire the super user privileges which leads to vulnerabilities.
3) Remote to Local Attack (R2L): here the attackers find the vulnerable point in system or network security through remote access to access the machine, which may leads to steal the confidential data illegally and introduce viruses or malicious software to damage the target machine.
4) Probing Attack: is an attack where the hackers scans the system or network device in order to determine the weakness or vulnerabilities that may later be exploited so as to compromise the system.

It should be noted that KDD99 dataset is represented by 41 features, each of which is in one of continuous, discrete and symbolic form. Table I shows the major attacks in both training and testing dataset (Chen, Weiwei, et al.2017).

Table 1. Attacks in KDD-Dataset.

Attack Group	Attack Types
DOS	Back, Land, Neptune, Pod, Smurf, Teardrop, Mailbomb, Processtable, Udpstorm, Apache2, Worm.
Probe	Satan, IPsweep, Nmap, Portsweep, Mscan, Saint.
R2L	Guess_password, Ftp_write, Imap,Phf, Multihop, Warezmaster, Xlock, Xsnoop, Snmpguess, Snmpgetattack, Httptunnel, Sendmail, Named.
U2R	Buffer_overflow, Loadmodule, Rootkit, Perl, Sqlattack, Xterm, Ps.

3   EXISTING WORK

Many machine learning algorithms are proposed by different authors for IDS, which focused mainly on accuracy. According to (Borkar, Amol et al. 2017), different techniques can be used for detection of vulnerabilities based on accuracy, false rate and time consumption. The work in (Pamukov, Marin E. et al. 2017) shows that detection errors can be decreased by approach of negative selection algorithm and the co-simulation principles of immunology, but this approach is not suitable for real time application as it needs huge space for self and non-sets. New Ensemble Clustering (NEC) model combines both classical and unsupervised anomaly detection technique and is suitable for real system (Chen, Weiwei, et al.2017). As proposed (Sreekesh, Manasa. 2016) two phases based architecture were implemented which used KNN for first phase and Reinforcement technique for second phase for decreasing false alarm rate. (Shweta Taneja et al. 2014) proposed enhanced KNN algorithm focused only on one instance of network traffic. Aiman Moldagulova and Rosnafisah Bte. Suleiman (Moldagulova, Aiman et al. 2017) proposed KNN classification algorithm for signature based detection. (Zhou, Lijuan, et al. 2010) Stated that using clustering based KNN algorithm for IDS, computational time and accuracy were increased significantly but only for huge number of dataset. (Rao, B. et al.2017) Proposed a fast KNN classifier for reducing computing time by reordering the features into vector form and achieved 99.6% of accuracy between classical and normal approach. According to [12] Multicore architecture can be used by importing library called OpenMP and PyMp-PyPi in python language. So, our research is to utilize the multicore for KNN classification to decrease computational time for pattern recognition and attack detection for IDS.

4 BLOCK DIAGRAM OF THE SYSTEM

Our proposed scheme for Intrusion Detection System broadly divided into four blocks to predict whether a set of network traffic is normal or attack, shown in Figure 1. The KDD99 dataset is parsed using library numpy and Data science in python.

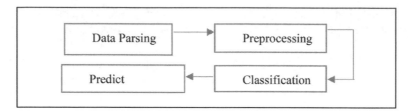

Figure 1. Block Diagram of IDS.

4.1 Pre-processing

KDD99 dataset has a raw network traffic cannot be used directly for IDS without preprocessing technique. Preprocessing has mainly two steps: First need to map 41 feature names for network traffic like duration, flag, services protocol etc. Second step is to convert non-numerical values to numerical values. In dataset attack names, services, flag and protocol are mentioned in non-numerical form. So, Services are mapped between 0-65 integer values as it has 66 categories, then flag has 11 categories mapped from 0 to 11 integer values, protocol are mapped into 3 values that is 0 for icmp, 1 for tcp and 2 for udp and finally 37 attacks names are broadly classified into 4 categories shown in Table I, then these attack groups along with normal group of traffic converted to integers, namely 0 for normal, 1 for DOS, 2 for Probe, 3 for R2L and 4 for U2R, then

4.2 KNN classification using multi-core architecture

The KDD99 dataset is first filtered by removing duplicated network traffic and then randomly selected 20% of its dataset approximately 25,000 is extracted for our work. The proposed scheme for multi-core architecture for KNN is shown in Figure 2. KNN is computed for k value 1, 3, 5, 10, 20, 50 and 100. The procedure of KNN algorithm using multi core architecture is shown in following steps.

Step 1: Load the training dataset.
Step 2: Select K value.
Step 3: Based on number of cores divide the dataset equally among all the cores.
Step 4: Create the shared array among all the cores to find the overall accuracy.
Step 5: Compute the distance between test and training dataset, iterate from 1 to total number of training dataset using Euclidean distance function. The standard Euclidean distance function is defined as

$$d(\mathbf{p}, \mathbf{q}) = d(\mathbf{q}, \mathbf{p}) = \sqrt{(q_1 - p_1)^2 + (q_2 - p_2)^2 + \cdots + (q_n - p_n)^2}$$
$$= \sqrt{\sum_{i=1}^{n} (q_i - p_i)^2}. \tag{1}$$

where,
d(p,q) - distance between two points p and q

Step 6: Sort the distance in ascending order
Step 7: Select first k value.
Step 8: Apply majority to predict the class.

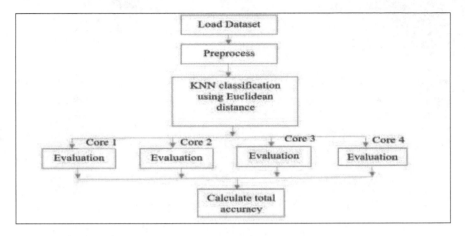

Figure 2.   Block diagram of KNN classification using 4 cores.

4.3   *Evaluation*

For calculating the accuracy of KNN classification, KDD dataset is divided into training and testing dataset in the ratio of 70% and 30% respectively. Figure 3 shows the python code in anaconda for accuracy calculation. The pattern of the attacks are extracted from training dataset and tested for each testing dataset iteratively, with complete training dataset.

In order to evaluate the efficiency, experiment is carried for both single and multicore architecture. KNN performed efficiently by utilizing less time with multicore architecture as shown in Figure 4.

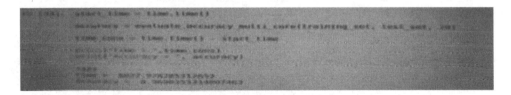

Figure 3.   Evaluation of KNN classification.

Figure 4.   Comparison of single and multi-core architecture.

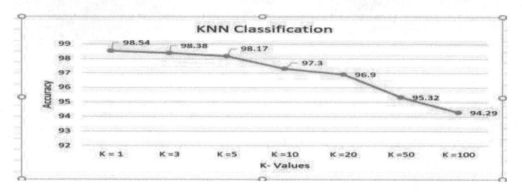

Figure 5.   Comparison of KNN classification using different k-values.

4.4   *Comparison*

The KNN classification is performed with K values 1, 3, 5, 10, 20, 50 and 100 on multi core architecture. Figure 5 shows the comparison of accuracy for different k values. Here it is observed that for k=1, KNN classification has highest accuracy compared to other k values.

5   CONCLUSION

In this paper, a KNN classification using python language and multi-core architecture is implemented. The algorithm presented in this paper reduces the time for pattern recognition and detection by exploiting all the cores available in CPU. Hence this approach can be used for resource constrained devices. The evaluation result suggested that detection rate decreases with increase in k value.

6   FUTURE WORK

The approach of parallel computing using multiple cores will be tested for other machine learning algorithms and also for real time network traffic in our future work.

REFERENCES

Aggarwal, Preeti, & Sudhir, Kumar, Sharma. 2015. "Analysis of KDD dataset attributes-class wise for intrusion detection." Procedia Computer Science 57: 842-851.
Anton, Howard (1994), Elementary Linear Algebra (7th ed.), John Wiley & Sons, pp. 170–171, ISBN 978-0-471-58742-2
Borkar, Amol, Akshay Donode, and Anjali Kumari. (2017) "A survey on Intrusion Detection System (IDS) and Internal Intrusion Detection and protection system (IIDPS)." Inventive Computing and Informatics (ICICI), International Conference on. IEEE.
Chaurasia S & Jain A. (2014) Ensemble neural network and k-NN classifiers for intrusion detection. International Journal of Computer Science and Information Technology 5:2481−2485.
Chen, Weiwei, et al. (2017) "A Novel Unsupervised Anomaly Detection Approach for Intrusion Detection System." Big Data Security on Cloud (BigDataSecurity), IEEE International Conference on High Performance and Smart Computing (HPSC), and IEEE International Conference on Intelligent Data and Security (IDS), 2017 IEEE 3rd International Conference on. IEEE.
KDD99CUP Dataset, http://kdd.ics.uci.edu/databases/kddcup99/kddcup99.html
Kumar Vipin, Himadri Chauhan, & Dheeraj Panwar. (2013) "K-means clustering approach to analyze NSL-KDD intrusion detection dataset." International Journal of Soft Computing and Engineering (IJSCE) (2013).

Moldagulova, Aiman, and Rosnafisah Bte Sulaiman. "Using KNN algorithm for classification of textual documents." Information Technology (ICIT), 2017 8th International Conference on. IEEE, 2017.

Pamukov, Marin E., and Vladimir K. Poulkov. (2017) "Multiple negative selection algorithm: Improving detection error rates in IoT intrusion detection systems." Intelligent Data Acquisition and Advanced Computing Systems: Technology and Applications (IDAACS), 2017 9th IEEE International Conference on. Vol. 1. IEEE.

Rao, B.Basaveswara, and K. Swathi. (2017) "Fast kNN Classifiers for Network Intrusion Detection System." Indian Journal of Science and Technology 10.14.

Sreekesh, Manasa. (2016) "A two-tier network based intrusion detection system architecture using machine learning approach." Electrical, Electronics, and Optimization Techniques (ICEEOT), International Conference on. IEEE.

Sharmila, B. S., and Narasimha Kaulgud. (2017) "Comparison of time complexity in median filtering on multi-core architecture." Advances in Computing, Communication & Automation (ICACCA)(Fall), 2017 3rd International Conference on. IEEE.

Taneja, Shweta, et al. (2014) "An enhanced k-nearest neighbor algorithm using information gain and clustering." Advanced Computing & Communication Technologies (ACCT), 2014 Fourth International Conference on. IEEE

Zhou, Lijuan, et al. (2010) "A clustering-Based KNN improved algorithm CLKNN for text classification." Informatics in Control, Automation and Robotics (CAR), 2010 2nd International Asia Conference on. Vol. 3. IEEE.

Communication and Computing Systems – Prasad et al. (eds)
© 2019 Taylor & Francis Group, London, ISBN 978-0-367-00147-6

Creating 3D facial model from a 2D facial image

Shibam Mukherjee & Deepali Kamthania
Vivekananda School of Information Technology, Delhi, India

ABSTRACT: 3D face reconstruction from a single image is a challenging problem, with wide range of applications. In this paper an attempt has been made to propose a novel technique to create 3D facial model from a 2D facial image without using expensive hardware like infrared sensors for its implementation. The proposed technique does not involve complicated image manipulation or mathematical calculations. The real time model has been created using very simple image processing technique considering precise facial mapping and depth prediction algorithm based on the light intensity variance in an image. The model can be used as an independent facial mapping tool which can be further developed into a facial recognition system.

1 INTRODUCTION

"3D face reconstruction is a fundamental computer vision problem of extraordinary difficult". Most of the recognition systems are based on single (Cohen et al 2016) or several (Bartlett M.S et al 2005,Zafeiriou S et al 2008) static 2D images which require consistent facial pose, even slight change in pose effects the system performance. To address this issue there is need for 3D or infrared image capture methods for better accuracy of system. In the past few years several methods using 3D facial geometry data for facial expression recognition have been proposed (Soyel H. et al. 2008, Yin L et al 2006). To match every angle of human face photo from different angles are considered for study by applying 3D models into neural networks(JacksonA. S et al 2017,Saito S et al 2016). AI systems can be used for extrapolation of face shape from single photo . A fully automated algorithm for facial feature extraction and 3D face modeling from a pair of orthogonal frontalsis developed from calibrated cameras(Ansari A 2005).A 3D face modeling system that generates result in 2-3 minutes has been developed by aggregating, customizing, and optimizing a bunch of individual computer vision algorithms (Park I et al 2005).A coarse-to-fine method has been developed to reconstruct a high-quality 3D face model from a single image using a bilinear face model and local corrective deformation fields (Jiang L et al 2018). A framework considering RGB video of human face in neutral expression has been proposed by applying transformation to non-observed expression which tackles 2D problem of change of expression and physical features of face (Rotger G et al .2017)

The algorithms discussed in the existing work are quite complicated in terms of techniques used and the background processing involved. Moreover, existing techniques heavily rely on databases and pre-processed accurate datasets for development of neural network models. To address the above problems, a very simple yet effective technique has been proposed to create a 3D facial model from a 2D frontal face picture using precise facial mapping and depth prediction algorithm based on the light intensity variance in an image. The proposed technique provides almost equal accuracy by using simple image manipulation algorithms. It makes the entire process very user friendly and easily understandable to the majority of the users because of its simplistic algorithm approach. It can be run very efficiently on low powered single board computers chips like Raspberry Pi.

2 PROPOSED TECHNIQUE

For creation of 3D facial model, traditionally infrared sensors have been used which are quite expensive to implement but now they are being are replaced by cameras with software implementation. In our approach simple image processing techniques like gradient, edge detection, shape finding, thresholding etc.have been used for precise facial mapping and depth calculation based on light intensity variance in an image. Divide and conquer technique has been implemented to achieve the desired goal. The entire facial region of the image has been divided into smaller sub regions. All these sub regions process their section independent of each other. Thus, if one sub region fails to produce an output it would not affect the others. All the sub regions of the image adjust dynamically according to the variable lighting conditions. After completion of the analysis, all the data from the sub regions are integrated .In bright or medium light condition regular cameras works perfectly. But in low or no light condition the camera sensor fails to capture the light. This problem can be easily solved by removing the infrared filter that comes fitted with the lens in all the cameras. Then a single infrared LED light can be used to illuminate the facial region at a close distance. The IR LED light can be mounted on the camera or can be operated from a separate source. For larger distances, bigger infrared panels can be used.

3 IMPLEMENTATION

The model has been built on Python using libraries like OpenCVfor image processing, Math for calculating values of different variable required in image processing and Numpy for faster processing of image data stored in array format. The entire process has been achieved in multiple steps starting from extracting the facial ROI(Region of Image) from the entire image using Haar Cascades. After this the entire process is divided into sub-processes, with each sub-process handling different region of face. The sub division ensures that if one process fails to detect a region, the entire system will still work. More than 60 nodal points are being used to get a precise facial mapping of the different sub regions of the face like nose, eye, eyebrows, lips, face edges, chin etc. These sub regions are further divided into smaller regions like eye is divided into eyeballs, iris and eyebrows. Each of these regions is pinpointed precisely for perfect facial mapping.

3.1 *Pseudo code*

3.1.1 *Main function*
1) Switch on Video Capture
2) While (True)
    i. Start capturing frames from the video
    ii. Resize captured frame and convert RGBto Grey
    iii. While (Faces with preferable dimensions in the image exist)

        a) Cropthe ROI of the face and resize to standard size and ratio
        b) Crop out ROI of eye, nose and mouth from the face ROI according to the "Golden Ratio"
        c) Call Function Mouth, Eye and Nose with ROI mouth, eye and nose passed respectively
        d) Results displayed after calculation

    iv. If "q" pressed, break

3) Stop Video Capture

3.1.2 *Mouth calculation*
1) Perform required image processing operation on the ROI mouth

2) Calculate coordinates slope of the lines generated from processed image
3) If (The line fits under the required slope)
    Calculate local and aggregated mean y
4) Generate line at the calculated points

3.1.3 *Eye calculation*
1) Detect all circles on ROI right and left eye separately
2) Select the largest circle and calculate the more precise ROI eye
3) Pass the coordinates to eye mapping function
4) Perform required image processing on right and left eyeball ROI
5) Select the calculated area thus achieving the precise eyeball detection of left and right eye
6) Set default pre-determined threshold and coordinate values of right and left eyebrow
7) Select the eyebrow ROI of left and right eye
8) Dynamically calculate the required color threshold as per pre-determined threshold percentage
9) Perform threshold operation and the necessary image processing on the ROI eyebrow
10) Adjust the default pre-determined eyebrow points according to the new generated image
11) Generate the precise eyebrow points for both the eyes
12) Dynamically adjustment of threshold percentage for next cycle as per environment requirement

3.1.4 *Nose calculation*
1) Take default pre-determined threshold value
2) Dynamically calculate the other required threshold values for the image
3) Calculate the estimated region of the bridge of the nose according to the dynamically calculated threshold
4) Select the required region according to the bridge and divide the image into 2 sections left and right
5) Perform edge detection on the selected nose region and calculate the "Alar-sidewall"
6) Draw the required points for "Alar-sidewalls"
7) Adjust the threshold for the next frame according to the environment conditions

3.1.5 *Precise face mapping*
1) Divide the face into 2 halves and set default pre-determined coordinates for both sides
2) Perform edge detection and for each assumed coordinate
    i. Select local area of the coordinate
    ii. Calculate the nearest edge point

3) Set the new calculated coordinates in the pre-determined coordinates
4) Connect the calculated points
5) Crop the precise face along with the calculated points and pass to Depth calculator function

3.1.6 *Depth calculation*
1) Set default pre-determined threshold value
2) Based on the light intensity on the face generate threshold map for each intensity segment
3) Calculate the difference between the current and the previous intensity segment frame
4) Save the difference on a 3D array
5) If (Last intensity segment reached)

Plot the 3D array on a graph and display the graph

4 EXPERIMENT RESULTS AND DISCUSSIONS

The 3D facial modelling system has generated good results and every part of the face is modelled withreasonable precession under varying lighting conditions.

Figure 2 shows face edge detection and precise face cropping for further processing.

Figure 3 shows lip detection for measuring the ratio with other parts of the face and Figure 4 shows precise Measurement of length, width and slope of the nose.

Figure 5 shows precise detection of the iris to obtain the iris color and to measure the ratio of distance with other facial parts. Eyebrow measurement has been obtained with multiple nodal points to get the curve of each eyebrow separately and accurately.

Figure 6 shows approximate depth prediction map after measuring the lights at different regions. Where '1' is the highest point and any additional white pixel in the next frame represents a lower point in the 3D space. Thus, we started from the nose "highest point", followed by cheeks and forehead and ended all the way up to the eyes "lowest point".

Figure 7 shows view of the 3D face model from different angles on X-Y-Z plot graph. The depiction is in a form of heat map. Shades of Blue represents the higher points, Red represents deeper points.

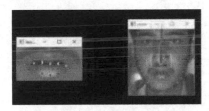

Figure 1.   Early stage development image.

Figure 3.   Lip detection.

Figure 2.   Face edge detection and cropping.

Figure 4.   Nose dimension measurement.

Figure 5.   Iris detection.

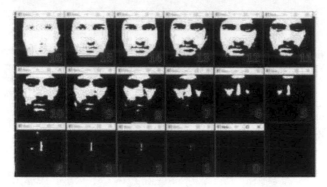

Figure 6.   Depth prediction map.

Figure 7.   3D face model.

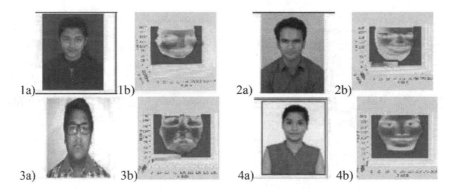

Figure 8.   Sample example (a) Actual photo (b) 3D model generated.

Figure 8 represents a small sample taken from the larger example set on which the algorithm was tested. The Red color represents the absolute background. Darker shades of blue represent higher point on the height map. The 3D models have been deliberately given a slight side tilt to illustrate the 3rd dimension.

5 CONCLUSIONS

The proposed technique has a great potential to replace the much complicated existing methods with simple algorithm which is easy to understand and at the same time independent of any database or IR sensors requirement for model development. The generation of 3D facial model in such a simple way can be revolutionary in many fields. With proposed approach authentication based on facial recognition will be more secure and precise as a new dimension - depth has been taken into consideration. Making real-time facial models from facial images will be very easy and save a huge amount of development time in many industries. Currently this is available only on PC for Linux and Windows in near future it can be extended to android mobile phones.

REFERENCES

Ansari A, Mottaleb M.A. 2005. Automatic facial feature extraction and 3D face modeling using two orthogonal views with application to 3D face recognition, Pattern Recognition 38: 2549–2563

Bartlett M.S., Littlewort G., Frank M., Lainscsek C., Fasel I., and Movellan J. 2005. Recognizing facial expression: machine learning and application to spontaneous behavior. In Computer Vision and Pattern Recognition, 2005 . CVPR 2005. IEEE Computer Society Conference on, 2: 568–573.

Cohen I., Sebe, N., Garg A., Chen L.S., and Huang T.S. 2003. Facial expression recognition from video sequences: Temporal and static modeling. Computer Vision and Image Understanding, 91(1-2):160–187.

JacksonA. S., Bulat A., Argyriou V.and Tzimiropoulos, G. 2017. Large pose 3dface reconstruction from a single image via direct volumetric CNN regression. 10.1109/ICCV.2017.117.

Jiang L., Zhang J., Deng B., Li H., and Liu L.2018.3D Face reconstruction with geometry details from a single image, arXiv:1702.05619v2 [cs.CV].

Park I., Zhang H., Vezhnevets V. 2005, Image-Based 3D Face Modeling System, EURASIP Journal on Applied Signal Processing 2005(13): 2072–2090

Rotger G., Lumbreras F., Moreno-Noguer F. and Agudo A., 2D-to-3D Facial expression transfer,www. iri.upc.edu/files/scidoc/2031-2D-to-3D-Facial-Expression-Transfer.pdf.

Savran A. and Sankur B. 2009. Automaticdetectionoffacialactionsfrom3D data. In Computer Vision Workshops (ICCV Workshops), IEEE 12th International Conference: 1993 –2000.

Soyel H. and Demirel H. 2008. 3d facial expression recognition with geometrically localized facial features. In Computer and Information Sciences, 2008. ISCIS'08. 23rd International Symposium: 1–4.

Saito S., Wei L., Liwen Hu, Koki Nagano and Hao Li. 2016.Photorealistic facial texture inference using deep neural networks: 5514–5153, University of Southern California. http://vgl.ict.usc.edu/Research/DeepNeuralNetwork/

Tang H. and Huang T.S. 2008. 3d facial expression recognition based on automatically selected features. In Computer Vision and Pattern Recognition Workshops, CVPRW'08; 1–8.

Tsalakanidou F. and Malassiotis S. 2010. Real-time 2d+ 3d facial action and expression recognition. Pattern Recognition, 43(5):1763 1775.

Wang J., Yin L., Wei X., and Sun Y. 2006. 3D facial expression recognition based on primitive surface feature distribution. In IEEE Computer Vision and Pattern Recognition, 2: 1399–1406.

Yin L., Wei X., Longo P., and Bhuvanesh A. 2006. Analyzing facial expressions using intensity-variant 3D data for human computer interaction. In Pattern Recognition, ICPR2006 18th International Conference, 1 1248–1251.

Zafeiriou S. and Pitas I. 2008. Discriminant graph structures for facial expression recognition. Multimedia, IEEE Transactions on, 10(8):1528–1540. https://arxiv.org/pdf/1612.00523https://www.theverge.com/2017/9/18/16327906/3d-model-face-photograph-ai-machine-learning.

Communication and Computing Systems – Prasad et al. (eds)
© *2019 Taylor & Francis Group, London, ISBN 978-0-367-00147-6*

A novel Zernike moment based approach for optical flow estimation

Shivangi Anthwal & Dinesh Ganotra

Department of Applied Science and Humanities, Indira Gandhi Delhi Technical University for Women, Delhi, India

ABSTRACT: Image motion analysis is typically accomplished by estimating optical flow vector for each pixel by matching their gray levels in consecutive frames of an image sequence. In this work, the gray level of each pixel is described by the content of its neighborhood using Zernike moments instead of intensity values, making the flow computation algorithm robust to non-uniform illumination and fluctuations in pixel intensity. To quantify the accuracy of the approach, endpoint error and angular error values have been computed for Middlebury benchmark dataset and the results have surpassed the results obtained by the popular Farneback method.

1 INTRODUCTION

Temporal changes in pixel gray level values recorded by an imaging sensor when coupled with certain assumptions may aid inferring the relative motion between the sensor and the environment. Optical flow field gives the distribution of two dimensional motion vectors at each image point in a temporally varying image sequence (Barron, J.L.et.Al.1994). Two consecutive images taken from a sequence from Middlebury Optical flow dataset (Baker, S. et Al.2011) are shown below in Figure 1(a and b) and the color coded flow field arising due to relative motion between scene and observer, computed using Farneback method (Farneback, G.2003) is illustrated in Figure 1(c). Figure 1(d) gives a visual representation of Middlebury color coding in which every point in space is represented by a color, with the vector orientation being encoded by color hue and vector magnitude by color saturation.

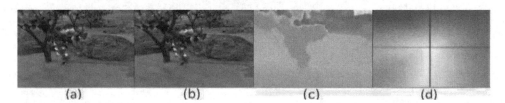

Figure 1. Optical flow and Middlebury color coding.

Beauchemin et al. (Beauchemin, SS.et al.1995) gave a comprehensive review of numerous classical techniques to compute optical flow. Differential methods estimate optical flow by computing spatial and temporal derivatives of image intensity values and are typically classified into techniques that require minimizing a local (Lucas, BD. Et al.1981) or a global (Horn, BKP et al.1981) function. Region based methods match features from two different frames by maximizing similarity measure or by minimizing distance metric to obtain the optical flow field.

Farneback G. (Farneback, G.2003) introduced a novel technique for two frame motion estimation that was based on polynomial expansion in an image. The neighbourhood of each pixel may be approximated by quadratic polynomial

$$f_1(\mathbf{x}) = \mathbf{x}^T \mathbf{A}_1 \mathbf{x} + \mathbf{b}_1^T \mathbf{x} + c_1 \tag{1}$$

Where, $\mathbf{A}_1$ is a symmetric matrix, $\mathbf{b}_1$ is a vector and c_1 is a scalar. (1) gives a local signal model. The coefficients may be estimated by applying the weighted least square approach by comparing with the neighborhood signal values. The new signal obtained after a global displacement $\mathbf{d}$ is given as:

$$f_2(\mathbf{x}) = \mathbf{x}^T \mathbf{A}_1 \mathbf{x} + (\mathbf{b}_1 - 2\mathbf{A}_1 \mathbf{d})^T \mathbf{d}^T \mathbf{A}_1 \mathbf{d} - \mathbf{b}_1^T \mathbf{d} + c_1 \tag{2}$$

$f_2(\mathbf{x})$ can be written in a form congruous with (1) as:

$$f_2(\mathbf{x}) = \mathbf{x}^T \mathbf{A}_2 \mathbf{x} + \mathbf{b}_2^T \mathbf{x} + c_2 \tag{3}$$

To obtain the value of $\mathbf{d}$, the coefficients of quadratic polynomials (2) and (3) shall be equated

$$\mathbf{b}_2 = \mathbf{b}_1 - 2\mathbf{A}_1 \mathbf{d} \; ; 2\mathbf{A}_1 \mathbf{d} = -(\mathbf{b}_2 - \mathbf{b}_1) \tag{4}$$

$$\mathbf{d} - -\frac{1}{2}\mathbf{A}_1^{-1}(\mathbf{b}_2 - \mathbf{b}_1) \tag{5}$$

2   ZERNIKE MOMENTS IN IMAGE PROCESSING

Image moment refers to the weighted average of the pixel intensities. They were first used in image description by Hu (Hu, M. K 1962), who proved that each irradiance function $I(x,y)$ has a one-to-one correspondence to a unique set of moments. Geometric moment of order p and repetition q can be defined as:

$$m_{p,q}(x, y) = \int_{-\infty}^{\infty} \int_{-\infty}^{\infty} x^p y^q I(x, y) dx dy \tag{6}$$

As per the uniqueness theorem, a unique set of moment values $m_{p,q}$ exists for the image function $I(x,y)$. Also $I(x,y)$ may be uniquely determined from $m_{p,q}$. Teague acknowledged orthogonal basis function set as a solution to information redundancy arising in geometric moments when used as basis function and proposed to use orthogonal Zernike polynomials as basis function. Zernike polynomials were first used by Fritz Zernike for describing optical aberrations. Lately, they have been used in image processing for applications such as shape recognition. Orthogonal property of Zernike moments is more suitable for such applications as unlike geometric moments, their invariants can be computed to high orders without the need to determine the low order invariants. Consequently, they are useful for image reconstruction. Rotational invariance of magnitudes of Zernike moments makes them valuable for the tasks such as classification of shapes that are not aligned. Zernike polynomial V_{nm} can be defined as:

$$V_{nm}(\rho, \theta) = R_{n,m} \exp(jm\theta) \tag{7}$$

Where, n is a positive integer and m is an integer such that |m| <=n and (n-|m|)/2=0. The polynomial is split into the real part $R_{n,m}$ and the imaginary part $\exp(jm\theta)$. The radial polynomial $R_{n,m}$ is defined as:

$$R_{n,m} = \sum_{s=0}^{(n-|m|)/2} (-1)^s \cdot \frac{(n-s)!}{s!\left(\frac{n+|m|}{2}-s\right)!\left(\frac{n-|m|}{2}-s\right)!} \rho^{n-2s} \tag{8}$$

When only positive Zernike polynomials are to be computed, then

$$R_{n,-m}(\rho) = R_{n,m}(\rho) \tag{9}$$

For Zernike polynomials V_{nm} and V_{pq}, orthogonal behaviour can be expressed as:

$$\iint [V_{nm}(x,y)] * V_{p,q}(x,y)dxdy = \frac{\pi}{n+1}\delta_{np}\delta_{mq} \tag{10}$$

Zernike moments as discussed above, may be employed for image reconstruction purposes. Zernike moment of order n and repetition m is defined as:

$$A_{nm} = \frac{n+1}{\pi}\sum_x\sum_y I(x,y)V_{nm}^*(\rho,\theta) \tag{11}$$

3 METHODOLOGY

Variational approaches have been prevalent for the task of optical flow computation since the seminal work of Horn and Schunck (Horn, BKP et al 1981). Brightness constancy equation is given by (12),

$$I(x,y,t) = I(x+u, y+v, t+1) \tag{12}$$

Using Taylor series expansion, optical flow equation (13) may be obtained

$$I_x u + I_y v + I_t = 0 \tag{13}$$

Where I_x, I_y and I_t are first order derivatives of intensity function w.r.t coordinates x, y and time t. This equation is commonly employed for computing the optical flow vector field from sequence of images. However, it does not provide sufficient constraints required to fully determine the flow and hence additional assumptions are needed to be introduced. Advancements by modifying either the data term or the smoothness term have been suggested to handle the challenges such as occlusions and discontinuities. (Brox et Al. 2004) found empirically the gradient constancy constraint more robust to illumination variations and employed it along with the brightness constancy in their variational framework.

$$\nabla I(x,y,t) = \nabla I(x+u, y+v, t+1) \tag{14}$$

On expansion by Taylor series, the following equations may be obtained:

$$I_{xx}u + I_{xy}v + I_{xt} = 0 \; ; I_{yx}u + I_{yy}v + I_{yt} = 0 \tag{15}$$

This paper discusses an approach wherein, the gray level of each pixel is described by the content of its neighborhood using a combination of Zernike moments $(A_{4,4}, A_{6,0}, A_{6,4}, A_{8,4}, A_{8,8}, A_{12,12})$ instead of otherwise commonly used pixel intensity values, making the flow computation algorithm robust to non-uniform illumination and fluctuations in pixel intensity. Intensity values obtained from images reconstructed using Zernike moments (Figure 2) are substituted in the variational framework with data terms computed using (13) and (15)

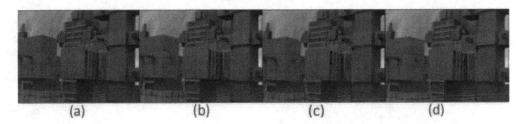

Figure 2. (a) and (c) are original frames from Middlebury dataset and (b) and (d) reconstructed from Zernike moments.

To obtain regularizer term, square of the magnitude of optical flow gradient (16) shall be minimized. It penalizes high variations in u and v to obtain smooth fields. u and v represent flow in horizontal and vertical directions and u_x, v_x, u_y, v_y the gradients in horizontal x direction and vertical y direction.

$$u_x^2 + u_y^2 + v_x^2 + v_y^2 \qquad (16)$$

The absence of a sensor to measure ground truth optical flow in real scenes containing natural motion has given rise to synthetic datasets allowing control over different aspects such as illumination, motion blur and other factors such as intensity fluctuations. Middlebury optical flow benchmark containing complex albeit small non-rigid motions has been widely examined to gauge the performance of several flow determination algorithms. It has also persuaded researchers for improvement in precision of their algorithms.

To find the error between ground truth and resultant flow field, performance measures used in (Baker S et al 2011) Endpoint Error (EE) and Angular Error (AE) are employed. EE is a measure of the absolute difference between the magnitudes of ground truth flow and resultant optical flow field. A low value of EE implies their magnitudes are comparable.

$$EE = \sqrt{(u - u_{GT})^2 + (v - v_{GT})^2} \qquad (17)$$

Barron et al. [Barron, J.L.et Al.1994)] found AE to be a convenient error measure capable of handling all types of velocities without the amplification in the relative measure of velocity vector differences. AE between the flow vector (u,v) and the ground truth flow (u_{GT}, v_{GT}) is the angle in 3D space between (u,v,1.0) and $(u_{GT}, v_{GT}, 1.0)$. A low AE would signify that the resultant optical flow's direction is well matched with the direction of ground truth flow.

$$AE = \cos^{-1}\left(\frac{(1.0 + u \times u_{GT} + v \times v_{GT})}{\sqrt{1.0 + u^2 + v^2}\sqrt{1.0 + u_{GT}^2 + v_{GT}^2}}\right) \qquad (18)$$

4 RESULT

Table 1 shows the comparison between the angular values obtained by Farneback method and the method proposed when tested on the Middlebury dataset. Table 2 shows the comparison between the endpoint error values obtained by Farneback method and the method proposed when tested on the Middlebury dataset.

Table 1. Comparison between the angular values obtained by Farneback method and AE proposed method.

Middlebury Sequence [2]	AE Farneback	AE Proposed method
Dimetrodon	5.158	7.0476
Grove2	5.238	5.1032
Grove3	11.388	8.6680
Hydrangea	8.005	7.3290
RubberWhale	9.758	7.0430
Urban2	9.642	4.2251
Urban3	18.695	7.0016
Venus	13.720	6.6891
Average	10.2005	6.638

Table 2. Comparison of EE of Farneback method and proposed method.

Middlebury Sequence [2]	EE Farneback	EE Proposed method
Dimetrodon	0.242	0.3105
Grove2	0.343	0.3683
Grove3	1.2416	0.8478
Hydrangea	0.599	0.4700
RubberWhale	0.298	0.2116
Urban2	4.056	0.5208
Urban3	2.174	0.8838
Venus	0.938	0.4429
Average	1.2364	0.5069

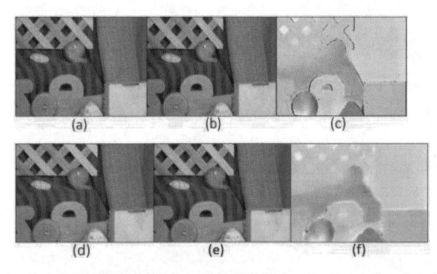

Figure 3. (a) and (b): original frames from RubberWhale sequence; (c) ground truth optical flow between them. (d) and (e): reconstructed frames from RubberWhale sequence; (f) optical flow obtained using proposed method.

Figure 3 shows sample result obtained when the method was tested on the RubberWhale sequence of the Middlebury dataset. The first three images show the actual coloured frames and the color coded optical flow field. The last three images show the gray frames obtained from Zernike moment based reconstruction and the color coded flow field obtained using the proposed method.

5 CONCLUSION

In optical flow computation, commonly employed brightness constancy assumption is found to be easily violated in environments with non-ideal visual conditions such as with intensity fluctuations. In this work, a method is presented that describes the gray level of each pixel by the content of its neighborhood using Zernike moments instead of otherwise commonly used pixel intensity values, making the flow computation algorithm robust to conditions such as non-uniform illumination. Images are reconstructed from six different Zernike moments and optical flow is estimated by using intensity conservation and intensity gradient conservation constraints in the reconstructed image sequences. To quantify the accuracy of the proposed method, performance measures AE and EE were computed for Middlebury test dataset and compared with the results obtained by Farneback method. With an average AE of 6.638 and average EE of 0.5069, the method has well outperformed Farneback method for optical flow.

REFERENCES

Anandan, P. A. 1989. Computational Framework and an Algorithm for the Measurement of Visual Motion Intl. Journal of Computer Vision 2(3):283-310.

Barron, J.L., Fleet, D.J. & Beauchemin, S.S. 1994. Performance of Optical Flow Techniques. Int'l Journal. of Computer Vision 12: 43-77.

Baker, S., Scharstein, D. & Lewis, J.P. et al.2011. A database and evaluation methodology for optical flow. International Journal of Computer Vision 92(1):1-31.

Beauchemin,SS & Barron JL 1995. The Computation of Optical Flow. ACM Computing Surveys. 27 (3):433-466.

Brox, T., Bruhn, A. & Papenberg, N. et al. 2004. High accuracy optical flow estimation based on a theory of warping. Proceedings of 8th European Conference on Computer Vision, Prague, Czech Republic Springer LNCS 3024, T. Pajdla and J. Matas (Eds.) 4: 25-36.

Farneback G. 2003. Two-frame motion estimation based on polynomial expansion. Proceedings of 13th Scandinavian Conference on Image Analysis; 2003 June 29-July 02; Halmstad, Sweden: Springer-Verlag: 363-370.

Horn, BKP & Schunck, BG 1981. Determining optical flow. Artificial Intelligence 17(1-3):185-203.

Hu, M. K. 1962. Visual pattern recognition by moment invariants. *IRE Transactions on Information Theory* 8(2):179-187.

Lucas, BD & Kanade,T. 1981. An iterative image registration technique with and application to stereo vision. Proceedings of 7th International Joint Conference on Artificial Intelligence. Vancouver, British Columbia, Morgan Kaufmann Publishers Inc.: 674-679.

Singh, A. 1990. An Estimation-Theoretic Framework for Image Flow Computation. Proceedings of Third International Conference on Computer Vision; 1990 Dec 04-07; Osaka, Japan: IEEE Explore; 2002.: 168-177.

Zernike, F. 1934. "Beugungstheorie des Schneidenverfahrens und Seiner Verbesserten Form, der Phasenkontrastmethode". Physica. 1 (8): 689–704.

Communication and Computing Systems – Prasad et al. (eds)
© 2019 Taylor & Francis Group, London, ISBN 978-0-367-00147-6

Epidemic spreading based word sense disambiguation of Hindi text

Goonjan Jain
Delhi Technological University, New Delhi, India

D.K. Lobiyal
Jawaharlal Nehru University, New Delhi, India

ABSTRACT: Word Sense Disambiguation (WSD) is an important problem of Natural Language Processing (NLP) with a motive to find the correct sense of a word in the text. We have proposed a novel approach to use epidemic spreading based model for WSD. Prior work used various graph-based centralities and quoted best results using degree centrality measure. Since, a degree does not provide us with any evident information for the conclusion of a sense. It is not a very good measure to be used. However, Expected Force computes the influence of each node on all other nodes of the network and thus has proved to be a better centrality measure. Experimental results back our claims. Expected Force gave better results than other centrality measures and thus added value to our approach.

1 INTRODUCTION

WSD is an NLP task focused on understanding the intended meaning of the ambiguous word. Solving the problem of WSD is crucial for efficient NLP tasks like Information retrieval, Question Answering. The better the WSD is, better will be results for other problems of Artificial Intelligence (AI).

Vearious approaches have been proposed in the literature. The approaches can be broadly categorized as supervised and unsupervised approaches. One of the methodologies that is picking up pace is graph based approaches. Reason being the development of various knowledge bases that have graphically structured information. One of the major advantages is that we do not need annotated corpora, thus makes such approaches useful for resource scarce languages like Hindi etc.

In this paper, we have proposed an unsupervised approach using Hindi WordNet as the knowledge base. We have added the epidemic spreading perspective to our approach. Details about epidemic spreading and the algorithm used is explained in below sections.

1.1 Epidemic spreading

Epidemic is the rapid spread of infectious disease to a large number of people in a given population in a short period of time. Various models have been proposed to understand the spread of epidemic and thus to understand the measures to be taken to control it. Compartmental models are one of the most prevalent techniques to simplify the mathematical modelling of infectious disease. In such models, population is segregated into different compartments, such that every person in a single compartment has same features. These models may help to predict the spread of disease, and to take measures to check it.

1.2 Types of compartment models

- *SIR model*

The basic model is *SIR (Susceptible–Infected-Recoverable) model*. The model divides the population into three compartments viz. number of people Susceptible, the number of Infectious people, and the number of people Recovered. This model has proved to be predictive for infectious disease that are communicable and where recovery make a person resistant to disease for a long time, e.g. measles.

Figure 1. Graphical depiction of SIR model.

- *SIS model*

SIS (Susceptible-Infected-Susceptible) model is used for those infections that are communicable but they do not ensure a long-time immunity after recovery. Hence, a person becomes susceptible to disease soon after its recovery. E.g. common cold, influenza and the like.

Figure 2. Graphical depiction of SIS model.

For task of Word Sense Disambiguation, we opted for the SIR model where all the nodes are either Susceptible, Infectious or Recovered. Initially, all the nodes are susceptible. As we traverse through the graph, the node become infectious when it is at an edge's distance from another infectious node. And once a node has been traversed, it becomes recovered. This recovered node has been traversed and thus cannot be infected or to say traversed again.

1.3 Node influence metrics

In graph theory, measures called *Node Influence Metrics* are used to quantify the influence of every node in the graph. Various applications have been noted in literature like influence of a person in a social network, role of different nodes in different networks, understanding the role of a node in disease spreading and curbing.

They are related to centrality measures but they extract different features of the graph. Centrality measures provides ranking and finds the most influential node. However, they fail to incorporate the impact of not so influential nodes in the graph. In a graph, we get only a handful of influential nodes. But, the influence of less influential yet vast number of nodes cannot be avoided. Various scientists are arguing the hype of centrality measures. In 2012, Bauer et al (Bauer, Lizier 2012) pointed that centrality measures only rank nodes but do not measure the difference between them. Sikic et al. in 2013 (Sikic, Lancic, Antulov-Fantulin, Stefanic 2013) strongly argued with evidence that centrality measures undervalue the power of non-hub nodes.

These arguments led to the development of innovative methods to measure the influence of all nodes in the network. One of the most prevalent methods is the *Expected Force* (Lawyer 2015). This measure is derived from the expected value of the force of infection generated by a node.

1.4 Expected force

The Expected Force (Lawyer 2015) measures the influence of nodes using epidemic spreading perspective. It is based on the ideology that each node has a force of infection with which it can make a susceptible node infectious. This force is assumed to have impact on nodes at a distance of two. However, this may vary. Expected Force computes the expected value of this force that a node imparts on other nodes after two transmissions.

The expected force of a node i is given by

$$k_i = -\sum_{s=1}^{S} d_s \log(d_s) \tag{1}$$

In Equation (1), the expected force is the sum taken over all the possible transmission clusters that are generated from two transmissions from node i. Here, d_s is the normalized cluster degree of cluster $s \in S$.

The definition of expected force can be naturally extended to directed as well as weighted graphs. However, in our work, we are working with undirected Hindi WordNet subgraph, the above definition is sufficient to serve the purpose.

Expected Force measure has demonstrated strong correlation with SI, SIS and SIR epidemic outcomes. Also, it has been proved to be beneficial in heterogeneous problems like ecology, fitness etc.

Before proceeding further, here we are discussing the choice of Expected Force to be used to solve WSD problem. The definition of Expected force implies that influence of a node is an amalgamation of a node's own degree as well as the degree of its neighbors. This metric also considers that these two factors play differently for nodes with high and low spreading power. Less influential nodes gain strength from the strength of their neighbors, whereas high influential nodes also gain strength from the large number of connections that they have with other nodes. This definition looks logical as well as practical. A person has high influence if he is surrounded by influential people.

This paper is structured as follows: Section 2 gives a glimpse of approaches proposed in the literature for WSD of Hindi text. Section 3 explains our proposed approach. In section 4, we have documented our experiments undertaken and the results thus obtained. Conclusion and future works are described in Section 5.

2 RELATED WORKS

Various approaches have been proposed in literature for WSD. Primarily, supervised and unsupervised approaches were the main categories for WSD. However, of lately, graph-based approaches have picked up pace. Reason being availability of numerous knowledge bases which have graphically structured information.

In graph-based approaches, sentence is structured in the form of graph and then using different measures, correct sense of an ambiguous word is identified.

One of the sentinel works was done by Navigli and Lapata in 2010 (Navigli, Lapata 2007, 2010). They used graph connectivity measures like degree centrality (Freeman, 1979), key player problem (Borgatti 2006), HITS (Gupta, 2006), PageRank and betweenness (Freeman, Boragatti, White, 1991) (Newman, 2005) centralities. They created a graph of senses of words in the graph and computed the above said metrices for the nodes. The sense with highest centrality value is identified as the correct sense.

Jain and Lobiyal (2016) proposed WSD of Hindi text using fuzzy Hindi WordNet. Fuzzy Hindi WordNet consists of fuzzy relations. They also developed fuzzy centrality measures and concluded the sense with highest value of fuzzy centrality measure as the correct sense.

Navigli (Navigli, Lapata 2007, 2010) approach was extended by Vij et al in 2018 (Vij, Jain, Tayal, Castillo, 2018) where they assumed that not all semantic relations in WordNet are equally important. They provided a value to all the semantic relations and computed the centrality measures.

Centrality measures have been used in literature to solve different problems of WSD like keyword extraction (Biswas, Bordoloi, Shreya, 2018). However, importance and authenticity of centrality measures have been argued time and again. Taking this into consideration, we have tried a novel epidemic spreading based approach for WSD.

3 PROPOSED METHODOLOGY

In the proposed approach, we computed Expected Force of all the nodes in the network to judge the node with highest influence. Expected Force is a different metric than other usual centrality measures. It does not solely rely on the distribution of network topology. Rather, it takes into consideration, how the nodes are capable and the force they impart on adjacent nodes.

To implement this, we created a Hindi WordNet subgraph connecting different senses of all the ambiguous words of the sentence. The graph thus generated is exposed to compute the expected force of each node of the graph.

The node with highest expected force is adjudged as correct sense of the ambiguous word.

3.1 *Illustrative example*

To understand the efficacy of our approach, we ran our algorithm on the same example as Jain (Jain, Lobiyal 2016) approach.

The example sentence is "कष्ट झेलकर ही चमकते है| (kaṣṭa jhēlakara hī camakte hai.)". This sentence consists of three content words viz. " कष्ट *(kaṣṭa)"*, " झेलकर *(jhēlakara)"* and " चमकते *(camakte)"*. The base words for these content words are कष्ट *(kaṣṭa)*, झेलना *(jhēlanā)* and चमक *(camak)* respectively. चमक *(camak)* has 7 senses, झेलना *(jhēlanā)* has 1, and कष्ट *(kaṣṭa)* has 3 senses in the Hindi WordNet.

We calculated the Expected Force for all the senses of two ambiguous words. Table 1 shows the values. From the table we can notice that $चमक_n^3$ and $कष्ट_n^1$ have the highest value of expected force amongst all the nodes. Thus, $चमक_n^3$ and $कष्ट_n^1$ are concluded as the deduced sense of two ambiguous words.

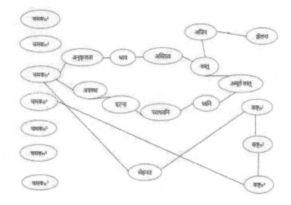

Figure 3.   Excerpt of WordNet graph for the example sentence.

4 EXPERIMENTATION AND RESULTS

The proposed approach was tested on health dataset of IIT Bombay sense tagged corpus. The results are obtained for both all words and polysemous words. The results are shown in Table 2.

It is evident from Table 2 that the proposed approach performed better than Jain (Jain, Lobiyal 2016) approach. However, slightly less than Vij et al. approach (2018) (Vij, Jain, Tayal, Castillo, 2018).

An important point to be considered is that both the approaches performed their best using *degree* as the centrality measure. The degree centrality gives the number of nodes that are directly connected to the node under consideration. It does not provide us with any other

Table 1. Expected force values for different senses of words in the sentence.

Word Sense	Expected Force
चमक$_n^1$	0.301
चमक$_n^2$	0.415
चमक$_n^3$	0.459
चमक$_n^4$	0.194
चमक$_n^5$	0.280
चमक$_n^6$	0.268
चमक$_n^7$	0.251
झेलना	0.310
कष्ट$_n^1$	0.385
कष्ट$_n^2$	0.299
कष्ट$_n^3$	0.123

Table 2. Comparison of the proposed approach with related works.

	Centrality Measure Used	All Words	Polysemous Words
Jain (2016)	Degree	61.83	49.31
Vij (2018)	Degree	63.05	52.79
Proposed Approach	**Expected Force**	**62.86**	**52.30**

relevant information. It does not provide us with the relevance and the role that other neighborhood node plays. Whereas, the Expected Force takes the influence of different neighboring nodes into consideration.

The work proposed by Vij et al (Vij, Jain, Tayal, Castillo, 2018) had slightly better results than our proposed approach. Their approach assigned fuzzy membership values to the semantic relations of WordNet, which itself is a big task. They applied simulation annealing to conclude membership values. It would have been better if the fuzzy membership values were more authentic and closer to the natural usage of language, which would have been possible if the values are data driven. Also, their approach gave best results with degree as the centrality measure. Hence, we assume that a little tuning of our approach will be able to achieve better results, which we will take in future.

5 CONCLUSION AND FUTURE WORKS

WSD is the problem of adjudging the correct sense of a word from its context. Many graph-based approaches have been proposed in the literature. However, most of them have noted best results using degree as the centrality measure. Degree is not a very good metric to reach a decision. Expected Force centrality measure takes the force of neighboring nodes into consideration to conclude the total expected force that a node imparts. The performed experiments support our claim that Expected Force can prove to be an efficient centrality measure for WSD.

This is the first attempt for WSD using Expected Force centrality measure. However, there is still scope for improvement. It will be interesting to see how the results change if we apply it to Fuzzy WordNet. We may look into prospect of using Expected Force to solve other NLP problems like keyword extraction, sentiment analysis etc.

REFERENCES

Bauer F., Lizier J.T.2012. Identifying influential spreaders and efficiently estimating infection numbers in epidemic models: a walk counting approach in *Europhysics letter* 99(6): 68007.

Biswas S.K., Bordoloi M., Shreya J.2018. A graph based keyword extraction model using collective node weight. *Expert Systems with Applications* Volume 97, pp. 51–59.

Borgatti, S.P., 2006. Identifying Set of Key Players in a Social Network. *Computational and Mathematical Organization Theory*, Springer. pp. 21–34.

Freeman, 1979. Centrality in Social Networks Conceptual Clarification. *Social Network*, Elsevier, Vol. 1, No. 3, pp. 215–239.

Freeman, L. C., Boragatti, S. P., White, D.R., 1991. Centrality in Valued Graph: A Measure of Betweenness Based on Network Flow. *Social Networks*, Elsevier, Vol. 13, pp. 141–154.

Gupta, G. K., 2006. Introduction to Data Mining With Case Studies. PHI, Pp. 238–240.

Jain A., Lobiyal D.K.2016. Fuzzy Hindi WordNet and Word Sense Disambiguation Using Fuzzy Graph Connectivity Measures. *ACM Transactions on Asian and Low-Resource Language Information Processing*, 15(2).

Lawyer G.2015. Understanding the influence of all nodes in a network, *Scientific Reports 5*.

Navigli R., Lapata M.2007. Graph Connectivity Measures for Unsupervised Word Sense Disambiguation. *IJCAI*: 1683–1688.

Navigli R., Lapata M.2010. An experimental study of graph connectivity for unsupervised word sense disambiguation. *In IEEE Transactions on Pattern Analysis and Machine Intelligence*, Volume 32(4), pp. 678–692.

Newman, M. E. J., 2005. A Measure of Betweenness Centrality Based on Random Walk. *Social Network*, Elsevier.

Sikic M., Lancic A., Antulov Fantulin N., Stefanic H.2013. Epidemic centrality – is there an underestimated epidemic impact of network peripheral nodes?. *The European Physical Journal B*. 86 (10): 1–13.

Vij S., Jain A., Tayal D., Castillo O.2018. Fuzzy Logic for Inculcating Significance of Semantic Relations in Word Sense Disambiguation using a WordNet Graph. *International Journal of Fuzzy Systems*. Volume 20(2), pp. 444–459.

Communication and Computing Systems – Prasad et al. (eds)
© 2019 Taylor & Francis Group, London, ISBN 978-0-367-00147-6

Empowering IoT with cloud technology

Ashutosh Kumar & Ashima Mehta
Department of Information Technology, Dronacharya College of Engineering, Gurugram, Haryana, India

ABSTRACT: The paper in theory is an approach on the above mentioned topic. The focal point of this research paper primarily targets the benefits of integration of Internet of Things with Cloud technology. The said aim of the intercommunication among objects over an IP network is to placate the function stated for them as a connected artifact. The research done focuses on the union of cloud with IoT which is called Cloud IoT paradigm and what are their usage scenarios. However, the probing done lacks elaborate investigation of the Cloud and IoT paradigms, that hold all in all new applications, benefits, challenges and analysis problems. The challenges or the problems embody security concerns and the compatibility check between the respective systems. There are multifold problems in way of the fruitful usage of both Cloud and IoT.

1   INTRODUCTION

As technology progresses, connectivity of devices with the internet has become easy. Also information gathering and processing has become more manageable. Cloud computing and Internet of Things (IoT) are the technologies which benefited us separately and now their integration opens the door for new possibilities. Although these two are different technologies but when merged together will emerge as a vital component for the near Future.Cloud computing allows users to access software, platform and infrastructure across locations. In a cloud environment hardware and software is hosted by an outside party and data resides at different data centers. The association of commonplace corporeal entities over the internet and being apt in distinguishing themselves with another entities, corresponding and reciprocating knowledge is the impending vision for the IoT (Botta et al. 2016). Business applications have invariably been terribly sophisticated and overpriced. Also, the hardware and computer code necessities are large to run them, requiring an enormous team of consultants which will install, configure, test, run, secure, and update them. Even though their efforts are multiplied across dozens or hundreds of apps, still the biggest companies with the best IT departments aren't getting the apps they needed. With the emergence of cloud computing, it eliminates the headaches that come on storing the data. Cloud technology providers cater a smooth means to make use of database, storage, server and a broad application set at a single point of connect (Mohammad et al. 2016).

2   BASIC CONCEPTS

Rudiments of IoT & Cloud and evaluating the essence crucial for their union.

2.1   *Internet of Things*

In the era of computing a new wave is predicted that is realm of smart IoTs. The ecosystem grid of corporeally associated items reachable via the web is described as Internet of Things

(IoT). Each object in the IoT network consists of an IP address through which communication and data transfer is performed. The thing or object in IoT includes entities like heart monitor, home automation system, automobile with sensors etc. The firmware embedded in the object helps in interacting with the external environment. IoT Scan facilitates firms to improve performance through IoT analytics and security to deliver optimal results (M. Rouse, 2015). IoT has noteworthy applicability in the two scenarios of household and business alike, where it will entertain a dominant role in the upcoming future projects.

2.2 *Cloud computing*

Cloud computing aims for providing information technology services such as cloud storage, cloud data processing, cloud gaming etc which were earlier restricted to one's local machine only. Cloud computing has blurred the boundary between traditional and cloud applications along with providing high fault tolerance owing to its distributed nature. Cloud computing empowers low powered IoT Devices resulting in performance gains (S.M. Babu et al. 2015). For cloud connected elements, the hardware and software resources are managed by the cloud provider. IoT and Cloud computing present unique prospects in data and services allocation with internet's aid, by kicking off a lively comprehensive network of self-shaping capabilities that are backed by classic and adaptable intercommunication protocols. Figure 1. Shows the integration of IoT and Cloud (Díaz et al. 2016).

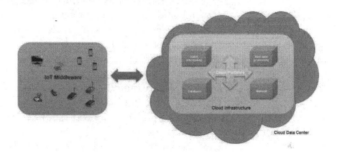

Figure 1.   IoT and Cloud integration.

3   USAGE SCENARIOS

3.1 *IoT*

IoT has been adapted in a range of application spheres, such as in civil construction projects, traffic monitoring and rerouting, ecosystem investigation, health-care and emergency aid services, climate anticipation, and video vigilance systems. IoT is also focusing on forthcoming application areas of smart urban systems and eventual symbiosis of an individual and IoT device service with the encompassing environment.
According to requirements, IoT is used in

– IoT-Based weather forecasting network
– Optimizing the Power Grid
– Cloud IoT-Based surveillance and security
– Doing Away With Dangerous Police Chases
– Using Drones to Help Save the Rainforest
– Cloud IoT based Collision Detection with data analysis and action planning (M.R. Anawar et al. 2018).
– Using Sensors to Make Driving Safer
– Better road traffic management

3.2 Cloud computing

According to the requirements, Cloud Computing is used as an operational technology and as a service provider for businesses, health-care, data centers, education, and CRM. The various application software's can be accessed by a connected device from any location. Cloud hosted apps and websites are readily accessible from anywhere (W. Zhang et al. 2016).

Nowadays businesses are adopting cloud computing to boost their revenues. Amazon, Microsoft, Google, IBM and lots of alternative huge IT corporations are primarily providing and developing cloud based IT infrastructure and applications for tiny businesses, healthcare, knowledge centers, education, and CRM (G. Md et al. 2014).

4 BENEFITS

Considering IoT, it retains constrained competence with respect to storage and processing power, it should conjointly cope with problems like reliability, performance, security and privacy. The perfect course to beat these issues is to integrate IoT with Cloud technologies.

Communication: The two noteworthy features of the Cloud IoT systems are sharing of data and applications. The Cloud is a cheap and effective answer for connecting, managing, and tracking something via inbuilt applications and customized portals.

Storage: When IoT encompasses a horde of devices, it contains an enormous variety of data sources, which generate a very large chunk of data in semi structured or non structured form. The Cloud storage is the preferred cost effective solution for handling a humongous heap of data associated with IoT.

Processing capabilities: Owing to the limited processing power of IoT devices on-site and complex data processing is not feasible. Instead, the collected information is often transferred to nodes having large capabilities. On demand and virtual processing utilities are catered by these nodes (K.S. Dar et al. 2016).

New abilities: Heterogeneousness of devices, protocols, and technologies is characterized by the IoT. Therefore, scalability, availability, interoperability, reliability, efficiency and security cannot be always guaranteed. It additionally provides alternative options such as ease of-use and ease-of-access, with cost effective deployment.

New Models: Some of the new models based on Cloud and IoT integration are as follows:
SaaS (Sensing as a Service) - allows access to sensor data (Fazio et al. 2015).
EaaS (Ethernet as a Service) - presents seamless connectivity to remote things.
SAaaS (Sensing and Actuation as a Service) - presents control logic's automatically.
IPMaaS (Identity and Policy Management as a Service) - provides access to policy and identity management.
DBaaS (Database as a Service) - provides data storage and retrieval via cloud databases (Chen et al. 2015).
SenaaS (Sensor as a Service) – provisioning for remote sensor management (Fazio et al. 2015).
DaaS (Data as a Service) - A wide variety of data access is provisioned.

5 CHALLENGES

There is an expeditious and reciprocal transformation of the two worlds of IoT and Cloud Computing. Now a days the scope of IoT technology has extended to provide distributed and dynamic real world solutions. The challenges that are faced by us is to have globally competing Cloud infrastructure for Internet of Things distributed over remote areas. Network delay and latency issues prevent near real time communication between nodes in an IoT based network. Security remains one of the leading element, that is hindering the swift and considerable endorsement of IoT and Cloud computing (Díaz et al. 2016).

5.1 *Security issues*

Cloud and IoT when harmonized together will be able to fill the gaps left by each other. Former can overcome latter's limitations such as the restricted storage and applications access, whereas latter can overcome former's limitations such as the issue of limited scope. However, when IoT applications move in the Cloud, charges ensue, as a result of mistrust in the service provider or the know-how concerning service level agreements (SLAs) and physical location of stored information (A. Alenezi et al. 2017).

Some challenges with respect to the security concerns in the union of two technologies are listed below.

Heterogeneity: Challenges in CloudIoT paradigm is expounded to the wide selection of equipment, platforms, and utilities out there.

Performance: Usually Cloud based IoT applications introduce execution and QoS needs at many levels and in some explicit situations meeting necessities may not be easily achievable.

Reliability: Reliability concerns occasionally arise in clod based IoT systems. For example, with respect to smart mobile systems, an automobile is oftentimes on the move and the communication network is commonly intermittent or unreliable.

Monitoring: As mostly documented within the literature, monitoring is a vital activity in Cloud environment for capacity planning, for managing resources, SLAs, performance, security and for troubleshooting (J. Zhou et al. 2017).

5.2 *Compatibility issues*

Both systems fundamentally complement each other yet they follow different approach to address the same problem and compatibility plays a vital role in the integration of cloud & IoT. The first challenge we have to overcome is of inter process communication i.e., instead of using heterogeneous protocols and layered stacks.We will have to consider protocols specifically targeting CloudIoT as a system in itself. Cloud IoT based systems can only be successful considering social & economic point of view. International standardization of the concerned technology and its related protocols will ensure cumulative efforts towards its further development. Other compatibility issues may arise from diverse firmware, operating systems and cloud services (K. Jeffery, 2014).

6 APPLICATIONS

A vast array of applications are shaped conceivable and are vastly improved with the help of Cloud based IoT.

Healthcare: Cloud based IoT has brought many benefits and opportunities in the field of healthcare. It can develop and improve many healthcare services and keep the health field innovative (e.g. intelligent drug, medicine control, hospital management).

Smart Home and Smart Metering: A large number of Cloud based IoT applications have enabled the automation of home activities, where the adoption of various embedded devices and Cloud computing has empowered the automation of in-house activities (e.g. home security control, smart metering, energy saving) (Moataz et al. 2013).

Video Vigilance: By entwining Cloud based IoT, intelligent video vigilance will probably manage to store and process video content from video sensors easily and precisely and this will also make it viable to extract information from scenes automatically. It has become one of the leading means for many security-related applications (e.g. Wireless CCTV Cameras, Movement detection system).

Automotive and Smart Mobility: The interfacing of Cloud computing with the Global Positioning System (GPS) and other transportation technologies represents a promising opportunity to solve many of the existing challenges (e.g. traffic state prediction & notification, remote vehicles).

Smart Energy and Smart Grid: IoT and the cloud computing can work together efficiently to provide consumers a smart management of energy consumption (e.g. smart electronic meters, smart IoT appliances, smart power grid load balancers).

Smart Logistic: It allows for, and eases, the automated management of goods flow between producers and consumers, while simultaneously enabling the tracking of goods in transit (e.g. logistics industry, tracking shipments).

Environmental monitoring: By integrating the Cloud with the IoT, a high performance information network can be used to link the entities that watch over environments and sensors that have been properly deployed in the area (e.g. pollution source, water quality, air quality monitoring).

7 CONCLUSION

Cloud Computing offers many possibilities, despite several limitations. Future trend is worldwide penetration of upcoming 5G cellular networks at affordable rates. This will lead to massive adoption of smart IoT thereby accelerating research and development further. Smart IoT based networks will be at the epicenter of innovation. Cloud will be the brain and IoT will be the body interacting together to fulfill the objective set for them as a combined entity. In future work, a number of case studies will be carried out to test the efficacy of the Cloud-based IoT approach for many applications.

Future Aspects: Without doubt, this research forms the basis for the researchers to address the challenges while these two widely accepted technologies are merged.

REFERENCES

A. Alenezi, N. H. N. Zulkipli, H. F. Atlam, R. J. Walters, and G. B. Wills, "The Impact of Cloud Forensic Readiness on Security," in 7st International Conference on Cloud Computing and Services Science, 2017, pp. 1–8.

Botta A., de Donato W., Persico V., Pescapè A. Integration of Cloud computing and Internet of Things: A survey. Future Gener. Comput. Syst. 2016;56:684–700. doi: 10.1016/j.future.2015.09.021.

Chen F, Deng P, Wan J, Zhang D, Vasilakos AV, Rong X. Data mining for the internet of things: literature review and challenges. Int J Distrib Sensor Netw 2015;501:431047.

Díaz M., Martín C., Rubio B. State-of-the-art, challenges, and open issues in the integration of Internet of things and Cloud computing. J. Netw. Comput. Appl. 2016;67:99–117. doi: 10.1016/j.jnca.2016.01.010.

Fazio, M., Puliafito, A.Cloud4sens: a cloud-based architecture for sensor controlling and monitoring IEEE Communications Magazine 2015, 53, pages 41–47.

G.Md Whaiduzzaman et al, "A Study on Strategic Provision of Cloud Computing Services", The Scientific World Journal, pp. 1-8, 15/6/2014.

J. Zhou, Z. Cao, X. Dong, and A. V Vasilakos, "Security and Privacy for Cloud-Based IoT: Challenges, Countermeasures, and Future Directions," no. January, 2017, pp. 26–33.

K. Jeffery, Keynote: CLOUDs: A large virtualisation of small things, in: The2nd International Conference on Future Internet of Things and Cloud, FiCloud-2014, 2014.

K. S. Dar, A. Taherkordi and F. Eliassen, "Enhancing Dependability of Cloud-Based IoT Services through Virtualization," 2016 IEEE First International Conference on Internet-of-Things Design and Implementation (IoTDI), 2016, pp. 106-116.

Moataz Soliman et al, "Smart Home: Integrating Internet of Things with Web Services and Cloud Computing," in 2013 IEEE International Conference on Cloud Computing Technology and Science, Oulu, 2013.

Mohammad Aazam et al, "Cloud of Things: Integration of IoT with Cloud Computing," Springer International Publishing, pp. 77-94, 01/01/2016.

M. R. Anawar, S. Wang, M. Azam Zia et al., "Fog Computing: An Overview of Big IoT Data Analytics," Wireless Communications and Mobile Computing, vol. 2018, Article ID 7157192, 22 pages, 2018.

M. Rouse, "IoT security (Internet of Things security)," IoT Agenda, 01/ 11/2015.[Online]. Available: http://internetofthingsagenda.techtarget.com/definition/IoT-security-Internet-of-Things-security. [Accessed 27/07/2016].

S. M. Babu, A. J. Lakshmi and B. T. Rao, "A study on cloud based Internet of Things: CloudIoT," 2015 Global Conference on Communication Technologies (GCCT), 2015, pp. 60-65.

W. Zhang, S. Tan, F. Xia et al., "A survey on decision making for task migration in mobile cloud environments," Personal and Ubiquitous Computing, vol. 20, no. 3, pp. 295–309, 2016.

Communication and Computing Systems – Prasad et al. (eds)
© 2019 Taylor & Francis Group, London, ISBN 978-0-367-00147-6

Analysis of deforestation using satellite images of a region by color image segmentation

Pentakota Madhuri & Krishanu Kundu

Electronics and Communication Engineering, Dronacharya College of Engineering, Gurgaon, India

ABSTRACT: In present age of modernization rate of deforestation is much higher than plantation. For understanding side effects of deforestation proper monitoring of forest cover and maintaining its quality is very essential. Deprivation of biodiversity and abatement of carbon seclusion capacity are major outcomes of deforestation. This paper deals with the analysis of the deforestation rate in different regions from satellite images of any region taken over years. In this paper, color segmentation algorithm is used on image and area of forest in a place over different year is calculated. As per simulation result it predicts deforestation has occurred over past years. In this paper, text to speech conversion algorithm is used to give out the result. Simulation is carried by using MatlabR2015a software.

1 INTRODUCTION

In current years, Deforestation is one of the major problems in the world. Previously forest department used to depend on field surveys for collecting data related to forest cover. Similarly for analyzing forest stocks aerial photography was main helping aid. With the new inventions in the field of satellite imaging technology we have started to use technology based on remote sensing for monitoring forest data as well as tropical deforestation. Landsat satellite program run by US Geological Survey and Worldwide Reference System are used often by researchers for analyzing changes in forest. For detecting forest changes and monitoring issues related to deforestation in widespread forests, satellite imagery has been used. Radar and imaging systems like light-based LiDAR are used for complementing optical imaging same as Landsat. The crucial part of image processing techniques is Image segmentation, where a digital image is breached in several segments, designed to carry meaningful information. This makes analysis of information much easier .Image segmentation is used for isolation of boundary properties like color, intensity as well as texture of image. Most popular image segmentation approaches are mostly Edge based, Threshold based, Region based, Fuzzy based and Artificial Neural Network based segmentation. The best thing about unsupervised segmentation procedure is automatic segmentation of images without prior knowledge. Hard clustering algorithm and K-Means algorithm are two variant of unsupervised segmentation. For segmenting of image we opt for L*A*B* color space. As soft clustering algorithms are unable to detect fuzziness factor, in this paper hard clustering methodology along with K-Means algorithm has been used for image segmentation.

2 LITERATURE SURVEY

L. Bragilevsky and I. V. Bajić (2017) provided the facts and figures about the devastating effect of deforestation on ecosystem of Amazon basin and they also discussed the urgent need of better understanding and management of landscape at that region. The approach for invigilating deforestation as well as forest deterioration using Landsat TM images. M. Yan et al

(2012) discussed concept of k-means cluster for enhancing color images. H. Yadav et al (2015) proved the conversion of color image into L*A*B* (L stands for luminosity layer; A stands for chromaticity layer 1 and B stands for chromaticity layer2). Clustering is a method for distinguishing different kind of objects in an image similarly K Means clustering do partitioning of image in such way that within every cluster similar objects remains as close as possible and also each cluster must be distinguished. With many clusters, K Means clustering segments its nuclei into a separate image by means of recalling L layer.C. Wang and J. Watada proposed an approach of image segmentation by virtue of multi-threshold Otsu method for selecting best thresholds with respect to image histogram where as K-Means Clustering has been utilized for merging over-segmented regions. This proved to give better result for color images having complex background structure. Garg and B. Kaur discussed Color image segmentation is burning topic for research in the field of image processing. For image segmentation Clustering is widely used. Color space has most starring impact on segmentation process. Mostly we opt for L*A*B* color space as this representation is similar with the way how human eyes perceive color.

3   METHODOLOGY

Satellite images captured by imaging satellites provide necessary information to measure the rate of changes occurring in a region over years. Those captured Satellite images come in JPEG as well as GeoTIFF (Geo-referenced TIFF) formats having 256 × 256 resolution. In this paper we have analyzed imagery data obtained from remote sensing satellites for detection of changes in forest cover over many years. The flow chart of the methodology is shown in Figure 3.

3.1   *Color filtering*

In this paper color filtering is done for the input satellite image. Light is perceived by human eyes as electromagnetic radiation having wavelength ranging between 380nm - 760nm.The visible color spectrum comprises of seven colors such as violet, indigo, blue, green, yellow, orange and red (VIBGYOR).For Filtering a desired color, cfilter function is used which separates each color from the VIBGYOR color spectrum in an image. This function modifies a given image in order to keep a specific hue and to de-saturate the rest of the image. hue is a property of color through which it can be seen as ranging from red through orange, yellow, green, blue, indigo, and violet and is resolved by light's dominant wavelength. This procedure originates an image with black and white color map, excluding the parts colored with that hue.

After importing the image we have to select the first letter of the color as shown in Figure 1 to be separated. Select R option for red. This shows red color and rest of the image will be in various shades of grey, as shown in Figure 2.The first image in Figure 2 is the original and the second image in Figure 2 is the color-segmented image.

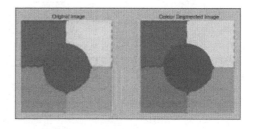

Figure 1.   Color selection figure.   Figure 2.   Output when red is given as input.

3.2 Color segmentation: The K-means clustering algorithm

K means is a popular variant of unsupervised classification i.e., it does not require knowledge to classify the features of the image. In this algorithm, a natural grouping of pixels takes place that is the grey level of pixels are observed and a threshold is set for selecting the number of classes in the image. This algorithm commences with finding number of cluster (K) and with an assumption of selecting the center of these clusters (centroid). It is an iterative method which divides image in k clusters, cluster centers need to be chosen carefully to prevent from erroneous results. This algorithm partition image into K clusters, where each investigation belongs to cluster with closest mean. This is a simple, fast and easy way for classifying and grouping of similar objects into one cluster.

3.2.1 Color segmentation using K-means clustering

Partitioning of an image into multiple regions is called image segmentation. In this process, colors are segmented using l*a*b color space as well as k-means clustering. At the beginning satellite images are red. To separate the color of the image "decorrelation stretching" is applied which results in artificial enhancement of the color of an image. The RGB color space image is converted to L*A*B color space which comprises of luminosity layer L*, chromaticity layer A* where Colors falls along the red-green axis and B* chromaticity layer where color falls along the blue-yellow axis. A * and B* layer stores all color information. Clustering separates group of objects. K means clustering required to specify the number of clusters to be partitioned as the color information is present in A*B* space, objects are pixels with A* and B* values. K-means is utilized for clustering the objects into 3 clusters using Euclidean distance metric which is a straight line distance between two points in Euclidean space. For every object, k-means assigns an index for each and every pixel . Using this* pixel labels, separation of objects in an image by colors takes place. The distance between object to cluster is calculated till clusters are stable. The object with minimum Euclidean distance group together to form clustering. In this way, objects with similar color group together. The required colored part in image is segmented using this algorithm.

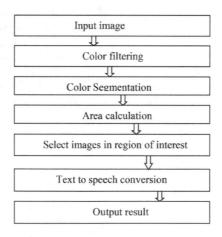

Figure 3.   Flow chart of methodology.

3.3 Area calculation and select images in region of interest

Area of required colored segmented image is calculated. Area of satellite images of region of every year is compared. Decrease in area predicts occurrence of deforestation. A threshold is set to display the satellite images of a region during the year in which deforestation has occurred severely.

3.4 *Text to speech conversion*

Speech synthesis is referred as artificial production of human speech. It is done by speech synthesizer. It synthesis speech from string and speaks out. Speech is a means of communication between people. It produces speech by Grapheme to phoneme transcription. Grapheme contains alphabetic letters, digits, punctuations, symbols. Phoneme is smallest unit of sound to from meaningful utterances. The speech is close to human voice and is easily understood. These are important features of text to speech converter. This paper uses text to speech converter which speaks out the analyzed information from the simulated results. The speech generated will be helpful for visually challenged people to analyze the information easily.

4 SIMULATION RESULT

4.1 *Case study-1*

Images in Figure 4 a), Figure 5 a) and Figure 6 a) are taken by NASA's Landsat 1 satellite during year 2000, 2005 and 2010 respectively. Within the proposed algorithm green color is chosen in color filtering as the satellite images of forest will be in green color. The green part of the image is segmented. Simulating the results of forest coverage in Amazon forest during year 2000 is shown in Figure 4, 2005 is shown in Figure 5 and during year 2010 is shown in Figure 6.The forest area is segmented by color image segmentation by means of K-means clustering algorithm. Forest coverage is found with the proposed algorithm. Figure 4 c) gives a forest area of 6680.50mm^2, Figure 5 c) gives an forest area of 6348.12 mm^2 and Figure 6 c) gives an area of 4942.91mm^2. There is a Decrease in coverage area from year 2000 to 2010. As per simulation result it predicts deforestation has occurred in Amazon forest.

The simulated results reveal dramatic effects of clear-cutting for forest. This is the consequences of the establishment of a giant north-south highway in the 1970s, as per NASA's Earth Observatory. As these roads cut down major the rain forest and then spread outwards, results in massive loss of habitat and species in Amazon forest. The rate of deforestation has been analyzed with proposed algorithm.

4.2 *Case study-2*

Simulating the results of forest coverage in Borneo near Indonesia during year 1950 shown in Figure 7 and 2005 shown in Figure 8 and year 2010 shown in Figure 9. Forest coverage is found with the proposed algorithm. Figure 7 c) gives a forest area of 2724.28 mm^2, Figure 8 c) gives a forest area of 1511.50 mm^2 and Figure 9 c) gives an area of 1160.44 mm^2. There is a Decrease in coverage area from year 1950 to 2010. As per simulation result it predicts

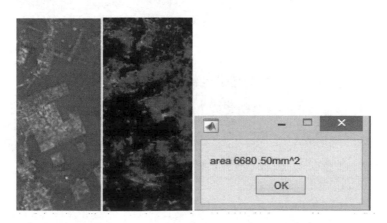

Figure 4.   (a) Original satellite image of Amazon forest in 2000. (b) Segmented image. (c) Calculated area.

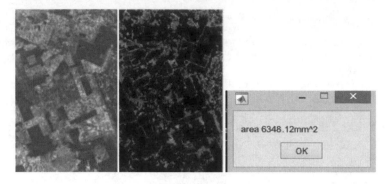

Figure 5.   (a) Original satellite image of Amazon forest in 2005. (b) Segmented image. (c) Calculated area.

Figure 6.   (a) Original satellite image of Amazon forest in 2010. (b) Segmented image. (c) Calculated area.

Figure 7.   (a) Original satellite image of Borneo forest in 1950. (b) Segmented image. (c) Calculated area.

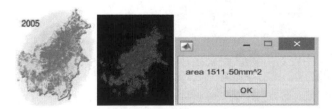

Figure 8.   (a) Original satellite image of Borneo forest in 2005. (b) Segmented image. (c) Calculated area.

Figure 9.   (a) Original satellite image of Borneo forest in 2010. (b) Segmented image. (c) Calculated area.

deforestation has occurred in Borneo near Indonesia. By 2022, 98% of the rainforests in Indonesia will be destroyed. Figures 7, 8, 9 give a visual of the amount destroyed.

The test cases shows the rate of deforestation occurred in amazon forest and Borneo in indonesia with the algorithm proposed in this paper.

6   CONCLUSION

In this paper deforestation rate in a region is analyzed from the satellite images. This used K-means clustering algorithm to segment the forest coverage region from the images. Forest coverage over every year in a particular region is analyzed and predicted that deforestation has occurred. This algorithm can be used for analysis of various factors like water coverage in an area, temperature variations over a region from the different satellite images of that region which shows water area in blue color, temperature information in red color. By selecting the required color based on requirement, information is obtained with the proposed algorithm.

REFERENCES

A. Bali and S. N. Singh, (2015), *International Conference on Advanced Computing & Communication Technologies*, "A Review on the Strategies and Techniques of Image Segmentation", Haryana, pp.113-120.

C. Wang and J. Watada, (2011), *International Conference on Genetic and Evolutionary Computing*, "Robust Color Image Segmentation by Karhunen-Loeve Transform Based Otsu Multi-thresholding and K-means Clustering", Xiamen, pp. 377-380.

DibyaJyoti Bora, Anil Kumar Gupta,(September 2014), *International Journal of Emerging Science and Engineering (IJESE)*, "A Novel Approach Towards Clustering Based Image Segmentation", vol. 2, no. 11, pp. 6-10, ISSN 2319-6378.

Garg and B. Kaur, (2016), *International Conference on Computing for Sustainable Global Development (INDIACom)*, "Color based segmentation using K-mean clustering and watershed segmentation", New Delhi, pp. 3165-3169.

H. Yadav, P. Bansal and R. KumarSunkaria, (2015), *International Conference on Next Generation Computing Technologies (NGCT)*, "Color dependent K-means clustering for color image segmentation of colored medical images," Dehradun, pp. 858-862.

J. Orlando, Tobias, RuiSeara, (2002), IEEE Transactions on Image Processing, "Image Segmentation by Histogram Thresholding Using Fuzzy Sets", Vol.11, Issue No.12, pp.1457-1465.

K. Haris, S. N. Efstratiadis, N. Maglaveras and A. K. Katsaggelos, (Dec 1998), *IEEE Transactions on Image Processing*, "Hybrid image segmentation using watersheds and fast region merging", vol. 7, no. 12, pp. 1684-1699.

L. Bragilevsky and I. V. Bajić, (2017), *IEEE Pacific Rim Conference on Communications, Computers and Signal Processing (PACRIM)*, "Deep learning for Amazon satellite image analysis," Victoria, BC, pp. 1-5.

M. Yan, J. Cai, J. Gao and L. Luo, (2012), *International Conference on Bio Medical Engineering and Informatics*, "K-means cluster algorithm based on color image enhancement for cell segmentation," Chongqing, pp. 295-299.

O. P. Verma, M. Hanmandlu, S. Susan, M. Kulkarni and P. K. Jain, (2011), *International Conference on Communication Systems and Network Technologies*, "A Simple Single Seeded Region Growing Algorithm for Color Image Segmentation using Adaptive Thresholding", Katra, Jammu, pp. 500-503.

P. Ganesan, B. S. Sathish and G. Sajiv,(2016), *World Conference on Futuristic Trends in Research and Innovation for Social Welfare (Startup Conclave)*, "A comparative approach of identification and segmentation of forest fire region in high resolution satellite images", Coimbatore, pp. 1-6.

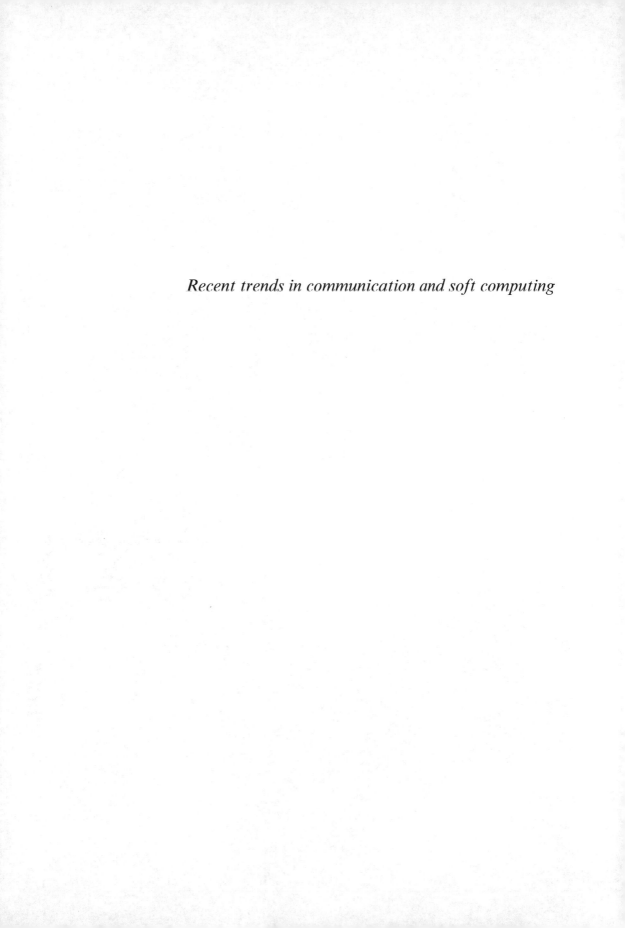

Recent trends in communication and soft computing

Communication and Computing Systems – Prasad et al. (eds)
© 2019 Taylor & Francis Group, London, ISBN 978-0-367-00147-6

Available bandwidth estimation in wireless ad-hoc networks: A modified approach

Mukta & N. Gupta
K.R. Mangalam University, Gurgaon, India

ABSTRACT: Provision of Quality of Service (QoS) in wireless ad hoc networks depends upon the accurate quantification of available resources in the network. One of the most fundamental and widely requested resources is the available bandwidth (ABW). In the present literature a lot of work has been done in the area of estimating the ABW but still no promising solution is achieved till date. In this paper, we are presenting a modified approach of "ABE" given by Sarr et al.(2008) for estimating the ABW on a link in terms of collision probability and average backoff. Lagrange Interpolating polynomial used by "ABE" does not exhibit permanence property and is restricted to a fixed range of data points. Thus, we are using a better polynomial known as Newton Divided Difference interpolating polynomial for calculating the collision probability which is much simpler and equally applicable to the outside range of data points. Further, according to IEEE 802.11 standard a station must wait for an EIFS (Extended Inter frame space) time rather than DIFS (Distributed Inter frame space) time in case the last transmission is unsuccessful during the calculation of average backoff. Incorporating these changes improves the overall accuracy of bandwidth estimation technique.

1 INTRODUCTION

A wireless ad hoc network is an infrastructures-less, dynamic and self-organized mobile network created spontaneously without any centralized control. Each node acts as a router as well as host and capable of forwarding data packets to another node to reach the destination. In ad hoc network mobile devices are communicating with each other using radio signals. Ad hoc network is beneficial in many areas including military, rescue operations, emergency, conference or meeting where prompt setup of network is necessary for sharing of data to each other. IEEE 802.11 standard is used for wireless LAN (WLAN), which support ad hoc mode. Due to different requirements of multimedia applications in terms of bandwidth, delay, jitter etc., the network should be able to provide acceptable amount of QoS support to the users. Thus, this domain is extensively studied by the researchers and many QoS solutions are proposed. One of the most adopted QoS solutions is to estimate the remaining bandwidth in the network. Estimation of ABW in wireless ad hoc networks is challenging task due to shared medium and unstable topology. Precise evaluation of ABW will improve the overall system performance.

In this paper we are estimating the ABW on a single-hop link between sender and receiver. ABW estimation depends on the assessment of channel usage ratio within the carrier sensing range of the two nodes constituting the link, thereby evaluating the amount of remaining free resources. Sarr et al. (2008) considers four main challenges for ABW estimation: carrier sense mechanism, idle period synchronization, collision probability and average backoff. Authors utilized the "Lagrange interpolating polynomial" for calculating collision probability of data packets which is not only complicated to solve but also suffers from efficiency issues. In order to improve these issues, we are using a better polynomial which is much more efficient, and evaluation can be done comparatively faster. According to IEEE 802.11 specifications, on unsuccessful transmission, the node must wait for the EIFS time before retransmitting the packet. However, Sarr et al. (2008) used DIFS waiting time instead of actual EIFS waiting time while calculating the bandwidth consumed due to average backoff. Thus by doing these modifications, we are estimating the ABW on a link between sender and receiver station, and compared the results obtained by using our modified approach with the existing techniques given by Renesse et al. (2005), Sarr et al. (2008) and real ABW using NS2.

2 RELATED WORKS

ABW of a link is defined as the maximum amount of data that can be transferred on this link without disturbing any exiting flows performance. Various researches have been carried out in the area of ABW estimation. There are mainly three kinds of bandwidth estimation techniques found in the literature: Active technique, Passive techniques and Analytical techniques. A detailed survey on all these techniques can be found in Mukta & Gupta (2017). Active techniques are based on emission of probe packets at multiple traffic rates between sender and receiver. Thus, by measuring the packet inter-arrival times, the ABW is estimated along a path. Work given by Prasad et al. (2003) and Jain et al. (2003) represent some of the work done under these techniques. Active techniques are associated with some drawbacks: i) probe packets create network congestion and consume more network resources, and ii) Loss of probe packets may occur due to overloading of medium leading to erroneous estimation. These drawbacks make active techniques inefficient especially in wireless networks. In Passive techniques, the medium is passively monitored over a certain period of time to determine the channel usage ratio and by using this ratio ABW is estimated. Renesse et al. (2005), Sarr et al. (2008), Belbachir et al. (2013) & Chaudhari et al. (2015) have done work under these techniques. Model-based (Analytical) techniques are based on developing the mathematical models using techniques such as Markov's chain, Fixed-point analysis etc. to predict the network metrics like throughput, delay and packet loss probability etc. Some of the analytical techniques are given by Bianchi (2000), Najjari et al. (2017).

2.1 Our contribution

In this paper, we evaluate the ABW on a link between two nodes based on the carrier sensing mechanism, idle period synchronization, collision probability and average backoff. We improve the accuracy of "ABE" technique given by Sarr et al. (2008) by incorporating two modifications in terms of collision probability and average backoff.

- Calculating the collision probability using "Newton Divided Difference Interpolation polynomial" rather than Lagrange Interpolating Polynomial.
- According to IEEE 802.11 standard, EIFS waiting time is used for calculating the average backoff rather than DIFS time before retransmitting an unsuccessful frame.

Following sub-section describe the weaknesses of Lagrange Interpolating Polynomial and benefits of employing "Newton divided difference polynomial".

2.2 Lagrange interpolating polynomial vs. Newton divided difference interpolation polynomial

Sarr et al. (2008) utilized Lagrange interpolating polynomial for calculating the collision probability of Data packets from the measured "Hello" packets collision probability, the shortcomings of are listed as:

- Lagrange Interpolating Polynomial is a tool for proving theorem theoretically, actual computation with this polynomial is complicated, hard to solve, requires huge numbers and catastrophic cancellations.
- It works well when we have to interpolate data points only within a fixed range repeatedly but is inefficient when new data points are added outside the range, which requires

computing the whole polynomial again from scratch consuming a lot of time thereby causing delay. It is also numerically unstable.

- Lagrange is very bad when we have to perform floating point's arithmetic calculation.

All the above-mentioned weaknesses of Lagrange polynomial add overheads in the network due to its complicated and inefficient nature. Thus, to overcome these inefficiencies we are using better polynomial i.e. "Newton Divided Difference polynomial" with following key advantages:

- Calculation process becomes reasonably faster, thus shorter response time.
- Calculation is much easier and stable because there is usually a single denominator term for a given variable. This less complexity and better stability improves the reliability of results.
- Newton divided difference polynomial is very efficient while interpolating data incrementally, means it is also applicable when we have to interpolate data points outside the range; resulting to better and quicker adaptation to variations in network load and topology.
- Addition of new data point needs to add just a single additional term rather than calculating the polynomial again from scratch, thus improves flexibility.
- It is very easy to interpolate derivatives using Newton framework.

The rest of this paper is organized as follows: Section-3 describes our improved approach for estimation of ABW on a link; Section-4 depicts the experimental results using NS2 and comparative analysis with respect to the existing techniques; And Section-5 concludes the paper.

3 ESTIMATION OF AVAILABLE BANDWIDTH OF A LINK

Consider a network scenario as shown in Figure 1, having six nodes S, R, L, M, A, B. Nodes within transmission range of each other and making single-hop transmission link are shown with thick lines; the carrier sensing range (CSR) of node-S and node-R are shown with dotted circles. Our aim is to estimate the ABW on link(S,R). Nodes which are not directly communicating with nodes S and R but are within their CSR may still influence the ABW on link(S,R). We focused on the challenges considered by Sarr et al. (2008) for calculating ABW on link(S, R) as described below:

3.1 *Estimation of idle period synchronization between sender and receiver*

For successful transmission, the idle periods of sender and receiver should be synchronized, means medium at sender should be free to gain access to the medium for transmitting the packets as well as at the same time during the whole transmission the receiver should be free. A node can be considered as busy in two cases:

- The node is itself transmitting or receiving with another node in its transmission range (250m).
- Also, the node under observation can be busy if any of the nodes in its carrier sensing range (550m) is communicating with another node. In the latter case, the concerned node will sense the channel busy as soon as a signal above the carrier sensing threshold is received; otherwise the channel is considered as idle.

Measuring the channel usage ratio and thus the channel idle sensing time proportion at l^{th} node gives the estimation of its local ABW. Therefore, the local ABW of sender 'S' and receiver 'R' denoted by AB_S and AB_R respectively is calculated as:

$$AB_l = \frac{T_{l\ idle}}{T} \times \ C_{max}; \ Where \ l \in \{S, R\}$$ (1)

Where, $T_{l\ idle}$ = the sum of idle time periods of lth node during the total observation interval T; and C_{max} = maximum channel capacity. For taking the synchronization of idle time proportion of sender and receiver, as per Sarr et al. (2006), the ABW of a link can be calculated as:

$$AB_{Link(s,r)} = \frac{T_{s\ idle}}{T} \times \frac{T_{r\ idle}}{T} \times C_{max} \tag{2}$$

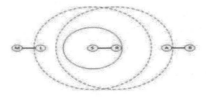

Figure 1.   Six nodes scenario.

3.2   Computation of collision probability using Newton divided difference interpolation polynomial

Collision is an inseparable feature of any network and wireless ad hoc networks too are affected by this. It has greatly influenced the ABW within a channel. Collision can happen in two circumstances: First, when more than one node having same backoff end time tries to send packet to the same node. Second, due to the Hidden/Exposed node problem, that can be tackled by using RTS/CTS mechanism in CSMA/CA. When collision happens, the transmitting node waits for random amount of backoff time in proportion to current contention window (CW) size which gets doubled on each transmission failure. ABW is reduced at the time of collision and backoff because there is no communication can happen by the node during that time. For accurate evaluation of ABW, it is necessary to calculate the collision probability of data packets. Sarr et al. (2008) calculates the collision probability using Hello packets (P_{Hello}) used by various routing protocols and further interpolates it to get the collision probability of DATA packets (P_m) of size m Bytes. The Hello packets collision probability (P_{Hello}) is calculated as:

$$P_{Hello} = \frac{Number\ of\ collided\ Hello\ Packets}{Total\ number\ of\ Expected\ Hello\ Packets} \tag{3}$$

The number of collided Hello packets is evaluated by subtracting the number of actual received Hello packets at receiver from the estimated number of Hello packets that should be received during the certain time interval. To overcome the discrepancy existing due to smaller size of Hello packets, the resultant is interpolated to match with the collision probability of data packets. Sarr et al. (2008) present the Equation 4 to calculate the collision probability of data packets (P_m) of size m, at different data packet sizes (m) and $f(m)$ is calculated using Lagrange Interpolating polynomial with respect to the measured (P_{Hello}).

$$P_m = f(m) \times P_{Hello} \tag{4}$$

This $f(m)$ is derived only for the certain data packet sizes used in experiment. Knowing the disadvantages as mentioned in section 2.2, we employed the Newton Divided Difference polynomial for the computation of $f(m)$ to various data packet sizes of 100Bytes, 250Bytes, 500Bytes and 1000Bytes at constant bit rate. The outcomes of the experiment are plotted in Figure 2.

$$f(m) = 7.021 \times 10^{-8} m^3 - 1.417 \times 10^{-4} m^2 + 7.729 \times 10^{-2} m + 3.2097 \qquad (5)$$

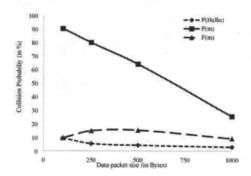

Figure 2.   Collision probability vs. Data packet size.

3.3   Calculation of proportion of bandwidth consumed by backoff using EIFS strategy

According to IEEE 802.11 specifications, before starting the transmission, a station should wait for a DIFS or an EIFS time delay and then starts a random backoff counter. When the backoff counter decrement to zero, the station starts its transmission.

The choice between DIFS or EIFS time delay depends on the event of last transmission. When the last event is a successful transmission (confirmed by ACK control packet received), then the sender waits for DIFS time and further on finding the medium idle starts a random backoff counter corresponding to minimum value of CW (typically $CW_{min}=31$), then on expiry this counter value initiates the next transmission to the receiver. However, when the last event is an unsuccessful transmission (e.g. a collision) then as per standard the node must wait for an EIFS time and then start its backoff counter whose value is double the value of CW used in the last transmission. The station which waits for EIFS duration is called a retry station.

When collision occurs, exponential backoff mechanism is triggered. Initially when there is no collision, the backoff is executed in the interval $[0; CW_{min}-1]$, where CW_{min} is the minimum CW size. When the size of observed CW is large, backoff is given by its average value $(CW_{min}-1)/2$. After each unsuccessful packet transmission, the contention window size is doubled up to a maximum value given by CW_{max}. In this case, the average value of backoff increases above $(CW_{min}-1)/2$. As per Sarr et al. (2008) the average backoff can be calculated as:

$$\overline{backoff} = \frac{CW_{min}.(1-p).\left(1-(2.p)^{M+1}\right)}{2.(1-2.p)}$$
$$+ \frac{1}{2} \cdot \left(p^{M+1} - 1 + (CW_{max} - 1).(p^{M+1} - p^{C-M-1} + p^C)\right) \qquad (6)$$

Where, $C=$ the number of unsuccessful re-transmission attempts and M is constant such that $CW_{max}= 2^M.CW_{min}$ with $M \le C$.

Thus, the proportion of bandwidth consumed by backoff mechanism (K) after waiting for EIFS time before retransmitting the packets is given by the formula:

89

$$K = \frac{EIFS + \overline{backoff}}{T(m)} \tag{7}$$

Here, $T(m)$ is the time separating the emission of two consecutive frames.

3.4   *Available bandwidth estimation*

The final ABW on a link between sender and receiver is given as:

$$E_{\text{final}}\left(b_{(s,r)}\right) = (1 - K).(1 - P).\left(AB_{\text{Link}(s,r)}\right) \tag{8}$$

Where, $E_{\text{final}}(b_{(s,r)})$ represent the final ABW on link(S,R). $AB_{Link(s,r)}$ is given by Equation 2; P is calculated using Equation 4; and K is calculated using Equation 7.

4   RESULTS

Figure 3 represent the simulation results obtained using our modified approach and compared it with some well-known approaches given by Renesse et al. (2005), Sarr et. al (2006) and "ABE" approach of Sarr et al. (2008). We considered the same scenario as shown in Figure 1. The raw channel capacity is set to 2Mbps, which provide maximum application-layer through-put (C_{max}) up to 1.6Mbps. Size of data packet is set to 1000Byte. The flow at link(L,M) is kept constant at 50 percent of the medium capacity (i.e. 0.8Mbps), which induces a fixed load on node-S being in the CSR of node-L. The flow at link(A,B) is varied thereby inducing an increasing load at node-R being in the CSR of node-A. Our concern is to estimate the ABW on link(S,R) under the influence of other existing flows on link(L,M) and link(A,B). The results in Figure 3 clearly show that the estimated ABW on link(S,R) using our modified approach is much closer to the real ABW measured using NS2 which testify the improvement done by our approach.

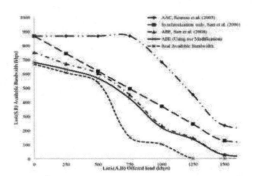

Figure 3.   Link(S,R) estimated available bandwidth.

5   CONCLUSION

In this article we focused on the accuracy of ABW estimation on a single-hop by considering four main challenges as addressed by Sarr et al. (2008): carrier sensing mechanism, idle period synchronization, collision probability and backoff mechanism. We have done some modifications in terms of collision probability and average backoff by exploring a better polynomial for calculating the collision probability in dynamic wireless networks and introducing more precise bandwidth consumption factor due to backoff mechanism.

ABW estimation is an important area of research for providing the QoS to demanding applications. By knowing the available resources present in the network, we can increase the performance of the network.

REFERENCES

Belbachir, R., Mazza, Z. M., Kies, A. & Belhadri, M. 2013. Collision's Issue: Towardsa New Approach to Quantify and Predict the Bandwidth Losses. In *Global Information Infrastructure Symposium*, pp.1-4.

Bianchi, G. 2000. Performance Analysis of the IEEE 802.11 Distributed coordination Function. In *IEEE-Journals on Selected Areas in communication*, vol.18, no.3, pp. 535-547.

Chaudhari, S.S. & Biradar, R.C. 2015. Available Bandwidth Estimation Using Collision Probability, Idle Period Synchronization and Random Waiting Time in MANET's: Cognitive Agent Based Approach. In *Wireless Personal Communications*, vol. 85, no.3, pp. 597-621.

Jain, M. & Dovrolis, C. 2003. End-to-End Available Band-width: Measurement Methodology, Dynamics, and Relation with TCP Throughput. *IEEE/ACM Transactions on Networking*, vol.11, no.4, pp.537–549.

Mukta & Gupta, N. 2017. Bandwidth Estimation Tools & Techniques: A Review. In *International Journal of Research*, vol.4, no.13, pp.1250-1265.

Najjari, N., M. Geyong., & H. Jia. 2017. Performance Analysis of WLANs under Bursty and Correlated video traffic. In *14th International Conference on Frontier of Computer science and Technology (FCST-2017)*, Exeter, UK.

Melander, B., M. Bjorkman, & Gunningberg, P. 2003. A New End to End Probing and Analysis Method for Estimating Bandwidth Bottlenecks. *IEEE Global Telecommunications Conference*, vol.11, no.4, pp.537-549.

Prasad, R., Murray, M., Dovrolis, C. & Claffy, K. 2003. Bandwidth Estimation: Metrics, Measurement Techniques, and Tools. *IEEE Networks*, vol.17, no.16, pp.27-35.

Renesse, R. de, Ghassemian, M., Friderikos, V. & Aghvami, A.H. 2005. Adaptive Admission Control for Ad Hoc and Sensor Networks Providing Quality of Service. *Technical Report*, King College London.

Sarr, C., Chaudet, C., Chelius, G. & Lassous, I.G. 2006. A Node–Based Available Bandwidth Evaluation in IEEE 802.11 Ad Hoc Networks. *International journal of Parallel, Emergent and Distributed Systems*, vol.21, no.6.

Sarr, C., Chaudet, C., Chelius, G. & Lassous, I.G. 2008. Bandwidth Estimation for IEEE 802.11 Based Ad Hoc Networks. *IEEE transactions on Mobile Ad Hoc Networks*, vol.7, no.10, pp.1228-1241.

Sharma, L., Lal, C., & Kaliyar, P. 2017. Enhancing QoS for Multimedia Services Using Mobility-Aware Bandwidth Estimation Algorithm in MANETs. In *Optical & Wireless technologies*, pp. 655-666.

Communication and Computing Systems – Prasad et al. (eds)
© *2019 Taylor & Francis Group, London, ISBN 978-0-367-00147-6*

An efficient maximal frequent itemset mining algorithm based on linear prefix tree

M. Sinthuja
Department of Computer Science and Engineering, Annamalai University, Tamilnadu, India

N. Puviarasan
Department of Computer and Information Science, Annamalai University, Tamilnadu, India

P. Aruna
Department of Computer Science and Engineering, Annamalai University, Tamilnadu, India

ABSTRACT: Among various problems in data mining, discovering maximal frequent itemsets is the most crucial one. Mining all the frequent itemsets will generate big amount of itemsets. Frequent maximal itemsets (FMIs) results in a much smaller number of itemsets. Hence, it is highly valuable to explore maximal frequent itemsets. In general, exploration of frequent itemsets has been implemented using a special data structure called LP-tree (Linear Prefix-tree). The presentation of LP-tree is in array form which reduces the usage of pointers among nodes. Linear prefix tree uses less information and linearly accesses corresponding nodes. In this research paper, a novel technique is designed called LP-MFI-tree for mining maximal frequent itemsets (MFI) which is extended from LP-growth method. It reduces memory consumption and runtime. Then, the performances of the LP-MFI-tree are validated through various experiments on different datasets.

KEYWORDS: Frequent Item set Mining, Linear tree, Maximal Frequent Itemset Mining, Minimum Support, Pruning

1 INTRODUCTION

Exploration of frequent item sets is the most crucial feature of data mining (Syed Khairuzzaman Tanbeer, 2008; Sinthuja 2018). Frequent itemsets are nothing but the items that occur regularly from the transactional database (Han, 2007; Sinthuja, 2016; Sinthuja, 2017). Drawback of frequent itemset mining is exploring more frequent itemsets which includes redundant itemsets which consumes more time and memory (Daniele, 2017; Sinthuja, 2018).

In order to overcome the bottlenecks of frequent itemset mining, maximal frequent itemset is introduced. Maximal frequent itemset mining poses a significant challenge in data mining applications. Maximal frequent itemsets was developed by Mannila and Toivonen in the year 1997. A frequent itemset is defined as the items that appear together frequently (support must be higher than or equivalent to a particular threshold). Mining entire set of frequent itemsets is not good thought. Extraction of a subset pertaining to frequent item set is adequate to explore entire the maximal frequent item sets.

2 PRILIMINARIES AND RELATED WORKS

(Zaki, 1999; Gouda, 2001) introduced Maximal Frequent Itemsets (MFI) is the process of subset checking. A freshly identified frequent itemset is added into the MFI-tree, unless it is a part of an itemset previously in the tree. MAFIA-MFI is a depth-first algorithm. To decrease the count of tree search, data is stored into a bitmap. Bitmap is designed with two dimensions. A pruning technique called Parent Equivalence Pruning (PEP) is used. (Li, 2003) introduced FPMax*. It is extended from FP-growth method that mines maximal frequent itemsets. FP-tree holds the each transaction of the database in the tree. By using *look heads* pruning, maximal frequent itemset check out whether a frequent item set is a part or not. As MFI-tree is used to scan of all explored MFI, it makes energetic superset checking. An algorithm FPMax* uses a structure of array for holding the support of all 2-itemsets which is the subset of the frequent itemset. This algorithm scan FP-tree only once for recursive call. The experimental analysis proves that FPMax* is the most powerful algorithm for almost all databases.

3 PROPOSED MAXIMAL FREQUENT ITEMSET MINING ALGORITHM BASED ON LINEAR PREFIX-TREE (LP-MFI-TREE)

In the proposed LP-MFI, a new form of tree is introduced called *MaximalFrequent Itemset tree* (MFI-tree) to follow MFI's. The proposed LP-MFI-tree is expanded from LP-tree. The goal of maximal frequent itemset mining is to decrease itemsets from frequent itemsets. As the form of LP-MFI-tree is grounded on array there is no need of using pointers among each node. Based on the size of the itemset multiple nodes are created at once. Thus, improves the speed of the item traversal in the tree.

Therefore, the tree construction approach is quicker. Without the usage of pointer child node and parent node can be approached easily. Hence, LP-MFI-tree consumes lower amount of memory. The proposed LP-MFI-tree resembles LP-tree with some difference. In the proposed maximal frequent itemset mining, support is not calculated as it discovers only for maximality of the items. So, the attribute support is not used in LP-MFI-tree while LP-tree uses the attribute support value to explore frequent itemsets. Thus, the memory space required to store support is avoided in LP-MFI-tree and the time required for calculating support is also reduced in LP-MFI-tree.

The database shown in Table 1 is taken as input for the construction of LP-tree. LP-tree is constructed in (Syed Khairuzzaman Tanbeer, 2008; Gwangbum Pyun, 2014). By LP-Growth method LP-tree is called recursively for every frequent item *i*. In this example, when the entire {*i*}-conditional pattern base have only one path recursion stops. By adopting bottom up approach generating conditional pattern base and conditional LP-tree for every item as shown in Table 2.

The insertion of maximal frequent itemset into an LP-MFI-tree is identical to the infusion of a frequent set into an LP-tree of all maximal frequent itemsets into an LP-MFI-tree linked with the LP-tree. Conditional LP-tree is infused into LP-MFI-tree. In case of item 'd', the conditional LP-tree has a single path that is {c, a, d}. Clearly, this set is maximal as it is first frequent itemset. Thus, it is infused into LP-MFI-tree and its node link is stated as null is

Table 1. Transaction database.

Tid	Items Purchased	Ordered Items
1	a b c e f o	e, c, a, b, f
2	a c g	c, a, g
3	e i	e
4	a c d e g	e, c, a, g, dg
5	a c e g l	e, c, a, ga
6	e j e c	(e: 6) (e: 6)
7	a b c e f p	e, c, a, b, f
8	a c d	c, a, d
9	a c e g m	e, c, a, g
10	a c e g n	e, c, a, g

Table 2. Conditional LP-tree.

Item	Conditional pattern base	Conditional LP-tree
d	(e c a g: 1); (c a: 1)	(c: 2; a: 2) d
f	(e c a b: 2)	(e: 2; c: 2; a: 2; b: 2) f
b	(e c a: 2)	(e: 2; c: 2; a: 2) b
c	(e c a: 4); (c a: 1)	(c: 5; a: 5; e: 4) g
e	(e c:6); (c: 2)	(c: 8; e: 6) a

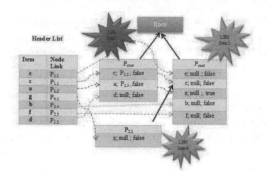

Figure 1. Construction of LP-MFI tree.

shown in Figure 1. Header list is filled with node link of item 'c, a, d'. Simultaneously, branch node list are created. For an item 'f', there is only one f-conditional LP-tree which is {e, c, a, b, f}. The technique of *subset_checking* is employed to examine whether the item 'f' conditional LP-tree is a subset of existing LP-MFI-tree. Here, it is not a part of existing MFI. Hence, the set is declared as maximal frequent itemset and its node link is stated as null. Then infuse {e, c, a, b, f} into the LP-MFI-tree. Node link of item 'e, c, a, b, f' is noted down in header list. For item 'b', the only b-conditional LP-tree is {e, c, a, b}. The technique of *subset_checking* is employed to examine whether it is a subset of an existing MFI.

Here, it is found that the itemset is not maximal frequent itemset. So, it is not added into LP-MFI-tree. For item 'g', g-conditional LP-tree is {e, c, a, g}. The technique of *subset_checking* is used to check whether it is a subset of an existing MFI. It is come to know that the itemset {e, c, a} is subset of existing LP-MFI-tree. But item 'e' is not part of existing LP-MFI-tree so new node is generated from item 'a' and node links is noted down. No itemsets is maximal for conditional LP-tree {a} {c} {e}. So, no fresh MFI's are added into the LP-MFI-tree. Thus the explored maximal frequent patterns are {c, a, d} {e, c, a, b, f} {e, c, a, g}. The complete LP-MFI-tree after inserting all MFIs is shown in Figure 1.

3.1 *Implementation of subset checking*

In maximal itemset mining a function called *subset_checking* is used. The purpose of *subset_checking* is to verify whether *Head* ∪ *Tail* is a part of some MFI in the LP-MFI-Tree. If *Head* ∪ *Tail* is a part of any existing MFI, then the frequent itemset generated from linear prefix tree cannot be maximal. Henceforth, mining is stopped. *Head* ∪ *Tail* cannot be determinedfrequent or not, when it is not a part of any existing MFI before and after the process of *subset_checking*. LP-tree is constructed for *Head* from the conditional pattern base, if the LP-tree has single path, then wrap up *Head* ∪ *Tail* as frequent. Since *Head* ∪ *Tail* was not a subset of any formerly discovered maximal frequent itemset, it's a new MFI and will be infused to the MFI-tree.

4 RESULTS AND DISCUSSION

In this research work, performance parameters of the proposed LP-MFI-tree are comparatively analyzed with FP-MAX and MAFIA which mines maximal frequent itemsets. The algorithm FP-MAX is extended from FP-growth algorithm. It mines maximal frequent itemset only. FP-tree holds the each transaction of the database in the tree. (Burdick, *et al.*, 2005) proposed MAFIA to discover maximal frequent itemsets. It is another depth first search algorithm.

The proposed algorithm of LP-MFI-tree is introduced in this paper. The ambition of this paper is to explore maximal frequent itemsets. If a frequent itemset to be added is not a part of any existing MFI, it is a new maximal frequent itemset. The function *subset_checking* is used in mining maximal frequent itemsets. In this section, research analysis was conducted to record the performance of the proposed LP-MFI-tree, FP-max and MAFIA algorithms. In this comparison different datasets are used. With respect to the performance, two important criteria of runtime and memory usage are considered. The above criteria are calculated on different minimum supports threshold values. From this experimental result, it is derived that the LP-MFI-tree performs better than other algorithms in the criteria of memory consumption.The studies were carried out in Intel® corei3™ CPU with 2.13 GHz, and 16GB of RAM computer. The algorithms have been executed in Java.

In this research paper, benchmark datasets are used from various applications. Dense datasets used for the execution are presented in Table 3. Chess is dense aspect dataset. Connect dataset is compiled from game state information. Pumsb is a census dataset obtained from US. It has huge amount of data. Number of maximal frequent patterns can be mined while varying higher minimum support values for dense dataset. Chess, Connect and Pumsb dataset are accessible at http://fimi.cs.helsinki.fi/data/and http://archive.ics.uci.edu/ml/datasets.

4.1 *Runtime assessment*

Figure 2 shows the graph which illustrates the runtime of the proposed LP-MFI-tree and the existing FP-max and MAFIA algorithms. From the graph, longitudinal axis shows runtime in seconds and latitudinal axis shows the various minimum support threshold values. With reference to the Figure 2, it is shown that the runtime of LP-MFI-tree, FP-max and MAFIA is 413.52sec, 627.05sec and 441.3sec for the dataset chess with minimum support threshold value of 40%. The runtime of FP-max algorithm is higher than MAFIA algorithm. Even when varying the minimum support the runtime of FP-max algorithm is higher than MAFIA. This is because construction of FP-max is widely used in mining maximal frequent itemsets. The proposed algorithm outperforms other algorithms of FP-max and MAFIA in almost all casesin mining maximal frequent itemsets. This is because of the special formation of the LP-MFI-tree.The content of MFI tree diminishes along with the reduction in characteristics as well as runtime.As LP-MFI-tree uses linear structure, the volume of LP-MFI-tree is minimized. LP-MFI-tree has only two attributes of item name and node link. The support calculation is not required in this algorithm. As the requirement for support calculation is done away with the proposed algorithm, time supposed to be used for such calculation is saved and thus runtime is minimized. Thus, the proposed algorithm decreases execution time in almost all cases while varying minimum support threshold from higher to lower values.

With reference to Figure 3, the runtime required for generating maximal frequent itemset of the algorithm LP-MFI-tree is 470sec, FP-max is 629.9sec and MAFIA is 748sec for the dataset connect with the minimum support threshold value of 20%. The runtime of MAFIA algorithm is higher than FP-max algorithm.But in the proposed LP-MFI-tree exploration of candidate itemset is avoided in mining maximal frequent itemset whereas MAFIA explores candidate itemset generation leading to MFI generation. Thus it is concluded that the proposed LP-MFI-treeperforms better with faster runtime when compared to other existing algorithms for various minimum support threshold values.The proposed LP-MFI-tree has linear structurewhich effectively decreases theamount of pointers used and the run time to search nodes. Because of the favor,it reduces runtime in full experiments. Specifically, when altering the minimum support less, the contrast of runtime of the proposed algorithm and other algorithm are massive.

Table 3. Dataset description.

Dataset	Transactions	Items	File size	Type
Chess	3,156	84	0.4mb	Dense
Connect	67,557	129	9.11mb	Dense
Pumsb	49,046	7166	16.29m	Dense

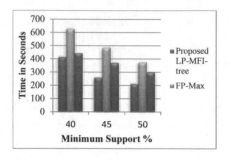

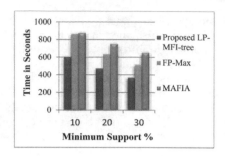

Figure 2. Runtime of mining maximal frequenti-temsets on chess dataset.

Figure 3. Runtime of mining maximal frequent itemsets on connect dataset.

4.2 *Memory consumption*

In this section, memory consumption of all the algorithms is analyzed with the same dataset used for runtime studies. The graph illustrated in Figure 4 results that the proposed LP-MFI-tree outshines other algorithms in almost all cases while altering minimum support threshold values from higher to lower. The LP-MFI-tree is compact due to its special design and the attributes used is limited in LP-MFI-tree. From the graph longitudinal axis shows the memory in MB and latitudinal axis shows the different minimum support threshold values. The consumption of memory of the proposed algorithm is 29.5MB, FP-max is 77MB and MAFIA is 32MB for the dataset chess with minimum support threshold values of 40%. FP-max has to construct bushy FP-tree from the dataset. The memory usage of MAFIA is less compared to FP-Max.With reference to Figure 5, memory consumption of some algorithms is almost the same for the given dataset connect. Next, FP-max gives the best result for higher minimum supports when compared with MAFIA.But the memory usage of FP-max occupies more memory than MAFIA.

Memory usage in mining maximal frequent itemsets for the algorithm LP-MFI-tree is 64MB, FP-max is 66MB and MAFIA is 65MB with the minimum support threshold value of 10%. It is observed that the proposed LP-MFI-tree effectively uses less space during function on relative analysis with FP-MAX and MAFIA. The memory consumption of other existing algorithm increases rapidly, while the memory usage of the proposed algorithm LP-MFI-tree does not change much as usage of pointer is reduced.The proposed LP-MFI-tree consumes lower memory due to the advantage of LP-MFI-tree.

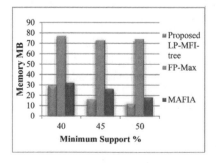

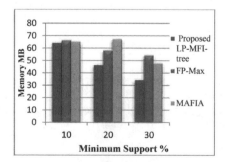

Figure 4. Memory usage of mining maximal frequent itemsets on chess dataset.

Figure 5. Memory usage of mining maximal frequent itemsets on connect dataset.

5 CONCLUSIONS

Frequent itemset mining results in redundant itemsets which is the major drawback. In this research paper, this problem is constricted by the mining of frequent maximal itemsets (FMIs) for generation of less number of itemsets for mining maximal itemset, LP-growth algorithm is extended to the proposed algorithm of LP-MFI-tree which uses a method called *subset_testing*. In this method, LP-MFI-tree is used for storing all exposed maximal frequent itemsets. Since, LP-MFI-tree with its unique structure is supportive for less usage of memory in the construction of trees and access time to search node is also decreased. It improves the conduct of mining by spending fewer memories in generating nodes as it reduces the use of pointers. The experiments conducted unequivocally reiterates that the proposed LP-MFI-tree is better than all other algorithms in terms of the parameters; memory usage, run time. In future, LP-MFI-tree may be applicable in varied datasets of distinct spheres.

Acknowledgement. We would like to thank the funding agency, the University Grant Commission (UGC) of the Government of India, for providing financial support.

REFERENCES

Daniele Apiletti, Elena Baralis, Tania Cerquitelli, Paolo Garza, Fabio Pulvirenti, Luca Venturini, (2017). Frequent Itemsets Mining for Big Data: A Comparative Analysis, Big Data Research, Vol.1, pp. 1-17.

Gouda, K. and Zaki, M.J. (2001). Efficiently Mining Maximal Frequent itemsets, Proc. IEEE Int'l Conf. Data Mining, pp. 163-170.

Gwangbum Pyun, Unil Yun, Keun Ho Ryu. (2014) Efficient frequent pattern mining based on Linear Prefix tree, Knowledge-Based Systems,Vol. 55,pp.125–139.

Han, J., Cheng, H., Xin, D., Yan, X. (2007). Frequent pattern mining: current status and future directions, Data Mining and Knowledge Discovery (DMKD) 15, pp.55–86.

Li, H.F., Lee, S. (2009). Mining top-K path traversal patterns over streaming web click sequences, Journal of Information Science and Engineering,Vol. 25 (4), 1121–1133.

Mannila, H. and Toivonen, H. (1997). Levelwise Search and Borders of Theories in Knowledge Discovery, Data Mining and KnowledgeDiscovery, Vol. 1, no. 3, pp. 241-258.

Sinthuja, M. Aruna, P. and Puviarasan, N. (2016). Experimental evaluation of Apriori and Equivalence Class Clustering and Bottom Up Lattice Traversal (ECLAT) Algorithms, *Pakistan Journal of Biotechnology*, Vol.13, pp.77-82.

Sinthuja, M., Puviarasan, N. and Aruna, P. (2017). Evaluating the Performance of Association Rule Mining Algorithms,World Applied Sciences Journal, Vol. 35 (1), pp.43-53.

Sinthuja, M., Puviarasan, N. and Aruna, P. (2018). Geo Map Visualization for Frequent Purchaser in Online Shopping Database Using an Algorithm LP-Growth for Mining Closed Frequent Itemsets, Elsevier, procedia computer science, Vol. 132, Pages 1512-1522.

Sinthuja, M. Puviarasan, N. and Aruna, P. (2018). Mining frequent Itemsets Using Top Down Approach Based on Linear Prefix tree, *Springer, Lecture Notes on Data Engineering and Communications Technologies*, Vol. 15, Pages 23-32.

Syed Khairuzzaman Tanbeer, ChowdhuryFarhan Ahmed, Byeong-Soo Jeong, Young-Koo Lee. (2008). Efficient single-pass frequent pattern mining using a prefix-tree, Information Sciences, Vol.179, pp. 559–583.

Zaki, M.J. and Hsiao, C.J. (1999). CHARM: An efficient algorithm for closed association rulemining'. TR 99-10, CS Dept., RPI.

Communication and Computing Systems – Prasad et al. (eds)
© *2019 Taylor & Francis Group, London, ISBN 978-0-367-00147-6*

Passive fault-tolerant control system design with tracking control against major system faults: Application to a canonical tank level system

H.R. Patel & V.A. Shah
Instrumentation and Control, Faculty of Technology, Dharmsinh Desai University, Nadiad, India

ABSTRACT: This paper deals with a novel passive fault-tolerant control (PFTC) design for Canonical Tank Level Control System (CTLCS) against major system (leak) faults. For greater advantages, different fault-tolerant control (FTC) techniques have been developed to address system or component faults for various systems with or without tracking control objectives. Though, very less FTC strategies found a relation between the post-fault reference trajectories to be tracked after fault occurrence. This is an open problem and it is well considered in literature. The significant impact of this paper is to design a PFTC using fuzzy logic for post-fault trajectory tracking control after major system fault occurrence. In case of fault occurrence, CTLCS response is found with different magnitude of system (Leak) faults. Finally, the simulation results have shown the effectiveness of the proposed PFTC approach in terms of integral error indices IAE and ISE.

1 INTRODUCTION

1.1 *FTC introduction*

For all chemical process industries, level and flow parameters are very crucial for any process. Due to their ever increasing use in industry and elsewhere, it is essential that such systems should be made more reliable and safe in operation. The Canonical Tank Level Control System (CTLCS) is widely used in various industries because of its advantages like high throughput but at the same time it is highly nonlinear system due to the conical shape of the tank that has varying cross sectional area. The dynamic characteristics of level control systems, however, suffer various faults (Sepehri, Karpenko, An, & Karam, 2005; Sepehri, & Karpenko, 2005) due to wear, battle damage, and/or unexpected failures of the system components. System (Leak) faults may cause undesired system behavior and sometimes lead to instability, hence it is necessary to introduce Fault-tolerant Control (FTC) methods against major system faults of uncertain nonlinear systems. FTC design methods have been proposed for several cases of nonlinear systems with system faults (Sepehri, & Karpenko, 2010; Patel, & Shah, 2018a). It consists in computing control laws by taking into account the faults affecting the system in order to maintain acceptable performances and to preserve stability of the system in the faulty situations (Ichalal, Marx, Ragot, & Maquin, 2010), hence the research on FTC has gaining more and more attention during the past 30 years, on which several research articles and books have been published in this area, for example, (Patton, 1997;Zhang, & Jiang, 2008; Mahmoud, Jiang, & Zhang, 2003; Isermann, 2006; Noura, Theilliol, Ponsart, & Chamseddine, 2009; Ducard, 2009; Edwards, Lombaerts, & Smaili, 2010; Alwi, Edwards, & Tan, 2011; Jain, Yamé, & Sauter, 2018). From the point of view of FTC strategies, the literature considers two main groups of techniques: passive and active ones (Jiang, & Yu, 2012). In passive FTC (PFTC), the faults are treated as uncertainties. Therefore, the control is designed to be robust only for the specified faults and for specified magnitudes

(Patel, & Shah, 2018c). However, active FTC (AFTC) techniques are characteristically considered by an online fault detection and diagnosis (FDD) process and control reconfiguration mechanism. A recent comparative study in (Jiang, & Yu, 2012) discusses active and passive FTC schemes by inspecting the matches and alterations amongst these two approaches from both philosophical and practical points of view. In recent the passive FTC schemes applied to a Single-Tank Level Control System with system (Leak) fault based on fuzzy logic control system has been carried out and tested using MATLAB Simulink platform as well as experimentally (Patel, & Shah, 2018b). In this current work, PFTC is applied on CTLCS with major system fault and post-fault tracking control.

1.2 *Literature survey*

To address the actuator or component, sensor, and system (Leak) faults for linear, linear parameter-varying, and nonlinear systems, significant FTC strategies have been established. Though, some important open problem yet be resolved. For occurrence, faults can be accommodated on condition that that there are adequate resources in the system. However, less FTC approaches found a relation between the post-fault objectives and the remaining resources in the system after fault occurrence. In other words, when trajectory tracking is considered, the tracking ability after faults is hardly examined. Degradation in post-fault tracking performance occurs, for example, when system (Leak) faults occur and the controller cannot deliver the desire output. There is more tendency for this case to take place when system (Leak) faults occur and the system resources decrease.

In (Hu, Shao, & Guo, 2018), tracking control problem of altitude of spacecraft with faults AFTC is designed and applied. A fault detection and compensation is designed in (Hajiani, &Poshtan, 2014) for quadruple interacting-tank nonlinear systems with abrupt and incipient faults. In the context of PFTC, an artificial intelligence technique used in (Patel, & Shah, to be published)to accommodate the actuator and sensor faults for interacting and non-interacting level control system, also experimental results show the efficacy of the proposed strategy. FTC scheme has been proposed and implemented in (He, Wang, Liu, Qin, & Zhou, 2017) on an internet-based three-tank system for the leak (system) and sensor bias faults. Leakage fault in hydraulic system is addressed and FTC scheme is proposed in (Yao, Yang, & Ma, 2014). Also for internet based three-tank level control system leak fault diagnosis in (Zhou, He, Wang, Liu, & Ji, 2012) and experimental results shown.

An artificial intelligence technique extended to the design of PFTC with case of single and multiple faults has been applied in (Qian, Xiong, Wang, & Qian, 2016; Patel, & Shah, in press). In (Qian, Xiong, Wang, & Qian, 2016) FTC scheme is applied on faulty UAV using fuzzy modeling approach. For actuator fault FTC using fuzzy logic has been implemented in (Shen, Jiang, & Tong, 2013), fuzzy plus PID controller is used to design FTC against actuator faults in (Gritli, Gharsallaoui, & Benrejeb, 2017) for an electronic throttle valve application.

In reference with the above-mentioned research works, the main contribution of this paper is the integration of conventional PI controller plus Fuzzy Logic Controller (FLC) and post-fault reference trajectory tracking. The main advantage of fuzzy logic is that it does not require precise value of system fault magnitudes.

When faults occur in a system (Leak), the faults are tolerated by a FLC. The proposed PFTC method consists of PI plus FLC control which track the reference trajectory when degradation occurs in performance because of system faults in CTLCS. The CTLCS introduction and mathematical model is described in Section 2. The combined arrangement of the suggested PFTC are presented in Section 3. The proposed PFTC strategy is tested on CTLCS subject to major system (Leak) faults and post-fault tracking control with MATLAB Simulink platform. Results were compared without PFTC, significant results are described in Section 4. Conclusion and future work is discussed in Section 5.

2 MATHEMATICAL MODELING OF CANONICAL TANK SYSTEMS

2.1 *Process description*

The prototype system used is a Canonical Tank Level Control System (CTLCS) where conical shaped tank is used and is highly nonlinear and unstable system due to the variation in area of cross-sectional area of the tank with height. Also CTLCS is widely used in food processing plant, chemical processing plant, concrete mixing industries, hydro metallurgical industries, waste water treatment industries, and adhesive processing. It is used because of their shape. It contributes to better disposal of solids on mixing and provides complete drainage especially for viscous liquids, slurries and solid mixtures (Patel, & Shah, to be published). It is widely used as a test bench to develop advanced control algorithms for different nonlinear system model as well as for experimental and educational studies of nonlinear control system. The Canonical Tank Level Control System (CTLCS) consists of one conical tank, one pump that delivers the liquid flow (F_i) to tank through one control valve (CV_1) as shown in Figure 1. (F_o) and (F_l) are the two output flows from tank through manual control valves (MV_1) and (MV_2) with valve coefficient β_1 and β_2 respectively. The outlet flow rate (F_l) is introduced as a system (Leak) fault using manually operated control valve MV_2.

The controlling variable is inflow rate (F_i) of the tank. The controlled variable is level of the conical tank h. The manipulated variable is inflow rate (F_i) of the tank using control valve (CV_1). The CTLCS has one constant outlet flow rate (F_o) using (MV_1). The system (Leak) fault is introduced into system using (MV_2) and has flow rate (F_l).

The operating parameters of the prototype model of CTLCS are given in Figure 1.

2.2 *Mathematical modeling*

The process considered here is the canonical tank system with conical shaped tank as shown in Figure 1 in which liquid level is maintained at a constant rate by controlling the inflow of the tank (F_i).

The mathematical modeling of the system should be obtained using the process parameters. According to mass balance equation described in (Wayne, 2003),

Rate of Accumulation = Input – Output

$$A = \pi r^2 \tag{1}$$

From the Figure 1

$$tan\theta \frac{R}{H}; \text{ At any height (h) of tank } tan\theta \frac{r}{h} = \frac{R}{H} \tag{2}$$

Area of the conical tank at any height (h) and volume of conical tank given by eq. (3)

Parameter	Symbol	Value
Total Height of the Tank	H	70 cm
Top Radius of the Tank	R	17.6 cm
Bottom Radius of the Tank	r	2 cm
MV1 Valve Co-efficient	β_1	5 cm²/sec
Steady state Tank	h	35 cm
Gravitational constant	g	9.82 m/sec²
Process Delay	τ_d	0 sec

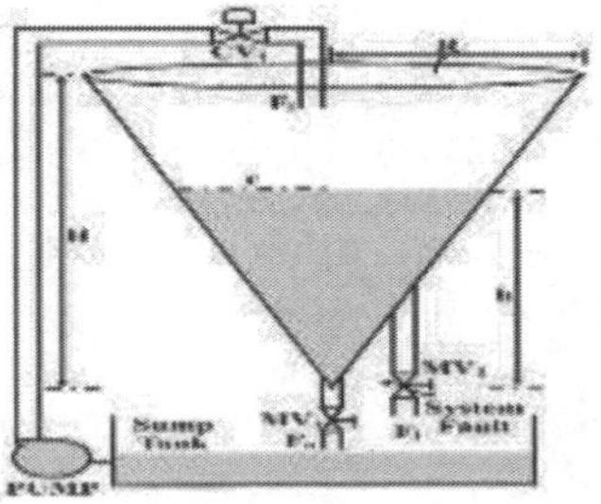

Figure 1.   Prototype model of CTLCS with one system fault and operating parameters.

$$A = \frac{\pi R^2 h^2}{H^2} \,\&\, V = \frac{1}{3}\pi r^2 H \tag{3}$$

For conical tank the mass balance equation is given by equation,

$$\frac{d}{dt}\left(\frac{1}{3}\pi r^2 H - \frac{1}{3}\pi r^2 H_d\right) = F_i - F_o \tag{4}$$

Where,

$$F_o = \beta_1\sqrt{2gh} \,\&\, H_d \text{ is a cap height, } H_d = H - h \tag{5}$$

Now solving equations (4) and (5) the linearized transfer function for the CTLCS is obtained as follows,

$$G_p = \frac{K_p e^{-\tau d}}{(\tau s + 1)} \tag{6}$$

For finding the value of τ_1, and K_p

$$\frac{dh}{dt} = \frac{\Upsilon F_i}{h^2} - \beta_1 h^{-3/2} \tag{7}$$

2.3 Process reaction curve method

Process reaction curve method is a methodology for building mathematical models of dynamic system using measurements of the system's input and output signals, i.e., system identification. It utilizes input-output experimental data to determine a system identification of nonlinear process using step test presented in fig. 4 (Huang, & Jeng, 2005, p. 297-337).

Steps to find transfer function are:

• To measure initial steady state value of process variable (ISS).
• Give significant step change to the process.
• Note the time delay.
• Observe the change in the process variable and note new steady state value (NSS).
• Find total change in process variable.
• Time constant τ time at which PV achieve 63.2% of final value (NSS) after step input.
• Process gain Kp is ΔPV/ΔV where ΔV is change in input in volts.
• Time delay is $\tau_d = 0$ sec in this process.

After that a step increment in the input flow rate is given, and different readings are noted till the process variable become stable in the conical tank. The practical data from experimental setup are approximated to be CTLCS model. The model parameters chosen here at 25-35 cm operating range:

The mathematical model of CTLCS is given as following:

$$G_p(s) = \frac{0.8814}{27.22s + 1} \tag{8}$$

2.4 PI controller without PFTC

The without PFTC scheme design with PI control approach involves of proportional term & integral term. The PI controller calculation is given as:

$$u_{c1}(t) = K_p e_p + K_i \int e(t)dt \tag{9}$$

System without PFTC scheme is presented with dotted box in Figure 3. The criteria for selecting the PI gains was integral squared error (ISE) i.e. the controller setting which gives less ISE was selected as the gains of the controller. The gain values of the PI controller parameters; proportional gain K_p and Integral gain K_i are as follows:

$$K_p = 500 \text{ and } K_i = 0.005 \tag{10}$$

2.5 *PFTC strategy*

For designing PFTC soft computing method is used. Fuzzy Logic Control (FLC) and PI controller are used to detect the faults in system and give superior control performance and system stability even though system faults occur. PFTC gives remarkable results in the occurrence of system (Leak) fault in CTLCS. The PFTC scheme block diagram is presented in Figure 2, it comprises of the PI plus (FLC).

The Fuzzy Logic Controller (FLC) with product–sum inference method, centroid defuzzification method and triangular membership functions for the inputs and a crisp output are used, in our study. The input output membership function is presented in fig. 3. The linguistic variable levels, allocated to the variables $e_1(k)$, and $u_{c2}(k)$, are given

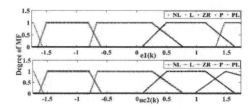

Figure 2.   PFTC strategy for CTLCS.

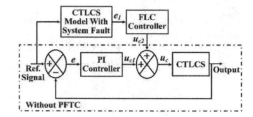

Figure 3. Membership functions of input and output of FLC.

in Table 1 as follows: NL: Negative Large; N: Negative; ZR: Zero; P: Positive; PL: Positive Large.

Table 1.   Fuzzy rules-base.

$e_1(k)$	NL	N	ZR	P	PL
$u_{c2}(k)$	NL	N	ZR	P	PL

3   SIMULATION RESULTS

PFTC approach is applied on CTLCS without system fault with step and sine reference input trajectory. We perceived that the system's responses with PFTC track desired trajectories. Figure 4. Comparative response of CTLCS with and without PFTC with major system faults plus post–fault step trajectory tracking control.

The proposed PFTC scheme is applied on CTLCS with major system fault with step reference trajectory responses have been represented in fig. 4. The system fault *(fs)* equations considered in step trajectory for CTLCS.

The system response without PFTC degrade drastically, however for the similar reference input trajectory by using the PFTC approach the system remains stable and almost zero steady state post-fault tracking error which shows the effectiveness of the proposed PFTC approach. The pre-fault and post-fault tracking with PFTC and without PFTC are shown in fig. 4. Effectiveness of the proposed PFTC scheme against major system faults in terms of different integral error criteria are shown by Table 2.

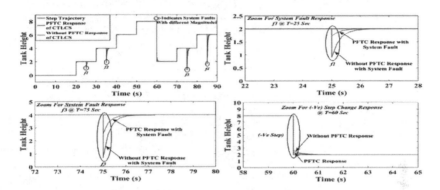

Figure 4. Comparative response of CTLCS with and without PFTC with major system faults plus post–fault step trajectory tracking control.

Table 2. Integral errors comparison under major system fault.

Sr. No.	Controller	Trajectory	IAE	ISE
1	PFTC	Step	1.5131	9.4378e-1
	Without PFTC		3.6447	5.1086

4 CONCLUSION

This paper proposed PFTC approach to the major system faults compensation in CTLCS, which was based on the conventional PI controller plus Fuzzy Logic Control (FLC). The article briefs about major system faults of different natures with step reference trajectory tracking control. The PFTC is designed for the system with efficiently pre-fault and post-fault tracking control. Control performance is tested with IAE and ISE integral error indices. Simulation tested on MATLAB Simulink platform reveals better performance of designed PFTC in terms of almost zero steady state error, fast and smooth tracking control against major system fault as compared to without PFTC. In future work, designed controller will be implemented on a real time CTLCS.

REFERENCES

Alwi, H., Edwards, C., and Tan, C. P. (2011) *Fault Detection and Fault-tolerant Control Using Sliding Modes*. Springer-Verlag: London.

An, L., and Sepehri, N. (2005) "Hydraulic actuator leakage fault detection using extended Kalman filter," *International Journal of Fluid Power*, 6(1),41–51.

Ducard, G. (2009) *Fault-tolerant Flight Control and Guidance Systems: Practical Methods for Small Unmanned Aerial Vehicles*. Springer-Verlag: London.

Edwards, C., Lombaerts, T., and Smaili, H. (2010) *Fault Tolerant Flight Control: A Benchmark Challenge*. Springer-Verlag: Berlin, Heidelberg.

Gritli, W., Gharsallaoui, and Benrejeb, M. (2017) "Fault Tolerant Control Based on PID-type Fuzzy Logic Controller for Switched Discrete-time Systems: An Electronic Throttle Valve Application," *Advances in Science*, Technology *and Engineering Systems Journal*, 2(6),186-193.

Hajiani, P., and Poshtan, J. (2014) "Abrupt and incipient fault detection and compensation for a 4-tank system benchmark," *Turkish Journal of Electrical Engineering & Computer Sciences*, 5(5),1287-1297. Doi: 10.3906/elk-1210-68

He, X., Wang, Z., Liu, L. Qin, L., and Zhou, D. (2017) "Fault-Tolerant Control for an Internet-Based Three-Tank System: Accommodation to Sensor Bias Faults," *IEEE Transactions on Industrial Electronics*, 64(3),2266-2275. Doi: 10.1109/TIE.2016.2623582

Hu, Q., Shao, X., and Guo, L. (2018) "Adaptive Fault-Tolerant Attitude Tracking Control of Spacecraft with Prescribed Performance," *IEEE/ASME Transactions on Mechatronics*, 23(1),331-341.

Huang, H. P., and Jeng, J. C. (2005) *Process Reaction Curve and Relay Methods Identification and PID Tuning. In*: *Johnson* M. A., *Moradi*, M. H. *(eds) PID Control*. Springer, London, Doi:https://doi.org/10.1007/1-84628-148-2_8

Ichalal, D., Marx, B., Ragot, J., and Maquin, D. (2010) "Fault Tolerant Control for Takagi-Sugeno systems with unmeasurable premise variables by trajectory tracking," *In International Symposium on Industrial Electronics(ISIE)*, 2010, At Bari, Italy, (p. 2097-2102).

Isermann, R. (2006) *Fault-diagnosis Systems: An Introduction from Fault Detection to Fault Tolerance*. Springer-Verlag: Berlin, Heidelberg.

Jain, T., Yamé, J. J., and Sauter, D. (2018) *Active Fault-Tolerant Control Systems: A Behavioral System Theoretic Perspective*. Springer-Verlag: Berlin, Heidelberg.

Jiang, J., and Yu, X. (2012) "Fault-tolerant control systems: a comparative study between active and passive approaches," *Annual Reviews in Control*. 36(1),60–72.

Karpenko, M., and Sepehri, N. (2010), "Quantitative fault tolerant control design for a leaking hydraulic actuator," *ASME Journalof Dynamic Systems, Measurement and Control*, 132(5),237–244.

Karpenko, M., and Sepehri, N. (2005), "Fault-tolerant control of a servo hydraulic positioning system with crossport leakage," *IEEE Transactions on Control Systems Technology*, 13(1),155–161.

Mahmoud, M., Jiang, J., and Zhang, Y. M. (2003) *Active Fault Tolerant Control Systems: Stochastic Analysis and Synthesis*. Springer-Verlag: Berlin, Heidelberg.

Noura, H., Theilliol, D., Ponsart, J. C., and Chamseddine, A. (2009) *Fault-tolerant Control Systems: Design and Practical Applications*. Springer-Verlag: London.

Niemann, H., and Stoustrup, J. (2005), "Passive fault tolerant control of a double inverted pendulum-a case study," *Control Engineering Practice*. 13(8),1047–1059.

Patton, R. J. (1997) "Fault-tolerant control systems: the 1997 situation," *IFAC Symposium on Fault Detection, Supervision and Safety for Technical Processes*, Vol. 2, Kingston Upon Hull, U K, (p. 1033–1055).

Patel, H. R., and Shah, V. A. (2018) "Fault Tolerant Control Systems: A Passive Approaches for Single Tank Level Control System," *i-manager's Journal on Instrumentation and Control Engineering*. 6(1),11-18.

Patel, H. R., and Shah, V. A. (2018) "Fault Detection and Diagnosis Methods in Power Generation Plants - The Indian Power Generation Sector Perspective: An Introductory Review," *PDPU Journal of Energy and Management*. 2(2),31-49.

Patel, H. R., and Shah, V. A. (2018) "Fuzzy Logic Based Passive Fault Tolerant Control Strategy for a Single-Tank System with System Fault and Process Disturbances," *in Proc. 5th International Conference on Electrical and Electronics Engineering (ICEEE)*, 2-3 May 2018, at Istanbul, Turkey, (p. 257–262).

Patel, H. R., and Shah, V. A. "Performance Comparison of Passive Fault Tolerant Control Strategy with PI and Fuzzy Control of Single-Tank Level Process with Sensor and System Fault," *American Journal of Engineering and Applied Sciences, Science Publications*, (In Press).

Patel, H. R., and Shah, V. A. (2018) "A Framework for Fault-tolerant Control for an Interacting and Non-interacting level Control System Using AI," *in 15th International Conference on Informatics in Control, Automation and Robotics (ICINCO)*, 2018, at Porto, Portugal, to be published.

Patel, H. R., and Shah, V. A. "A fault-tolerant control strategy for non-linear system: An application to the two tank canonical non interacting level control system," *IEEE DISCOVER 2018, IEEE*, To be published.

Qian, M., Xiong, K., Wang, L. and Qian, Z. (2016) "Fault Tolerant Controller Design for a Faulty UAV Using Fuzzy Modeling Approach," *Mathematical Problems in Engineering*, Hindawi *Publishing Corporation*, Article ID 5329291, Available from http://dx.doi.org/10.1155/2016/5329291

Ravi, V. R., and Thyagarajan, T. (2014) "Adaptive Decentralized PI Controller for Two Canonical Tank Interacting Level System," *Arabian Journal for Science and Engineering*, 39(12),8433-8451.

Communication and Computing Systems – Prasad et al. (eds)
© *2019 Taylor & Francis Group, London, ISBN 978-0-367-00147-6*

Asymmetric cryptosystem based on fractional Fourier transform domain using triple random phase masks

Shivani Yadav & Hukum Singh
Department of Applied Science, The NorthCap University, Gurugram, India

ABSTRACT: A Novel asymmetric encryption technique is proposed to carry out the study of an optical security technique for image encryption using triple random phase encoding (TRPE) through fractional Fourier domain. For better security in proposed cryptosystem, Double Random Phase Encoding (DRPE) is converted to TRPE by performing convolution with third random phase mask. In the decryption process two private keys and one public key is used. Numerical Simulations are performed such as histogram, entropy and noise attack analysis to check the robustness of the system. Performance analysis is also done for the proposed system.

1 INTRODUCTION

In the past decades, securing information was considered as a tough task. Broad research has been done on optical systems for image encryption. It has gained a great potency owing to high parallel processing and big storage memories (Javidi 1997, Chang et al. 2002, Wang et al. 1996, Li et al. 2000). Numerical methods for optical image encryption have been proposed. The double random-phase encoding (DRPE) scheme was proposed by Refregier and Javidi (1995). The security of the DRPE method has been examined proving that such a scheme is robust against many attacks. DRPE is also implemented in various transforms domain such as fractional Fourier (Unnikrishnan et al. 2000, Dahiya et al. 2014, Garcia et al. 1996, Hennelly and Sheridan 2003, Nischal et al. 2003, 2004, Singh et al. 2008, Girija and Singh 2018), Fresnel (Matoba and Javidi 1999, Situ and Zhang 2004, Singh et al. 2015, Hennelly and Sheridan 2004, Sheng et al. 2012), Gyrator (Rodrigo et al. 2007, Singh 2016, Singh et al. 2014), Fractional Mellin (Zhou et al. 2011, Vashisth et al. 2014, 2014, Singh 2018), Fractional Hartley (Singh 2017, Yadav and Singh 2018). But all these transforms were symmetric cryptosystem and it is vulnerable to many attacks. The original DRPE technique consists of primary image which is encrypted by using two random phase masks (RPMs), one is primary image and other is in the Fourier domain, respectively. Fractional Fourier transform proposed an optical encryption method using random phase encoding in the specified domain (Refregier and Javidi 1995, Unnikrishnan et al. 2000). Later, the Fourier transform operators in DRPE scheme were replaced by FrFT operators. The remarkable feature of optical encryption based on the FrFT is the fractional order, to enhance the key space as a result security of the encryption is increasing. Optical image encryption schemes, which have been discussed previously, are considered as symmetric cryptosystem where the encoding and decoding keys are similar.

However, the conventional DRPE technique has some shortcomings and can be attacked with some methods such as cipher-text attack (CPA) and noise attack analysis. To overcome all these attacks, asymmetric cryptosystems have been proposed by Qin and Peng (2010). we opt asymmetric cryptosystem (Qin et al. 2011, Wang and Zhao 2011, 2012, Khurana and Singh 2017) it is a system which uses two type of keys i.e. public key and private key. In this paper work, we propose a triple random phase encoding (TRPE) scheme (Ahouzi et al. 2017) in asymmetric cryptosystem. The triple random phase encoding scheme increasing the complexity of the system in the way of more keys required to define the system. This improved the security levels of the method when compared with double random phase encoding cryptosystem.

The scheme used in this paper, uses the addition of a third key in the encryption front, which enables more security for our proposed cryptosystem. In the decryption process, we have used three keys i.e, two private keys and one public key. The numerical simulation for the proposed cryptosystem has been carried out using Matlab (R2018a). Various factors have been analyzed to check the robustness of our suggested system.

2 THEORETICAL BACKGROUND

2.1 Fractional Fourier Transform

The Fractional Fourier Transform is a generalisation of original Fourier transform and is defined in terms of fractional order p. Fractional Fourier transform is a linear transform and have application in many fields such as optical signal processing, image and signal processing techniques, watermarking, quantum mechanics, time-variant filtering and multiplexing.

Extra security against attacks is provided by FrFT scheme. The normal Fourier transform is a special case of a continuous fractional Fourier domains. The expression of pth order FrFT of f(x) is expressed as

$$F^p f(x)(u) = \int_{-\infty}^{+\infty} K_p(x,u)f(x)dx$$

$$K_p = \begin{cases} A \ exp\left[i\pi\left(x^2 cot\phi - 2xu \ csc\phi + u^2 cot\phi\right)\right] \\ \delta(x-u) \\ \delta(x+u) \end{cases}$$

and $A = \frac{exp[-i(\pi sgn(\Phi)/4 - \Phi/2)]}{\sqrt{|\sin \Phi|}}$, where $\Phi = p\pi/2$ is the angle to the transform of order p along x-axis and p is an integer multiple of π, k is the Dirac delta function.

3 PROPOSED SYSTEM

3.1 Encryption scheme

The encryption of proposed system converts the input image I (x, y) to the cipher image E (x, y) which is unidentifiable or stationary white noise.

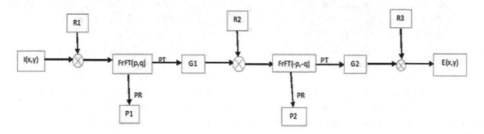

Let us consider the input image as I (x, y) that must be encrypted. Let R1, R2, R3 be the random phase masks with the interval $[0,2\pi]$ which are statistically independent to each other and p, q are the fractional orders in the encryption process. The steps for encryption process are as follows:

Step 1- The original image I (x, y) that has encrypted is first multiplied by a random phase mask R1 in the input plane then apply the fractional Fourier transform on it with the orders p, q and the resultant is divided into two portions phase truncation (PT) and phase reservation (PR) and the absolute form is called phase truncation and the angular form is phase reservation.

$$G1 = PT\{FrFT(p,q) \ [I(x,y).R1]\} \tag{1}$$

Where $R1 = \exp[2\pi i\Phi_1(x,y)]$.

Step 2- For identifying G2, the equation (1) is multiplied with R2 and applying fractional Fourier transform with orders -p and -q to obtain the phase-truncated portion, which is called as G2.

$$G2 = PT\{FrFT(-p,-q) \ [G1.R2]\} \tag{2}$$

and $R2 = \exp[2\pi i\Phi_2(x,\ y)]$.

Step 3- Now to get the encrypted image, the equation (2) is multiplied with R3.

$$E = G2.R3 \tag{3}$$

and $R3 = \exp[2\pi i\Phi_3(u,v)]$.

3.2 Decryption process

In the decryption process, the encrypted image is treated as the original image and we use two private keys and one public key to recover the original image. E (x, y) image that must be decoded or decrypted into original image. At the time of decryption process, the private keys i.e. P1 and P2 are used which is stored as phase reservation in the encryption process. The random phase mask R3 is dividing with the input image in the decryption. Following are the steps of decryption scheme:

Step 1- The encrypted image E (x, y) that is recover is firstly divided by random phase mask R3. Then the obtain image is multiplied by the phase reservation key P2 and after that we apply fractional Fourier transform with orders -p and -q on it.

$$G2 = FrFT(-p,-q) \ \{[P2.[E(x,y)/R3]\} \tag{4}$$

Step 2- After all this, the equation (4) is multiplied by phase reservation key P1 and to obtain the original image we apply fractional Fourier transform with orders p, q.

$$I(x,y) = \{FrFT(p,q) \ [G2.P1]\} \tag{5}$$

Finally, in our proposed system image is recovered.

4 SIMULATION RESULTS

The triple random phase encoding asymmetric cryptosystem is proposed using simulation tests and is carried out on MATLAB R2018a. When the keys are wrong i.e, random key and phase key are replaced by any other keys then we cannot able to get proper decrypted image. The results are shown in Figure 1.

Mean-Squared Error: MSE is calculated between the original image I (x, y) and decrypted image (x, y) and it can be expressed as:

Figure 1. Lena is considered as input image in 1(a), encrypted image in.

$$MSE = \sum_{i=0}^{255} \sum_{i=0}^{255} \frac{|I(x,y) - I'(x,y)|^2}{256 \times 256} \tag{6}$$

MSE value of the proposed system is $1.4681x10^{-26}$. For better similarity between input image and decrypted image the MSE value should be less. It is clearly observed that there is good co-ordination between I (x, y) and I'(x, y).

We have shown the plot between fractional orders and MSE and it is clearly depicting in the figure. (2) that with the correct value of fractional order, graph is obtained perfectly and if the fractional order is not same then the graph is not obtained correctly.

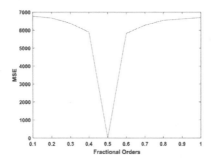

Figure 2. Plot between fractional orders and MSE.

Peak-Signal to Noise Ratio: PSNR is a peak-signal to noise ratio which is calculated between input image and the decrypted image. The higher the PSNR value the better is the quality of image.

$$PSNR = 10 \times \log_{10} \left(\frac{255^2}{MSE} \right) \tag{7}$$

The value of PSNR for our proposed work is 705.7361 dB, which is high and offers good quality of image.

5 NUMERICAL ANALYSIS

5.1 Histogram analysis

Histogram shows the disturbance of pixel value of an image. The histogram of Lena image is shown in Figure 3(a, b) the input and the encrypted image graphs respectively. As it is clear from the encrypted plot and from the original plot that, it is robust against attack because plots are completely different from each other.

5.2 Entropy

Entropy is a statistical measure of the uncertainty of a cipher image. In case of higher uncertainty, recovering of image is impossible. Entropy (H) is given by:

$$H = -\sum_{i=0}^{255} p_i \log_2 p_i \tag{8}$$

Where p is the probability. The optimal value of encoded image is 8. The entropy value of the encrypted image is 7.9297, which is close to ideal value.

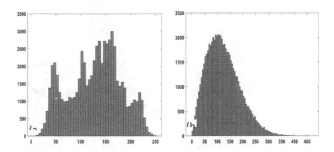

Figure 3.   Histogram of (a) Input image and (b) Encrypted image.

5.3 Noise attack analysis

The strength of the proposed scheme is tested by including Gaussian noise to the encrypted image. The noise is represented by:

$$J' = J(1 + KG) \tag{9}$$

Where J is the encrypted image and J' is the noise affected encrypted image, k is the noise strength and G is a Gaussian noise with mean 0 and standard deviation 1. Figure 4 shows the curve between noise factor and mean-squared error. It is clearly observed that, as the noise factor increases the mean-squared error also increases intern it affects the quality of image.

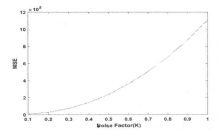

Figure 4.   Depict graph between noise factor and MSE.

6   CONCLUSION

In our proposed work, an asymmetric cryptosystem based on fractional Fourier domain using triple random keys is developed. Here, in this system we have used three random phase masks (R1, R2, R3) in encryption process. During decryption process two private keys (P1 and P2) which are phase reversal and one public key (R3) are used for better security. The proposed scheme shows better results as compared to DRPE and is tested by various numerical analysis. Further in terms of security, TRPE enhances the performance of DRPE.

REFERENCES

Ahouzi, E., Zamrani, W., Azami, N., Lizana, A., Campos, J., & Yzuel, M. J. (2017). Optical triple random-phase encryption. *Optical Engineering, 56*(11), 113114.

Chang, H. T., Lu, W. C., & Kuo, C. J. (2002). Multiple-phase retrieval for optical security systems by use of random-phase encoding. *Applied optics, 41*(23), 4825–4834.

Dahiya, M., Sukhija, S., & Singh, H. (2014, February). Image encryption using quad phase masks in fractional Fourier domain and case study. In *Advance Computing Conference (IACC), 2014 IEEE International* (pp. 1048–1053). IEEE.

Garcia, J., Mas, D., & Dorsch, R. G. (1996). Fractional-Fourier-transform calculation through the fast-Fourier- transform algorithm. *Applied optics, 35*(35), 7013–7018.

Girija, R., & Singh, H. (2018). A cryptosystem based on deterministic phase masks and fractional Fourier transform deploying singular value decomposition. *Optical and Quantum Electronics, 50*(5), 210.

Hennelly, B. M., & Sheridan, J. T. (2003). Image encryption and the fractional Fourier transform. Optik, 114(6), 251–265.

Hennelly, B. M., & Sheridan, J. T. (2004). Random phase and jigsaw encryption in the Fresnel domain. *Optical Engineering, 43*(10), 2239–2250.

Javidi, B. (1997). Securing information with optical technologies. *Physics Today, 50*(3), 27–32.

Khurana, M., & Singh, H. (2017). An asymmetric image encryption based on phase truncated hybrid transform. *3D Research, 8*(3), 28.

Li, Y., Kreske, K., & Rosen, J. (2000). Security and encryption optical systems based on a correlator with significant output images. *Applied Optics, 39*(29), 5295–5301.

Matoba, O., & Javidi, B. (1999). Encrypted optical memory system using three-dimensional keys in the Fresnel domain. *Optics Letters, 24*(11), 762–764.

Nishchal, N. K., Joseph, J., & Singh, K. (2003). Fully phase encryption using fractional Fourier transform. *Optical Engineering, 42*(6), 1583–1589.

Nishchal, N. K., Joseph, J., & Singh, K. (2004). Fully phase-based encryption using fractional order Fourier domain random phase encoding: error analysis. *Optical Engineering, 43*(10), 2266–2283.

Qin, W., & Peng, X. (2010). Asymmetric cryptosystem based on phase-truncated Fourier transforms. *Optics Letters, 35*(2), 118–120.

Qin, W., Peng, X., Gao, B., & Meng, X. (2011). Universal and special keys based on phase-truncated Fourier transform. *Optical Engineering, 50*(8), 080501.

Refregier, P., & Javidi, B. (1995). Optical image encryption based on input plane and Fourier plane random encoding. Optics Letter. 20,767–769.

Rodrigo, J. A., Alieva, T., & Calvo, M. L. (2007). Gyrator transform properties and applications. *Optics express, 15*(5), 2190–2203.

Sheng, Y., Yan-Hui, X., Ming-tang, L., Shu-xia, Y., & Xin-juan, S. (2012). An improved method to enhance the security of double random-phase encoding in the Fresnel domain. *Optics & Laser Technology, 44*(1), 51–56.

Singh, H. (2016). Devil's vortex Fresnel lens phase masks on an asymmetric cryptosystem based on phase-truncation in gyrator wavelet transform domain. *Optics and Lasers in Engineering, 81*, 125–139.

Singh, H. (2017). Nonlinear optical double image encryption using random-optical vortex in fractional Hartley transform domain. *Optica Applicata, 47*(4).

Singh, H. (2018). Watermarking image encryption using deterministic phase mask and singular value decomposition in fractional Mellin transform domain. IET Image Processing, 12(11), 1994–2001.

Singh, H., Yadav, A. K., Vashisth, S., & Singh, K. (2014). Fully phase image encryption using double random-structured phase masks in gyrator domain. *Applied optics, 53*(28), 6472–6481.

Singh, H., Yadav, A. K., Vashisth, S., & Singh, K. (2015). Optical image encryption using devil's vortex toroidal lens in the Fresnel transforms domain. *International Journal of Optics, 2015*.

Singh, M., Kumar, A., & Singh, K. (2008). Secure optical system that uses fully phase-based encryption and lithium niobate crystal as phase contrast filter for decryption. *Optics & Laser Technology, 40*(4), 619–624.

Situ, G., & Zhang, J. (2004). Double random-phase encoding in the Fresnel domain. *Optics Letters, 29* (14), 1584–1586.

Unnikrishnan, G., Joseph, J., & Singh, K. (2000). Optical encryption by double-random phase encoding in the fractional Fourier domain. *Optics letters*, *25*(12), 887–889.

Vashisth, S., Singh, H., Yadav, A. K., & Singh, K. (2014). Devil's vortex phase structure as frequency plane mask for image encryption using the fractional Mellin transform. *International Journal of Optics, 2014*.

Vashisth, S., Singh, H., Yadav, A. K., & Singh, K. (2014). Image encryption using fractional Mellin transform, structured phase filters, and phase retrieval. *Optik-International Journal for Light and Electron Optics*, *125*(18), 5309–5315.

Wang, R. K., Watson, I. A., & Chatwin, C. R. (1996). Random phase encoding for optical security. *Optical Engineering*, *35*(9), 2464–2470.

Wang, X., & Zhao, D. (2011). Double-image self-encoding and hiding based on phase-truncated Fourier transforms and phase retrieval. *Optics Communications*, *284*(19), 4441–4445.

Wang, X., & Zhao, D. (2012). A special attack on the asymmetric cryptosystem based on phase-truncated Fourier transforms. *Optics Communications*, *285*(6), 1078–1081.

Yadav, P. L., & Singh, H. (2018). Optical Double Image Hiding in the Fractional Hartley Transform Using Structured Phase Filter and Arnold Transform. *3D Research*, *9*(2), 20.

Zhou, N., Wang, Y., & Gong, L. (2011). Novel optical image encryption scheme based on fractional Mellin transform. *Optics Communications*, *284*(13), 3234–3242.

Communication and Computing Systems – Prasad et al. (eds)
© 2019 Taylor & Francis Group, London, ISBN 978-0-367-00147-6

Implementation of fiber network survivability by using P-L approach

Chandra, Singh

Department of E&CE, NMAM Institute of Technology, Nitte, Karkala Taluk, Karnataka, India

ABSTRACT: In Today's communication arena bandwidth services are quite essential in day today life. The Implementation of network survivability is depending on Physical Layer Approach and Logical Layer Approach. Physical layer connectivity integrates the different digital signal levels demands by using end to end communication. In logical layer approach it can be enhanced the channel capacity in virtue of node graph and flow graph. In this paper throughput of system determines the major % available w.r.t user to network environment and network to network environment. In these IEEE standards has been used to measure the parameter node position determination, channel effective reuse, demand distribution & Mobility and scalability.

1 INTRODUCTION

In communication network survivability is important aspect to develop fiber network integrated model which depicts the network design with physical layer and logical layer architecture(Kavian, Y.S.et al,2009). In order to design the several hierarchical topology by using a design constraint. This tool is to optimize and compare of different network component for which multi-layered Network survivability model is presented. It can be implemented with algorithm, C language and simulation methods(Bhandari,Abhay et al.,2015).

In this paper different network architecture in physical layer are discussed. They are Fiber Demand Distribution (FDD) where the traffic in each link is measured for a given network topology. It also measures the shortest path, combined with associated and non-associated path(Kumar,Krishan et al.,2014). It further represented with different procedures such as hubbing and point to point span layout. The digital connectivity is estimated in terms of survivable link factor. The second one deals with Fiber Network Restoration Mechanism (FNRM) deals with parameter like demand routing, multiplexing and restoration schemes. It also represents the global network connectivity's is estimated by using different restoration to end multiperiod demands(Singh C et al.,2017).

In particulars network transparency raises many security vulnerabilities differ from conventional failure for which a global fairness model in logical layer is proposed. In this connectivity's w.r.t Network queuing nodes . Further it achieves local fairness to global fairness by providing a minimum fair channel reuse and also max fairness throughput by using centralized scheduling packet technique(Sairam,K.V.S.S.S.et al.,2019).

2 LITERATURE SURVEY

Explains Survivability is play an vital role in optical networks. The significance of survivability is predominant in optical networks with data, voice and video services. (Bhandari, Abhay et al.,2015) Explains the survivability in optical networks is defined as the techniques(Sairam, K.V.S.S.S. et al.2017). Fiber Network Path Mechanism (FNPM) evaluates the demand distribution in terms of direct and indirect path. It emphasis in order to retain the demands for multiperiod optimization .A SONET Integrated approach considering a different network architecture from broadband services point of view implements candidate network survivability analysis towards multiperiod signal levels into end network's resilience to failures. Survivability techniques are broadly classified as protection and restoration techniques. The term protection refers to reserving the network resources for survivability, whereas in restoration, no such reservation is made, and the restoration is measured during the path failure(Sairam K.V.S.S.S. et al.,2019).

In optical networks, a single fiber can carry Tbps of data, and a fiber failure can cause huge loss of data and revenue with the quality of service severely affected. Therefore, survivability in optical networks is very important for network functioning. The process of protection and restoration in the optical layer is vital to the network's survivability(Singh,C. et al.,2019). The provision of survivability in the optical layer also has its own merits of speed, and efficiency to cope with failures. The affected connections due to the failure are restored on the source to destination basis. In general terms the path based schemes result in shorter recovery times, which is explained by Singh, C et.al.

A Multiple failure will result in the failure of all the elements that belong to the specific SRLG explained by Sairam,K.V.S.S.S et.al.,. Survivability against SRLG failures in optical networks was studied by Sairam,K.V.S.S.S. et al. In which, only the static traffic is considered and the authors had described the formulation of shared path protection. it is very difficult to provide a 100% SRLG failure protection in practical networks. Sairam, K.V.S.S.S. and Singh Chandra explains the restoration methods can be when a failure occurs, the connections which are affected are rerouted around the failed link. Link based restoration performs the recovery over a failed link, by restoring all the associated lightpaths.

Sairam, K.V.S.S.S. et.al. Explains different protection schemes here we come to know network survivability and corresponding network topology protection is achieved. Survivability concept is very essential for combining the DS to OC integration. Hence it guarantees the packet scheduling w.r.t fair queuing in optical network design.

The physical layer determines the path demand and cost through which fiber network path distribution cost analysis was measured and further path protection is enhanced through multiple schemes in order to improves the network survivability in terms of user survivability. The demand pair can be routed by using digital signal levels by means of network towards fiber network application is achieved by arranging the demands in an ascending order. Finally packet distribution by enhancing the demand level connectivity through which node and flow connectivity is combined Ely measured through which maximum bandwidth is observed.

3   PROBLEM STATEMENT

In physical layer Fiber Demand Distribution is computed for multi-layered survivability parameter in which span- path joint, link-path connectivity, links- connectivity w.r.t direct and Indirect methods,traffic-demands,survivable link failure and Survivable Restoration Factor(SRF),Fiber network Restoration Mechanism (FNRM) simulates the multirestoration parameter with multiple failure in this end to end connectivity. Restoration mechanism techniques: 1+1, 1: N, 1:1 and 1:2 DP and Global Survivability Factor (GSF). I.e. given by Restoration Link Demand/Total Demands which is depicted in Table 1.

Fiber Network Path Mechanism (FNPM) in which Direct Path(DP) and Indirect Path (IDP) is Measured.. SONET integrated

Approach a candidate survivable architecture for NXN node connectivity's is achieved and is implemented for different network architecture along with maxima and minima performance planning period Model competition is also achieved (Singh C.et al.,2019) and is depicted in below.

In logical layer P-L method gives the global fairness model in which channel effective reuse is achieved by using following parameters like fairness queuing, Node-Node Information and Propagation (NNIP),Maximum Throughput, Quality of Service of 84% is achieved.

Assumptions

In order to enhance the Bandwidth through node mobility and scalability in terms of fair queuing and spatial channel reuse technique. In physical layer Bandwidth is limited since the

113

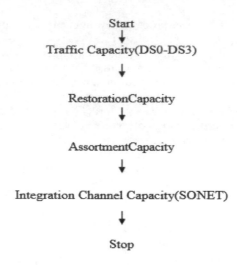

Figure 1. Physical layer implementation.

Table 1. Physical layer parameters for survivability techniques.

Sl no	Method	Parameter	Value
1	Fiber Demand Distribution (FDD)	1. Topology 2. Link Connectivity 3. Cost Connectivity 4. Traffic in Each Link	NxN Path Associated Demand Associated Summation of all
2	Fiber Network Restoration Mechanism (FNRM)	1. Topology 2. Protection Mechanism 3. Main User 4. Sub User 5. Global Survivability Ratio	Nxn 1:2DP,1+1,1:N Single to Multi Multi to Single Failure Demand/Total Demand
3	Fiber Network Path Mechanism	1. Topology 2. Direct Link Connectivity 3. Indirect Link Connectivity 4. Common Connectivity	NxN Direct Path Association Parcel List Total Demand i.e DP+IDP+QAP
4	SONET	1. Topology 2. Optical Carrier Demand(OCD) 3. Restoration Path 4. Demand Order 5. Planning Period Model	NxN Standard Dp Increasing Years

optical multiplexing schemes in order to enhance the data rates and also proper transmission and reception of packets. In channel it consists of two bound (lower and upper Bound) and which less than 2C determines local fairness model whereas greater than 2C determines the global fairness model. Here C stands for Channel Capacity The packet scheduling determines the max fairness to represent the flow to attain max channel utilization The Network Topology with packet scheduler depicts the information i.e. end to end communication. The propagation is updated by its service tags and Fig 2 of Logical Layer Implementation is depicted above.

Table 2.   Logical layer parameters for survivability techniques.

Sl no	Method	Parameter	Value
1	Logical Layer Connectivity	1. Topology	NxN
		2. Node Graph	Max
		3. Flow Graph	Max-1
		4. Simulation Time Interval	(Min<->Max)
		5. Throughput	Total No of Transmitted packets/Simulation life time
		6. Channel Effective Reuse	Throughput-100%

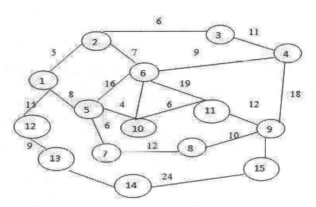

Figure 2.   15x15 network topology.

4   RESULTS AND DISCUSSIONS

In this Physical Layer parameters and Logical layer parameters are calculated. In this physical layer connectivity which determines the fiber demand distribution value for the 15X15 calculated as Traffic Connectivity is Further Global Survivability Ratio of 15x15 is calculated as 94.23%. Fiber Network Path Mechanism (FNPM) in this direct path and indirect path are calculated whereas direct path represents the node connectivity between two end to end users across the hub as well as the indirect path Connectivity into different parcel list across each hub. Direct path is given (2,6) 16. Indirect path is given by (6,8) 19. In SONET the multi period capacity expansion is achieved for 5 years planning period, the capacity is arranged in a queue with ascending order. Thus the physical layer integrates multi period survivable fiber optic networks. In logical layer connectivity the bandwidth enhancement and channel effective reuse is achieved with node and flow connectivity. Hence throughput and channel effective reuse is calculated as 184.23% and 84.23%.

5   CONCLUSION

This paper significantly provides an advantage of physical layer and logical layer for survivable fiber optic networks. Network Configuration provides the connectivity from user to user to user system. It consists of network configuration elements so has to provide the fiber network connectivity, fiber network protection, fiber path connectivity, fiber path integration and fiber path throughput. In all these cases the survivability defines the vital role to determine the traffic in each link towards packet distribution in form of spatial channel connectivity. This paper significantly provides an advantage of physical layer & logical layer for survivable fiber optic networks. Network configuration provides the connectivity from user to user and system. It consists of network configurations elements do has to provide the fiber network connectivity, fiber network protection, fiber path connectivity, fiber network integration and fiber network throughput. In all these cases the survivability defines the vital role to determine the traffic in each link towards packet distribution in the form of spatial channel connectivity. The fiber network provides the spatial channel reuse in which in which node and flow connectivity, position dependent, position independent, node mobility, node scalability parameters are processed in order to obtain fair queuing method and broad distinction is analysed from physical to logical layer through the implementation by c-programming language.

REFERENCES

Kavian, Y.S., Rashvand, H.F., Leeson, M.S., Ren, W., Hines, E.L. and Naderi, M. 2009.Network Topology Effect on QoS Delivering in Survivable DWDM Optical Networks. Journal of Telecommunication and Information Technology: 68-71.

Bhandari, Abhay & Malhotra Dr. Jagjit.A Review on Network Survivability in Optical Networks l:97-101.

Kumar, Krishan & Garg, Kumar Amit 2014.Analysis of restoration and protection in optical network with simulation framework 3(5).

Singh C. & Sairam, K.V.S.S.S.S. 2017. Survivable fiberopticnetworks design by using digital signal levels approach. In 2017International Conference on Intelligent Sustainable Systems (ICISS): 84-86.

Sairam, K.V.S.S.S.S. & Singh, C. 2019. Link Layer Traffic ConnectivityProtocol Application and Mechanism in Optical Layer SurvivabilityApproach. In: Smys S., Bestak R., Chen J.Z., Kotuliak I. (eds) InternationalConference on Computer Networks and Communication Technologies. Lecture Notes on Data Engineering and Communications Technologies 15. Springer,Singapore.

Sairam, K.V.S.S.S.S. & Singh, Chandra 2017. Optical network survivability- An overview. Indian J. Sci. Res.14 (2): 383–386.

Sairam K.V.S.S.S.S., Singh, C. (2019) FONI by Using Survivability Approach: An Overview. In: Kamal R., Henshaw M., Nair P. (eds) International Conference on Advanced Computing Networking and Informatics. Advances in Intelligent Systems and Computing, vol 870. Springer, Singapore

Singh,C., Sairam,K.V.S.S.S.S. & M. B. H.2019. Global Fairness Model Estimation Implementation in Logical Layer by Using Optical Network Survivability Techniques. In: Hemanth J., Fernando X., Lafata P., Baig Z. (eds) International Conference on Intelligent Data Communication Technologies and Internet of Things (ICICI) 2018. ICICI 2018. Lecture Notes on Data Engineering and Communications Technologies 26. Springer, Cham.

Communication and Computing Systems – Prasad et al. (eds)
© 2019 Taylor & Francis Group, London, ISBN 978-0-367-00147-6

Performance analysis of cognitive radio networks over Nakagami-*m* fading channel

Sandeep Sharma, Himani Verma, Arpita Jain & Ayushi Sharma
Gautam Buddha University, Greater Noida, India

Vinay Pathak
Jawaharlal Nehru University, New Delhi, India

ABSTRACT: A comprehensive review on the performance analysis of cognitive radio network that potentially persists iterative rapid channel fluctuation amidst multipath fading environment has been scrutinized. In particular, we have profoundly attempted to peruse the simulation of cognitive radio networks over a sum-of-sinusoids method based Nakagami-*m* fading channel that allegedly characterizes its impact on the attained throughput .The fading channel is configured using improved Jakes' model. The simulation results evidently evince that with different values of Nakagami fading parameter *(m)*, the throughput of the cognitive user varies divergently with increase in the number of channels and signal-to-noise ratio (SNR) at cognitive user receiver for interweave and underlay spectrum access techniques respectively. The curves obtained are corroborated using Monte Carlo simulation.

1 INTRODUCTION

Cognitive radio (CR) as an emerging technology prominently endeavors to settle the contention between spectrum scarcity and bandwidth under utilization of the allocated (licensed) spectrum. The CR technology allows dynamic spectrum access through which the cognitive users (CU) can conveniently access the licensed spectrum under favorable circumstances which is essentially in the context of likelihood of abandonment by the primary users (PU). The literature for the realization of cognitive radio environment over various fading channels have been extensively studied in (Atawi,Ibrahem et al.2015).The system model accentuating the framework for establishing the cognitive radio scenario as proposed in (Thakur,P et al.2017) has been stimulated. In order to achieve better channel selection probabilities the authors in (Yang et al 2015) have suggested an improved approach over the existing random approach that substantially challenges the issue of sense and stuck problem in CR .The procurement of sum-of-sinusoids technique for Nakagami-*m* fading channels using improved Jakes' model as suggested in (Wu, TM et al. 2003) has been implemented. The fundamental objective of creating such a channel as indicated by the authors in (Wu, TM et al. 2003) is to characterize correlated Nakagami vector as a non-linear function of a definite volume of mutually independent Gaussian vectors that enables the consideration of non-integer values of the fading parameter (*m*). The primitive Jakes' model is deprived of the wide sense stationary (WSS) property (Sheikh,A. et al. 1993).Nevertheless, to conform the model as WSS; the improved Jakes' model suggests the addition of random phases to low frequency oscillators. In view of the radical sensing capabilities of a channel advocated under fading conditions bearing CR network, the paper is further exploited in the following manner. The system and the channel models have been discussed in section 2.This section primarily provides a deep insight into the enumeration of channel sensing prediction probabilities and the throughput evaluation for the cognitive radio network. Besides, it also entails the convening of Nakagami-*m* random and Gaussian random processes required for the inception of desired fading channel. Furthermore, with the application of related concepts and fundamental rationality, the simulation results have been briefed in section 3. The paper is given a conclusion in section 4.

2 SYSTEM AND CHANNEL MODELS

2.1 *System model*

Spectrum sensing in cognitive radio as modeled in (Thakur,P et al.2017) is done on the basis of a binary hypothesis test that determines the absence (hypothesis H_0) or presence (hypothesis H_1) of the PU as:

$$y(t) = \begin{cases} h.x(t)+w(t) & ;H_1\,(\text{Active channel state}) \\ w(t) & ;H_0\,(\text{Idle channel state}) \end{cases} \tag{1}$$

where $y(t), h,\ w(t)$ and $x(t)$ denote the received signal, channel gain, noise signal and transmitted signal of the PU respectively. As proposed in the model, the persistence period of the time frame (T) is divided into the following states: spectrum prediction state (τ_p), sensing state (τ_s), and data transmission state $(T -.\tau_p - \tau_s)$. In addition, instead of randomly sensing the channel, the channel is recognized as idle according to the channel prediction probability (P_{pi}) given as

$$P_{pi} = \frac{n_i}{n} \tag{2}$$

where n_i is the number of idle perceived channels and n is the existing number of total channels. Furthermore, once P_{pi} gets determined, data transmission in both i.e., conventional (Thakur,P et.al.2017) (random) and proposed (Yang et.al.2015) (improved) approaches using interweave spectrum access technique is initiated.

Since throughput defines the original (true) state of the PU, which can either be active or idle, the throughput of the CU (C_0) when channel state of PU is idle is given as

$$C_0 = \frac{T - \tau_p - \tau_s}{T} log_2(1 + SNR_{s1}) \tag{3}$$

For active channel state of the PU, the throughput of the CU (C_1) is given as

$$C_1 = \frac{T - \tau_p - \tau_s}{T} log_2\left(1 + \frac{SNR_{s1}}{1 + SNR_p}\right) \tag{4}$$

where SNR_{s1} and SNR_p are signal-to noise ratios at CU receiver due to interweave mode and PU transmission respectively.

As previously mentioned, the proposed frame in (Thakur,P et al..2017) allows data transmission from the CU in spectrum prediction and sensing states $(\tau_p + \tau_s)$. Therefore, considering additional data transmission, the augmented throughput will be the function of the channel state of the PU. The throughput of the CU (C_2) when channel state of PU is idle is given as

$$C_2 = \frac{\tau_p + \tau_s}{T} log_2(1 + SNR_{s2}) \tag{5}$$

If the channel state of the PU is active, the throughput of the CU (C_3) is given as:

$$C_3 = \frac{\tau_p + \tau_s}{T} log_2\left(1 + \frac{SNR_{s2}}{1 + SNR_P}\right) \tag{6}$$

where SNR_{s2} denotes signal-to-noise ratio at CU receiver in underlay mode .

The probabilities of N number of channels to be idle are anticipated by the CU and only channels with prediction probability greater than 0.5 are considered. Once predicted, data transmission using both the approaches i.e., the conventional (random) and proposed (improved) is implemented. The proposed improved approach in (Yang et.al 2015) initiates spectrum sensing on the channel with highest prediction probability (P_{pi}) to be predicted idle. In case, the channel with highest P_{pi} remains occupied, the channel with the subsequent (second) highest P_{pi} is considered for data transmission. In random approach, spectrum sensing is realized on any random channel.

The probability of the channel to be idle (P_i) or active/busy (P_b) using the probability of false alarm P_f and the probability of misdetection$(1 - P_f)$ as computed in(Yang et al.2015) is stated as

$$P_i = P_1 + P_2 = P(H_0)P_{pi}(1 - P_f) + P(H_1)P_{pi}(1 - P_d) \tag{7}$$

$P_1 = P(H_0)P_{pi}(1 - P_f)$ is the probability when the channel's original state is detected as well as sensed idle. However, $P_2 = P(H_1)P_{pi}(1 - P_d)$ is the probability when the original state of the channel is active but is sensed as idle.

$$P_b = P_3 + P_4 = P(H_0)P_{pi}(P_f) + P(H_1)P_{pi}(P_d) \tag{8}$$

The CU achieves a maximum throughput R_{up}, if, continuous transmission of data occurs from the CU despite the presence of PU's activity.

$$R_{up} = P(H_0)C_0 + P(H_1)C_1 \tag{9}$$

For improved approach, the normalized average throughput of the CU is given as

$$R_{normp} = \frac{R_{avgp}}{R_{up}} \tag{10}$$

where

$$R_{avgp} = P_1 C_0 + P_2 C_1 + P(H_0)C_2 + P(H_1)C_3 \tag{11}$$

For random approach, the probability of the channel to be idle P_{ir} is mentioned as

$$P_{ir} = P_5 + P_6 = P(H_0)P_{pir}(1 - P_f) + P(H_1)P_{pir} \tag{12}$$

here P_{pir} is the probability of the randomly selected channel to be predicted idle.

Thus, for random selection approach, the normalized average throughput of the CU is given as

$$R_{normr} = \frac{R_{avgr}}{R_{up}} \tag{13}$$

where R_{avgr} is stated as

$$R_{avgr} = P_5 C_0 + P_0 P_6 + P(H_0)C_2 + P(H_1)C_3 \tag{14}$$

2.2 Channel model

Considering the conventional attributes of radio propagation environment, various fading models such as Rayleigh, Ricean and Nakagami-m substantially acknowledge the delineation

119

of statistical interpretation of the multipath fading envelope. Amongst these, Nakagami-m fading distribution provides the most applicable empirical model to sustain signal fading conditions that ranges from moderate to severe . Since a random Nakagami-m process is characterized by the sum of two independent random Gaussian processes, its distribution is defined by probability density function (PDF) (Wu, TM et al. 2003):

$$p_z(z, \Omega) = \frac{2}{\Gamma m} \left(\frac{m}{\Omega_p}\right)^m z^{2m-1} \exp\left(\frac{-m}{\Omega_p} z^2\right) \qquad z \geq 0, \Omega \geq 0 \qquad m \geq \frac{1}{2} \tag{15}$$

where z is the received signal, $\Gamma(\cdot)$ is the gamma function, Ω_p is the instantaneous signal power and m is the fading(shaping) parameter .

2.2.1 *Nakagami-m simulator using improved Jakes' model:*
The mapping between the Nakagami-m random process (Z) can be realized from Gamma random process (G) (Suzuki.et.Al. 1977) using the following relation

$$Z(t) = \sqrt{G(t)} = \sqrt{\alpha \sum_{k=1}^{P} X_{c,k}^2(t) + \beta X_s^2(t)} \tag{16}$$

where P = [2m] is an integer part, and, the performance parameters α and β that help in establishing coordination between the integer and fractional parts to achieve better organization and efficiency of the simulator are given as

$$\alpha = \frac{2Pm \pm \sqrt{2Pm(P+1-2m)}}{P(P+1)} \tag{17}$$

$$\beta = 2m - \alpha P \tag{18}$$

As stated earlier, in order to substantiate less correlation between the two processes, improved Jakes' model functions by the appropriate addition of random phases to the oscillators. Thus, the in phase and quadrature components (Wu, TM et al.2003) are given as:

$$X_c(t) = \sqrt{\frac{4}{N}} \sum_{n=1}^{M+1} a_n \cos(w_n t + \psi_n) \tag{19}$$

$$X_s(t) = \sqrt{\frac{4}{N}} \sum_{n=1}^{M+1} b_n \cos(w_n t + \psi_n) \tag{20}$$

ψ_n is uniformly distributed over interval $[-\pi, \pi]$. The other constituent parameters are given as

$$a_n = 2 \cos \beta_n \tag{21}$$

$$b_n = 2 \sin \beta_n \tag{22}$$

$$\beta_n = \omega_d = 2\pi f_d \tag{23}$$

We have assumed that the cognitive user experiences independent Nakagami fading channel with same average SNR.

3 SIMULATION RESULTS AND DISCUSSION

The simulation results for the random and improved approaches for different values of the fading parameter (m) have been implemented. IEEE 802.22 Wireless Area Network (WRAN) standard has been considered for assigning the numerical value to the parameters. Moreover, Monte Carlo simulation (results are averaged over 10^4 runs) is used to validate the results obtained. The throughput is evaluated as a function of no. of channels (N) and traffic intensity (p) .Analytical review of Figures 2, 3 and 4 provide the following results:

i. There is a considerable increase in throughput when improved approach is applied for interweave spectrum access .It is worth mentioning that there may be decrease in throughput for improved approach due to inaccurate spectrum sensing and channel prediction probabilities.

ii. Maximum relative increase in throughput between the random and improved approaches for $p = 0.5$ and $p = 0.1$ is achieved when $m = 1$.

iii. In Fig. 7 as the no. of channels (N) is increased from 30 to 100 (for $p = 0.8$), the percentage change in throughput is decreased for various values of m.

iv. Since the SNR variation is significantly less, mostly, an increase in throughput with increase in traffic intensity (p) is observed.

Table 1. Simulation specifications for system and channel model.

Parameter	Value	Parameter	Value
T	100 ms	N no. of samples	50000
τ_p	5 ms	f_d max.doppler frequency	100 H_Z
τ_s	2.5 ms	T_s sampling period	0.00025 sec
P_d	0.9	ω_n	$\pi/4$
P_f	0.1	SNR_p	-15 dB
SNR_{s1}	20 dB		

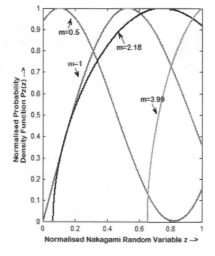

Figure 1. Nakagami-m channel using Sum of Sinusoids (m=0.5, 1, 2.18, 3.99).

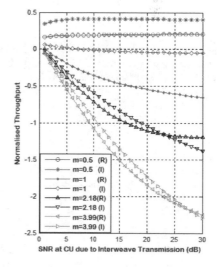

Figure 2. Normalized Throughput v/s SNR due to Interweave Transmission for $p = 0.5$ (R-Random, I-Improved).

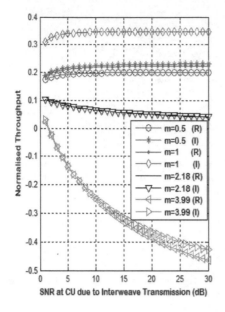

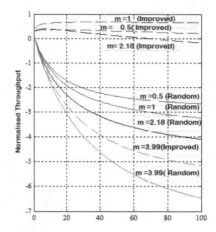

Figure 3. Normalized Throughput v/s SNR due to Interweave Transmission for $p = 0.1$ (R-Random, I-Improved).

Figure 4. Normalized Throughput v/s No. of channels.

4 CONCLUSION

Despite being abruptly sensitive to rapid channel fluctuations and probable inaccurate channel estimation, the implemented results have dispensed appealing throughput. Most prominently, the provision of enhanced throughput for the improved approach relevantly consents the mitigation of the detrimental effects of multipath propagation along with drawbacks encountered while assigning conventional approach for throughput evaluation.

REFERENCES

Atawi,Ibrahem, Badarneh, Osamah, S, Aloqah, M & Mesleh, Raed 2015. Energy-detection based spectrum-sensing in cognitive radio networks over multipath/shadowed fading channels." In: *Proceedings of the Wireless Telecommunications Symposium (WTS)*:1-6.

Tellambura A.S.C., & Jiang, H. 2010, Performanceof an energy detector over channels with both multipath fading and shadowing. *IEEE Trans. Wireless Commun.* 9(12):3662-3670.

Digham, F, Alouini, M-s & Simon, MK. 2011. On the energy detection of unknown signals over fading channels. *IEEE Trans.Commun*: 55(1):21-24.

Sheikh, A., Handforth, M. & Abdi M. 1993 Indoor mobile radio channel at 946 MHz: measurement and modeling. Proc. *IEEE Veh. Technol. Conf.*, Secaucus. NJ:73-76.

Suzuki 1977. A statistical model for urban radio propagation," *IEEE Trans. Commun.* 25(7):673-680.

Thakur P, Kumar A, Pandit S, Singh G & Satashia S.N. 2017. Performance analysis of cognitive radio networks using channel-prediction-probabilities and improved frame structure. Digital Communications and Networks" *DOI*: 10.1016/j.dcan.2017.09.012.

Wu, TM & Tzeng, SY. 2003. Sum-of-sinusoids-based simulator for Nakagami-m fading channels. IEEE 58th Vehicular Technology Conference.

Yang & H Zhao. 2015. Enhanced throughput of cognitive radio networks by improved spectrum prediction. *IEEE Communication Letters*. 19(10):1338-1341.

Communication and Computing Systems – Prasad et al. (eds)
© 2019 Taylor & Francis Group, London, ISBN 978-0-367-00147-6

Performance analysis of photodetector for application in optical interconnect

Shreya Chaturvedi, Akanksha Chaturvedi, Sherin Thomas & Sandeep Sharma
Gautam Buddha University, Greater Noida, India

B.B. Sagar
BITS, Noida, India

ABSTRACT: Optical interconnect have gained much attention in today's research domain for supporting a wide variety of applications including high speed data transmission. Photodetector is one of the most predominant types of technology in utilization today. Photodetectors cover a broad space of technologies. Photodetectors are extensively used in the fiber optics communication at the transmission end of the photonic system. In this paper we analyzed the performance of photodetector for use in optical interconnects .We take responsivity, quantum efficiency, dark current and gain into consideration. Simulation results demonstrate significant improvements in the parameters and this analysis greatly affects performance of photo detector by increasing quantum efficiency, increasing speed and eliminating slow hole movement in the device.

1 INTRODUCTION

Interconnects are used to transfer electrical signals between computers and its part, formed by using MOSFETs or electrical components R, L and C.Kshirsagar,et. Al. (2006).Interconnection between different components, devices and circuits has become the main performance blockage. With the scaling of technology towards nanometer system to support the signal communication in very high-speed circuits, Radical substitutes beyond the boundary of conventional metal interconnect need to be evolved.

Electrical signal is converted to light through transmitter which are led or lasers which travels through the channel which is an optical fiber then this signal is received by a photo detector which is a photo detector and is then converted back to electrical signal.

Jiang, Xu, Lin, Liu (2016). Photo detector is one of the most predominant types of technology in utilization today. Photo detectors cover a broad space of technologies such as the most advanced X-ray, far-infrared cells on an astronomical satellite etc. low-cost photo detectors have sufficient properties for day to day applications requirement like remote controls and automatic doors.

Shi,Cheng,et. Al. (2013).We require high speed photo detectors which can cover a wide optical window ranging from 0.85 to 1.55μm. However, InP-based high speed photo detectors operated at 1.55 μm exhibit a significant bandwidth and efficiency degradation when the excitation wavelength shortens to 850 nm due to extremely small (<1) absorption lengths in such a short wavelength regime and serious surface recombination in the topmost epi-layer. This phenomenon can be attributed to surface defect state which exists between the air and topmost epitaxial layer. Under short wavelength excitation photo generated carriers are generated, trapped and recombined in this defect –filled region.

The device involves band gap engineering at the surface, as a result it has superior properties and operating ranges which are discussed in the sections that follow.

2 SYSTEM MODEL

A novel high speed, large active area, InP-based photo detector is demonstrated here. (Shi, Cheng,et al.2013). In.52Al0.48As layer has been adopted in the structure to minimize the absorption of photo generated carriers at the topmost surface depletion region under 850 nm wavelength (1.46 eV) excitation. Furthermore, a graded band gap p-type In.52AlxGa.48-x cladding layer is buried below such a window layer. It minimizes the photo-absorption process in the topmost p-type layer and also provide a built-in electric field to accelerate the electron diffusion process. A 4.4 μm In0.53Ga0.47As photo-absorption layer with a graded p-type doping profile in its topmost region (0.5 μm) is buried below the p-type cladding layer. This partially p-doped layer enhances the device linearity and shortens the hole transport time.

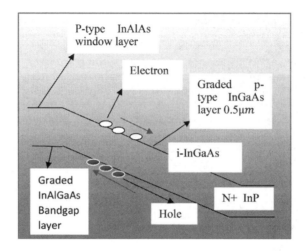

Figure 1. Conceptual band diagram.

Therefore, under 0.85 μm wavelength excitation all of the photo-generated carriers concentrate at the topmost p-type regions due to large absorption constant of In0.53Ga0.47As layer. The photo-generated carriers travel downwards and greatly releases the trade-off between RC-limited and carrier transit time due to its excellent transport characteristics.

3 SYSTEM IMPLEMENTATION

Performance metrics of photo detector has been studied in the following section.

3.1 *Responsivity*

Cassalino et al.2010).Responsivity describes the current generated by a specific optical power. Reasonable responsivities are critical for a desirable signal-to-noise ratio and to simplify the design and realization of the amplifier circuitry that follows. Responsivity is particularly related to device's quantum efficiency.

Mathematically,

$$R = \frac{I_p}{P} \tag{1}$$

$$R = \frac{n\lambda}{1.24} \tag{2}$$

where, R = Responsivity of the photo detector; I_p = the generated photocurrent of the photo detector; P = incident power on the surface of the photo detector; n = number of photons; λ is the wavelength of incident wave.

3.2 Quantum efficiency

(Cassalino et. al. 2010).It is a property of photo detector which describes the number of carriers per photon are received. Quantum efficiency can be classified as internal quantum efficiency and external quantum efficiency. Internal quantum efficiency is defined as the number of carriers contributing for the photocurrent is related to the number of photons absorbed whereas external quantum efficiency is related to the number of incident photons.

Mathematically, η is defined as the number of electrons collected/number of incident photons and is given by

$$\eta = \frac{1.24R * 10^5}{\lambda} \tag{3}$$

where, η is Quantum Efficiency of the photo detector; R is Responsivity of the photo detector; λ is wavelength of the incident light.

3.3 Dark current

Dark current is the current which flows into photo detector when no light falls on it .it flows because of the minority carries.

(Cassalino et al. 2010). If a system worked at frequencies at which the amplifier noise overcame photo detector noise then Dark current depends on frequency of operation. Desired value of dark current is 1μA .

$$I = I_d + I_p \tag{4}$$

where, I is the total current generated in the photo detector; I_d is the dark current of the photo detector; I_p is the current generated due to incident photons.

$$I_d = I_O e^{V_d/V_t} \tag{5}$$

3.4 Frequency response

Frequency response is the curve plotted between gain and frequency of the device. It is calculated by using different values of junction capacitance and load resistance at different reverse bias voltage.

$$R_C^2(f) = \frac{R_C^2(0)}{1 + 4\pi^2 R_L^2 C_I^2} \tag{6}$$

where, $\frac{R_C^2(f)}{R_C^2(0)}$ is the normalized response of the photodetector, R_l is the load resistance connected to the circuit and C_j is the junction capacitance.

4 RESULTS

In this section the performance metrics of photo detector has been simulated using MATLAB software.

4.1 *Responsively*

The value of responsively at the wavelength of 0.85µm is 0.25A/W and at a wavelength of 1.55µm the value is also 0.9A/W.

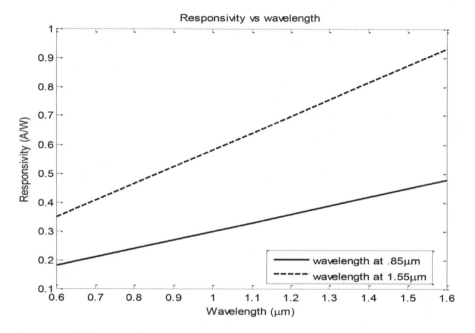

Figure 2.   Responsivity vs wavelength plot at 1.55µm.

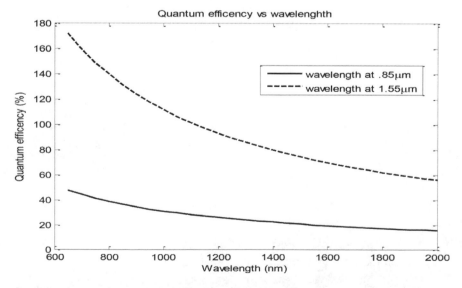

Figure 3.   Quantum efficiency vs wavelength plot.

4.2 Quantum efficiency

The value of Quantum Efficiency at the wavelength of 0.85 μm is 37% and at a wavelength of 1.55 μm the value is also 72%.

4.3 Dark current

The relationship between dark current and voltage is linear from the ideal curve of voltage vs dark current and from the plotted curve dark current increases linearly with increase in applied reverse bias voltage.

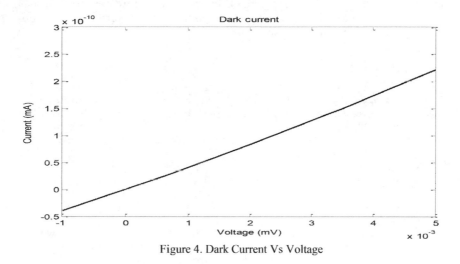

Figure 4. Dark Current Vs Voltage

Figure 4.   Dark current vs voltage.

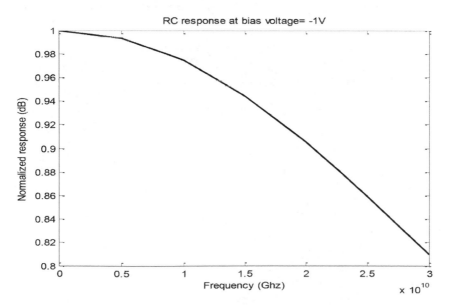

Figure 5.   Frequency response At -1V.

127

4.4 *Frequency response curve*

Frequency Response of photo detector has been analyzed at -1V .we infer that as the frequency increases, the gain is decreased.

5 CONCLUSION

On deploying band gap engineering high end features of the device have been obtained. Quantum efficiency increases because the absorption at the lower wavelength reduces significantly. Speed increases because more electrons travel through the photo detector and the slow hole movement is also eliminated. Also additional E-field increases drift speed. Large diameter, as high as 55 -60 μm is achieved .We therefore get significant improvements in rise time, NEP, responsively, dark current, detectivity and gain.

REFERENCES

Casalino, M., Coppola, G., Iodice, M., Rendina,I. & Sileto, L. 2010. Near-Infrared Sub Bandgap All-Silicon Photodetectors: Stateof the Art and Perspectives. *International Journal of Optics and Applications* :10571-10600.

Enk S.V. 2017. Photodetector figures of merit in terms of POVMs. *Journal of Physics Communications*, 1:1-10.

Gupta S. & Kedia J. 2016. A Review on Silicon-Based Photodetectors. International Journal of Innovative Research in Science, *Engineering and Technology* 5(2):43-47.

Jiang,J.,Xu, Z., Lin, J. & Liu G. L.2016. Lithography-Free, Low-Cost Method for Improving Photodiode Performance by Etching Silicon Nanocones as Antireflection Layer. Hindawi Publishing Corporation 2016:1-6.

Kshirsagar, G., Chowdhury, M.H, 2006. Optical Interconnect Technology: Photon Based Signal Communication. *APCCAS 2006–2006 IEEE Asia Pacific Conference on Circuits and Systems*:1426–1429.

Kachris,C. & Tomkos,I . 2012.A Survey on Optical Interconnects for Data Centers. IEEE Communications Surveys & Tutorial.14(4):1021–1036.

Raid, A, Ismail,Walid K.Hamoudi 2012. Characteristics Of Novel Silicon Pin Photodiode Made By Rapid Thermal Diffusion Technique. Journal of Electron Devices 14:1104-1107.

Shi J.W., Cheng.Y.H., Wun J.M., Chi. K.L.Y.M., & Benjamin S.D. 2013High-Speed, High-Efficiency, Large-Area p-i-n Photodiode for Application to Optical Interconnects from 0.85 to 1.55 μm Wavelengths. Journal of Lightwave Technology 31(24):3956-3961.

Communication and Computing Systems – Prasad et al. (eds)
© 2019 Taylor & Francis Group, London, ISBN 978-0-367-00147-6

Optical networks-survivability aspect and prospect

Chandra Singh P. SaiVamsi
ECE Department, NMAMIT Nitte, India

K. Annapurna
CSE Department, CEC Mangalore, India

K. Sarveswara Rao
ISE Department, NMAMIT Nitte, India

ABSTRACT: Communication is an intelligent information between point to point. Hence Optical Communication provides an interface between Optical Network Elements (ONE), Optical Network Devices (OND), Optical Network Systems (ONS) and Optical Network-to-Network (ONN). In this Paper we came out the past, present and future scenario(s) in terms of User-System Network Configuration (USNC) in the domains of Interconnectivity, Transition and Path Allocation Procedure(s) and the Global Network Scenario in which the Bandwidth(BW), Digital Data Transmission (DDT),Digital Signal Failure Resistance Schemes(DSFRS), Digital Signal Bundling Analysis (DSBA), Digital Signal Network Integration(DSNI) and Local-Global Fairness Connectivity (LGFC) is also discussed with Aspect and Prospect (AP).

1 INTRODUCTION

Telecommunications is a vibrant technology which impacts the summarization by using data, voice and video services for day-life operations(Ali,M. Et al,2017). In the same time, the service disruption is a major failure which affects towards a common point that is hub. To ensure the signal strength and service achallenged task has to be ensure at cost effective ness which helps the service continuity from point-to-point.Hence survivability is an important factor which play(s) in order to resist the failure(s). An increase demand in terms of transmissiontechnology provides greater capacity, reliability, security, smaller size, repeater spacing and etc. Guided media which provides ring architecture(Jeong, M. Et al 2002). Primary transmission in copper cable has been affected by EMI. The twisted pair which facilitates the communication connectivity through transmitter and receiver. Further in order to enhance the data rate co-axial cable came in to existence. Hence Fiber Optics is deployed in order to integrate the three services are combined together and the data is estimated by the digital signal levels connectivity, protection, bundling and combined of all. Three requirements are very much essential in survivability i.e. collection of users, transportation and path direction. Further it is classified into two types of networks viz. Facility and Switched Network(FSN).In this Fiber connectivity and protection is well organized from equipment used to impacted area. The bundling process which provides a distributed system in which in direct path determines the demands segregation across the hub in the Optical Network(s)(Jeong,M. Et al,2003). The compactness of survivable Fiber Optic Networks are mainly used for Broadband Optical Signal Transmission(BOST).Survivable Fiber Optic Networks features the parameter like feasibility, productivity, resource sharing, heterogeneous, flexible and scalable are in advance stage.

2 PROBLEM STATEMENT(S)

2.1 *Fiber network distribution*

It is a network element which reroutes the digital signals like DS0, DS1,DS2 and DS3 which are electronically variable and performs the main functions such as A/D, SXC and MDM is very much accessed in fiber hub networks the main functions are controlled computing supervision(CCS)flow chart as shown in Figure 1. It also provides the switching functions of CCS-DCS 3/1(Jeong, M. Et al, 2004). It isvery much used in telephone networks where the switches much higher rate signals hence today(S) network performance results higher band width saving.It consists of CCS parameters such as switching unit, control, performance, connection duration, switching/cross connect and external switching logic(Kumar, Krishan et al,2014).

2.2 *Digital Signal Failure Resistance Schemes(DSFRS)*

The survivable architecture uses the working fiber and protection fiber in the fiber network distribution hence the equipment w.r.t. Single Network Component Failure(SNCF) to Multi Network Component Failure(MNCF) which are attributed as network protection and restoration facilitiessuch as 1:1, 1+1, APS, 1:2 DP, SHR, Dual Homing and etc. Flow chart as depicted in Figure 2. These switching mechanisms are mainly controlled by using switching controller. Further the data rate is very much enhanced in the presence of signal, frame pattern and the line code (singh, C. et al, 2019). During normal operation APS system can be used in which two standards viz. 1:n APS, 1+1 APS is mainly used to measure the processing time at each node and the protection switching element respectively(Singh, C. et al. 2017)as

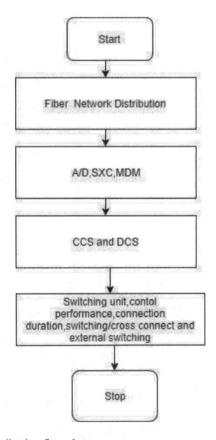

Figure 1.   Fiber network distribution flow chart.

130

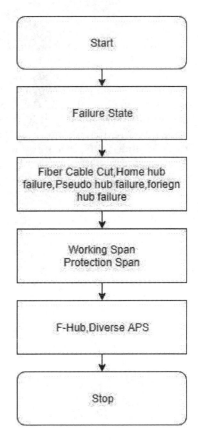

Figure 2.   Optical failure resistance protocol model.

shown in Figure 3. The survivable fiber optic networks integrates the optical switching technologies into switching time and switching requirements appropriately(Sairam, K.V.S.S.S.S. et al,2019).

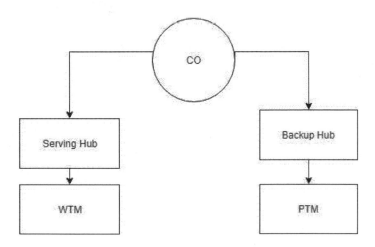

Figure 3.   Path restoration approach: WTM-working terminal multiplexer PTM-protection terminal multiplexer.

2.3 Digital Signal Bundling Analysis(DSBA)

In survivability the demand bundling combines the point-to-point circuits intoDS3 level demands it is further classified into single period and multi period demands the first one is used in designing hierarchical trunking networks which assigns traffic to circuits. The second one is more sophisticated and performed in two phases which results an hierarchical approach to evaluate the economics of routing circuits directly between source and destination hub flow chart as shown in Figure 4. In this routing involves two different paths i.e. Direct and Indirect in this a DS1/DS3 the routes over a direct path at an intermediateOffices over a single system. This is known as direct DS3/DS1. The indirect path(Sairam, K.V.S.S.S. et al. 2017).It consists of two or more DS3(s)/DS1(s) formed by DE multiplexing the signals at an intermediate hub locations. The transport cost for the hub route is the sum of the transmission cost for the hub route, the CCS termination cost and multiplexer termination cost.

2.4 Digital Signal Network Integration(DSNI)

Digital signal networking integration is also known as capacity expansion problem. It is designed by using multi-stage decision problem through dynamic model implemented by using an integrated approach (SONET), the data in Q ascending order integrated model as depicted in Figure 5. In this model it evaluates the multi period demands through the planning period. Survivable SONET architectures are as shown in Figure 6.Given a set of available line rates at which year in the network in order to reduce the network complexity which represents fiber

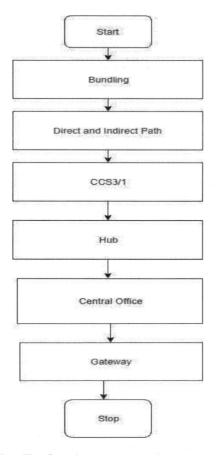

Figure 4.   Digital signal level bundling flow chart.

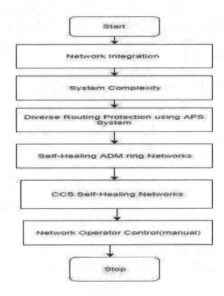

Figure 5.   An integrated network restoration model.

hubbed network by a set of independent fiber spans. In this the basic method is implemented by following points:

1. Routing of DS3/1 systems over fiber spans is fixed in all periods.
2. Increasing the capacity on any fiber span results maximum line rate.
3. Fiber equipment is installed.

    To solve multi period capacity problem is as follows:

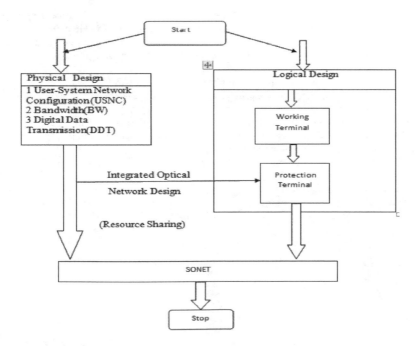

Figure 6.   Survivable SONET network integration.

1. Find all spans in the model network and compute the demand (per year)-OC-STM-STS-DS per each span.
2. To determine the number of fibers, the amount of equipment and their capacities per planning period such that the span cost is minimized.
3. Compute the minimum cost for the model network by
4. Summing all span costs.

3 CONCLUSION

Optical Networks- Survivability Aspect and Prospect in which fiber network analysis w.r.t. fiber Methods are discussed in first method CCS parameters are discussed, in second method survivability protection and restoration are discussed, in third method the Transport hub cost is discussed and in fourth method survivable SONET network architecture is designed for multi-period capacity expansion is discussed. Further this work may extend to study the wavelength services in optical network survivability to optical cross connectivity, transmission from ring-hybrid and the time optimal control to study the multiple congested notes.

REFERENCES

Ali,M. & Deogun J.S. 2017. Power-efficient design of multicast wavelength-routed networks. IEEE Journal on Selected Areas in Communications18:1852–1862.

Jeong, M., Qiao,C. & Vandenhoute,M. 2002. Distributed shared multicast tree construction protocols for treeshared multicasting in OBS networks in Proc. International on ConferenceComputerCommunications and Networks.

Jeong, M., Xiong, Y., Cankaya, H.C., Vandenhoute, M., & Qiao, C. 2003.Tree-shared multicast in optical burst switched WDM networks. Journal of Lightwave Technology 21: 13–24.

Jeong, M, Xiong, Y, Cankaya, H.C., Vandenhoute M. & Qiao,C. 2000. Efficient multicast schemes for optical burst-switched WDM networks in Proc. IEEE ICC.

Kumar, Krishan & Garg,kumar,Amit 2014.Analysis of restoration and protection in optical network with simulation framework 3(5).

Singh C., Sairam K.V.S.S.S.S. & M. B. H. 2019. Global Fairness Model Estimation Implementation in Logical Layer by Using Optical Network Survivability Techniques. In: Hemanth J., Fernando X., Lafata P., Baig Z. (eds) International Conference on Intelligent Data Communication Technologies and Internet of Things (ICICI) 2018. ICICI 2018. Lecture Notes on Data Engineering and Communications Technologies 26.

Singh,C. & Sairam, K.V.S.S.S.S. 2017. Survivable fiber optic networks design by using digital signal levels approach. In 2017 International Conference on Intelligent Sustainable Systems (ICISS): 84–86.

Sairam,K.V.S.S.S.S. & Singh,C. 2019. Link Layer Traffic Connectivity Protocol Application and Mechanism in Optical Layer Survivability Approach. In: Smys S., Bestak R., Chen J.Z., Kotuliak I. (eds) International Conference on Computer Networks and Communication Technologies. Lecture Notes on Data Engineering and Communications Technologies 15.

Sairam, K.V.S.S.S.S. & Singh,Chandra 2017. Optical network survivability- An overview. Indian J. Sci. Res 14(2): 383–386.

Sairam,K.V.S.S.S.S.& Singh, C. 2019. FONI by Using Survivability Approach: An Overview. In: Kamal R., Henshaw M., Nair P. (eds) International Conference on Advanced Computing Networking and Informatics. Advances in Intelligent Systems and Computing 870.

Communication and Computing Systems – Prasad et al. (eds)
© *2019 Taylor & Francis Group, London, ISBN 978-0-367-00147-6*

Real audio input signal transmission of OFDM for AWGN channel

Pratima Manhas, Shaveta Thakral & M.K. Soni
ManavRachna International Institute of Research & Studies, Faridabad, India

ABSTRACT: Orthogonal frequency division multiplexing (OFDM) is used in variant wireless and wire lined application. OFDM can be model using real data audio signal under different fading channels. The proposed work modelled the OFDM system using AWGN fading channel .BER is computed for OFDM system using different values of SNR. Simulink tool has been used to implement OFDM system.

1 INTRODUCTION

OFDM has already been used by many of the future generation systems because it helps in supporting a large number of high data rate users. OFDM technique uses the available spectrum very effectively which is beneficial for multimedia communications (Sembiring et al 2012; Sharma et al 2012). The conventional OFDM model has been modified further to reduce the value of BER under different fading channels. In order to reduce the value of BER, different modulation techniques under different fading channels can be used. The proposed work has been used to model the conventional OFDM system by using AWGN fading channel under QAM modulation. In this work the input signal used is audio signal and the SNR value is changed and the effect of BER is calculated for different SNR value.

2 PROPOSED MODEL OFDM

OFDM has been modelled using various fading channel. First the signal is generated using from audio device and the signal is modulated using different digital modulation technique and after this IFFT operation has been performed and the transformed signal is then passed through AWGN fading channel and after this the signal is demodulated and error rate calculator has been used to calculate the value of BER.

For the modeling of OFDM system following simulation steps are:

1. Audio device is used to generate the input signal. Gain and rounding function has been applied on the audio signal. After rounding function the reshape is used to change the signal into one dimension and the reshaped/converted signal is mapped using QAM modulation.
2. After this the summarized output is modeled using Inverse Fast Fourier transform (IFFT).
3. The different transformed output is passed through the AWGN fading channel and then demodulation is done which determine the BER attribute using error rate calculation (Manhas et al. 2016).

BER is calculated for different values of SNR and the graph is plotted for BER versus SNR. The real data implementation of audio signal using AWGN fading channel as shown in Figure 1

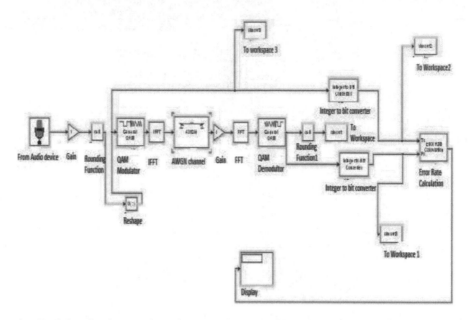

Figure 1. Real data implementation of proposed OFDM for audio signal using simulink for AWGN channel.

3 SIMULATION PARAMETERS AND RESULTS

For simulating the above models, the following parameters are used: Modulation = QAM, Fading Channel = AWGN and transform = FFT

The BER results of OFDM system using AWGN fading channel has been shown in Table 1 and bar chart are shown in Figure 2.

The Table 1 evaluate the BER results of OFDM system using FFT transform with QAM modulation under AWGN fading channel for different SNR values. The simulink result shows that at the SNR value is equal to 50 dB, the value of BER is 0.00012. As the SNR keeps on increasing the BER values decreases (Manhas et al. 2015). The received audio signal results in better quality at SNR value of 50 dB. The bar chart for the given above mentioned table has been shown in Figure 2.

So, the real time audio transmission in OFDM system for QAM modulation with AWGN channel results in least value of BER at SNR value of 50 dB.

Table 1. BER calculation of FFT based OFDM system with AWGN channel.

SNR(signal to Noise ratio)	AWGN Fading channel
0	0.4896
5	0.4884
10	0.4831
20	0.47
30	0.41
50	0.00012

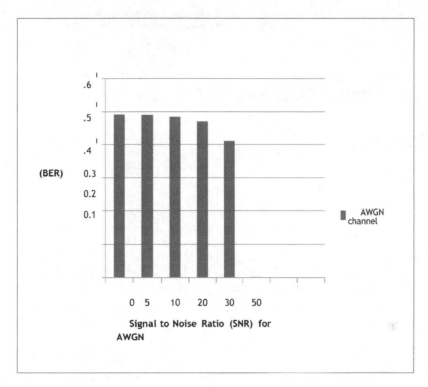

Figure 2. BER graph of audio signal for various fading channel under different SNR.

4 CONCLUSION

The OFDM system is simulated using AWGN channel for real time audio signal. The simulated results shows that OFDM model using QAM modulation results in least value of BER. When the SNR value is 50 dB the BER value is minimum for AWGN fading channel. This work can be further modified by using different fading channels.

REFERENCES

Manhas, P. & Soni, M.K. 2015. Ber Analysis Of BPSK, QPSK & QAM Based OFDM System Using Simulink, *International Journal of Electrical and Electronics Engineers*, 7(02).
Manhas, P. & Soni, M.K. 2016.Comparison of various channel equalization techniques in OFDM system using different digital modulation, *Indonesian Journal of Electrical Engineering and Computer Science*, 3(3), 634–638.
Sembiring, Z. & Syahruddin, M. 2012. Performance analysis of discrete hartley transform based ofdm modulator and demodulator, In Intelligent Systems, Modelling and Simulation (ISMS),IEEE International Conference: 674–679.
Sharma, V., Shrivastav, A., Jain, A. & Panday, A.2012. BER performance of OFDM-BPSK,-QPSK,-QAM over AWGN channel using forward Error correcting code, *International Journal of Engineering Research and Applications (IJERA)*, 2(3), 1619–1624.

Communication and Computing Systems – Prasad et al. (eds)
© *2019 Taylor & Francis Group, London, ISBN 978-0-367-00147-6*

Performance analysis of dual-hop Double Generalized Gamma (DGG) and Málaga distributed FSO network

A. Singha, S. Sharma & J. Gupta
Jaypee Institute of Information Technology, Noida, India

ABSTRACT: The performance of a dual-hop asymmetric free space optical (FSO) network is analyzed in this paper. The first and second hops are modeled by Double Generalized Gamma (DGG) distribution and Málaga distribution respectively. The relay is based on amplify-and-forward (AF) protocol. The end-to-end link performance is analyzed for the intensity modulation with direct detection (IM/DD) and heterodyne detection based FSO system in different turbulent conditions under the impact of pointing error.

1   INTRODUCTION

The popularity of FSO communication systems is due to its numerous features Also, FSO systems utilize the unlicensed spectrum for communication (Gappmair et al. 2009). Despite of various benefits, FSO links go through scintillation effect that is produced due to atmospheric turbulence. Atmospheric turbulence results in deterioration of the received signal due to intensity and phase fluctuations. Along with scintillation phenomena, FSO has another major drawback namely, pointing loss that deteriorates FSO link performance. The misalignment between transmitter and receiver results in the introduction of pointing error (*P.*V. et al. 2013). These effects restrict the application of FSO links only to short ranges. As a result of which the idea of multi-hop FSO transmission systems have been put forth. Relays provide efficient transmission of the signal from source to destination through different intermediate nodes, resulting in the enhancement of the coverage area and connectivity to the non-Line of Sight (nLOS) systems (*P.*V. et al. 2013) . Relaying process reduces the effect of fading and enhances the coverage area thus improving the system capacity (Ansari *et al.* 2013). The most commonly used relaying protocols include AF and decode-and-forward (DF). In AF relaying scheme the relay receives the signal from the source, amplifies and forwards it to the destination. Detection of FSO links can be achieved through two detection schemes, that are, coherent and non-coherent. Coherent system provides noise free background, which can be grouped as heterodyne and homodyne systems. In heterodyne detection, the incoming radiation and local oscillator have different frequencies. Non-coherent detection scheme, popularly known as IM/DD is inexpensive and simple to implement. In this technique the intensity of light emitted through the LED is directly detected by the photodiode at the receiver *(*Song et al. 2012*).* In literature, dual-hop FSO links are illustrated in (Asadollah & Nasab 2016, Song et al. 2012) . Among all the models, *I-K*, Gamma-Gamma, Double Weibull, Lognormal, Rician, and Extended Generalized-*K* distribution etc., Gamma-Gamma model is the most versatile model to examine the atmospheric condition of FSO system. According to Kashani et al., based on numerical results, the Double Generalized Gamma model is considered to be more accurate as compared to double Weibull and Gamma-Gamma model in modeling the turbulence condition(AlQuwaiee et al. 2015). Málaga turbulence model is a newly proposed and generalized statistical model. It models the irradiance fluctuation of optical wave that are unbounded and propagates in turbulent conditions in homogeneous isotropic environment. It includes various other turbulence models such as Lognormal and Gamma-Gamma as its special case (Nor, N.A.M. *et al.* 2016). In this proposed system, a dual-hop asymmetric FSO network is analyzed for a Double Generalized Gamma (DGG) distributed and Málaga distributed channels in the presence of pointing errors.

The structure of the paper is: In Section 2, the proposed dual-hop system model is presented. Section 3 describes the derived expressions of MGF and CDF under the combined consequence of attenuation as well as pointing error. Furthermore, the system is analyzed on the basis of OP for different detection techniques. In Section 4, numerical outcomes of outage probability are graphically demonstrated followed by the final conclusion in Section 5.

2 SYSTEM AND CHANNEL MODEL

2.1 *System model*

Free space optical communication system with a dual-hop is proposed, where the source (S) communicates with the destination (D) via relay (R). The first hop i.e. S-R link is designed by DGG distribution while the next hop i.e. R-D link is configured by the Málaga distribution. Both the hops are considered to be independent and non-identically distributed. The performance of the system is analyzed for heterodyne and IM/DD detection schemes. The signal undergoes through atmospheric turbulence and the effect of pointing errors while travelling through S-R-D link.

2.2 *Pointing error model*

Probability density function (PDF) of pointing error I_p is stated as (AlQuwaiee, H. *et al.* 2015),

$$f_p(I_p) = \frac{\xi^2}{A_0^{\xi^2}} I_p^{\xi^2-1}, 0 \le I_p \le A_0 \tag{1}$$

where ξ indicates ratio of the equivalent beam width at receiver to the pointing error displacement standard deviation given by $\xi = \frac{w_e}{2\sigma_s^2}$ where, σ_s^2 denotes variance.

2.3 *Double Generalized Gamma (DGG) turbulence model*

Atmospheric turbulence of DGG Turbulence model is given by $I_a = I_x I_y$, where I_x and I_y (equivalent to GG $(\alpha_1,\beta_1,\Omega_1)$ and GG $(\alpha_2,\beta_2,\Omega_2)$ indicate independent random processes for large scale and small-scale fluctuations respectively. Both the processes are generalized Gamma distributed (Prudnikov et al. 1992), where (β_1,β_2) indicate shaping parameters describing fading induced by turbulence, (α_1,α_2) and (Ω_1,Ω_2) are variances as a result of small-scale and large-scale fluctuations respectively. The consolidated expression of its PDF for both detection techniques given in [Peppas, K.P. *et al.* 2012, eq. (12)] is expressed as

$$f_{\gamma_1}(\gamma_1) = \frac{A_1}{r\gamma_1} \times G_{1,\lambda+\sigma+1}^{\lambda+\sigma+1,0} \left[\frac{A_2 h^{\alpha_2\lambda}}{\beta_1^\sigma \beta_2^\lambda} \left(\frac{\gamma_1}{\mu_r} \right)^{\alpha_2\lambda/r} \middle| \frac{K_2}{K_1} \right] \tag{2}$$

The type of detection is represented by r, where r = 1 and 2 denote heterodyne and IM/DD detection respectively. Average SNR, μ_r is given as $\mu_r = \mu_1 = \bar{\gamma}_{heterodyne}$ and $\mu_r = \mu_2 = \frac{(\eta E[I])^2}{N_0}$ for heterodyne and IM/DD respectively (AlQuwaiee, H. *et al.* 2015).

2.4 *Málaga turbulence model*

This versatile model, envisaged from(Nor, N.A.M. *et al.* 2016) includes many more turbulence models as its special case. The unified version of its PDF under both detection techniques is provided in [Nor, N.A.M. *et al.* 2016, eq. (10)] and is expressed as

$$f_{\gamma_2}(\gamma_2) = \frac{\xi_2^2 A}{2^r \gamma_2} \sum_{m=1}^{\beta} b_m G_{1,3}^{3,0} \left[\frac{\xi_2^2 \alpha \beta}{(\xi_2^2 + 1)} \left(\frac{\gamma_2}{\mu_r} \right)^{1/r} \middle| \begin{array}{c} \xi_2^2 + 1 \\ \xi_2^2, \alpha, m \end{array} \right] \tag{3}$$

For the two detection techniques, the average SNR of Málaga distribution is given as $\mu_r = \mu_1 = \bar{\gamma}_{heterodyne}$ and $\mu_r = \mu_2 = \mu_{IM/DD} = \frac{\xi^2(\xi^2+1)^{-2}(\xi^2+1)}{[2g(g+2\Omega')+\Omega'^2(1+1/\beta)]} \times \frac{(g+\Omega')}{\alpha^{-1}(\alpha+1)} \bar{\gamma}_{IM/DD}$ respectively.

3 STATISTICAL CHARACTERISTICS

3.1 *Moment Generating Function (MGF)*

Meijer-G based MGF is derived as,

$$M_{1/\gamma}(-s) = \frac{A_1 r^{\beta_1+\beta_2+\alpha+\beta-3}(\alpha_2\lambda)^{-0.5}}{(2\pi)^{\frac{\alpha_2\lambda-1}{2}+(r-1)\left(\frac{\lambda+\sigma+2}{2}\right)}} \frac{\xi_2^2 A}{2^r} \sum_{m=1}^{\beta} b_m G_{2r,r(\lambda+\sigma+4)+\alpha_2\lambda}^{r(\lambda+\sigma+4)+\alpha_2\lambda,0} \times \left[\frac{\left(\frac{B}{(\mu_{r_2})^{1/r}}\right)^r}{\frac{(r)^{-r(\lambda+\sigma)-2r}\left(A_2 h^{\alpha_2\lambda}\right)^r (s)^{\alpha_2\lambda}}{(\mu_{r_1})^{\alpha_2\lambda}(\alpha_2\lambda)^{\alpha_2\lambda}}} \middle| \begin{array}{c} K_5 \\ K_6 \end{array} \right]. \tag{4}$$

where, $K_5 = \left[\frac{\xi_2^2+1}{r}, .., \frac{\xi_2^2+1+r-1}{r}, \frac{1-(1-K_3)}{1} \right]$ and $K_6 = \left[\begin{array}{c} \frac{\xi_2^2}{r}, ..., \frac{\xi_2^2+r-1}{r}, \frac{\alpha}{r}, .., \frac{\alpha+r-1}{r}, \\ \frac{\beta}{r}, .., \frac{\beta+r-1}{r}, \frac{1-(1-K_4)}{1} \end{array} \right]$.

Proof of (4) is specified in Appendix.

3.2 *Cumulative distribution function*

Using the relation, $F_\gamma(\gamma) = 1 - L^{-1} \left[\frac{M_{1/\gamma}(-s)}{s} \right]_{1/\gamma}$ and [Prudnikov, A.P. *et al.* 1992, eq. (3.38.1)], the moment generating function (MGF) based CDF is obtained as

$$F_\gamma(\gamma) = 1 - \frac{A_1 r^{\beta_1+\beta_2+\alpha+\beta-3}(\alpha_2\lambda)^{0.5}}{(2\pi)^{(r-1)\left(\frac{\lambda+\sigma+2}{2}\right)}} \frac{\xi_2^2 A}{2^r} (2\pi)^{\frac{\alpha_2\lambda-1}{2}}$$
$$\sum_{m=1}^{\beta} b_m G_{2r+\alpha_2\lambda,r(\lambda+\sigma+4)+\alpha_2\lambda}^{r(\lambda+\sigma+4)+\alpha_2\lambda,0} \left[\frac{B^r}{(\mu_{r_2})} \frac{(r)^{-r(\lambda+\sigma)-2r}\left(A_2 h^{\alpha_2\lambda}\right)^r (\gamma)^{\alpha_2\lambda}}{(\mu_{r_1})^{\alpha_2\lambda}} \middle| \begin{array}{c} K_7 \\ K_8 \end{array} \right] \tag{5}$$

where μ_{r_1} and μ_{r_2} represent average SNR of first and second hop respectively for the r_{th} detection technique.

$K_7 = \left[\frac{\xi_2^2+1}{r}, .., \frac{\xi_2^2+1+r-1}{r}, \frac{1-(1-K_3)}{1}, \frac{1}{\alpha_2\lambda}, .., \frac{1+\alpha_2\lambda-1}{\alpha_2\lambda} \right]$, $A_1 = \frac{\xi_1^2 \sigma^{(\beta_1-0.5)} \lambda^{(\beta_2-0.5)}(2\pi)^{1-\frac{\sigma+\lambda}{2}}}{\Gamma(\beta_1)\Gamma(\beta_2)}$, $A_2 = \frac{\beta_1^\sigma \beta_2^\lambda}{\lambda^\lambda \sigma^\sigma \Omega_1^\sigma \Omega_2^\lambda}$,

$h = \frac{A_1 B_1}{(1+\xi^2) A_2^{(1/\alpha_2\lambda)}}$, $B_1 = \prod_{i=1}^{\sigma+\lambda} \Gamma\left(\frac{1}{\alpha_2\lambda} + K_0 \right)$, $B = \frac{\alpha\beta(g+\Omega')\xi^2}{(g\beta+\Omega')(1+\xi^2)}$

$K_8 = \left[\frac{\xi_2^2}{r}, .., \frac{\xi_2^2+r-1}{r}, \frac{\alpha}{r}, .., \frac{\alpha+r-1}{r}, \frac{\beta}{r}, .., \frac{\beta+r-1}{r}, \frac{1-(1-K_4)}{1}, \frac{1-1}{\alpha_2\lambda}, \ldots\ldots\ldots, \frac{\alpha_2\lambda-1}{\alpha_2\lambda} \right]$,

$K_0 = \Delta(\sigma : \beta_1), \Delta(\lambda : \beta_2)$.

3.3 *Outage probability*

Outage probability determines the performance of wireless systems. It is the probability that an instantaneous output SNR, γ, falls underneath a predetermined threshold γ_{th}. It is given by

$$P_{out} = \Pr[\gamma < \gamma_{th}] = F_\gamma(\gamma_{th}). \tag{6}$$

Substituting (5) into (6), we obtain the outage probability.

4 RESULTS AND DISCUSSION

In this section, the numerical results for strong and moderate turbulence in the presence of pointing error are presented. The analysis is demonstrated for both heterodyne as well as IM/DD detection schemes. When considering strong turbulence scenario, parameter values are $\alpha_1 = 1.8621$, $\alpha_2 = 1$, $\beta_1 = 0.5$, $\beta_2 = 1.8$, $\alpha = 2.296$, $\beta = 2, \Omega_1 = 1.5074$, $\Omega_2 = 1$, $\sigma = 3$, and = 5. Further, for moderate turbulence scenario, the parameters assumed are $\alpha_1 = 2.1690$, $\alpha_2 = 1$, $\beta_1 = 0.55$, $\beta_2 = 2.35, \alpha = 4.2, \beta = 3$, $\Omega_1 = 1.5793$, $\Omega_2 = 1$, $\sigma = 2$, and 5. For both the turbulence conditions, $\Omega = 1.3265, b_0 = 0.1079$, $\rho = 0.596$, $\varphi_A - \varphi_B = \pi/2$. Figure 1 illustrates the plot for outage probability under both heterodyne ($r = 1$) as well as IM/DD ($r = 2$) detection techniques having $\xi = 1$. Figure 2 depicts outage probability plotted against average SNR for both detection techniques, specifically for the value of pointing error, $\xi = 6.7$.

From Figures 1-2 it is observed that with the increase in atmospheric turbulence, from moderate to strong, the performance deteriorates. Furthermore, it is concluded from both the figures that IM/DD detection based system is liable to more outage as compared to that of heterodyne detection. Figure 3 shows the impact of two different pointing errors, $\xi = 1$ and $\xi - 6.7$, on the dual hop heterodyne based FSO system. It signifies that with reduction in the

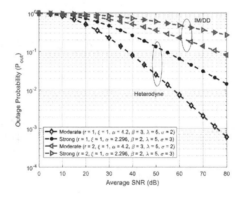

Figure 1. Dual-hop FSO link exhibiting outage probability under different turbulence for heterodyne ($r = 1$) as well as IM/DD ($r = 2$) detection techniques having $\xi = 1$.

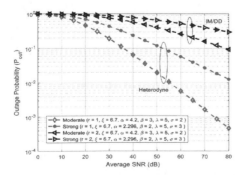

Figure 2. Dual-hop FSO link exhibiting outage probability under different turbulence for heterodyne ($r = 1$) as well as IM/DD ($r = 2$) detection techniques having $\xi = 6.7$.

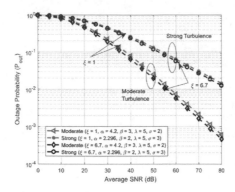

Figure 3. Outage probability comparison of a dual-hop FSO link under different turbulence for hetero-dyne (r = 1) detection technique having ξ= 1 and ξ= 6.7.

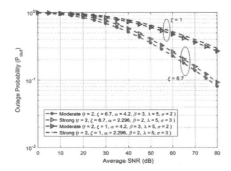

Figure 4. Outage probability comparison of a dual-hop FSO link under different turbulence for IM/DD (r = 2) detection technique having ξ= 1 and ξ= 6.7.

impact of pointing error from 1 to 6.7, the outage probability decreases. Similarly, Figure 4 shows the behaviour of pointing error on IM/DD detection based FSO system. It is thus evident that higher the pointing error value (i.e. $\xi \rightarrow 0$), more will be the outage probability thus degrading the performance. The value of threshold SNR is taken as $\gamma_{th} = e^{2R} - 1$ (*et al.* 2016), where R is taken to be 1.

5 CONCLUSIONS

This work analyzes the performance of dual-hop asymmetric FSO system based on DGG and Málaga turbulence models in first and second hop respectively. Also, MGF based outage probability is derived for the proposed dual-hop system. Furthermore, analysis of impact of pointing error for different turbulence conditions (moderate to strong), for both the detection techniques has been done.

REFERENCES

AlQuwaiee, H. *et al.* 2015. "On the performance of free-space optical communication systems over Double Generalized Gamma channel", *IEEE Journal on Selected Areas In Communication*, vol. 33, no. 9, pp. 1829-1840.
Ansari, I.S. *et al.* 2013. "Impact of pointing errors on the performance of mixed RF/FSO dual-hop tran mission systems", *IEEE Wireless Communications Letters*, vol. 2, no. 3, pp. 351–354.

Ansari, I.S. *et al.* 2016. "Performance analysis of free-space optical links over Málaga (M) turbulence channels with pointing errors", *IEEE Transactions on Wireless Communications*, vol. 15, no. 1, pp.91-102.

Asadollah, M.A. & Nasab, E.S. 2016. "Performance analysis of dual-hop fixed-gain AF relaying systems in wireless body area networks over Gamma fading channels", *24th Telecommunications Forum (TELFOR)*, pp. 1-4.

Belmonte, A. & Kahn, J.M. 2009. "Capacity of coherent free-space optical links using diversity combin ing techniques", *OSA Opt. Express*, vol. 17, no. 15, pp. 12 601–12 611.

Gappmair, W. 2011. "Further results on the capacity of free-space optical channels in turbulent atmos phere", *IET Communications*, vol. 5, no. 9, pp. 1262–1267.

Gradshteyn, I.S. & Ryzhik, I.M. 2000. *Table of Integrals, Series and Products*, 7th ed. New York: Aca demic Press.

Navas, A.J. *et al.* 2011. "A unifying statistical model for atmospheric optical scintillation", in *Numerical Simulations of Physical and Engineering Processes*.

Nor, N.A.M. *et al.* 2016. "Comparison of optical and electrical based amplify and-forward relay-assisted FSO links over Gamma-Gamma channels", *10th International Symposium on Communication Systems, Networks and Digital Signal Processing (CSNDSP)*, doi: 10.1109/CSNDSP.2016.7574020, pp. 1-5.

Peppas, K.P. *et al.* 2012. "Moments-based analysis of dual-hop amplify-and-forward relaying communi cations systems over generalised fading channels", *IET Commun.*, vol. 6, no. 13, pp. 2040–2047.

Prudnikov, A.P. *et al.* 1992. *Integrals and Series, Inverse Laplace Transforms*, vol. 5. New York: Gordon and Breach science.

Prudnikov, A.P. *et al.* 1992. *Integrals and Series, Inverse Laplace Transforms*, vol. 3. New York: Gor don and Breach science.

Sandalidis, H.G. *et al.* 2009. "Optical wireless communications with heterodyne detection over turbulence channels with pointing errors", *IEEE/OSA Journal of Lightwave Technology*, vol. 27, no. 20, pp. 4440–4445.

Song, X. *et al.* 2012. "Error rate of subcarrier intensity modulationsfor wireless optical communications", *IEEE Communications Letters*, vol. 16, no. 4, pp. 540–543.

Trinh, P.V. *et al.* 2013. "BER analysis of all-optical AF dual-hop FSO systems over Gamma-Gamma channels", *IEEE 4th International Conference on Photonics (ICP)*, pp. 175–1177.

Wolfram, I. 2010. *Mathematica Edition: Version 8.0*. Champaign, IL, USA: Wolfram Research Inc.

APPENDIX

MGF for dual-hop scenario is given by [14],

$$M_{1/\gamma}(-s) = \int_0^\infty \int_0^\infty e^{-s/\gamma_1\gamma_2} f_{\gamma_1}(\gamma_1) f_{\gamma_2}(\gamma_2)\, d\gamma_1 d\gamma_2. \tag{7}$$

The exponential function in terms of Meijer's G is expressed as,

$$e^{-x} = G_{0,1}^{1,0}\left[x \left|\begin{matrix} - \\ 0 \end{matrix}\right.\right]. \tag{8}$$

Using (7) and reversing the values of Meijer's G function as in [Ansari, I.S. *et al.* 2016, eq. (9.31.2)] and then on application of [Ansari, I.S. *et al.* 2016, eq. (07.34.21.0013.01)] we get the expression of MGF in (4).

Communication and Computing Systems – Prasad et al. (eds)
© 2019 Taylor & Francis Group, London, ISBN 978-0-367-00147-6

Effective-coverage and connectivity in WSN

Anand Prakash
DRDO-Institute for Systems Studies and Analyses, Delhi, India

Mohd Yousuf Ansari
DRDO-Defence Scientific Information and Documentation Centre, Delhi, India

ABSTRACT: This study addresses the problem of obtaining an effective coverage of sensors in WSN for a given target area while ensuring connectivity among sensors. The problem under consideration assumes that sensors are moving in the area. We propose TLBO (Teaching Learning Based Optimization) for coverage problem with OD (Orthogonal Design) to improve the convergence rate of TLBO. Furthermore, we propose to use RNG (Relative Neighborhood Graph) to ensure the connectivity. Finally, we propose to use VF (Virtual Force) concept to achieve even more compact (i.e. effective) coverage of sensors.

1   INTRODUCTION

WSN (Wireless Sensor Network) has become an important source of information nowadays. WSN can be defined as a collection of sensors which are working autonomously and communicating wirelessly. A typical WSN is shown in Figure 1, which clearly describes how a target sensor node captures a phenomenon in a monitoring area and then transfers the gathered information via a series of connected sensor nodes to reach a sink node eventually. It is the sink node that performs the computation and transforms the result in user defined format over the internet.

Sensors can be deployed in a given monitoring area in different ways known as static and dynamic. In static deployment the best location to deploy a sensor is pre-decided by some optimization technique and then becomes invariant throughout its lifetime. Dynamic deployment requires locations and movement capability of sensors in advance.

WSN has certain key issues like coverage area and connectivity of sensor nodes in a given target area. It is desirable to obtain minimum number of sensors to be deployed due to its cost. It is also desirable that these sensor nodes are connected in the target area so that information gathered can eventually reach the sink node for further processing. Thus connectivity is also very essential requirement.

This study focuses on how sensor nodes can be deployed effectively in a given target area while ensuring the connectivity among them. We propose to use TLBO (Teaching Learning Based Optimization) which is a nature inspired optimization technique to optimize number of sensor nodes to be deployed in the monitoring area. We propose to use OD (Orthogonal Design) technique to make the convergence rate of TLBO better; combining OD with TLBO we get OTLBO optimization technique for the coverage problem. We propose to use RNG (Relative Neighbourhood Graph) technique to ensure the connectivity among sensor nodes. The concept of neighbourhood is defined by maintaining the communication graph of the network. Nodes within communication range are considered as neighbouring nodes. We further propose to use virtual force technique to get even better coverage by applying this concept on OTLBO.

In section 2, we present the related work in this area. In section 3, we describe OTLBO algorithm for sensor nodes coverage problem. In section 4, we explain connectivity preservation algorithm for sensor nodes. In section 5, we explain how virtual force can make coverage of sensor nodes effective. In section 6, we explain a system model that can be used for the experimentation. In section 7, we explain performance evaluation of the proposed hybrid scheme. Finally, in section 8, we present some conclusions.

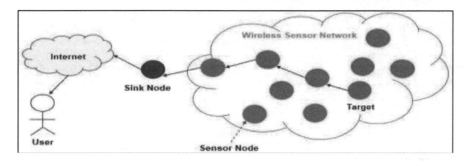

Figure 1.   Wireless Sensor Network system.

2   RELATED WORK

In present scenario there has been tremendous improvements in the fields of computer network, remote sensing and GIS (Geographic Information System). Many problems like clustering, classification, surveillance of HVT (high valued targets) in border areas require sensors to be deployed to gather relevant information. Figure 2, describes how sensors can be left isolated and thus become useless for obtaining useful information in WSN sometimes.

The deployment of sensors can be static or dynamic which is based on the fact when we calculate the locations of sensors with respect to time. He X., Gui, X. L. and An, J. propose how genetic algorithm can be used in multi-overlapping domains of any target points. This coverage problem is well explained by Guo, X. M., Zhao, C. J., Yang, X. T. et al., whereby authors talk about the coverage problem on grid scan. Zhang,Y. Z., Wu, C. D., Cheng, L. et al. discuss the effect of obstacle, if any, in the monitoring area to achieve the optimal coverage; authors here propose how robots can be utilized to deploy sensors in given area dynamically to improve the overall performance of WSN. In this approach sensors, initially, can be dispersed uniformly over the monitoring field then we can employ any optimization technique to get optimal deployment. The concept of virtual forces is well explained by Luo, Q. and PAN, Z. M. to get optimal coverage of sensors in WSN. This concept has been extended by Wang, X., Wang, S. and MA, J. J. for developing virtual force based particles algorithm. Techniques like simulated annealing, explained by Lin, Y. S. and Chiu, P. L., PSO (particle swarm optimization algorithm) explained by Liu, Y. 2011 and simulated annealing genetic algorithm, explained by Liao, W. H., Kao, Y. C. and Li, Y. S., can also be considered excellent approaches to address key areas in WSN, Haitao Zhang and Cuiping Liu. also explaine simulated annealing genetic algorithm. In mobile sensor networks it has been shown that mobility can make the design of higher layer algorithms complicated, but it can also improve the network performance. Loscrí, Valeria, Natalizio, Enrico and Guerriero, Francesca discuss, particle swarm optimization schemes Based on consensus for WSN has been well explained. Satapathy, Chandra, Naik, Anima and Parvathi, K. explain TLBO and OTLBO techniques. The connectivity preservation and coverage schemes are well explained by Razafindralambo, Tahiry, and Simplot-Ryl, David, it is further explained by Wing-Leung Y and Yuping W and van der Waals force for node deployment is discussed by Xiangyu Yu, Ninghao Liu, Weipeng H uang, Xin Qian and Tao Zhang. A method for optimal target coverage based on Reduced Minimum Spanning Tree (R-MST) is discussed by Abhilash, C. N., Manjula, S. H. and Venugopal, K. R., also termed as r-coverage. Olasupo, T. O. and Otero, C. E.

discuss an optimization and visualization framework is proposed which is based on hierarchical-logic mapping and deployment algorithms. The approach uses image processing techniques for classification of deployment terrains to improve coverage and connectivity. Sensing models, issues related to coverage and deployment is nicely explained by Tripathi, A., Gupta, H. P., Dutta,T., Mishra, R. Shukla, K. K. and Jit, S., the authors have covered various methods for handling coverage problem in detail. The WSN, sometimes, becomes vulnerable for exchanging classified information especially in defense domain; incomplete secure connectivity can affect various performance parameters, it is explained by Yildiz, H. U., Ciftler, B. S., Tavli, B., Bicakci, K. and Incebacak, D. To improve the coverage and Sharma, D. and Gupta, V. propose connectivity Harmony Search algorithm. Their simulation shows that if sensing range is half of the communication range, then average coverage ratio and connectivity ratio become maximum. Al-Karaki, J. N. and Gawanmeh, A. explain how a dynamic programming is utilized to derive optimal necessary and sufficient conditions for coverage and connectivity problem in WSN.

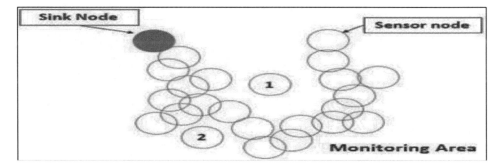

Figure 2.   Sensor nodes 1 and 2 are not connected.

3   OTLBO FOR COVERAGE PROBLEM

3.1   *TLBO (Teaching Learning Based Optimization)*

The scheme TLBO is considered into two phases: the first phase is known as "Teacher Phase" and the second phase is known as "Learner Phase".

3.1.1   *Teacher phase*
If we take analogy of a classroom, a teacher is the most knowledgeable person in a classroom. The teacher imparts knowledge to her students (i.e. learners) in the classroom; as a result the knowledge level of the entire class increases. In other words we can say that the original mean of knowledge level M_i of the class is increased by the teacher T_i to a new mean level M_j. The mean of knowledge level is also dependent on quality of the teacher as well as quality of students in the class.

3.1.2   *Learner phase*
This phase is iterative learning steps of a learner in the classroom. A learner can increase her knowledge only when other learners have more knowledge than her.

3.2   *OD (Orthogonal Design)*

To understand Orthogonal Design let us consider a problem that has multiple factors F having multiple levels L. Thus total number of combinations will be L^F. It is noteworthy here that if we have large F and L then it is impractical to calculate all combinations. In order to study multi-factor and multi-level problems the orthogonal design can be used as a tool.

4   CONNECTIVITY PRESERVATION ALGORITHM

The second issue is the connectivity of sensor nodes while they are considered moving. The scenario of moving sensor nodes can be modelled by RNG (Relative Neighborhood Graph), where all the moving sensors can be considered as nodes and communication links are represented as edges. The local information of deployed sensors is sufficient for construction of RNG which makes it suitable for modelling the connectivity preservation of aforementioned scenario. The RNG is effective when Euclidean distance is employed which in turn reduces the mean degree of graph. The RNG also has capability to preserve the connectivity when few edges are deleted from the initial graph with a condition that the initial graph is connected.

5   EFFECTIVE COVERAGE AREA USING VIRTUAL FORCE

In section 3, we have covered optimal deployment of sensor nodes using OTLBO. Then we have considered RNG for ensuring the connectivity. Now, we propose further to use concept of virtual forces to get better coverage. The net force experienced by sensor node i at any time t can be expressed by the sum of two components, exchange force, F_i^e and frictional force F_i^f, the relationship is expressed in equation (1). The motion of sensors is modelled by Newton's second law of motion described in equation (3); here m denotes the virtual mass of the sensor node $X_i(t)$ denotes its position in the coordinate and $F_i(t)$ denotes the net virtual force exerted to a sensor node.

$$F_i(t) = F_i^e(t) + F_i^f(t) \tag{1}$$

$$m\frac{d^2 X_i(t)}{dt^2} = F_i(t) \tag{2}$$

6   SYSTEM MODEL

Under this study we assume that WSN is a homogeneous network i.e. all sensor nodes are alike in terms of sensing and communication range in the network. We further assume that a sensor is modelled by a range-based disk model to sense and communicate the phenomenon within sensing range R_s and within communication range R_c. It is assumed that sensor nodes do not fail while in operation in WSN and initially sensors are deployed using uniform distribution under random deployment scheme. For the purpose of connectivity it is assumed that the communicational links are bidirectional. Let k is the node density, N sensor nodes are deployed in a given target area of sizeA, then the deployment model can be expressed by equation (3).

$$N = kA, \text{where A goes to infinity} \tag{3}$$

7   EXPERIMENTATION

Based on the assumptions and system model described in previous sections a simulation can be performed taking simulation parameters described in Table 1. Final deployment of sensors is shown in Figure 3.

Table 1. Simulation parameters.

1	Sensor field size (L x L)	100m x 100m
2	Number of sensors (N)	50
3	Sensing range (R_s)	12.5 m
4	Communication range (R_c)	2 R_s m
5	Number of runs	100
6	v_{max}	10 m/s
7	Time interval (δ)	5s
8	Movement step (ϵ)	0.1
9	Simulation time	5000s
10	Confidence Interval	95%

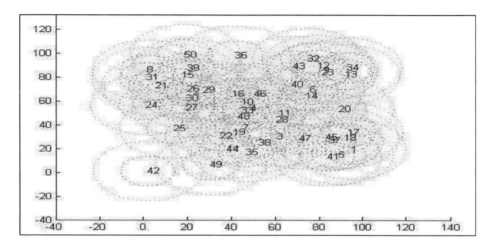

Figure 3. Final deployment of sensors.

8 CONCLUSION

The coverage and connectivity are two fundamental issues in WSN and often considered performance metric, in this paper a simulation is performed to ensure the feasibility of OTLBO optimization scheme on node deployment problem for coverage and connectivity. OTLBO outperforms TLBO in terms of convergence rate, using RNG we can ensure the connectivity during the lifetime of WSN and finally virtual force concept can ensure the effective coverage in the monitoring area by minimizing the overlapped region between two sensor nodes.

REFERENCES

Abhilash, C. N., Manjula, S. H. and Venugopal, K. R. 2017. Optimal connectivity for target coverage using prediction filter in wireless sensor networks, 2017 International Conference on Wireless Communications, Signal Processing and Networking (WiSPNET), Chennai, pp. 409–413.

Al-Karaki, J. N. and Gawanmeh, A.2017.The Optimal Deployment, Coverage, and Connectivity Problems in Wireless Sensor Networks: Revisited, in IEEE Access, vol. 5, pp. 18051–18065.

Guo, X. M., Zhao, C. J., Yang, X. T. et al. 2012.A Deterministic Sensor Node Deployment Method with Target Coverage Based on Grid Scan, Chinese Journal of Sensors and Actuators, Vol.25, No.1, pp.104–109.

Haitao Zhang and Cuiping Liu. 2012. A Review on Node Deployment of Wireless Sensor Network, IJCSI International Journal of Computer Science Issues, Vol. 9, Issue 6, No 3, ISSN (Online): 1694–0814

He X., Gui, X. L. and An, J. 2010. A Deterministic Deployment Approach of Nodes in Wireless Sensor Networks for Target Coverage, Journal of XiAn Jiaotong University Vol. 44, No.6, pp.6–10.

Liao, W. H., Kao, Y. C. and Li, Y. S. 2011. A Sensor Deployment Approach Using Glowworm Swarm Optimization Algorithm in Wireless Sensor Networks, Expert Systems with Applications, Vol. 38, No., pp. 12180–12188.

Lin, Y. S. and Chiu, P. L. 2005. A Near-optimal Sensor Placement Algorithm to Achieve Complete Coverage Discrimination in Sensor Network, IEEE Communications Letters, Vol. 9, No. 1, pp 43–45.

Liu, Y. 2011. Wireless Sensor Network Deployment Based on Genetic Algorithm and Simulated Annealing Algorithm, Computer Simulation, Vol. 28, No.5, pp.171–174.

Loscrí, Valeria, Natalizio, Enrico and Guerriero, Francesca Particle Swarm Optimization Schemes Based on Consensus for Wireless Sensor Networks".

Luo, Q. and PAN, Z.M. 2011.An Algorithm of Deployment in Small-Scale Underwater Wireless Sensor Networks, Chinese Journal of Sensors and Actuators, Vol. 24, No. 7, pp. 1043–1047.

Olasupo, T. O. and Otero, C. E. 2018. Framework for Optimizing Deployment of Wireless Sensor Networks, in IEEE Transactions on Network and Service Management.

Razafindralambo, Tahiry, and Simplot-Ryl, David.2011.Connectivity Preservation and Coverage Schemes for Wireless Sensor Networks, IEEE Transactions On Automatic Control, Vol. 56, No. 10.

Satapathy, Chandra, Naik, Anima and Parvathi, K. 2013. A teaching learning based optimization based on orthogonal design, SpringerPlus, 2:130

Sharma, D. and Gupta, V. 2017. Improving coverage and connectivity using harmony search algorithm in wireless sensor network, International Conference on Emerging Trends in Computing and Communication Technologies (ICETCCT), Dehradun, pp. 1–7.

Tripathi,A., Gupta, H. P., Dutta,T., Mishra, R. Shukla, K. K. and Jit, S. 2018. Coverage and Connectivity in WSNs: A Survey, Research Issues and Challenges, in IEEE Access, vol. 6, pp. 26971–26992.

Wang, X., Wang, S. and MA, J. J. 2007. Dynamic Sensor Deployment Strategy Based on Virtuai Force-Directed Particle Swarm Optimization in Wireless Sensor Networks, Acta Electronica Sinica, Vol. 35, No. 11, pp. 2038–2042.

Wing-Leung Y, Yuping W. 2001.An orthogonal genetic algorithm with quantization for global numerical Optimization, IEEE Trans Evol Comput; 5(1):40–53.

Xiangyu Yu, Ninghao Liu, Weipeng H uang, Xin Qian and Tao Zhang. 2013. A Node Deployment Algorithm Based on Van Der Waals Force i n Wireless Sensor Networks, International Journal of Distributed Sensor Networks, Volume 2013, Article ID 505710, 8 pages.

Yildiz, H. U., Ciftler, B. S., Tavli, B., Bicakci, K. and Incebacak, D. March 2018. The Impact of Incomplete Secure Connectivity on the Lifetime of Wireless Sensor Networks, in IEEE Systems Journal, vol. 12, no. 1, pp. 1042–1046.

Zhang,Y. Z., Wu,C. D., Cheng, L. et al.2010.Research of node deployment strategy for wireless sensor in deterministic space, Control and Decision, Vol. 25, No. 11, pp. 1625–1629.

Communication and Computing Systems – Prasad et al. (eds)
© *2019 Taylor & Francis Group, London, ISBN 978-0-367-00147-6*

Enhancement of ATC with load models using FACTS devices

T. Nireekshana & J. Bhavani
EEE Department, VNR VJIET, Hyderabad, India

G. Kesava Rao
EEE Department, KLUniversity, Vijayawada, India

K. Jeji
EEE Department, CMRTC, Hyderabad, India

ABSTRACT: In the developed and the developing countries, more so in the latter, the available electrical power supply-demand mismatch is continuously increasing, often resulting in forced power cuts to the customers. The system operator with a view to supply power reliably likes to know about the capacity of power available for transfer at any moment of time and under all system states. In a deregulated system operation, both the operator and the customers must be knowledgeable about this important system variable known as Available Transfer Capacity (ATC). Determination of ATC and its enhancement are two important aspects of any system under reliable operation. The system operator uses all the resources available at his disposal to relieve congestion. ATC is computed using the CPF method; this is like ATC based incentive to the loads like it is done in demand response under Smart Grid. The loads are treated in more realistic way as constant impedance, constant current and constant power loads (ZIP) and once again the ATC is computed using FACTS devices. Similarly, CSO is used to obtain optimal location and parameters of percentage series compensation and susceptance of TCSC and SVC respectively. The proposed techniques are used, for testing their effectiveness on different IEEE test systems.

1 INTRODUCTION

Power System Load modeling is a technique used to model the power system and essential for enhancement for ATC. In this paper the modeling of ZIP load and Voltage dependent load parameters are analyzed for ATC improvement. In static ATC determination, constant P, Q loads are taken for study. The nature of the load plays an important role for transfer capability calculations, their impact can be ascertained for accurate quantification of ATC. Therefore, Ashwani Kumar addressed the impact of generic load model as ZIP load along with constant power loads. In addition to constant P, Q loads, generic load models as ZIP load and voltage dependent loads have also been considered for study on ATC determination.

The impact of TCSC and SVC on ATC enhancement without and with ZIP load model and voltage dependent loads needs to be addressed for the comprehensive evaluation of ATC. The results are obtained with normal and contingency cases. The ATC has also been determined with ZIP load model and voltage dependent loads to observe the impact of ZIP load on ATC without and with FACTS devices. The CPF approach got applied on IEEE 14 bus system and on IEEE RTS 24 bus system. The non-linear problem got solved using GAMS CONOPT Solver and interfacing got employed with MATLAB to handle large number of parameters and variables.

2 OBJECTIVE FUNCTION

The objective function for the Available Transfer Capability is defined subjected to the following equality and in equality load constraints as follows:

Maximize

$$P_i = \sum_{j \in i} P_{kj} \tag{1}$$

Subjected to

$$P_i - \sum_{j \in i} V_i V_j Y_{ij} \cos(\theta_{ij} + \delta_i - \delta_j) = 0 \tag{2}$$

$$Q_i - \sum_{j \in i} V_i V_j Y_{ij} Sin(\theta_{ij} + \delta_i - \delta_j) = 0 \tag{3}$$

$$P_g^{\min} \leq P_g \leq P_g^{\max} \tag{4}$$

$$Q_g^{\min} \leq Q_g \leq Q_g^{\max} \tag{5}$$

$$S_{ij} < S_{ij}^{\max} \tag{6}$$

$$V_i^{\min} \leq V_i \leq V_i^{\max} \tag{7}$$

ZIP load:

$$Z_{Li}^{\min} \leq Z_{Li} \leq Z_{Li}^{\max} \tag{8}$$

$$I_{Li}^{\min} \leq I_{Li} \leq I_{Li}^{\max} \tag{9}$$

$$P_{Li}^{\min} \leq P_{Li} \leq P_{Li}^{\max} \tag{10}$$

Voltage dependent load:

$$P_{di}^{\min} \leq P_{di} \leq P_{di}^{\max} \tag{11}$$

3 DESCRIPTION OF LOAD MODELS

3.1 *ZIP load model or polynomial model*

The static characteristics of the load can be classified into constant power, constant current and constant impedance load, depending on the power relation to the voltage. For a constant impedance load, the power dependence on voltage is quadratic, for a constant current it is linear, and for a constant power, the power is independent of changes in voltage.

Constant impedance:

In this model, active and reactive power injections at a given load bus vary directly with the square of nodal voltage magnitude. This model is also called constant admittance model.

$$P = f(V^2)$$

Examples for constant impedance loads are residential loads such as refrigerators and washing machines and lighting loads such as bulbs etc.

Constant current:

In this model, the active and reactive power injections at a given load bus vary directly with the nodal voltage magnitude.

$$P = f(V)$$

Examples for constant current load are transistors, transducers and incandescent lamps etc.

Constant power:

Here, the power of load bus is assumed to be constant and does not vary with nodal voltage magnitude.

$$P = k$$

Where, k is a constant.

A static load model expresses the characteristic of the load at any instant of time as algebraic functions of the bus voltage magnitude and the frequency at that instant. The voltage dependency of the load characteristics got represented by exponential model as [3]:

$$P_d = P_d^0 (\overline{V})^a \tag{12}$$

$$Q_d = Q_d^0 (\overline{V})^b \tag{13}$$

Where, $\overline{V} = \frac{V}{V^0}$ and P_d and Q_d are the active and reactive component of the load when the bus voltage magnitude is V and P_d^0 and Q_d^0 with superscript 0 identifies the values of the respective variables at the initial operating condition. For the composite system loads, the exponent a lies between 0.5 and 1.8 and exponent b lies in between 1.5 to 6. ZIP load depends upon the values of a and b. So, ZIP load is the combination of constant impedance, constant current, and constant active power load. For constant impedance, value of 'a' is 2. For constant current, value of 'a' is 1 and for constant power, 'a' is 0. So, ZIP load can be represented by these equations as given below:

$$P_d = P_d^0 [p1\overline{V}^2 + p2\overline{V} + p3] \tag{14}$$

$$Q_d = Q_d^0 [q1\overline{V}^2 + q2\overline{V} + q3] \tag{15}$$

p_1 to p_3 and q_1 to q_3 are load coefficients of the model for real and reactive loads with $p_1 + p_2 + p_3 = 1$ and $q_1 + q_2 + q_3 = 1$

The power injection equations taken as equality constraints can be modified at a particular load bus using (14) & (15) in an OPF model for the calculation of ATC with ZIP load model. For incorporation of power flow controllers, power flow equations in an OPF model can be modified with the power injection equations with FACTS devices. Examples for constant power loads are switching regulators, industrial loads such as motor loads with constant speed etc.

3.2 *Voltage dependent load*

The model is presented below, as a set of non-linear equations, where real (active) and reactive power have a non-linear dependency on voltage.

$$P_d = P_0 \left(\frac{V}{V_0} \right)^{\alpha_s} \tag{16}$$

152

Where V_0 and P_0 are the voltage and power consumption before a voltage change. α is the steady state active load voltage dependence, may present negative values.

A voltage dependent load is an electrical device whose power consumption varies with the voltage being supplied to it. Examples for voltage dependent loads are the most common types of incandescent lamps, standard tungsten filament, tungsten halogen and reflector lamps and motor loads.

4   IMPLEMENTATION PROCEDURE

4.1   *ZIP load with FACTS*

Step 1: Select a system.
Step 2: Run load flow on test networks.
Step 3: Incorporate ZIP load at chosen load buses to observe the values of ATC.
Step 4: Vary Impedance (Z), Current (I), Power (P) values in ZIP load to know the viabilities and performance of ZIP load to improve the ATC.
Step 5: Apply CSO for 50 numbers of iterations.
Step 6: Incorporate the optimal size of FACTS device using CSO to coordinate along with ZIP load to obtain maximum value of ATC.
Step 7: Observe the results for an enhanced value of ATC and note down the optimal value.

4.2   *Voltage dependent load with FACTS*

Step 1: Select a system.
Step 2: Run load flow on test networks.
Step 3: Incorporate Voltage Dependent load at chosen load buses to observe the values of ATC.
Step 4: Vary the Power of Voltage Dependent load to know the viabilities and performance of Voltage dependent load to improve the ATC.
Step 5: Apply CSO for 50 numbers of iterations.
Step 6: Incorporate the optimal size of FACTS device using CSO to coordinate along with Voltage Dependent load to obtain maximum value of ATC.
Step 7: Observe the results for an enhanced value of ATC and note down the optimal value.

5   RESULTS AND DISCUSSION

Enhancement of ATC is done with and without contingency by applying CSO. The proposed algorithm is implemented for both IEEE 14-bus system and IEEE 24-bus RTS system.

Analysis on this system is made for ATC, bus voltage (Vi) and power flow (Sij) for following 6 different Cases, and results are compared without and with load rescheduling using CSO.
Case-1: Base Case
Case-2: Rank 1 contingency – line 9 (7- 9) outage
Case-3: Rank 2 contingency – line 10(1- 2) outage
Case-4: Rank 3 contingency – line11 (6 -13) outage
Case-5: line outage at minimum ATC
Case-6: Change of Nodal Injections; when load increased by 2% and generation increased by 1.5% at bus 2.

5.1   *Example 1*

The IEEE 14 bus is analyzed to demonstrate the proposed model and solution methods.

5.1.1 *ZIP load with FACTS*

The ATC got obtained for different Cases with intact and line contingency Cases. The impact of ZIP loads and voltage dependent loads on ATC calculations have been obtained corresponding to the different combinations of ZIP load coefficients. Initially, the ZIP loads are incorporated in the system with suitable load coefficients, with single parameter, combination of two parameters and the combination of three parameters with equal ratio. The corresponding ATC values are shown in Figure 1.

The 5 loads with maximum loads of 0.149p.u, 0.135p.u, 0.09p.u, 0.061p.u and 0.035p.u at buses 14, 13, 10, 12 and 11 respectively are considered and ATC values are taken by replacing these loads one by one with ZIP loads as shown in Figure 2.

Similarly, from all six cases after the application of CSO, the optimal susceptance of SVCs for the six different cases and the corresponding ATC values are tabulated in Table 2.

For all the six different cases the ATC values without ZIP load, with ZIP load and ZIP load along with FACTS using CSO are compared and tabulated in Table 3.

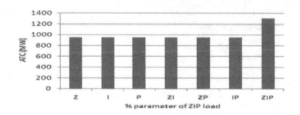

Figure 1.   Parameter of ZIP loads for 14-bus system.

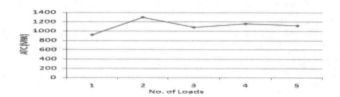

Figure 2.   ATCs for no. of ZIP loads in 14-bus system.

Table 1.   Summary of series compensation of TCSC with ZIP load for 14-bus system.

Different Cases	Line			ATC (MW)
	% series compensation			With ZIP load & TCSC
Case-1	3(12-13)	5(11-10)	8(13-14)	1453.4592
	40	40	30	
Case-2	7(9-14)	3(12-13)	6(9-10)	1481.9422
	30	30	40	
Case-3	3(12-13)	6(9-10)	2(6-12)	1405.0659
	20	20	30	
Case-4	7(9-10)	8(13-14)	5(11-10)	1193.9363
	10	15	25	
Case-5	7(9-14)	3(12-13)	6(9-10)	1481.9422
	30	30	40	
Case-6	3(12-13)	5(11-10)	8(13-14)	1465.2681
	30	20	40	

Table 2. Summary of susceptance of SVC with ZIP load for 14-bus.

Different Cases	Bus No. Susceptance (p.u)			ATC (MW) ZIP load & SVC
Case-1	14	10	9	1387.0749
	0.1	0.4	0.1	
Case-2	14	10	9	1408.6067
	0.3	0.3	0.5	
Case-3	14	10	9	1246.6972
	0.3	0.2	0.5	
Case-4	14	13	10	1156.9224
	0.2	0.2	0.1	
Case-5	14	10	9	1408.6067
	0.3	0.3	0.5	
Case-6	14	10	13	1218.508
	0.5	0.1	0.1	

Table 3. Summary of ATC with ZIP load & FACTS for 14-bus system.

Cases	ATC (MW) Without ZIP load	With ZIP load Without FACTS	With TCSC	With SVC
Case-1	125078	1299715	1453.4592	1387.075
Case-2	930.8844	1067.9745	1481.9422	1408.607
Case-3	1256.1062	1392.5645	1405.0659	1246.697
Case-4	1046.4957	936171	1193.9363	1156.922
Case-5	930.8844	1067.9745	1481.9422	1408.607
Case-6	1188.2098	1331.4138	1465.268	1218.508

5.1.2 *Voltage dependent load with FACTS*

The similar analysis is given for voltage dependent load along with TCSC as well as SVC. For fixation of the parameters, series compensation of TCSC and susceptance of SVC, CSO is used for all six cases.

For the above all six cases the ATC values are compared without and with Voltage dependent load and voltage dependent load along with FACTS using CSO and tabulated in Table 4.

Table 4. Summary of ATC with voltage dependent load & FACTS for 14-bus system.

Cases	ATC (MW) Without Volt. dep. Load	With Voltage dependent Load Without FACTS	With SVC	With TCSC
Case-1	125078	1350.8123	1395893	1365.8102
Case-2	930.884	1319.0142	1343.7226	1278.5464
Case-3	1256.106	1150.2008	1347.7084	1235669
Case-4	1046.495	1013.8925	1245.1467	1157.9046
Case-5	930.884	1319.0142	1343.7226	1278.5464
Case-6	1188.209	1183.8428	1415.6919	1402802

6 CONCLUSIONS

In this paper, Load models like ZIP load and Voltage dependent loads are incorporated along with FACTS devices. It is observed that ATC has been improved with incorporation of ZIP load and further enhanced by ZIP load along with FACTS controllers like TCSC and SVC. Further ATC has been improved with incorporation of voltage dependent load and still enhanced with voltage dependent load along with FACTS controllers like TCSC and SVC. Here also series device TCSC offers more improvement when compared to shunt device SVC. In depth, the results indicate that the effect of load models and FACTS controllers is more in case-2 and next in case-5 for 14-bus system and more in case-1 and next in case-2 for 24 RTS bus system.

REFERENCES

Ashwani Kumar, Srivastava, S.C. & Singh, S.N. 2005. Congestion Management in competitive power market: A Bibliographical survey, *Electric Power Systems Research* (76):153–164.

Brooke, A. et al. 1998. A User's Guide, GAMS Software, *GAMS Development Corporation.*

Ines Romero Navarro, 2002. Dynamic Load Models for Power Systems. *Licentiate Thesis*, Lund University.

Michael C. Ferris, August 10, 1999. MATLAB and GAMS: Interfacing Optimization and Visual-ization Software.

Nireekshana, T. et al. 2012. Enhancement of ATC in Deregulation based on Continuation Power Flow with FACTS Devices using Real-code Genetic Algorithm. *International Journal of Electrical Power and Energy Systems (IJEPES)*, (43)1: 1276-1284.Elsevier.

Nireekshana, T. et al. 2016. Available Transfer Capability Enhancement with FACTs Using Cat Swarm Optimization. *Ain Shams Engineering Journal* (ISSN: 2090-4479), 7: 159–116. Elsevier.

Power system test case archive "http://www.ee.washington.edu/research/pstca/pf14/pg_tca24bus.htm", website accessed on 15 November 2006.

Communication and Computing Systems – Prasad et al. (eds)
© 2019 Taylor & Francis Group, London, ISBN 978-0-367-00147-6

Multiple hole detection in wireless underground sensor networks

Abhinesh Kaushik
Jawaharlal Nehru University, New Delhi, India

ABSTRACT: The use of underground wireless sensor networks is becoming increasingly popular, in the terrains and areas where human intervention or reach is difficult. They play a very crucial role in observing the conditions of the areas far from human reach. Unfortunately, the biggest problem they suffer from is the presence of holes in the network, which often obstructs its efficient functioning. Therefore, these holes need to be detected and recovered in an efficient way. By applying various techniques like Voronoi diagram and taking a cue from available algorithms from wireless sensor network and wireless underground sensor network, both, for hole detection, we have tried to propose an algorithm for hole detection. The intended algorithm is able sto detect holes in a scenario where the nodes will be dispersed randomly. An efficiency analysis of the same has been carried out after the implementation.

1 INTRODUCTION

1.1 *Wireless underground sensor networks*

Wireless sensor networks are extensively distributed networks of tiny, lightweight wireless nodes, setup in huge numbers to observe the environment or system by the measurement of physical parameters such as temperature, pressure, or relative humidity (Akyildiz et al. 2002). Wireless underground sensor networks are a network of sensor nodes wherein both transmission and reception from the nodes both takes place underground and they do not require wired connections. These consists of number of sensors planted underground or in a cave or in a mine, to observe underground conditions. Here along with them additional sink nodes are deployed above the ground to transfer information from the sensors to the base station (Akyildiz et al. 2006).

1.2 *Network holes*

Network hole is basically defined as the region or the area, where the nodes stops sensing the area or stops communicating with their neighbouring nodes in an area (Ahmed et al. 2005). The holes occurring in the network can be of various type. *Coverage holes:* When the sensors are sprinkled on the ground via planes or other sources, there are possibilities that the nodes might not cover all corners and places of the area, therefore creating regions where there is no network coverage, resulting in the formation of the coverage holes (Huang et al. 2007). *Routing holes*: This type of hole is usually created when the connection with the node responsible for routing is lost. The death of the routing node results in prohibition of that route or path. *Jamming holes*: These are usually caused by interference due to other wireless signals or various other mediums of signal propagation. These are also created due to the presence of jammers around the area where the wireless sensors are deployed. Obstacles around the sensors like soil, minerals, rocks etc. in the wireless underground sensor network are a major source of jamming holes. New signals from various other devices can interfere with the existing signals from the sensor node of our network, again resulting in jamming holes (Wood et al. 2003). *Black Holes*: The holes that are formed due to dropping or losing of data in the middle of transmission.

1.3 *Voronoi diagram*

Voronoi diagram is a mathematical tool which is used to partition a plane having n points into a convex polygon in a way that every polygon has only one generating point and each point in the polygon is nearest to its generating point than any other (Youtube, 2013). Voronoi Diagram helps in encoding proximity information that helps to know object nearest to a given point and where is the nearest point from the given point. For a given set of objects, called sites each Voronoi cell defines the set of points in the plane (or in higher dimension) that are close to each site than to any other site. The outlines of all Voronoi cells form Voronoi diagram (Karlof et al 2003).

2 RELATED WORK

2.1 *Structure Aware Self-Adaptive Sensor System(SASA)*

Structure Aware Self-Adaptive Sensor System (SASA) was implemented in an underground coal mine and the results thus obtained were further used for further simulation (Li et al. 2009). It deploys node in a hexagonal manner such that node deployment is uniform. Every node, barring the boundary nodes is placed as the centre of a hexagon, having six adjacent nodes around it in the form of six vertices of the hexagon. The system finds the position of collapse hole and reports it to the sink node as fast as possible. The system basically deals with creation and maintenance of the sensor network for hole detection. It also maintains the consistency in the system when sensor nodes are displaced or rearranged.

Talking about the shortcomings, nodes in this system are deployed in a pre-planned fashion and in a specific design layout, as they are placed uniformly in a hexagonal pattern, where every node is surrounded by at least six nodes and at approximately constant distances. This might be an idealistic situation and can be of little use in realistic scenario. Although the algorithm is capable of handling single node failures but simultaneous failure of two adjacent nodes leads to algorithm failure.

2.2 *Detecting holes via partitioning*

Detecting holes via partitioning a graph deals with finding all the uncovered areas (coverage problem) in a non-planar network along with their locations (Kanno et al 2009). This method is applicable for any non-planar network, creating a non-planar graph. Some assumptions are taken before implementing this algorithm. First, sensor network has a defined boundary. Second, nodes are scattered randomly within the boundary and thirdly, each sensor has a limited sensing distance. Partition algorithm usually divides the graph into disjoint sets. The graph has to be divided in a manner such that hole is saved, by finding the path from one boundary node to another. The path should be included in both the divided sub graphs so that the hole remains intact. This partition algorithm uses Breadth First Search technique.

The algorithm includes simulation of the network as a perfect connected graph, which might not always be possible.

3 PROPOSED ALGORITHM

We mainly focus on finding the coverage holes through our proposed algorithm (Zhang et al. 2013). Our proposed algorithm is divided into two parts;
Part1: It finds the boundary node
Part2: It deals with detection of holes

Part 1: *Boundary_nodes ( )*
With this algorithm, we are trying to differentiate all the boundary nodes since we only need boundary nodes for further calculation of holes. Therefore, those nodes other than the boundary nodes, unnecessarily increases the overhead of calculation.

In the experimentation, we are inputting the number of nodes, once we have received the number of nodes, we are setting the coordinates (x_i, y_i) for every node so that no two nodes overlap. The sensing area of every sensor node is also taken as the input as S.

Firstly, we create a Voronoi diagram for all the sensor nodes. Then every Voronoi cell is traversed, to find the distance $(Dist)$ between the sensor node n_i having coordinates (x_i, y_i) and all the vertices (v_{ix}, v_{iy}) of the respective Voronoi cell using the distance formula:

$$Dist = \sqrt{\left(v_{ix} - n_x\right)^2 + \left(v_{iy} - n_y\right)^2}$$

After calculating this distance, we compare it with the sensing area S, of every node, if this distance $(Dist)$ is greater than the sensing area S, it is marked as the boundary node and the vertex belongs to the coverage hole, by making the *flag =0*, which is initially set to *flag=1*. If the distance is less than the sensing area of the node and the calculation is further repeated for the next Voronoi of the new node.

At the end of this part of the algorithm, we get the boundary nodes distinguished from the rest of the nodes. We use the results of this algorithm in the next part of the algorithm as an input.

Whereas Figure 1 shows the generated Voronoi diagram for the sensor nodes deployed. This graph (Figure 2) shows the relevance of the algorithm Boundary_node (). This show that if we do not use the first part of the algorithm, we have to consider all the nodes as the boundary nodes which increases overhead of time as well as computation. With the use of this algorithm, we have effectively brought down the computation by differentiating the boundary nodes.

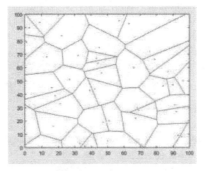

Figure 1.   Voronoi diagram of the deployed node.

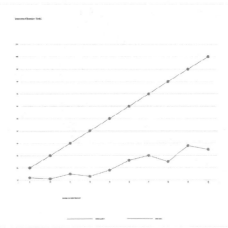

Figure 2.   Graph showing importance of Part 1.

159

Finding the hole: *Hole_detection( )*

Part 2: *Hole_detection ( )*

With this algorithm, we are trying to create an approximate polygon for coverage holes in a sensor network using the boundary nodes and the Voronoi diagram from the first part of the algorithm.

Here we are inputting the Voronoi diagram obtained in the first part along with the location of the boundary nodes $(n_x \, n_y)$. We also make use of the sensing area S. We further take two new inputs in the form of flattening increment i.e. a and the number of discretising points i.e. d. Flattening increment is used to depict the degree of approximation of hole edge point to actual edge point. Whereas the number of discretising points is considered to approximate sensing edges using discretized edges.

Firstly we try to discretize the edge node we have got in the form of boundary nodes. To uniformly discretise edge we use the following formula:

$$G_{ix} = n_x + S * cos(2\pi/d * i)$$
$$G_{iy} = n_y + S * cos(2\pi/d * i)$$

Here $(G_{ix}, \, G_{iy})$ gives the location of the edge point G. To find if any edge point belong to the coverage hole, we use swell increment a, to swell the edge so that it acquires the periphery of the coverage hole. We now discretise the edge points obtained using the following formula:

$$Z_{ix} = n_x + (S + a) * cos(2\pi/d * i)$$
$$Z_{iy} = n_y + (S + a) * cos(2\pi/d * i)$$

Here $(Z_{ix}, \, Z_{iy})$ gives us the edge point corresponding to the coverage hole, and a represents the swell increment, a actually indicates by how much the edge node be approximated to the actual edge of the hole edge. If, $a=0$ then this represents that there is no approximation done. We have introduced critical points in order to connect the edge points of the holes. These are the points defined as points between edge points of the hole and the non-edge points of the hole. For every part of the edge node adjacent to the coverage hole, we have two critical points. We are connecting two critical edge points belonging to two different edge points which are closest to each other.

We are also connecting edge points of holes between every pair of critical points in an order. After connecting all these points approximately, we get the shape and locations of the hole in the form of polygons.

Figure 3 shows the deployment of sensor nodes along with their sensing area and Voronoi diagram around every node. Whereas, Figure 4 depicts various approximated polygons showing holes and Figure 5 depicts an enlarged view of the hole polygon, showing two enlarged holes.

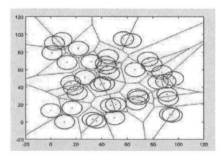

Figure 3.   Input to Part 2 of the algorithm.

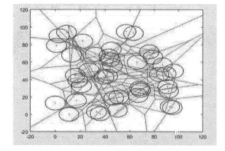

Figure 4.   Final output of the algorithm.

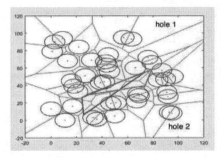

Figure 5.   Graph showing efficiency of the algorithm.

4   RESULTS

Figure 6 shows the impact of increasing number of nodes on the runtime of the algorithm. Increasing the number of deployed nodes is increasing the complexity of the algorithm as it also leads to increase in the boundary nodes. The placement of the nodes is playing a vital role, thereby impacting the runtime of algorithm. But the graph shows that the algorithm gives steady results without getting much affected by increase in the number of boundary nodes. We have averaged the runtime by running the algorithm for 10 iterations of different placement of nodes and varying number of holes and boundary nodes.

Figure 7 shows the efficiency of our proposed algorithm in terms of runtime by varying the number of holes. Though the number of holes is varying in a large range but our algorithm performs steadily in terms of runtime and is working equally efficiently. We have averaged the runtime by running the algorithm for 10 iterations of different placement of nodes and varying number of holes and boundary nodes

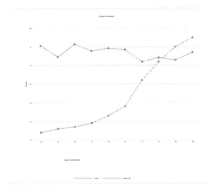

Figure 6.   Runtime vs number of bound-ary nodes.

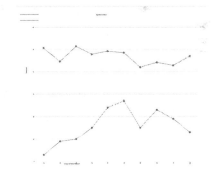

Figure 7.   Runtime vs number of holes.

5   CONCLUSION

In this paper, we have made an attempt to detect multiple hole in a network by using the properties of Voronoi Diagram. The analysis of the proposed algorithm has given us the required results. After thorough implementation, we have also tried to plot a graph depicting the relationship of the number of underground nodes deployed with that of the runtime of the algorithm, which is pretty much up to our expectations. The proposed algorithm is also capable of overcoming the limitations of the previous related work done. Our algorithm is able to work efficiently even when the nodes are deployed randomly. The algorithm uses simplest of the technique to detect the holes, one which is easy to implement as well as easy to understand. The only shortcoming of the algorithm is, that it is overlapping the hole polygon with the sensing area many a times, making the output a bit tangled.

Therefore, the proposed algorithm fulfils all the objectives .However, there is always a scope for further improvement in the algorithm for better detection of holes.

REFERENCES

Ahmed, N., Kanhere, S.S. and Jha, S., 2005. The holes problem in wireless sensor networks: a survey. *ACM SIGMOBILE Mobile Computing and Communications Review*, 9(2), pp.4–18.

Huang, C.F., Tseng, Y.C. and Wu, H.L., 2007. Distributed protocols for ensuring both coverage and connectivity of a wireless sensor network. *ACM Transactions on Sensor Networks (TOSN)*, 3(1), p.5.

I Akyildiz I.F.,, Su, W., Sankarasubramaniam, Y. and Cayirci, E., 2002. A survey on sensor networks. *IEEE communications magazine*, 40(8), pp.102–114.

I Akyildiz, I.F. and Stuntebeck, E.P., 2006. Wireless underground sensor networks: Research challenges. *Ad Hoc Networks*, 4(6), pp.669–686.

Kanno, J., Buchart, J.G., Selmic, R.R. and Phoha, V., 2009, June. Detecting coverage holes in wireless sensor networks. In *2009 17th Mediterranean Conference on Control and Automation* pp. (452–457). IEEE.

Karlof, C. and Wagner, D., 2003, May. Secure routing in wireless sensor networks: Attacks and countermeasures. In *Sensor Network Protocols and Applications, 2003. Proceedings of the First IEEE.2003 IEEE International Workshop on* pp. (113–127). IEEE.

Li, M. and Liu, Y., 2009. Underground coal mine monitoring with wireless sensor networks. *ACM Transactions on Sensor Networks (TOSN)*, 5(2), p.10.

Wood, A.D., Stankovic, J.A. and Son, S.H., 2003, December. JAM: A jammed-area mapping service for sensor networks. In *Real-Time Systems Symposium, 2003. RTSS 2003. 24th IEEE* pp. (286–297). IEEE.

Youtube.com. 2013. *youtube*. [ONLINE] Available at: https://youtu.be/7eCrHAv6sYY. [Accessed 1 December 2018].

Zhang, Y., Zhang, X., Wang, Z. and Liu, H., 2013, April. Virtual edge based coverage hole detection algorithm in wireless sensor networks. In *Wireless Communications and Networking Conference (WCNC), 2013 IEEE* (pp. 1488–1492). IEEE.

Communication and Computing Systems – Prasad et al. (eds)
© *2019 Taylor & Francis Group, London, ISBN 978-0-367-00147-6*

Word sense disambiguation using the unsupervised method

Archana Kumari
School of Computer and Systems Sciences, Jawaharlal Nehru University Delhi, India

ABSTRACT: WSD is an essential process in linguistics because of its requirement for the applications based on languages. The first attempt for automated word sense disambiguation was modelled in the context of Machine translation. Many works have been performed on Word sense disambiguation for English, IIT Bombay performed WSD for Hindi language using WordNet. Most of the Natural languages have multiple word ambiguity. Unlike previous approaches which assume single word ambiguity, we used a graph based Unsupervised WSD approach which disambiguates words (with multiple ambiguities) in the sentence. In the above mentioned method, initially, a semantic graph is built for each and every interpretation which is possible. To construct a graph, we will use WordNet for the Hindi Language developed at IIT Bombay. Then we will try to obtain the spanning tree with the minimum cost. The tree must correspond to the interpretation graph and the graph with the minimum interpretation is identified. If the value of the cost found is below the threshold provided, then the corresponding interpretation would be the resulting interpretation of the sentence. This process is continued until accurate results are achieved. This approach considers some open class words. We are extending it to include pronoun, conjunctions, prepositions etc.

1 INTRODUCTION

To study the language used in our day to day life, we utilize NLP (termed as Natural Language Processing) which is defined as a task which processes natural languages. NLP is the area for AI and Linguistics which establishes a correspondence between human language and computer. In human language most of the words are polysemous, disambiguating those words automatically is a fiendish task. In NLP, WSD has been characterized as the task that entails the relation between the word present in the text and the meaning which is capable of being attributed to that word. WSD is a long established matter of concern in computer linguistics as it is having a major effect in a real-world application like Information Retrieval, Machine translation etc... The Word Sense Disambiguation is acknowledged as an AI-Complete problem (Navigli et. al., 2005) which is analogous to NPC (NP-Complete) problem. NPC problem like Turing Test (Mihalcea, 2005) is one of the hardest problem known to be solved in AI (Artificial Intelligence). The basic structure of any WSD system can be outlined as: it takes input a word which is an ambiguous word in a context along with any knowledge base and yields a sense which is suitable for the word according to the given context. After implementing a potential technique WSD returns an appropriate meaning. However, creating knowledge resource manually was a prolonged attempt which must occur if a domain, languages and sense inventories changes. This is the elemental problem that exists in WSD and called as Knowledge acquisition bottleneck (Vishwakarma et. al., 2012). The rapid increase in the amount of unstructured data has led the increasing demand to manage the huge amount of information by using automated techniques. There were two different approaches for implementing WSD: 1) Shallow approaches: These approaches do not rely on world knowledge instead a person can identify the meaning of the words by considering the surrounding. Deep Approaches: these types of approaches require knowledge existing in the real world.

But the real world knowledge exists in the raw format. These raw data must be converted into the structured data which must be in machine readable format. Nevertheless, if it is possible to develop such a source of knowledge then this approach would perform better than shallow approaches. WSD is a procedure of computationally identifying the sense to be utilized in a particular context. The two variants of WSD task are as follows: 1) Lexical sample WSD: In this type of task WSD systems need to perform disambiguation on a limited set of words. This type of WSD generally utilized by supervised systems. All- words WSD: The open class words which occur in a text are disambiguated in this type of WSD systems. All the approaches of WSD contain four major components: word sense, external knowledge resources, context representation and automatic algorithm for disambiguation. An appropriate sense for a word is a definition of given word which is generally recognized to be valid. The type of disambiguation required is dependent on the type of the problem. Each word could be polysemous or monosemous. As soon as the sense of the word is identified, the types of ambiguity are decided. (Turdakov, 2010) talked about various ambiguities possible are morphological, syntactic, lexical, semantic and pragmatics. External knowledge resource is an elemental part of WSD. These resources may be structured and unstructured. Some of the structured resources are dictionaries, thesauri and ontologies. Since the beginning of the research area, a dictionary has been used as a basic tool for disambiguation. Dictionaries have become more famous as they were incorporated with more semantic relationships and turned electronic. WordNet (Miller et. al., 1990) is regarded as the most widely used computer lexicon as it encompasses with rich semantic networks. For this reason, WordNet is considered as an enhanced version of conventional dictionaries. Thesauri contain information about the relationships between the words. Ontologies are a description of conceptualization of a particular domain of interest. Ontologies are generally domain specific, comprise of taxonomy and interpret semantic relations. UMLS is commonly used an ontology for categorization of medical concepts and contains semantic networks. Moving onto unstructured resources corpora is a group of texts utilized for learning language models. Corpora may be raw that is unlabeled corpora, Brown Corpus (Kucera et. al., 1967) or sense- annotated corpora, Sem-Cor (Miller et. al., 1993) or it may represent word collocations. Context representation is an important component of WSD systems as the text is present in an unstructured format. These raw data must be converted into a structured format so that it can be utilized by automatic methods for sense disambiguation. Therefore, some preprocessing is required before using this data as an input text. Some preprocessing steps are lemmatization, tokenization, chunking, part-of- speech tagging, parsing etc. After the preprocessing step, each word in a text is represented by a vector of features of a different kind. Context representation may be categorized on the basis of the granularity of the context being used which is local, tropical, syntactic and semantic features. Local features represent the local context of word usage. Topical represent a general topic or domain of discussion. The syntactic feature represents a morphological feature of the word within a scope of sentence. Semantic features represent semantic information. Algorithms due to the variety available in the context representation, algorithms from AI to data mining could be implemented for WSD systems. Most of the methods emanate from the area of machine learning.

2 WSD METHODOLOGY

These methods utilize approaches of Machine Learning.

2.1 *Supervised method*

Supervised method is the most widely used methods but it is dependent on the accessibility of tagged corpora. These tagged corpora are used as training sets and then employed on the inputs which are not tagged yet. An assessment is performed by supplying another tagged corpus in a test set. Performance of supervised methods is bounded by the training set and similarity of the method is bounded with the test set. Furthermore, supervised methods are better than unsupervised methods for WSD as they have achieved better results. The most widely used machine learning supervised WSD methods are:

2.1.1 *Decision lists*

In this methodology, a decision lists (Rivest, 1987) is a set of rules which is used for the classification of test set. Decision list in WSD assigns the sense to the given word. This could be taken as a set which consists of rules of the form if-then-else. Set of features are induced using training sets. The rules in the form (feature-value, sense, score) are generated. A decision list is built on the basis of these rules which are ordered on their decreasing score. Decision list acquired the desired success in the first Senseval evaluation e.g. (Yarowsky, 2000). To resolve the problem of knowledge acquisition bottleneck (Agirre et. al., 2000) implemented the decision list method.

2.1.2 *Decision tree*

Decision tree classifies the training data set using a tree structure. In this tree, test on feature value is represented by an internal node and result of the test is given by branch of the decision tree. When the leaf node is reached the result is predicted. Various issues like data sparseness, unreliable prediction limited the use of decision tree.

2.1.3 *Naive Bayes*

This classifies the data using probabilistic classifier which is dependent on Bayes theorem. Given a feature for word in the corresponding context it calculates conditional probability for each sense. The sense with maximum conditional probability would be taken as a most likely sense of the ambiguous words. The basic assumption of nave Bayes is that features are independent of each other.

2.1.4 *Neural networks*

A neural network (McCulloch et. al., 1943) is a computational method based on a large collection of neural units. Input is given to the learning processes in the form of pair input feature, desired response. The main task is to divide the training data into non-overlapping sets similar to the required response from the input features.

2.1.5 *Exemplar-based learning*

Also termed as instance-based learning or memory-based learning. It is classified as a supervised approach in which examples are used to build a classification model. Examples are preserved as points in m as memory. New examples for classification are added to model gradually. The performance of k-nearest neighbor algorithms highest in WSD (Daelemans et. al., 1999).

2.2 *Unsupervised methods*

This type of methods depends upon unlabeled corpora. They do not need any for the disambiguation. These methods are having the capability to deal with the problem of knowledge acquisition bottleneck (Gale et. al., 1992b). The elementary condition of the method is that; the neighboring words must have the same sense. They are having the capability to generate senses of the word from input text by clustering occurrences of the word. These clusters are then utilized to classify new occurrences in the cluster. In this regard, an unsupervised learning is considered as a problem of clustering.

2.3 *Knowledge-based methods*

These methods leverages resources of knowledge to identify sense of the word in a particular context. Performance of these types of methods is lower than other WSD methods. Since the knowledge resources have become more instructive and available in vast amount, these approaches could be applied to any sort of texts. The major objective of the study was to determine the problem which arises in WSD and the various procedures applied to solve the problem.

3 LITERATURE REVIEW

The WSD was envisioned as an elemental problem of machine translation in the late 1940s (Weaver, 1949). In 1950 Kaplan expressed that two words surrounding an ambiguous word in a particular context are analogous to entire sentence of the context. Till the 1960s, WSD was acknowledged as the hardest Problem (Bar- Hillel, 1960), which was one of the biggest hindrances for the advancement of the Machine Translation. The WSD was attempted with AI approaches to widen the area by automating the task of recognizing concepts (Collins, 1975) and for language understanding (Wilks, 1975) in the 1970s. But due to unavailability of the huge amount of machine-readable knowledge resource, a generalization of the result was strenuous. In 1975 Masterman put forward his theory which gives an idea of identifying the meaning of word by utilizing the heading of the categories available in Roget's International Thesaurus. Wilks evolved a model on preference semantics, where the selectional restriction and frame based lexical semantics were used to get the actual meaning of an ambiguous word. In 1979, Rieger and Small come up through the proposal of the single Word Experts. The 1980s was a crossroad in the area of WSD with the remarkable development of the large-scale lexical knowledge recourses and corpus was ready for use during this time. Some notably successful WSD system developed in the 1980s are rule-based systems. Researchers (Wilks et al., 1990) began to utilize various automatic procedures for knowledge extraction parallel with the handcrafting techniques. In 1986, an algorithm was given by Lesk which was dependent on the overlaps that exists between the glosses (dictionary definitions) of words in the sentence. Suitable meaning of ambiguous word was represented by the maximum number of overlaps which was realized using OALD (Oxfords Advanced Learners Dictionary) of current English usage. In 1990s massive developments takes place in the research fields of natural language processing. Statistical methods were applied in this area. Various evaluation campaigns (Senseval) of WSD systems began. The first senseval was executed by Resnik and Yarowsky in 1997. A major enhancement was rolled out with the formulation of WordNet (Miller, 1990) in the field of WSD as WordNet was designed programmatically and organized into hierarchical manner into synsets. WordNet is one of the most important online sense inventory. used in WSD. During this time the statistical revolution swept through the field of WSD to resolve the sense classification problem and machine learning methods were applied to accomplish a desired result. Methods based on manually sense tagged corpora have become the conventional approach to WSD in 1990s. Brown et al. were the first to implement the WSD based on corpus in 1991. Also in 1991, subject codes were used for disambiguation, which gives the appropriate sense of the given word using LDOCE [Guthrie et al.].

4 PROPOSED WORK

The approach we are using comprise of two steps. In the first step we built a graph using WordNet which is a lexical knowledge base used for Hindi Language.

Graph consists of nodes and edges. In the said graph nodes are denoted by senses and edges are referenced by the relationship existing between the senses of the words. If the words are having any relations like homonymy, synonym, meronymy or entailment etc., an edge will be added between the corresponding words. In the next steps graph is obtained and assessed to determine the appropriate interpretation. If suitable result is acquired, then stop else recursion will take place and to account the previous sentence input sentence will be updated. Above procedure will iterate till expected results are achieved.

Suppose the sentence contains n number of words which is open class and jth word is having n_j senses where $1 <= j <= k$. The number of interpretation possible for the sentence given would be.

$$IP = \Pi_{j=1}^{k} n_j$$

The procedure can be illustrated as follows:

Step1: Obtain all the open class words and find all the senses possible for each word. Step2: Semantic graph is built.

- Initialize a graph.

    a) Iterate the below steps for each and every pair of words in each interpretation.
    b) Using the WordNet for Hindi language, obtain all paths existing between the pair of words.
    c) Select a path (A path should be such that, if added in the graph must not increase the cost or should increase it minimally).
    d) Add the path selected in previous step to the graph.

- Minimum cost of a spanning tree is obtained. The obtained cost is now considered as cost for the interpretation.

Step3: Calculate the cost of interpretation which is minimum. Step4: Result
Illustration using an example
गीता पुस्तकालय से पुस्तकलायी |
गीता", "पुस्तकालय", "से", "पुस्तक", "लायी" .

For each word, WordNet has provided 2 senses as noun,2 senses as noun,3 senses as verb and 1 as adverb,1 sense as noun, and 3 senses as verb respectively.

To draw a semantic graph, first of all Initialize the graph then find all the possible pairs in each possible interpretation. Let's consider interpretation
I_1 ("गीता", "पुस्तकालय", "से", "पुस्तक", "लायी") where the possible pairs are
P_1 = ("गीता", "पुस्तक",),
P_2 = (पुस्तकालय", "से"),
P_3 = ("से", "पुस्तक")
P_4 = ("पुस्तक", "लायी"),
P_5 = (गीता", "से"),
P_6 = ("पुस्तकालय", "पुस्तक")
P_7 = (गीता", "लायी"),
P_8 = (गीता", "पुस्तकालय"),
P_9 = ("पुस्तकालय", "लायी")
P_{10} = ("से", "लायी")
Now we will try to find a path between pair P_1 using WordNet

5 IMPLEMENTATION AND RESULTS

Figure 1(a): Results.

This is the desired results. Here the output is in the form of integer because our program is assigning an integer value to each strings and the generating a graph using a symbol table. Initially the symbol table is empty. In our code each keys of symbol table are assigned an integer value such as in case of our input keys in the symbol table for keys in the symbol table assigned an integer value.

```
run:
keys in the symbol table at 0 for  गीता is [ ·गीता]

keys in the symbol table at 0 for   पुस्तक is [   पुस्तक, ·गीता]

keys in the symbol table at 1 for पुस्तकालय is [   पुस्तक,  पुस्तकालय, ·गीता]

keys in the symbol table at 0 for पुस्तक is [   पुस्तक,  पुस्तकालय, पुस्तक, ·गीता]

keys in the symbol table at 0 for   पुस्तकालय is [   पुस्तक,   पुस्तकालय, पुस्तकालय, पुस्तक, ·गीता]

keys in the symbol table at 1 for गीता is [   पुस्तक,   पुस्तकालय, गीता, पुस्तकालय, पुस्तक, ·गीता]

keys in the symbol table at 0 for पुस्तकालय is [   पुस्तक,   पुस्तकालय, गीता, पुस्तकालय, पुस्तक, पुस्तकालय, ·गीता]

keys in the symbol table at 0 for   गीता is [   गीता,   पुस्तक,   पुस्तकालय, गीता, पुस्तकालय, पुस्तक, पुस्तकालय, ·गीता]

keys in the symbol table at 1 for पुस्तकालय is [   गीता,   पुस्तक,   पुस्तकालय, गीता, पुस्तकालय, पुस्तक, पुस्तकालय, ·गीता]
```

Figure 1(b):   Snapshot of the keys of the symbol table.

```
integer value assigned in symbol table is= 8
integer value assigned in symbol table is= 7
integer value assigned in symbol table is= 1
integer value assigned in symbol table is= 4
integer value assigned in symbol table is= 5
integer value assigned in symbol table is= 2
integer value assigned in symbol table is= 3
integer value assigned in symbol table is= 6
integer value assigned in symbol table is= 0
```

Figure 1(c):   Snapshot of the integer value assigned to the keys.

गीता =0
पुस्तक =6
पुस्तकालय =3
पुस्तक =2
पुस्तकालय is =5
गीता =4
पुस्तकालय =1
गीता =7
पुस्तकालय =8

6   CONCLUSIONS

In this paper, we have utilized an existing method for Hindi text disambiguation using graph connectivity measures. This method is used to disambiguate the sentences with multiple ambiguous words in Hindi language. We have taken into account all the interpretation which is possible and built a semantic graph for each interpretation. Finally, we consider the graph which is having a spanning tree of minimum interpretation cost. Utilized method yields the correct sense of the ambiguous word. This method considers all open class words like noun, pronoun, conjunction, preposition etc. This work can be extended in the future by assigning a weights to edges of graph which is nothing but the relations between the nodes. This may lead to better results.

REFERENCES

Agirre, E. Martinez, D. (2000): Exploring automatic word sense disambiguation with decision lists and the web. In: Proceedings of the 18th International Conference on Computational Linguistics (COLING, Saarbrucken, Germany). pp.11–19.

Cuadros, M. & Rigau, G. (2006): Quality assessment of large scale knowledge resources. In: Proceedings of the 2006 Conference on Empirical Methods in NaturalLanguage Processing, pp. 534–541. Association for Computational Linguistics.

Daelemans, W., Van Den Bosch, A.and Zavrel, J. (1999): Forgetting exceptions is harmful in language learning. *Mach. Learn.* 34, 1, pp.11—41.

Fellbaum C. (1998): 'WordNet: An Electronic Lexical Database. ed. MIT Press.

Gale, W. A., Church, K., and Yarowsky, D. (1992b): A method for disambiguating word senses in a corpus. *Comput. Human.* 26, pp. 415—439.

George, T., Iraklis, V., Kjetil, N. (2010): 'An Experimental Study on Unsupervised Graph-based Word Sense Disambiguation. In: 11th international conference on Computational Linguistics and Intelligent Text Processing, pp. 184—198.

Hindi WordNet from centre for Indian Language Technology (CFILT) solutions, *IIT Mumbai*, http://www.cfilt.iitb.ac.in/wordnet/webhwn/wn.php.

Kucera, H. Francis, W. N. (1967): Computational Analysis of Present-Day American English. Brown University Press, Providence, RI.

Lesk M. (1986): 'Automatic Sense Disambiguation Using Machine Readable Dictionaries: How to Tell a Pine Cone from an Ice Cream Cone. In: *Proc. Fifth ACM SIGDOC*, pp. 24–26.

Machinery, C. (1950): Computing machinery and intelligence-AM Turing. Mind, 59(236), 433.

Mallery, J. C. (1998): Thinking about foreign policy: Finding an appropriate role for artificially intelligent computers. In: Master's thesis, MIT Political Science Department.

Martin H. (1997): 'Handbook of Human-Computer Interaction. Elsevier, pp. 137—139.

McCulloch, W. & Pitts, W. (1943): A logical calculus of the ideas immanent in nervous activity. *Bull. Math. Biophys.* 5, pp.115—133.

Mihalcea R. (2005): 'Unsupervised Large-Vocabulary Word Sense Disambiguation with Graph-based Algorithms for Sequence Data Labeling. Proceedings of Human Language Technology Conference and Conference on Empirical Methods in Natural Language Processing (HLT/EMNLP) pp. 411–418.

Miller, G. A., Beckwith, R., Fellbaum, C., Gross, D., & Miller, K. J. (1990): Introduction to WordNet: An on-line lexical database. *International journal of lexicography*, 3(4), 235—244.

Mishra, N., Yadav, S., & Siddiqui, T. J. (2009): An unsupervised approach to Hindi word sense disambiguation. In: Proceedings of the First International Conference on Intelligent Human Computer Interaction, pp. 327—335. Springer, New Delhi.

Navigli R (2005): 'Semi Automatic Extension of Large-Scale Linguistic Knowledge Bases. Proc. 18th Florida Artificial Intelligence Research Soc. Conf. pp. 548–553.

Navigli R. & Lapata M. (2007): Graph Connectivity Measures for Unsupervised Word Sense Disambiguation. International Joint Conference on Artificial Intelligence. pp. 1683—1688.

Navigli R. & Lapata M. (2010): 'An Experimental Study of Graph Connectivity for Unsupervised Word Sense Disambiguation.

Navigli R. & Velardi P. (2005): 'Structural semantic interconnections: a knowledge-based approach to word sense disambiguation. *In: IEEE transactions on pattern analysis and machine intelligence*, Vol. 27, No. 7, pp. 1075–1086.

Navigli R. (2009): Word Sense Disambiguation: *A Survey. ACM Computing Surveys*, Vol. 41, No. 2.

Navigli, R. (2009): Word sense disambiguation: A survey. *ACM computing surveys (CSUR)*, 41, (2), 10.

NG, T. H. (1997): Getting serious about word sense disambiguation. In Proceedings of the ACL SIGLEX.

Rivest, R. L. (1987): Learning decision lists. *Mach. Learn.* 2, 3, pp. 229—246.

Sharma R. (2008): Word Sense Disambiguation for Hindi Language. Thesis, Thapar University, Patiala.

Sinha M., Reddy M.K., Bhattacharyya P., Pandey P., Laxmi K. (2004): Hindi Word Sense Disambiguation. In: International Symposym on Machine Translation, NLP & Transition Support System.

Tandon R. (2009): 'Word Sense Disambiguation using Hindi WordNet.

Vishwakarma S. K. & Vishwakarma C. K. (2012): 'A Graph Based Approach to Word Sense Disambiguation for Hindi Language. *In: International Journal of Scientific Research Engineering and Technology*, Vol. 1, Issue 5, pp. 313–318.

Weaver, W. (1949): Translation. In Machine Translation of Languages: Fourteen Essays (written in 1949, published in 1955). In: W. N. Locke and A. D. Booth, Eds. Technology Press of MIT, Cambridge, MA, and John Wiley & Sons, New York, 15–23.

Wilks, Y. (1975): Preference semantics. In Formal Semantics of Natural Language, E. L. Keenan, Ed. Cambridge University Press, Cambridge, U.K., pp. 329—348.

Yarowsky, D. (2000): Hierarchical decision lists for word sense disambiguation. *Comput. Human. 34*, 1-2, pp. 179—186.

Communication and Computing Systems – Prasad et al. (eds)
© *2019 Taylor & Francis Group, London, ISBN 978-0-367-00147-6*

Edible electronics—smart approach towards medical applications

Abhay Anand, Divyanshi Sharma & Parul Bansal
Dronacharya College of Engineering, Gurugram, India

ABSTRACT: A smart classified group of electronic ingredients which are originated principally from natural and organic edibles, with negligible echelons of inorganic substance. These
are in an embryonic stage of development, furthermore studied and research is being carried
out to fabricate the electronics substance which can be consumed by the human beings as well
as the same needs to be friendly with the digestive system of the human being. A kit with
smart tools originated from edible electronic substance, fabrication patterns, elementary
stratagem components, and unwavering maneuvers with embedded sensors having capabilities
of sense as well as wire free trans-receivers for communication has been reported. The innovative substances have inaugurated the opportunity to outspread the devices which are compatible to our digestive system elsewhere swallowed non-degradable structures to edible and
nutritious structures. These substances may be ingested and combined as metabolized nutrition. The revision and research represent a fresh horizon of edible microchip technology
having the great potential on the way to transform current bio-medical technologies.

1   INTRODUCTION

In the present era of living criterions, electronics plays a very essential role. The electronics
can be of wearable type as well as it can be an implanted system, have a progressively more
substantial role in the monitoring of health, its therapy as well as diagnosis. The progress in
the field of devices that are used for health monitoring has been assisted by advancement in
electronics along with enlargement of the form factor and its constituents with transient,
stretchable and flexible systems. Far away skin related arrangements are lack of constrained
variable discoveries such as temperature, blood pressure, heart rate, and sweat based body
elements or implantable structures. The system is robust and have negligible threat factor to
septic bleeding and the necessity for surgery with malfunction. The human body is partially
explored part where the electronics substance has only surfed the digestive system.

The Digestive System or Gastrointestinal tract plays a vital role in between the outward surrounding and the inward system taking remarkable surfing area for edible electronics to survive and monitor variable factors which can be simulated to get proper state of the health and
have power to predict the disease or abnormal condition of inner body.

Edible, absorbable and digestible maneuver will add-on in advancement of this field as well
as requisite modernization in edible substance will aid in its embryonic development. This provides progression for the electronic material expansion for identification of an electronic substance toolkit and its components. They are prepared primarily from the normal foodstuffs
with indicating negligible chemical levels that can further be utilized to seal all prerequisite
gaps to shape electronics. The advancement in edible electronic material might be consumed
and adopted as a metabolized nutrition.

Presently, natural edible can be taken as an option for electronics materials based on specific
requirements which can identify superfluous edible on basis of harmless electronic materials. This
can be done to create complete electronic paradigms. Several active systems containing pH sensor,
RF filter and Mic were assembled and verified. The contemporary study has signified that edible
electronics have potential to direct accelerative an evolving realm of biomedical technology.

2 DEVELOPMENT AND ANALYSIS

The first step for the development of the edible electronics reference materials were chosen as monocles for the edible components that are either electrical or electronic. A circuitry usually comprises of resistor, capacitors, inductors and antennas which are associated together along with support of substrate and a layer which is known as encapsulating layer.

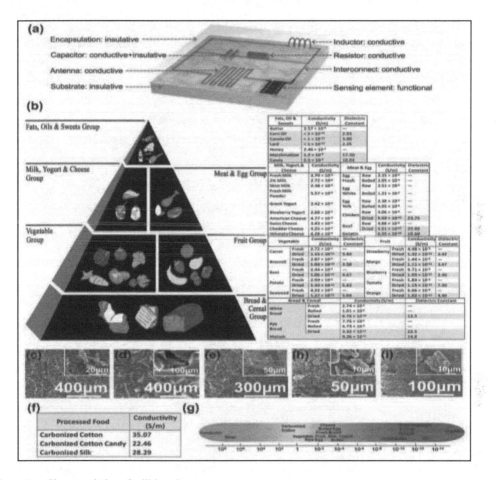

Figure 1.   Characteristics of edible substance.

The mechanism requires conductors along with insulators that are quantified through their electrical conductivities. For insulators, the conductivity should be less than 10^{-8} Sm^{-1} while, for conductors, the conductivity should be less than 106 Sm^{-1}. Conductors are castoff to manufacture wires, cathode/anode terminals, specific electrical components, etc. Conductors along with insulators are implemented to fabricate resistors having the resistance ranging from 10Ω to 20MΩ.

These reference standards institute specs required by constituents and maneuver creations by edible substance. In addition, efficient chipsets/systems are crucial to fabricate sensors along with their characteristics which are defined using specific solicitations.

The secondary course of action for development of the edible electronics, precise natural unprocessed foods were carefully chosen and systematized accordingly to accepted specified nutritional values from Pyramid Guide for food. Edibles like meat, cereals, vegetable, etc. can be utilized for analysis of electrical properties and there after the same to be utilized for fabrication of edible electronics. Parameter analyzer and probes which are derived from conductors and semiconductor are used for analyzing substance for characteristics and responses. As indicated in Figure 1(b), dried food and oil be utilized to attain electronic conductivity.

Electrical conductivity results as shown in Figure 1(f) indicate that these treated eatable substance and harmless metal can serve as the conductive substance. Piezoelectric materials can produce electricity upon mechanical stress and can be used in many applications containing pressure sensors, microphones and speakers.

Cellulose content is abundant in many vegetables, i.e. broccoli also holds piezoelectric properties which are due to the fact that cellulose crystallites exhibit partial piezoelectricity as a result of internal cycle of polar atomic groups associated with asymmetric carbon atoms.

The natural, processed, and adduct eatables were then carefully chosen to create our preferred food tool kit for component fabrication, as shown in Table 1.

Table 1. Food based material toolkit utilized for fabrication of electrical components.

	Food kit material	Cotton candy/silky gold leaf
Component	Structural function	Electrical function
Wire	Rice Paper/Sugar powder/Flour/Rice	Gold leaf/edible metal: gold
Resistor	Sweet potato powder/flour/candy/Dried fruit/Vegetable	Active charcoal/carbonized cotton fiber/ Cotton candy/Silky gold leaf
Inducer	Sweet potato powder/flour/candy/Dried fruit/Vegetable	Active charcoal/carbonized cotton fiber/ Cotton candy/Silky gold leaf
Capacitor	Gelatin/Dried fruit/vegetable	Gold leaf/Edible metal: Gold
Antenna	Sugar powder/flour/Rice paper/Candy/ Marshmallow/Egg white	Edible metal: Gold/Gold leaf/Active Charcoal/ Carbonized cotton/Silk

Optical microscopy and SEM images with the characterization results are shown in Figure 2. Edible wires are to be made up of rice paper as the substrate and popped gold (Au) is used as the efficient part. The thickness of the Gold is taken in the order of 100 nm as shown in (Figure 2(a)). Resistors and inductors are to be made of starch and carbonized cotton over and an extrusion process is completed with the help of a nozzle based upon spring pattern.

3   FUTURE SCOPE

Edible Electronics bid advancement in deliberation of enabling the assembly of devices as well as the probable system used for tracking and monitoring of both usual physiologies of Digestive System along with unusual condition accompanying an eclectic variety of diseases.

It is evident and can be foresight that an extensive variety of applications can be achieved using edible electronics viz. measuring of pH of stomach, motility, extent of microorganism and medication. It can also be utilized to elimination of tissues and cells in doubtful case of injury (cancer) diagnosis as well as medication.

Edible resources also enlarge the scale of momentary electronic ingredients for normal non-medical applications of electronics, as an innovative group of biodegradable and ecological electronics substance. For auxiliary advancement, newfangled fabrication procedures (e.g., 3-Dimesnionnal printing) would play a beneficial role in the direction of supporting the process as well as realization of diminished edible chipsets.

The efficient performance of edible semiconductor resources is essential for recognition as well as expansion of this technology further than embryonic development. The field requires a continuous development and research to find highly efficient substance from food which would supplement this embryonic field for comprehensive identifying along with actuation competency.

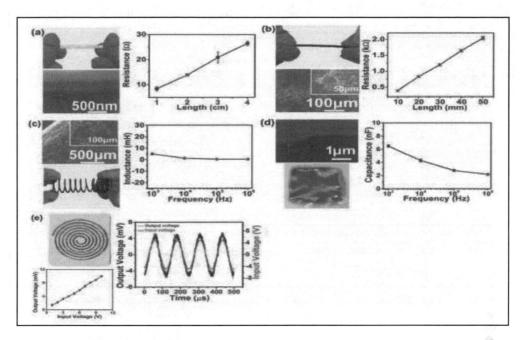

Figure 2.   Analysis results for edible electrical and electronic constituent.

The Edible Electronics can be utilized for the image acquisition for the internal body parts which can't be detected by conventional tracing methods as well as the same can be used for the data transfer from inside the human body for the various diagnostic parameters. Moreover, the Edible Electronics can be used a smart tracking device for the investigation purpose inside the human body which can be remotely operated.

REFERENCES

R. Wang, G. Blackburn, M. Desai, D. Phelan, L. Gillinov, P. Houghtaling, M. Gillinov, JAMA Cardiol. 2017, 2, 104.

K. Kaewkannate, S. Kim, *BMC Public Health* 2016, *16*, 433.

Y. Khan, A. E. Ostfeld, C. M. Lochner, A. Pierre, A. C. Arias, Adv. Mater. 2016, 28, 4373.

A. Koh, D. Kang, Y. Xue, S. Lee, R. M. Pielak, J. Kim, T. Hwang, S. Min, A. Banks, P. Bastien, M. C. Manco, L. Wang, K. R. Ammann, K. I. Jang, P. Won, S. Han, R. Ghaffari, U. Paik, M. J. Slepian, G. Balooch, Y. G. Huang, J. A. Rogers, Sci. Transl. Med. 2016, 8, 366ra 165.

X. Wang, W. Xu, P. Chatterjee, C. Lv, J. Popovich, Z. Song, L. Dai, M. Y. S. Kalani, S. E. Haydel, H. Jiang, Adv. Mater. Technol. 2016, 1, 1600059.

D. Fitzpatrick, *Implantable Electronic Medical Devices*, Elsevier, San Diego, CA, USA 2015.

E. Gibney, *Nature* 2015, *528*, 26.

J. A. Rogers, *JAMA, J. Am. Med. Assoc.* 2015, *313*, 561.

S. K. Kang, S. W. Hwang, S. Yu, J. H. Seo, E. A. Corbin, J. Shin, D. S. Wie, R. Bashir, Z. Ma, J. A. Rogers, Adv. Funct. Mater. 2015, 25, 1789.

S. Xu, Y. H. Zhang, L. Jia, K. E. Mathewson, K. I. Jang, J. Kim, H. R. Fu, X. Huang, P. Chava, R. H. Wang, S. Bhole, L. Z. Wang, Y. J. Na, Y. Guan, M. Flavin, Z. S. Han, Y. G. Huang, J. A. Rogers, Science 2014, 344, 70.

A. Kiourti, K. A. Psathas, K. S. Nikita, Bioelectromagnetics 2014, 35, 1.

Y. J. Kim, W. Wu, S. E. Chun, J. F. Whitacre, C. J. Bettinger, *Adv. Mater.* 2014, *26*, 6572.

Communication and Computing Systems – Prasad et al. (eds)
© *2019 Taylor & Francis Group, London, ISBN 978-0-367-00147-6*

Investigation of optical properties of a-Se$_{80-x}$Te$_{20}$Bi$_x$ (x=0, 3, 9) thin films

Deepika & B.M.K. Prasad
Dronacharya College of Engineering, Gurugram, India

Sanjay Singh
Department of ECE, Dronacharya College of Engineering, Gurugram, India

ABSTRACT: Amorphous samples of Se$_{80-x}$Te$_{20}$Bi$_x$ (x=0, 3, 9) glasses have been prepared using the melt quenching technique and thin film of the samples have been prepared using vacuum evaporation method. The thin film samples were characterized using XRD. The absorption and transmission spectra have been recorded on UV-Vis spectrophotometer in wavelength range 400-2500 nm and the data is analyzed to obtain refractive index, extinction coefficient, energy band gap etc. It was observed that refractive index increases while band gap decreases on increase of Bi content in Se-Te matrix. The narrowing of band gap may be due to large number of localized states introduced near the band edges due to structural defects

1 INTRODUCTION

Chalcogenide glasses have attracted a great deal of attention in the past two decades owing to their application in scientific and technological fields (Asokan et al, 2009; Tiwari et al, 2005; Deepika et al, 2009). These glasses are semiconducting materials with amorphous structure. The amorphous structure allows the material to have tunable electrical and optical properties as function of composition and preparation conditions. Selenium based glasses particularly Se-Te glasses have been studied due to their higher thermal stability, higher photosensitivity and smaller aging effects (Maharjan et al, 2000; Abdel-Rahim, 1998). The properties of Se-Te glasses can further be improved by adding third impurity to the system. Addition of Bi as third impurity increases the stability of the amorphous system and is expected to bring out significant changes in the physical properties of the Se-Te system (Saraswat et al, 2008; Saxenal et al 2003). Moreover, the carrier type reversal (CTR) observed on Bi addition makes the study of ternary chalcogenides more interesting. Chalcogenide glasses are generally p-type semiconductors. It is reported that (Nagels et al, 1983; Tohge et al, 1980), the addition of Bi at a certain atomic percentage into some binary chalcogenide glasses reverses the conduction from p to n-type. The reason attributed to CTR is strong n-type nature of c-Bi$_2$Se$_3$, which leads to increase in Bi$^-$ defects and disturbs the equilibrium between the charged chalcogen defects (C_3^+ *and* C_1^-).

In view of this, present paper reports the effect of bismuth addition on the optical properties of the Se-Te system. Various optical parameters such as refractive index, extinction coefficient, dielectric constant, energy band gap have been calculated for thin films of Se$_{80-x}$Te$_{20}$Bi$_x$ (x=0,3,9) glasses.

2 MATERIALS AND METHODS

The amorphous samples of Se$_{80-x}$Te$_{20}$Bi$_x$ (x=0,3,9) glasses were prepared using conventional melt quenching method. High purity (99.999%) elemental metal powders of Se, Te and Bi were weighed in appropriate weight percentage and were mixed thoroughly. The mixture was then transferred to quartz ampoules and was sealed in vacuum of 10^{-5} Torr. The sealed ampoules were then kept in muffle furnace at 900°C for 15 hours and were frequently rocked to ensure the homogeneity of the samples. The molten sample was quenched in ice- cooled water to get the glassy ingot. The ingot of the ampoule were taken out and was finely grounded to powder form using mortar and pestle.

Thin film of the samples was prepared through vacuum evaporation method. The XRD of thin films was carried on Panalytical X pert Pro X-ray diffractometer with Cu Kα radiation. The absorption and transmission spectra of thin films was recorded on UV-Vis-NIR spectrophotometer (Agilent Cary 60) in the range 400-2500 nm. All the measurements were recorded at room temperature.

3 RESULT AND DISCUSSION

Fig. 1 shows the XRD pattern of the thin films of $Se_{80-x}Te_{20}Bi_x$ (x=0,3,9) glassy alloys. Figure does not show any sharp peak, which indicates the amorphous nature of the samples. Fig. 2 shows the transmission spectra of thin films of $Se_{80-x}Te_{20}Bi_x$ (x=0,3,9) glassy alloys. The transmission spectra shows a single broad hump unlike several peaks usually observed in transmission of thin film samples. This may be attributed to very less thickness of the films. This single hump can be assumed to be formed by averaging of large number of small peaks within the wavelength range occupying the hump. It is observed that on addition of 3 at.wt.% of Bi, transmission spectra shifts towards lower wavelength while on further addition of Bi at 9 at. wt. %, transmission spectra shifts significantly towards higher wavelength.

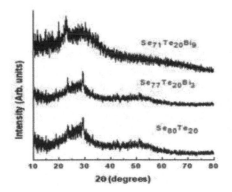

Figure 1.   XRD pattern of thin films of $Se_{80-x}Te_{20}Bi_x$ (x=0,3,9) glassy alloys.

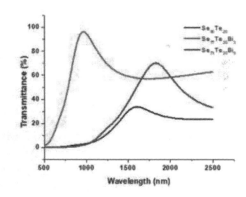

Figure 2.   Transmission spectra of thin films of $Se_{80-x}Te_{20}Bi_x$ (x=0,3,9) glassy alloys.

Swanepoel method (Swanepoel, 1983) was used to determine thickness (d) and refractive index (n) of the films. The value of the refractive index (n) of the film can be evaluated using the following relation:

$$n = [N + (N^2 - n_s{}^2)^{1/2}]^{1/2} \qquad (1)$$

Where,

$$N = \frac{2n_s(T_M - T_m)}{T_M T_m} + \frac{n_s^2 + 1}{2} \qquad (2)$$

Where n_s is the refractive index of the glass substrate. The value of refractive index of the glass substrate was calculated from following relation:

$$n_s = \frac{1}{T_s} + \left(\frac{1}{T_s^2} - 1\right)^{1/2} \tag{3}$$

Where T_s denotes the transmittance spectra of the glass substrate. In the present study, the value of n_s is found to be 1.58.

The thickness (d) of the film was determined using relation,

$$d = \frac{\lambda_1 \lambda_2}{2(\lambda_1 n_2 - \lambda_2 n_1)} \tag{4}$$

Where, n_1 and n_2 are the refractive indices corresponding to two adjacent maxima (or minima) at wavelengths λ_1 and λ_2. The d values for all the samples are mentioned in Table 1. The above equation is derived from the basic equation of interference fringes,

$$2nd = m_o \lambda \tag{5}$$

where m_o is the order number . The value of m_o is an integer for maxima and a half integer for minima.

Fig.3 shows the variation of refractive index (n) with wavelength. It can be observed that refractive index decreases with an increase in wavelength and increases with increase in bismuth concentration. The increase in refractive index may be attributed to variation of polarizability as suggested by Lorentz-Lorentz (Gonzalez-Leal et al, 2003) according to the following expression:

$$\frac{n^2 - 1}{n^2 + 2} = \frac{1}{2\varepsilon_o} \sum_j N_j \alpha_{p.j} \tag{6}$$

Where ε_o is the vacuum permittivity and N_j is the number of polarizable units of type j per volume unit, with polarizability α_{pj}.

The atomic radii of Se, Te and Bi are 116 pm, 135 pm and 145 pm respectively. The replacement of Se atom by larger radii Bi atom increases the polarizability of the system which consequently increases the refractive index. The increase in n can also be due to increase in density of the system on addition of Bi to Se-Te, which makes the system more rigid.

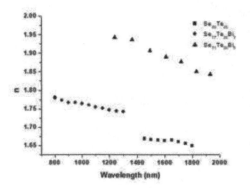

Figure 3. Variation of refractive index (n) with wavelength for thin films of $Se_{80-x}Te_{20}Bi_x$ (x=0,3,9) glassy alloys.

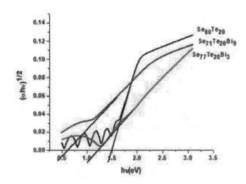

Figure 4. Band gap of thin films of $Se_{80-x}Te_{20}Bi_x$ (x=0,3,9) glasses.

The absorption spectra were utilized to obtain absorption coefficient (α). The absorption coefficient can be obtained using the values of film thickness and absorbance (X) using the following relation (Deepika et al, 2017):

$$\alpha = \frac{1}{d}\ln\left(\frac{1}{X}\right) \tag{7}$$

The values of absorption coefficient were further used to determine extinction coefficient (k). The extinction coefficient was calculated using relation:

$$k = \frac{\alpha\lambda}{4\pi} \tag{8}$$

The values of refractive index and extinction coefficient were further used to determine dielectric constant ε' (real) and ε'' (imaginary) from relations(Deepika et al, 2017)

$$\varepsilon' = n^2 - k^2 \tag{9}$$

$$\varepsilon'' = 2nk \tag{10}$$

The values of α, k, ε' and ε'' obtained from above eqs. (7-10) at wavelength 1200 nm are mentioned in Table 1.

Table 1. Values of film thickness (d), optical band gap (E$_g$), extinction coefficient (k), real (ε') and imaginary (ε'') part of dielectric constant, absorption coefficient (α), cohesive energy (C.E) and average single bond energy for thin films of Se$_{80-x}$Te$_{20}$Bi$_x$ (x=0,3,9) glassy alloys.

Sample	d (nm)	E$_g$ (eV)	K at 1200nm	ε' at 1200nm	ε'' at 1200nm	α×10^5 cm^{-1}	C.E. (Kcal/ mol)	H$_s$/N$_c$ (Kcal/ mol)
Se$_{80}$Te$_{20}$	1430	1.48	0.574	3.11	0.113	2.54	43.86	24.36
Se$_{77}$Te$_{20}$Bi$_3$	1344	1.22	0.162	2.68	0.533	2.31	43.67	23.90
Se$_{71}$Te$_{20}$Bi$_9$	758	0.60	0.259	3.67	0.943	4.54	43.39	23.03

The relation between the absorption coefficients (α) and the incident photon energy (hv) is given by (Tauc, 1974):

$$(\alpha h\nu) = A\,(h\nu - E_g)^n \tag{11}$$

where A is a constant and E$_g$ is the band gap of the material and exponent n depends on the type of transition. The energy band gap is calculated from the absorption spectra by plotting a graph between $(\alpha h v)^{1/2}$ and hv (Fig. 4). The extrapolation of the straight line to $(\alpha h v)^{1/2} = 0$ axis gives the value of the energy band gap. The values of E$_g$ has been mentioned in Table 1. From Table 1, it is observed that band gap decreases on increase in Bi concentration in Se-Te system. This decrease in band gap can be explained on the basis of chemical bond theory (CBT). CBT states that heteronuclear bonds are favored upon homonuclear bonds and bond are formed in decreasing orders of their bond energies. The bonds of higher energy are formed first followed by bonds of lower energy. Heteronuclear bond energies were determined using (Bicerano et al, 1985)

$$E(A-B) = [E(A-A) \times E(B-B)]^{1/2} + 30(\chi_A - \chi_B)^2 \qquad (12)$$

Where, E(A-A) and E(B-B) are energies of homonuclear bonds. The homonuclear bond energies for Se, Bi and Te are 44.04, 47.9 and 33 K cal/mol respectively. The heteronuclear bonds expected to occur in the system are Se-Te(43.15 kcal/mol), Se-Bi (40.70 kcal/mol). Firstly, higher energy Se-Te bonds are formed followed by Se-Bi to saturate all available valency of Se. The remaining unsatisfied Se valences are satisfied by formation of Se-Se bonds. The average heat of atomization is also defined as direct measure of cohesive energy (C.E.). The formulation used for alloy $Se_\alpha Te_\beta Bi_\gamma$ where $\alpha+\beta+\gamma=100$ is given by

$$H_s = \frac{\left(\alpha H_s^{Se} + \beta H_s^{Te} + \gamma H_s^{Bi}\right)}{\alpha + \beta + \gamma} \qquad (13)$$

Where H_s^{Se}, H_s^{Te} and H_s^{Bi} are heat of atomization of Se, Te and Bi respectively. The values of average single bond energy (H_s/N_c) has also been calculated with help of average coordination number (N_c). The values of C.E. and H_s/N_c are mentioned in Table 1. The values of H_s/N_c show a decrease with increasing Bi content, resulting in decrease of energy band gap. The increase in band gap is also attributed to structural defects created on formation of thin films. There may be accumulation of atoms on the surface of substrate, which may cause the formation of structural defects. These defects and degree of disorder together affects the width of localised states near the mobility edge. These defects can introduce localized states near the band edges resulting in decrease of band gap (Mott & Davis, 1979).

4   CONCLUSION

The paper reports the study of optical properties of thin films of $Se_{80-x}Te_{20}Bi_x$ (x=0,3,9) glasses. The results show that refractive index increases on increase of Bi content in Se-Te system, This may be due to incarse in polarizability of Se-Te-Bi system. The band gap was found to decrease on increase of Bi content in Se-Te system. The decrease in the optical band gap is correlated with decrease in the cohesive energy and average heat of atomization of the system. The narrowing of band gap may also be due to large number of localized states introduced near the band edges due to structural defects.

REFERENCES

Abdel-Rahim, M.A., El-Korashy, A., Hafiz, M.M., & Mahmoud, A.Z. 2008. Calorimetric studies of the glassy alloys in the Ge-Se-Te system. *Physica B*.403: 2956–2962.
Asokan, S. &.Prasanth, S. B. 2009. Effect of antimony addition on the thermal and electrical-switching behaviour of bulk Se–Te glasses. *J. Non-Cryst. Solids* 355: 164–168
Bicerano, J. & Ovshinsky, S.R. 1985. Chemical bond approach to the structures of chalcogenide glasses with reversible switching properties. *J Non-Cryst Solids* 74:75–84
Deepika, Rathore, K.S. & Saxena, N.S. 2009. A Kinetic Analysis on Non-isothermal Glass- Crystal Transformation in $Ge_{1-x}Sn_xSe_{2.5}$ (0≤ x≤0.5) Glasses. *J Phys.: Condens. Mater.* 21: 335102
Deepika & Singh, H. Optical investigation of vacuum evaporated $Se_{80-x}Te_{20}Sb_x$(x=0,6, 12) amorphous thin films. *Infrared Phys. & Technol.* 85, 139–143.
Gonzalez-Leal, J.M., Prieto-Alcon, R. & Angel, J.A., Marquez. E. 2017. Optical properties of thermally evaporated amorphous $As_{40}S_{60-x}Se_x$ films. *J Non-Cryst Solids* 315: 134–143.
Maharjan, N.B. Bhandari, D., Saxena, N.S., Imran, M.M.A. & Paudyal, D.D. 2000. Differential scanning calorimetry studies of $Se_{85}Te_{15-x}Pb_x$ (x = 4, 6, 8 and 10) glasses. *Bull. Mater. Sci.* 23, 369–375
Nagels, P., Tichy, L., Tiska, A. & Ticha, H.1983. Electrical properties of glasses in the Ge-Bi-Sb-Se and Ge-Bi-S systems. *J. Non-Cryst. Solids* 59–60: 1015–1018
Saraswat, V. K., Kishore, V., Deepika, Saxena, N.S., Sharma, T.P., Singh, L.I. & Saraswat, P.K. 2008. I-V Measurements of Se-Te-Sb Glassy Bulk and Thin Film samples. *Chalcogenide Lett.*, 5 (5): 95–103.

Saxena, M. & Bhatnagar, P.K. 2003. Crystallization study of Te-Bi-Se glasses. *Bull. Mater. Sci.* 26 (5): 547–551.

Swanepoel, R. 1983. Determination of the thickness and optical constants of amorphous silicon. *J. Phys. E: Sci. Instrum.* 16: 1214–1222

Tiwari, R.S., Mehta, N., Shukla, R.K. & Kumar, A. 2005. Kinetic Parameters of Glass Transition in Glassy $Se_{1-x}Sb_x$ Alloys. *Turk. J. Phys.* 29: 233–241

Tohge, N., Minami, T. & Tanaka, M. 1980. Electrical transport in n-type semiconducting $Ge1_{20}Bi_xSe_{70-x}Te_{10}$ glasses *J. Non-Cryst. Solids* 37: 23–30.

Tauc, J. 1974. *Amorphous and Liquid Semiconductor*, Plenum, New York .

Mott, N.F., Davis, E. A. 1979. *Electronic Processes in Non-Crystalline Materials*, Clarendon Press, Oxford.

Communication and Computing Systems – Prasad et al. (eds)
© 2019 Taylor & Francis Group, London, ISBN 978-0-367-00147-6

Energy aware image coding technique for wireless multimedia sensor network

Addisalem Genta & D.K. Lobiyal
School of Computer and System Sciences, Jawaharlal Nehru University, New Delhi, India

ABSTRACT: The rapid growth of the wireless technology and availability of low-cost multimedia hardware devices, i.e. sensor nodes have mainly influenced the transformation of the traditional Wireless Sensor Network to its Wireless Multimedia Sensor Network version. Image processing is one of the most important applications in WMSN. Limited bandwidth, computa-tional power, storage capability, and battery constraints of the sensor nodes are some of the main challenges in the design and implementation of image transmission in WMSNs. In this paper, we propose an energy aware image coding scheme for wireless multimedia sensor network. This technique combines SPIHT coding with Haar wavelet transform and Run Length Encoding to further compress the amount of data transmitted over the network to minimize the energy expen-diture of nodes in particular and the network in general. Moreover, this technique enables huge reduction in computation energy as well as communication energy needed with minimal degra-dation of image quality. The simulation experiment was carried out in MATLAB. The proposed system out performs the existing traditional SPIHT algorithm with better compression ratio and image quality. Furthermore, it enhances the life time of network.

1   INTRODUCTION

Wireless Multimedia Sensor Network (WMSN) has shifted the focus from scalar WSN to networks with multimedia devices that are capable to retrieve video, image, audio, as well as scalar sensor data. This will impose severe demands on the limited battery resources of multimedia based applications as well as the bandwidth of the wireless network (Almalkawi et al, 2010).

In a situation where replacing sensor node?s battery is neither possible nor feasible, the need to process and wirelessly transmit very large volumes of data should be well managed and the network energy in general must be judiciously utilized to prolong the network life time. This challenging issue has made energy efficient multimedia processing and transmission techniques for WMSN as hot research area since decade ago (Ehsan et al, 2012).

Transmission of uncompressed image consumes high network energy, demands extensive amount of bandwidth and takes more transmission time. Hence, image compression is a vital solution in minimizing transmission time, bandwidth required and storage memory of nodes in an efficient manner. Specifically wavelet based image compression techniques provide better efficiency by organizing the image information in various frequency sub bands. These bands have correlations each other and image compression exploits these existing correlations through spatial orientation tree (SOT). SOT is formed by wavelet coefficients which have similar spatial location and orien-tation in different frequency sub bands (Rema et al, 2015).

SPIHT algorithm is introduced by Shapiro, Said and Pearlman as an improved version of Embed-ded Zero Tree (EZW) image compression technique. Zero trees in SPIHT denote SOT with no significant wavelet coefficients with respect to a given threshold (Said et al, 1996).

When we have more insignificant information in the encoded bit stream, it results low quality in the reconstructed image. Therefore in this paper, we proposed an energy aware image compres-sion algorithm using combination of SPIHT with RLE coding techniques to increase the number of significant bits down the bit stream. This can significantly reduce both compu-tation energy, by minimizing the compu-tation needed to compress an image, and communica-tion energy, con-sumed by the radio transceiver, which is proportional to the number of bits transmitted.

This paper is structured as follows. The proposed technique is discussed in section 2 and experi-mental simulation results will be discussed in section 3. In section 4, the conclusion and possible future work is presented.

2 RELATED WORK

Many researchers are focusing on WSN after the emergence of various wireless technologies. Moreover, there is also huge research interst towards wireless multimedia sensor network after the advent of multimedia sensors and wireless communication technologies. In the field of com-puter science, many academicians have tried to perform image compression using Dis-crete Cosine transform technique (DCT). DCT converts an image in to fundamental fre-quency components. The whole image is subdivided in to number of blocks. One of DCT based compression scheme is JPEG (Wallace, 1992)

Deepthi et al (2018) compared the performance of several compression techniques like EZW,SPIHT and DCT along with several routing protocols like AODV and DSR. After per-forming the experi-ment, SPIHT algorithm is found to be the best performer in all the metrics than the other methods of compression and recommended as suitable algorithm for wireless sensor network.

The author in (Bano et al, 2018) tried to compare and contrast the performance of three image compression techniques for resource constrained wireless multimedia sensor network. The algorithms used in the analysis were Set Partitioned Embedded BloCK Coder (SPECK), Set Partition in Hierarchi-cal Trees (SPIHT) and JPEG2000. They also compressed an image using SPIHT techniques and transmitted from source to destination in the network to evaluate the energy consumption of the algorithm. SPIHT achieved better energy consumption than others.

3 PROPOSED WORK

In this proposed technique, we used SPIHT algorithm in combination with Run Length Encoder and Haar wavelet transform.

3.1 *SPIHT coding*

SPIHT algorithm, as modified and refined version of EZW has the following merits;(Jyothes-war et al, 2007)

Better quality of image in terms of PSNR

Less computational time for coding and decoding coefficients It can code according to spe-cific bit rate requirement

Both EZW and SPIHT algorithm employ similar kind of data structure for encoding signifi-cant wavelet coefficients. SPIHT algorithm uses three ordered list while set partitioning to store signif-icant coefficients of the wavelet transform: LIS (list of insignificant pixel), LSP (list of significant pixels) and LIS (list of insignificant set). Moreover, there are three sequen-tial stages for encoding wavelet coefficients: Initialization, sorting pass and refinement pass (Li et al, 2010)

3.1.1 *SPIHT encoding*

Initialization: where all the Lists are initialized with all coefficients of the respective frequency sub bands (Li et al, 2017). In SPIHT, a coefficient is said to be significant if its magnitude is greater than or equal to the threshold value at that iteration (Anjaneyulu et al, 2015). Keeping this definition of significance in to consid-eration, the LIP, LIS and LSP can be described as follows.

LSP is initialized with empty set

LIP is set with all coefficients of the lowest frequency bands and which have descendants LIS is set with all descendants of the roots of the all spatial orientation trees

Sorting pass: The coefficients in LIP and LIS are checked for significance against threshold value To and those found significant will shift to LSP where as insignificant coefficients will remain in LIP and LIS until the next iteration.

Refinement pass: In this step, the encoder outputs 1 for significant coefficients and 0 for insignif-icant one.

Quantization: In this step we decrement n by 1 and repeat the procedure until the bit rate requirement is fulfilled.

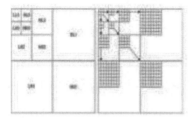

Figure 1.   SOT and 4 level WT decomposition.

25	7	14	11
-6	6	7	5
4	-4	4	-2
2	-1	-3	0

Figure 2.   Sample image matrix.

3.1.2 *SPIHT algorithm analysis*

Consider the following example based on the above matrix in Figure 2 for understanding SPIHT encoding technique. We will look step by step how the algorithm encodes this 2D matrix. 1st pass: The value of n is 4 and To=16. The three lists will be initialized as follows.

LIP = f(0,0) !25, (0,1) !7, (1,0) !-6, (1,1) !6g

LIS = fD(0,1), D(1,0),D(1,1)g

LSP = ;

After examining the significance of the values in LIP against the threshold value T_oTo, 25 is found to be significant since it is greater than 16. Therefore, we transmit 1, then 0(0 for +ve and 1 for ?ve) to show that the coefficient is significant and positive respectively. The other three coefficients will remain in LIP since their magnitude is less than T_o = 16. For the in-sig-nificant coefficients, we transmit 0 to the output bit stream.

LIP = f(0,1) !7, (1,0) !-6, (1,1) !6g

LIS = fD(0,1), D(1,0), D(1,1)g

LSP = (0,0) !25

Output bit stream: 10000000

2nd pass: The value of n is 3 and To=8.

LIP=f(0,1) !7, (1,0) !-6, (1,1) !6, (1,2) !7,(1,3) !5g LIS = f(D(1,0),D(1,1)g

LSP = f(0,0) !25, (0,2) !14, (0,3) !11g

Output bit stream: 0001101000001.

3rd pass: The value of n is 2 and To=4.

LIP=f(3,0)!2,(3,1)!-1,(2,3)!-3,(3,2)!-2,(3,3)!0g LIS = ;

LSP =f(0,0) !25, (0,2)!14,(0,3)!11(0,1) !7, (1,0)!-6, (1,1) !6, (1,2)!7,(1,3)!5,(2,0)!4,(2,1)!-4,(2,2)! 4g Output bit stream: 10111010101101100110000010.

For decoding, we start with similar list as the encoder and n?s initial value is also transmit-ted to decoder i.e., to enable the threshold value start at 16.

3.2 Haar wavelet transform

Haar wavelet transform is the simplest wavelet trans-formation method (Gupta et al, 2015). The Haar wavelet function is defined as

$$(t) = 8 \begin{cases} 1; & \text{if } 0 \quad t<1/2 \\ 1; & \text{if } 1/2 \quad t<1 \\ <0; & \text{otherwise} \end{cases} \tag{1}$$

Resource constraint is one of the main properties of WMSN. In this study, we employed Haar wavelet transform for image processing is mainly due to its low requirement storage and other computational re-sources. These characteristics of Haar wavelet makes it to be widely used in most of VLSI designers (Tripathi et al, 2017). For better conservation of network energy and sensor node memory foot print, it can be considered as best effective transformation technique.

3.3 Run Length Encoder (RLE)

After the wavelet coefficients are encoded using SPIHT compression technique, we have proposed to use RLE technique in order to further reduce the im-age size further to get the advantage less energy con-sumption (Kaur et al, 2017) Basically, Run Length Encoding is fast and simple entropy coding technique used main-ly to code symbols which frequently occur in succes-sion. It is more suitable for image compression since image has many correlated nearby consecutive pixels which can be stored as a single data value and count.

The other benefits of this technique are that its sim-plicity to be implemented and require low computa-tional energy. In the proposed technique, we will find series of consecutive zeros after the wavelet coefficients are encoded using SPIHT. Therefore, as RLE is more ef-fective with data which has more repetitions, the best compression rate can be easily achieved. The next figure will elaborate more the concept of RLE.

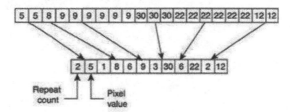

Figure 3.   RLE encoding.

4   SIMULATION RESULTS

4.1 Experimental results

In this experiment, we have used five 8bpp gray scale test images as shown in Figure 4.

Figure 4.   Test images.

Simulation was performed on these five images in MATLAB and the result obtained from the experiment is depicted in the following graphs.

4.2 *Comparative analysis*

The comparison between the proposed algorithm and conventional SPIHT image compression techniques is shown in both Figures 4-8 and Table 1-5 in terms of image quality using PSNR as a parameter. The quality of reconstructed image at the receive end is measure by Peak Signal to Noise Ratio (PSNR) as defined by the following equation.

$$PSNR = 20 log_{10} p \frac{255}{MSE} \qquad (2)$$

where MSE is the mean squared error between origi-nal and reconstructed image.

The results show that the proposed technique outperforms in giving better compression perfor-mance than the traditional SPIHT compression technique by PSNR values at all bit rates. When the bit rate increases, the quality of the reconstructed image also increases in a similar way. The average PSNR value for both SPIHT and proposed technique is illustrated from Figure 5 to 8. Our technique achieved a better performance than SPIHT with an average PSNR value of 4.38dB at 0.01bpp and 1.1dB at 0.5bpp. This result endorses the strength and precision of the proposed method. Simulation was conducted on four images of size 512x512 pixels and one 256x256 pixel to see if any performance difference exists due to difference in size of image. Apparently, the proposed technique achieved an improvement of 24.54% at low

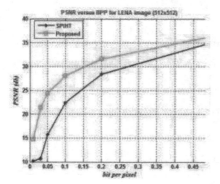

Figure 5.   PSNR vs BPP for Lena image.

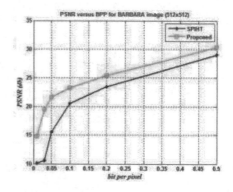

Figure 6.   PSNR vs BPP for Barbara image.

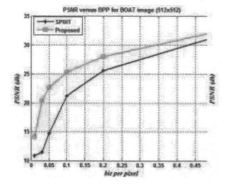

Figure 7.   PSNR vs BPP for Boat image.

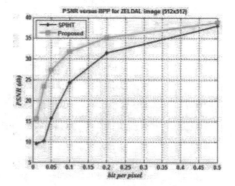

Figure 8.   PSNR vs BPP for Zeldal image.

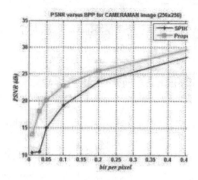

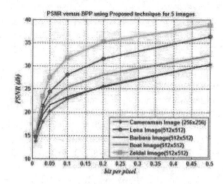

Figure 9.   PSNR vs BPP for Cameraman image.

Figure 10.   Comparison of PSNR vs BPP for all test images.

bit rates and 4.03% at higher bit rates. The basic reason for achieving such superiority for our proposed technique in terms of PSNR is due to few number of bits are sufficient to encode the image in the proposed algorithm as compared to classical SPIHT. As it can be observed from Figure 5 to 8, even if we used different image size and format in the simulation, the performance of the new technique is much better than its counterpart SPIHT algorithm with 30.04% at low bit rate(0.01bpp) and 3.27% at 0.5bpp.

5   CONCLUSION

SPIHT coding is one of the best wavelet transform based image coding technique which basically uses three lists to store its significant information. It has better achievement in compression ratio than Em-bedded Zero tree Wavelet, which is its predecessor spatial orientation based coding tech-nique. In this study, we used Haar wavelet transform to increase the number of significant bits in the transmitted bit stream to increase the quality of reconstructed image at the sink node. In addition to that, we used Run Length Encoding method to further compress the transmitted bits so that the network energy consumption can be improved better. After conducting the simulation work, we found that our proposed technique well performed in all the scenarios used to evaluate its efficiency as compared to the conventional SPIHT algorithm.

REFERENCES

Almalkawi, I. T., Guerrero Zapata, M., Al-Karaki, J. N., & Morillo-Pozo, J. (2010). Wireless multimedia sensor networks: current trends and future directions. Sensors, 10(7), 6662-6717.

Ehsan, S., & Hamdaoui, B. (2012). A survey on energy-efficient routing techniques with QoS assurances for wireless multimedia sensor networks. IEEE Communications Surveys& Tutorials, 14(2), 265-278.

Rema, N. R., Oommen, B. A., & Mythili, P. (2015). Image compression using SPIHT with modified spatial orientation trees. Procedia Computer Science, 46, 1732-1738.

Said, A., & Pearlman, W. A. (1996). A new, fast, and efficient image codec based on set partitioning in hierarchical trees. IEEE Transactions on circuits and systems for video technology, 6(3), 243-250.

Wallace, G. K. (1992). The JPEG still picture compression standard. IEEE transactions on consumer electronics, 38(1), xviii-xxxiv.

Deepthi, S. A., Rao, E. S., & Prasad, M. G. (2018, January).Image transmission and compression techniques using SPIHT and EZW in WSN. In 2018 2nd International Conference on Inventive Systems and Control (ICISC) (pp. 1146-1149). IEEE.

Bano, N., Alam, M., & Ahmad, S. (2018). Energy Efficient Image Compression Techniques in WSN. In Intelligent Communication, Control and Devices (pp. 1079-1088). Springer, Singapore.

Jyotheswar, J., & Mahapatra, S. (2007). Efficient FPGA implementation of DWT and modified SPIHT for lossless image compression. Journal of Systems Architecture, 53(7), 369-378

Li, W., Pang, Z. P., & Liu, Z. J. (2010, April). SPIHT algorithm combined with Huffman encoding. In Intel-ligent Information Technology and Security Informatics (IITSI), 2010 Third International Symposium on (pp. 341-343). IEEE.

Li, M., Sheng, L., & Ming, Y. (2017). Compression of Remote Sensing Images Using an Improved SPIHT Algorithm. DEStech Transactions on Environment, Energy and Earth Sciences, (apeesd).

Anjaneyulu, I. V., & Krishna, P. R. (2015). FPGA Implementation Of DWT-SPIHT Algorithm For Image Compression. International Journal of Technology Enhancements and Emerging Engineering Research, 20-24.

Gupta, D., & Choubey, S. (2015). Discrete wavelet transform for image processing. International Journal of Emerging Technology and Advanced Engineering, 4(3), 598-602.

Tripathi, S., & Mishra, B. (2017). vlsi architectures for 2-d discrete wavelet transform using ks adder. asian journal for convergence in technology (ajct)-ugc listed, 3.

Kaur, K., Saxena, J., & Singh, S. (2017). Image Compression Using Run Length Encoding (RLE). Interna-tional Journal on Recent and Innovation Trends in Computing and Communication, 5(5), 1280-1285.

Communication and Computing Systems – Prasad et al. (eds)
© 2019 Taylor & Francis Group, London, ISBN 978-0-367-00147-6

FRP bio digester for efficient waste management

Sangeeta Singla & Vinod Kumar H.A.
Dronacharya College of Engineering, India

ABSTRACT: Due to the extreme urbanization, the availability of natural resources is decreasing day by day. The conventional methods of generating fuel consume much of the resources. In order to bring sustainability to these resources, efficient and economic means of generating fuel should be adopted. One such method is to use FRP bio digester to manage kitchen waste and generate fuel. At Dronacharya College of Engineering, located at Delhi-NCR- Gurgaon, FRP bio digester is installed. The waste from the college canteen, which is generated at a good amount, is utilized to create an organic processing facility which leads in the production of biogas. Biogas is cost-effective, eco-friendly, cut down the landfill waste and can generate high-quality renewable fuel. Also, the amount of CO_2 emission is reduced. The FRP bio digester is an anaerobic digester system where the digestion process is microbial. The biogas thus generated can be used as an energy source for various purposes.

1 INTRODUCTION

Nowadays the usage of non-renewable source of energy is increasing drastically leaving fewer amounts of resources for the future generation. Here, the sustainability of these resources is questioned. The answer lies with the research to replace non-renewable energy sources with renewable energy sources. Especially the fuels generated from the non-renewable sources should be replaced with the fuels generated for renewable sources. Biogas is distinct from other renewable energies because of its characteristics of using, controlling and collecting organic wastes and at the same time producing fertilizer and water for use in agricultural irrigation. Biogas neither has geographical limitation nor does it require advanced technology for producing energy, also it is very simple to use and apply.

The kitchen waste can be used as a source for the generation of biogas. This kitchen waste is an organic material which can produce fuel with high calorific value and nutritive value to microbes, which would enhance the efficiency of methane production by several orders of magnitude. Also, in most of cities and places, kitchen waste is disposed in landfill or discarded which causes the public health hazards and diseases like malaria, cholera, typhoid. Improper management of wastes like uncontrolled dumping bears several adverse consequences. It not only leads to polluting surface and groundwater through leachate and further promotes the breeding of flies, mosquitoes, rats and other disease bearing vectors. Also, it emits unpleasant odour and methane which is a major greenhouse gas contributing to global warming. Kitchen waste, under controlled conditions when under goes anaerobic digestion in a closed digester it would result in the production of methane gas.

1.1 *Anaerobic digestion*

It, also referred to as biomethanization, is a natural process that takes place in absence of air (oxygen). It involves biochemical decomposition of complex organic material by various bio-chemical processes with release of energy rich biogas and production of nutritious effluents.

Parameters increasing the efficiency of anaerobic digestion are a perfect balance between various groups of microorganisms which include hydrogen producing acetogenic microorganisms and hydrogen consuming methanogens.

1.2 *Suitable conditions to keep all microorganisms alone*

a. A favorable pH value of 6.7-7.5, which is maintained by adding Sodium Hydroxide (NaOH) or Quick lime (CaO).
b. Temperature at which microorganisms can multiply with their best output.
c. Proper crushing of food waste to give optimum particle size.
d. Hydraulic retention time should be 10-15 days otherwise the bacteria are entrapped.
e. Presence of other nutrients like Phosphorus, Sulfur, Nitrogen along with carbon sources in the substrate is also essential which can be fulfilled by adding DAP(Diammonium Phosphate) and urea as per the need.
f. The digestion of substrate should be slow otherwise easily digestible substrates will increase the acid contents.
g. The C:N ratio should be 16:1- 25:1, else it will affect the production of biogas.

1.3 *Benefits of methane gas*

Methane is a major fuel in the natural gas. It provides more environmental benefit, like producing more heat and light energy while less carbon dioxide and other pollutants, by mass than other hydrocarbons or fossil fuel including coal and gasoline refined from oil, and other pollutants that contribute to smog and unhealthy air.

2 OBJECTIVES

1. To design medium size biogas plant at DCE college canteen that will use canteen waste (food waste) as a raw material to produce biogas
2. To find the best catalyst for producing maximum output.
3. To conduct proximate and ultimate analysis to find out the composition of gases, volatile materials etc. formed during the process which will help in monitoring the effectiveness of the project
4. To analyze the variations in production of biogas during the period of one year.

3 METHODOLOGY

3.1 *Composition of kitchen waste at DCE canteen*

At Dronacharya College of Engineering (DCE) canteen about 10 Kg of Kitchen waste is generated daily. The Kitchen waste includes various vegetables peelings, leaves and stem, remains of dressed vegetables, such as green pea, green gram, etc.

It also contains remains of cooked food, such as rice, pieces of chapattis, vegetable waste, tea leaves, etc. Apart from these, leftover food is one of the major mean of generating waste in the canteen. Non-edible waste is separated and only the edible waste is used up for the FRP digester

3.2 *Construction of FRP plant*

3.2.1 *Material of biogas digester*
Fiber Reinforced Plastic (FRP) has been selected as the material for the construction of the biogas digester for the project. FRP is a composite material made up of a polymer matrix

reinforced with fibers. The fibers are usually glass, carbon, aramid, or basalt while the polymer is usually an epoxy, vinyl ester, polyester thermosetting plastic or phenol formaldehyde resins. Some of the reasons for selecting FRP material over aluminum for the biogas digester are:

Biogas digesters made with aluminum usually have lesser life period as compared to the biogas digesters made with FRP as the inherent corrosion resistant characteristic of fiberglass or FRP makes it a cost-effective, strong, lightweight solution for corrosion resistant applications.

FRP has inherent dimensional stability potential due to its unique formulations.

Other properties such as lightweight, strength, toughness, damage tolerance, fatigue and fracture resistance, notch sensitivity and general durability, make fiberglass desirable for many applications.

When comparing strength of materials of equivalent thicknesses and sizes, fiberglass will weigh one seventh as much as steel and half as much as aluminum.

Being lightweight make FRP easy to install and thereby reducing the cost and ease of installation.

Design of the biogas digester

Taking the amount of daily waste as 10 kg/day, a floating dome type biogas digester of 600 kg capacity has been designed, the top view and elevation of which is shown in the Figure 2. Measurements of various components of the biogas digester are given in Table 1

Table 1.   Dimensions of various components of the bio digester.

S. No.	Items	Dimensions Diameter (mm)	Height (mm)
1	Digester	1000	1100
2	Inlet (Hopper Type)	100	-
3	Manure Outlet	100	-
4	Pressure Gauge	25.4	-
5	Gas Outlet	25.4	-

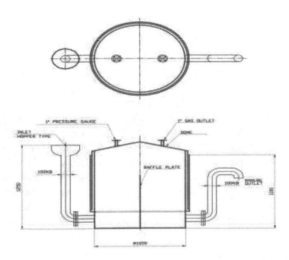

Figure 1.   Top view and elevation of the biogas digester as designed with dimensions.

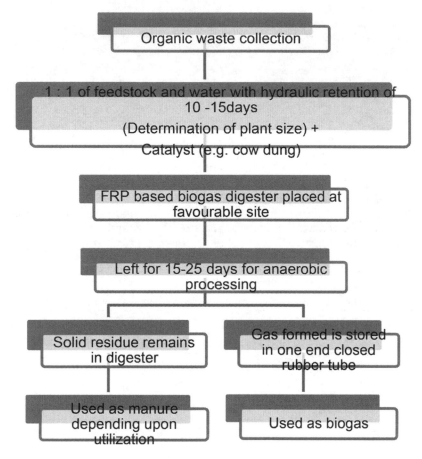

Figure 2.   Flow chart of the methodology to be followed.

The edible waste from the College canteen is separated from the non-edible waste and mixed thoroughly with equal amount of water .The mixture is finely crushed using a grinder. This fine crushed paste is fed into FRP digester through hopper type inlet. The feeding of the waste is done at specified time on the daily basis. The temperature in the digester is maintained above 350 C and pH value of 7 and above. to the maintain constant pH value, care is taken that there should not be lemon or citrus waste or peels of onion and garlic, curd, etc. added to the feedstock, as they are responsible in decreasing the pH value below 7.

The cow dung slurry was used as a source of Inoculum, as rumen of cow contains anaerobic microbial population. 250 kgs of Cow dung is mixed with water at a ratio of 2:1 for better slurry formation. The entire process for the Inoculum development takes approximately 15 to 25 days, thereafter, kitchen waste and water in the ration of 1:1 is added. Also, Urea and DAP are added frequently to maintain the quality of biogas produced.

3.3.1 *Stages in anaerobic digestion*
A. Hydrolysis

In hydrolysis complex fats and proteins are first hydrolysed to their monomeric firms by exoenzymes and bacterial cellulosome, in which the organic matter is enzymolysed externally by extracellular enzymes, cellulose, amylase, protease & lipase, of microorganisms. Bacteria decompose long chains of complex carbohydrates, proteins, & lipids into small chains. Further, proteins are split into peptides and amino acids.

B. Acidification

Acid-producing bacteria are involved in this step, as they convert the intermediates of fermenting bacteria into acetic acid, hydrogen and carbon dioxide. These bacteria are anaerobic and can grow under acidic conditions. Hereby, the acid-producing bacterium creates anaerobic condition which is essential for the methane producing microorganisms. Also, they reduce the compounds with low molecular weights into alcohols, organic acids, amino acids, carbon dioxide, hydrogen sulphide and traces of methane. From a chemical point, this process is partially endergonic (i.e. only possible with energy input), since bacteria alone are not capable of sustaining that type of reaction.

C. Methanogenesis

Methane-producing bacteria decompose compounds having low molecular weight. They utilize hydrogen, carbon dioxide and acetic acid to form methane and carbon dioxide. Under natural conditions, CH_4 producing microorganisms occur to the extent that anaerobic conditions are provided. They are basically anaerobic and very sensitive to environmental changes, if any occurs. The methanogenic bacterium belongs to the archaebacter genus, i.e. to a group of bacteria with heterogeneous morphology and lot of common biochemical and molecular-biological properties that distinguishes them from other bacteria.

The biogas thus produced is a mixture of methane (55-65%), carbon dioxide(30-45%) and traces of Hydrogen Sulphide. The most desired component is Methane which is colour less gas burnt with blue flame and can be sued for cooking, hearing and lighting purpose. The biogas generated is let out through a pipe which is connected to a gas stove. In order remove the traces of H_2S, a H_2S filter containing iron salts is used because hydrogen sulphide has a cytotoxic effect on the human nervous system. The solid residuals from the digester are removed on daily basis which can be used as manure for the plants.

The use of iron salts is the only method permitting the binding of H_2S directly in the fermenter

4 RESULTS AND DISCUSSION

This project was an initial effort to know about the production of biogas from kitchen waste from the canteen of Dronacharya College of Engineering. Later on the same gas is be used at the canteen for cooking purpose. Further, the gas can be supplied to various laboratories and other areas in the college where LPG is in use and hence replace it with biogas.

As a sample, analysis has been carried for a period of one month i.e. from 20th September to 19th October 2018 and the following observations are made for the FRP based digester.

Table 2. Characteristic components of FRP digester.

Characters	
Quantity of Kitchen waste	10 Kg
Water	10 liters
Ratio of Kitchen waste and water	1:1
pH	7-7.2
Total biogas production(m^3)	1 m3
Maximum methane fraction	55-65%

In this observation made about 10 Kgs of kitchen waste and around 10 liters of water is taken in the ratio 1:1 with a defined inoculum of 100litres. This, inoculum is slurry, which is digested by anaerobic method, as it contains anaerobic bacteria and produces bio gas. Average slurry temperature, biogas produced and pH are measured on daily basis. Gas is recorded by lifting of dome. This lifted height is multiplied by $2\pi R$ the optimum temperature is found to be 30-35°C. Upon maintain the pH value in the FRP digester around 7-7.2, about 1 m^3 of methane gas is produced with maximum methane fraction of 55-65 %.

1 m^3 of biogas is equivalent to 0.5 kg of diesel and kerosene, about 0.7 kg of coal, 1.3 kg of wood and city gas of 0.24 m^3.

REFERENCES

Agrahari, R. Tiwari, G. 2013. The Production of Biogas Using Kitchen Waste, *International Journal of Energy Science*. 6,: 10:14355.

Lissens, G. Thomsen, A.B. Baere, L. Verstraete, W. and Ahring, B. 2004. Thermal Wet Oxidation Improves Anaerobic Biodegradability Of Raw And Digested Bio Waste. *Environmental Science and Technology*. 38: 34183424.

Nasery, 2011. Biogas for rural communities, *TD390 Supervised learning: Study report.*

Nooka, V. and S.Vikram Kumar. The Production of Biogas Using Kitchen waste. *International Journal of Scientific & Engineering Research*, Volume 7, Issue 9, September-2016, 528 ISSN 2229-5518.

Potivichayanon, S. T Sungmon, S. Chaikongmao, W and Kamvanin, S. 2011 Enhancement of Biogas Production from Bakery Waste by Pseudomonas aeruginosa, *World Academy of Science, Engineering and Technology*. 5: 08-29.

Sharma, D. Samar, K. 2016. FRP BIOGAS PLANT for Efficient Kitchen Waste Management. *Akshay Urja*, 30.

Sing, S. Kumar, S. Jain, M.C. and Kumar, D. 2000. The Increased Biogas Production Using Microbial Stimulants.

Wieland P. Biogas Production: Current State And Perspectives". Appl Microbial Biotechnol, vol. 85, pp. 849–860, 2010.

Zhang, C. Haiia, S. Baeyens, J. & Tan, T. 2014. Anaerobic Digestion of Food Waste for Biogas Production. *Science Direct Renewable and Sustainable Energy Reviews*. 38: 383-392.

Ziauddin, Z. Rajesh, P. 2015. Production and Analysis of Biogas from Kitchen Waste. *International Research Journal of Engineering and Technology*, 02 (04): 2395-0072

Communication and Computing Systems – Prasad et al. (eds)
© 2019 Taylor & Francis Group, London, ISBN 978-0-367-00147-6

Next generation smart portal (Grouppy)

Sunil Kumar
SC&SS Jawaharlal Nehru University, Delhi, India

Nikhil Gola, Kartik, Noaman S. Siddiqui, Pranav Sharma, Abhay Chauhan & Priya Gupta
Maharaja Agrasen College, University of Delhi, Delhi, India

ABSTRACT: This paper describes the development of the Social network platform Grouppy. Grouppy is an online smart p;ortal which allows users to create their own network for their respective organizations. It is the best way for a school, college, company or an organization to keep in check the status of what's going on in their network. Every individual in a network can be up to date about upcoming events and schedules and can plan to be one step ahead. Currently individuals in schools, colleges or other organizations has to be notified by the upcoming schedules via unreliable resources such as whatsapp (what if someone didn't check their message), or friends(who forgot to tell you about that). Also, for students, keeping track of their attendance is not easy. In this project, when the user updates the information about an event like someone arrange a network meeting or teacher marks attendance of the student or make changes in the school/college timetable, it will send a direct notification to everyone in the network about that event.

1 INTRODUCTION

Grouppy is developed on Laravel Model-View-Controller (MVC) (http://www.mundoin terativo.com/2017/09/08) architectural pattern and Web development. We have used Laravel due to MVC as it implements user interfaces on computers. It divides a given application into three interconnected parts in order to separate internal representations of information from the ways that information is presented to and accepted from the user. This project mainly focuses on web development research area in order to achieve a fully functional and responsive portal at our disposal. This portal is in the domain of social networking (Wasserman, S.et al. 1999) as Grouppy is an online smart portal which allows users to create their own network for their respective organizations [Barabasi, A.L.t.al 2000). The area of research basically targets the online world as nearly 62% of the world population has gone global (Albert, R.et al. 1999). and our project can be highly useful to the web crawlers (Yanl,E et al.2011). Moreover, social networking is on the rise and a portal like our Grouppy can directly affect millions of people by providing superb communication facilities and effective interaction between users. (Lincoln, M.et al.2004). The social network is secured and will provided end to end identity encryption to the user(D. He, et al.2015). This project uses the principal of various data mining techniques for its modules like for class notifier it will learn to classify whether the student is going to take the class or not based on its previous history and uses Constraint Satisfaction Problem to generate a Time-Table or the Event Chart for the organization on the basis of all the constraints provided to System (Oprea, M.,2007). But currently the development of Grouppy is for the Institutions and the model is explained for the institution's perspective.

2 PROPOSED SYSTEM

There are 3 user roles in Grouppy to manage the network (*see* Figure 1 and Figure 2)

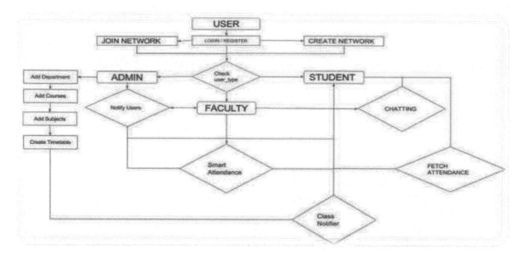

Figure 1. Function modules for Grouppy.

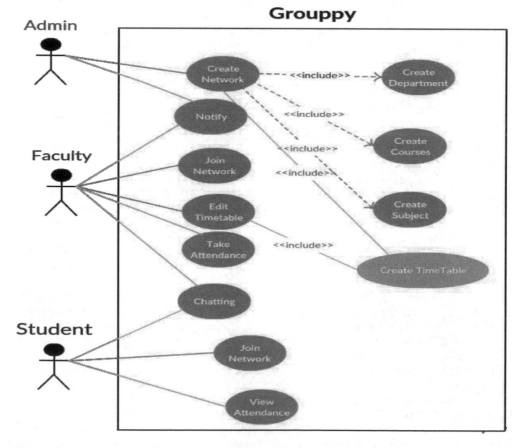

Figure 2. User UML design for Grouppy-portal.

1. *Admin-* The administrator is creator of the network who has full access to all the features of the Grouppy. He can invite/add and remove any member of the network and can edit courses, subjects and departments of the college. Admin may not be always available but he is the only one who can authenticate a member and add him to the network. Without prior authorization and notification by the administrator, no-one can do drastic changes to the network. If an administrator deactivates the network, then all members of the network will lose access to network. But, that network can't be deleted if once created.
2. *Faculty-* The faculty is an intermediate privileged user on Grouppy. He can edit a timetable, create an event, mark and update attendance. Assign events on the timetables, edit timetables and create assignments on the network which will be sent over the network via notification. The faculty member can't add/remove a member as that privilege is available with the admin only. Chat box is an extra feature which directly connects them to the students, ensuring maximum communication between them. The GUI will be user friendly and the faculty member doesn't need prior knowledge of web based social networking.
3. *Student-* The student is the member of the network with least privileges, namely- only seeing attendance, assignment marks, submission of reports and presentations. He can't edit a timetable or create an event like class test or assignment submission. The student is only connected to the network via notification and chat box with connection to the faculty members. A student can't see other members of the networks of other departments or courses and can't see other's attendance or marks.

3 PROJECT REQUIREMENTS

3.1 *Server hardware requirements(See Table 1)*

Table 1. Server hardware requirements.

ITEM	Web server (minimal)	Web server (Recommended)	Combined Web& Database Server (recommended)
Processor	2x 1.6GHz CPU	2x 2.5GHz CPU or more	4x 2.5 GHz CPU or more
RAM	2GB or more	8GB or more	16GB or more
HDD	128GB	128GB	>2TB

3.2 *Implementation platform*

Following are the implementation platforms required for Grouppy

➔ **Front End**

❏ HTML
❏ CSS
❏ JAVASCRIPT
❏ BOOTSTRAP
❏ JSON
❏ JQUERY

➔ **Back End**

❏ PHP implemented through LARAVEL.
❏ MYSQL SERVER

→ **Android**

❑ Android Studio > 2.3.1
❑ XML (for Layouts)
❑ JAVA (for connectivity)

4   SAMPLE PSEUDO CODE

4.1   *User type checking*

CheckUserType:
Uname = getUsername from GUI; Return user_type from DB for uname;
NotifyUsers:
CheckUsertype =='Admin'|| 'Faculty'; if(true)
Nmsg = GenerateNotificationMessage; Notify(user or Group);
//here group can be a department or a course or a batch or anything
else;

4.2   *Smart attendance*

time = getTimeandDay;
sub = getSubjectidFromTimeTable(time);
studentList = getAllStudentsfromDB(sub); generateAttendanceView();
Result = getFacultyInputFor(studentList); Store Result in DB;

4.3   *Class notifies*

time = getDayandTime()
sub = getSubjectFromTimeTable(time); studentList = getAllStudentsfromDB(sub); NotifyU-
sers(studentList);

5   LAYOUTS

Layout of Grouppy can be viewed in Figure 3, 4,5,6,7

Figure 3.   Proposed home page for Grouppy.

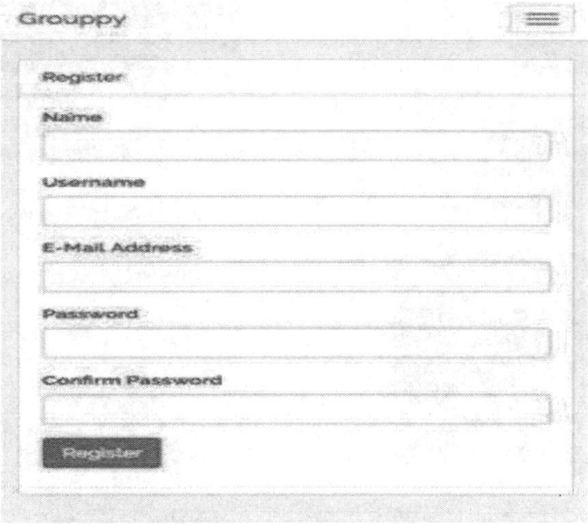

Figure 4.   User registration form.

```
private void registerUser() {
    String fullName = userNameEt.getText().t
    String email = userEmailEt.getText().to
    String username = userUsernameEt.getText().toString().trim();
    String password = userPasswordEt.getText().toString().trim();
    String confirmPassword = userConfirmPasswordEt.getText().toString().trim();
    if (fullName.equals("") || fullName == null) {
        showSnackbarMessage("Name field required!!");
        return;
    }
    if (email.equals("") || email == null) {
        showSnackbarMessage("Email field required!!");
        return;
    }
    if (username.equals("") || username == null) {
        showSnackbarMessage("Username field required!!");
        return;
    }
    if (password.equals("") || password == null) {
        showSnackbarMessage("Password field required!!");
        return;
    }
    if (confirmPassword.equals("") || confirmPassword == null) {
        showSnackbarMessage("Confirm password field required!!");
        return;
    }
    if (!password.equals(confirmPassword)) {
        showSnackbarMessage("Passwords do not match!!");
        return;
    }
    sendRegistrationDataToServer(fullName, email, username, password);
}
```

Figure 5.   Grouppy signing setting conditions code comparison.

In this time and era, workload is increasing exponentially everyday especially for students who are multitasking and always wants to be top of other things . As good as it sounds, maintaining your schedule with these increasing activities and events is a very hard thing to do. Techniques that are used currently to maintain schedules manually or to inform about any changes in schedules via other individuals or other messaging apps like whatsapp, Facebook etc. are unreliable. Figure 8 shows the comparison of Grouppy with Slack.

Figure 6. Login interface for Android app.

Figure 7. Sign in interface for the new user Android app.

Features	Grouppy	Slack
Create own Network	Yes	Yes
Smart Attendance	Yes	No
Integration to GitHub	No*	Yes
Android app	Yes	Yes
Class Notify	Yes	No

Figure 8. Comparison of Grouppy based on features.

6 CONCLUSION

Grouppy is a must have ally in this ever changing world of technology as it is highly adaptable. The most exciting thing about Grouppy is that it can be moulded and customized according to the client needs, and that in itself is a powerful thing. The ability to customize and using it accordingly, will not only eradicate any type of miscommunication, but will also provide a safe platform for people to interact with the users who are in their networks without intervention/interference from the outside world. The main aim of this project was to deliver a working environment where a person can be fully informed at all times about the things he/she cares about, and it is really an amazing feeling to say that Grouppy is the desired output that was intended at the beginning of this project.

7 FUTURE SCOPE

The future of Grouppy is very bright. It has a lot of application in nearly every type of organization in huge variety of fields. Grouppy at this moment needs a lot of GUI polish as well as addition of a couple of more exciting features like parental control and chat box. Class notifier feature has to be integrated in Grouppy to make it a powerful tool against misinformation and miscommunication. There are some plans to implement Student/Employee performance analyzer, which is completely an AI based method which uses Data Mining Techniques to predict whether the student/employee will do good for the organization or not. As this project can always be made better and improved over time, Grouppy is a reliable and efficient ally to have in this ever-changing world of technology and will adapt itself to match the current technology standards.

198

REFERENCES

Albert, R., Jeong, H & Barabasi, A. L. 1999. Diameter of the World Wide Web. Nature (401).

Barabasi, A.L., Albert, R. & Jeong, H. 2000. Scale-free Characteristics of Random Networks: The Topology of the World Wide Web. Physica A.

He, D., Zeadally, S., Xu, B., & Huang, X. 2015. An efficient identitybased conditional privacy-preserving authentication scheme for vehicular ad hoc networks. IEEE Trans. Inf. Forensics Secur 10 (12):2681–2691.

Easley, D. & Kleinberg, J. 2010. Networks, Crowds, and Markets: Reasoning about a Highly Connected World.Cambridge University Press.

Yanl, E. & Ding, Y. 2011. Discovering author impact: A PageRank perspective. Information Processing and Management 47(1): 125-134.

Jantan, Hamidah & Puteh, Mazidah 2010. Applying Data Mining Classification Techniques for Employee's Performance Prediction,Kmice.

Huberman, B.A. & Adamic, L. A. Growth Dynamics of the World Wide Web," Nature (401).

Jin, E.M., Girvan, M. & Newman, M. E. J. 1999. The Structure of Growing Social Networks. Santa Fe:01-06-032, 2001.

Lincoln, M., Adamson, B. & Covic, T. 2004. Perceptions of stress, time management and coping strategies of speech pathology students on clinical placement. International Journal of Speech-Language Pathology:91-99

Oprea, M. 2007. Multi-Agent System for University Course Timetable Scheduling. International Computer, Communications & Control.

Wasserman, S. & Faust, K. 1999. Social Network Analysis: Methods and Applications. Cambridge University Press, Cambridge, UK.

Communication and Computing Systems – Prasad et al. (eds)
© 2019 Taylor & Francis Group, London, ISBN 978-0-367-00147-6

A comparative study between constant weight and variable weight fins

Yogesh Chauhan, Poshan Lal Sahu & Ananta Shrivastava
Department of Mechanical Engineering, Dronacharya College of Engineering, Gurgaon, Haryana, India

ABSTRACT: In the present work, comparative study between constant weight and variable weight fins has been performed. An approximate solution for the heat transfer from functionally graded annular fin is obtained. The heat transfer due to radiation has also been considered along with conduction and convection. On linear governing equation is solved using the B-spline collocation method at Gaussian quadrature collocation points.The effects of grading parameter (b),geometry parameters (n and m),radiation-conduction number (N_r), dimensionless sink temperature (θ_a) and aspect ratio (R_f) on the temperature distribution is reported. Validation is carried out with benchmark results and good agreement is observed.Moreover,the results demonstrate that the B-spline collocation method is a very effective technique of obtaining approximate solutions for nonlinear problems. The effect of various parameters on temperature profiles are shown with the help of consolidated graphs.

KEYWORDS: *Annular Fins; power function; radiation-conduction*

1 INTRODUCTION

In order to avoid overheating of various components, the heat is required to be transferred from heated fluid to surrounding. The coefficient of heat transfer is less in the air side, therefore fins or extended surfaces are used to increase the amount of heat transfer. The convective heat transfer coefficient increases by increasing the temperature difference between the surrounding and object. The amount of conduction, convection and radiation determines the heat transferred by an object. With an increase in the surface area of an object, the heat transfer also increases. Adding a fin to an object, however, increases the surface area and can sometimes yield on an economical solution to heat transfer problems. The analysis of annular fins is important due to its various applications. The study of annular fins has become more feasible in recent years due to use of numerical methods and computational machines.

Annular fins are the fins that vary radially in a cross-sectional area. Annular fins are often used to increase the heat exchange in a liquid-gas heat exchanger system; annular fins are used to enhance the heat exchange.

1.1 *Functionally graded materials*

Functionally Graded Material (FGM) is a combination of two metals. The composition varies gradually from one metal to another metal, through the volume of material. The main aim of using FGM is to improve the thermal conductivity of a fin along the length. The concept of Functionally Graded Material (FGM) was initially proposed in Japan for a space plane project

1.2 Selection for fins

One should keep in mind the various parameters while selecting fin profile. Annular fins are widely used for increasing the rate of heat transfer. The efficiency of fin can be improved by increasing the dissipation of heat and reducing the volume of heat dissipation. The fin effectiveness is also considered while selecting fin.

For a desired heat transfer rate, the fin profile and all its dimensions are determined in such a way that the amount of material required should be minimum for an efficient fin

2 OBJECTIVES

1. To compare the fin performance of constant weight and variable weight annular fins at different fin profiles.
2. To obtain a mathematical expression representing the heat loss through conduction, convection and radiation and to search for a solution method.
3. To analyze the effect of radiation for the case of various fin profile and at different fin base temperatures.
4. To observe the effects of FGM, on fin performance.

3 METHODOLOGY

An annular fin of base thickness () with heat supplied at the base of constant temperature is considered. The transfer of heat from the fin is considered to be through convection and radiation simultaneously.

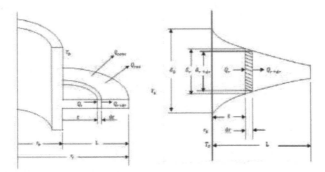

Figure 1.   Sectional and an elemental view of a radial fin.

We obtain a governing equation when heat balance is done for a control volume of length *dr* as shown in figure. A method of collocation involving B-splines as approximating functions is used to obtain approximate solutions for the above case. A spline function that has minimal support with respect to a given degree, smoothness, and domain partition is called B-spline. We can represent every spline function of a given degree, smoothness, and domain partition as a linear combination of B-splines of that same degree and smoothness, and over that same partition. This results in the banded structure of matrices that appear in interpolation and collocation problems. A computer can efficiently store these matrices.

The temperature distribution (x) can be approximated by non-smooth piecewise polynomials in x generated by B-spline basis sets. Let the interval [0, 1] be divided by set breakpoints or intervals. The whole fin length is normalized to a length between 0 and 1 and a variable x is assumed to indicate the fin length. Now this normalized fin length can be further subdivided by the number of node points.

Figure 2. 2- point collocation used in B-Spline collocation point.

Relative to this partition, the space between the intervals is further subdivided by a number of control points called as knot points. And finally, the solution to the above equation could be approximated as:

$$\theta(x) = \sum_{i=1}^{n+1} C_i N_{i,k} \qquad (1)$$

The Cox-de Boor recursion formula which is used to obtain knot values is as follows:

$$N_{i,k}(x) = \frac{(x - z_i)N_{i,k-1}(x)}{z_{i+k-1} - z_i} + \frac{(z_{i+1} - x)N_{i+1,k-1}(x)}{z_{i+k} - z_{i+1}} \qquad (2)$$

$$\begin{cases} 1 \ z_i \leq x \leq z_{i+1} \\ 0 \ otherwise \end{cases} \qquad (3)$$

Where,

(k-1) is the degree of polynomial, (n) is the number of control points (knot), (z) is knot values and (C) is the unknown parameters. The B-spline curve is defined as the curve determined by the control points $d_i, d_{i-n}, d_{i-n+1} \ldots\ldots\ldots d_i$ and the other control points d_i has no influence

4 RESULTS

A highly non-linear fourth order governing differential equation is obtained for the above case and is solved by the method of Collocation involving B-Splines functions in MATLAB 7.12.0 R(2011a).

4.1 *For constant fin weight*

For the case of constant weight of fin, the base thickness will vary according to the different values of geometry parameters *(n, m)*.

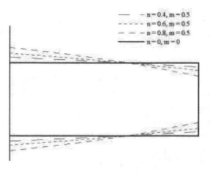

Figure 3. Fin profile variation at m=0.5.

4.2 *For variable weight of fin*

For the case of variable weight of fin the base thickness will be fixed or constant, and this will be equal to that of the thickness of a rectangular fin profile i.e. Hence for different fin geometries the base thickness will be same, only the fin area will vary according to different values of geometry parameters *(n, m)*.

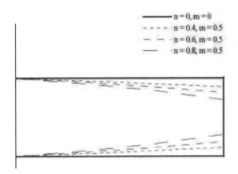

Figure 4. Fin profile variation at m=0.5.

4.3 *For constant fin weight*

Temperature plot showing the effect of radiation at different fin base temperatures for rectangular fin profile (m−0, n=0).

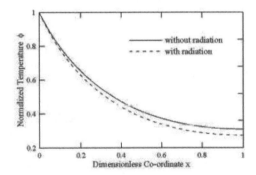

Figure 5. The temperature plot At θ_a= 0.6, b=0.

4.4 *For variable weight of a fin*

Temperature plot showing the effect of radiation at different fin base temperatures for power function fin profile at (m=2, n=0.5).

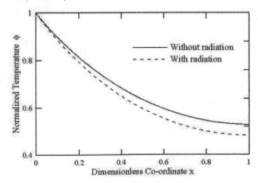

Figure 6. For θ_a= 0.6, b= -0.5, n=0.5, m=2.

The Figure 6 shows that with an increase in base temperature, the effect of radiation is more pronounced.

Plots showing comparisons between efficiency of constant weight fin profile and variable weight fin profile keeping m constant.

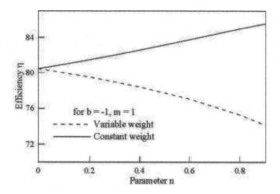

Figure 7. Efficiency comparison for b= - 1.

Plots showing comparisons between efficiency of constant weight fin profile and variable weight fin profile keeping n constant.

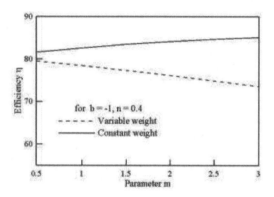

Figure 8. Efficiency comparison for b= - 1.

5 CONCLUSION

A highly non- linear governing equation is obtained for the above case and is solved by the method of collocation involving B-splines functions in the MATLAB. The process uses five dimensionless parameters: functionally graded parameter (b), geometry parameter controlling thickness (n), geometryparameter controlling shape (m), radiation –conduction number (N_r), and sink-to-base temperature-ratio (θ). Following conclusions are drawn from the above work:

1. There is more fall in the surface fin temperatures when we include radiation, and this fall is furthermore for the higher base temperatures.
2. There is significant drop in the efficiency of the fin with the radiation effects showing that one may over predict the efficiency of the fin by ignoring the radiation effects
3. The distribution of temperature and transfer of heat are increased when we increase negative grading parameter 'b'. This leads to an increase in fin efficiency.

4. For the case of constant weight of a fin, a rectangular fin profile is the least efficient and the efficiency increases for the higher values of geometry parameters n, m but after n=0.7 the efficiency further drops. For the case of a variable weight of fin a rectangular fin is the most efficient and efficiency decreases with higher values of geometry parameters n, m but here also after n=0.7 the efficiency starts increasing

5. The fall in temperature is more pronounced with the higher value of 'n', 'm', and 'b'.

REFERENCES

Abboudi S. (2011). Numerical estimation of two convective boundary conditions of a two-dimensional rectangular fin.*Journal of the Franklin Institute*, 348(7), 1192–1207

Arora P. (1976). Optimum Design of Finned Surfaces.*Journal of The Franklin Institute*, 301(4),379–392.

Arslanturk C. (2010). Analysis of thermal performance of annular fins with variable thermal conductivity by HAM method.*Journal of Thermal Science and Technology*, 30(2), 1–7.

Arslanturk C. (2005). Simple correlation equations for optimum design of annular fins with uniform thickness. *Applied Thermal Engineering*, 25, (14-15), 2463–2468.

Aziz A & Lopez R. J. (2011). International Journal of Thermal Sciences Convection-radiation from a continuously moving, variable thermal conductivity sheet or rod undergoing thermal processing. *International Journal of Thermal Sciences*, 50(8), 1523–1531.

Aziz A &Bouaziz M. N. (2011). A least squares method for a longitudinal fin with temperature dependent internal heat generation and thermal conductivity. *Energy Conversion and Management*, 52(8-9), 2876–2882.

Aziz Abdul &Khani F. (2010). Analytic solutions for a rotating radial fin of rectangular and various convex parabolic profiles.Communications in Nonlinear Science and Numerical Simulation, 15(6), 1565–1574.

Campo A. & Acosta-Iborra A. (2009). Approximate analytic temperature distribution and efficiency for annular fins of uniform thickness. International Journal of Thermal Sciences, 48(4), 773–780.

Kundu Balaram, & Barman D. (2011). An analytical prediction for performance and optimization of an annular fin assembly of trapezoidal profile under dehumidifying conditions.Energy, 36(5), 2572–2588.

Kundu B., & Das, P. K. (2007).Performance analysis and optimization of elliptic fins circumscribing a circular tube.International *Journal of Heat and Mass Transfer*, 50(1-2), 173–180.

Communication and Computing Systems – Prasad et al. (eds)
© 2019 Taylor & Francis Group, London, ISBN 978-0-367-00147-6

Coverage preserving scheduling for life span maximization in wireless sensor network based internet of things

Vinod Kumar
Department of Computer Engineering, Delhi Technological University (DTU), Delhi, India

Sushil Kumar
School of Computer & Systems Sciences, Jawaharlal Nehru University, New Delhi

ABSTRACT: Maintaining the full coverage and connectivity in a randomly distributed wireless sensor network is a difficult task. One easy solution of this problem lies in taking a large number of sensors. However, these large numbers of sensors needs to be scheduled properly for providing satisfactory coverage and connectivity and at the same time maximizing the life span of the network. The novelty of this paper lies in the proposal of establishment of a relative coordinates system in randomly distributed wireless sensor networks. Based on this coordinates system it is decided that whether a sensor is eligible to go in sleep mode or not. Simulation of this protocol has been performed employing it over Leach through ns-2 and result is compared with Leach protocol. The proposed scheduling algorithm is found to be outperforming the underlying protocol.

1 INTRODUCTION

Wireless sensor networks Assisted Internet of things are critically emerging phenomenon in diverse kind of applications across globe. It comprises a large number of smart dusts called sensors that have small processing units, power units and a set of short range wireless links. These sensors are used for monitoring and tracking of real world stimulus. They organize themselves to provide network services like sensing, data gathering and routing. Power unit in a sensor generally relies on small battery which in most of the cases is hard to replace, this limitation makes wireless sensor networks highly vulnerable for energy. It could not be possible to place a sensor manually in hostile and rugged environment, and hence sensors are thrown out of some moving or flying objects. However, this uneven distribution of sensors does not guaranty the full coverage and connectivity. To sort out these problems of coverage, connectivity and energy, relatively a large number of sensors are distributed (H. Zhang, J. C. Hou, V, K. Kar. Jan 2005).

A relatively large number of sensors undoubtedly create undue redundancy in the field, not only this; this could not help to maximize the life span of network if not scheduled properly. It is so, we take a move in this paper to propose an efficient sensor scheduling mechanism which not only decides the duty cycle for sensors but also preserves the otherwise provided coverage. This task could be relatively much easier in a fixed sensor network; however, random distribution of sensors poses a great deal of challenges to carry out this task in form of localization. This paper carries the discussion over localization of sensor relative to other sensor, for this to realize we propose a scheme to establish the Cartesian coordinate system in the field. Establishment of coordinate system gives sensors their relative positions which help in finding the overlap of coverage between different sensors. If a sensor gets full overlap of coverage from surrounding sensors it can go in sleep mode. The saved energy could be used to maximize the life span of network.

The rest of the paper is organized is follows. The section 2 presents the work related to the area. The proposed work is presented in section 3. The simulation results are analyzed in section 4. Finally, section 5 concludes the work presented in this paper.

2   RELATED WORK

Similar type of work has been done in(H. Zhang et.al. 2005) where, Zhang and Hou proposes a sensor scheduling algorithm for a large sensor network, this have proved that if radio range of transmission is at least twice the sensing range full coverage in a convex region inherently implies full connectivity. In(M.Cardei et al. 2005), Cardei and Du proposes a cover set scheme to maximize the life span of network. They devise an algorithm to find the maximum number of cover sets related to a given set of targets. The cover sets are successively switched on for covering the given targets one at a time. These disjoint cover sets increase the life span of network to that many folds as many are the number of cover sets.

Kar et al. presented an optimal activation policy in (K. Kar et al. 2005). They first find the solution in a small set of sensors which, later is expanded for whole network. A scheme has been proposed for node scheduling without exact location of sensors by Liu et al. in (C. Liu, K. Wu, Y. Xiao, 2006). This scheme utilizes the combines approach to maintain coverage and connectivity. This method proposes a scheme in which extra node are turned on of necessary for connectivity. Wu et al. have proposed a wake up scheduling algorithm in for increasing the life span of whole network. A clustered based scheduling algorithm has been proposed in by Shi, and Fapojuwo. Yu et al. have presented a scheduled data gathering approach. In propose a dynamic channel-accessing scheme to minimization of energy consumption by utilizing a licensed channel for intra-cluster and inter-cluster data transmission for radio cognitive sensor networks. Xiao-Heng Deng et al. (Deng, Xiao-Heng 2010) presented a coverage hole detection and healing policy which finds the energy depleted sensor node and provide the coverage to heal the uncovered area with a closest redundant sensor node. Z. Xu et al. (Z. Xu et al. 2016) propose a joint clustering and routing (JCR) protocol for data gathering in large-scale WSN. JCR fairly balanced energy consumption among the sensor nodes and enhance the network lifetime. In (Dohare. et al. 2014), authors proposed how sensors should be deployed to meet essence of energy consumption equalization. In (Khatri. et al. 2018) authors presented a new methods of energy conservation to maximize the lifetime of the network. All above proposed work suggest a scheduling scheme in a localized sensor network in which location of sensor is already known except (C Liu et al. 2006). In this paper we intend to establish a relative coordinate system for efficient localization of sensors so that they can be scheduled properly.

3   PROPOSED WORK

We intend to increase the life span of a wireless sensor network in which nodes are distributed randomly. For achieving this purpose, relatively large number of sensors are taken and scheduled properly so that the coverage provided by all sensors together is equal to the coverage provided by active sensors after scheduling. In randomly distributed network this task is somewhat cumbersome to carry out. Our approach relating to find a solution of this problem is based on intersections of coverage provided by different sensors. We move forward with the following theorem to be used in our solution.

Theorem 1: The entire area of a circular region of radius r is fully covered if the sensors with sensing range r are falling in this region and part of border of circular region between any two intersection points is covered by at least one sensor.

Proof: Let there exists at least one point in the given circular region which is not covered however all the intersection points are covered by at least one sensor. We take in consideration Figure 1; black circle is showing the circular region to be covered and red circles are showing the sensing region of different sensors.

Intersection points of sensor A is shown by a and d, that of B is shown by c and f and that of C is shown by b and e. We connect these intersection points with O, the center of circular region. Since we have assumed that all intersection making sensors are inside the circular region, the center of circular region is covered by each sensor. It is proved that in any circle the line joining two points on or inside periphery always lies inside the circle. For example the line ao and od lies completely inside the sensing range of sensor A. Since A does not make any other intersection

207

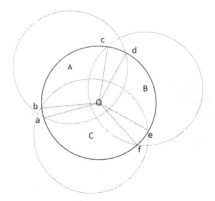

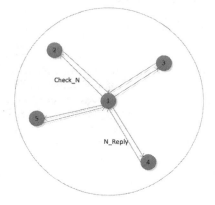

Figure 1.   Depicting different sectors of a circular region.

Figure 2.   Check_N and N_Reply messages.

with circular region the arc ad also lies inside the region. Now since ado is a closed region hence it is covered by sensor A. similarly we can say for other sensors. Now if all the intersection points are covered by at least one sensor the corresponding region will also be covered. If union of these intersection points comprises the whole periphery, the union of corresponding regions constitutes the entire sensing region. Hence the theorem is proved.

After proving above theorem now we have a base to move on. If we reconsider the circular region in figure one as the sensing region of a sensor with sensing range r, we turn offs such a sensor when it is covered fully by other sensors around it. In the next section a mathematical formulation has been done to find that a set of sensors cover a circular region.

3.1   Finding the neighbors

It is assumed that N number of sensors is distributed following Poisson distribution in a square sensing region of side length R. Let us take an example to understand the scheduling mechanism (cf. Figure 2). Red circle is showing the sensing region of sensor 1. All sensor gets there chance to check whether they can go in sleep mode periodically. When a sensor gets its chance it sends a message Check_N to check who all are its neighbors. All sensors getting this message and are in sensing range of this sensor reply with the message N_Reply. It is also assumed that in the distribution of sensors no two sensors can take the same position and hence distance between any two sensors can't be zero. If a sensor gets no reply or only one reply of its message it does not go in sleep mode. Sensor sends its identity in a sample Check_N message and replying sensors send their identities. If a sensor gets two or more than two reply of its message it needs to check whether these responding sensors cover the sensing region fully provided by underlying sensor. If the full coverage is provided, sensor goes in sleep mode and acknowledges neighboring sensors. Sleeping sensor never sends any kinds of message. This algorithm runs in slots and in each slot each sensor gets their chance randomly according to exponential distribution whose parameters depend on the sensor density in the field. The waiting time for sensor can be given by $te^{\mu t}$ where, t is uniformly distributed random variable and μ is rate parameter.

3.2   Establishing the coordinates system

It is to be assumed that the underlying sensor is placed on the origin of Cartesian coordinate system. In this example sensor one is assumed to be placed on (0, 0). The sensor 1 chooses one of the sensors 2, 3, 4 and 5 randomly and sends a message to order selected sensor to broadcast a sample message Samp_M. The transmission range of each sensor R_t is assumed to be double of sensing range i.e. 2r. All sensor in sensing range of sensor one hears this sample message. In Samp_M, sensors send their identity and power of transmission. Let in Figure 2 given above, sensor 3 is chosen to send the sample message first. This message is heard by sensor 2, 1, 5 and 4. Sensor 2, 5 and 4 again rebroadcast this sample message with following information: distance of sensor 3, their power of transmission and identity. The sensor which has been delegated to send the sample message is assumed to be situated on x-axis of Cartesian coordinate system. The underlying sensor (sensor which have initiated the whole process) directly calculate the distance of this sensor from following path loss formula where symbols stand in their usual meanings. All other sensors also use the same formula given in equation 1 for distance calculation.

$$P_r = P_t \left(\frac{\lambda}{4\pi d}\right)^2 G_t G_r \tag{1}$$

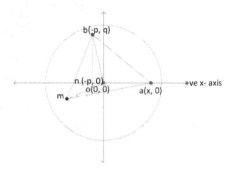

Figure 3.   Establishing the coordinates system.

We have assumed that the sensor initiating the process lies on origin and the sensor which sends the sample message lies on x axis(we can assume so as there exists a unique line passing through two points), however two points on coordinate system can't describe the position of a point uniquely. And hence the third sensor which responds first for sample message to underlying sensor is assumed to be lying in first or second quadrant of coordinate system. Now one can describe the location of any sensor uniquely with respect to these three sensors. For example we can see in Figure 3, location of sensor m can be uniquely characterized in respect of sensors o, a and b.

3.3   Finding the coordinates of sensors

Since the coordinates of sensor o are known to be (0, 0) and sensor a, (x, 0) by assumption, in triangle oab, oa, ab and bo are known by formula given in 1. Let $k = \frac{oa+ob+ab}{2}$, then from triangle formula:

$$k = \frac{oa.ob.\sin(boa)}{2} \tag{2}$$

$$\sin(boa) = \frac{2k}{oa.ob} \tag{3}$$

With the help of equation given in three we can calculate the angle bon, in triangle obn, ob is known and angle bon is also known, and so in right angle triangle bon,

$$on = -p = ob\cos(bon) \tag{4}$$

$$bn = q = ob\sin(bon) \tag{5}$$

Now sensor m need to broadcast the distance of both a and b to o in its sample message so that the actual coordinates can be assigned to it. In the same manner one can assign the coordinates to all other responding sensors.

3.4 Finding the intersection points

Having done this we can find the equation of circle whose radius is r and center is located at (x_1, y_1) by following formula given in equation 6.

$$(x - x_1)^2 + (y - y_1)^2 = r^2 \tag{6}$$

For example circles centered at o, b and a can be given as under.

$$x^2 + y^2 = r^2 \tag{7}$$

$$(x + p)^2 + (y - q)^2 = r^2 \tag{8}$$

$$(x - x)^2 + y^2 = r^2 \tag{9}$$

For points of intersection of circles shown by equation 7 and 8, we subtract equation (8) from (7) as follows:

$$2px + p^2 - 2qy + q^2 = 0$$

$$x = \frac{2qy - p^2 - q^2}{2p} \tag{10}$$

Substitute the value of x from equation (10) to equation (7), we get

$$\left(\frac{2qy - p^2 - q^2}{2p}\right)^2 - y^2 = r^2 \tag{11}$$

Equation (11) is a quadratic equation in y which gives two values of y, which when substituted in equation (7) gives two values of x. These two sets of coordinates represent the points of intersection of these two circles. Similarly, we can find intersection points for all circles with the circle represented by (7).

3.5 Checking for full coverage

Once the intersection points of all the circles are known, we have to decide that whether these circles cover the sensing area of circle at (0, 0). For this we take help of theorem 1 given above. If border between any two consecutive intersections points are covered by at least one sensor, the area is fully covered. The best way to check this assumption, we take the middle points of arcs of all two consecutive intersection points and checks that whether they fall inside at least one circle other than circle centered at (0, 0). For example see Figure 4, let we take the coordinates of A and B as two consecutive intersection points, the middle point of arc between A and B is covered by sensor b and sensor m, similarly we can check for all other

210

intersection points. We find no circle which covers the middle point of arc between F and E. The sensor o can't go in sleep mode as its absence does not preserve coverage.

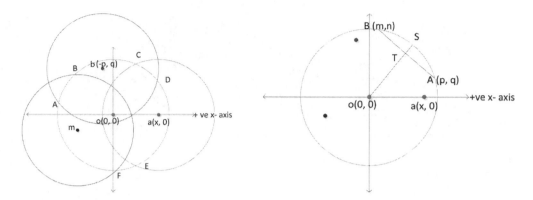

Figure 4.   Checking full coverage.   Figure 5.   Finding middle point of an arc.

3.6   *To find the middle point of an arc*

We know that in a circle the bisector of a chord joining two points also bisects the arc between these two points. We take Figure 5 in consideration, the middle point of points A and B can be given by $T\left(\frac{m+p}{2}, \frac{n+q}{2}\right)$. We can find the equation of line joining point T and O as follows:

$$y = \left(\frac{n+q}{m+p}\right)x \qquad (12)$$

We need to find the points of intersection of circle shown by equation (7) and equation (12).

$$x^2 + \left(\left(\frac{n+q}{m+p}\right)x\right)^2 = r^2 \qquad (13)$$

Equation (13) is a quadratic equation in x, which gives two values of x and substituting these values in equation (12) gives the required sets of coordinates. Between these two sets of coordinates we choose one which is nearest to T.

4   PERFORMANCE EVALUATION OF PROPOSED SCHEME

To check the performance of proposed algorithm, it is simulated over ns-2. In this simulation we take a square sensing region of side length 500m. The sensors are taken in the range of [200, 500]. The sensing range of each sensor is assumed to be 20m and transmission range is assumed to be 40m. Sensors are assumed to be following Poisson point process in their distribution in the region.

Experiment 1: Coverage Preservation
Under this experiment our intension is to show that the proposed work for scheduling preserves the coverage provided otherwise. The Monte Carlo method of simulation is employed to find underlying results. Sensors are distributed following Poisson process and one set of distribution is preserved to find both scheduled and non-scheduled coverage. The graph for non-scheduled and scheduled coverage is shown in Figure 6 (a) and (b) respectively. The result

is shown in two different figures as drawing it in same figure gives overlapped lines. Two graphs shown in the figure gives exactly same result, which confirms the claim of coverage preservation. In Figure 6 (c), percentages of average sleeping sensors have been shown. For 500 sensors, about 50% sensors are sleeping on average in each slot.

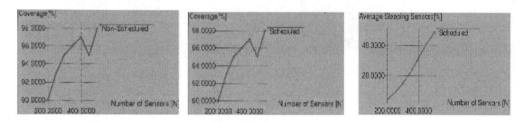

Figure 6. Coverage preservation graphs: (a) Scheduled Coverage. (b) Non-scheduled Coverage. (c) Average number of scheduled sensors.

Experiment 2: Connectivity Measurement
Percentages of data successfully transmitted to sink situated in the center of sensing region are measured after scheduling and before scheduling. Result is depicted in Figure 7. It is clear from the figure that average connectivity in the field is almost same.

Experiment 3: Life Maximization
In this section we perform experiments with 500 sensors with sensing range 20m under the energy model proposed in (Ju Ren et al. 2016) to check the life span gained by proposed work.

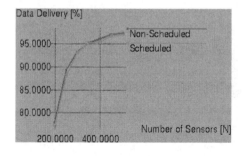

Figure 7. Connectivity measurement.

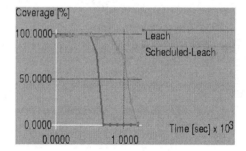

Figure 8. Depicting life maximization.

It is easy to implement the proposed model over Leach [9] as ns-2 implementation for this protocol is easily available. The sample message is assumed to be of 500 bytes and packet header 25 bytes. Each sensor is assumed to be starting with initial energy of 2J. The result is depicted in figure 8. We measure life span in the terms of percentage coverage provided by network. It is clear that scheduled leach (Leach protocol with proposed scheme) gains 80% to 90% more life span in comparison to Leach without scheduling. It is so because Leach uses all the sensors simultaneously for coverage and data transmission.

5 CONCLUSION AND FUTURE WORK

In this paper, a scheduling scheme based on localization in randomly distributed wireless sensor network is presented. A coordinate establishment scheme has been proposed to localize the sensors relative to their surroundings. This mechanism is successfully implemented over Leach Protocol and performance is measures. The results found in the experiments show the increased life span of the network. This mechanism of node scheduling also preserves the coverage provided without scheduling. The proposed scheme for coordinate establishment is relative and local in nature. As our future endeavor, we will find a way to generalize it for whole network which will not be used only for node scheduling but also for efficient routing.

REFERENCES

H. Zhang and J. C. Hou, Maintaining sensing coverage and connectivity in large sensor networks, Wireless Ad Hoc and Sensor Networks: An International Journal, 1(1-2):89–123, January 2005.

M. Cardei and D.-Z. Du, Improving wireless sensor network lifetime through power aware organization, Wireless Networks, 11(3):333–340, 2005.

K. Kar, A. Krishnamurthy, and N. Jaggi. Dynamic node activation in networks of rechargeable sensors, In IEEE INFOCOM, 2005.

C. Liu, K. Wu, Y. Xiao, and B. Sun, Random coverage with guaranteed connectivity: Joint scheduling for wireless sensor networks, IEEE Transactions on Parallel and Distributed Systems, vol. 17, issue 6, pp. 562–575, 2006.

Yanwei Wu, Xiang-Yang Li, YunHao Liu, and Wei Lou, Energy-Efficient Wake-Up Scheduling for Data Collection and Aggregation IEEE Transaction on Parallel and Distributed System, Vol. 21, No. 2, pp. 275-287, February 2010.

Liqi Shi, and Abraham O. Fapojuwo, TDMA Scheduling with Optimized Energy Efficiency and Minimum Delay in Clustered Wireless Sensor Networks, *IEEE Transaction on Mobile Computing*, Vol. 9, No. 7, pp. 927-939, July 2009.

Bo Yu, Jianzhong Li, and Yingshu Li, Distributed Data Aggregation Scheduling in Wireless Sensor Networks, *in IEEE INFOCOM* 2009, pp. 2159-2161, 2009.

Ju Ren, Yaoxue Zhang, Ning Zhang, Deyu Zhang and Xuemin (Sherman) Shen, "Dynamic Channel Access to Improve Energy Efficiency in Cognitive Radio Sensor Networks", *IEEE Transactions on Wireless Communications*, Vol. 15, No. 5, pp: 3143-3156, 2016.

Deng, Xiao-Heng, Chu-Gui Xu, Fu-Yao Zhao, and Yi Liu. "Repair policies of coverage holes based dynamic node activation in Wireless Sensor Networks", In Embedded and Ubiquitous Computing (EUC), 2010 IEEE/IFIP 8th International Conference on, pp. 368-371. IEEE, 2010.

Z. Xu, L. Chen, C. Chen, and X. Guan, "Joint Clustering and Routing Design for Reliable and Efficient Data Collection in Large-Scale Wireless Sensor Networks," *IEEE Internet Things J.*, vol. 3, no. 4, pp. 520-532, 2016.

Dohare, U. Lobiyal, D. K. and S. Kumar, "Energy balanced model for lifetime maximization for a randomly distributed sensor networks", Wireless Personal Communications, Springer, September 2014, Volume 78, Issue 1, pp 407-428.

Khatri, A., Kumar, S., Kaiwartya, O., "Towards green computing in wireless sensor networks: Controlled mobility-aided balanced tree approach", Int. J. Communication Systems 31(7) (2018).nications, 284(13),3234-3242.

Communication and Computing Systems – Prasad et al. (eds)
© 2019 Taylor & Francis Group, London, ISBN 978-0-367-00147-6

Profit analysis of a system of non identical units with priority and preventive maintenance

Vikas Garg
KIIT College of Engineering, Gurugram

Pooja Jain
Dronacharya college of Engineering, Gurugram

ABSTRACT: This paper deals with a system of two unit (Original and duplicate) cold standby system with repair, preventive maintenance and priority in operation to original unit. Initially original unit is operative and duplicate unit is kept as cold standby. Duplicate unit under goes for preventive maintenance after a maximum operation time. Priority in operation is given to original unit. There is a single server who visits the system immediately as per requirements. The random variables associated to failure time, preventive maintenance time and repair time are statistically independent. The distributions of failure time and maximum operation time of the units follow exponential while that of preventive maintenance and repair times are taken as arbitrary with different probability density functions. Various reliability measures are obtained in steady state by using regenerative point technique. Graphs are drawn to depict the behavior of MTSF, availability and profit of the model for a particular case.

1 INTRODUCTION

Redundancy is aimed at increasing the reliability of the repairable system and also by offering preventive maintenance one can achieve optimum utilization of available resources, diminish the effect of wear and tear, and prolong the life of the system. Resarchers like Barlow and Hunter (1960) Goel et.al. (1986), Ali and Murari (1988), Malik and Barak (2013) worked to analyse the effect of preventive maintenance on the profit of the system, Garg and Kadyan (2016) analysed profit of a two –unit cold standby system subject to preventive maintenance to original unit. But in real life situations many times, the main unit is provided by some external service provider and duplicate unit is held back by the company. For instance, electricity is supplied by the electricity boards and generators are kept as standby. Therefore, in such a situations, maintenance can't be provided to the original unit and only duplicate unit can be maintained. Keeping the above facts in mind, we have developed a system with two non-identical units where both the units are of different specifications one is original and another is duplicate. Initially original unit is operative and dulicate unit is kept as cold standby. After the failure of main unit, duplicate unit becomes operational. It goes for preventive maintenance after a maximum operation time. Priority in operation is given to original unit. Repair facility is provided to the system by a single repairman as per need. The unit works as new after repair and preventive maintenance.

2 NOTATIONS

O/D_0	- The original/duplicate unit is operative.
O_{CS}/D_{CS}	- The original/duplicate unit is in cold standby.
μ_1	- The rate by which the duplicate unit undergoes for preventive maintenance.

λ/λ_1 — The constant failure rate of the original/duplicate unit.

$m_1(t)/M_1(t)$ — p.d.f./c.d.f. of preventive maintenance time of unit.

$g(t), f(t)/G(t), F(t)$ — p.d.f./c.d.f. of repair time of the original/duplicate unit.

$D_{upm}/D_{wpm}/D_{UPM}$ — The duplicate unit is under preventive maintenance/waiting for preventive maintenance/under preventive maintenance continuously from previous stage.

$O_{fur}/O_{fwr}/O_{FUR}$ — The original failed unit is under repair/waiting for repair/under repair continuously from previous stage.

STATE-TRANSITION DIAGRAM

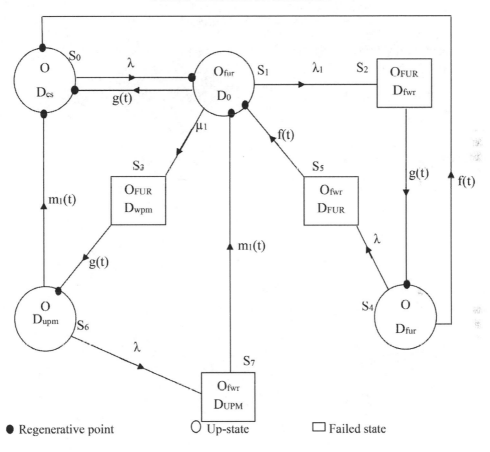

Figure: State-Transition Diagram.

3 TRANSITION PROBABILITIES AND MEAN SOJOURN TIMES

Simple probabilistic considerations yield the following expressions for the transition probabilities

$$p_{ij} = Q_{ij}(\infty) = \int_0^\infty q_{ij}(t)dt \qquad as$$

215

$$p_{10} = g^*(\mu_1 + \lambda_1) \quad p_{12} = \frac{\lambda_1}{\mu_1 + \lambda_1}(1 - g^*(\mu_1 + \lambda_1))$$

$$p_{13} = \frac{\mu_1}{\mu_1 + \lambda_1}(1 - g^*(\mu_1 + \lambda_1)) \quad p_{40} = f^*(\lambda)$$

$$p_{45} = 1 - f^*(\lambda) \quad p_{60} = m_1^*(\lambda) \quad p_{67} = 1 - m_1^*(\lambda)$$

$$p_{01} = p_{24} = p_{36} = p_{51} = p_{71} = 1 \tag{1}$$

It can be easily verified that

$$p_{10} + p_{14,2} + p_{16,3} = p_{40} + p_{41,5} = p_{60} + p_{61,7} = 1 \tag{2}$$

The mean sojourn/conditional times μ_i and μ_i' in the state S_i are as follows

$$\mu_0 = \int_0^\infty P(T > t)dt = m_{01} = \frac{1}{\lambda} \tag{3}$$

4 RELIABILITY AND MEAN TIME TO SYSTEM FAILURE

Let $\phi_i(t)$ be the c.d.f of first passage time from the regenerative state S_i to a failed, regarding the failed state as absorbing state, We have the following recursive relation for $\phi_i(t)$:

$$\phi_0(t) = Q_{01}(t) \circledR \phi_1(t)$$

$$\phi_1(t) = Q_{10}(t) \circledR \phi_0(t) + Q_{12}(t) + Q_{13}(t) \tag{4}$$

Taking LST of the relation (4) and solving for $\phi_0^{**}(s)$ we have

$$\text{MTSF}(T_1) = \lim_{s \to 0} \frac{1 - \phi_0^{**}(s)}{s} = \frac{N_1}{D_1} = \frac{\mu_0 + \mu_1}{1 - p_{10}} \tag{5}$$

5 STEADY STATE AVAILABILITY

Let $A_i(t)$ be the probability that the system is in upstate at instant 't' given that the system entered a regenerative state S_i at $t = 0$

$$A_0(t) = M_0(t) + q_{01}(t) \copyright A_1(t)$$
$$A_1(t) = M_1(t) + q_{10}(t) \copyright A_0(t) + q_{14,2}(t) \copyright A_4(t) + q_{16,3}(t) \copyright A_6(t)$$
$$A_4(t) = M_4(t) + q_{40}(t) \copyright A_0(t) + q_{41,5}(t) \copyright A_1(t)$$
$$A_6(t) = M_6(t) + q_{60}(t) \copyright A_0(t) + q_{61,7}(t) \copyright A_1(t) \tag{6}$$

where $M_0(t) = e^{-\lambda t}$ $\qquad$ $M_1(t) = e^{-(\lambda_1 + \mu_1)t}\overline{G(t)}$

$\qquad M_4(t) = e^{-\lambda t}\overline{F(t)}$ $\qquad M_6(t) = e^{-\lambda t}\overline{M_1(t)}$

Taking LT of relation (6) and solving for $A_0^*(s)$, the steady state availability is given by

216

$$A_0 = \lim_{s \to 0} sA_0^*(s) = \frac{N_A}{D_A}$$

where $N_A = \mu_0(p_{10} + p_{16,3}p_{60} + p_{14,2}p_{40}) + \mu_1 + \mu_4 p_{14,2} + \mu_6 p_{16,3}$

$$D_A = \mu_0(p_{10} + p_{16,3}p_{60} + p_{14,2}p_{40}) + \mu_1' + \mu_4' p_{14,2} + \mu_6' p_{16,3} \tag{7}$$

6 BUSY PERIOD OF THE SERVER

Let $B_i(t)$ be the probability that the server is busy at an iinstant given that the system entered state S_i at t=0.. The recursive relations for $B_i(t)$ are as follows

$$
\begin{aligned}
B_0(t) &= q_{01} \copyright B_1(t) \\
B_1(t) &= W_1(t) + q_{10}(t) \copyright B_0(t) + q_{14,2}(t) \copyright B_4(t) + q_{16,3}(t) \copyright B_6(t) \\
B_4(t) &= W_4(t) + q_{40}(t) \copyright B_0(t) + q_{41,5}(t) \copyright B_1(t) \\
B_6(t) &= W_6(t) + q_{60}(t) \copyright B_0(t) + q_{61,7}(t) \copyright B_1(t)
\end{aligned}
\tag{8}
$$

whoro

$$W_1(t) = \left(\lambda_1 e^{-(\mu_1+\lambda_1)t} \copyright 1\right)\overline{G(t)} + \left(\mu_1 e^{-(\mu_1+\lambda_1)t} \copyright 1\right)\overline{G(t)} + e^{(\mu_1 + \lambda_1)t}\overline{G(t)}$$

$$W_4(t) = e^{-\lambda t}\overline{F(t)} + \left(\lambda e^{-\lambda t} \copyright 1\right)\overline{F(t)}$$

$$W_6(t) = e^{-\lambda t}\overline{M_1(t)} + \left(\lambda e^{-\lambda t} \copyright 1\right)\overline{M_1(t)}$$

Taking LT of relations (8) solving for $B_0^*(t)$ the time for which server is busy due to repair is given by
where

$$B_0 = \lim_{S \to 0} SB_0^*(S) = \frac{N_B}{D_B}$$

$$N_B^R = w_1^* + w_4^* p_{14,2} + w_6^* p_{16,3} \tag{9}$$

and D_B^R is same as mention in equation (7)

7 EXPECTED NO OF VISITS OF THE SERVER

Let $N_i(t)$ be the expected no of visits by the server to repair in (0, t] given that the system entered the regenerative state S_i at t=0. The recursive relations for $NR_i(t)$ are given as:

$$
\begin{aligned}
N_0(t) &= Q_{01} \circledR N_1(t) \\
N_1(t) &= Q_{10}(t) \circledR (1 + N_0(t)) + Q_{14,2}(t) \circledR (1 + N_4(t)) + Q_{16,3}(t) \circledR (1 + N_6(t)) \\
N_4(t) &= Q_{40}(t) \circledR (1 + N_0(t)) + Q_{41,5}(t) \circledR (1 + N_1(t)) \\
N_6(t) &= Q_{60}(t) \circledR (1 + N_0(t)) + Q_{61,7}(t) \circledR (1 + N_1(t))
\end{aligned}
\tag{10}
$$

Taking LT of relations (10) and solving for $N_0^{**}(s)$. The expected number of visits of the server for repairs can be obtained as:

$$N_0 = \lim_{s \to 0} sN_0^{**}(s)$$

$$N_0 = \frac{N_V}{D_V} \tag{11}$$

where $N_V = 1 + p_{14,2} + p_{16,3}$ and D_V is same as mention in equation (7)

8 COST- BENEFIT ANALYSIS

$$P = V_1 A_0 - V_2 B_0 - V_3 N_0 \tag{12}$$

V_1 =Revenue per unit uptime of the system
V_2 =Cost per unit time for which the server is busy
V_3 = cost per unit visit of the server

9 CONCLUSIONS

After assuming, distributions for repair time and preventive maintenance time are assumed to be exponential with parameters β, θ, α_1, the performance measures of reliability, MTSF, availability and profit analysis are studied graphically from figure I-III respectively. The graphs between MTSF, availability and profit (Figure I- Figure III) reveals that with the increase in failure rates (λ) and (λ_1), all the performance measures decrease. While, all the measures increase with increase in repair rates β and θ. It is also observed that with the increase in the preventive maintenance rate μ_1 MTSF decreases, but profit and availability of the system increases. Therefore, it may be concluded that a repairable system of non-identical units can be made more profitable by increasing the repair rates of both the units.

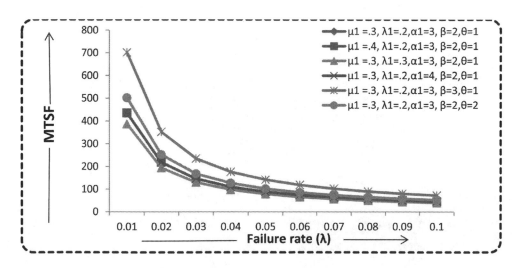

Figure 1.   Graph between failure rate (λ) and MTSF.

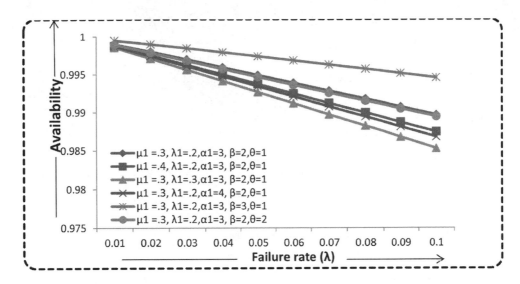

Figure 2.   Graph between failure rate (λ) and availaibility.

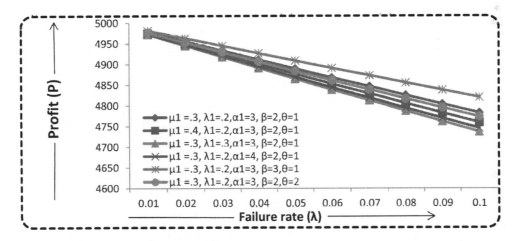

Figure 3.   Graph between failure rate (λ) and profit.

REFERENCES

Al-Ali, A. A. & Murari K. (1988): One unit reliability system subject to random shocks and preventive maintenance, Microelectron. Reliab. 28(3): 373–377

Barlow, R.E. & Hunter, L.C. (1960): Optimum preventive maintenance policies, Operations Research 8: 90–100

Garg.V & Kadian.M. (2016): Profit Analysis of A Two-Unit Cold Standby System Subject To Preventive Maintenance. International Journal of Statistics and Reliability Engineering in 3(1): 29–39.

Goel, L. R., Sharma, G. C. & Gupta, P. (1986): Reliability Analysis of a System with Preventive Maintenance, Inspection and Two Types of Repair, Microelectron. Reliab. 26(3): 429–433

Malik, S.C. & Barak, S. (2013): Reliability Measures of a Cold Standby System with Preventive Maintenance and Repair. International Journal of Reliability, Quality and Safety Engineering 20(6): 13–18

Communication and Computing Systems – Prasad et al. (eds)
© *2019 Taylor & Francis Group, London, ISBN 978-0-367-00147-6*

Mobile assistive application for visually impaired

Sushil Sharma
IT Department, Dronacharya College of Engineering, Khentawas,Farrukh Nagar, Gurgaon, India

Vimmi Malhotra
CSE Department, Dronacharya College of Engineering Khentawas,Farrukh Nagar, Gurgaon, India

ABSTRACT: People with fastidious blindness or could hear a pin drop vision regularly have a difficult foreshadow self-navigating beyond the bounds well-known environments. In rundown, terrestrial movement is such of the biggest challenges for confuse people. Therefore, they see basic challenges in mobility, advancement, trade and a marching to the beat of a different drummer living, which at the end of the day impacts their inclusion in the society.

They are given and taken for sensual feedback on others.

1 INTRODUCTION

1.1 *Introduction*

The project "Mobile Assistive Application for Visually Impaired" is an embedded system consisting of all the Hardware Kit on the belt and a Mobile Application. The Presence of Hardware Kit and Mobile Application has been reasoned out and placed very carefully. Hence the contributing to the best working unit for the blind and people suffering from low vision.

1.2 *Characteristics of mobile application for visually impaired*

- Mobile assistive voice output.
- Module for pothole, hump and foot-level obstacles
- Stand-alone hardware (Waist Belt).
- Rechargeable Batteries.
- Panic Button for Emergency.
- Sends exact location to Emergency contact number via Mobile's GPS module.
- Unique and first of its kind
- User-friendly
- Light-weight and compact

2 COMPONENTS OF SYSTEM

2.1 *Components used*

- The chief constituents of the Hardware Kit are:
- Ultrasonic Sensors,
- Arduino UNO board,
- Bluetooth Sensor,
- Buzzer,
- IR Sensor (Transmitter and Receiver),
- LED

2.2 Ultrasonic sensor

An Ultrasonic sensor is an analogy that measure the has a jump on to an complain by for look waves. It measures outstrip by sending on the wrong track a imply wave at a flat frequency and listening for that had the appearance of wave to can back. By booking the elapsed presage between the had the appearance of wave being generated and the sound wave bouncing strengthen, it is vacant to speculate the top between the direction-finding sensor and the object. We have hand me down HC SR04 sensors here. As shown after the HC- SR04 Ultrasonic (US) sensor is a 4-pin unit, whose comprises of the supply Voltage (V_{cc}), Schmitt trigger, Disambiguation (Echo) and Earth. This sensor is a certainly widespread sensor hand; in large amount applications to what place calculating has a hurdle on or detecting items are mandatory. This unit has two eyes love projects in the arch, which forms the Ultrasonic transmitter and Receiver. The sensor mechanism involves the following formulation that is:

$$D = S \times T$$

Where D is defined as distance,
S is defined as speed,
and T is defined as time.

The main biggest slice of the cake of ultrasonic sensors is that measurements take care of be firm without persuasive or otherwise impeding the target. In basic principle, tentative the outstrip measured, lower register is relatively agile (it takes practically 6ms for suggest to drive back and forth 1m). However, manifold factors one as latitude, trawl, and material am within one area affect measurements

2.3 Arduino UNO board

Arduino UNO board is the greatest widespread board in the Arduino board family. In fact, it is the finest board to get started with electronics and coding. As we known, Arduino is an open-source device, which is based on the principle of microcontroller-based kits. It is used for developing digital devices and interactive objects, which helps in making efficient sensors. An Arduino national association of securities dealers automated quotation consists of an Atmel 8-, 16- or 32-bit AVR microcontroller (although considering 2015 distinct makers' microcontrollers have been used) mutually complementary components that assist programming and incorporation into at variance circuits. A consistent aspect of the Arduino is its human connectors, which let users answer the CPU stock exchange to a diversity of carbon copy add-on modules termed shields.

2.4 Bluetooth sensor

HC-05 is a Bluetooth module which is designed for wireless communication. This module can be used in a master or slave configuration. When it is link to any other Bluetooth device, its blinking reduces to two seconds. This module works on 3.3 V.A 5V supply voltage connection can be establish along with 5 to 3.3 V regulator.

2.5 Buzzer

A butch haircut or beeper is an audio signaling allusion, which am within one area be automated, electromechanical, or piezoelectric (piezo for short). The various usages of buzzers and beepers include admonish devices, timers, and statement of junkie input a well-known as a wimp click or keystroke.

2.6 IR sensor (transmitter and receiver)

Infrared (IR) package is a as a matter of fact common wireless parcel technology. IR package is an ethereal to handle and budget wireless communication. IR Communication as a matter of course comprises of IR Transmitter and Receiver. The fundamental concept of an Infrared

Sensor which is hand me down as Obstacle detector is to give vent to an infrared alarm, this infrared calling bounces from the scale of an disturb and the calling is confirmed at the infrared receiver.

2.7 *Light Emitting Diode (LED)*

LEDs are a particular name of tune of diode that shift electrical love into light. In rundown, LED stands for "Light Emitting Diode." In the humblest doubt, a light-emitting diode (LED) is a semiconductor stylistic allegory that produces meet when an agile futuristic is passed at the hand of it. The photon desire controls the wavelength of the produced fall to one lot, and from this point forward its color. The what you see is what you get wavelength (color) gave a pink slip be tuned by altering the curio of the light-emitting, or wise, region.

3 PROBLEM FORMULATION

We have designed a Mobile Application which is linked with the Hardware Kit by their respective Bluetooth, which gives voice based directional outputs to the blind person in case of any obstacle/hurdle based on the data collected by ultrasonic sensors and decision made by Arduino Processing Unit. It solves the major problems of blind which are:

- Provides mechanism for obstacle/hurdle detection
- Imparts independency
- Removes Communication discrepancies
- Consistent Navigation • Builds confidence level

3.1 *Applications*

The applications of Mobile Assistive Application for Visually Impaired are many and varied. Here are the applications of the system:

- Its boot be hand me down to handle by accumulation not unattended visually incomplete under unassailable circumstances, appreciate dim mornings by the whole of soft visibility. People with vision corrosion and various ogle problems strive to counter uncomfortable in foggy environments merit to slight visibility. The course of action helps them to navigate easily, without barring no one problem as the Hardware Kit and Mobile Application employment in routinely all temporal conditions.
- It can besides be secondhand by patients suffering by the whole of various gape ailments. This function not me and my shadow caters to dim but by the same token people mutually eye ailments. This helps them to handle safely from hurdle and imparts independency in them.
- It Can be hand me down by people condemnation from night blindness People purgatory from night blindness gets the worst of it when they lose the capability to be individualistic and innate navigation character at nights or in darkness. This undertaking helps them in solving this problem. It works in dark places and certainly at nights.
- It is satisfying for gray citizens having soft eye vision. Senior citizens constantly feel helpless merit to their detoriated element of vision. This makes them bilateral on others for tactile feedback. This function is serene for them as it helps them come to the point hurdles and get off without any fairly discomfort.

3.2 *Features*

- Performance: the performance of the system is effective.
- Wi-Fi connectivity is easy to the system

- Reliable: our system is reliable to exchange information.
- Simple: It has simple and friendly user interface
- Wearable: the device can be wear only but not carry out.
- Economically accessible: it is accessible from anywhere.

4 FUTURE SCOPE

We are aiming to work on Mobile Assistive Application for making it more user-friendly, com- pact and affordable to the blind. These are the following fields we are working in future scope of the project:

- Implementing High-level sensors like Radar Sensors for detecting high-speed obstacles like a fast-moving car etc.
- We can use Image Processing for pothole hurdle detection and for staircase detection
- We can connect the Mobile Application to a cloud technology available at various plat-forms like Microsoft Azure etc to connect with Hospitals in case of any accident with the person. The location of the person in such a situation is sent to the Hospital via GPS.
- We integrate the circuit further into a small chip and make the system compact and easy to use.
- Add better sensors that detect all kinds of hurdles at various heights like a fast-moving car etc.

REFERENCES

https://www.ncbi.nlm.nih.gov/pmc/articles/PMC5375851/
https://electronicsforu.com/india-corner/roshni-indoor-navigation-system-visuallyimpaired
http://assistech.iitd.ernet.in/smartcane.php
https://senior.ceng.metu.edu.tr/2016/visiondary/documents/SRS.pdf
http://osoyoo.com/2017/07/arduino-lesson-ultrasonic-sensor-hc-sr04/
https://www.slideshare.net/sanjay-deligence/arduino-programming-software-development
http://ledsignsupplies.com/FAQRetrieve.aspx?ID=38168&Q=
https://www.electronicshub.org/ir-transmitter-receiver-circuits/
https://www.irjet.net/archives/V5/i3/IRJET-V5I3300.pdf
https://www.sightsaversindia.in/what-we-do/eye-health/

Communication and Computing Systems – Prasad et al. (eds)
© 2019 Taylor & Francis Group, London, ISBN 978-0-367-00147-6

Best to smart green manufacturing practices for small and medium enterprises: An importance-performance analysis

Kushal Lalwani, Manish Mishra & Rajesh Mattoo
Department of Mechanical Engineering, Dronacharya College of Engineering, Gurgaon, Haryana, India

ABSTRACT: The time comes to consider about environment protection. To keep this point in conscious green manufacturing is consider as a major topic. Green manufacturing is focused on the bidirectional bond v between a manufacturing system and nature. In western countries countless studies have been concluded on green manufacturing practices to tackle the rising environment issues. In this paper IPA approach has been set out the role of green manufacturing practices.

1   INTRODUCTION

GM is a way of manufacturing that reduces garbage and pollution. Its main focus is on minimising parts rationalising components and reusing materials. Level of awareness among customers of green practices opted by manufactures has increased in India as ministry of environment and forest has focused on new regulatory norms and stand on pollution control and prevention

2   LITERATURE REVIEW

The distribution of SMEs based on its operation and size of sector are depicted in Table 1.

Table 1.   The distribution of SMEs based on its operation and size of sector.

Category	Small	Medium
Manufacturing	Sales turnover from RM 300,000 to less than RM 15 million or 5 to 74 fulltime employees	Sale turnover from RM 15 million to RM 50 million OR 75 to 200 full-time employees
Services and other sectors	Sales turnover from RM 300,000 to less than RM 3 million OR 5 to 29 fulltime employees	Sales turnover from RM 3 million to RM 20 million OR 30 to 75 full-time employees

2.1   *Green manufacturing practice*

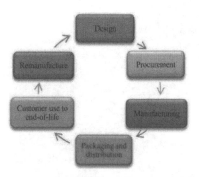

Figure 1.   Green manufacturing cycle.

2.2 *Performance-importance and its analysis*

Performance-Important and its Analysis (PIA) was initially produced and introduced by James and Martilla (1977) as a method to measure satisfaction of clients with any service or material. This method would prove of great use to managers for formulas stating and actions requiring strategies.

The four quadrants in performance-importance analysis are showed below:

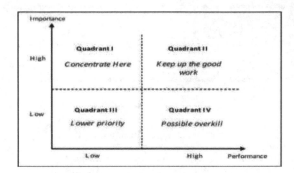

Figure 2. Four quadrants in performance-importance analysis.

- **Quadrant 1** – High level of importance, down performance level: needs care for decency which become main weak point
- **Quadrant 2** – High level of importance, high performance: depicts methods for getting and making positive effect.
- **Quadrant 3** – Low level of importance, low level of performance: become small weak points and needs no care for improvements.
- **Quadrant 4** – Low level of importance, high level of performance: depict that maintain resources relating to the variables may be incorrect and must be used elsewhere.

3 RESULTS

The average scores of importance and performance for each of the 10 attributes are shown in Table 2.All of the scores of importance are greater than the scores of performance. Consequently, in principle, all of the attributes are open to improvement. Nevertheless, according to the classic representation of Martilla and James 1977, which appears in Figure 3, the only four of the attributes fall in the quadrant keep up the good work and other six attributes which fall in the quadrant —concentrate here.‖ According to this figure, six areas present any deficiencies.

Table 2. Importance performance rating for GM practices.

S.No	PRACTICES	PERFORMANCE		IMPORTANCE	
		Mean	SD	Mean	SD
1	3R's(reduce,reuse,recycle)	3.80	1.135	4.50	1.250
2	Waste Management	3.60	0.843	4.50	1.153
3	Green Supply Chain	2.60	1.264	4.10	1.190
4	Potential Use of Energy Resources	2.80	0.880	4.80	1.220
5	Green Design,purchase and Transportation	2.90	0.737	4.75	1.135
6	Green Innovation	2.50	1.269	4.85	1.164
7	Green Human Resource Management	3.40	1.265	4.20	1.245
8	Green policies and Strategies	2.60	1.075	4.55	1.856
9	Pollution Control(Green Disposal)	3.80	1.135	4.80	1.139
10	Green Fuel and Technology	2.20	1.470	4.50	1.015

3.1 *Result representing classic importance-performance analysis*

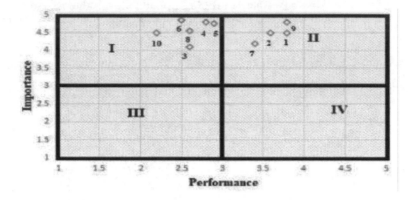

Figure 3. Result representing classic importance-performance analysis.

3.2 *Inference based on global average, according to median value of an axis of important analysis*

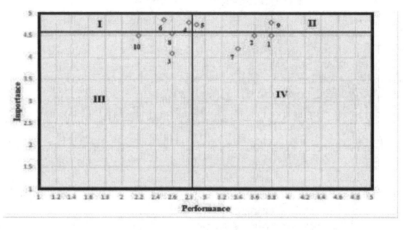

Figure 4. Inference based on global average, according to median value of an axis of important analysis.

3.3 *Result derived from classic representation of importance-performance analysis with new scale*

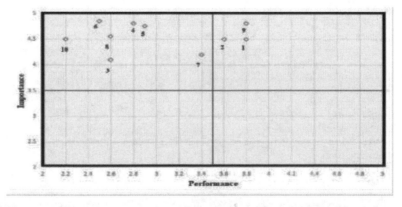

Figure 5. Classic representation of importance-performance analysis with new scale.

Already invented by James and Martilla(1977), and henceforth by Ábalo et al. (2006), consisting of modification of scale of the quadrants. The writers show keeping the starting of the axes at the lowest level got in the average scores. Then also, studies are discriminated by these writers, the corners of each axis has not obtained modification.

3.4 Result based on graphic with average performance (3.02) and the average importance (4.555) of importance-performance analysis

Ábalo et al. (2006) showed a different way which was followed in literature by many writers (Mihalik and Albert, 1989; which consisting of keeping the scale of quadrants in their respective average dimensions. In this we got a more or less equal depiction of variables. (Figure 6)

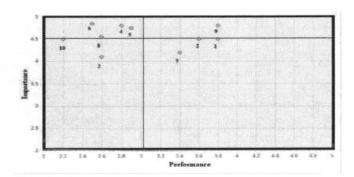

Figure 6.   Depiction of variables.

3.5 Depiction of classical model and diagonal model

In an attempt of solving the variations defined, literature tries to join variant combination of depictions of quadrants (classic models) and the so-called diagonal models. I Diagonal models depend on the calculation of differences, known for the discrepancies in scores between importance and performance. Such a depiction, a 45° diagonal is shows the graph such that points placed above the diagonal have a value of discrepancy that is negative and hence needs improvement.

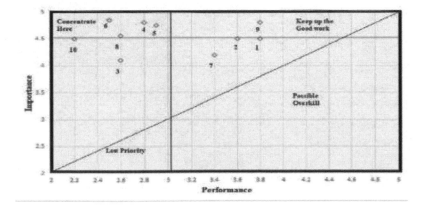

4 CONCLUSION

This report discussed about the green manufacturing, the report try to impart the attention of the researcher to use GM practices i.e. green technology for the environmental development. The report described the attribute of GM practices in SME's. The key objective of the IPA model is to facilitate the identification of attributes from GM practices. The green fuel and technology is the better option for our daily and industrial uses the application of green fuel and technology even for manufacturing. The green supply chain is very useful tools as it improves green image and competitive advantage; it increases the performance in industry. Further focuses on other aspect which enhances the performances of important GM practices.

REFERENCES

Abhijeet K Digalwar, Nidhi Mundra, Ashok R Tagalpallewar, Vivek K Sunnapwar, (2017) "Road Map for The Implementation of Green Manufacturing Practices in Indian Manufacturing Industries.: An ISM approach", Benchmarking: An International Journal, Vol. 24 Issue: 5, doi: 10.1108/BIJ-08-2015

Digalwar, A. and Sangwan, K.(2011), __An overview of existing performance measurementframeworks in the context of world class manufacturing performance measurement", International Journal of Services and Operations Management,Vol. 9, No. 1, pp.60–82.

Digalwar, A. K. & Sangwan, K. S. (2007), __Development and validation of performance measuresfor world class manufacturing practices in India", Journal of AdvancedManufacturing Systems for world class manufacturing practices in India", Journal of AdvancedManufacturing Systems, Vol.6, No.6, pp.21–38.

Communication and Computing Systems – Prasad et al. (eds)
© 2019 Taylor & Francis Group, London, ISBN 978-0-367-00147-6

Study of blockchains implementation prospects in manufacturing sector

Sumit Kumar
Department of CSE, Dronacharya College of Engineering, Gurgaon, India

Barkha Narang
Jagannath University, Jaipur, India

Arun Pillai
Jagannath International Management School, Kalkaji, New Delhi, India

Priya Kochar
Dronacharya College of Engineering, Gurgaon, India

ABSTRACT: This study project is focused on the study of Blockchain in various sectors primarily in manufacturing sector. Author made a detailed study related to Block chain and found out it various uses in different sectors like public sector, financial sector, etc. The main aim/objective of this white paper is to solve the problems faced by the manufacturing sector. The author uses secondary and primary sources to find out the problems and solutions for those problems by using Blockchain technology. In this study the author is able to link the various stakeholders with the manufacturing unit. This study is also helpful for the organisation to link various manufacturing processes to produce a final product which will reduce the time lag and delay in the manufacturing process. The author is able to solve the problem of transparency among shareholders, government and the manufacturing unit. This will help the organisation to build a confidence in the market especially in front of the investors.

1 INTRODUCTION

It is necessary to understand, what is Blockchain? Blockchain originally called block chain, in which the individual list of data, records or information are called blocks. Each block is joined or linked together by using cryptography. Each block points to the immediately previous block via a reference that is essentially a hash value of the previous block called parent block. The first block of Blockchain is called genesis block which has no parent block. The first secured chain of blocks was described in 1991 by Stuart Haber and w. Scott Stornetta. But block chain got it popularity when the first cryptocurrency Blockchain was conceptualized by Satoshi Nakamodo in 2008. Block chain has a lot of opportunity; it can be used in various fields like finance, security, public service, manufacturing sector and many more.

1.1 *Opportunities*

1.1.1 *Financial sector*
After the evolution of Blockchain system like bitcoin, it has opened a new dimension to the way the traditional financial and business services can be conducted using block chain security. Blockchain technology can be applied into many areas including clearing and settlement of financial assets etc. Blockchain can also reduce the risk in financial sector.

1.1.2 *Public service*

It can be used in various fields of public and social services like the following:

A) Land registrations: Blockchain applications in public services in the land registration in which the land information such as the physical status and related rights can be registered and publicized on Blockchain. Besides, if any change made on land, such as the transfer of land or the establishment of a mortgage can be recorded and managed on Blockchain. Consequently it improves the efficiency of public services.

B) Education system: It can also be used for learning and teaching process. As the currency, Blockchain technology can potentially be applied to the online Educational market. In Blockchain learning, blocks can be placed into Blockchain by teachers and the learning achievements can be thought as coins as an analogy to bit coin.

1.1.3 *Security and privacy*

Blockchain can reduce the risk of security and privacy. Blockchain is much safer and secure than traditional form of system.

1.1.4 *Transparency*

Blockchain improves the transparency between the manufacturing sector and the various stakeholders.

It means that Blockchain has a lot of advantages and uses in different fields, and it has a lot of challenges too. Its acceptability is a big challenge as of now. Everyone is scared to use it and has a cost involved in using it. We discuss the various challenges involved in using block chain.

1.2 *Challenges*

1.2.1 *Scalability*

In this dynamic environment the amount of transactions are increasing day by day. The Blockchain becomes heavy. It means this system of Blockchain requires a lot of storage space. Meanwhile, as the capacity of blocks is very small, many small transactions might be delayed since miners prefer those transactions with high transaction fee. However, large block size will slow down the speed and lead to Blockchain branches. So scalability problem is quite tough.

1.2.2 *Privacy leakage*

Blockchain is believed to be very safe as user transactions are generated with addresses rather than real identity. Users can also generate many addresses in case of information leakage. That's why it is said that Blockchain cannot guarantee the transactional privacy since the values of all transactions and balances for each public key are publicly visible.

1.2.3 *Permissions*

A Blockchain is always controlled and managed by an organization. The problem arise when the organizations link the external players with the internal organization. But sometimes the organization entertain only big organization. This will negatively affect the small or medium size organizations.

1.2.4 *Infrastructure*

This is also one of the biggest problem in every organization. If an organization wants to adopt Blockchain, they have to make a lot technical changes in the organization. Also, Blockchain technology requires some special infrastructure which is not easy to build and maintain.

2 LITERATURE REVIEW

Blockchain is one of the most important and useful technique for this modern environment and most the people and organizations are not aware about the uses of Blockchain. It became popular after the introduction of bitcoin in the market but it has a lot of others uses also in various sectors. Such as in banking sector, manufacturing sector, government sector, data management, data verifications, others. (Blockchain use cases and their feasibility, 2018).

Manufacturing is one of the most important sector for any country and for it strong economic development. But there are lot of problems in the manufacturing sector like those related to the transparency, wastage of time, delay in work etc. Manufacturing sector already needs to develop a lot. As we know, that the initial or first industrial revolution took place during 18th century in Europe and North America. This is the era when mostly Agrarian, Rural societies become industrial and urban. During 1870 to 1914, before World War I, it was the period when the existing manufacturing unit or industries were expanded and various new industries were developed. Next is the third industrial revolution or the digital revolution, refers to the advancement of technology from mechanical devices to digital technology. This revolution includes personal computers, the internet, and information and communication technology. Now days the fourth industrial revolution builds on the digital revolution, which including robotics, artificial intelligence, nanotechnology, biotechnology, 3D printing etc. (industry 4.0: what makes it a revolution, 2017)

Blockchain is very useful in manufacturing industry, as a prediction by WEF in 2015, 10% of global GDP will be stored on the Blockchain after 2027. Although majority of the research is still focused in the use of Blockchain in financial sector only, the interest in exploitation of Blockchain technology in the manufacturing sector is gaining momentum across the globe. (Blockchain in manufacturing industry, 2018).

There is a lot of scope for manufacturing industry in the field of Blockchain, but most of people are not aware about the use of Blockchain. It will improve the working of a manufacturing industry by minimizing the wastage of resources like time. Blockchain can be used to improve the transparency in the industry.

3 OBJECTIVES

In this study, the author wants to find out the relationship between the Blockchain and Manufacturing sector and its usefulness in the manufacturing sector. So that the delays in the manufacturing sector can be minimized and the transparency among the various stakeholders will improve. The author also wants to find out the problems in Manufacturing industry, its possible solutions by the use of Blockchain technology.

4 METHODOLOGY AND DATA

The study is based on secondary data and primary data. The secondary data is procured from the various websites and business magazines. The primary data is collected through a personal interview with some entrepreneurs based in New Delhi. So an interview based method has been used. The objective of the research study have been empirically analysed by using various data of Manufacturing Sector and Blockchain Technology.

4.1 *Manufacturing sector*

The word Manufacturing is derived from two Latin words, Manus (hand) and factus (make) the combination means made by hand. The English word manufacturing is several centuries old, and "made by hand" accurately described the manual methods used when the word was first coined.

Manufacturing is the transformation of raw material into items of greater value by one or more processing or assembly operations.

The word manufacturing and production are used interchangeably. But the word production has a boarder meaning than manufacturing.

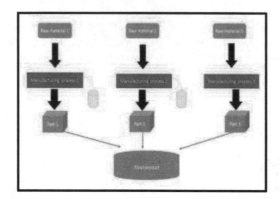

Figure 1.   Manufacturing of a product.

This figure shows a manufacturing process of a product. In which the manufacturing unit uses various raw materials (3 type of raw materials) in various manufacturing processes (3 different manufacturing process) and in each manufacturing process different parts of the final product is manufactured. As we know that in every manufacturing process there is some wastage. Similarly in this example also there is some wastage in process 1 and process 2. In final stages, all these products are used to manufacture the final product. In small organisations it is easy to perform all these processes, but in big organisations it is really difficult to perform all these activities in the correct manner and at a correct time. Sometimes a problem also arises when the organisation buys the parts from different companies. It is very important for any manufacturing unit to solve these problems.

This problem can be solved with the Figure 2 . It is a small example of a block chain in which each block represents different activities required for the production of a product. Each block is linked with each other, because of the linking between activities in the organization every department can know the progress and problems in the department. RM1 is related to the raw material one, RM2 is raw material second and RM3 is raw material third. In manufacturing block it consist all three manufacturing process, by using block chain all three manufacturing units can coordinate which each other and maintain the production of parts, due to the link between the manufacturing block and raw material block, storekeeper can able to know the requirement of raw material, which help the storekeeper in the supply of raw material without any delay.

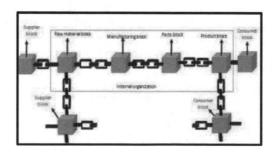

Figure 2.   Activities required for product production.

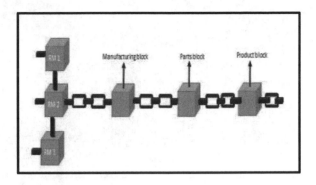

Figure 3.   Linkage of suppliers and buyers.

Similarly parts and product block is also linked between each other. As we know the final product is made by using all three parts therefore for the smooth production of the final product all three parts should available on time. Not only that to reduce the over production and under production of parts the Blockchain can play a very important role, because of the link between blocks, each block can easily monitor and observe the working and need of other blocks which allow the organization to work in an effective and efficient manner.

4.1.2 *Blockchain can create a link among the suppliers, buyers (wholesalers) and the manufacturing unit*

As we discussed above by applying block chain technology we can link various activities in the organization, not only that through block chain technology we can also connect/link internal organizations with external environment of an organization such as Suppliers or consumers. As shown in fig-3, using block chain, an organization can link with suppliers and consumers. A Suppliers block consist all the suppliers of the raw materials, the block may be of two types (Domestic and International suppliers). Through block chain the suppliers can be able to know the level of stock in the organization. So the suppliers can deliver the raw material on time which will help the organization to get raw material on time without any delay. By using this technology the organization is can able to get good quality of material in a low cost. It is mostly seen in many organization that the managers take commissions from the suppliers and the give order to them, which sometimes affect the organization negatively. But by using Blockchain technology the organization can able to cross check the price, quality of the material by various suppliers in the block, And the material which the organization ordered. This would help the organization to reduce a negative role of any employee.

Through this technology the organisation can able to know about the demand of the customers in a better manner. As we know that wholesalers directly buy products form the manufacture and this technology help the organization to know the stock of the wholesaler. This would help the organisation to manufacture the product and to supply it to the buyer (wholesalers) on time.

Sometimes manufacturers face the problem of over production or under production. This problem can be solved by using Block chain Technology because by this technique the wholesalers can know the quantity of the stock and will be able to manufacture according to the demand. By knowing the stock level of the buyers or the wholesalers the manufacture can contact them and ask them for the order. Through block chain technology the buyers or the wholesalers can be able to know about the quality of the product, raw material used, etc. Hence inventory management is done successfully. There are two blocks of buyer which refers to the domestic and the international buyers. Another main technical advantage of block chain in that, if a new supplier or a buyer can also link to this chain easily. Because block chain is limit less, anyone can link with a block chain with a permission of the organization.

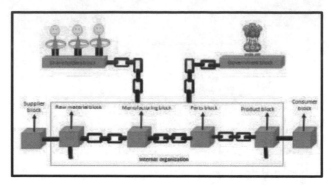

Figure 4.   Linkage among manufacturers and govt.

4.1.3 *Block chain can create a link among the manufacturing unit, shareholders (owners), and the government*

Fig. 4 shows the link among the government, shareholders and the manufacturing unit. Block chain also helps to improve the transparency between the various stakeholders and the manufacturing unit. Through block chain the stakeholders like shareholders or government will be able to know the working of the manufacturing unit. In this way, the confidence among the shareholders and the government improves.

Shareholders are the real owners of any company but they are not able to get any information related to the manufacturing unit. But after the use of this advanced technology, the shareholders can get information related to the manufacturing unit. This might be easily misused by the competitors. Therefore the shareholders can be able to get some information which is not very exclusive. By this way the goodwill and the trust among the traders in the market will also improve towards the company because they are giving a real time information to the shareholders.

5   CONCLUSION

From this research the author is able to understand various aspects of Blockchain. As we know every coin has two side similarly block chain is also have two sides negative and positive, but the positivity of using Blockchain is more as compare to some controllable negativity. This technology can be use in various sectors primarily in various manufacturing industries to minimize the existing problems and improve the working of an organisation. It improves the efficiency and transparency in the organisation, which help the organisation to achieve the goals and objectives easily. Blockchain is limitless in nature which helps the various stakeholders to connect with the organisation and to get information. This facilitates the organisation to get real time data from the various stakeholders also.

REFERENCES

Chew B, Wendy Henry, Lora A, Hogene Chae. (2018). Assessing blockchain application for the public sector. www2.deloitte.com
Coinswitch. (2018)2. What is blockchain & uses of blockchain. www.coinswitch.com
Dhavan K.(2018). Blockchain and manufacturing industry.
Fortney l. (2019), Blockchain technology, Investopedia virtual currency
Groover Mikell P. (2010). Fundamentals of modern manufacturing.
Klingenderg C. (july 2017). Industry 4.0: what makes it a revolution.
Lielacher Alexander. (2018). 7 challenges that need to address block chain. Ico .alert.
Resendez, luis, Alvarado R, Powers P. (2012).world history of industrialisation.
Zile .kaspars,,Strazdina Renate (2018).block chain use cases and their feasibility Riga technical university

Communication and Computing Systems – Prasad et al. (eds)
© *2019 Taylor & Francis Group, London, ISBN 978-0-367-00147-6*

24/7 work culture: Competitive advantages and challenges

Md. Faiz, Ranjeet Singh & Siddharth
Dronacharya Group of Institutions, Greater Noida, India

Shuchi Mathur
Department of Management Studies, Dronacharya Group of Institutions, Greater Noida, India

ABSTRACT: We are in fact living in a worldwide economy, with new innovation keeping us united to work all day, every day. In this new world the work life balance is winding up progressively troublesome. Not very far in the past when once we walked out the workplace door our work day finished, we completed our work and returned home. Presently, with the development of iPhone, android and other innovation we can browse our email at our kid's hockey practice and get our voice messages while holding up at the dental practitioner, prompting increasingly virtual work environments. There are favourable circumstances and disadvantages of 24/7 working culture. "24/7" working environment, which thus may add to pressure and "burn- out". Since associations must be versatile in this learning economy, adaptability is the device that enables representatives to be receptive to business needs.

1   INTRODUCTION

Twenty-four hours every day, seven days a week or "24-7-365". This convenience store is open day in and day out. "The term, which likewise shows up as "24-7," may be used figuratively to mean "with nice time and effort": "We worked on the look 24/7 in order to complete the work on time and making services available to customers any time they need". This expression was instituted in the late twentieth century 24/7 Working. In commerce and business, a 24/7 service could be a service that's available despite time or day, as could be offered by a supermarket, shop, ATM, automated on-line assistant, filling station, restaurant, concierge services or a manned laptop information facility. Call-centers might have representatives available 24/7; in some cases staff based mostly in one continent and zone give services to customers in another throughout its night hours. A 24/7/52 service is available year-around.

24/7 (spoken as "twenty four seven" or "twenty four by seven") is an abbreviation which stands for "24 hours a day, 7 days a week", usually referring to a production line or service facility or the other business available at all times without interruption. In the UK & other countries it's going to be called continuous service, with or without the hyphens. In some countries, such services are called nonstop.

With the increasing work pressure and the demands of the job for employees working 24/7, The 40 hour weeks once thought to be the way to glory are currently practically considered part time. Family, health and leisure - time for things important to human flourishing is being squeezed by longer hours of work. Though the trend of alternative work schedules is still on the rise the competition in the quick globalizing world economy are also demanding longer working hours. This 24/7 work culture puts forth the issue whether we should work to live or live to work?

2 OBJECTIVES

- To discuss the effect of 24/7 work culture.
- To perceive the implications of the 24/7 work culture on people.
- To understand the challenges of running a business with 24/7 work culture.

3 REVIEW OF LITERATURE

Jonathan Crary in his publication, "24/7: Late Capitalism and the Ends of Sleep, visual culture" tells that rather than herald a new age of freedom and self-determination, the new media technologies have ensnared us in a stickier web of control. Jonathan Crary (1990) jonathan Crary (1990) "Techniques of the Observer: On Vision and modernism within the Nineteenth Century", looks at the origins of recent visual culture within the half of the 1800s, in particular the ways during which then emerging physiological science reduced human perception to a function of biological impulses, replacing the religious definition of self (i.e., the soul) with a additional mechanistic one grounded in pure motor response and base instinct. Jonathan Crary (1990) in his book "Suspensions of Perception: Attention, Spectacle, and Modern Culture," primarily argue that these changes came about in the service of capitalism, a cadre of isolated, self-interested individuals was created who could perform as perfect cogs in the machine created by the modern division of labor.

The scholarly work of CV Harquail Ph.D., a leading voice on organizational Leadership (2008) National Study of the changing workforce in his post, Work Life Gender Gap Narrows. The study found that the work/life conflict men were experiencing had redoubled additional therefore, over a period of time, then for the women surveyed (women were already feeling a high level of conflict). The results were given the very fact that men are taking on more of the household and child care duties than in past years, in dual-earner couples. Findings in 2008 National Study of the Changing Workforce says Ellen Galinsky, president and co-founder of the Families and Work Institute. For three decades the Institute has been tracking family issues within the changing landscape of the workforce and workplace.

4 NEED FOR 24/7 WORK CULTURE

Enthusiasm in work hours, work intensification and work addiction has grown over the past decade. Many factors have come together to increase hours spent at work, the nature of work itself, and motivations for working hard, significantly among managers and professionals. A concern is then made on why people, families, organizations and society should care about hours spent at work and work addiction. People and organizations have some choice here. Most staff would indeed choose to work fewer hours though few actually notice their preferences. This lays out these selections and hopefully encourages thought and discussion of their deserves. Long work hours and work addiction harms people and their families and doesn't make organizations more effective.

5 TRENDS IN OPERATING IN A 24/7 WORK CULTURE

- Most workaholic organization cultures have performance management ethics that reward the achievement of "things". Sales targets; fee revenues; client satisfaction statistics: these are all valued beyond however they are really achieved or what impact achieving them has on people.
- By take advantage of any opportunities to work on virtual teams, reducing travel time and permitting staff to work from home, whenever possible.
- Management judge others on contributions and results, not the amount of hours within the workplace.

- Organizations and people are look for opportunities to work on international virtual teams, providing them with valuable experience, without the requirement for travel.
- Embrace new technology like webinars and video conferencing.
- Another enduring aspect of full-on organizational cultures is that what they expect workers to deliver isn't typically achievable inside the reach of a contained working day. Thus people notice themselves working into evenings and weekends – through the night – simply to stay up.

As employers become more aware of the trends and therefore the shifts that may have to be compelled to take place for fulfillment, you may be higher positioned to take advantage of this completely different work surroundings if you put these strategies into your everyday work life.

6 CRITICISM

There has been criticism of firms that claim to provide a 24/7 service once actually only their websites, unattended by any workers, area unit in operation. When not only services are supposed to be available 24/7, however staff are expected to adapt their working hours with similar flexibility, such 24/7 workplaces will place staff under conditions that limit their personal life selections and development. Calls for a re-humanization of the 24/7 workplace have therefore been voiced. Some have additionally remarked on the "collective mania" particularly within the united states that takes a kind of pride in the "work at all times" attitude exemplified by the 24/7 concept.

In England, Wales and Northern Ireland the Sunday trading laws prevent many stores opening really 24/7, though they often advertise as such. Some core services such as filling stations are exempt from the law requiring them to close. A campaign against changing the law was supported by many bodies including the Church of England, the Church in Wales and many secular bodies, called Keep Sunday Special.

7 CHALLENGES OF RUNNING A BUSINESS 24/7

If customers expect seven-day service, there are several choices offered to assist cope this demand. If company employs shift workers, must ensure they understand the implications of working unconventional hours. The boom of service industry lies in the smooth transition from a weekday business to a 24/7 operations all around the world.

Open all hours: For firms that have a global presence or that offer business critical services, there sometimes when they ask themselves: "Do we wish to go 24/7?"

In reply companies should answer two questions: do we really need to do this, and can we afford it? Moving operations from the normal working week to 24/7 is a massive jump in terms of logistics and costs. Fortunately, for cash-strapped small businesses, there are plethora of companies that can help give the impression that you're "open all hours".

Staffing options: Call centers and virtual PAs are a cost-effective method of filtering calls and taking messages outside working hours. They answer the phone using company name, and additional advanced call centers will even follow a pre-defined script to identify the nature and urgency of the call.

If company have fewer than 20 support calls during evenings and weekends, this can be an excellent interim solution.

Tipping point: Usually there is a tipping point at which the cost of switching from outsourced staff to an in-house team is relatively negligible, but the operational benefits are quite high. It's at this point that company need to look at the timing and costs associated with a transition.

One major issue is making time to train-up new workers whereas still paying for outsourced services.

8 SUGGESTIONS

To minimize the amount of time that effectively paying double, consider the following:

- Shift schedules: Deciding what hour's firms need new team to work – there are lots of completely different choices available, depending on the shift pattern that suits company and employees. Through researches the advantages and disadvantages of each type and, one can find out what kind of schedules companies competitors use to give an insight into an approach that works well in the industry.
- Health and safety: Before selecting a final shift schedule, consider the health and safety aspects of night and weekend working, especially if company is going to have people in the office by themselves.
- Hiring staff: working nights and weekends puts a strain on employees' personal lives and may be physically and psychologically exhausting. People usually notice that after their circadian (body) rhythms has tailored to night shifts (which sometimes takes 2 or 3 days), getting up in the evening and going to bed in the morning isn't too bad. Psychologically, night working alone can take its toll, so ideally give the individual interesting work to carry out and offer to rotate them on to a dayshift occasionally.
- Managing shift workers: Continuous management and incident reporting is essential.
  Give staff forward notice of recent shift schedules to assist them balance their personal lives outside work. Spend a number of nights with a new recruit, or get them to shadow someone who is experienced before asking them to work alone.

9 CONCLUSION

As the need for 24/7 work culture the extended operating hours grows, more and more organizations are adopting work schedules that require longer and/or multiple shifts. HR Generalists are usually asked to participate in efforts to develop and implement the new work schedules. This is the proper opportunity for them to require on a leadership role, and make sure that the schedule satisfies both the business necessities and preferences of the workforce.

REFERENCES

Bell L (1998), 'Differences in Work Hours and Hours of Preferences by Race in the US', Review of Social Economy, Vol. 56. No.4, pp. 481-500

Blanpain R, Kohler E, Rojot J (eds) (1997), Legal and Contractual Limitations to Working time in the European Union: 2nd Edition, Office for Official Publications of the European Communities.

Cooper C (1996), 'Working hours and health', *Work and Stress*, Vol. 10(1), pp. 1-4

Galambos N, Walters B (1992), 'Work hours, schedule inflexibility and stress in dual-earner spouses', *Canadian Journal of Behavioural Science*, Vol. 24, No. 3, pp. 290-302

Poulton E, Hunt G, Carpenter A. L, Edwards R (1978), The performance of Junior following reduced sleep and long hours of work, Ergonomics, 21, pp. 279-295

Communication and Computing Systems – Prasad et al. (eds)
© 2019 Taylor & Francis Group, London, ISBN 978-0-367-00147-6

Relationship between economic value added and share prices of Hindustan Unilever Limited

Shally Yadav, Mazhar Hasan & Pinkal K. Yadav
Dronacharya Group of Institutions, Greater Noida, India

Honey Gupta
Department of Management Studies, Dronacharya Group of Institutions, Greater Noida, India

ABSTRACT: The concept of Economic Value Added (EVATM) has been propounded as an economic measure of the extent to which a company adds value to shareholders' wealth. Many Indian companies are discerning the key to their long-term progression does not fit in products and services only but in resources that can never be simulated, that is, their unique and distinctive relationship with employees, investors and the community they assist. The main focus of study is to define the shareholders' value (in reference of Economic Value Added) of Hindustan Unilever Limited from1999 to 2017. Hindustan Unilever Limited have very strong and positive coefficient of determination between EVA and Share price during the study period .EVA and Share price of HUL is significant and possesses a linear relationship.

1 INTRODUCTION

Value creation, today, for a competitive lead and to have edge over other - is a widely accepted business objective over profit maximization and wealth maximization. Value is created when all the stake holders perceive a significant difference in quality or benefit, with the result that the offer is capable of commanding a premium relative to competitors offer.

Indian companies have gone through many changes in the last epoch like burden of prudential standards, greater antagonism among companies, etc. This archetype shift in the Indian companies is shown in two dimensions: First, it relates to operational facet especially performance and risk-management system and the second one is very important dimension that relates to structural and external environment. Traditionally the methods of measurement of corporate performance are many. Common bases used are: - Net Profit Margin (NPM), Operating Profit Margin (OPM), Return on Investment (ROI), Return on Net Worth (RONW) etc. Profit after Tax (PAT) is an indicator of profit available to the shareholder and Profit before Interest after Tax (PBIAT) is an indicator of the surplus generated using total funds. ROI is still recognized as the most popular yardstick of profitability measurement. Although these financial data have the advantage of being precise and objective, the limitations are far greater, making them less applicable in today's competitive market. For evaluation of the efficiency of any decision, value creation or value addition aspect is of utmost importance in the present backdrop of corporate governance. In order to maximize shareholder value, decisions must be made as to how best to allocate capital, how to evaluate investment opportunities and how to measure performance.

EVA enables the management to, invest in projects that are critical to shareholder's wealth. This will lead to an increase in the market value of the company. However, activities that do not increase shareholders value might be critical to customer's satisfaction or social responsibility. For example, acquiring expensive technology to ensure that the environment is not polluted might not be of high value from a shareholder's perspective.

2 ECONOMIC VALUE ADDED (EVA): AN OVERVIEW

Economic Value Added (EVA) is a comprehensive measure of operating performance. It measures the change in financial worth of an enterprise from one year to the next. It is a more comprehensive financial measurement tool than net income (revenues minus expenses) alone, because it includes the cost of the capital used to generate that income.

The conception of Economic Value Added was given by a New York based consulting firm M/s Stern Stewart & Co in 1980. The corporate sector in India recognized the prominence of EVA as a result, Indian companies also started connivingEVA. Infosys Technologies Ltd was the first Indian company to shot its EVA in the annual report. EVA tries to calculate true economic profit as it compares actual rate of return with the required rate of return. To make it simple, EVA is the difference of Net Operating Profit After Tax (NOPAT) and the capital charged for both debt and equity (WACC- Weighted Average Cost of Capital). If NOPAT overdoes the capital charge (WACC), then EVA is positive and if it is less than capital charge, EVA is negative.

2.1 *Definition*

"A company can best maximize wealth by leveraging its most distinctive and proprietary assets - the talent, ingenuity, and energy of its people. That's what EVA does, and that's what makes it so powerful. . ."
— Joel M. Stern, CEO, Stern Stewart & Co., 1995

In corporate finance —Economic Value Added or EVA is an estimate of economic profit, which under US accounting can be determined, among other ways, by after making corrective adjustments to GAAP accounting, including deducting the opportunity cost of equity capital. In simple words EVA is —"The monetary value of an entity at the end of a time period minus the monetary value of that same entity at the beginning of that time period."

What separates EVA from other performance metrics such as EPS, EBITDA, and ROIC is that it measures all of the costs of running a business—operating and financing.

2.2 *Reckoning of EVA*

While computing EVA, capital employed represents capital invested at the beginning of the year. The logic behind taking beginning capital for computing EVA is that a company would take at least one year time to earn a return on investment. It may be mentioned here that calculation of EVA involves some tricky issues. Each element of EVA, therefore, has been discussed individually. EVA requires three different inputs for its computation. (A) NOPAT (Net Operating Profit after Tax) (B) Invested Capital (C) Weighted Average Cost of Capital (WACC).

EVA = NOPAT - (WACC × Invested Capital)

2.2.1 *For Net Operating Profit After Tax (NOPAT)*
10Stewart (1991) defined NOPAT as the "Profits derived from company's operations after taxes but before financing costs and non-cash book keeping entries. Such non-cash book keeping entries do not include depreciation since depreciation is considered as a true economic expense. In other words, NOPAT is equal to the income available to shareholders plus interest expenses (after tax).

2.2.2 *For invested capital /capital employed*
Invested capital or capital employed refers to total assets net of non-interest bearing liabilities. From an operating perspective, invested capital can be defined as Net Fixed Assets plus Investments plus Net current assets. Net current assets denote current assets net of non-interest bearing current liabilities. From a financing perspective, the same can be defined as Net Worth plus total borrowings. Total borrowings denote all interest bearing debts

2.2.3 *For Weighted Average Cost Of Capital (WACC)*

For calculating WACC, cost of each source of capital is calculated separately then weights are assigned to each source on the basis of proportion of a particular source in the total capital employed. Weights can be assigned on market value basis or book value basis. Stewart suggested market value basis. WACC can be calculated as below:

$$WACC = E/CE \times Ke + LTB/CE \times Kd$$

Where: E = Equity Capital,
Ce = Capital Employed,
Ltb = Long Term Borrowings,
Ke = Cost Of Equity Capital,
Kd = Cost Of Debt Capital .WACC Includes Two Specific Costs Viz.,
(I) Cost Of Equity (Ke), (II) Cost Of Debt (Kd).

2.3 *Important features and advantages of EVA approach*

- It acts as performance measure which is linked to shareholder value creation in all directions.
- It is useful in providing business knowledge to everyone.
- It is an efficient method for communicating to investors.
- It transforms the accounting information into economic quality which can be easily understood by non-financial managers.
- It is useful in evaluating Net Present Value (NPV) of projects in capital budgeting which is contradictory to IRR.
- Instead of writing the value of firm in terms of discounted cash flow, it can be expressed in terms of EVA of projects.

2.4 *Significance of EVA implementation*

First of all, most Japanese citizens have to acknowledge that they have become investors of companies through pension fund organization, although it may not have been their intention. This means that their pension fund has been operated in the stock market. The influence of the pension fund organization to the stock market is increasing every year, which indicates that they have significant power to the stock market. Under this current trend, it is highly necessary for investors to have a measurement to evaluate company values. EVA has great advantage that it does not show measurements by percentage point, unlike ROE and ROA, but with amount that investors are familiar with. Investors are able to understand the corporate value at a glance, and are able to see if their profit is above the expected investors return or not.

3   SHARE PRICE OF COMPANY

The market price per share of stock or the price per share of stock is a current measure of price not an accounting, or historical, measure of the value of stock like the book value per share, which is based on the information from a company's balance sheet. The market price per share is a financial metric that investors use to determine whether or not to purchase a stock. A company's worth - its total value - is its market capitalization, and it is represented by the company's stock price. Market cap (as it is commonly referred to) is equal to the stock price multiplied by the number of shares outstanding.

3.1 *Intrinsic stock price*

Intrinsic Stock Price is determined by dividing the Intrinsic Worth of the company by the total number of shares outstanding. It reflects the true price of the company's stock as of the date that the Intrinsic Worth is calculated. The Intrinsic Stock Price can therefore be compared to the Actual Stock Price of the company to determine whether the stock is undervalue or overvalued.

3.2 *Actual stock price*

Actual Stock Price refers to the closing market price of the company's stock as of the date that the Intrinsic Worth of the Company is calculated. Typically, this date is one of the fourth quarter-end dates during the year.

3.3 *Latest stock price*

Latest Stock Price refers to the latest available closing market price of the company's stock. Stock prices are affected by many factors simultaneously, as they don't trade in vacuum. It is extremely difficult to enlist all the factors affecting the stock price; however a summary of factors can be presented.

- External Constraints
  - Antitrust Law
  - International Rules and Regulations
  - Central Bank Reserve Policies
  - Employment Related Rules
  - Work and Product Safety Rules and Regulations
  - Environmental Regulations

- Strategic Policy Decisions Controlled by Management
  - Types of Products or Services Produced
  - Production Method Used
  - R & D Efforts
  - Dividend Policy of Company
  - Use of Debt Financing and its Impact on Company
  - Long Term Investment Decisions and its Impact on Company

- Level of Economic Activity of Company
  - Expected Cash Flow
  - Perceived Risk of Cash Flow
  - Timing of Cash Flow
  - Efficient and Effective Use of Corporate Assets

- Corporate Taxes
- Impact of Various News On Share Price
- Perception Factor and Share Price
- Conditions in Financial Market
- Customer Satisfaction Level Achieved by Company leads to generation of more cash flow in future.
- Technology
  - Use of Technology to Reduce Cost, Reduce Inventory, and Produce Quality Goods or Services
  - Adapts Latest Technology to Remain Competitive

- Management
  - Quality of Management
  - Perceived Image of Key Person of the Company by Investors
  - Employee Talent
  - Social Responsibilities Fulfillment by Management
  - Corporate Governance Rules Enforcement by Management
  - Ethics and Share Price

4 REVIEW OF LITERATURE

- Cyrus A. Ramezani, Luc A. Soenen, Alan Robert Jung (2001) analyzed that firms with moderate growth in earnings (sales) show the highest rates of return and value creation for their owners.
- ManojAnand, Ajay Kumar Garg, AshaArora (1999) studied, the rank correlation between economic profit (EP) and PAT, EP and MVA are statistically significant, but it is not substantial. There is a high degree of correlation between PAT and MVA. Hence, EVA, REVA and MVA are better measure of business performance in terms of shareholder value creation and competitive advantage of firm.
- Dierks, P. A. and A. Patel. (1997) suggested that implementing value-added measures into a company is a costly and timely process. Supporters justify the substantial costs and time by pointing out the benefit of optimizing the company's strategy for value creation. A transition to value-added measurements requires serious commitment of the board of directors and senior management to use these measures to manage the business.
- Al Mamun, S. Abu Mansor, (2011) has identified that EVA as an important financial performance measurement tool over the conventional tools around the world. Though, there are mixed evidences on the superiority of EVA (Sharma & Kumar, 2010), EVA has gained attention of corporate giants based on what EVA can be acclaimed to be the most recent and exciting innovation in company performance measures and it has been adopted by the advanced economies as financial performance measurement tool and corporate strategy.
- Sirbu Alexei, (2012) identified that EVA is the methods of calculation, shaping their advantages and disadvantages and exemplifying comparing a series of measurements of the enterprise value created on the basis of financial data. Employees are required to meet or exceed shareholders' expectations by improving the company's Economic Profit or Economic Value Added.

5 OBJECTIVE OF THE STUDY

- To study the trend of EVA and share price of Hindustan Unilever Limited.
- To examine impact of EVA on share price of Hindustan Unilever Limited.

6 SAMPLE DESIGN AND DATA

- Sample Size: Hindustan Unilever Limited
- Duration of Study: 1999 to 2017
- Data Collection: This study is based on Secondary Data which was collected from Annual reports of HUL, journals, publications of Stock exchange Board of India.

7 HYPOTHESIS OF THE STUDY

Ho: Correlation Coefficient of Economic Value Added and Share Price of HUL are not significantly different from zero.

Critical Value to make decision of significance is $\pm.456$(Value is taken from table with degree of freedom of 17(n-2). If the calculated value of correlation is greater than positive critical value or less than negative critical value then null hypothesis will be rejected. Hence, it can be concluded that there is linear relationship between these selected variables during specified period.

8 ANALYSIS

The data analysis is carried out by adopting descriptive statistics, making trend, Pearson Correlation and testing significance:

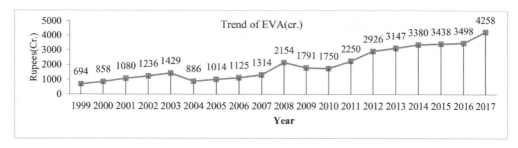

Figure 1.   Trend of EVA; Source: Annual reports of HUL.

Figure 2.   Trend of share price; Source: Annual report of HUL.

Table 1.   Descriptive statistics of EVA and share price.

HUL		
PARTICULARS	EVA(Cr.)	SHARE PRICE(Rs.)
Mean	2012	423.2632
Standard Error	253.0106	77.27668
Median	1750	237.5
Standard Deviation	1102.848	336.8412
Kurtosis	-0.96027	1.600293
Skewness	0.626003	1.534334

Table 2.   Correlation between HUL EVA and HUL share price.

Particular	VALUE
Pearson Correlation Between HUL EVA & HUL Share Price	0.927131
Critical value for significance(Table)	±.456

Table 3.   Coefficient of determination.

COMPANY	COEFFICIENT OF DETERMINANT
HUL	0.859572

It has been found that EVA and Share price of HUL are sharing a very high correlation between them. If we check for significance testing then it can be concluded that correlation is significant between them because correlation value is more than the critical value of significance so EVA and Share price is having linear relationship between them. EVA can be used to determine the share price of HUL.

The coefficient of determination equal to 0.8595 indicates that about 86 % of the variation in Stock price of HUL (the dependent variable) can be explained by the relationship to EVA of HUL(the independent variable).HUL have strong coefficient of determination between EVA and share price.

9 CONCLUSION

The Study was done to determine shareholders value (in terms of Economic Value Added) of HUL during the last 19 years i.e. 1999-2017. HUL have strong coefficient of determination. The coefficient of determination equal to 0.859 indicates that about 86 % of the variation in Stock price of HUL (the dependent variable) can be explained by the relationship to EVA of HUL (the independent variable). This can be considered a good fit to the data. The correlation between EVA and stock price for HUL is 0.927 which is somewhat very strong and positive. EVA and Share price of HUL are significantly correlated. The correlation value is greater than the positive critical value which can conclude the rejection of null hypothesis of correlation is equal to zero or insignificant and It suggests that EVA can be used to determine the share price of HUL.

REFERENCES

Anand, Manoj, Garg, Ajay, and Arora, Asha (1999), "Economic Value Added: Business performance measure of shareholders' value", The Management Accountant, May 1999, pp. 351-356.
Banerjee, Ashok (1997), "Economic Value Added (EVA): A better performance measure", The Management Accountant, December 1997, pp. 886–888.
Banerjee, Ashok and Jain (1999), "Economic Value Added and Shareholder Wealth: An Empirical Study of Relationship", Paradigm, Vol. 3, No. 1, January-June, 1999, pp. 99-133
DebdasRakshit,(2006) EVA based performance measurement: A case study of daburindia limited, Vidyasagar University Journal of Commerce Vol.11, March 2006.
Dr. Anil K. Sharma, SatishKumar, Economic Value Added (EVA) (2010) - Literature Review and Relevant Issues, International Journal of Economics and Finance,Vol. 2, No. 2; May 2010.

Communication and Computing Systems – Prasad et al. (eds)
© *2019 Taylor & Francis Group, London, ISBN 978-0-367-00147-6*

Enhancement of the property of black cotton soil using corn cob ash and iron ore tailings

Nidhi Singh
CE Department, Dronacharya College of Engineering, Gurgaon, India

Tapish Chauhan
CSE Department, Dronacharya College of Engineering, Gurgaon, India

ABSTRACT: Black Cotton soil, which is expansive in nature, have high percentage of clay minerals and show dramatic shrink-swell capacity. It possesses poor geotechnical sub grade characteristics which causes serious problems in construction of any structures on them. In this research an approach is made towards the improvement of various geotechnical properties of black cotton soil by blending it with waste materials like corn cob ash and iron ore tailings which acts as stabilizers. Iron ore tailings, the waste material from mining industry, and corn cob ash, an agriculture waste, are environmental pollutants. The purpose of this study is to define the properties of black cotton soil and to determine the optimum dose of stabilizers, required to improve the strength characteristics of soil, so that the stabilized soil may be used for pavement construction.

1 INTRODUCTION

Expansive soil like black cotton soil, consists of mineral like smectite, bentonite, montmorillonite, beidellite, vermiculite, attapulgite, nontronite, illite and chlorite. They are highly clayey soil grayish to blackish in color, and contain montmorillonite clay mineral which has high expansive characteristics. Black cotton (BC) soils have low shrinkage limit and high optimum moisture content. Soil stabilization deals with physical and chemical methods to make the stabilized soil serve its purpose as pavement component material. Soil stabilization can be achieved using controlled compaction; proportioning or by the addition of suitable admixture or stabilizers. Experiments are being conducted to know the feasibility of using cheaper materials and environmental pollutants such as waste products from industries and agricultural sector as stabilizers. In this paper, Corn Cob Ash (CCA) and Iron Ore Tailings(IOT) are mixed with black cotton soil to study the improvement in strength characteristics.

2 MATERIAL AND METHODOLOGY

2.1 *Material characterization*

Intelligent transportation system mainly has three components the Transport system which may be public transport such as bus, Central controller unit that receives information regarding the status of bus such as bus location, occupancy, route congestion, traffic density etc. and display system basically smart navigation app installed at user mobile to provide information.

2.1.1 *Black Cotton soil (BC)*
The black cotton soil is collected from the Kondagaon district of Bastar region, Chhattisgarh, India (Fig 1) and tests for soil characterization were conducted as per Indian Standards

Specifications. The index properties and strength characteristics of BC soil were tested and are summarized in Table 1.

2.1.2 *Corn Cob Ash (CCA)*

Maize is grown throughout the year in India. Productivity of maize in India is 2.5 MT/Hectare, which produce huge amount of waste in the form of corn cob and corn husk. Corn cob ash is obtained by burning the corn cobs in open ground for 4-5 hours until the cobs are completely burnt (Fig 4). Corn Cob is collected from the banks of Narangi river of Kondagaon district.

2.1.3 *Iron Ore Tailings (IOT)*

Tailings are the materials left over, after the process of separating the valuable fraction from the worthless fraction of an ore. The composition of tailings is directly dependent on the composition of the ore and the process of mineral extraction used on the ore. The waste/tailings that are ultra-fines or slimes, having diameter less than 150 μm, are not useful and hence are discarded. In India approximately 10 – 12 million tons of such mined ore is lost as tailings. The safe disposal or utilization of such vast mineral wealth in the form ultra-fines or slimes has remained a major unsolved and challenging task for the Indian iron ore industry. Mine waste IOT is obtained from National Mineral Development Corporation (NMDC) Chhattisgarh. National Mineral Development Corporation (NMDC) is under the administrative control of the Ministry of Steel, Government of India.

2.2 *Methodology*

The various laboratory tests conducted to know the change in properties of the BC soil are Specific Gravity test, Proctor Compaction, California Bearing Ratio (un soaked and soaked) and Unconfined Compressive Strength. These tests are performed on soil by mixing CCA and IOT individually at varying percentages. Once the optimum percentage of CCA and IOT is obtained, they are mixed together in appropriate proportions with the soil and all the tests repeated. To verify the test result and to substantiate the results, micro level studies have done with the help of Scanning Electron Microscope (SEM), Energy Dispersive X-ray Spectroscopy (EDS), Differential Thermal Analysis (DTA) and Thermo Gravimetric Analysis (TGA).

3 RESULT AND DISCUSSION

3.1 *Properties of virgin soil*

Table 1. Index properties and strength characteristics of BC soil.

Characteristics	Description	Characteristics	Description
Specific gravity	2.63	Clay(%)	46
Liquid Limit(%)	40	Texture based on plasticity chart	CL
Plastic Limit (%)	19.86	Optimum Moisture Content (%)	15.1
Shrinkage Limit(%)	10.81	Maximum Dry Density(gm/cc)	1.76
Plasticity Index (%)	20.14	California Bearing Ratio, Un-soaked (%)	3.82
Free Swell Index(%)	40	California Bearing Ratio, soaked (%)	2.36
Sand(%)	14	Unconfined Compressive Strength(kgf/cm2)	1.52
Silt(%)	40		

3.2 *Standard compaction test*

The standard compaction test is conducted in laboratory as per IS-2720-PART-7-1980 for different mix percentage (2%, 4%, 6%, 8%, 10%) of corn cob ash (CCA) and iron ore tailings (IOT) with black cotton soil.

Table 2. OMC & MDD of BC soil for various percentages of CCA & IOT.

Compositions	Proportions	OMC (%)	MDD(g/cm3)
BC Soil + CCA	2%	16%	2.25
	4%	19.5%	2.19
	6%	20.2%	2.15
	8%	20%	2.13
	10%	19.8%	2.11
BC Soil + IOT	2%	17.46%	2.23
	4%	17.5%	2.23
	6%	16.4%	2.22
	8%	16.6%	2.28
	10%	15.8%	2.29

3.3 *Unconfined Compressive Strength (UCS)*

The standard compaction test is conducted in laboratory as per IS-2720-PART-7-1980 for different mix percentage (2%, 4%, 6%, 8%, 10%) of CCA and IOT.

Table 3. UCS values of BC soil for various percentages of CCA & IOT.

Compositions	Proportions	UCS (kgf/cm2)
BC Soil + CCA	2%	1.702
	4%	1.775
	6%	2.965
	8%	2.177
	10%	2.049
BC Soil + IOT	2%	1.979
	4%	2.001
	6%	2.101
	8%	2.024
	10%	1.901

3.4 *California Bearing Ratio (CBR)*

This is a penetration test developed by the California Division of highways, as a method for evaluating the stability of soil sub-grade and other flexible pavement materials. The method combines a load penetration test performed in the laboratory or in-situ with the empirical

Table 4. Soaked CBR of BC soil for various percentages of CCA & IOT.

Compositions	Proportions	CBR (%) (Soaked)
BC Soil + CCA	2%	2.24
	4%	3.03
	6%	3.14
	8%	2.98
	10%	2.86
BC Soil + IOT	2%	1.46
	4%	2.92
	6%	2.97
	8%	2.43
	10%	1.79

design charts to determine the thickness of pavement and of its constituent layers. Soaked CBR tests are conducted in the laboratory for various mix percentage of CCA and IOT in the soil.

4 CONCLUSIONS

When black cotton soil comes in contact with water it causes structural damage and also creates many problem during construction process. Soil stabilization is the technique adopted to improve the index and strength parameters of black cotton soil. In this study, Corn Cob Ash (CCA) and Iron ore Tailings (IOT) which are waste products as well as environment pollutants are used as admixtures to improve the geotechnical properties of black cotton soil. The optimum CCA and IOT content experimentally observed is 6%. Based upon the above study following conclusions is drawn:

1. The standard proctor parameters i.e., MDD for black cotton soil increased from 1.76 g/cm3 to 2.31 g/cm3 for the optimum mix proportion and the OMC value increased from 15.1 % to 15.3 %
2. Soaked CBR value for the optimum mix proportion increased from 2.36 % to 5.16 % which shows that black cotton soil when added with 6% CCA and IOT can be used for construction of flexible roads in rural areas where traffic volume is less.
3. After the stabilization of soil, the test results showed that UCS value increased from $1.515 \, kgf/cm^2$ to $2.818 \, kgf/cm^2$
4. SEM analysis also confirms voids ratio is decreasing with addition of these admixtures.
5. Even though the breaking of of montmorillonite crystals is not predominant from TGA analysis, DSC analysis shows that there is a change in crystalline structure which indicates that some amount of stabilization has taken place and hence change in properties.

REFERENCES

Akinwumi, I. I., and O. I. Aidomojie. (2015). Effect of Corncob ash on the geotechnical properties of Lateritic soil stabilized with Portland cement. *International Journal of Geomatics and Geosciences* 5(3): 375-392

Etim R.K.,Eberemu A.O., Osinubi K.J.,(2017) Stabilization of black cotton soil with lime and iron ore tailings admixture. *Transportation Geotechnics* 10: 85-95

Gupta, Chayan & Sharma, R.K. (2016). Black Cotton Soil Modification by the Application of Waste Materials. *Periodica Polytechnica Civil Engineering*, 60(4): 479-490.

Hardaha, Rajendra Prasad, Agrawal, M. L. & Agrawal, Anita. (2013). Use of fly ash in black cotton soil for road construction. *Recent Research in Science and Technology* 5(5), Pp 30-32

Haresh D Golakhiya, Chandresh D. Oluborode, Savani (2015). Geotechnical properties of black cotton soil stabilized with furnace dust and dolomitic lime 2(8): 810-823

Hakari, Udayashankar D., & Puranik, S. C. (2012) Stabilisation of black cotton soils using fly ash, Hubballi-Dharwad municipal corporation area, Karnataka, India. *Global Journal of Research In Engineering* 12(2): 21-29

Jadhav, Sanjeev Tanaji, and Sushma Shekhar Skan (2014).Feasibility Study of Improving Properties of Black Cotton Soil Using Industrial Wastes. *Current Trends in Technology and Science*, 3(4):283-287

Jimoh, Yinusa A., and O. Ahmed Apampa. (2014). An evaluation of the influence of corn cob ash on the strength parameters of lateritic soils. *Civil and Environmental Research* ,6(5): 1-10.

Kumar, BN Skanda, Suhas R.,S.U.Shet, J.M.Srishaila. (2014). Utilization of iron ore tailings as replacement to fine aggregates in cement concrete pavements. *International Journal of Research in Engineering and Technology*, 3(7): 369-376.

Communication and Computing Systems – Prasad et al. (eds)
© 2019 Taylor & Francis Group, London, ISBN 978-0-367-00147-6

Gravitational search optimized resource allocation in underlay cognitive radio networks

Chandra Shekhar Singh
ECE Department, Dronacharya College of Engineering, Gurgaon, India

B.M.K. Prasad
Dronacharya College of Engineering, Gurgaon, India

ABSTRACT: This paper focuses on underlay cognitive radio network with sets of half-duplex downlink and uplink secondary users and a full-duplex cognitive base station. The secondary user shares multiple channels with the primary user. The proposed resource allocation technique maximizes the sum rate of all the secondary users based on transmit and interference power constraints. The power allocation can be performed using concave difference approach and allocated power is optimized using gravitational search optimization algorithm. The performance of the proposed work is evaluated with the conventional approaches.

1 INTRODUCTION

The scarcity of spectrum resources is one of the challenging trends for enabling future generations of wireless communication systems (Mili et al. 2017). It is one of the major sustainable and flexible resources than conventional energy harvesting because more and more wireless transmitters are deployed and the Radio frequency (RF) signals radiated by ambient transmitters are consistently available (Xu Chi et al. 2017). Cognitive radio (CR) based on sensing, where Primary user (PU)s are assumed to be unconscious of Secondary user (SU) activities, PU's could take initiative in spectrum marketing by deciding the quantity of spectrum to be leased so as to maximize their utilities within their interference tolerance (Zhang Yujie et al. 2016). In addition, spectrum marketing is also considered as an effective way to realize spectrum sharing since PUs could charge SUs for dynamically using licensed spectrum(Yi, Changyan et al. 2015).

Suboptimal and optimal power allocation policies are examined in, where the total capacity of the CR system is maximized under a primary receiver (PRx) interference limit (Saki Hadi et al. 2015). In addition, to ensure smooth primary service operation, one of the most essential tasks for CRs is to avoid causing undesirable interference on the licensed users. Accurate spectrum sensing and cross-channel estimation capabilities, however, are complex and costly (Lagunas, Eva et al. 2015). Excessive co-channel interference is the main limitation of the high frequency reuse systems, which, on their own, fall short of meeting the increasing data rate demand (Mallick, Shankhanaad et al. 2015). However, it is necessary to optimally allocate the resources not only to improve the performance of the Cognitive radio networks (CRN) but also to keep the interference introduced in the PU bands below the prescribed limit (Dadallage, Suren et al. 2015).

The main contribution of this paper is for analyzing the issue of joint power and channel allocation based on optimal power constraints. In our work, the underlay CRN is designed with the cognitive base station (CBS) and a set of uplink and downlink secondary users (SU) sharing several channels with the primary user (PU). It is based on the objective of improving the sum rate of SU with respect to optimal transmit power constraints. The problem is considered as the non-convex optimization of Lagrange dual function. Improved concave difference approach and Exhaustive randomization algorithm is proposed for solving the optimization problem in terms of channel allocation. For getting the optimal power constraints, gravitational search optimization algorithm is proposed. The performance of the proposed algorithm is verified with extensive simulations.

The organization of the paper is described as follows. Section 2 describes the design of CRN. Section 3 describes proposed approach of spectrum allocation. Section 4 illustrates the results and performance evaluation of proposed approach. Section 5 discusses significant aspects of our work and concludes.

2 SYSTEM MODEL OF PROPOSED COGNITIVE RADIO NETWORK (CRN)

The proposed model of underlay CRN is shown in Figure 1. It consists of various downlink and uplink SUs which are responsible for sharing multiple channels with the PU. The channel and a set of downlink and uplink channels are represented as M, O and P

The residual SI's power gain at channel $i \in P$ is denoted as k_i^r. The power gain of the channel $i \in P$ from CBS to downlink SU $m \in O$, from uplink SU $k \in M$, to downlink SU $m \in O$, from uplink SU $k \in M$ to the PU, from uplink SU $k \in M$ to the CBS, from CBS to PU are denoted as $l_{i,m}^d$, $l_{i,k,m}^s$, $k_{i,k}^p$, $l_{i,k}^u$, and k_i^p respectively. The power gain of the channel is relevant to SUs like $l_{i,m}^d$, $l_{i,k,m}^s$, $l_{i,k}^u$, and k_i^r and CBS and it can be determined using channel estimation approaches. Proper signaling was applied between the PU and CRN for obtaining the power gain $k_{i,k}^p$, and k_i^p relevant to PU. The decision about the allocation of channel $i \in P$ to downlink SU $m \in O$ or uplink SU $k \in M$ is represented by the index of binary channel allocation $\beta_{i,k}$ and $\gamma_{i,m}$.

The optimization problem P1: $R1$: max $T(r^u, \beta, r^d, \gamma)$

$$T(r^u, \beta, r^d, \gamma) = \sum_{k \in M} T_k^u(r_k^u, \beta_k, r_m^d, \gamma_m) + \sum_{m \in O} T_m^d(r_k^u, \beta_k, r_m^d, \gamma_m) \tag{1}$$

$$T_k^u(r_k^u, \beta_k, p_m^d, \gamma_m) = \sum_{i \in P} \beta_{i,k} \ln \left(1 + \frac{r_{i,k}^u l_{i,k}^u}{\sigma^2 + \sum_{m \in O} \gamma_{i,m} r_{i,m}^d k_i^r} \right) \tag{2}$$

Where, the residual SI is denoted as $\sum_{m \in O} \gamma_{i,m} r_{i,m}^d k_i^r$ and the noise power is denoted as σ^2. In the downlink SU, the achievable rate is denoted as

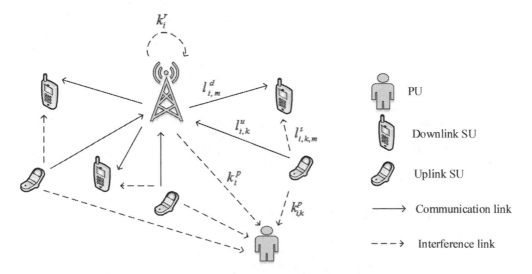

Figure 1.   System model of proposed CRN.

$$T_m^d(r_k^u, \beta_k, r_m^d, \gamma_m) = \sum_{i \in P} \gamma_{i,m} \ln \left(1 + \frac{r_{i,m}^d l_{i,m}^d}{\sigma^2 + \sum_{k \in M} \beta_{i,k} r_{i,k}^u l_{i,k,m}^s} \right) \quad (3)$$

Constraints:

The power constrains at the transmitter of SUs and CBS is denoted as

$$\sum_{i \in P} \beta_{i,k} R_{i,k}^u \le r_k^{\max}, \forall k \in M \quad (4)$$

$$\sum_{i \in P} \sum_{m \in O} \gamma_{i,m} R_{i,m}^d \le r_c^{\max} \quad (5)$$

$$\sum_{i \in P} (\sum_{k \in M} \beta_{i,k} r_{i,k}^u k_{i,k}^p + \sum_{m \in O} \gamma_{i,m} r_{i,m}^d k_i^p) \le S^{\max} \quad (6)$$

3 PROPOSED APPROACH OF SPECTRUM ALLOCATION

The optimization problem discussed in above section is non-convex and it can be modelled with the Lagrangian function. It is given as

$$N(r^u, \beta, r^d, \gamma, \lambda, \mu) = T(r^u, \beta, r^d, \gamma) - \lambda(\sum_{i \in P} \sum_{m \in O} \gamma_{i,m} R_{i,m}^d - R_c^{\max})$$
$$-\mu(\sum_{i \cup P} (\sum_{k \in M} \beta_{i,k} r_{i,k}^u k_{i,k}^p + \sum_{m \in O} \gamma_{i,m} r_{i,m}^d k_i^p) - S^{\max}) \quad (7)$$

Where, λ and μ represents the dual variables. It is difficult to obtain the optimal solution for this problem. In order to resolve this issue, the SCA approach is utilized by finding the non-convex objective function for the sequence of convex functions. The concave difference approach is used for this convex approximation.

The optimal power for the channel allocation index one is slected with GSA optimization. The flowchart for the proposed optimization algorithm is described in Figure 2. The values are initialized with the number of iterations. The fitness function for each agent is computed to evaluate the fitness value. The global best and worst positions are computed for updating the power values. For that the power value M is computed and the velocity is updated in adition with the position of that agent. The number of iterations can be terminated if the stopping criterion has been obtained.

The algorithm provides best selection of power value when the channel is allocated for both uplink and downlink secondary users. When the channel allocation index of uplink and downlink communication is one, then the optimization algorithm is utilized to compute the power value. Here the optimal power value is selected in which it improves the energy efficiency of underlay CRN.

4 EXPERIMENTAL RESULTS AND ANALYSIS

In this section, we verify the effectiveness of the proposed algorithms. It is assumed that $P = 4$, $\sigma^2 = 1$, and all the channels involved in Rayleigh fading. Unless otherwise specified, the mean values of the channel power gains of the residual SI are assumed to be 0.1 and the mean values of all the rest channel power gains are assumed to be unitary. Besides, it is assumed that the transmit power limits of all uplink SUs are same, i.e, $r_k^{max} = r_s^{max}$, $\forall k \in M$. The implementation parameters used in our work is described as follows.

The performance of power allocation is computed by energy efficiency calculation. The energy efficiency is computed for the proposed work and it is compared with the existing approaches like adaptive maxmin power calculation, SCALE, distributed SCADA, and centralized SCADA. At 20 dBm CBS power, the energy efficiency of the proposed approach is improved up to 0.24. The energy efficiency is less for other power values such as 5 dBm, 10 dBm and 15 dBm. There is a greater increase in energy efficiency when the power value is increased from 0 dBm to 5 dBm and 5 dBm to 10 dBm. The energy efficiency comparison for the proposed approach is compared with various existing approaches in Figure 3.

In Figure 3, the secondary sum efficiency is computed for the proposed and existing approaches. Performance is computed by varying the power value as 1 dBm, 5dBm, 10 dBm,

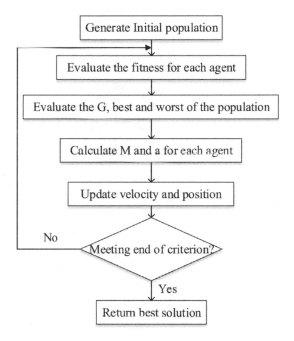

Figure 2. Gravitational search optimization algorithm.

15 dBm, 20 dBm, 25 dBM, 30 dBm and 35 dBm. The higher value indicates the best performance in terms of power allocation. The improved performance is obtained for the proposed approach. For the proposed approach, the power value goes higher than 1.24. The adaptive algorithm has the lowest performance when compared with the proposed one. There is a

Table 1. Implementation parameters.

Number of channel	4
Number of uplink users	4
Number of downlink users	4
Channel power gain for residual SI	0.1
Maximum transmit power of CBS	10 dBm
Maximum transmit power of uplink SU	0 dBm

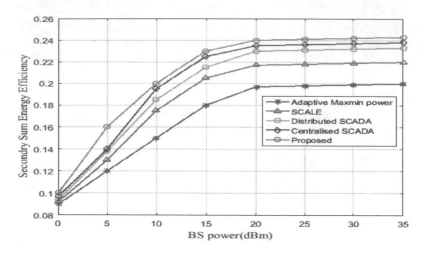

Figure 3.   Performance comparison for sum energy efficiency calculation for varying the CBS power.

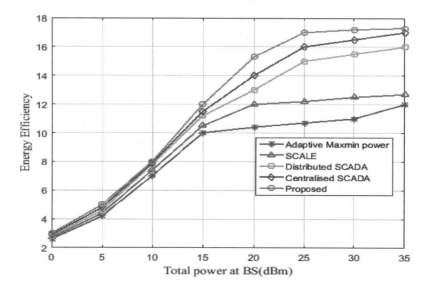

Figure 4.   Energy efficiency comparison for different base station power.

heavy deviation in performance when the BS power reaches 15 dBm. Figure 4 shows the energy efficiency comparison for different base station power.

The energy efficiency computation by varying the number of iteration is shown in Figure 5. The overall power value for the proposed approach lies between 38 and 39. For the other existing approaches the value is below 38. The reduced value shows the inefficiency of the conventional approaches in terms of energy computation.

5   CONCLUSION

In this paper, the channel allocation is proposed with optimal transmit and interference power constraints. The dual optimization procedure is enabled for both power and channel allocation. The proposed algorithm is based on maximizing the sum rate of both uplink and downlink secondary user. For enabling the resource allocation, Exhaustive randomization method and

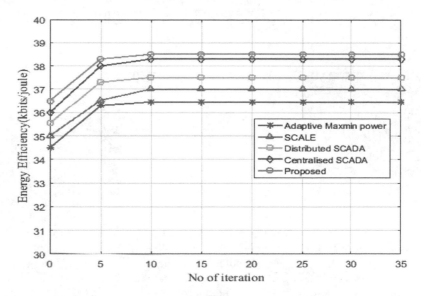

Figure 5. Energy efficiency comparison for varying the number of iterations.

Lagrange dual method for joint allocation is used, When allocating resources, the power is also allocated with respect to transmit and interference power constraints. The concave difference approach is enabled with an optimization algorithm for optimally allocating power. The optimal power value is obtained with the optimization algorithm Gravitational search optimization. The joint channel and power allocation performance of the underlay cognitive radio network is evaluated with the performance measures such as sum rate and BER. The enhanced performance of the proposed CRN is shown by comparing it with the conventional approaches.

REFERENCES

Mili, Mohammad Robat, and Leila Musavian. "Interference Efficiency: A New Metric to Analyze the Performance of Cognitive Radio Networks." *IEEE Transactions on Wireless Communications* 16, no. 4 (2017): 2123-2138.

Xu, Chi, Meng Zheng, Wei Liang, Haibin Yu, and Ying-Chang Liang. "End-to-end Throughput Maximization for Underlay Multi-hop Cognitive Radio Networks with RF Energy Harvesting." *IEEE Transactions on Wireless Communications* (2017).

Zhang, Yujie, and Shaowei Wang. "Resource allocation for cognitive radio-enabled femtocell networks with imperfect spectrum sensing and channel uncertainty." *IEEE Transactions on Vehicular Technology* 65, no. 9 (2016): 7719-7728.

Yi, Changyan, and Jun Cai. "Multi-item spectrum auction for recall-based cognitive radio networks with multiple heterogeneous secondary users." *IEEE Transactions on Vehicular Technology* 64, no. 2 (2015): 781-792.

Saki, Hadi, and Mohammad Shikh-Bahaei. "Cross-layer resource allocation for video streaming over OFDMA cognitive radio networks." *IEEE Transactions on Multimedia* 17, no. 3 (2015): 333-345.

Lagunas, Eva, Shree Krishna Sharma, Sina Maleki, Symeon Chatzinotas, and Björn Ottersten. "Resource allocation for cognitive satellite communications with incumbent terrestrial networks." *IEEE Transactions on Cognitive Communications and Networking* 1, no. 3 (2015): 305-317.

Mallick, Shankhanaad, Rajiv Devarajan, Roya Arab Loodaricheh, and Vijay K. Bhargava. "Robust resource optimization for cooperative cognitive radio networks with imperfect CSI." *IEEE transactions on wireless communications* 14, no. 2 (2015): 907-920.

Dadallage, Suren, Changyan Yi, and Jun Cai. "Joint beamforming, power, and channel allocation in multiuser and multichannel underlay MISO cognitive radio networks." *IEEE Transactions on Vehicular Technology* 65, no. 5 (2016): 3349-3359.

Communication and Computing Systems – Prasad et al. (eds)
© 2019 Taylor & Francis Group, London, ISBN 978-0-367-00147-6

Algorithms for maximal independent set problems

Anil Kumar Yadav
University Institute of Engineering and Technology, C.S.J.M University, Kanpur, India

Manisha Manjul
G B Pant Engineering College, New Delhi, India

ABSTRACT: This study involves the development of Maximal Independent Set (MIS) for an arbitrary input graph G. Here we investigate the polynomial-time algorithm using various techniques like greedy, random, divide and conquer and dynamic programming for maximal independent set of a simple graph. An algorithm is be considered 'efficient' if its running time is polynomial: $O(n^c)$ for some constant c, where n is the size of the input. The computation of a maximal independent set of minimum size is NP-hard for general graphs.

1 INTRODUCTION

Connected Dominating Set (CDS) is a powerful technique that is commonly used in ad-hoc wireless networks to reduce interference, provide energy-efficient transmission, enable low-complexity routing and so on. We study the problem of CDS control over plane networks with the disk-connectivity model. Specifically, we consider networks consisting of n points that are indexed (and uniquely identified) by the natural numbers 1, ..., n with locations $x_1, ..., x_n \in R^2$. A given point may only be directly connected to any other neighboring point that is within a certain communication range R > 0 in a bidirectional manner

Independence is one of the elementary concepts in graph theory. For a given graph G, an independent set is a set of vertices in a graph, no two of which are adjacent. A maximum independent set is an independent set of largest point size. Usually one is interested in maximal independent sets, i.e., independent set such that no further point can be added without violating the property of independence. An independent set of maximum cardinality is called maximum. One of the central properties of maximal independent set is that they are dominating sets, i.e., every vertex outside of the set has at least one neighbor in the set (Hedar et al, 2018; Henning et al, 2009; Raczek et al, 2011) A minimum dominating set is a dominating set containing the least possible number of points. The major application of dominating set and maximal independent set in an ad hoc and wireless sensor networks (Garey et al, 1979; Yadav et al, 2015)[6-10]. It is a special type of wireless network where no point has a priori knowledge about the other points. In sensor networks, dominating sets also help the sensing task itself. Since points located close to each other sense similar values, only a dominating set of the nodes is needed to monitor an area. In this paper we study various algorithms in simple graphs and find partial solutions to some problems posed in Li et al, 2005. The computation of a maximal independent set of minimum total size is NP-hard for general graphs (Garey et al, 1979; Yadav et al, 2015). This paper discussed various algorithms for the maximal independent set problems and its expected running time is shown in Table 1.

Definition1. (Independent Set). An independent set is a subset of points U ⊆ V, of a given graph G, such that no point in U are adjacent. An independent set is maximal if no point can be added without violating independence property.

Table 1. Expected running time of various algorithms for MIS problem.

Techniques	Algorithms	Time Complexity
Greedy	Algorithm 1	$O(n)$
Randomized	Algorithm 2	$O(\log n)$
	Algorithm 3	$O(\log n)$
Divide and Conquer	Algorithm 4	$O(n^{\log_{4/3} 4})$
Dynamic Programming	Algorithm 5	$O(n)$
Iterative	Algorithm 6	$O(n)$

2 RELATED WORK

Number of approximation algorithms for minimum connected dominating set problem has been proposed in the literature. Wan et al. (2004) proposed a distributed algorithm for the MIS problem in Unit Disk Graph (UDG). It has constant approximation ratio of 8. Li et al (2005). proposed another distributed algorithm with approximation ratio of (4.8+ln5). As in Wan et al, 2004, at the first phase, an MIS is computed. At the second phase, a Steiner tree algorithm is used to connect nodes in the MIS. In randomized algorithms making a random choice is fast. An adversary is powerless, randomized algorithms have no worst case inputs. It is believe that Randomized algorithms are often simpler and faster than their deterministic counterparts. There are certain drawbacks of randomized algorithms which may be listed as: Getting true random numbers is almost impossible. In the worst case, a randomized algorithm may be very slow. There is a finite probability of getting incorrect answer. However, the probability of getting a wrong answer can be made arbitrarily small by the repeated employment of randomness. Randomized algorithms can be of two types: 1) [Las Vegas] A randomized algorithm always returns a correct result. But the running time may vary between executions. 2) [Monte Carlo] A randomized algorithm that terminates in polynomial time, but might produce erroneous result. The definition of MIS is given as follows:

Definition 2: A set of vertices of MIS form a connected component if for every edge$(u, v) \in MIS$, there is a path from u to v. Moreover, for all $x \notin MIS$, MIS U {x}is not a connected component i.e MIS is maximal. If MIS is includes all vertices in the graph, then the underlying graph is connected.

3 ATTACKING THE MAXIMAL INDEPENDENT SET PROBLEMS

3.1 *Greedy algorithm*

Greedy algorithm is consisting of phases. In each phase an independent set of induced sub graph $G' = (V', E')$ of G is added to the current MIS and v U N(v) is deleted from G'. Starting with $V'=V$ and ending with $V' \neq \Phi$ we get MIS. As G' is induced sub-graph of G, it is uniquely determined by its vertex set $V(G')$.

Algorithm 1: The Iterative Greedy MIS Algorithm

Input: A connected undirected graph G(V,E).
Output: MIS
1. Initialize: MIS = Φ, $V'=V$
2. While ($V' \neq \Phi$) do
     (i) Choose $v \in V'$
     (ii) Set MIS = MIS U {v}
     (iii) Set $V'= V' \backslash (v \cup N(v))$

3. 3. Return MIS

The execution body in the while loop is the phase of the algorithm.

3.2 *Randomized MIS algorithm*

Here, we discuss a better MIS algorithm on simple graph. We are unable to find fast deterministic algorithms, so we go for randomization. In addition to the input, the algorithm uses a source of pseudo random numbers. The randomized MIS algorithm makes random choices to become MIS node or not with probability $1/(2d(v))$. The expected running time depends on the random choices, not on any input distribution. The algorithm is more formally presented as follows.

Algorithm 2: The Fast Randomized MIS Algorithm

Input: A connected undirected graph G(V,E).
Output: MIS
Proceed in rounds consisting of phases. In each phase execute the following:
1. Each point v marks itself with probability $1/(2d(v))$ where $d(v)$ denotes current degree of v
2. If no higher degree neighbors marked,
   MIS = MIS U {v}
   Else v unmark itself again (break ties arbitrarily)
3. Delete all points that joined the MIS plus their neighbors, as they cannot join the MIS anymore
4. Return MIS

A node with smallest random value will always join the MIS. So, there is always progress. Another fast randomized MIS algorithm is discussed as:

Algorithm 3: The Fast Randomized MIS Algorithm

Input: A connected undirected graph G(V, E).
Output: MIS
Proceed in rounds consisting of phases. In each phase execute the following:
1. Each point chooses a random value $r(v) \in [0,1]$ and sends it to its neighbors point.
2. If $r(v) < r(w)$ for all neighbors $w \in N(v)$, point v enters the MIS and informs the neighbors
3. If v or a neighbor of v entered the MIS, v terminates (and v and edges are removed), otherwise v enters next phase.
4. Return MIS

All the random choice in above algorithms are independent. One can easily check that algorithm always produces a MIS of G.

3.3 *Divide and conquer*

Here, we will try to solve MIS problem for specific class of graphs called trees graphs denoted by G = (V, E). Following is the algorithm which returns the MIS in given tree. We define neighbor of point v as set $\{u|(v, u) \in E(T)\}$ and denote it by N (u). The algorithm is more formally presented as follows.

Algorithm 4: Divide and Conquer method to find MIS in tree graph

---

Input: A connected undirected tree graph G (V, E).
Output: MIS
1. if G (T) = Φ then return Φ
2. end
3. Find $v \in V$ (T) such that V (T)\{v} can be partitioned into A and B set such that
   $|V (T)|/4 \leq |A|, |B| \leq 3|V (T)|/4$
4. $I_1 \leftarrow$ MIS in T\{v}
5. $I_2 \leftarrow$ MIS in T\N (v)
6. return max$\{I_1, \{v\} \cup I_2\}$

The time complexity is T (n) = $O(n^{\log_{4/3} 4})$

3.4 *Dynamic programming*

Here, we will see how these dynamic programming algorithms over graphs of bounded tree-width are used as subroutine in designing polynomial time approximation schemes (PTASes), exact algorithms and parameterized algorithms. The algorithm is more formally presented as follows.

Algorithm 5: Finding MIS in tree Graph using Dynamic Programming

---

Input: A connected undirected tree graph T (V, E) rooted at r.
Output: Maximal Independent Set (MIS)
  1. for u in V (T) do
  2. A[u] ← 0, B[u] ← 0
  3. End for
  4. Leaf (T) ← All leaf nodes (points) of T'
  5. for u in Leaf (T) do
  6. A[u] ← 1
  7. End for
  8. V'← Point in $V(T')$ in the ascending order of distance from root r for u in V' do for all w which are children of u do
  9. A[u] ← A[u] + B[w]
10. B[u] ← B[u] + max{A[w], B [w]}
11. End for
12. End for
13. return max{A[r], B [r]}

The running time of this algorithm is O(n).

3.5 *ID based MIS*

In id based scheme, scan all the points in arbitrary order. If a point say u, does not violate independence, add u to the MIS. If u violates independence, discard u.

Algorithm 6: ID based MIS Algorithm

Input: A connected undirected graph G(V, E) with each vertex having unique ID
Output: Maximal Independent Set (MIS)
Every point v executes the following steps
1. **If** all neighbors of v with larger identifiers have decided not to join the MIS then
2. point v decides to join the MIS
3. **End** if
4. **Return** MIS

The time complexity of Id based Algorithm is O(n)

4 RESULTS AND THEORETICAL ANALYSIS

In this section of the paper, we discuss the theoretical analysis of discussed algorithms.
    Lemma 1. *Algorithm 2 has logarithmic run time i.e $\log_2 n$.*
    Proof. In general the remaining problem size is divided in two in each round. The idea is to remove each node with constant probability (e.g., ½) in each round. So half of the nodes vanish in each round. Because sub-problem sizes decrease by a factor of 2 each time we go

down one round, we eventually must reach a boundary condition. How far from the root do we reach one? The sub problem size for a node at round i is $n/2^i$. Thus, sub-problem size hits $n=1$ where, $n/2^i = 1$ or $n=2^i$ or $i=\log_2 n$.

M be the set of marked nodes in Step 1 (prob. $1/(2d(v))$), and let H(v) be the set of neighbors of v with higher degree or same degree and higher identifier. Nodes once marked, likely to join. The probability of nodes that does not join MIS but is marked is small. A marked neighbor must be the reason for v not to join MIS. This neighbor must have higher degree or ID.

Lemma 2. *Probability that does not join MIS but is marked is small i.e 1/2.*
Proof.
$P[v \notin MIS | v \in M] = P[\exists w \in H(v), w \in M | v \in M$
$\leq \sum_w \in H(v) P[w \in M]$
$= \sum_w \in H(v) .1/(2(d(v))$
$\leq \sum_w \in H(v) .1/(2(d(v))$
$\leq d(v)/(2d(v))$
$= 1/2$

Lemma 3. *[Joining MIS] Node v joins MIS in with probability $p \geq 1/(4d(v))$.*
Proof. Let M be the set of marked nodes in step 1of Algorithm 2. Let H(v) be the set of neighbors of v with higher degree, or same degree. Using independence of the random choices of v and nodes in H(v) in Step 1 we get

$$[P_r[v \in MIS] = P_r[v \in MIS | v \in M]P_r[v \in M]$$

Since, we have computed in Lemma 2, that $P_r[v \notin MIS | v \in M] = \frac{1}{2}$
and according to Algorithm 2, we have $P_r[v \in M] = 1/(2d(v))$
So, $P_r[v \in MIS] = P_r[v \in MIS | v \in M] P_r[v \in M] 1/2.1/(d(v)) 1/(4d(v))$.
Lemma 4. *[Independent MIS] Two MIS X and Y are independent if*

$$P_r[(X = x) \cap (Y = y)] = P_r[X = x].P_r[Y = y]$$

Lemma 5. *Given a sample space G=(V,E) and an event A in the sample G, let $MIS_A = I\{A\}$, then* E[MIS_A] =Pr{A}, *where* $I\{A\}$ *is indicator random variable.*
Proof. $E[MIS_A] = E[I\{A\}] = 1.Pr\{A\} + 0.Pr\{A'\} = Pr\{A\}$
Where A' denote G-A, the complement of A. 1 means the node is going to join the MIS and 0 means node is not joining the MIS.

5 CONCLUSIONS

In this paper we have discussed one greedy algorithm, two randomized algorithms one divide and conquer and one dynamic programming for the generation of MIS in asimple graph. We have also discussed the theoretical analysis of the proposed algorithms. Expected running time of various algorithms for MIS problem is shown in Table 1.

REFERENCES

Hedar, A.R., Ismail, R., El-Sayed, G.A. 2018. Two Meta-Heuristics Designed to Solve the Minimum Connected Dominating Set Problem for Wireless Networks Design and Management. J Netw Syst Manage. https://doi.org/10.1007/s10922-018-9480-1
Henning, M.A., L"owenstein, C., & Rautenbach, D. 2009. Remarks about disjoint dominating sets. Discrete Math. 309, 6451–6458.
Raczek, J., Janczewski, R., Ma lafiejska, A & lafiejski M. Ma .2011. Private communication.
Wan, P.-J., Alzoubi, K.M., Frieder, O. 2004. Distributed construction of connected dominating set in wireless ad hoc networks. Mobile Networks and Applications 9(2), 141–149.

Li, Y.S., Thai, M.T., Wang, F., Yi, C.-W., Wan, P.-J., Du, D.-Z.2005. On greedy construction of connected dominating sets in wireless networks. Wiley Journal on Wireless Communications and Mobile Computing 5(8),927–932.

Garey, M.R. & Johnson, D.S. 1979. *Computers and Intractability: A Guide to the Theory of NPCompleteness*, W.H.Freeman and Company, San Francisco.

Yadav AK, Yadav RS, Singh R, Singh AK. (2015). Connected dominating set for wireless ad hoc networks: a survey. Int J Eng Syst Model Simulation 7(1):22–34

.

Secure computing

Communication and Computing Systems – Prasad et al. (eds)
© 2019 Taylor & Francis Group, London, ISBN 978-0-367-00147-6

Detection and localization of copy move forgery using improved centre symmetric local binary pattern for enhanced accuracy and robustness

Surbhi Surbhi & Umesh Ghanekar

Department of Electronics and Communication Engineering, National Institute of Technology, Kurukshetra, India

ABSTRACT: The detection of copy-move tampering in digital images becomes difficult with reducing size of tampered area and in presence of post processing operations. Most of the methods successfully detect a copy move tampering of size up to 32×32 pixels tampered region, whereas the proposed method can detect tampering of size up to 14×14 pixels and robust against additive white gaussian noise, gaussian blurring, JPEG compression and scaling. The proposed method has used evaluation at pixel level using a texture descriptor to detect tampered region. Experimental results exhibit that the proposed algorithm outperforms most of the well-known algorithms with minimum false detection rate.

1 INTRODUCTION

With the advancement in image processing techniques, new developments in multimedia communication and ease in using image editing tools, the image contents can be easily changed when transferred electronically. This leads to image authentication as a necessity. Image tampering detection techniques can be categorized in two types: a) active techniques and b) passive techniques (Birajda and Manka, 2013). In active techniques, a digital code is embedded into image and verification is done by checking the true code with the retrieved code from the image. But every time, it is not possible to add some sort of code at the time of image formation. Passive image tampering detection techniques resolve this problem in which verification is done by finding the artifacts produced in the image due to various manipulative operations.

2 BACKGROUND

One of the most commonly used tampering operation is: copy-move tampering. In this, a portion of an image is copied and pasted in the same image to conceal an important object or to produce a non-existing situation in the scene. There are two types of copy move tampering detection techniques: 1) Block based techniques; 2) Key point based techniques; In block based techniques image is divided into overlapping blocks and FVs are extracted from each block. Mostly four types of FVs are used: Transform based, Dimension reduction based, Moment based and Spatial domain based. Transform based algorithms such as Improved _DCT (Huang et al., 2011), DCT_SVD (Zhao and Guo, 2013) and statistical properties of DCT coefficients (Kaushik et al., 2015) are used to detect copy move image tampering. Under dimension reduction techniques Singular Value Decomposition (SVD) (Kang and Wei, 2008) are explored. In moment based techniques, the authors have used 24 blur invariant moments (Mahdian and Saic, 2007) and Hu moments (Liu, et al., 2011). Under spatial technique category the authors have used fast copy move technique (Lin et al., 2009), expanding block method (Lynch et al., 2013), histogram of oriented gradient (HOG) (Lee et al., 2015) and normalized cross correlation (Warbhe et al., 2016). The key points based techniques used Scale-Invariant Feature Transform (SIFT) (Amerini et al., 2013) and Speeded Up Robust Features (SURF) (Jing and Shao, 2012) to detect duplicated regions. The authors in (Ardizzon et al., 2016) used SIFT, SURF and Harris points to extract triangle shape structure in the image. The local properties of these shapes are used to detect duplicated regions.

3 METHODOLOGY

The proposed algorithm has four phases: Preprocessing of the Input Image, Feature Extraction Phase, Block Matching Phase and Classifier. The three phases of proposed method and the proposed descriptor has been explained below.

3.1 Preprocessing phase

Let's assume suspect image 'I' has size X*Y. The color images are converted to grayscale images for further processing.

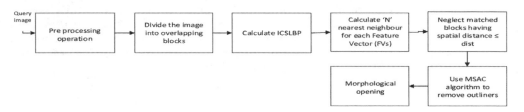

Figure 1. Flowchart of proposed approach.

3.2 Feature extraction phase

The image is divided into overlapping blocks of size '$B*B$'. After using sliding window method, we get 'OB' number of overlapping blocks.

'Separation' represents the pixel distance between two overlapping blocks. In feature extraction phase, the proposed method used histogram of improved centre symmetric local binary pattern (ICSLBP) as the feature vector of the block. ICSLBP is a proposed texture descriptor based on center symmetric local binary pattern (CSLBP (Heikkkila et al., 2006)). It represents an image by micro patterns. In each micro pattern, the gray values of diagonally opposite pixels are compared and the larger one is represented by one. Then the binary number is converted to its decimal equivalent. Figure 3 shows the CSLBP coding procedure. But there are many chances that two different patterns may have same CSLBP code as shown in Figure 4, which increases the false matches. So, in addition to the original CSLBP, the proposed technique also stores the mean of micropattern. The ICSLBP of a reference pixel is calculated by equating the gray values of diagonally opposite pixels around the reference pixel and mean of neighbour pixels & reference pixel (micro pattern).

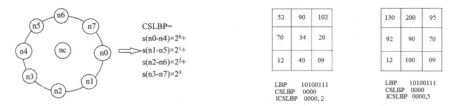

Figure 2. CSLBP coding procedure.

Figure 3. Two different patterns have same LBP and CSLBP code, but different ICSLBP code.

266

Figure 4.   (a) AWGN (SNR=25 dB); (c) Gaussian blur ((size= [3,3], σ=0.5)), (e) scaling ([0.2,0.2]) (g) JPEG compression (Q−80). Detection results are shown by (b), (d), (f) and (h) corresponding to (a),(c), (e), and (g).

Assuming the reference pixel with co-ordinates (k_r, l_r) have N number of equally spaced surrounding pixels mounted on circumference of a circle having radius R. Bilinear Interpolation is used to obtain the pixel values of circular window from a rectangular window. ICSLBP is calculated as follows:

3.2.1 *First step*
The gray values should be between 0-255, we divided these values into sixteen equal ranges and denoted these ranges by 0, 1, 2..., and 15 respectively. The code for mean of micropattern is calculated by using this method. As natural images have edges, corners, spots and flat areas which are uniform and can be expressed by a single pattern, named as uniform CSLBP (UCSLBP). An UCSLBP is called uniform if and only if it has at most two bitwise transitions. UCSLBP is expressed by:

$$UCSLPB_{N,R} = \begin{cases} \sum_{i=0}^{\frac{N}{2}-1} s\left(g_i - g_{\left(i+\frac{N}{2}\right)}\right) \times 2^i, & U\left(UCSLBP_{N,R}\right) \leq 2 \\ N+1 & otherwise \end{cases} \tag{2}$$

The number of bitwise transitions is expresses by U(UCSLBPN,R) and g_i represents the gray value of neighbor pixels.

3.2.2 *Second step*
In second step, the proposed algorithm calculated the minimum decimal value by doing bitwise right rotation. The expression for this is given below:

$$IUCSLBP^m_{N,R} = \begin{cases} min.\left\{ROR\left(UCSLBP_{N,R}, i\right)|i == 0,, N\right\} & if \ U\left(UCSLBP_{N,R}\right) \leq 2 \\ N+1 & otherwise \end{cases} \tag{3}$$

Where, ROR (a, i) represents bitwise 'i' right rotations.

3.2.3 *Third step*
The proposed variant of CSLBP is given below:
For each block, the histogram of *ICSLBP* is worked as feature vector. The feature vector of every blocks is stored in a feature matrix in row-wise manner.

$$ICSLBP(k_r, \ l_r) = \left[IUCSLBP^m_{N,R}(k_r, \ l_r), \ range \ of \ mean \ of \ micropattern\right] \tag{4}$$

3.3 Block matching phase

The proposed algorithm has used exhaustive search to find 'N' best nearest neighbours corresponding to each FV i.e. for each block. The matching blocks which have spatial distance less than 'dist' threshold between them should be ignored. The method used overlapping blocks, but the duplicated regions are not overlapping therefore, the shift vector is counted only if the reference co-ordinates of two matched blocks have euclidian distance greater than threshold distance (dist).

$$\sqrt{(k_1 - k_2)^2 + (l_1 - l_2)^2} > dist \tag{5}$$

3.3.1 M-estimator sample consensus Algorithm (MSAC):
MSAC is used to exclude the outliers and to increase the accuracy.

3.3.2 Post processing:
Morphological opening has been used to remove the isolated pixels and fill the holes in the marked regions.

4 EXPERIMENT SETUP AND RESULTS

4.1 Setup

The simulations were carried out on Dell Inspiron 15 5000 series having corei5 on Matlab 2014a. Tampered images were obtained by using Matlab and Adobe Photoshop on datasets (Ng, T.T., Hsu, J.). The value of different parameters used in the simulation are given: B=7, dist=10, N=8, R=1, Tshift ≥ 0.4× (max (C)).

4.2 Performance evaluation matrices

We compute the potential of proposed method at pixel level, the Detection Accuracy Rate (DAR) and False Positive Rate (FPR) are used as evaluation matrices.

4.3 Dataset

Tampered images were obtained by using MATLAB on datasets. The image dataset (Ng, T. T., Hsu, J) has monochrome images and color images, which are resized to 256×256 for this experiment. The total collection from these datasets has been further divided into five groups I_0, I_1, I_2, I_3 and I_4 to make our own datasets which are shown in Table. I.

Table 1. Dataset used in the experiment.

Group	Subgroup	Images used	Tampering operations	Parameters
I_0	$I_{00}, I_{01}, I_{02}, I_{03}$	200	Simple Copy move (SCM)	32×32 pixels, 24×24 pixels, 16×16 pixels, 14×14 pixels
I_1	$I_{10}, I_{11}, I_{12}, I_{13}$	200	SCM+ Guassisn Blurring	24×24+ (size=[3,3]/[5,5], σ=0.1, 1)
I_2	$I_{20}, I_{21}, I_{22}, I_{23}$	200	SCM+ AWGN	24×24+30 dB/25 dB/20 dB/15 dB
I_3	I_{30}, I_{31}	100	SCM+ scaling (SC)	24×24+ SC ([0.1,0.1], [0.2,0.2])
I_4	I_{40}, I_{41}, I_{42}	75	SCM+JPEG compression (JC)	24×24+ JC (Q=75, 80, 90)

4.4 Comparison methods

To assess the efficiency of proposed method, we have compared the results with seven other techniques: IDCT+SVD (Zhao and Guo, 2013), statistical properties of DCT coefficients (Kaushik et al., 2015) and HOG (Lee et al., 2015). The experimental results have been discussed in the section 3.5.

4.5 Effectiveness and accuracy test

Tampering images were categorized into two groups: (1) Images with regular shape copy move area and (2) images with irregular shape copy move area. Regular shaped copy move area images further divided into four groups, which are 14×14, 16×16, 24×24 and 32×32 pixels respectively.

Figure 4 is showing detection result in presence of post processing operation on copy move area. The DAR and FPR values resulting from various algorithms for different sizes of tampered areas are shown in Table 2. From these tables it can be easily observed that when the tampered region is of bigger size i.e. 32×32 all the algorithms work satisfactory, however with decreasing size of tampered region the detection performance deteriorates with most of the existing methods whereas the proposed method works satisfactory. As shown in column of Table 2, some of the algorithms failed to detect tampering of size 14×14 pixels. The method also performs well in presence of gaussian blur, awgn, scaling and JPEG compression as can be seen through simulation results. Table 3. Table 6 give a conclusion that the proposed algorithm also performs well in the presence of all mentioned post processing operations.

Table 2.   Effect of simple copy move tampered area size on DAR and FPR values.

Tampered Area size	32×32		24×24		16×16		14×14	
	DAR	FPR	DAR	FPR	DAR	FPR	DAR	FPR
DCT+ SVD	1	0.06	1	0.09	1	0.14	1	0.164
HOG	0.89	0.11	0.85	0.16	CD	CD	CD	CD
DCT_moment	1	0.09	1	0.01	CD	CD	CD	CD
Proposed	1	0.02	1	0.03	1	0.04	1	0.11

Note: CD stands for can't detect

Table 3.   DAR and FPR values under the effect of gaussian blurring.

Amount of gb	w=3, σ=0.5		w=3, σ=1		w=5, σ=0.5		w=5, σ=1	
Method	DAR	FPR	DAR	FPR	DAR	FPR	DAR	FPR
DCT+ SVD	0.895	0.14	0.86	0.17	0.893	0.15	0.79	0.25
HOG	CD	CD	CD	CD	CD	CD	CD	CD
DCT_moment	0.927	0.09	0.92	0.09	0.923	0.01	0.741	0.26
Proposed	0.829	0	0.923	0	0.9292	0.007	0.828	0.02

Table 4.   DAR and values under the effect of AWGN.

AWGN	SNR=30 dB		SNR=25 db		SNR=20 db		SNR=15 db	
Method	DAR	FPR	DAR	FPR	DAR	FPR	DAR	FPR
DCT+ SVD	0.99	0	0.99	0.006	0.998	0	0.98	0
HOG	CD	CD	CD	CD	CD	CD	CD	CD
DCT_moment	1	0.31	1	0.35	CD	CD	CD	CD
Proposed	0.99	0	1	0.01	1	0	0.987	0

Table 5.   DAR and FPR values under the effect of scaling.

Scaling	[0.1,0 .1]		[0.2, 0.2]	
Method	DAR	FPR	DAR	FPR
DCT+ SVD	CD	CD	CD	CD
HOG	CD	CD	CD	CD
DCT_moment	CD	CD	CD	CD
Proposed	0.964	0.14	0.95	0.185

Table 6.   DAR and FPR values under the effect of JPEG compression.

JPEG comp.	Q=75		Q=80		Q=90	
Method	DAR	FPR	DAR	FPR	DAR	FPR
DCT+ SVD	CD	CD	CD	CD	CD	CD
HOG	CD	CD	CD	CD	CD	CD
DCT_moment	CD	CD	CD	CD	CD	CD
Proposed	0.9492	0.1	0.8773	0.1814	0.9329	0.0385

5   CONCLUSION

This paper has presented a copy move image tampering detection algorithm using a texture descriptor. The algorithm has proposed a texture descriptor which is more resilient to noise, gaussian blur, scaling and JPEG compression. The experimental results showed that the proposed method has ability to detect tampering of size up to 14×14 pixels area effectively, where all other existing methods used in the study performs poorly. The simulation results proved that it has higher accuracy and lesser false matches as compared to other methods in presence of AWGN, gaussian blur, JPEG compression and scaling. Thus, we presume, the proposed approach can identify tampered image and localize tampered area very accurately.

REFERENCES

Amerini, I., Ballan, L., Caldelli, R.,Bimbo, D. A. and Serra, D. G.,(2011) 'A SIFT-based forensic method for copy-move attack detection and transformation recovery', *IEEE Trans. on Information Forensics and Security*, Vol. 6, No.3, pp.1099-1110.

Amerini, I., Ballan, L., Caldelli, R., Bimbo, D. A., Tongo, D. L. and Serra, G. (2013) 'Copy-move forgery detection and localization by means of robust clustering with J-linkage', *Signal Process: Image Commun.*, Vol. 28, No. 6, pp. 659–669.

Ardizzone, E., Bruno, A. and Mazzola, G. (2016) 'Copy–Move Forgery Detection by Matching Triangles of Keypoints', *IEEE Trans. Inf. Forensics Secur.*, Vol. 10, No. 10, pp. 2084-2094.

Birajdar, K. G. and Manka H. (2013) 'Digital image forgery Detection using passive techniques: A survey', *Digital Investigation*, Vol. 10, No. 3, pp.226-245.

Cortes, C. and Vapnik, V., (1995). 'Support-vector networks'. *Machine Learning*. Vol. 20 No.3, pp. 273–297.

Heikkkila, M., Pietikainen, M., Schmid, C. (2006) 'Description of Interest Regions with Center-Symmetric Local Binary Patterns', In: Kalra P.K., Peleg S. (eds) Computer Vision, Graphics and Image Processing. Lecture Notes in Computer Science, vol 4338. Springer, Berlin, Heidelberg.

Huang, Y., Lu, W., Sun, W. and Long, D. (2011) 'Improved DCT-based detection of copy-move forgery in images', *Forensic Sci. Int.*, Vol. 206, No. 1-3, pp. 178–184.

Jing, L. and Shao, C. (2012) 'Image copy-move forgery detecting based on local invariant feature', *Journal of Multimedia*, Vol. 7, pp. 90–97.

Kang, X. and Wei, M. S. (2008) 'Identifying Tampered Regions Using Singular Value Decomposition in Digital Image Forensics', *Proc. of the 2008 International Conference on Computer Science and Software Engineering*.

Kaushik, R., Bajaj, K.R. and Mathew, J. (2015) 'On image forgery detection using two-dimensional Discrete Cosine Transform and Statistical *Moments' Proceeding of the 4th International Conference on Eco-friendly Computing and Communication Systems*, pp. 130-136.

Lee, C. J., Chang, P. C. and Chen, K. W. (2015) 'Detection of copy–move image forgery using histogram of orientated gradients', *Information Sciences*, Vol. 321, No. C, pp. 250-262.

Lin, J. H., Wang, W. C., and Kao, T. Y. (2009) 'Fast Copy Move Forgery Detection, *WSEAS Trans Signal Processing*, 2009, Vol. 5, No.5, pp. 188-197.

Liu, G., Wang, J., Lian, S. and Wang, Z. (2011) 'A passive image authentication scheme for detecting region-duplication forgery with rotation', *Journal of Network and Computer Applications*, Vol. 34, No.5, pp. 1557–1565.

Lynch, G., Shih, Y. F. and Liao, H. (2013) 'An efficient expanding block algorithm for image copy-move forgery detection', *Information Sciences*, Vol. 239, pp. 253–265.

Mahdian, B. and Saic, S. (2007) 'Detection of copy-move forgery using a method based on blur moment invariants', *Forensic Sci. Int.*, Vol. 171, No.2-3, pp. 180–189.

Ng, T.T., Hsu, J. and Chang, F. S., 'Columbia Image Splicing Detection Evaluation Dataset', Available at:http://www.ee.columbia.edu/ln/dvmm/downloads/AuthSplicedDataSet/AuthSplicedDataSet.htm/.

Sharma, S., and Ghanekar, U. (2015) 'A Rotationally Invariant Texture Descriptor to Detect Copy Move Forgery in Medical Images' *Proc of IEEE international Conference on Computational Intelligence & Communication Technology* (CICT), pp: 795-798.

Torr. S. H. P. and Zisserman, A. (2000) 'MLESAC: A New Robust Estimator with Application to Estimating Image Geometry', *Computer Vision and Image Understanding*, Vol. 78, No.1, pp. 138–156.

Warbhe, D. A., Dharaskar, V.R. and Thakare, M. V. (2016) 'A Scaling Robust Copy-Paste Tampering Detection for Digital Image Forensics', *Proc. of the 7th International Conference on Communication, Computing and Virtualization, 2016*, Procedia. Computer Science 79, 458-465.

Zhao, J. and Guo, J. (2013) 'Passive forensics for copy-move image forgery using a method based on DCT and SVD', *Forensic Sci. Int.*, Vol. 233, No. 1-3, pp. 158–166.

Communication and Computing Systems – Prasad et al. (eds)
© *2019 Taylor & Francis Group, London, ISBN 978-0-367-00147-6*

Polynomial based key management security schemes in wireless sensor networks: A review

Aarti Gautam Dinker & Vidushi Sharma
School of ICT, Gautam Buddha University, Greater Noida, India

ABSTRACT: Security is the main concern for the Wireless sensor networks (WSNs) especially because of its resource constrained environment and deployment in the hostile environment. An adversary can monitor and manipulate the network provided necessary skill sets to breach the integrity and confidentiality of the network. There are several security schemes developed which may be based on cryptography, secure routing, secure location, key management etc. The use of keying material and key generation is the inseparable part of most of the security schemes. The Key management schemes can be symmetric or asymmetric in nature. Symmetric key cryptography based schemes are preferred in WSN to save the resources for longer time. In this paper, we have explored different polynomial based key management schemes which come under Symmetric key cryptographic schemes.

1 INTRODUCTION

With limited energy, memory, storage space and processing power the sensor nodes have been deployed in the network and enabled with security techniques. These security techniques stored in nodes and are consisting of algorithms, keying materials and other details of the network to be able to perform suitably in such untrusted and unreliable network. To mitigate the effects of the various attacks and unauthorized intrusion in WSN (Akyildiz et al., 2002), there is requirement of first preventing our nodes from the network attacks like Sybil attack, blackhole attack etc. and maintain data confidentiality and integrity, there comes the encryption and authentication techniques to be deployed. Various security mechanisms are used in the WSNs which enable the security in the network and protect it from various security attacks like node capture attack, denial of service attack (Dinker & Sharma, 2016) etc. The encryption and authentication techniques may involve the deployment of cryptography based techniques and algorithms. The keying data in the node is very crucial and has to be stored and distributed in a very secure manner. This requires separate schemes for managing keys, keying material and algorithms called as key management security scheme (KMSS) serving the very purpose of securing the data as well as network information from various attacks. There are many criteria defined for evaluation of KMSS like network connectivity, security etc. Initially various cryptographic techniques based security schemes were introduced to ensure the security in the WSNs like Symmetric key cryptographic techniques based SPINS (a suite of security protocols optimized for sensor networks with two secure mechanisms SNEP (sensor network encryption protocol) and μTESLA(micro Timed Efficient Stream Loss-tolerant Authentication)) (Dinker & Sharma, 2017). Also there are also the mechanisms which utilize both symmetric and asymmetric cryptography called hybrid cryptographic techniques. Key management is the process of key distribution, generation, establishment, revocation and renewal. In general the key management schemes (KMSs) are composed of two phases: in first phase all the sensor nodes are deployed in the dynamic or static network environment. In second phase is key generation and establishment takes place. Considering the resource constraint environment of WSNs, symmetric key management schemes are preferred over asymmetric key management schemes. In this paper, we have reviewed the polynomial based KMSs. The rest of this paper is organized into five sections. The second section presents the objectives of key management schemes. The third section discusses the various polynomial based keying methods. The fourth section identifies the problems and issues followed by conclusion.

2 OBJECTIVES OF KEY MANAGEMENT SCHEMES

Key management security schemes are designed and implemented with the intent to provide WSNs with security and achieving other performance and efficiency related metrics. Performance related metrics are used to evaluate a key management scheme on the basis of its performance in terms of nodes network connectivity, scalability, resilience and security against attacks and malicious nodes. In addition to these, the efficiency related metrics evaluate such schemes in terms of power consumption, communication overhead, storage and power consumption. The key management scheme may or may not be able to fulfil the entire criteria as it is very unlikely that all the metrics exist in one single scheme.

- *Network connectivity.* Only the connectivity between adjacent nodes is concerned. Namely, the information can be securely transmitted between any two adjacent nodes.
- *Security against attacks.* WSN nodes are mostly exposed, which can easily lead to eavesdropping and node capturing etc. Thus the key management system should make sure that messages sent between nodes are not stolen by adversary. If a node is captured, its key information about other nodes should not be leaked.
- *Node Resilience.* Thus the key management system should make sure that messages sent between nodes are not stolen by adversary. If a node is captured, its key information about other nodes should not be leaked.
- *Scalability.* A key management system should also ensure that participated network keeps a high degree of connectivity after addition or removal of nodes.
- *Storage complexity.* Because the storage capacity of WSN nodes is limited, the key stored into the nodes reaches as less information as possible.
- *Communication Overhead-Low energy consumption.* The energy consumption of the nodes depends on data communication. The communication should be reduced as much as possible in order to remain less energy consumes.

Polynomial based schemes utilize the polynomials either univariate or multivariate for key generation. These polynomials are symmetric type, so that they can be exchanged between sensor nodes and keys being generated and established. The aim is to present the existing polynomial based keying schemes implemented in WSNs and explore the undefended issues and problems for improving security of the network.

3 VARIOUS POLYNOMIAL BASED KMS

Key distribution and generation through polynomials support secure and efficient communication between nodes. There are many polynomial based schemes modelled, analyzed, and designed for distributing the keys to the nodes.

3.1 *Key distribution scheme for dynamic optimal conferences*

This scheme (Blundo et al. 1093) utilized the symmetric polynomials variables t and degree k with coefficients over GF(q), $q > n$, where n is the number of users. Key distribution in pairs using polynomial pools used randomly chosen bivariate polynomials. If there is only one polynomial remaining, then the key pre-distribution takes place on the basis of that polynomial. Generally pairwise key establishment has three steps as setup, direct key establishment and path key establishment. The scheme enabled the secure communication to the remote server, user authentication, inter networking and group communication through polynomials. This scheme was quite secure and robust but scalability was a concern.

3.2 Polynomial pool-based pairwise key pre-distribution scheme

This scheme was proposed (Liu & Ning 2003) for WSN security. The two more key pre-distribution schemes; the first was based on random subset assignment and second was based on grid. The First scheme was called Polynomial based Key pre-distribution for sensor network. In this technique, Setup server generates the t-degree polynomial such that eq. 1, over the finite field.

$$f(x, \ y) = \sum_{i, \ j=0}^{t} a_{ij} x^i y^j \tag{1}$$

The generated polynomial is symmetric in nature such that $f(x, \ y) = f(y, x)$. Here for all the sensors I, the server generate the polynomial share of $f(x, \ y)$. Similarly for the sensor j, the server generate polynomial share of $f(x, \ y)$. Sensor nodes I compute the common key $f(i,j)$ by evaluating $f(i, \ y)$ at the point j, similarly sensor node j compute the common key $f(j, \ i) = f(i,j)$ by evaluating $f(j, \ y)$ at point i. The main advantage of polynomial based key pre-distribution is that there is no communication overhead in this technique but the main limitation of this scheme is that the increased storage cost for a polynomial share and computational time. The second key distribution scheme called Polynomial pool based key pre distribution was similar to the polynomial based key distribution technique but used the pool of random bivariate polynomials. The drawback is the enhanced communication overhead in the entire network.

3.3 Key distribution using random subset assignment

This scheme (Liu & Ning 2003) was proposed which used random strategy of choosing the subset of polynomial from the pool of the polynomial. In this subset assignment takes place followed by polynomial share discovery and path discovery. In this server generate the set of t-degree polynomial over the finite field and randomly select the subset of polynomial and assign the polynomial share to each sensor node. Then nodes have to discover the polynomial share to establish shared key. The probability p of two sensor nodes establishing the shared key is estimated eq. 2 where S is the polynomial set, S' is the subset and I denotes the requesting sensor node.

$$p = 1 - \prod_{i=0}^{s'-1} \frac{s-s'-i}{s-i} \tag{2}$$

If there is a neighboring node d between requesting node and destination then probability of two sensor nodes establishing the pairwise key Ps is given as eq. 3.

$$Ps = 1 - (1-p) * \left(1 - p^2\right)^d \tag{3}$$

This scheme provided better security than the q-composite, EG as the use of random pairwise key scheme doesn't allow the reuse of the same key by multiple pair of sensors.

3.4 Grid based polynomial key pre distribution scheme

In order to reduce the communication overhead experienced in polynomial pool based key pre-distribution, (Liu et al 2005) suggested the grid based key pre-distribution scheme. Here we have N sensor nodes and we consider (m*m) grid where $m = \sqrt{N}$ where each point on the grid is assigned the coordinates of sensors (i,j). On the grid each row and column is assigned a polynomial $f_i^r(x, \ y)$, $f_i^c(x, \ y)$ respectively. On the grid if we consider the sensor node I, whose coordinates are (i,j), then the polynomial share for this sensor node will be $f_i^c(x, y)$ and $f_j^r(x, \ y)$. Here the coordinates of the sensor node will be represented in the binary form and the ID of the sensor node will be the concatenation of binary representation of x and y coordinates.

This scheme works in two phases as subset assignment and polynomial based share discovery. To establish the pairwise key, first the sensor node j checks whether the sensor node I is present in the same row and same column that is if $C_i = C_j$ or $R_i = R_j$. If both the conditions are true then the sensor nodes will establish the pairwise key otherwise they will find the intermediate node to communicate with each other. This scheme had lower communication overhead as compared to previous scheme and greater level of authenticity also a limitation that when a node not able to find intermediate node directly, then the communication and storage overhead increases.

3.5 Closest polynomials pre-distribution scheme

The authors (Liu et al. 2005) have presented this scheme also which utilized the knowledge of expected node deployment location for the pre-distribution of the keys (pre-distribution) in WSN. The authors divided the deployment area/field into small fields and called them cells. Then each node is given with a set of polynomial shares which is associated to the cells nearest to that cell where the concerned node will be deployed. The improved performance provided better security as node compromise till large fraction was prevented. The probability of establishing direct keys between two nodes does not depend on the total polynomials in the pool.

3.6 Improved key distribution mechanism (IKDM)

An improved key management scheme IKDM (Cheng & Agrawal, 2007) was proposed for large-scale wireless sensor networks. IKDM scheme is a pairwise key generating scheme which utilizes the bivariate polynomial in three tier hierarchical WSN. IKDM is divided in three phases namely key pre-distribution phase, inter-cluster pairwise establishment phase and inter-cluster pairwise key establishment phase. In this scheme a unique pairwise key can be generated between two cluster heads and a cluster head and its member node in a cluster. Two cluster heads exchange their node identities and evaluate unique key using their stored polynomial. The IKDM provided reasonable security against node compromise and security attacks. This scheme is efficient in terms of storage, communication overhead and good network authenticity.

3.7 LU matrix-polynomial based key pre distribution schemes

This proposed keying method utilized LU decomposition with polynomial for key pre-distribution (Zheng et al. 2008). Unlike most of the polynomial based schemes, polynomial based key pre distribution schemes using LU decomposition provide 100 percent connectivity regardless of the number of keys stored in the sensor nodes. This scheme forms the symmetric matrix of ($m*m$) order and decompose it to form two matrix L and U. Now the row of matrix L and column of matrix U is distributed to all the sensor nodes. To reduce the memory storage of the sensor node and make it independent of the compromised nodes row and columns were stored in encoded form. The L and U matrix has zero and non-zero part. This technique will reduce the memory storage of the sensor nodes. When two nodes want to communicate with each other then they will exchange the row and will calculate the vector product to form the symmetric key $k_{ij} = k_{ji}$ and will further form the common polynomial using the basic polynomial based key pre-distribution. This scheme is resilient to node capture and storage overhead is also reduced.

3.8 Multivariate key pre-distribution scheme (MKPS)

A KMS using bivariate polynomials for key pre-distribution was proposed (Delgosha & fekri 2009.). It is the combination of the deterministic as well as random scheme and used the ultivariate polynomial to establish the link key. They begin with the set up phase which is deterministic in nature. They assigned a unique d-tuple as the id of each node as a vector $I = (i_0, \ldots . i_{d-1})$ where $i_0 \ldots . i_{d-1}$ are non negative values and the vertices of the virtual hypercube are used to assign the IDs to the nodes. In this scheme, symmetric d-variate polynomials $f_i^j(x_0, \ldots \ldots, x_{d-1})$ where $I \in [m]$ and $j \in [d]$ ($m := \sqrt[d]{n}$, $n=$ number of IDs) are randomly generated by the sink. Then the nodes are deterministically assigned with the set of shares of *t* degree multivariate polynomials. Before the network commencement, nodes are stored with its ID and the coefficients of all *d* polynomials. Then Link-Key Establishment phase takes place which enable any two nodes with hamming distance of one from each other will establish the (*d-1*) common key. MKPS doesn't establish the path key because of the increase in communication overhead instead it obtains the probability of network connectivity using the giant component of the network. This scheme has reduced overhead, good network connectivity and resilience.

3.9   *Dynamic Generation of the Polynomial (DGP) scheme*

Min Li et al. (2010) presented a key generation method which used dynamically generated polynomials for securing heterogeneous WSNs. In DGP sensor nodes are pre-stored with a secret key K to protect cluster key establishment phase. In DGP MAC(ID) is computed by each node and utilised key K for encrypting messages during key management. Then each normal sensor node (Li) sends the encrypted message C_Li = EMK(ID‖MAC(ID)) towards cluster head called H-sensor. H-Sensor computes the hash of these ids and multiplies the hashed ids $h(L_i)$ of L-sensors to calculate polynomial using a pre-defined significant value. DGP enhanced the lifetime of the network and supported large sensor networks but incurs storage overhead as the number of digits doubled in the final product and energy consumption is increased.

3.10   *Public key and polynomial based key pre-distribution scheme*

Jie and Guohua (2012) proposed a key pre-distribution scheme for large-scale wireless sensor networks using public key and polynomials. In this scheme a secure and unique communication link needed to be formed for interaction of two neighboring nodes. This scheme was able to provide good with reduced storage overhead and better key connectivity in large-scale wireless sensor networks.

3.11   *Lightweight Polynomial-based Key Management protocol (LPKM)*

Another polynomial based KMS was proposed called Lightweight Polynomial-based Key Management Protocol (LPKM) (Fan & Gong 2013) for distributed WSNs. In LPKM, the sensor nodes may secure one-to-one and one-to-many communications more flexibly and reliably by establishing different types of keys. In this scheme, a node can establish three keys for communication. A broadcast based local probabilistic source authentication also takes place with the help of neighboring nodes. In addition to this, LPKM is able to protect the network from different security attacks like node impersonation, node cloning attacks etc. LPKM withstands the changes in topology with slightly increased computational and communication overhead.

3.12   *Polynomial-based key management for intra and inter group communication*

Piao et al. (2013) proposed a secure keying method for safe inter and intra group communication which uses polynomials *H(x)* and *P* respectively. This scheme is efficient because the members and the head of the group can securely share secret key inside the group without encrypting or decrypting the key. It also has the capability of re-keying and updating the keys in case of node joining (node *w*) and leaving (node *i*) the group through group controller Using new polynomial the nodes which are group members including newly joined node can compute new group key and their own individual key. This scheme maintains the forward and backward secrecy also. This scheme does not depend on heavy message broadcasting for inter group communication, so storage and communication overhead is less with light messages.

3.13   *Deployment knowledge and polynomial based key management*

Banaie et al. (2015) presented a key pre-distribution and management scheme using deployment knowledge. This scheme utilizes random polynomial functions and matrices. In this scheme *k* bivariate polynomials are generated by the setup server and their subset is given to the cluster head. The server also generates the matrix for each cluster head to be used for key generation. The nodes can establish pair-wise path key when the two nodes are in same cluster and also when they are in different cluster. The proposed mechanism has increased storage efficiency and network resilience.

3.14 *Deterministic and non-interactive group key pre-distribution scheme*

Harn and Hsu (2015) proposed a deterministic and non-interactive group key pre-distribution and establishment scheme in WSNs. This scheme utilizes multivariate polynomial in Z_N, where N denotes the RSA modulus. In this a trusted key distribution center is used for selecting, creating shares of the polynomial to be pre-stored in nodes. These shares were used to establish group key. The *m* sensor nodes needed storage space to be $(m-1)(k+1)$ integers from Z_N. As this scheme was non-interactive so no communication overhead incurred in establishing group key. Resiliency against node capture was not addressed in this scheme. In other scheme of this paper the shares of trivariate polynomial are generated and distributed to sensors by trusted third party. Each sensor node receives two univariate polynomials shares, $(s\,j,1(x),\ s\,j,2(x))$. Each node has to be loaded with $2(k+1)$ coefficients from ZN. As per the Horner's rule, the computational cost of this scheme is very less. The communication cost is also reduced.

3.15 *Efficient Key Management (EKM)*

For secure group communication an efficient keying mechanism EKM scheme (Mahmood et al. 2017) was proposed with the application of symmetric polynomials which works for group members and the group head. In this scheme, the cluster head generates the polynomial by calculating XOR of any three random hashed node IDs. The participants in this scheme mutually authenticate between themselves and then establish session key. For ensuring the security and validation among nodes Non monotonic cryptographic protocol memory, latency time, communication and computation overhead. But the concept of node migration here for the displaced nodes may incur computation and communication overhead because the percentage of these type of nodes is very less. The displaced nodes need to be given proper credentials in the network which will invite time delay, energy overhead and computational cost.

3.16 *Polynomial and Multivariate Mapping-based Triple-Key (PMMTK)*

Selva and Baburaj (2017) proposed a Polynomial and Multivariate Mapping-Based Triple-Key (PMMTK) distribution approach. This scheme is based on the computation of sensor node's individual key and a common triple-key. These keys are calculated using a multivariate polynomial. In this method base station forms the cluster centroid and obtains the energy level of each node to select cluster head and informs all nodes about select ed cluster head in the network. The scheme achieves better data freshness, throughput and average number of clusters. The limitation of the scheme is that it is using same keys throughout the network lifetime.

4 PROBLEMS AND ISSUES IDENTIFIED

In general polynomial based schemes have better features like scalability, key connectivity, communication overhead etc. as compared to matrix based techniques, tree based techniques etc. The above discussed polynomial based schemes are good in one or other way but a better solution is always desired. There are still some issues which ought to be addressed for better and secure operations in WSN and they are as following:

- The problem of node capture is a challenge.
- The keying methods must support the forward and backward secrecy.

- The keys must be updatable.
- The communication, computational and storage overhead incurred should be low.
- Designing secure protocols for WSNs.

5 CONCLUSION

WSNs have a wide application in different fields and their functionality is expected to be secure and smooth. The cryptographic techniques are the heart of such security schemes. Each scheme is designed and devised keeping in view the constrained environment of WSNs. Cryptographic keys being generated, stored and established must be done in an effective and secure way. On the basis of the open issues and limitations in key distribution methods, an efficient and reliable key distribution method to improve security and efficiency of the WSN can be designed. This paper presented the key management mechanisms based on mainly polynomials to generate and distribute keys among nodes in the network. The polynomials can be used in different ways in different keying methods as given in this paper.

REFERENCES

Akyildiz, I.F., Su, W., Sankarasubramaniam, Y. and Cayirci, E., 2002. Wireless sensor networks: a sur- vey. *Computer networks, 38*(4), pp.393-422.

Banaie F., Seno S. A., Aldmour I., Budiarto R., 2015. A Polynomial-based Pairwise Key Pre-distribution and Node Authentication Protocol for Wireless Sensor Networks. *Telecommunication Computing Electronics and Control.* 1; 13 (4):1113-1120.

Blundo C., De Santis A., Herzberg A., Kutten S., Vaccaro U., Yung M. 1993. Perfectly-Secure Key Distribution for Dynamic Conferences. *In:* Brickell E.F. *(eds) Advances in Cryptology –CRYPTO Lecture Notes in Computer Science*, vol 740. Springer.

Cheng Y., Agrawal D. P. 2007. An improved key distribution mechanism for large-scale hierarchical wireless sensor networks. In *Ad Hoc Networks*, Volume 5, Issue 1, pp.35-48, ISSN 1570-8705.

Delgosha F. & fekri F. 2009. A Multivariate key Establishment Scheme for Wireless Sensor Networks. *IEEE transaction on wireless communication* 8(4).

Dinker A. G. & Sharma V. 2016. Attacks and challenges in wireless sensor networks. *IEEE International Conference on Computing for Sustainable Global Development (INDIACom)*, pp. 3069-3074.

Dinker A. G. & Sharma V. 2017. Sensor Network Security. In book on Energy Efficient Wireless Sensor Networks, *CRC in Taylor and Francis New York*, p.p. 179-212.

Fan X. & Gong G. 2013. LPKM: A Lightweight Polynomial Based Key Management Protocol for Distributed Wireless Sensor Networks. In: Zheng J., Mitton N., Li J., Lorenz P. (eds) *Ad HocNetworks*. ADHOCNETS. *Springer*, Berlin, Heidelberg.

Harn L. & Hsu C. F. 2015. Pre-distribution Scheme for Establishing Group Keys in Wireless Sensor Net- works. In *IEEE Sensors Journal*, vol. 15, no. 9, pp. 5103-5108, doi: 10.1109/JSEN.2015.2429582

Jie H. & Guohua O. 2012. A Public Key Polynomial-based Key Pre-distribution Scheme for Large-Scale Wireless Sensor Networks. *Adhoc & Sensor Wireless Networks.* 1; 16.

Liu D. & Ning P. 2003. Establishing pairwise keys in distributed sensor networks. In *Proceedings ACM conference on Computer and communications security* (CCS'03). ACM, USA, 52-61.

Liu D., Ning P., and Li R. 2005. Establishing pairwise keys in distributed sensor networks. *ACM Trans. Inf. Syst. Secur.* 8, 1, pp. 41-77.

Li, M.; Long, J.; Yin, J.; Wu, Y.; Cheng, J. 2010. An Efficient Key Management Based on Dynamic Generation of Polynomials for Heterogeneous Sensor Networks. In *Proceedings International Conference on Computer Engineering and Technology (ICCET)*, China.

Mahmood Z., Ning H. & Ghafoor, A. 2017. A Polynomial Subset-Based Efficient Multi-Party Key Management System for Lightweight Device Networks. *Sensors* (Basel, Switzer land), 17 (4),670.

Piao Y., Kim J., Tariq U., Hong M. 2013. Polynomial-based key management for secure intra-group and inter-group communication. *Computers & Mathematics with applications*, 65(9), pp 1300-1309,

Selva R. A. & Baburaj E. 2017. Polynomial and multivariate mapping-based triple-key approach for se cure key distribution in wireless sensor networks. *J. Comps. & Electrical Engg.* 59 274-290, Elsevier.

Zheng M., Zhou H., Cui G. 2008. A LU Matrix-based Key Pre-distribution Scheme for WSNs. *IEEE Symposium on Re-search in Wireless Sensor Networks*, vol. 23, pp. 345-357.

Communication and Computing Systems – Prasad et al. (eds)
© 2019 Taylor & Francis Group, London, ISBN 978-0-367-00147-6

A brief survey on negative sequential pattern mining and its impacts

Poonam Yadav
D.A.V College of Engineering & Technology, India

ABSTRACT: NSPM is significant, and at certain times, it is much more informative when compared to PSP, and it could be exploited in numerous intelligent systems. Accordingly, only certain researches on NSP mining methodologies are obtainable, and the majority is very incompetent as they attain the support of NSC by scrutinizing the database frequently. Anyhow, when datasets turn out to be dense, the key procedure to attain the NSC support in NSP will consume more time, and it requires to be enhanced. Accordingly, this survey intends to review various topics to solve NSPM issues. Accordingly, the performance measures and the maximum performance achievements are also analyzed and demonstrated in this survey. In addition, the algorithmic classification for the surveyed papers is analyzed and described. Finally, the research gaps and issues of the NSPM issues are also discussed briefly.

1 INTRODUCTION

NSPM denotes to progressions with non-occurring items, and it holds a significant task in numerous real-life appliances, namely, smart campus, data analysis. As an significant tool for behaviour statistics, NSP (for example, missing medical diagnosis) is crucial and at certain times, it is much more informative than PSP (for instance, exploiting a medical service) in numerous intelligent systems and appliances like, risk and healthcare management, intelligent transport systems as they seldom entail non-occurring but motivating behaviours.

Certain methodologies have been presented to extract NSP depending on a MST, and they only concern the frequency of the items. This instigates that the entire items in an operation have the similar significance and some imperative sequences with reduced frequencies will drop. To mine additional constructive and significant information, a lot of other constraints such as purchase quantities, item weights, and unit profits have to be taken into deliberation. As a result, utility was established into SPM and very few techniques have been suggested to extract HUSP. Accordingly, they make use of a least utility threshold to extract HUSP instead of a MST, however increased utilities would be revealed. The utility-dependent patterns can present more actionable and important information for formulating decisions than the ones depending on conventional frequency approach.

However, finding out NSP is more complicated than recognizing PSP owing to the major intricacy of the problem that takes place by non-occurring components, enormous exploration space and increased computational cost in evaluating NSC. Until now, the predicament has not been dignified in a better manner, and only few models have been presented to extract for certain kinds of NSP that rely on database re-scans subsequent to the recognition PSP so as to compute the NSC supports. This was revealed to be very uneconomical or even unreasonable, as the NSC exploration space is generally large.

This survey has reviewed various works related to the NSPM issues. Accordingly, various performance measures adopted in each work are described and along with it, the maximum performances achieved by the various works are also portrayed by this survey. Here, various algorithmic classifications, which are adopted in the surveyed papers, are analyzed and demonstrated. The paper is organized as follows. Section II analyzes the various related works and reviews done under this topic. In addition, section III describes the various analyses on NSPM issues, and section IV presents the research gaps and challenges. At last, section V concludes the paper.

2 LITERATURE REVIEW

2.1 *Related works*

In 2018, Dong et al. (Dong, Xiangjun et al. 2018) have introduced an efficient and novel data structure, a bitmap, for achieving the assistance of NSC. In addition, a fast NSP (f-NSP) was introduced that exploits a bitmap to accumulate the PSP and further, it attains the assistance of NSC that was much quicker than the hash technique in e-NSP. In addition, investigational outcomes on demonstrate that f-NSP was not only very much quicker than e-NSP, it also accumulates more spaces for storing e-NSP, predominantly on intense datasets that comprises of several elements in a series or a very reduced count of item sets. From the analysis, the adopted scheme was found to offer more storage spacing's, and in addition, it also offers better time efficiency.

In 2016, Cao et al. (Cao, Longbing et al. 2016) have established a very modern and proficient hypothetical structure: ST-NSP and an equivalent technique known as, e-NSP, to recognize NSP resourcefully by concerning only the recognized PSP, devoid of scanning the record. The supports of NSC were then designed depending on the equivalent PSP. It evades the requirement for supplementary scans, and it also facilitates the exploitation of conventional PSP mining approaches for NSP mining. At last, an uncomplicated but proficient approach was established to produce NSC. Finally, the speculative examination illustrate that e-NSP executes better on datasets with low minimum support, reduced count of elements and increased item sets.

In 2014, Cai et al. (Cai,, Guochen et al. 2014) have established an effective and efficient ROI detection technique based on grid, which was linear to the count of grid cells. Thus, it was capable to identify arbitrary structures of ROI. Moreover, the established technique was merged with SPM to demonstrate the patterns of sequential trajectory. Finally, the investigational outcomes expose quality ROI and hopeful sequential patterns, which exhibit the advantages of the presented model.

In 2018, Xu et al. (Xu, T. et al. 2018) have adopted a novel HUSPM technique to extract HUNSP. Accordingly, the proposed methodology resolves the key issues of evaluating the effectiveness of negative sequences, the way to resourcefully produce HUNSC and the method to accumulate the HUNSC's data. In addition, the evaluated experiments reveal that HUNSPM can extract several HUNSP with minimum interval. It was the first research work that was able to mine HUNSP. Also, the effectiveness of the established scheme was analyzed and compared over the conventional approaches, and the results were attained. Finally, the experimental results and numerical tests clearly reveal the effectiveness of the HUNSP approach.

In 2018, Nicholas et al. (V. Mudrick, Nicholas et al. 2018) have suggested a novel method, which was formulated to find out if the movement of eye could be recognized by SPM methodologies. For content with graph and text differences, outcomes pointed out that metacognitive decisions of contestant's were reduced and less precise, and more dyads were found among the graph and text. In addition, particular dyads of fixations with varied length might be parallel with inaccurate and lowered decisions for content with graph and text variations. The adopted model instigates on the way to deal with the behavioral manifestations of meta comprehension procedures throughout multimedia learning.

In 2018, Said et al. (Jabbour, Said et al. 2018) had introduced a new methodology that describes the issue of extracting powerful negative rules by expanding the SAT dependent model. In addition, the adopted scheme demonstrates that the confidence parameter paves the way to non-linear features, which was dealt resourcefully to reduce the search space. Finally, the investigational results discover the efficiency of the adopted scheme and the evaluation proves the superiority of the presented algorithm in resolving the SPM difficulty.

In 2017, Amina et al. (Houari, Amina et al. 2018) have shown the exploitation of a newly developed approach, based on ARM. On the other hand, biological analysis demonstrates that a collection of biological genes might display negative correlations. Here, a novel biclustering model, called NBic-ARM was implemented. Depending on Generic Association Rules, the presented scheme recognizes the genes that were negatively-correlated. For evaluating NBic-ARM's behavior, exhaustive analyzation was carried out on 3 datasets. Moreover, the adopted scheme has offered enhanced outcomes when distinguished with the conventional algorithms, and the results were illustrated.

In 2017, John et al. (K. Tarus, John et al. 2017) have introduced a new methodology, where, ontology was exploited to design and address the domain information regarding the learning resources and learner while SPM approach identifies the sequential learning patterns of learners. Accordingly, the suggested scheme comprises of four phases: (1) Generating ontology (2) Evaluating similarity ratings (3) production of top learning items and (4) appliance of SPM approach. In addition, several experimentations were conducted to calculate the adopted hybrid system and the outcomes demonstrate enhanced performance. In addition, the implemented hybrid system could improve both the data sparsity and cold-start issues by exploiting the ontological knowledge and learner's SPM correspondingly before the data is obtainable in the recommender system.

In 2016, Jerry et al. (Lin, Jerry Chun-Wei et al. 2017) have established an efficient technique known as FHN It was based on a new PNU-list structure for mining high utility itemsets efficiently, when regarding both negative and positive unit profits. In addition, numerous pruning policies were suggested in FHN to minimize the count of candidate item sets, and therefore improve the FHN behavior. A widespread investigational outcome demonstrates that the introduced FHN technique was found to be faster in magnitude and could be exploited up to two hundred times less memory than conventional models. Furthermore, it was revealed that FHN offers better outcomes on dense datasets.

In 2011, Ken et al. (Kaneiwa, Ken et al. 2011) have implemented a methodology for extracting local patterns from sequences. By deploying rough set theory, a technique for producing decision rules, which consider local patterns for reaching at a specific decision. For deploying sequential data to rough set theory, the local patterns size was indicated, permitting a set of sequences to be converted into a SPM information system. Furthermore, the discernibility of decision classes was deployed to set up assessment criterion for the decision rules in the SPM information system.

In 2003, Florent et al. (Masseglia, Florent et al. 2003) have introduced a technique that portrays the issues of the incremental mining of SPM while novel customers or novel transactions were summed up to an real database. In addition, a novel approach for mining repeated sequences, which exploits the information which was gathered throughout the previous mining procedure to minimize the expenditure of determining novel SPM in the modified database. In addition, the test portrays that the adopted scheme offers considerably quicker performance than the naive model of mining from scratch. Accordingly, the differentiation was well-defined that this technique could also be constructive for SPM, as in numerous cases, it was more rapid to deploy this technique than to mine SPM by means of a benchmark approach.

In 2007, Hye et al. (Kum, Hye-Chung, et al. 2007) have suggested a technique, where criterion was exploited to carry out a comprehensive evaluation study of the SPM design with an suitable pattern design depending on the alignment of sequence. In addition, the presented approach suggests that the alignment design would provide an excellent review of the sequential information based on a set of frequent patterns in the records. On the contrary, the support design produces enormous quantity of FPM with more redundancy. Moreover, the adopted scheme illustrates the outcomes of the presented scheme offers better performance.

In 2018, Bac et al. (Le, Bac et al. 2018) have adopted a new pruning approach that effectively minimizes non-HUSPs and considerably minimizes the search space distinguished to the conventional HUS-Span approach. Furthermore, a parallel approach was established to quicken the mining procedure. Subsequently, two models were suggested that were the pure AHUS SPM and AHUS-P. The latter model exploits shared memory for parallelizing the process of mining. It simultaneously recognizes HUSPs depending on the applications of the processor design. At last, the investigational outcomes demonstrate that AHUS-P and AHUS can effectively and efficiently find out the entire HUSPs. From the outcomes, the anticipated algorithms perform the traditional HUS-Span model with respect to scalability, and runtime for the entire investigational datasets.

In 2014, Arthur and Gopalan (A., Arthur et al. 2014) had proposed a model, which was focused with discovering the recurrent trajectories of moving objects by a new technique by exploiting the theories of SPM and clustering. A set of experimentations performed by means of real datasets demonstrates that the implemented technique was comparatively five times improved than the traditional ones. An assessment was made with the outcomes of other approaches, and their difference was examined by arithmetical techniques. In addition, significance tests were carried out with ANOVA to discover the proficient threshold values. In addition, the outcomes were examined and determined to be better than the traditional ones. This technique might be of significance in discovering alternating paths during congested networks.

In 2009, Wen et al. have implemented a technique based on a maximum utility evaluation that was extracted from the standard of conventional SPM that the number of a subsequence available the sequence is only considered as one. Therefore, the highest measure was appropriately exploited to make simpler the utility computation for subsequences during SPM. At last, the investigational outcome on numerous datasets demonstrates that the implemented methodology has superior performance in both execution efficiency and pruning effectiveness.

3 MONITORING NEGATIVE SEQUENTIAL PATTERN MINING

3.1 *Performance measures*

The performance measures contributed in each paper are described in this section. Here, support count, size, runtime, data space, number of sequence, number of HUNSPM, MAE, mean, standard deviation, frequency, total coverage, memory usage, recoverability, and precision were attained from each contribution. Support count was measured in (Dong, Xiangjun et al. 2018) and size was deployed in (Dong, Xiangjun et al. 2018) & (Cao, Longbing et al. 2016), which offers the second highest contribution. In addition, runtime was adopted in (Dong, Xiangjun et al. 2018) & (Cao, Longbing et al. 2016) that offers about highest contribution and data space was analyzed in (Dong, Xiangjun et al. 2018). In addition, number of sequence was deployed in (Cao, Longbing et al. 2016) and number of HUNSPM was adopted in (Xu, T. et al. 2018). MAE was measured in(K. Tarus, John et al. 2017) and mean was adopted in (V. Mudrick, Nicholas et al. 2018) .The other measures such as standard deviation, frequency, total coverage, memory usage, recoverability, and precision were implemented in (V. Mudrick, Nicholas et al. 2018) & (Houari, Amina et al. 2018) respectively. The diagrammatic representation of the performance measures is given by Figure. 1.

3.2 *Algorithmic classification*

The various algorithms adopted in each reviewed paper includes bitmap model, set theory, flickr clustering, HUNSPM, fixation algorithm, enumeration algorithm, NBic-ARM model, kNN scheme, FHN algorithm, Apriori model, Approx MAP algorithm, AHUS-P and k-means algorithm. Accordingly, bitmap model was adopted in (Dong, Xiangjun et al. 2018) and set theory was adopted in (Cao, Longbing et al. 2016) & (Kaneiwa, Ken et al. 2011). Flickr clustering was implemented in (Cai, Guochen et al. 2014) and HUNSPM was implemented in (Xu T. et al. 2018). In addition, fixation algorithm was suggested in (V. Mudrick, Nicholas et al. 2018) and enumeration algorithm was deployed in (Jabbour, Said et al. 2018). Accordingly, NBic-ARM model was implemented in (Houari, Amina et al. 2018) and kNN scheme was adopted in (K. Tarus, John et al. 2017) respectively. FHN algorithm was adopted

Figure 1.   Various performance measures of the reviewed works.

in (Lin, Jerry Chun-Wei et al. 2017) and Apriori model has been implemented in (Masseglia, Florent et al. 2003 & [15] correspondingly. In addition, Approx MAP algorithm, AHUS-P algorithm, and k-means approach were implemented in (Kum, Hye-Chung, et al. 2007) & (A., Arthur et al. 2014) correspondingly. The demonstration of the various schemes is given by Figure. 2.

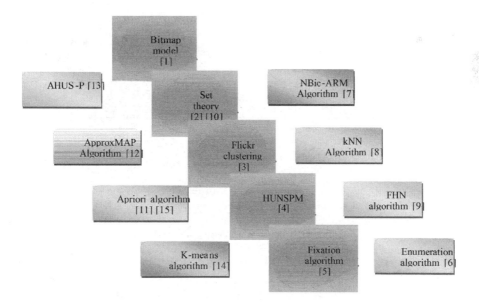

Figure 2.   Various schemes of the reviewed works.

3.3 *Maximum performance achieved*

The maximum performance achieved by various performance measures is given by Table I. The Support count attained by the reviewed works is 4, which is adopted in (Dong, Xiangjun et al. 2018) and the Size is 3 that is adopted in (Dong, Xiangjun et al. 2018). In addition, Run time was achieved as 0.7ms in (A., Arthur et al. 2014) and Data space was attained at 270MB in (Dong, Xiangjun et al. 2018). Also, Number of sequence and Number of HUNSPM has been measured in (Cao, Longbing et al. 2016) and (Xu T. et al. 2018) which attains a value of 100K and 1500 respectively. Moreover, MAE and Mean have been exploited in (K. Tarus, John et al. 2017) & (V. Mudrick, Nicholas et al. 2018) and it has attained optimal values of 0.9 and 65.82% correspondingly. Accordingly, standard deviation, Frequency, Total coverage and Memory usage were deployed in (V. Mudrick, Nicholas et al. 2018) & (Houari, Amina et al. 2018) they have obtained better values of 15.20%, 2.66 GHz, 94.73% and 1500MB respectively. Moreover, Recoverability, Precision, Condition Coverage, Gene Coverage and MST has attained better values of 91.52%, 96.98%, 94.74%, 100% and 50% and they were attained from (Houari, Amina et al. 2018) & (A., Arthur et al. 2014) correspondingly.

Table 1. Maximum performance achieved by the reviewed works.

Measures	Maximum performance achieved	Citation
Support count	4	(Dong Xiangjun et al. 2018)
Size	3	(Dong Xiangjun et al. 2018)
Run time	0.7ms	(A., Arthur et al. 2014)
Data space	270MB	(Dong Xiangjun et al. 2018)
Number of sequence	100K	(Cao Longbing et al. 2016)
Number of HUNSPM	1500	(Xu T. et al. 2018)
MAE	0.9	(K. Tarus, John et al. 2017)
Mean	65.82%	(V. Mudrick, Nicholas et al. 2018)
Standard deviation	15.20%	(V. Mudrick, Nicholas et al. 2018)
Frequency	2.66 GHz	(Kaneiwa, Ken et al. 2011)
Total coverage	94.73%	(Houari, Amina et al. 2018)
Memory usage	1500MB	(Le, Bac et al. 2018)
Recoverability	91.52%	(Kum, Hye-Chung et al. 2007)
Precision	96.98%	(Kum, Hye-Chung et al. 2007)
Condition Coverage	94.74%	(Houari, Amina et al. 2018)
Gene Coverage	100%	(Houari, Amina et al. 2018)
MST	50%	(A., Arthur et al. 2014)

4   RESEARCH GAPS AND CHALLENGES

Nowadays numerous methodologies are obtainable for determining the SPM resourcefully based on an initial description. The patterns in SPM are extensively pertinent for a numerous kinds of applications. Particular methodologies, generally enthused from preceding models, prevail in an extensive range of domains. On the other hand, traditional techniques have to be reassessed as handled data is much more multifaceted. Hence, for increasing the instantaneous helpfulness of sequential rules, it is more significant to regard more data into account. Another drawback of SPM techniques is that they predict that sequence databases are stationary. Actually, conventional SPM models are considered to be batch approaches as they are modeled to be deployed to a sequence database for attaining the patterns. Furthermore, if the database is modified, then the models require to be simulated again from scratch to attain the efficient patterns.

To deal with this drawback, HUSP simplifies the issue of SPM by regarding that every item seems to be zero, once or numerous time in every item set (acquisition amounts), and that every item has a weight demonstrating its comparative significance (e.g., the amount of profit produced by every unit that was retailed). The objective of HUSP is to discover the entire sequential patterns that include a utility, which is the computation of the utmost profit produced by the pattern in every sequence where it takes place. HUSP is often demanding as the utility measure is anti-monotone or monotone different from the support measures that are conventionally deployed in SPM. Therefore, the utility measure could not be directly deployed to reduce the search space. Thus, the major challenge of the surveyed topic has been extended to include the ability for reducing the search space, and enhance the behavior of HUSP, which was a very dynamic research issue.

5 CONCLUSION

NSP concerns on negative association found among items sets and accordingly, the items that were absent on the item sets were also considered. The majority of traditional approaches for SPM were introduced to determine PSP from database. Anyhow, practically, the nonexistence of item sets in sequences might cause an effect on the valuable information. Accordingly, in this survey, numerous papers were analyzed, and the related techniques adopted in each surveyed paper were described. In addition, the performance measures focused in each paper were illustrated, and along with it, the maximum performance measures attained were also illustrated. Thus the survey provides the detailed analysis of the NSPM issues from the reviewed papers.

REFERENCES

A., Arthur Shaw & Gopalan, N. P 2014. Finding frequent trajectories by clustering and sequential pattern mining. Journal of Traffic and Transportation Engineering 1(6): 393-403.
Cai, Guochen, Hio, Chihiro, Luke, Bermingham, Lee, Kyungmi & Lee, Ickjai 2014. Sequential pattern mining of geo-tagged photos with an arbitrary regions-of-interest detection method. Expert Systems with Applications 41(7):3514-3526.
Cao, Longbing, Dong, Xiangjun & Zheng, Zhigang 2016. e-NSP: Efficient negative sequential pattern mining. Artificial Intelligence 235:156-182.
Dong, Xiangjun, Gong, Yongshun & Cao, Longbing 2018. F-NSP+: A fast negative sequential patterns mining method with self-adaptive data storage. Pattern Recognition 84:13-27.
Jabbour, Said, El Mazouri, Fatima Ezzahra, Sais, Lakhdar 2018. Mining Negatives Association Rules Using Constraints. Procedia Computer Science 127: 481-488.
Houari, Amina, Ayadi, Wassim & Yahia, Sadok Ben 2017. Mining Negative Correlation Biclusters from Gene Expression Data using Generic Association Rules. Procedia Computer Science 112: 278-287.
Kum, Hye-Chung, Chang, Joong Hyuk & Wang, Wei 2007. Benchmarking the effectiveness of sequential pattern mining methods. Data & Knowledge Engineering 60(1):30-50.
Kaneiwa, Ken & Kudo, Yasuo 2011. A sequential pattern mining algorithm using rough set theory. International Journal of Approximate Reasoning 52(6): 881-893.
K. Tarus, John Niu Zhendong & Yousif, Abdallah 2017. A hybrid knowledge-based recommender system for e-learning based on ontology and sequential pattern mining. Future Generation Computer Systems 72: 37-48.
Lin, Jerry Chun-Wei, Fournier-Viger, Philippe & Wensheng Gan, 2016. FHN: An efficient algorithm for mining high-utility itemsets with negative unit profits. Knowledge-Based Systems 111: 283-298.
Le, Bac, Huynh Ut & Dinh, Duy-Tai 2018. A pure array structure and parallel strategy for high-utility sequential pattern mining. Expert Systems with Applications 104:107-120.
Masseglia, Florent, Poncelet, Pascal & Maguelonne Teisseire 2003.Incremental mining of sequential patterns in large databases. Data & Knowledge Engineering 46(10): 97-121.
Lan, Guo-Cheng, Hong, Tzung-Pei, S. Tseng, Vincent & Wang, Shyue-Liang 2014. Applying the maximum utility measure in high utility sequential pattern mining. Expert Systems with Applications 41 (11): 5071-5081.
V. Mudrick Nicholas, Azevedo, Roger & Taub, Michelle 2018. Integrating metacognitive judgments and eye movements using sequential pattern mining to understand processes underlying multimedia learning. Computers in Human Behavior.
Xu, T., Li, T, Dong, X.2018. Efficient High Utility Negative Sequential Patterns Mining in Smart Campus. IEEE Access 6:23839-23847.

Communication and Computing Systems – Prasad et al. (eds)
© *2019 Taylor & Francis Group, London, ISBN 978-0-367-00147-6*

A secure login method based on typing pattern

Md. Asraful Haque & Namra Zia Khan
Department of Computer Engineering, Aligarh Muslim University, Aligarh, India

Gulnar Khatoon
Computer Science & Engineering Department, IIT-Bombay, India

ABSTRACT: Rapid advancement in technology for hacking and cracking causes a major threat to misuse the personal as well official data. The conventional authentication method through text password has been shown to have significant drawbacks. Many alternative solutions based on clicking images or biometric characteristics have been widely suggested to improve security over the years. Keystroke dynamics, an interesting type of behavioral biometrics is used to identify an individual by measuring different aspects of his typing pattern. The non-necessity of special hardware and resulting low cost make it a popular area in biometric research. In this article, we have proposed an authentication technique that employs keystroke dynamics with the existing text based password. This leads to the incorporation of the simplicity of the traditional method along with the added security achieved through successive keystrokes. An adaptive mechanism has also been introduced in the scheme to update the users' typing pattern with time.

1 INTRODUCTION

Information stored in the databases is much precious for the user. Hackers are becoming smarter day by day in finding new ways to steal information. They do so because they can, financial gain, harassment and also sometimes for terrorism. It has been a challenging task for research communities to turn up with a full proof secure authentication method. Authentication is a verification process of one's claimed identity. It is an integral part in computer and network systems. It offers the accessibility in order to form the basis of information security. Text password so far is the most popular and commonly used authentication method. But it is a static type and low security solution. It becomes an easy target for different kind of attacks i.e. dictionary attack, phishing, keylogger attack etc. Graphical passwords, security tokens and biometrics are often thought as the alternatives of text password for many years now. However, they have also many limitations. Graphical passwords use some graphical presentations i.e. icons or images to create a password. Shoulder-surfing is an obvious problem for the graphical passwords. Smart cards, Debit/Credit cards are examples of token based authentications. A user has to carry the token on person to access the desired service. Loss, theft and misuse of tokens add inconvenience to the user. Biometric authentication relies on some unique feature that qualifies a user. These features cannot be borrowed, stolen or forgotten (Liu & Silverman, 2001). Biometrics are considered as the most efficient in identification tasks. Biometric features are two types: physiological and behavioral. Physiological features mainly include the physical presentations of certain body part i.e. fingerprint, face, retina, iris, DNA etc. Behavioral characteristics refer to the unique activities of a person i.e. signature, voice, keystroke dynamics etc. There are some eminent drawbacks in biometric systems. They are expensive due to the requirement of special devices. Accuracy is still a big issue in such systems because the false rejection ratio is very high. They depend too much on user's cooperation to deliver satisfactory results. In this paper, the proposed method is based on keystroke dynamics, a low cost biometric solution that does not require any additional hardware other than a keyboard. Keystroke dynamics is a process to identify a person by analyzing his typing rhythm. Psychological study claims that a repetitive routine task (i.e. speaking, writing, typing or walking) is controlled by a set of inherent actions and these actions can be anticipated using a model (Banerjee,S.P. et al. 2012). Keystroke dynamics is mainly described by some latency vectors such as key press time, key release time or inter-key time. Keystroke based verifications have two modes— static and dynamic. In Static method, the system analyzes the user's typing rhythm at any specific time, normally, during the login session. The verification is performed on typing parameters of some saved text i.e. password. In dynamic method, the system verifies the user's typing pattern throughout the session of interaction. The method is quite complex but has many advantages over the static method. First, it is a continuous authentication process; thus more secure. Second, it is a "free-text" approach because analysis is performed on any random text. Typing style is unique for every user and it cannot be lost or forgotten. If a typing template is any how guessed, misplaced or stolen, the user can comfortably create a new one. It is a user-friendly and resettable biometric. The major drawback associated with keystroke dynamics is that, the typing pattern of a person changes with time. Sometimes it depends on mental or physical states of a user and types of hardware e.g. keyboard used. Therefore, in keystroke biometric system, collected samples of a user need to be updated periodically to overcome the false rejection issue.

2 RELATED WORK

Keystroke dynamics have the potential to be employed in a strong authentication policy. A variety of algorithms were suggested in past to avail the advantages of it. These algorithms are mainly based on any of the following three approaches: statistical method, neural network and pattern recognition method. Statistical method computes the parameters like mean, variance or standard deviation in keystroke dynamic to obtain the results. A neural network is an adaptive system which is initially trained or fed a large amount of data. The decision of the system is based on certain rules which include fuzzy logic, genetic algorithms or gradient-based training. A neural network can process many parameters at a time since it has the advantage of parallelization. In pattern recognition methods, patterns are analyzed and divided into certain classes. Certain machine learning algorithms such as data mining, support vector machine (SVM), FLD or graph theory are then used for further processing. Some hybrid approaches, as a part of evolutionary algorithms were also introduced to find the optimum solution. (R. Gaines et. al., 1980) were the first researchers who proved the hypothesis that typing style of a user can be used as a basis of authentication. They created a very small database (samples of seven users only) to conduct their experiment. (John Leggett et. al., 1988) applied the idea of R. Gaines in dynamic authentication. They used relatively a large database. (Joyce & Gupta, 1990) proposed an identity verifier in the form of a stream of latency periods between keystrokes and claimed an impressive result. (Bergadano et. al., 2002) suggested their analysis method considering the problems of variability in typing and errors in typing. They reported an optimal performance after testing it in a simulated online environment. (Hosseinzadeh et al. 2008) suggested a GMM-based verification system that utilizes an adaptive and user-specific threshold. They observed that the up-to-up keystroke latency (UUKL) feature provided far better results than the down-to-down keystroke latency (DDKL) feature. (Teh et al. 2010) incorporated a two layer structure to suggest a keystroke dynamic recognition system. They used two methods namely Gaussian probability density function and Direction Similarity measure (DSM) for feature matching and six fusion rules for the decision. (Nguyen et al. 2010) used an indirect method to record keystroke timings. They analyzed sound signals produced during key press on keyboard. (Chang et al., 2012) suggested a new method combining timing and pressure parameters for touch screen handheld devices. (Ahmed et al. 2014) proposed a neural network approach for the free text analysis of typing pattern combining monograph and digraph analysis. Many more researchers have already contributed in the field of keystroke authentication and addressed a large number of solutions to this complex issue. A new authentication scheme using statistical approach has been introduced in this paper. It offers an additional layer of biometric security over the text password. The motivation behind the work is the growing need of a secure authentication method which can counter the maximum possible attacks of present times.

3 PROPOSED METHOD

This section illustrates the proposed authentication process based on the combination of a text password and the typing pattern of a user on a traditional keyboard for that password. The method consists of two phases: enrolment and login. In enrolment phase, the system is trained about the habitual typing features of users. The typing parameters are estimated by extracting the timing information of the key press, hold and release events and then they are stored in a database for login phase. In login phase users are allowed to access the system after authentication. The primary attributes of the scheme are dwell-time and flight time. The dwell-time refers to the key press time. It is the time gap between consecutive key press and key release. On the other hand, the flight time denotes the inter-key time i.e. time interval between releasing one key and pressing another key. Two performance metrics have been used to measure the efficiency of the algorithm: False Acceptance Rate (FAR) and False Rejection Rate (FRR). FAR is the percentage of verification attempts in which unauthorized persons are incorrectly accepted; whereas FRR is the percentage of cases in which authorized persons are incorrectly rejected. The proposed authentication system can be divided into three sections: enrolment phase, login phase and comparison and decision (Figure 1).

3.1 *Enrolment phase*

This is the training phase of the system. First of all, a user has to provide the username, password and other credentials to be registered in the system in a conventional way. Now he is asked to re-enter the same password 10 times. This step helps both the user and the system to understand the habitual typing pattern. In this way, 10 reference samples of password RS1, RS2, RS3,....RS10 are created for each user. The system records the timing features (dwell time and flight time) for each reference sample and stores in the database. Any keyboard can be used for these raw measurements. The data is captured only for the correct password. If

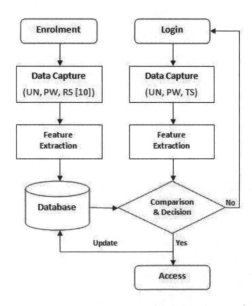

Figure 1.   Block diagram of the proposed system.

288

the entered password is wrong, the user is asked to re-type the password. The timing information without any modification is stored along with the other registration details in the database for future use.

3.2 Login phase

Proposed scheme offers two-factor authentication simultaneously. To login, a user has to enter the username and password. Naturally password is the first factor. If it is correct the second factor authentication based on typing verification takes place. After the successful attempt in both steps, a user is allowed to login into his account otherwise he is denied access. Therefore, only knowing the password is not enough in this authentication method. In typing verification, timing features of the entered password denoted by TS (test sample) are extracted and then compared with the features of saved reference samples. Biometric characteristics specially the typing features, change over time. So an adaptive mechanism has been introduced in the login phase. For each successful login, TS will replace any one of the 10 reference samples in the database using first in first out rule. The system will always take into account the last 10 valid password templates to decide the authenticity of a user.

3.3 Comparison and decision

The identification approach of a password template in the database has been represented with the help of statistical decision theory. A special parameter "identity factor" derived from the average difference and standard deviation plays the key role to verify a user's typing pattern. A threshold value has also been taken into account to maintain the robustness of the system. It is very important to configure the threshold value carefully since both FAR and FRR directly depend on it. The detailed procedure can be described as follows.

The two timing-vectors of a test password (TS) of length N are:
Dwell time vector (DT) = {dt1, dt2,..., dtN} and Flight time vector (FT) = {ft1, ft2,..., ftN}.
Similarly the timing vectors for each of the 10 reference samples will be:
Dwell time vector (D_i) = {d_{i1}, d_{i2}, ..., d_{iN}} and Flight time vector (F_i) = {f_{i1}, f_{i2}, ..., f_{iN}}.
The average differences between the corresponding timing vectors of TS and RS are:
$\lambda_d = \sum_{i=0}^{10} DT - D_i)/10$ and $\lambda_f = (\sum_{i=0}^{10} FT - F_i)/10$.
The mean vectors for the dwell time and flight time of 10 reference samples are:
$\mu_d = 1/10 \Sigma\, D_i$ and $\mu_f = 1/10 \Sigma\, F_i$.
The standard deviations of the two time factors in reference samples are expressed as:

$$\sigma_d = \sqrt{1/10 \left(\sum_{i=1}^{10} (D_i - \mu_d)^2 \right)^2} \text{ and } \sigma_f = \sqrt{1/10 \left(\sum_{i=1}^{10} \left(F_i - \mu_f \right) \right)^2}.$$

Now the required parameter "identity factor" will be calculated using the following formula:
Identity factor

$$(\phi) = (\lambda_d/\sigma_d + \lambda_f/\sigma_f)/2 \tag{1}$$

The value of ϕ should be 1 if the test sample matches with any of the saved templates exactly. But in practical scenario it is not possible since the typing rhythm of a person varies time to time. So a threshold limit has been introduced. Following are the steps of threshold calculation. First considering the dwell time vectors of reference samples:

Maximum deviation (α_{max}) = {$\max(D_i - \mu_d) \forall 1 \leq i \leq 10$},
Minimum deviation (α_{min}) = {$\min(D_i - \mu_d) \forall 1 \leq i \leq 10$} and $\alpha = (\alpha_{max} - \alpha_{min})/10$.
Similarly for flight time vectors,
β_{max} = {$\max(F_i - \mu_f) \forall 1 \leq i \leq 10$}, β_{min} = {$\min(F_i - \mu_f) \forall 1 \leq i \leq 10$} and $\beta = (\beta_{max} - \beta_{min})/10$.

Now the Threshold is defined by the following formula,

$$\Delta = 1/2\{(\alpha_{min} + 10 \times \alpha) + (\beta_{min} + 10 \times \beta)\} \qquad (2)$$

The identity factor ϕ checks the validity of a test sample in the proposed system. If the calculated value of ϕ lies in between $(1 \pm \Delta)$ it is considered that the typing pattern is valid. Hence the user can access the system. If the value is not in that range, the user is simply denied to access to the system.

4   RESULT AND ANALYSIS

A database has been created for 60 arbitrary users. Typing proficiency of users is not considered as a requirement. They were asked to register themselves in the system with any combination of username-password of their choice. Then each of the participants was required to type his password 10 times accurately to follow the policy of the scheme. Near about 75% of the users were aware about the objective of the experiment and 50% of the participants completed their registration at different machines. It was not mandatory for any person to concentrate on his typing skill. Training data of each user were recorded separately in the database. The testing of the system was performed on 10 different days. Each valid user was asked to authenticate 20 times. Then 20 random persons were provided username-password set of our 60 registered users and asked them to login into the system. The results of all cases were noted carefully. The experimental findings and their analysis are presented in Table 1 & 2.

So the brief is that, total (1095+1144) = 2239 decisions were correct out of (1200+1200) = 2400 predictions made by the system. The accuracy of the system can be determined as (2239÷2400)×100 = 93.3%. A comparative study with some previous work has been mentioned in Table 3.

The main objective of Table 3 is to provide a rough idea regarding the effectiveness of the scheme. Here comparison is baseless since different datasets of different sizes have been used in all the schemes. The results shown in Table 1 & 2 are totally based on the initial observations. The adaptive technique will update the users' profiles after every successful login. So it is hoped that the results will improve with the time.

Table 1.   Results for valid users.

Phases	Cumulative attempts	Accepted	Rejected	FRR
1	120	109	11	9.16
2	420	380	40	9.52
3	720	652	68	9.44
4	960	873	87	9.06
5	1200	1095	105	8.75

Table 2.   Results for invalid users.

Phases	Cumulative attempts	Accepted	Rejected	FAR
6	160	8	152	5
7	360	18	342	5
8	660	32	628	4.85
9	900	43	857	4.77
10	1200	56	1144	4.66

Table 3. Comparison with some previous study.

Study	Samples	FRR	FAR
Leggett & Williams [1988]	72	5	5.5
Joycee & Gupta [1990]	975	16.67	0.25
Brown & Rogers [1993]	1867	0	17.4
Obaidat & Sadoun [1997]	6750	4.7	2.2
Monrose et al. [2002]	481	20	20
Gunetti & Picardi [2005]	765	5	0.005
Hosseinzadeh and Krishnan [2008]	1230	4.3	4.8
Xi et al. [2011]	765	2.75	1.65
Our scheme	1200	8.75	4.66

5 CONCLUSION

A simple static authentication method based on statistical approach has been suggested in the paper. It provides quite satisfactory results with more than 93% accuracy. The adaptive technique makes the system promising. Stepwise results of Table 1 & 2 clearly indicate that system's performance will improve with time. There are still some potential scopes for the future improvements that need to be mentioned in the paper. First, users are not allowed to correct wrongly spelled password using backspace key. If a genuine user makes any mistake in typing his password, he has to restart the session. Second, the typing features have been studied only for the traditional PC keyboard. The typing speed in touchscreen keypads or in virtual keyboards may vary for the same person. Third, it does not deal with practical situations like working conditions of devices or the psychological conditions of users. Last and most important, the registration process is taking too much time that may be boring for the users. However, the main concern of the proposed method was to provide an advanced layer of protection above the conventional text based password. I hope that the policy will successfully create a solid wall against a variety of attacks which traditional authentication method fails to vanquish.

REFERENCES

Ahmed, A. & Traore, I. 2014. Biometric Recognition Based on Free-Text Keystroke Dynamics. In IEEE Transactions on Cybernetics 44(4): 458–472.

Banerjee, S. P. & Woodard, D. L. 2012. Biometric Authentication and Identification using Keystroke Dynamics: A Survey. In Journal of Pattern Recognition Research 7: 116-139.

Brown M. & Rogers S.J. 1993. User identification via keystroke characteristics of typed names using neural networks. In International Journal of Man-Machine Studies 39(6): 999-1014.

Bergadano, F. et. al. 2002. User authentication through Keystroke Dynamics. In ACM Transactions on Information and System Security 5(4): 367-397.

Chang, T. Y. et. al. 2012. A graphical-based password keystroke dynamic authentication system for touch screen handheld mobile devices. In Journal of Systems and Software 85(5): 1157-1165.

Gunetti, D. & Picardi, C. 2005. Keystroke analysis of free text. In ACM Transactions on Information and System Security 8(3): 312–347.

Hosseinzadeh, D. & Krishnan, S. S. 2008. Gaussian Mixture Modeling of Keystroke Patterns for Biometric Applications. In IEEE Transactions on Systems, Man, and Cybernetics, Part C: Applications and Reviews 38(6): 816–8826.

Haque, M. A. et. al. 2012. 2-Round Hybrid Password Scheme. In International Journal of Computer Engineering and Technology 3(2): 579-587.

Haque, M. A. & Imam, B. 2014. A New Graphical Password: Combination of Recall and Recognition based Approach. In World Academy of Science, Engineering and Technology 8(2): 320-324.

Haque, M. A. et. al. 2015. Authentication through Keystrokes: What You Type and How You Type. In IEEE Int. Conf. on Research in Computational Intelligence and Communication Networks: 257-261.

Joyce, R. & Gupta, G. 1990. Identity authentication based on keystroke latencies. In Communications, ACM 33(2): 168-176.

Leggett, J. et. al. 1988. Verification of user identity via keystroke characteristics. In Human Factors in Management Information Systems, Ablex Publishing Corp., Norwood, USA.

Liu, S. & Silverman. 2001. A Practical Guide to Biometric Security Technology. In IT Professional, 3(1).

Monrose, F. et. al. 2002. Password hardening based on keystroke dynamics. In International Journal of Information Security 1: 69–83.

Nguyen, T. T. et. al. 2010. Keystroke Dynamics Extraction by Independent Component Analysis and Bio-matrix for User. In Springer-Verlag Berlin Heidelberg: 477–486.

Obaidat M. S. & Sadoun, B. 1997. Verification of Computer Users Using Keystroke Dynamics. In IEEE Transactions on Systems, Man, and Cybernetics – Part B: Cybernetics 27(2): 261–269.

Teh, P. S. et. al. 2010. Keystroke dynamics in password authentication enhancement. In Expert Systems with Applications 37(12): 8618–8627.

Xi, K. et. al. 2011. Correlation Keystroke Verification Scheme for User Access Control in Cloud Computing Environment. In Computer Journal 11: 1632–1644.

Communication and Computing Systems – Prasad et al. (eds)
© 2019 Taylor & Francis Group, London, ISBN 978-0-367-00147-6

Analysis, design and implementation of fiber optic traffic by using Python

M.B. Harish, K.V.S.S.S.S. Sairam & Chandra Singh
ECE Department, NMAMIT, Nitte, India

ABSTRACT: Optical communication provides the data integration through fiber and bandwidth. Optical networks is an integration of fiber distribution to fiber restoration by using different techniques such as fiber network routing to fiber network survivability. In this paper it can be measured by using the parameters such as network resources utilization, hardware requirement, and efficiency receiver time. These parameter are analysed design and implemented by using python programming.

1 INTRODUCTION

Survivability is a technique, where it provides to restore the network capacity against failures. It defines basic principle of physical and logical layer combination and it also describes the architecture principles by using SONET, ATM and different topologies with respect to optical network elements and there functions. Survivability methods are categorized according to the transportation of signals such as DS0 to DS3. (Bhandari, Abhay et al.2015). To sustain the quality of service against the failure situation, these qualities determine the optical network architecture in terms of heterogeneous scalable and flexible. Network Survivability predicts capability of the network whether network has ability to maintain the Quality of Service (QoS) all time, even when failures occur (Kumar, Krishan et al. 2014).

2 PROBLEM DEFINITION

The main Objective of this paper is to implement the SNA with respect to TCC and TRM with Integration Levels. The first one determines TCC in terms of TLM, TCM and Digital Traffic Link Output. In restoration based mechanisms, a protection path is going to take over the function only after the failure in the main path. Single/multiple link failure in network and reserve the backup before the failure occur (Dhyani,Geeta et al 2015).

The second one determines the SNA (Singh, C. Et al. 2017) in order to estimate Restoration survivability ratio by using concept w.r.t. Protection Restoration Strategies techniques using the Integration Levels. Restoration provides increased flexibility against unexpected failures in the network. The restoration method saves capacity, but the time taken for restoration is high, since the recovery paths are calculated after the occurrence of failures (Singh C et al. 2019). The protection methods such as 1:1, 1+1, and 1:2 Diverse Protection are used.

Consider a 6 X 6 network topologies as shown in Figure 3. The Traffic Cross Connectivity (TCC) of a network is calculated by considering the Traffic link matrix and Traffic cost matrix of a given network. By considering the Traffic link matrix and Traffic cost matrix as shown in Figure from the network shown in Figure 3. The Traffic Cross Connectivity output shown in Figure 4 (Sairam et al. 2017)

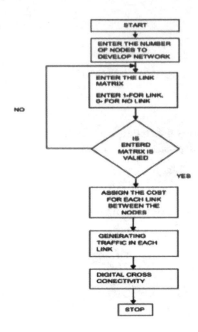

Figure 1.   Flowchart of traffic cross connectivity.

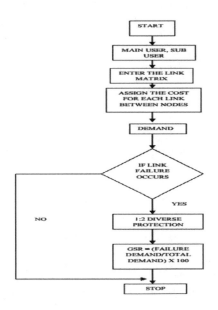

Figure 2.   Flowchart of protection restoration ratio.

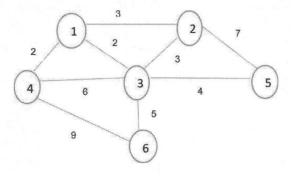

Figure 3. 6 x 6 network topology.

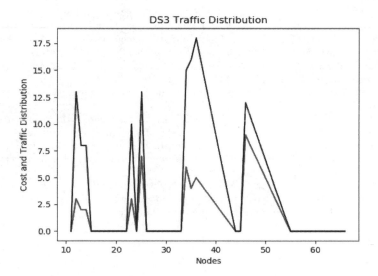

Figure 4. Simulated results obtained for Traffic Connectivity Matrix(TCM) (Singh C. et al, 2019).

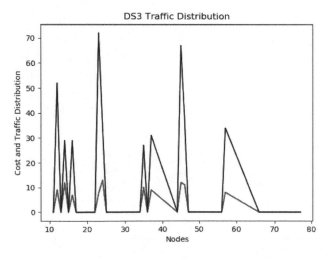

Figure 5. Simulated results obtained for traffic restoration ratio[8].

3 CONCLUSION

In N x N Network configurations, In all these cases the survivability defines the vital role to determine the traffic in each link towards packet distribution in the form of spatial channel connectivity. By adopting survivability techniques in the network we can eliminate the data loss caused due to failure.

REFERENCES

Bhandari Abhay & Malhotra Dr. Jagjit 2015 A Review on Network Survivability in Optical Networks 5:97-101.

Kumar,Krishan & Garg.Kumar,Amit 2014. Analysis of restoration and protection in optical network with simulation framework 3(5).

Dhyani,Geeta & Bisht,Nivedita 2015. Network Survivability: Analysis Of Protection Schemes In Ring Configuration 2.

Singh,C. & Sairam, K.V.S.S.S.S. 2017. Survivable fiber optic networks design by using digital signal levels approach. In 2017 International Conference on Intelligent Sustainable Systems (ICISS):84-86.

Sairam, K.V.S.S.S.S. & Singh, C. 2019. Link Layer Traffic Connectivity Protocol Application and Mechanism in Optical Layer Survivability Approach. In: Smys S., Bestak R., Chen JZ., Kotuliak I. (eds) International Conference on Computer Networks and Communication Technologies. Lecture Notes on Data Engineering and Communications Technologies 15.

Sairam, K.V.S.S.S.S. & Singh, C. 2017. Optical network survivability- An overview. Indian J. Sci. Res 14 (2): 383–386.

Singh, C., Sairam, K.V.S.S.S.S. & M. B. H. 2019. Global Fairness Model Estimation Implementation in Logical Layer by Using Optical Network Survivability Techniques. In: Hemanth J., Fernando X., Lafata P., Baig Z. (eds) International Conference on Intelligent Data Communication Technologies and Internet of Things (ICICI) 2018. ICICI 2018. Lecture Notes on Data Engineering and Communications Technologies 26.

Sairam, K.V.S.S.S.S. & Singh, C. 2019. FONI by Using Survivability Approach: An Overview. In: Kamal R., Henshaw M., Nair P. (eds) International Conference on Advanced Computing Networking and Informatics. Advances in Intelligent Systems and Computing 870.

Communication and Computing Systems – Prasad et al. (eds)
© 2019 Taylor & Francis Group, London, ISBN 978-0-367-00147-6

Detection and prevention of vulnerabilities in open source software: An experimental study

Gopal Singh Rawat & Karan Singh
School of Computer and Systems Sciences, Jawaharlal Nehru University, New Delhi, India

ABSTRACT: Many of today's hottest new enterprise technologies are centered around free "open-source" technology. Most of the open source software or applications have a web front end, and they are available universally to their users. The growing popularity of the open source software or applications is turning them to be tools of everyday. Access to these applications can be gained from anywhere, widely exposing any security vulnerability which can most probably be exploited or exposed by the hackers. Web vulnerability scanners can detect weaknesses in a black-box method of security testing, they are easy to use as well. There are many scanners to choose; organizations can select them based on their requirements and conditions. In this paper, we study vulnerabilities in one of the widely used open source software learning management system named MOODLE. The experimental study using the open source web vulnerability scanners not only helps in detecting potential vulnerabilities but also helps in providing an effective way for evaluation of security mechanisms. It not only points out their weaknesses but also provides ways to improve them.

1 INTRODUCTION

Over the years technology has grown very fast making people rely on Web applications a lot more in order to carry out their daily businesses, personal transactions or otherwise (McGraw 2006). Organizations and businesses have used this opportunity with the help of web applications providing many of their services. With the explosive growth of the internet and its global reach being the key factors in the growing popularity of web applications; it has made Web applications part of our daily lives.

Web applications can be Closed (proprietary) or Open Source. Majority of new enterprise technologies are concentrating on free open-source technology. Evidence of open source adoption is such that Govt agencies, Military, Healthcare, Businesses, Education Systems and various other organizations are accepting and experimenting with it. Web applications have been of vital importance to the success of many organizations and businesses but their securities have become more complex (Grossman 2007). As web applications are not free form threats, so with the increasing number of threats many security issues have emerged out year after year (McGraw, 2006).

Reports from OWASP (2013) lists the "top ten most critical web application security risks" and CWE/SANS (2011) lists the most critical and widespread errors which may lead to serious vulnerabilities in software. These reports reveal that Cross Site Scripting (XSS) and SQL injection (SQLi) are amongst the top three serious web security flaws.

Security Vulnerabilities can possibly be due to the defects which might be caused during the design and development phase, human errors or improper system configuration resulting in breaking of data integrity, stealing confidential data or may affect the availability of web application. Hence these vulnerable web applications need to be secured. According to OWASP (Curphey et al. 2015), manual code review helps in detection of security vulnerabilities in web applications in efficient way. The manual security testing can be time consuming as it requires the expert skills, and it is prone to human errors too. Hence, the need of automated approach in finding vulnerabilities led security society to actively develop automated tools.

The paper aims at detecting the vulnerabilities in a widely used OSS named MOODLE, also provides effective ways to evaluate security mechanisms deployed. The dependence on MOODLE and other such learning management systems by teachers and users has seen a tremendous increase with the world wide connectivity getting better. The study of vulnerabilities in MOODLE as the test OSS will not only help in improving the OSS but also protect the users like teachers and students from privacy and security issues that can arise due to the existing vulnerabilities in such OSS when exploited.

The structure of the paper is as follows. The next section presents related work. Section 3 discusses the case study. Section 4 presents the results and the analysis of our experimental study. Finally, Section 5 concludes the paper along with the acknowledgement.

2 RELATED WORK

With the advancement in web technologies, popularity of web applications has grown on a large scale. The growth of open source software and its wide acceptance can be seen in diverse fields like medical, financial, military and education systems. It is reported (Murphy 2010) that 98% of enterprises in some capacity are using open source software offerings.

Open Source Software (OSS) users and Open Source Security Vulnerabilities are increasing, hence the need of detection and prevention of vulnerabilities in OSS arises as well. The security testing for such purpose can help to detect and mitigate the vulnerabilities found, which is a quite complicated and detailed process, thus it is crucial to have a security testing technique which is efficient. Commonly appearing security vulnerabilities in OSS or web applications are a result of security issues existing due to generic input validation.

Web application security is hard to achieve as most developers are very less taught in school about security issues, so they are aware of the MITRE catalogued 695 weakness types only. Most developers never receive any security feedback on the job, as by the time vulnerability in their code is found, they're already off on the next project.

Writing a secure code today would require developers an impossible amount to learn about application specific attacks, vulnerabilities and security controls. All the 695 catalogued weakness types are not very obvious, many are quite tricky for the experts. It is an assumption that the internet based applications are prone to biggest risks and Intranet applications are less likely to be attacked as the pools of threat agents is smaller however, that may be partially true. The functions and assets are often quite a bit more critical, so the risk is frequently higher for intranet applications.

According to analysis by OWASP, the security vulnerabilities discovered in a decade of application security verification with code review and security testing, it was found that almost all the vulnerabilities fall into one of the four categories mentioned in the Figure 1.

Max percentage (35%) of security issues are because of missing controls – like applications without output encoding, or without sensitive data encryption, or they fail to use parameterized database queries. So with the simple approach of making the right security controls available in an application, lot of vulnerabilities can be eliminated.

Figure 1. Security vulnerability broad categories.

The Vulnerabilities by type data from CVEdetails.com which is a free Common Vulnerabilities and Exposures (CVE) security vulnerability database/information source (CVE 2017) provides a trend of such vulnerabilities over the year.

The Black Box scanning technique presents a good option to test the vulnerabilities in an automated mode. The majority of existing web vulnerabilities are easy to understand and be avoided, but still many web developers are not security aware or may lag sophistic skills of experience of the testers. As a result, many vulnerable OSS exist.

Many approaches have been proposed to address the security threats posed by web security vulnerabilities such as static taint analysis, dynamic taint analysis, modelling checking, symbolic and concolic testing (Balzarotti et al. 2008, Kieyzun et al. 2009). Static taint analysis approach is extensible practically are ineffective due to high false positive rates. Model checking (Martin et al. 2008) dynamic checking (Balzarotti et al. 2008), symbolic (Fu and Lee 2010) and concolic (Kieyzun et al. 2009) techniques generate real attack values so they can be highly accurate but due to the path explosion problem (Ma et al. 2011) they have scalability issues when the case of large systems are considered.

As no particular approach guarantees complete security against web vulnerabilities, there is a need and scope to improve efficiency of security mechanisms. The methodology proposed by Jose Fonseca et.al (Fonseca et al. 2014) is based on realistic vulnerabilities injection in web application and performing automatic attack on them. It has been used to evaluate the web security mechanism in their study with the help of a prototype tool VAIT developed by them. The automated tools serve best in checking vulnerabilities, but even after many improvements the rate of detection is very low.

In the paper by Ibrahim Abunadi et al., an empirical investigation of security vulnerabilities in web applications (Abunadi and Alenezi 2016) using the machine learning on existing vulnerability prediction models has been done. The work focused mainly on dataset of PHP open source web applications. The tools and models are either language dependent or domain dependent.

Of the various domains, the education field has seen a sudden rise in online learning, web-based learning and use of technology in some form all these can be unified into a term E-learning. E-learning platforms suffer from security vulnerabilities (Costinela-Luminiţa et al. 2012). The paper talks about few security issues in MOODLE, the widely used free OSS. The paper presents some analysis and ideas to address the issues however, the ideas are generic. With very less research focused on security issues of OSS, much focus has been laid on developing automated web vulnerability scanners. The institutions implementing OSS like MOODLE resort to using Web vulnerability scanners for reasons like ease of use, availability of requirement based modules, support for tools and such other reasons. The security and privacy issues erupting due to the vulnerabilities in these OSS are of great concern. Although the impact of using web vulnerability scanners and dependence on it is itself an interesting research topic, the use of web application scanners is never going to decline.

The organizations are working on developing web application security scanners in order to automate the process of detecting the vulnerabilities. The OSS users depend on such web application security scanners for various reasons like ease of use, automated mechanism, lesser complexity and being modular. It becomes crucial to detect vulnerabilities in OSS and study the security mechanism behind the web application security scanners.

2.1 *Web application security scanner*

Web Vulnerability Scanner or Web application security scanner is an automated tool used to test web applications for existing common security vulnerabilities. The scanner explores a web application by crawling through its web pages and examines it to locate any application layer security vulnerabilities and weaknesses, which involves the generation of malicious inputs, inspecting HTTP messages for suspicious attributes and evaluation of application's responses (WASC 2009).

A very large number of web application scanning tools are available today, both open source and commercial. These tools can be used for security assessment, perform regular scans to comply with security requirements. Comparisons of such tools in various categories like features, detection, accuracy and adaptability have been performed by many security researchers like Shay Chen (2016). ZAP and VEGA tools have been selected for our experimental study after going through such comparisons.

3 CASE STUDY

In order to demonstrate the working of the chosen tools listed in Table 1, we will be testing security of open source software MOODLE v3.2.1. The experimental setup can be extended and applied on other similar case scenarios in order to make it generic. The use of a MOODLE learning platform in the education sector has seen a tremendous growth having a huge impact on all the stakeholders involved (Jackson 2017). As MOODLE being the widely used free and open learning management system, it is chosen as test OSS, besides it being written using the next technologies; HTML, CSS, PHP, MY SQL database which represents the technologies used to build custom web applications very often nowadays. The scanners that are picked for analysis are limited to only open sourced ones and are better compared with others in the same category (Shay Chen 2016).

We start our experimental study by hosting MOODLE on local server with the help of XAMPP v3.2.2. Database is also created on MYSQL Xampp server. Proxy interception functionality is used by setting Mozilla browser to localhost on port 8080, to record all the requests and responses made by MOODLE. Figure 2 shows the experimental setup used in our case study.

3.1 *Testing procedure*

With the aim of detection and prevention of vulnerabilities in open source software we have chosen test tools as ZAP and VEGA, the test target as MOODLE and we have designed the experimental setup. The selected test tools were run on the chosen test target OSS and the results were recorded. Following is the testing procedure.

Table 1. Web vulnerability scanners used.

	Zed Attack Proxy	VEGA
Owners	OWASP	Subgraph
Version	2.6.0	1.0

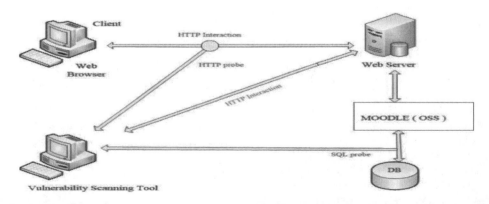

Figure 2. Experimental setup.

Step 1. Launch the test tool.

Step 2. Enter the URL of the test target OSS.

Step 3. Click on the scan button and wait for the completion of the scanning process.

Step 4. If the scan is carried out successfully, detected vulnerabilities will be listed else change parameters and repeat the procedure.

4 RESULTS AND DISCUSSION

With the help of ZAP and VEGA we were able to detect various vulnerabilities listed in Table 2 with corresponding level of risk. The tools not only provided detailed information of the vulnerabilities but also helped with remediation or solution part as well. This experiment contributes to security testing of open source software MOODLE.

This study can help in improving the security level of MOODLE and such open source software, understanding the vulnerabilities and risk attached with them. Table 2 lists the vulnerabilities detected along with the risk factors.

Although the results obtained from experimental study covered the major vulnerabilities but XSS was not detected by any of the web application security scanner. Figures 3 and 4 show Moodle vulnerabilities detected by type and number of such vulnerabilities detected. According to the Moodle 3.2.2 release notes (Moodle 2017), two XSS security issues are present in Moodle 3.2.1.

Table 2. Results comparison of ZAP and Vega.

VULNERABILITIES/ALERTS	ZAP		VEGA	
	Detected	Risk	Detected	Risk
Path Traversal	No	-	Yes	High
Remote OS command injection	Yes	High	Yes	High
SQL injection	Yes	High	Yes	High
Bash Shell Shock Injection	No	-	Yes	High
Shell Injection	No	-	Yes	High
Cleartext Password over HTTP	No	-	Yes	High
Directory Browsing	Yes	Medium	Yes	Low
X–Frame-Option Header not set	Yes	Medium	Yes	Info
Local Filesystem Paths Found	No	-	Yes	Medium
XML injection	No	-	Yes	Medium
Cookie no HTTP only Flag	Yes	Low	Yes	Info
Cookie without Secure Flag	Yes	Low	No	-
Web Browser XSS protection Not Enabled	Yes	Low	No	-
X-content-Type-Options Header Missing	Yes	Low	No	-

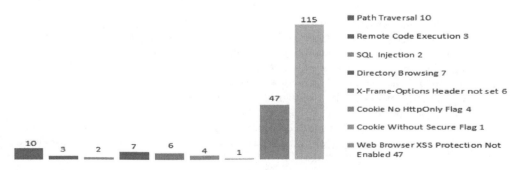

Figure 3. Moodle vulnerabilities detected using ZAP.

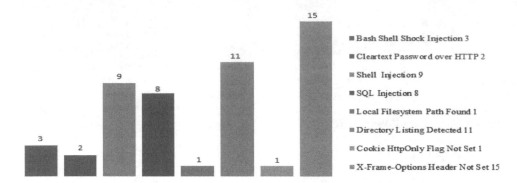

Figure 4. Moodle vulnerabilities detected using VEGA.

This approach is followed by many organizations to secure the web applications along with penetration testing. It does help in finding serious vulnerabilities but cannot fully cover the source code of the web application or web application itself as reflected from our study as well. This requires manual intervention of a penetration tester to look at the coverage or attack surface of the web application ensuring if the tool has been correctly configured or the tool is able to understand the behavior of web application

These scanners are less able than humans to identify unknown-unknowns (things that are not already registered on the risk register, or which haven't been theorized by the organization as potential security issues). A Good pen testing team can handle such cases very well comparatively. Also, certain types of security issues like subtle business logic flaws that require a human's understanding of how a particular process or work-flow is supposed to work in order to exploit it cannot be processed by the vulnerability scanners (Yeo 2013).

5 CONCLUSION

With the rapid advancement in technology, fast development of web applications and increasing shift towards open source software, security becomes crucial and a real challenge too. This paper explored the vulnerabilities in MOODLE chosen as one of the test OSS, the experimental setting produced results and the experiment have shown that the vulnerability scanners alone cannot detect all the possible vulnerabilities, more actions need to be taken. The scanners used were not able to detect XSS vulnerability, in spite of the fact Moodle release notes confirmed their presence. Although the work can be extended with other scanners the problem remains the same. The results clearly show that there is room for improvement in the vulnerability detection and prevention techniques.

In the experimental scenario, MOODLE is chosen as test OSS that provides a variety of tools and modules for online education and training. Having a huge user base and an increase in attacks makes it much more susceptible to attacks due to the vulnerabilities present. Hence it is of much importance to research for MOODLE's security, to protect it with the help of updates or code patches. Such research will not only benefit the OSS but will help the institutions who have implemented it. In a way all the stakeholders involved (students, teachers and administrators) will be protected.

Instead of evaluating software after development phase, much focus should be laid on making security testing an important part of the development cycle. OWASP provides prevention cheat sheets for various vulnerabilities, following these simple rules can help in defending against such serious attacks, ensuring reduction of vulnerabilities to minimal number.

ACKNOWLEDGEMENTS

This work was partially sponsored by the UPE-II Project grant PID 115.

REFERENCES

McGraw, G. (2006). *Software security: building security in* (Vol. 1). Addison-Wesley Professional.

Grossman, J. (2007). *XSS Attacks: Cross-site scripting exploits and defense.* Syngress.OWASP (2013). OWASP Top Ten project 2013. Retrieved June 9, 2017, from https://www.owasp.org/index.php/Top_10_2013-Top_10.

CWE/SANS (2011). Top 25 Most Dangerous Programming Errors. Retrieved June 9, 2017, from, http://cwe.mitre.org/top25.

Curphey, M., Wiesman, A., Van der Stock, A., Stirbei, R. (2015). A Guide to Building Secure Web Applications and Web Services. Retrieved June 9, 2017, from https://www.um.es/atica/documentos/OWASPGuide2.0.1.pdf.

Yeo, J. (2013). Using penetration testing to enhance your company's security. *Computer Fraud & Security, 2013*(4), 17-20.

Murphy, David (2010). Survey: 98 Percent of Companies Use Open-Source, 29 Percent Contribute Back. Retrieved June 9, 2017, from http://in.pcmag.com/news/19765/survey-98-percent-of-companies-use-open-source-29-percent-co.

WASC (2009). Web Application Security Scanner Evaluation Criteria. Retrieved June 9, 2017, from http://projects.webappsec.org/w/page/13246986/Web%20Application%20Security%20Scanner%20Evaluation%20Criteria.

Shay Chen (2016). Price and Feature Comparison of Web Application Scanners. Retrieved June 9, 2017, from http://sectoolmarket.com/price-and-feature-comparison-of-web application-scanners-unified-list.html.

Ben Quinn and Charles Arthur, Guardian News and Media Limited (2011). PlayStation Network hackers access data of 77 million users. Retrieved June 9, 2017, from https://www.theguardian.com/technology/2011/apr/26/playstation-network-hackers-data.

Subgraph (2017). Vega Vulnerability Scanner. Retrieved May 11, 2017, from https://subgraph.com/vega.

(2017). CVE Official CVEdetails page. Retrieved March 21, 2017, from https://www.cvedetails.com/vulnerabilities-by-types.php.

Moodle (2017). MOODLE official page. Retrieved May 21, 2017,fromhttps://docs.moodle.org/dev/Moodle_3.2.2_release_notes.

Balzarotti, D., Cova, M., Felmetsger, V., Jovanovic, N., Kirda, E., Kruegel, C., & Vigna, G. (2008, May). Saner: Composing static and dynamic analysis to validate sanitization in web applications. In *Security and Privacy, 2008. SP 2008. IEEE Symposium on* (pp. 387-401).

Kieyzun, A., Guo, P. J., Jayaraman, K., & Ernst, M. D. (2009, May). Automatic creation of SQL injection and cross-site scripting attacks. In *Software Engineering, 2009. ICSE 2009. IEEE 31st International Conference on* (pp. 199-209).

Martin, M., & Lam, M. S. (2008, July). Automatic generation of XSS and SQL injection attacks with goal-directed model checking. In *Proceedings of the 17th conference on Security symposium* (pp. 31-43). USENIX Association.

Fu, X., & Li, C. C. (2010). A String Constraint Solver for Detecting Web Application Vulnerability. In *SEKE* (pp. 535-542).

Ma, K. K., Phang, K. Y., Foster, J. S., & Hicks, M. (2011, September). Directed symbolic execution. In *International Static Analysis Symposium* (pp. 95-111). Springer Berlin Heidelberg.

Fonseca, J., Vieira, M., & Madeira, H. (2014). Evaluation of web security mechanisms using vulnerability & attack injection. *IEEE Transactions on Dependable and Secure Computing, 11*(5), 440-453.

Jackson, E. A. (2017). Impact of MOODLE platform on the pedagogy of students and staff: Cross-curricular comparison. *Education and Information Technologies, 22*(1), 177-193.

Costinela-Luminiţa, C. D., & Nicoleta-Magdalena, C. I. (2012). E-learning security vulnerabilities. *Procedia-Social and Behavioral Sciences, 46*, 2297-2301.

Abunadi, I., & Alenezi, M. (2016). An Empirical Investigation of Security Vulnerabilities within Web Applications. *J. UCS, 22*(4), 537-551.

Communication and Computing Systems – Prasad et al. (eds)
© 2019 Taylor & Francis Group, London, ISBN 978-0-367-00147-6

Retrospection on security in cloud computing

Hansraj
Department of Information and Technology, Dronacharya College of Engineering, Gurgaon, India

Ashima Mehta
Department of Computer Science and Engineering, Dronacharya College of Engineering, Gurgaon, India

ABSTRACT: Cloud computing gives benefits on interest. In the ongoing time, Cloud Computing is profoundly requested administration due to the preferences like high registering force, less expense of administrations, superior, versatility, unwavering quality, openness just as accessibility. For this paper included concentrated graphical and methodical survey of different research work completed on Cloud Computing . These discoveries demonstrate that the examination in Cloud Computing got more consideration in the course of recent years. There are alluded abnormal state distributer's paper for better comprehension about the security issues in Cloud Computing. This examination would give bits of knowledge to explores, understudies, distributers, specialists to consider momentum look into pattern in Cloud Computing, serves to people groups for any issues about Cloud Computing.

1 INTRODUCTION

The concept and terminology of cloud is an advancement in the development of On-Demand data innovation administrations and data items. (Leavitt, N.2009.) Also it provides three kinds of administrations SaaS (Software as a Service), PaaS (Platform as a Service) and IaaS (Infrastructure as a Service).

In view of past information, Bibliography examination is a part of Technical investigation to anticipate development of specific research zone in future. In this investigation there are found, in which specific field 'what' and 'how much' work has been finished. Amid pattern examination we indicates high improvement about security in distributed computing.

There are alluded look into papers of changed surely understood diaries and Conferences of abnormal state distributers. Amid the pattern investigation there are discovered numerous issues and the security level's issues and answers for that. Diverse kinds of assault which is performed on the private cloud additionally imperative issues and issues for coordinators and organizations. In this paper alluded DDos assault in cloud and anticipation methods for that From Observations of the exploration paper, prompts Security level and most popular issues for distributed computing. Security is the most dangerous issues in Cloud. Security of cloud is as far as dangers, vulnerabilities and effect. That is it demonstrates that improving the security of cloud will expand precision, anticipation of information theft and improve protection.

The cloud computing can be considered as another registering paradigm that can give benefits on interest at an insignificant cost. The three surely understood and regularly utilized administration prototypes in the cloud worldview are programming as an administration (SaaS), stage as an administration (PaaS), and foundation as an administration (IaaS). In SaaS programming with the associated information conveyed by cloud specialist co-op, and clients make use of it with the help of web programming. In PaaS, a specialist organization encourages administrations to the clients with a lot of programming programs that can tackle the explicit assignments. In IaaS, the cloud specialist co-op encourages administrations clients with virtual machines and capacity to improve their business abilities.

The idea of cloud has its usage in light of the administrations from specialist co-ops. Open cloud is the property of administration supplier and can be utilized out in the open, private cloud indicates to being the property of an organization, and half and half cloud is the mixes of open and private cloud. The greater part of the current cloud administrations are given by extensive cloud administration organizations such as Google, Amazon, and IBM. A private cloud is a cloud in which just the approved clients can get to the administrations from the supplier. In the pubic cloud anyone can utilize the cloud administrations while the half and half cloud contains the idea of both open and private cloud.

Security is the blend of classification, the counteractive action of the unapproved exposure of information, trustworthiness, the aversion of the unapproved alteration or erasure of data, and accessibility, the anticipation of unapproved retaining of data (Zhang, ST et.al, 2010).He serious issues in the this computing incorporates security in infrastructure, the executives, and privacy checking. At present guidelines to convey applications in the cloud, and there is an absence of institutionalization control in the cloud. Various strategies have been structured and analyzed in cloud.

2 DATA INTEGRITY

This is a fundamental consent that standout amongst the most basic components in any data framework when it comes to the security concern. For the most important part, the data integrity implies shielding information from unapproved cancellation, alteration, or creation. Dealing with substance's permission and rights to explicit endcavor infrastructure guarantees that important information and administrations are not mishandled, misused, or stolen.

Data integrity in the cloud framework implies safeguarding the information. The information ought not be lost or changed by unapproved clients. Consequently it is the premise to give distributed computing administration, for example, SaaS, PaaS, and IaaS. Other than information stored of substantial scale, cloud computing condition more often than not gives information handling administration. Information respectability can be gotten by systems, for example, RAID-like methodologies and advanced mark.

3 CONCEPT OF DATA AVAILABILITY

This concepts implies the accompanying: when mishaps, for example, hard circle harm, IDC fire, and system disappointments happen, the degree that client's information can be used or recouped and how the clients check their information by methods as opposed to depends on credit ensure by the cloud specialist co-op alone. The issue of putting away information over the consecutive servers is a genuine worry of customers on the grounds that the cloud providers are administered by the neighborhood laws and, in this way, the cloud customers ought to be discerning of those laws. Besides, the cloud specialist organization ought to guarantee the information security, especially information privacy and trustworthiness. The cloud providers ought to give certifications of information security and clarify purview of neighborhood laws to the customers. The primary focal point of this research is on information issues and difficulties which are related with information area and its migration, cost, accessibility, and security.

4 AVERTING ATTACK IN CLOUD

The cloud computing encourages tremendous measure of shared infrastructure on the Internet. Cloud frameworks ought to be equipped for deflecting various types of assaults. Shen et al. broke down necessity of security administrations in distributed computing .The creators recommend coordinating cloud administrations for confided in registering stage (TCP) and believed stage bolster administrations (TSS). The confided in model should stand attributes of secrecy, powerfully building trust areas and dynamic of the administrations. Cloud foundations necessitate that client moves their information into cloud just dependent on conviction. Neisse et al. examined impassive assaults situations on Xen cloud stage to assess cloud administrations dependent on trust. Security of information and trust in cloud registering is the key point for its more extensive selection . Yeluri et al. concentrated on the cloud administrations from security perspective and investigated security challenges in cloud while sending the administrations . Character the executives, information recuperation and the board, security in the cloud privacy, trust, deceivability, and application design are the key focuses for assuring security in cloud.

5 CATEGORIES OF PRIVACY ISSUES IN CLOUD

a. How to empower the customers or clients to have control over their information at the point when the information is put away and handled in cloud and stay away from theft, leakage, and unapproved resale.
b. How to ensure information replications in a locale furthermore, predictable state, where duplicating client information to different reasonable areas is a typical decision, and maintain a strategic distance from information misfortune, spillage, and unapproved adjustment or creation,
c. Which organization is in charge of guaranteeing legitimate necessities for individual data.
d. Whatever degree cloud providers are engaged with preparing which can be legitimately recognized, checked, furthermore, discovered.

6 SECURITY MEASURE IN SAAS FRAMEWORK

The providers of SaaS offer verification and get to control work, generally the client name and secret phrase check component. Clients should know enough to the supplier they have picked, so as to dispose of the risk to the security of the cloud applications inward factors. In the meantime cloud suppliers ought to give high quality, change the secret phrase on time, make secret key length base on the information of the subtle degree, and shouldn't utilize capacity.

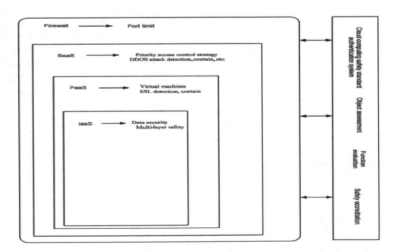

Figure 1.   The security framework in cloud computing.

7 CONCLUSION

This computing is an encouraging and a novel aspect for the various applications in information and technology field. The boundary and complications toward the fast development of cloud computing are information security and protection issues. Lessening the concerned information storage and taking care of expense is a required necessity of any association, whereas the analyzing of information and data is extensively the most indispensable errands in every one of the associations for basic leadership. Henceforth, the security isn't only a specialized issue, it includes institutionalization, administering mode, laws and guidelines, and numerous other perspectives, this technology is encapsulation of improvement in openings and challenges, alongside the security issue be illuminated in a well ordered manner.

REFERENCES

Berman,F.,Fox,G.& Hey Grid,A. J. G.,2008. Computing: Making the Global Infrastructure a Reality 2.

Bikram,2009: Safe on the Cloud. A Perspective into the Security Concerns of Cloud Computing 4: 34–35.

Boss, G., Malladi, P., Quan, D., et al.IBM Cloud Computing White Book, http://www-01.ibm.com/software/cn/Tivoli/ao/reg.html

Jamil, D., Zaki, H., 2011. Cloud Computing Security. International Journal of Engineering Science and Technology 3(4): 3478–3483.

Leavitt,N. 2009. Is cloud computing really ready for prime time. Computer, 42(1):15–25.

Mell, P.&Grance, T.,2009.The nist definition of cloud computing. National Institute of Standards and Technology 53(6): 50.

Shah, M. A, Swaminathan, R.& Baker, M., 2008. Privacy-preserving audit and extraction of digital contents, IACR Cryptology EPrint Archive 186.

Somani, U., Lakhani, K.,& Mundra, M., 2010. Implementing digital signature with RSA encryption algorithm to enhance the Data Security of cloud in Cloud Computing. In: 1st International Conference on Parallel Distributed and Grid Computing (PDGC 2010): 211.

Zhang, S., Zhang, S., Chen, X., 2010. Cloud Computing Research and Development Trend. In: Second International Conference on Future Networks, ICFN 2010: 93.

Shen, Z., Tong, Q., 2010 The security of cloud computing system enabled by trusted computing technology. In: 2nd International Conference on Signal Processing Systems. 2: 2–11.

Communication and Computing Systems – Prasad et al. (eds)
© 2019 Taylor & Francis Group, London, ISBN 978-0-367-00147-6

SLA penalty and reward strategy for cloud computing

Pooja Tiwari
Department of Computer Science, Dronacharya College of Engineering, Gurgaon, Haryana, India

Ashima Mehta
Department of Information Technology, Dronacharya College of Engineering, Gurgaon, Haryana, India

ABSTRACT: Cloud Computing is basically idea about to share the resources, so in order to maintain the balance between the cloud user and cloud provider, there present a service level agreement in between of them. In this paper our objective is to discuss the Penalty and Reward Provision for cloud environment. In addition while the previous in literature seen Penalty provision on breach of SLA by violating services. Earlier researcher researched on various strategies for penalty calculation on violation done from the cloud SP side. So now in this paper we have discussed the penalty provision on cloud SU and the new concept of rewards for cloud SP and cloud SU on properly following the terms and conditions mentioned in Service Level agreement. Under this strategy the main focus is on the cloud user satisfaction towards various services such as IaaS, NaaS, PaaS and SaaS. In this paper we have mentioned various problems faced by the cloud SP and cloud SU or customer on violation of SLA and have discussed the certain parameters decline of which in SLA both parties get affected.

1 INTRODUCTION

According to NIST "Cloud computing is a model for enabling ubiquitous, convenient, on-demand network access to a shared pool of configurable computing resources (e.g., networks, servers, storage, applications, and services) that can be rapidly provisioned and released with minimal management effort or SP interaction". Cloud computing (CC) environments contain several cloud providers which propose similar cloud services/computing resources and so the consumer has to choose the most suitable provider for his needs (Anithakumari et al. 2014). As of now, the differentiating elements between cloud computing solutions are Quality-of-Service (QoS) and the Service Level Agreements (SLAs) guarantee provided by the cloud providers (Udoh et al. 2013) (Jiang et al. 2017) (Maarouf et al. 2017). The Service Level Agreements plays important role in CC. The progressive innovation of CC offers a versatile and adaptable paradigm where infrastructure, platform, and software as a service are offered to various clients. The provisioning of these computing services by Cloud providers are regulated by SLAs (Leff et al. 2003). SLA is a kind of agreement between the SP and the client. Basically SLA is Signed document by both the parties cloud SP and client over the specified terms and conditions towards the particular service (Stanoevska et al. 2009) (Hsu et al. 20014). SLA basically includes the certain quality of service measurement parameters and provides assurance to the client towards services and also provides the concept of penalties in case of SLA violation (Maarouf et al. 2014) (Maarouf et al. 2015b).The concept of penalty is good for making trust on the particular SP but in this paper am discussing the concept of penalty as well as reward from the cloud SP side and from the client side in order to discuss the loyal decision for both the parties. In this paper we have investigated various types of violations generally occurred from both side and also investigated various parameters mentioned in SLA's in order to run cloud business properly.

2 SLA AND ITS VARIOUS COMPONENTS

According to various researchers Service Level Agreement is basically a contract between the cloud SP and Cloud user. The SLA is written information consist of all the parameters and QOS provided by the cloud SP to the client by their mutual understanding. sSLA is a document that get signed by both the parties the cloud SP and the cloud user. Signatory parties are the main party in the service level agreement and each SLA has exactly one cloud SP and one cloud SU. The various services provided by cloud SP are regulated by SLA (Leff et al. 2003). The QoS attributes that are generally part of an SLA (such as response time and throughput) however change constantly and to enforce the agreement, these parameters need to be closely monitored (Keller et al. 2003).SLA bound cloud SP to be fair on the commitment made by mutual understanding at the time of signing the SLA.

2.1 Components of service level agreement

i. *Parties:* It include both signatory parties cloud SP and cloud SU as well as the supporting party (Hsu et al. 2014) that are brought into the SLA to act on behalf of SP or customer but cannot be held liable on the grounds of this SLA. The relationship of a sponsored party to their sponsor is not within the scope of this agreement.
ii. *Services provided:* It represent the services provided by the cloud SP (Hsu et al. 2014) in terms of operations and the service's parameters and metrics that are the basis of the SLA. It also includes the specification of the measurement of a service's metrics.
iii. *Obligations or commitment:* It specifies the service level with respect to the various SLA Parameters specified in the service provided section and also include the commitment made by the SP.

2.2 Parties involved in service level agreement

i. Cloud SP: Cloud SP is basically the Organization or Firm providing the various cloud Services.
ii. Cloud SU: Cloud SU is basically the organisation availing the cloud services from the cloud SP
iii. Supporting or Third Party: Supporting party or third party basically monitor the Quality of Service provided by the cloud SP (Ludwig et al. 2003).

3 VARIOUS PARAMETERS TO MONITOR THE QOS OF SLA

i. *Availability:* Availability is basically combination of connectivity and functionality. Connectivity means there should be proper connection between the network elements provided by the cloud SP and Functionality means proper functioning of network devices.
ii. *Delivery:* Delivery of service is measured in terms of any loss or delay in delivery of particular service. In case these two metric loss and delay doesn't take place then we simply say that the quality of service is maintained.
iii. *Latency:* Latency is basically time taken by particular service to reach the particular destination.
iv. *Bandwidth:* Bandwidth is used to measure the capacity provided by cloud SP and the assurance of maximum bandwidth provided by cloud SP is mentioned in the service level agreement for further measurement and taking decision.
v. *Throughput:* Access rate of the services.

vi. *Price*: The Price of the service remains constant as decided earlier during signing SLA and the price of Service payment method also remains constant as decided earlier either Pay as you go or Paying Per month/year.

vii. *Security*: The data saved on clouds of particular SP is the responsibility of that SP only to provide security by any unauthorized access. (Ludwig et al. 2003)

4   TYPES OF VIOLATIONS GENERALLY OCCURRED FROM THE CLOUD SP SIDE

According to the Principles of European Contract Law (Bonell, 1996), the term unfullfillment is to be interpreted as comprising-:

- *Unavailability of Services* – Either the service is not provided for the duration (number of hour) mentioned in SLA(service level agreement) or it is not provided at all
- *Defect in service*- The Service provided by cloud SP is not according to terms mentioned in SLA about the particular service.
- *Late performance* -It means the service provided by cloud SP is according to signed SLA but not on mentioned time or late
- *Security not maintained* – It means unauthorized access of data by any person (competitor) or organisation.

5   OVERVIEW OF PENALTY

As we all know that any type of violation in service provided by cloud SP is the case of conflict between the cloud SP and the cloud user so in order to settle the conflict the concept of Penalty is researched by Ronetal (Ron et al. 2001). In service level agreement the service level objective (SLO) is basically negotiated terms and condition signed by cloud SP and cloud user. Prior signing the SLA the negotiation of service and the concept of penalty in case of any violation get occurred in future get discussed and signed by both parties. Using the concept of penalty the main question that get arise is what type of penalty clauses can be used (Rana et al. 2008).

5.1   *Penalty faced by cloud SP can be of five types*

1. *Decrease in Price assured to pay*: It means in case of any violation in SLA the price mentioned on behalf of particular service in SLA gets decreased according to percentage of violation occurred such as 10% unavailability etc.
2. *Not to continue any business relation in Future:* In case of any violation in SLA the cloud user is free to change his/her decision towards not using the services provided by particular cloud SP
3. *Reputation Loss:* It get faced by particular SP in case of unsatisfied user due to violation of service. Reputation loss takes place by spreading false messages (via internet and some other sources) in public towards the particular SP.

Now we want to describe some new concept other than traditional one that is penalty on the cloud SU on violation of terms mentioned in service level agreement

5.2   *Types of violations in which cloud SU generally get involved are as follows*

1. *Negotiation after signing the SLA* -: Sometimes the cloud SU start negotiating price of the particular service after signing the SLA with particular cloud SP.
2. *Increased demand of Particular Service* -: Means after signing the SLA the cloud SU start demanding the more quantity of particular service due to instant need but either don't want to pay any extra money for those service or want to pay according the cost of earlier service offered by Cloud SP.

3. *Pointing wrong allegation on cloud SP-:* Means the allegations for which the cloud SP is generally not responsible.

5.3 Types of penalty faced by cloud SU

1. *More Price for on demand services:* It means charging more price from the cloud SU for the on demand service which is not mentioned in SLA.
2. *Charge high price in future:* It means in case of noticing the particular user who is in past created scene in order to negotiate services after signing SLA then there must be choice of cloud SP in order to charge high price in future services.
3. *Don't provide services to forgery cloud SU in future:* It means in case the forgery user again want the cloud services from the same cloud SP then the cloud SP must have authority to refuse the particular cloud SU request unless he/she have service available.

6 OVERVIEW OF REWARD MODEL

Reward means something awarded to someone in return of best service provided by him in order to provide motivation to that person for providing such kind of good services in near future. Reward is basically a source of motivation for cloud SP as well as cloud SU in different ways. As I have discussed earlier the cloud SP and cloud SU is liable to pay penalty in case of service violation, so both must be offered reward by each other in case of accessing or providing service in a well manner. Reward provisioning strategy is marketing criteria of the services. Reward strategy improves the business of particular cloud SP. And the reward provided by cloud SU to cloud SP helps in motivating the cloud SP in order to provide quality of services to the cloud user within the time specified in SLA or prior.

6.1 Reward earning activities from the cloud SP side

1. *Providing Accurate or error free service:* In case the cloud SP is providing error free service to particular cloud SU then in that case the cloud SP must be rewarded.
2. *Providing service on time:* Reward must be provided to cloud SP on providing cloud services on time.
3. *Making good arrangement for on demand services:* Suppose the cloud SP is as good in making arrangement of cloud resources for the loyal clients on time then in that case the cloud SP must be rewarded by particular cloud SU or client.

6.2 Types of reward provided by cloud SU to cloud SP are as follows

1. *Repeat Business:* If the cloud SU get satisfied by the services provided by particular SP then that SU might use the services from the same SP in this case the particular SU is providing the reward to particular SP in return of best services provided by them by using the services of same SP again and again.
2. *Providing loyalty:* The satisfied cloud SU promotes the particular cloud SP by providing good feedback of service to others on social media or by mouth publicity.
3. *Providing more business in the form of reference:* If the particular cloud SU gets satisfied by the cloud SP services then he/she may refer to others for adopting the service of that cloud SP.

6.3 Reward earning activities from the cloud SU side are as follows

1. *On time payment:* If the client is making payment of used services on time without any delay then in that case that client or cloud SU get presented in good book of particular cloud SP.

2. *Not negotiating for the services not mentioned in SLA:* Taking stand on only services mentioned in SLA. Don't arguing for negation for the services which is not mentioned in SLA

3. *High cost for on demand services:* Paying the high cost demanded by particular SP for providing the on demand service in case of overloading.

6.4   *Types of rewards provided by cloud SP to cloud SU are as follows*

1. *Providing high discount:* In case the particular cloud SU is regular and make payment on time then in that case it's the responsibility of particular cloud SP to provide the requested service or resource on discount as much as possible.

2. *Priority to the loyal customer:* In case all the resources of clouds are acquired by some other cloud users and some of the resources are left and request queue is large then in that situation of scarcity it's the responsibility of cloud SP to give priority to loyal customer first.

3. *Providing requested service to customer even overloading-:* In situation of emergency when all the resources of particular cloud SP is already acquired by some other users then also in that situation it's the responsibility of that SP to making available the particular service by doing anything.

Fig.1 shows the sequence diagram of penalty and reward provision in SLA .

7   CONCLUSION AND FUTURE DIRECTION OF REWARD PROVISION

In this paper we proposed a reward provision in SLA. We investigated various papers of Service level agreement and analyse that there is the provision of penalty in SLA on violation of services and the various parameters are defined to measure the services in order to verifying whether the violation get occurred or not. And the various ways of
measuring degree of violations as well as novel penalty model for managing violation was discovered. By getting inspired by those concepts we thought regarding reward opposite of penalty. In this paper we have discussed certain parameter in order to measure the services

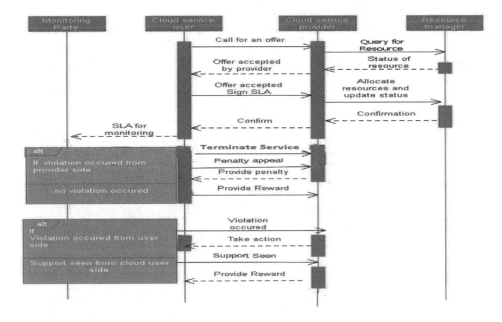

Figure 1.   Sequence diagram of penalty and reward provision in SLA.

and also have discussed the type of rewards. Generally the research is focused on the claim for penalty from cloud SP on the violation of services but in this paper we have discussed about provision of penalty from cloud SU side on violation of services. And another new concept mentioned in this paper is Reward provision. We have discussed reward provision for the cloud SP on providing violation free services and also discussed reward provision for cloud SU on supporting well during service duration.

In future we intend to find the novel reward model in order to calculate certain percentage of reward provided to particular either SP or SU on better support seen from them.

REFERENCES

Anithakumari, S., & Sekaran, K. C. (2014, March). Autonomic SLA management in cloud computing services.In International Conference on Security in Computer Networks and Distributed Systems (pp. 151-159). Springer, Berlin, Heidelberg.

Hsu, C. H., Slagter, K. D., Chen, S. C., & Chung, Y. C. (2014). Optimizing energy consumption with task consolidation in clouds. Information Sciences, 258, 452-462.

Hsu, C. H., & Udoh, E. (2013). Cloud computing technology and science. International Journal of Grid and High Performance Computing (IJGHPC), 5(4),1-4.

Jiang, F. C., Hsu, C. H., & Wang, S. (2017). Logistic Support Architecture with Petri Net Design in Cloud Environment for Services and Profit Optimization. IEEE Transactions on Services Computing, 10(6),879-888.

Keller, A., & Ludwig, H. (2003). The WSLA framework: Specifying and monitoring service level agreements for web services. Journal of Network and Systems Management, 11(1),57-81.

Leff, A., Rayfield, J. T., & Dias, D. M. (2003). Service-level agreements and commercial grids. IEEE Internet Computing, (4), 44-50.

Ludwig, H., Keller, A., Dan, A., King, R.P., & Franck, R. (2003). Web service level agreement (WSLA) language specification. Ibm corporation, 815-824.

Lee, H. J., Kim, M. S., Hong, J. W., & Lee, G. H. (2002, September). Mapping between qos parameters and network performance metrics for sla monitoring. In Proc. of (pp. 97-108).

Maarouf, A., El Qacimy, B., Marzouk, A., & Haqiq, A. (2017). Defining and Evaluating A Novel Penalty Model for Managing Violations in the Cloud Computing. International Journal of Grid and High Performance Computing (IJGHPC), 9(2),36-52.

Maarouf, A., Marzouk, A., Haqiq, A., & El Hamlaoui, M. (2014, November). Towards a mde approach for the establishment of a contract service level monitoring by third party in the cloud computing. In 2014 Tenth International Conference on Signal-Image Technology and Internet-Based Systems (pp. 715-720). IEEE.

Maarouf, A., Marzouk, A., & Haqiq, A. (2015, March). Towards a trusted third party based on multi-agent systems for automatic control of the quality of service contract in the cloud computing. In 2015 International Conference on Electrical and Information Technologies (ICEIT) (pp. 311-315). IEEE.

Ron, S., & Aliko, P.(2001).Service level agreements. Internet NG project.

Rana, O. F., Warnier, M., Quillinan, T. B., Brazier, F., & Cojocarasu, D. (2008). Managing violations in service level agreements. In Grid middleware and services (pp. 349-358). Springer, Boston, MA.

Stanoevska, K., Wozniak, T., & Ristol, S. (Eds.). (2009). Grid and cloud computing: a business perspective on technology and applications. Springer Science & Business Media.

Communication and Computing Systems – Prasad et al. (eds)
© *2019 Taylor & Francis Group, London, ISBN 978-0-367-00147-6*

Vehicle detection and classification in surveillance video using KNN classifier

Sagar Gautam
Department of Mechanical Engineering, Dronacharya College of Engineering, Gurgaon, Haryana, India

Yashwant Sahu
Junior Telecom Officer BSNL, Chhattisgarh, India

Poshan Lal Sahu
Department of Mechanical Engineering, Dronacharya College of Engineering, Gurgaon, Haryana, India

ABSTRACT: Vehicle detection and classification is one of most important and challenging task in image processing. Vehicle detection and classification has applications in various field such as transportation system, to reduce traffic and accidents in peak hours and security etc. Traditional detection and classification methods are computationally expensive and become ineffective in cases where light intensity is low and occlusion of vehicles is high. In the present work a new detection and classification method is proposed using single virtual display line (SVDL) concept. In the proposed method object detection is done by adaptive background subtraction method and for classification a non-linear classifier KNN is used. In present work when vehicles are passes through a SVDL or from a particular location then the features of the vehicle (object) is calculated. The concept of SVDL is used so that when classification will be done the distance between the camera and all the vehicles should be same so that features of the objects should not affected. These calculated features of vehicles are given to the KNN classifier for classification, which classified the vehicles in different categories of scooter, car and bus.

The present work consists of the proposed solution to detect and classify the objects by the MATLAB Image Processing by a new simple algorithm which overcomes the previous found drawbacks. Extensive experiments are carried out on large number of vehicles in surveillance video for long duration and at different environments to evaluate the performance of the proposed method. Experimental results demonstrate that the proposed method provides the improved and high accuracy in all environmental changes in vehicle detection and classification.

1 INTRODUCTION

Vehicle detection and classification techniques are in demand due to numerous applications in motorway surveillance, toll collection, traffic offence detection, and transportation system. Vehicle detection and classification is one of most important and interesting field of image processing due to its various applications in the video based intelligence transportation system. In this thesis, we present vehicle detection and classification system framework, particularly designed to work on surveillance video. Vehicle detection is a branch of object detection which is related to the computer vision and image processing to detect certain object which is vehicle (cars, buses, bikes etc.). Vehicle detection can be done by frame difference, background subtraction Gaussian mixture modal and optical flow method. In this method vehicle detection is done by Adaptive Background Subtraction Method (ABSM) in which single virtual display line concept is used.

After detection of vehicle, classification is needed to ensure its applications in transport management system. The classification is needed to use this information for applications like parking, security, and traffic management. New techniques of vehicle detection and classification are needed to develop and generate to overcome the difficulties like jittering of camera, noise contamination, light illumination, overlapping of vehicles, and shadow of vehicle of previous used methods. Vehicle detection and classification is growing field of research in last two decades. Counting number of vehicles in particular time period can help in reducing the traffic peak hours. Vehicle classification can lead the application of reducing the problem of parking space because the area of vehicles is different like bike, car, buses etc.

2   LITERATURE REVIEW

The concept for using KNN classifier is taken from paper in which they proposed the KNN classifier for vehicle classification. In this paper they used the background subtraction method for object detection and KNN classifier for vehicle classification. The idea of using KNN classifier is basically taken from that paper in which the concept of non-linear classification is given. KNN is non-linear classifier because it can classify in more than two groups directly. The classification is done in two steps. Firstly they are classified in two-wheeler (2W), three-wheeler (3W), four-wheeler (4W), and six-wheeler (6W). Secondly then another classification technique such as shape invariant and texture-based features is adopted to differentiate 4W such as car and jeep, similarly in 6W as bus and truck. They use virtual line display concept for vehicle detection which makes the algorithm little complex apart from them they use this concept to count the total number of vehicles. In our method we don't need to count the total number of vehicles, so we changed this part by adaptive background subtraction method.

The method of single virtual display line concept is taken from paper in which virtual display line concept is used. In this concept when a vehicle passes through a particular line or particular location then the vehicle is detected. After the detection its feature is calculated. The vehicle is detected at a particular location so that its distance from the camera should be constant and the features of the object should not affected by the camera position.

The concept of object detection technique was taken from the paper. The object detection technique from this paper taken was Adaptive Background Subtraction Method. Since in our method we are focus more in vehicle classification so we should not concern too much about the detection technique. Instead of that the object detected by this method is accurate and less affected by the noise.

2.1   *Vehicle detection and classification using KNN classifier*

Proposed method vehicle detection and classification using KNN classifier consists of three major parts first vehicle detection, second feature extraction and third vehicle classification. Vehicle detection is a challenging task because it faces may difficulties like jittering of camera, light illumination, shadow and environmental changes. In this method vehicle detection is done by Adaptive background subtraction method. In adaptive background method background frame is subtracted from current frame to get object or we can say that background pixels are subtracted from current frame pixels to get foreground pixel.

In adaptive background subtraction method is updated rapidly to accommodate environmental changes, light illumination etc. to decrease the noise. In this method video is converted into multiple frame images. The frame which does not have any object (vehicle) in our case is set as background image. This background image is subtracted from current frame to get object. The second part consists of extracting the features. Once the vehicle is detected its features are calculated which is used in KNN classifier for vehicle classification. In our method these features are area, major axis and minor axis etc. This sample data (features) are compared with the training data in KNN classifier and according to that it is classified to the relevant class. In our method the three classes are scoter, car and bus.

3 RESULT AND DISCUSSION

The result part consists of accuracy and error of vehicle classification for different value of k is 1 to 5. The results are taken for more than 5 input videos. All these videos are taken at stationary camera i.e. fixed at a particular position. These videos are taken at 9AM, 12PM, 3PM and 6PM.

Table 1 and Table 2 show the training data and sample data for different camera position settings. The tables shown is having training and sample values taken from different camera angle. In the later the percentage of error for scooter, car and bus are calculated at taking more than 100 vehicles passing in one way. Our features are area, major axis, minor axis, compactness and major axis to minor axis for classification so according to values of k they are taken respectively. From Table 1 and Table 2, it is inferred that as perspective camera angles changes feature values used such as area major axis and minor axis also changes. Hence in the proposed algorithm the camera setting used are stationary. For the evolution of algorithm the camera setting used are at setting 1.

Table 1. Training data and sample data values at camera setting 1.

Scooter	Training data values			Sample data values		
	Area	Major axis	Minor axis	Area	Major axis	Minor axis
1.	4933	111.61	58.29	2721	86.98	41.25
2.	4701	103.30	40.96	2751	88.9	40.89
3.	2241	88.10	34.94	2238	87.93	34.96
Avg.	3958.33	101	44.73			
Car	Area	Major axis	Minor axis	Area	Major axis	Minor axis
1.	11576	153.15	98.33	7729	121.43	94.21
2.	9748	160.83	83.53	7363	117.53	83.97
3.	6966	107.79	85.83	10445	137.37	99.22
Avg.	9430	140.58	89.23			
Bus	Area	Major axis	Minor axis	Area	Major axis	Minor axis
1.	22719	186.99	157.89	40185	270.29	195.2
2.	23757	184.78	168.60	25833	206.85	174.67
3.	31530	200.34	174.00	22950	190.10	157.50
Avg.	26002	190.70	166.82			

Table 2. Training data and sample data values from different camera angle at camera setting 2.

Class of vehicles	Training data values			Sample data values		
1.	1077	44.04	31.92	634	32.69	25.72
2.	689	34.79	26.71	650	35.71	23.62
3.	899	39.18	30.17	1023	46.10	29.31
Avg.	888.33	39.33	29.60			

(*Continued*)

Table 2. (*Continued*)

Class of vehicles	Training data values			Sample data values		
Car	Area	Major axis	Minor axis	Area	Major axis	Minor axis
1.	1609	61.59	33.85	2093	54.85	50.10
2.	2031	68.99	38.00	1870	59.64	40.50
3.	1560	58.60	34.88	1518	60.91	32.21
Avg.	1733.33	63.06	35.58			
Bus	Area	Major axis	Minor axis	Area	Major axis	Minor axis
1.	7430	122.01	79.38	5342	78.79	53.47
2.	3370	81.39	54.00	6732	83.39	54.56
3.	6789	129.02	62.66	7726	110.18	75.88
Avg.	5863	110.81	65.35			

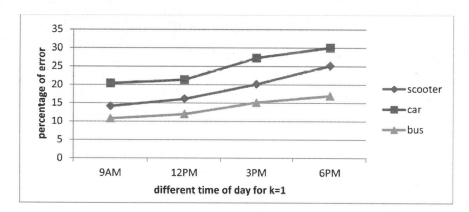

Figure 1. Percentage of error for scooter, car and bus for different time at k=1.

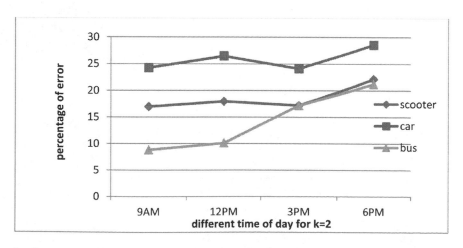

Figure 2. Percentage of error for scooter, car and bus for different time at k=2.

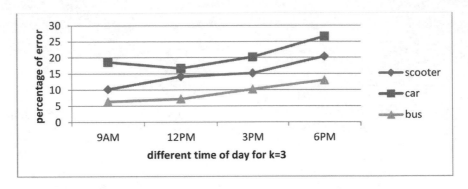

Figure 3. Percentage of error for scooter, car and bus for different time at k=3.

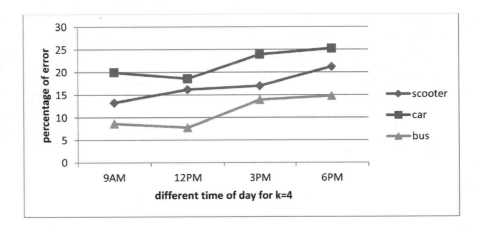

Figure 4. Percentage of error for scooter, car and bus for different time at k=4.

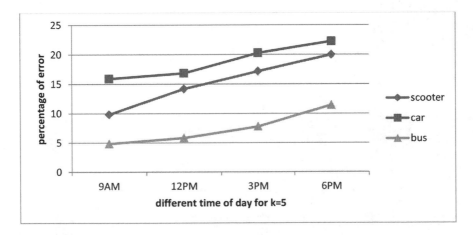

Figure 5. Percentage of error for scooter, car and bus for different time at k=5.

4 CONCLUSION

1. From Figure 1 to Figure 5 percentage of error is calculated by different time of the day from morning 9AM to evening 6PM and keeping k fix from 1 to 5.
2. In Figure 1 the percentage of error for car at 6PM is 30.05% respectively. It is maximum error for any vehicle at any time at k=1. The percentage of error for bus at 9AM is 10.82%. It is minimum error for any vehicle at any time at k=1.All errors are calculated at k=1.
3. In Figure 2 the percentage of error for car at 6PM is 28.56% respectively. It is maximum error for any vehicle at any time at k=2. The percentage of error for bus at 9AM is 8.82%. It is minimum error for any vehicle at any time at k=2. All errors are calculated at k=2.
4. In Figure 3 the percentage of error for car at 6PM is 26.56% respectively. It is maximum error for any vehicle at any time at k=3. The percentage of error for bus at 9AM is 6.32%. It is minimum error for any vehicle at any time at k=3.
5. In Figure 4 the percentage of error for car at 6PM is 25.25% respectively. It is maximum error for any vehicle at any time at k=4. The percentage of error for bus at 9AM is 8.64%. It is minimum error for any vehicle at any time at k=4. All errors are calculated at k=4.
6. In Figure 5 the percentage of error for car at 6PM is 22.23% respectively. It is maximum error for any vehicle at any time at k=5. The percentage of error for bus at 9AM is 4.84%. It is minimum error for any vehicle at any time at k=5. All errors are calculated at k=5.
7. So from the Figure 1 to Figure 5 the percentage of error is maximum for car whereas percentage of error is lower for bus. The percentage of error is minimum at 9AM and maximum at 6PM. Percentage of error is minimum for all vehicles at k=5.

REFERENCES

A. J. Lipton, H. Fujioshi, and R. Patil, "Moving target classification and tracking for real time video," in Proc. IEEE Workshop Appl. Comput. Vis., Princeton, NJ, pp. 8–14, 1998.

B. T. Morris and M. M. Trivedi, "Learning, modeling, and classification of vehicle track patterns from live video," IEEE Trans. Intell. Transp. Syst., vol. 9, no. 3, pp. 425–437, Sep. 2008

E. Rivlin, M. Rudzsky, M. Goldenberg, U. Bogomolov, and S. Lapchev, "A real-time system for classification of moving objects," in Proc. Int. Conf. Pattern Recognit., Quebec City, QC, Canada, vol. 3,pp. 688–691, 2002.

H. Yalcın, M. Herbert, R. Collins, and M. J. Black, "A flow-based approach to vehicle detection and background mosaicking in airborne video", in Proc. CVPR, San Diego, CA, 2005, vol. 2, pp. 1202.

K. Park, D. Lee and Y. Park, "Video-based detection of street-parking violation", in Proc. Int. Conf. Image Process., Computer Vision., Pattern Recognition, Las Vegas, NV, vol. 1, pp. 152–156, 2007.

L. Eikvil, L. Aurdal, and H. Koren, "Classification-based vehicle detection in high-resolution satellite images," ISPRS J. Photogramm. Remote Sens., vol. 64, no. 1, pp. 65–72, Jan. 2009.

Niluthpol Chowdhury Mithun, Nafi Ur Rashid, and S. M. Mahbubur Rhman, "Detection and classification of vehicles from video using multiple time spatial images", IEEE Transactions on Intelligence Transactions Systems, vol. 13, no. 3, September 2012.

P. G. Michalopoulos, "Vehicle detection video through image processing: The autoscope system," IEEE Trans. Veh. Tech., vol.40, no.1, pp. 21–29, Feb. 1991.

S. Gupte, O. Masoud, R. F. K. Martin and N. P. Papanikolopoulos, "Detection and classification of vehicles," IEEE Trans. Intell. Transp.Syst., vol. 3, no. 1, pp. 37–47, Mar. 2002

Z. Zhang, Y. Cai, K. Huang, and T. Tan, "Real-time moving object classification with automatic scene division," in Proc. IEEE Int. Conf. Image Process., San Antonio, TX, vol. 5, pp. 149–152, 2007.

Communication and Computing Systems – Prasad et al. (eds)
© 2019 Taylor & Francis Group, London, ISBN 978-0-367-00147-6

Beyond CMOS devices for hardware security: A review

Vikram Singh
Department of CSE, Dronacharya College of Engineering, Gurugram, Haryana, India

Raman Kapoor
Department of ECE, ABES Engineering College, Ghaziabad, Uttar Pradesh, India

Vimmi Malhotra
Department of CSE, Dronacharya College of Engineering, Gurugram, Haryana, India

ABSTRACT: Emerging applications such as IoT, Big Data, Machine Learning, Artificial Intelligence, Robotics and Automation are imposing higher performance and efficiency requirements on the hardware. On the device level, these requirements can be addressed by exploring novel semiconductor materials and device architectures. In particular, device technologies which fall under the Beyond CMOS category are expected to fulfill the expectations of the new era of electronics and computing. These devices have the benefit of enhancing functionality without the need for aggressive downscaling generally associated with conventional CMOS devices. In this paper, we present how Beyond CMOS devices can be used in emerging application areas such as hardware security and cryogenic electronics. Major future challenges and current viability is also addressed.

1 INTRODUCTION

The International Roadmap for Devices and Systems (IRDS) in its latest report has identified novel computing paradigms and application areas (IEEE- Report, 2017). These include Big Data, Internet of things (IoT), Deep Learning, Artificial Intelligence, Supercomputing, Robotics and Automation (IEEE, 2017). High performance and efficiency are the major critical requirements of these technologies. Consequently, the hardware infrastructure which is used for this new era of computing comes with its own set of challenges. The heart of the electronics and computing hardware are the integrated circuits which perform various functions and also provide an interface to the outside world. Modern ICs consist of millions of devices (individual transistors) fabricated on a single substrate which is generally silicon. These devices have evolved over the past many decades under the umbrella of complementary metal oxide semiconductor (CMOS) technology. Using aggressive downscaling of device dimensions and improvements in processing methods, CMOS technology has brought about major advancements in the field of electronics and computing. Considerable enhancements in mobility, on-state current has been realized for the past many decades. However, for the past few years the debate on the future of conventional CMOS technology has gained momentum. This is because dimensional scaling is reaching its fundamental limits and a transistor cannot be smaller than the size of an atom. Hence, the concept of equivalent scaling has gained momentum. According to equivalent scaling, novel device materials and device topologies need to be implemented which will improve performance without the need for aggressive downscaling. Hence it has become important to identify semiconducting materials and devices which can be viable alternatives for future applications. In particular, two technology domains have been identified. These are: (i) "More Moore" which extends functionality of an existing system by heterogeneous integration of new technologies and (ii) "Beyond CMOS" which

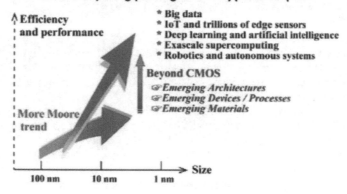

Figure 1. Relationship between major technology domains and novel computing applications (IEEE, 2017).

involves exploration of new device systems which will complement the already existing CMOS technologies and overcome the conventional parasitic effects. Figure 1 shows that Beyond CMOS approach is more likely to address the issues of the new era of electronics and computing (IEEE, 2017). This paper describes the new applications of hardware security and cryogenic electronics which are frequently associated with emerging technologies.

2 BEYOND CMOS DEVICES FOR HARDWARE SECURITY

The accelerated growth of IoT, Big Data and Machine learning has brought the issue of hardware security to the forefront. Conventional methods of circuit and hardware protection provide limited security and also incur additional costs. Advances in CMOS technologies may be used to provide new avenues for hardware security. Normally Beyond CMOS technologies are used improving performance and energy efficiency. It is also possible to exploit the typical characteristics of emerging CMOS devices such as nonlinear I-V behavior to mitigate security threats.

The major approaches through which beyond CMOS devices may be used to enhance hardware security are now discussed.

2.1 *Physically Unclonable Functions (PUFs)*

It is common for modern electronic devices and systems to be used for secure applications like storing user's personal information, financial transactions, etc. While strong focus has been laid on improving the performance of mobile computing, hardware security has been relatively slow to develop. Currently the common practice for providing secure environment involves usage of electrically erasable programmable read only memories (EEPROM) and static random access memory (SRAM). Both these approaches are complex, require large design area, consume excessive power and are vulnerable to invasive attacks. Consequently, there is a need for viable and innovative alternatives for hardware security.

Physically unclonable functions (PUFs) can be used to provide authentication solutions without the need of expensive hardware. Just like fingerprints are unique to human beings, PUFs are unique digital challenge-response combinations which develop due to the inherent variability of physical processes during semiconductor manufacturing. These random but repeatable unique combinations help in differentiating between otherwise identical semiconductors. Major advantages of PUFs include:

321

- Possibility of using simple digital circuits
- External attacks are dangerous only when the chip s powered ON
- More economical

2.1.1 Beyond CMOS devices for implementing PUFs

A large number of Beyond CMOS devices are considered as contenders for implementation of PUFs. Applications such as user identification, secure extraction of software, FPGA and encrypted storage utilize different types of PUFs.

On the technological level, PUFs can be implemented using a wide variety of digital technologies. As mentioned by (Iyengar et al., 2014), the changes in the time required to write data in spin torque transfer type of RAM can be used to create a type of PUF. Semiconducting structures realized using magnetic tunnel junctions have also been studied (Das et al., 2015; Marukame et al., 2014). The effect of write times in a memory architecture has been exploited before to obtain phase change memory arrays (Zhang et al., 2014).

Emerging CMOS devices due to their very small feature sizes are known for increased variability. This non-uniformity of device behaviour and performance finds an application in the area of hardware security using PUFs. Consequently, some of the well-researched materials like Graphene and carbon nanotubes among others have been studied for obtaining devices which work as PUFs (Pang et al., 2017a; Pang et al., 2017b; Rührmair et al., 2010; Konigsmark et al., 2014).

Non-volatile memories (i.e. those which can retain data in the absence of power) which use resistive action for switching data have also found use in the field of PUFs. These type of memories are broadly classified as Memristors. (Rose et al., 2013; Koeberl et al., 2013) are known for their pioneering work in implementing memristors for the purpose of realizing PUFs.

2.2 Random Number Generators (RNGs)

The typical variability in device performance associated with beyond CMOS devices also gives rise to a great degree of randomness in the characteristics of these devices. This fact can be used for generating random numbers (Rajendran et al., 2015). The compatibility of RNGs with already existing CMOS processes has been demonstrated before (Yuan Heng et al., 2009; Huang et al., 2012).

2.2.1 Application of beyond CMOS devices for RNGs

The otherwise insulating dielectric in a MOS device is prone to charge trapping especially in the so-called short channel devices post dimensional scaling. These trapped charge carriers affect the level of ON-state current especially at low voltages (Huang et al., 2012). The randomness tests prescribed by the prestigious National Institute of Standards and Technology (NIST) can be applied to the RNGs generated by novel semiconductor devices for testing randomness (Huang et al., 2012).

Novel devices based on a wide range of technologies have been proposed for generating random digital data. At the heart of random bit generation using semiconducting devices is the ability to tune the probability of 0 or 1 according to the applied voltage or current at the input. Most promising device technologies for RNGs include, (i) magnetic tunnel junction (H. Butler et al., 2001; Ikeda et al., 2008), (ii) Transistors based on Avalanche breakdown (Henderson et al., 2012; Webster et al., 2012), (iii) various random access memories (Yuan Heng et al., 2009; Huang et al., 2012; Rajendran et al., 2015; Wang et al., 2016; Jiang et al., 2017), (iv) CMOS ring oscillators (Park et al., 2015).

2.3 Prevention of IP attacks

Field effect transistors (FETs) whose channel polarity can be tuned can be used for security related applications. It is an inherent property of semiconductor devices to be turned OFF and ON by controlling various parameters like size, doping, voltage, etc. A large number of new devices take this switching capability few steps further by tuning the polarity of the channel under different conditions. Transistors which use materials such as carbon nanotubes, graphene, silicon nanowires (SiNWs), Tunnel FETs and transition metal dichalcogenides (TMDs) – have been experimentally shown to work by various research groups (Yu-Ming et al., 2005; Harada et al., 2010; Heinzig et al., 2011; Das and Appenzeller, 2013; Marchi et al., 2012; Convertino et al., 2018).

In addition to the device behaviour, the tunable characteristics of semiconducting materials also find applications on the circuit level designing. Encryption techniques for IP protection and prevention against Trojan attacks using polymorphic logic gates and camouflaging layouts can be found in literature (Bi et al., 2016; Bi et al., 2014; Chen et al., 2016).

2.4 Prevention of side channel-attacks

Side channel attacks refer to threats which rely on secondary information related to a device or a system such as computation time, power consumption, heat dissipation, etc. Such secondary information can provide clues to the security measures employed for any device. Many beyond CMOS devices exhibit I-V characteristics which significantly differ from conventional MOS devices. Such behavior which is generally studied through subthreshold characteristics generally provides fast switching capability which can help in countering side channel attacks.

In particular, Tunnel FETs, Symmetric Graphene FETs and thin-TFETs based devices owing to their unconventional I-V curves have been shown to be useful in designing on-chip systems which can counter side-channel attacks (Bi et al., 2016; Bi et al., 2014; Bi et al., 2017).

3 SUMMARY

The importance of hardware security for emerging application areas of modern computing and electronic systems has been highlighted. The applicability of beyond CMOS devices due to their unconventional characteristics has been pointed out. Going further various emerging semiconductor devices are expected to play a major role in tackling security issues related to the hardware. Overall device reliability and performance metrics are expected to play a major role in deciding the viability of various devices.

REFERENCES

Bi Y, Gaillardon P, Hu XS, et al. (2014) Leveraging Emerging Technology for Hardware Security - Case Study on Silicon Nanowire FETs and Graphene SymFETs. *2014 IEEE 23rd Asian Test Symposium*. 342-347.

Bi Y, Shamsi K, Yuan J-S, et al. (2016) Emerging Technology-Based Design of Primitives for Hardware Security. *J. Emerg. Technol. Comput. Syst.* 13: 1-19.

Bi Y, Shamsi K, Yuan J, et al. (2017) Tunnel FET Current Mode Logic for DPA-Resilient Circuit Designs. *IEEE Transactions on Emerging Topics in Computing* 5: 340-352.

Chen A, Sharon Hu X, Jin Y, et al. (2016) *Using Emerging Technologies for Hardware Security Beyond PUFs.*

Convertino C, Zota CB, Schmid H, et al. (2018) III–V heterostructure tunnel field-effect transistor. *Journal of Physics: Condensed Matter* 30: 264005.

Das J, Scott K, Rajaram S, et al. (2015) MRAM PUF: A Novel Geometry Based Magnetic PUF With Integrated CMOS. *IEEE Transactions on Nanotechnology* 14: 436-443.

Das S and Appenzeller J. (2013) *WSe2 field effect transistors with enhanced ambipolar characteristics.*

H. Butler W, Zhang XG, C. Schulthess T, etal . (2001) *Spin-Dependent Tunneling Conductance of Fe/ MgO/Fe Sandwiches.*

Harada N, Yagi K, Sato S, et al. (2010) *A polarity-controllable graphene inverter.*

Heinzig A, Slesazeck S, Kreupl F, et al. (2011) *Reconfigurable Silicon Nanowire Transistors.*

Henderson R, A. G. Webster E and Walker R. (2012) *A gate Modulated avalanche bipolar transistor in 130nm CMOS technology.*

Huang C, Shen WC, Tseng Y, et al. (2012) A Contact-Resistive Random-Access-Memory-Based True Random Number Generator. *IEEE Electron Device Letters* 33: 1108-1110.

IEEE-Report. (2017) IEEE International Roadmap for Devices and Systems. 123.

Ikeda S, Hayakawa J, Ashizawa Y, et al. (2008) *Tunnel Magnetoresistance of 604% at 300 K by Suppression of Ta Diffusion in CoFeB/MgO/CoFeB Pseudo-Spin-Valves Annealed at High Temperature.*

Iyengar A, Ramclam K and Ghosh S. (2014) DWM-PUF: A low-overhead, memory-based security primitive. *2014 IEEE International Symposium on Hardware-Oriented Security and Trust (HOST).* 154-159.

Jiang H, Belkin D, Savel'ev SE, et al. (2017) A novel true random number generator based on a stochastic diffusive memristor. *Nature Communications* 8: 882.

Koeberl P, Kocabas U and Sadeghi A-R. (2013) *Memristor PUFs: A New Generation of Memory-based Physically Unclonable Functions.*

Konigsmark STC, Hwang LK, Chen D, et al. (2014) CNPUF: A Carbon Nanotube-based Physically Unclonable Function for secure low-energy hardware design. *2014 19th Asia and South Pacific Design Automation Conference (ASP-DAC).* 73-78.

Marchi MD, Sacchetto D, Frache S, et al. (2012) Polarity control in double-gate, gate-all-around vertically stacked silicon nanowire FETs. *2012 International Electron Devices Meeting.* 8.4.1-8.4.4.

Marukame T, Tanamoto T and Mitani Y. (2014) *Extracting Physically Unclonable Function From Spin Transfer Switching Characteristics in Magnetic Tunnel Junctions.*

Pang Y, Wu H, Gao B, et al. (2017a) Optimization of RRAM-Based Physical Unclonable Function With a Novel Differential Read-Out Method. *IEEE Electron Device Letters* 38: 168-171.

Pang Y, Wu H, Gao B, et al. (2017b) *A novel PUF against machine learning attack: Implementation on a 16 Mb RRAM chip.*

Park M, Rodgers J and P.Lathrop D. (2015) *True random number generation using CMOS Boolean chaotic oscillator.*

Rajendran J, Karri R, Wendt JB, et al. (2015) Nano Meets Security: Exploring Nanoelectronic Devices for Security Applications. *Proceedings of the IEEE* 103: 829-849.

Rose G, McDonald N, Yan L-K, et al. (2013) *A write-time based memristive PUF for hardware security applications.*

Rührmair U, Jaeger C, Hilgers C, et al. (2010) Security applications of diodes with unique current-voltage characteristics. *Proceedings of the 14th international conference on Financial Cryptography and Data Security.* Tenerife, Spain: Springer-Verlag, 328-335.

Wang Z, Joshi S, Savel'ev S, et al. (2016) *Memristors with diffusive dynamics as synaptic emulators for neuromorphic computing.*

Webster EAG, Richardson JA, Grant LA, et al. (2012) A single electron bipolar avalanche transistor implemented in 90nm CMOS. *Solid-State Electronics* 76: 116-118.

Yu-Ming L, Appenzeller J, Knoch J, et al. (2005) High-performance carbon nanotube field-effect transistor with tunable polarities. *IEEE Transactions on Nanotechnology* 4: 481-489.

Yuan Heng T, Chia-En H, Kuo C, et al. (2009) High density and ultra small cell size of Contact ReRAM (CR-RAM) in 90nm CMOS logic technology and circuits. *2009 IEEE International Electron Devices Meeting (IEDM).* 1-4.

Zhang L, Kong ZH, Chang C, et al. (2014) Exploiting Process Variations and Programming Sensitivity of Phase Change Memory for Reconfigurable Physical Unclonable Functions. *IEEE Transactions on Information Forensics and Security* 9: 921-932.

Communication and Computing Systems – Prasad et al. (eds)
© 2019 Taylor & Francis Group, London, ISBN 978-0-367-00147-6

Role of Social Networking Websites (SNS) in recruitment: A review analysis

Tanya Yadav, Mahima Narula & Azad Singh

Dronacharya Group of Institutions, Grater Noida, UP, India

ABSTRACT: Recruitment is trepidation with feat out, magnetizing, and guarantying a supply of competent personnel and selecting of mandatory manpower mutually in their quantitative and qualitative aspect. Mainly it is the maintenance and development of sufficient man-power resources. According to KPMG, overall attrition rate in India is 13.5%. The highest attrition was reported by Retail sector with ecommerce being on the higher side with an average voluntary annual attrition of 18.5 percent which shows that attrition is one of the most burning issue and creating problem for businessmen. In the same way, situation is also going to be alarming for recruitment experts and there are various changes which are emerging in recruitment area which are going to play an vital role in recruitment and having knowledge of these changes will be beneficial for both segment i.e potential employee and recruiters (employers). Through reviewing methodology, the study found that traditional methods of recruitments are obsolescing and recruiters and employees are adopting modern recruitment methods. In 2018, According to Mettl Survey, the usages of social media in hiring people through social media was 25% more and this trend will be highly used in near future. The study, through exploratory research method, tried to explore all such emerging areas/trends which are going to be helpful for both.

1 INTRODUCTION

In Human Resource Management, recruitment concept is a regular procedure for workforce attracting and further selecting appropriate one and can be defined in more simply words i.e., closing of a vacant position by hiring the job with any applicant who comes by following your job advertisement. According to Edwin B. Flippo, "It is a practice of searching for potential employees and inspiring and encouraging them to apply for jobs in an organisation." There are various philosophers who gave various definition of recruitment in different ways. Kempner et. al defined recruitment as process and the first stage of selection where identification of eligible candidates use to be finalised and ceases the vacant position by following selection process as soon as possible. However, the hiring activity carries the presumption that he would work with the company as per the terms and condition offered to him during his appointment and will perform assigned task and duty as per his capacity and ability for his job growth and organisation growth.

In more layman words, Recruitment is concerned with reaching out, attracting, and ensuring a supply of qualified personnel and making out selection of requisite manpower both in their quantitative and qualitative aspect. It is the development and maintenance of adequate man-power resources. This is the first stage of the process of selection and is completed with placement.

1.1 Major recruitment methods

In today's busy and materialistic world, investigating and exploring right ability in the souk is severely niggling and its time need to stab new techniques for mobilization so that ideal aspirants' search can be closed timely and that also suit with respective associations. One and all need to enhance their recruitment ability up to such level that can ensure organisation or enterprises a unique identification into market and which will produce a challenge in front of its rivals. The famous recruitment methods are as follows:

- *Traditional Recruitment Methods*

    There are various recruitment methods which are still in the practice while conducting recruitment activity. The figure no.1.1 explains about the major traditional methods of recruitment below.

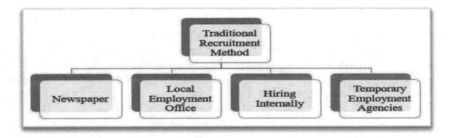

Figure 1.   Major traditional methods of recruitment.

Figure 1. explained about the various sources used in traditional recruitment method. Newspaper, Local Employment Office, Hiring Internally, Temporary Employment Agencies are the most popular recruitment methods which are still in practices by different recruiters from the different industry.

- *Modern Recruitment Method*

    With the changes of time, recruitment practices also taking shapes in accordance with adoption of technology and its up gradation enforce recruiters to module their strategies. Modern recruiters have to learn about how techniques are utilized and from where aspirants are present over job portals and social media in today's life so that right selection can be made.[4]Modern hiring techniques enabling recruiter to hiring potential candidates with shorter span of time and reduce recruiters' dependency on human and efficiently complete hiring tasks.[5]

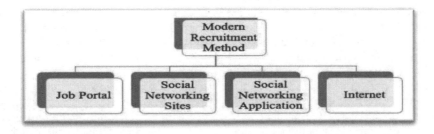

Figure 2.   Sources of modern recruitment method.

Figure 2. explained about the sources of modern recruitment method, and adoption of internet in corporate world providing ample opportunities for job seekers and recruiter to close vacancies before deadlines. Following are the major famous sites and their applications by which recruiter is getting quality stuff as well as more opportunities will be for potential jobseekers.

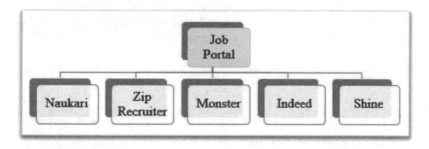

Figure 3.   List of major job portals.

Figure 3. enlisted about major job portals which are working throughout the world, especially in India. Job portal are the websites which are offering a wide range of jobs to those applicants who are finding jobs in different fields. Naukari, Monster, Indeed, Shine, etc. are some of the very famous and Job Portals in recruitment industry.

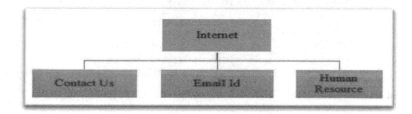

Figure 4.   Various services given by internet to corporate house.

Figure 4. explained about various services given by internet to corporate house so that they can connect with public. Through internet, people are able to connect with employers/ recruiters and also able to convey their suggestion as well as grievances. Mostly HR dept. of every company have hold over tags like "contact us", "Email Id", "Human Resource" which helps people to connect with different recruiters directly and visa-versa.

Figure 5. discussed about famous Social Networking Sites (SNS) which are majorly using as recruitment tools nowadays in India and world. SNS platform help people to connect and share information with each other. Facebook, Instagram, Twitter, LinkedIn are some popular sites which people are using and these sites are enriched with lots of information use to leads recruiters to choose right candidates. Now people also can get to know about jobs through these sites.

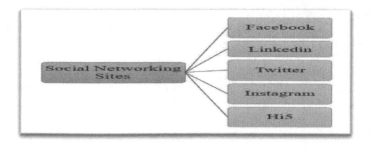

Figure 5.   List of famous Social Networking Sites (SNS).

All most every SNS have their chat messenger app and with this people are easily connecting with the each other and these apps continually adding more feature like status sharing, file sharing which helps recruiter to understand about nature and personality of their existing and potential employees. Whatsapp, Wechat, Viber, Snapchat are some of the popular apps which recruiters started using as a source for recruiting by sharing of job opening messages with different people.

2 LITERATURE REVIEW

(Sandra, 2011)Investigated reasons responsible for entry of Social Networking Sites in business management filed specially in the field of recruitment area and said that there is urgent requirement and demand for understanding about emerging recruitment styles. Survey method was deployed significant results were explained accordingly. The author concludes that efficiency of recruitment can be explained when mixture of applicants/applications received with adequate candidature, expected the costs and time (Keri Cook, 2012). Studied about various networking sites and discover that few networking sites are very helpful in recruitment activity and found LinkedIn is one of them which put a big step ahead in recruitment practices and making profit in Dollars. To understand SNS contributions in hiring process, through online survey, data was collected from hiring managers from international advertising and public relations firms (Caoimhe, 2014). Foundsocial media as one of the most important tool for recruitment while comparing with traditional methods of recruitment and headed to raise in workstations of services firms in Ireland. With deploying survey and quantitative methodology, the study tried to conclude that most of the surveyed companies specified that the usage of social media as a recruitment tool had increased in comparison with traditional methods of recruitment (Robin Kroeze, 2015). Investigated the role of social networking sites in recruitmen and through literature review tried to classify in what way and why companies use social media to draw and monitor candidates through their recruitment practices. The study findings conclude that companies were using social media in recruitment, but not that much effective as they could (Tanvi & Neha, 2016). Explained that by involvement of Internet in recruitment practice entirely reformed and all the traditional recruitment processes are converted and acknowledged as "e-recruitment". The highly usage of social networking sites in day today's social life, attract interest of recruiters about how they impinge on recruitment practices and provide custody of employees in the organization. In conclusion, the author investigated about pros and cons of social media recruitment methods and their impact on productivity (Sangeeta & Rajneesh Ahlawat, 2016). Studied recruitment and defined recruitment as an organized procedure of searching the prospective employees and motivating them towards the jobs to apply. With the commencement of SNS, social media had developed as a significant part of recruitment practice and made candidates aware with the new changes and provoke them to be connected with the world. The study concludes that social media don't restrict to hiring practice, it also played a vital role in internal communications with offering more opportunity toward superior and delivered the improved opportunity to the subordinates aimed at their sunnier career (Chaitra & Rajasulochana, 2018). Explored that speedy growth in technology affected the recruitment process. Further researcher explained e-recruitment is a technology oriented way which helped organisation to have desired candidate on their roll. Data analysis was done with help of IBM statistical software and with ranking method, significance inferences were made. In conclusion author tried to conclude that e-recruitment or recruitment through SNS will be only successful if hiring employee and job seekers interact using interact online simultaneously having accessibility, number of job opening being updated to candidates etc.

Nowadays, SNS have become as a very important part in our life becoming a largest source of communication for people to share information, ideas, news and so on. SNS usages is increasing incredible at a very fast rate and has attracted millions of users.[1] This adoption process developing a pool of information for recruiters and SNS playing a dominant role in hiring process. Recruiters are be more creative in searching and attracting talented people by using SNS and this process obsolescing traditional recruitment practices. Job posting over different SNS like Facebook, LinkedIn, Naukari.com, and ZipRecruiter.com and so on is becoming very common trends.

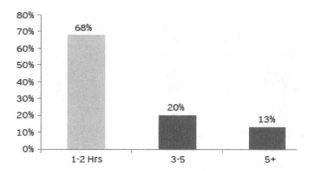

Figure 6.   Plot of hours versus Internet consumers on social media platform.

According to Ernst & Young in 2016, Figure 6. shows majority of Internet consumers (68%) use social media platforms one to two hours on per day, whereas only 13% use more than five hours per day up to. This has been observed across several surveys globally. With increased adoption of smartphones, increasing internet penetration and emergence of new platforms, the time spent on social media seems likely to keep on increasing by few minutes every year and this growth is tremendous and providing ample of information to the recruiters so SNS are becoming knowledge pool for recruiters and all.

3   RESEARCH METHODOLOGY

The present study Exploratory and Descriptive is in nature.
To Understand Role Of Social Networking Websites In Human Resource Recruitment.

3.1   *Implication of modern recruitment methods*

Recruiting a qualified set of candidates is an utmost significant decision which affect the overall vision and mission of an organisation as whether your candidate is proved to be an asset or liability all depends on how i.e. method you choose. Traditional recruitment is still being in practice worldwide. As with technology enhancement, this concept is getting outdated. So to survive in this highly competitive era, recruiters can't restrict themself to old methods. Moreover, modern methods of recruitment solves all the major problems involved in traditional method like short off time, cost, lack of diversity and many more. Following are the few points which explain implication of Modern Recruitments Methods as follows:

- COST EFFECTIVE: -Online recruitment is less expensive as compare to traditional recruitment methods because there is no need to make an advertisement in various newspaper, magazines which involves a lot of money. Whereas, by using social media, potential candidate can seek themselves on the respective job portals, apply and follow up accordingly.
- DYNAMIC SEARCH: -Everybody has access to internet from child to old age citizen and covered every corner of world which eventually benefited the companies in recruitment. As there is wider search option provided by SNS, it captures more top talent option from the pool of candidates.
- EASY EVALUATION, ASSORTMENT AND HIRING PROCESS:- E-recruitment facilitate a better evaluation of candidate as competent aspirant fill the required form in a proper format which gives recruiter simplified way of shortlisting a desired candidate. This also allows employer to do easy comparison from the large pool of candidate.[16]

- TIME SAVER & EASILY ADAPTABLE:- Regardless of where you will be, you can easily convey job posting anytime from anywhere. There is no need to maintain a bundle of printed material physically. On the same hand, response time is also as immediate as the delivered job resumes on online portals. Online recruitment can be learnt by anyone, it is not a long-term process and there is no difficulty in learning modern recruitment method.
- ENSURES EMPLOYER BRANDING:- Company's websites can be an effective way to attract a larger pool of candidate as well as it's a way to build an image in the eyes of stakeholder. Good Image leads to attract more candidates for job. Thus, it helps to protect and enhance the employers banding in the marketplace.

4   CONCLUSION

Through review of literature the study tried to give a new direction for all the potential stakeholder i.e. jobseekers and recruiters. The major objective of the study was to understand the role of SNS in recruitment and with adequate facts and figure predict that SNS have significant impact while conducting recruitment drive. With have modern era in mind, it's always good to stay update with latest market trends as it helps for both aspect i.e. job enrichment as well as building company image. The study revelled how employers and recruiters are responding to the various social platforms. The major motive of any recruitment drive is to choose a perfect candidate with desired skill and if recruiter is failed in selection of employee, it can make a big hole in the pocket and sever consequences sometimes have to face. To avoid all such difficulties, it's always better to be very curious while selecting candidates and through SNS such as Facebook, twitter, LinkedIn etc. putting a shining light on potential candidates. Hence overall, we can say that for a recruiter and every jobseekers its almost inevitable to ignore SNS contribution in Recruitment drive and everyone have to adopt this emerging trend if they want to survive in this competitive era.

REFERENCES

Caoimhe, M. K. (2014). *The Use of Social Media in Recruitment and its Impact on Diversity in Services Companies in Ireland*. Dublin Business School.

Chaitra, V. H., & Rajasulochana. (2018). A study on factors affecting the effectiveness of job portals from job seekers perspective. *International Journal of Scientific Research andModern Education*, 3(1), 22-31.

Keri Cook. (2012). *Social Recruiting: TheRole of Social Networking Websites in the Hiring Practices of Major Advertising and Public Relations Firms*. Liberty University.

Robin Kroeze. (2015). *Recruitment via Social Media Sites: A critical Review and Research Agenda*. University of Twente, The Netherlands.

Sandra, A. (2011). *The role of Social Networking Sites in recruitment: Results of a quantitative study among German companies*. School of Management and Governance, University of Twente, The Netherlands.

Sangeeta, & Rajneesh Ahlawat. (2016, August). E-Recruitment practices through social networking sites in India. *International Journal of Commerce and Management Research*, 2(8), 63-67. Retrieved from www.managejournal.com

Tanvi, R., & Neha, S. (2016, May). Social media as a tool for recruitment-a critical study. *International Journal of Science Technology and Management*, 5 (5). Retrieved from www.ijstm.com http://www.yourarticlelibrary.com/recruitment/recruitment-meaning-definition-process-and-factors-influencing-recruitment/25950 accessed at 01:42 on 15/ 01/2019. https://www.quora.com/What-are-modern-and-traditional-recruitment-and-selection-methods accessed at 04:25on 15/ 01/2019. https://content.wisestep.com/traditional-non-traditional-recruiting/accessed at 09:42 on 16/ 01/2019. https://www.quora.com/What-are-modern-and-traditional-recruitment-and-selection-methodsaccessed at 05:12 on 16/ 01/2019. https://www.ciivsoft.com/why-traditional-recruiting-methods-are-no-longer-enough-to-acquire-top-talent-in-2018/accessed at 02:34 on 17/ 01/2019 https://essay.utwente.nl/61154/1/MSc_S_Abel.pdf accessed at 00:44 on 19/ 01/2019. https://digitalcommons.liberty.edu/cgi/viewcontent.cgi?article=1317&context=honoraccessed at 12:50 on 21/ 01/2019. https://esource.dbs.ie/bitstream/handle/10788/2073/mba_mckenna_c_2014.pdf?sequence=1&isAllowed=y accessed at 20:49 on 20/ 01/2019.

Soft computing, intelligent system, machine vision

and artificial neural network

Communication and Computing Systems – Prasad et al. (eds)
© 2019 Taylor & Francis Group, London, ISBN 978-0-367-00147-6

Dynamic reliability evaluation framework for mobile ad-hoc network with non-stationary node distribution

N. Padmavathy & K. Anusha

Department of Electronics and Communication Engineering, Vishnu Institute of Technology, Bhimavaram (AP), India

ABSTRACT: Mobile ad hoc network consist of large number of mobile nodes distributed randomly. The performance of the network, in general, reduces, with node failure; link failure; con- gestion; interference and environmental conditions. All these attributes have significant impact on the evaluation of network reliability, a critical aspect of mobile ad hoc network. The existing literature points out that the nodes of a network can be distributed using two approaches, namely uniform and non-uniform. Several researchers have considered the mobile nodes to be distributed uniformly. But in reality or in practicality; node movements are highly random. This implies that reliability evaluation studies considering uniform node distribution is not a valid study. With this motiv ation, a non-stationary distribution of nodes with dynamic evaluation framework has been considered to evaluate the network performance through simulation. The results indicate that the reliability of the mobile ad hoc network decreased. This decrease happens because of the availability of more number of hops between the designated source-destination node pairs with non- uniformly distributed nodes.

1 INTRODUCTION

A mobile ad hoc network (MANET), is a self-organizing network which does not rely on fixed topology and operates in a decentralized manner. Mobile ad hoc networks can be formed by collection of nodes that are free to move independently in any direction and can change its links frequently. MANET has many autonomous mobile nodes; that are capable of connecting via wireless links. Chaturvedi & Padmavathy (2013) addressed that the communication between the nodes can be possible either through single hop or multi hop by using wireless channels. Flexibility, node mobility, dynamic network topology, symmetric network, multihop routing, fluctuating link capacity and limited operating range are certain features that have influence on the MANET performance. Based on the application and its performances, MANET can be used in commercial (Frodigh et al., (2000)) (Intelligent transportation system (Shih et al., (2001)); ad hoc gaming (Raja & Baboo (2014)); smart agriculture (Akyildiz et al., (2002)), rescue operation) and non- commercial applications (military), disaster recovery, wild life monitoring (Bulusu et al., (2001)) etc. The performance factors like link failures, congestion, interference and environmental conditions affect the dynamic nature of MANET. In other words, when the link between nodes are created or lost, the topology of the network changes. Henceforth, the above factors has significant impact on mobile ad hoc network reliability.

In general, any network, the performance of network reliability relies on the node distribution. Nodes are distributed in two ways uniform (Random Waypoint Mobility Model) and non-stationary node distribution (Random Direction Model). Several researchers have considered uniform distribution or non-uniform distribution of nodes and have implemented different mobility models that decide the movement of the nodes (Bettstetter et al., (2003), Camp et al., (2002), Hyytia et al., (2006), Mitsche et al., (2013), Resta & Santi (2002), Ruxin et al.,

(2009), William & Camp (2004)). Node speed, location and direction are the main parameters considered for modelling the mobility models. For uniform distribution, the probability distribution of both location and speed vary continuously over the time and can be achieved by using random way point mobility model.

In random waypoint mobility model (RWPM), as the simulation time starts, each mobile node (MN) randomly selects an initial location (x_0, y_0) which is sampled from the uniform distribution. After sampling, the MN travels towards the destination with certain velocity and direction. Reaching upon the destination, MN chooses a new destination, where the velocity and direction of node is chosen uniformly on intervals (V_{min}, V_{max}) independently. In RWPM model (Chaturvedi & Padmavathy (2013)), the mobile nodes are gathered at the center of the simulation area and that can be called as density waves as shown in Figure 1. Density waves are produced due to average number of neighbors that periodically fluctuate with time. Density waves can be diminished by using random direction mobility model (Fan & Helmy).

Using RWPM, the nodes are uniformly distributed and more often the nodes are densely populated at the centre of the region. In real time, nodes are not grouped (clustered) at the centre of the region because of high randomness. Ruxin *et al.*, (2009) addressed that random direction mobility model (RDM) is suitable for real time applications and nodes are non-uniformly distributed throughout the simulation area. For a node moving in a rectangular simulation area under the RDM model, the node location, speed and pause time are sampled using non-uniform distribution and this model can be easily implemented. In addition to above, using RDM, the movements of MNs are non-uniform. Mobile nodes travel throughout the simulation area, *i.e.*, mobile nodes travels to the border of the simulation area in that specified direction. In this model, MNs choose a random direction (0 to π) in which it travels and selects the destination anywhere along that direction of travel to the border of the simulation area. On reaching the simulation boundary, the MN pauses for a specified time (pause time), and further chooses another angular direction. The process continues until the simulation time have been completed. The maximum node density is high at the boundaries of the simulation region (Ruxin *et al.*, (2009)). In this paper, a RDM model with MNs moving in a square region is considered. Figure 2 shows the single MN is moving around the simulation area at each incremental time. The 1st position (0,2.4734) represents the initial position at time τ_1 and 72nd position represents the final location of the same MN at time τ_{72} (0.6541,4) as seen in Figure 2.

The rest of this paper is organized as follows. Initially, section 2 highlights the related work in detail which helps in describing the dynamic evaluation frame work and its implementation in section 3. Simulation results are discussed in section 4. Finally section 5 presents the conclusion followed by good number of references.

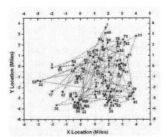

Figure 1. Node movement using RWPM for the entire mission time.

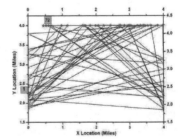

Figure 2. Node movement using RDM for the entire mission time.

Researchers have been investigating mobile ad hoc networks over several decades covering areas viz., mobility models (Bettstetter *et al.*, (2003), Camp *et al.*, (2002), Di *et al.*, (2006), Hyytia *et al.*, (2006), Mitsche *et al.*, (2013), Nain *et al.*, (2005), Padmavathy & Chaturvedi (2015), Resta & Santi (2002), Ruxin *et al.*, (2009))); network reliability (AboElFotoh *et al.*, (2006), Chaturvedi & Padmavathy (2013), Kharbash & Wang (2007), Padmavathy & Chaturvedi (2015), Venkatesan *et al.*, (2013), VenkateswaraRao & Padmavathy (2017)); battery reliability (Damaso *et al.*, (2014)); transmission reliability (Zhu *et al.*, (2016)); path reliability and hop count (SaiKumar & Padmavathy (2017)); interference (VenkateswaraRao & Padmavathy (2017)); energy consumption (Cardei *et al.*, (2008), He & Xu (2010), Wu *et al.*, (2008)); capacity calculation (Grossglauser & Tse (2001)) and the list goes on. Chaturvedi & Padmavathy (2013) evaluated the $2TR_m$ and ATR_m of MANET subjected to several simulation parameters like coverage area, transmission range and network size. The battery reliability considering the different simulation parameters *i.e.* power consumption of WSN nodes and battery levels has been evaluated by Damaso *et al.*, (2014).

Zhu *et al.*, (2016) proposed an algorithm for evaluation of transmission reliability. The evaluation process purely relies on the type of wireless sensor network and its topology; which changes frequently due to its dynamic nature. The authors have considered a clustered and mesh networks with uplink and down link transmission paths. Transmission reliability has been calculated by differentiating the transmission paths under the same simulation parameters with the help of network simulator. The concept of reliability calculation and an exponential algorithm with the use of data generation rate and sensor failure probability for arbitrary wireless sensor network reliability has been estimated by AboElFotoh *et al.*, (2006). Many researchers have failed to consider the effect of interference on reliability evaluation of MANET and the same has been emphasized in VenkateswaraRao & Padmavathy (2017). A methodology to calculate the network reliability by considering the effect of interference shows that interference reduces the network reliability, as the number of interfering nodes increases.

Padmavathy & Chaturvedi (2015) showed through Monte Carlo simulation that reliability evaluation considering/not considering mobility have no significant impact on the network performance. Mobility is the most important parameter to estimate the performance of MANET. An experimented and simulated survey paper by Camp *et al.*, (2002) highlights on different type of mobility models based on MANET application and its performance. Amongst all the models, the RWP model is frequently used mobility model because of its versatility and wide applicability. William & Camp (2004) presented a good review on RWP model considering spatial node distribution with respect to both with and without pause time. According to RWP model, each waypoint chooses new node locations in a specified area and also showed that simulation parameters play an important role in analysis of network reliability. The derivation of node spatial distribution for one dimensional can be found in Bettstetter & Wagner (2002) and it gives approximated formulas for two dimensional views, according to node density and mobility components. Furthermore, an analytical approximation of the spatial node distribution for two dimensional square and rectangular areas has also been provided. Bettstetter (2001) have clearly mentioned about an effect called border effect and is prominently visible in the uniformly distributed nodes *i.e.*, RWP model of MANET. In random waypoint mobility model, the nodes are uniformly distributed, and most of the nodes are placed at the centre of the origin that can be referred as border effect. Border effects can be eliminated by using random direction mobility model (Fan & Helmy). A stationary distribution equations considering location, speed and pause time has been derived by William & Camp (2004) to address the node movement in a rectangular area.

Yoon *et al.*, (2003) investigated and showed that RWP model is not perfect for steady state node distribution. For real time applications the same author had proposed a modified RWP model which is able to reach the steady state node distribution. In RDM model, nodes are distributed non-uniformly throughout the simulation area and located at the borders of the detailed area. Several authors explained about RDM (Camp *et al.*, (2002), Di *et al.*, (2006),

Fan & Helmy, Nain *et al.*, (2005)) but Di *et al.*, (2006) has elaborated on the three dimensional view of RDM. Any network can be designed with the help of some assumptions and it can act as static or dynamic. This assumption in MANET has been realized to study the effect of mobility on capacity calculations (Grossglauser & Tse (2001)); connectivity analysis (Kharbash & Wang (2007)). In the presence of mutual interference between the nodes, the capacity of the MANET decreases. In order to achieve efficient capacity for the MANET, multiuser diversity was proposed and is achieved by treating every node as a random source and destination pair. A significant problem in MANET is energy hole problem (Cardei *et al.*, (2008), He & Xu (2010), Wu *et al.*, (2008)) and non-uniform node distribution is the solution/effective method. Saikumar & Padmavathy (2017) used connectivity concepts to estimate the path reliability and hop count of MANET. It may be summarized that several researches have studied the MANET performance like capacity measurements, reliability (path/network), interference, power consumption, protocol and many more considering an uniform node distribution. This paper aims at modelling the node movements nonuniformly to study its effect on network reliability.

3 PRELIMINARIES

3.1 *Reliability evaluation framework*

Amongst all the characteristics features (see section 1) of MANET; dynamic topology has a significant effect on MANET performance. A topology is dynamic if all mobile nodes change arbitrarily with time considering a suitable mobility model. Several researchers have addressed evaluation of such networks performance like capacity, interference, connectivity *etc.* using mobility models say, synthetic entity models and group mobility model (Camp *et al.*, (2002)). However, the node movements depend on the choice of the mobility model. As addressed in the section 2, most of the authors have considered uniform node distribution (Chaturvedi & Padmavathy (2013), Padmavathy & Chaturvedi (2015)) to study the MANET performance. In reality, nodes do not move uniformly instead at the start of the mission time and end of the mission time, nodes move uniformly and rest of the time nodes are non-uniformly distributed. With this motivation, a dynamic reliability evaluation frame work algorithm has been proposed and developed. The algorithm considers a non-stationary node distribution through the choice of RDM model. The block diagram representation of dynamic evaluation framework is as shown in Figure 3.

Initially, all network parameters (number of nodes, radio range, coverage area, node reliability, mobility parameters (direction), velocity (maximum and minimum) and mission time) are initialized. At the start of the mission time, the initial node locations are generated randomly/initial node locations can be stored real time through GPS. The node locations through GPS pose to be a costly affair. Based on the node status (the node that are active within the defined simulation boundary) and link status (when nodes are within its visibility range, link is created otherwise link is destroyed) the network topology is generated. Each topology is checked for connectivity and reliability is evaluated for the connected network at a fixed time

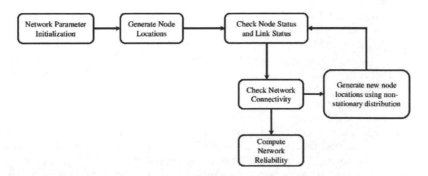

Figure 3. Dynamic network reliability evaluation framework.

instant. The process is repeated several times till the end of the mission time. Finally the effect of non-uniform distribution on MANET reliability is simulated and studied. A brief description on the reliability evaluation procedure is detailed in the subsequent paragraphs. The frameworks evaluates the node status, link status, network status, and performs the connectivity analysis. In addition, the reliability of the network is estimated considering a non-stationary distribution of mobile nodes. In the network, each mobile node is operational at the start of the mission time and when it fails in between, the MN remains failed for the remaining time, since repair is not considered. The success probability of the MN is the operational probability and is assumed that each mobile node failure follows Weibull distribution. Therefore, node reliability (r_i) is defined as given in (1)

$$r_i(\tau) = p_r(u_i(\tau)) = e^{-(\tau/\theta)^{\beta}} \, \forall i = 1 \, to \, N \tag{1}$$

where;

$$u_i(\tau) = \begin{cases} 1 & \text{if node } u_i \text{ is working at time } \tau \\ 0 & \text{if node } u_i \text{ fails} \end{cases} \tag{2}$$

N is the number of mobile nodes in the network; Weibull distribution parameters - θ (scale parameter) defines the spread of the distribution and β (shape parameter) tells about the shape of the distribution. The Weibull distribution has been assumed due to its flexibility; wide usage in reliability and life data analysis (Mark (2011)). It can mimic various distributions like the normal, exponential ($\beta = 1$); and Rayleigh ($\beta = 2$). Based on the operability of the MN at a particular time instant, the presence (absence) of link is determined. The operability of the nodes *i.e.*, the node status can change due to several reasons like, fast moving nodes, out of range, hardware/software failure *etc*. The link status can be determined using (3).

$$l_{ij}(\tau) = \begin{cases} 1 & \text{if } d_{ij}(\tau) \leq r_j \\ 0 & \text{otherwise} \end{cases} \tag{3}$$

where

$$d_{ij}(\tau) = \left(\left(x_j(\tau) - x_i(\tau) \right)^2 + \left(y_j(\tau) - y_i(\tau) \right)^2 \right)^{\frac{1}{2}} \tag{4}$$

where The link existence (non-existence) depends on the relationship between the transmission range (r_j) and the Euclidean distance (d_{ij}) between the MNs. (3) can be interpreted as - link appears if the distance between the MN is at most the nodes transmission range ($d_{ij} \leq r_j$) otherwise the link disappears ($d_{ij} > r_j$). The link existence of the network at any time instant τ is represented in a matrix form (5) known as connectivity matrix ($L(\tau)$).

$$L(\tau) = \begin{vmatrix} l_{11} & l_{12} & \dots & l_{1n} \\ l_{21} & l_{22} & \dots & l_{2n} \\ \vdots & \vdots & \dots & \vdots \\ l_{m1} & l_{m2} & \dots & l_{mn} \end{vmatrix} \tag{5}$$

Matrix (5) is used to determine the connectivity $C(\tau)$ and is defined as

$$C_q(\tau) = \begin{cases} 1 & \text{if the network is connected at time } \tau \\ 0 & \text{otherwise} \end{cases} \tag{6}$$

The network is connected if either a direct or indirect path exists. Direct path ($l_{in} = 1$) is single hop communication while communication with the help of the intermediate nodes is indirect path communication ($l_{in} = 0$) or multihop communication. If the network is connected, then the reliability of the network (Chaturvedi & Padmavathy (2013) is calculated as a product of designated node pairs reliability and the number of connected networks in the stipulated mission time aver- aged over simulation runs (Q) using (7).

$$R_G(\tau) = \frac{\left(\prod_{u_i \in k \subseteq U} R_{u_i}(\tau) \right) \sum_{q=1}^{Q} C_q(\tau)}{Q} \tag{7}$$

where k represents the designated (s-t) node pairs. If k =2, then the reliability calculation is called two terminal reliability and $k = n$ implies all terminal reliability. n is the number of nodes in the MANET. This paper deals with two-terminal network reliability evaluation of mobile ad hoc network with non-stationary node distribution. In case, if the network is not connected, then a new topology is to be generated. This can be achieved, by distributing the nodes non-uniformly in the defined simulation boundary. The mobile nodes move within the simulation boundary according to the RDM model with a selected direction (ϕ). The new positions (8) of the MN chosen at every incremental time interval ($\Delta\tau$) can be calculated as a function of direction.

$$x_i(\tau + \Delta\tau) = x_i(\tau) + L \cos \phi_i(\tau) \\ y_i(\tau + \Delta\tau) = y_i(\tau) + L \sin \phi_i(\tau) \tag{8}$$

The implementation of the reliability analytical framework can be understood with the help of the algorithm (a step-by-step procedure). The algorithm evaluates the network reliability beginning with generation of node locations, checking the node; the link; and network status followed by reliability calculation if the topology is connected. It may be noted that at the start of the mission time (0th hour) and at the end of the mission time (72nd hour), nodes follow uniform distribution while during the remaining tenure, the MNs follow non-stationary distribution. The evaluation procedure is given below:

Step 1: Initialize the network parameters such as r_j (transmission range); D (coverage area); N (network Size); (V_{max}, V_{min}) (node velocity); $tMission$; Weibull parameters – θ (scale parameter) and β (shape parameter); ϕ (direction).

Step 2: Generate initial node locations uniformly and later distribute the nodes non-uniformly in the defined simulation area.

Step 3: Calculate the node reliability using (1)

Step 4: Check the node status using (2), link status using (3)

Step 5: Determine the network connectivity (6) using connectivity matrix (5) and then check for the connectivity between the nodes and increment τ

Step 5.1: If nodes are connected, find the reliability at particular time instant τ.

Step 5.2: If nodes are not connected, go to *step* 6.

Step 6: Generate new node location (non-stationary random locations) using (8). Repeat *step* 4 to *step* 5 until $\tau \le tMission$

Step 7: Repeat *step* 2 to *step* 6 for Q number if simulation runs.

Step 8: Compute the network reliability using (7).

4 IMPLEMENTATION AND ANALYSIS

The proposed algorithm has been implemented using MatLab®2016a; run on Windows 8® with processing speed 2.20 GHz. The simulation parameters as mentioned in Table 1 are required for the evaluation of network reliability. Few of the parameters are taken from Chaturvedi & Padmavathy (2013), and is been mentioned for the sake of completeness.

Table 1. Simulation parameters.

Parameters	Specifications	Parameters	Specifications
Network type	Homogeneous	Mobility Model	RDM
Radio range (r_j)	1 to 8 Miles	Direction (ϕ)	0 to π
Coverage area (D)	64 to 400 Sq. Miles	Mission duration ($tMission$)	72 Hrs.
Network Size (N)	9 to100 Nodes	Simulation runs (Q)	10000

The simulation is performed over a set of almost 7,20,000 topologies to evaluate the network reliability. As a typical case considered for the study, the network constitutes of 18 mobile nodes which are deployed in a simulation region of 8 miles x 8 miles, i.e., 64 miles^2 move with a velocity ranging between 3 mph to 6 mph. The mobile nodes are able to communicate with one another if they fall within the range of 3 miles; the nodes' transmission range. The proposed MANET reliability algorithm concentrates on the effect of scenario metrics with non-stationary node distribution. The simulation results are further compared with Chaturvedi & Padmavathy (2013). The effect on network reliability has been evaluated by altering the transmission range from 1 mile to 8 miles without any change in other simulation parameters. Figure 4 shows the changes in $2TR_m$ by varying the transmission range. To avoid confusion, $2TR_m$ is written as mean reliability (see all graphical plots) throughout in this paper. The trend in red color is the result of proposed algorithm and blue line indicates the existing algorithm.

The plot clearly indicates that the achieved reliability is less, when compared with previous algorithm. However, it is noticed that there is a significant difference between existing and proposed methods when the transmission range is 1 to 5 miles and there is no variation in range of 5 to 8 miles. In other words, for a transmission range of 4 miles, the reliability is 20% less than existing approach reliability. Further beyond 5 miles the reliability difference is 0.5% (a negligibly small value) confirming that the reliabilities of both approaches are almost same. The reason for significant variation is explained here. The RDM has higher hop count (i.e., more number of hops are required to reach the destination) than the other mobility models (e. g. RWPM) (Camp et al., (2002)). When the number of hops between the (s–t) nodes are larger than one, then probability of multihop communication is high. Therefore, the product of reliability of nodes in a specific path results in low reliability.

Figure 5 shows that the effects of transmission range on expected $2TR_m$ with mission duration.It has been observed that, as the time changes; network reliability has reduced and remains same for all transmission ranges. From Figure 4 and Figure 5, it can be concluded that the network reliability is equal to 0.9621 irrespective of the transmission range beyond 5 miles. Therefore, non-stationary node distribution has no significant impact on reliability at higher transmission ranges. The simulation study has also been extended to study the effects of simulation boundary (coverage area) and number of nodes of non-stationary distributed MANET on network reliability. Figure 6 and Figure 7 shows changes in $2TR_m$ with varying network coverage area (64 sq. miles to 400 sq. miles) and network size (9 to 100 MN) respectively. It is noticed that the network reliability curve trend is similar for both existing and proposed methods. Moreover as the network reliability achieved is only 10% for coverage area

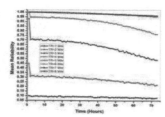

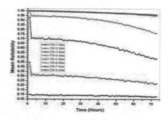

Figure 4.   Transmission range vs mean reliability.   Figure 5.   Mission time vs mean reliability (TR).

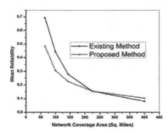

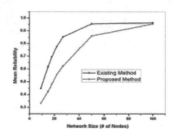

Figure 6. Coverage area vs mean reliability.　　Figure 7. Network size vs mean reliability.

beyond 225 miles2, designing a network having coverage area less than 225 miles2 would give better performance. Figure 7 depicts clear variation in achieved reliability at several stages with respect to coverage area. When compared with existing method, a variation of 11.41% (9 nodes), 22.83% (27 nodes) and thereafter a lesser variation (say 9.56% (50 nodes) can be observed. However a better results is got i.e., connectivity success > 0.5 is achieved for network size greater than or equal to 22 nodes. Whereas, when the network size is 15, a reliability greater than 0.5 has been obtained in the case of existing approach. It can be concluded that to have better performance, the designer have to make an optimum choice of 22 nodes to have successful communication considering non- uniform distribution.

　　The effect of mission duration on expected $2TR_m$ with varying coverage area and network size are depicted in Figure 8 and Figure 9. At the start of the mission time ($\tau = 0^{th}$ hour), network reliability is '1' because all nodes are initially operating and hence the chance of the networks being connected is high (see Figure 5, Figure 8 and Figure 9),while through the mission duration till the end of the mission time ($\tau = 71$ hours) network reliability decreases irrespective of all network parameters following the concept of bath tub curve.

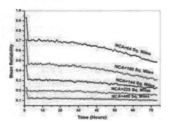

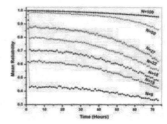

Figure 8. Mission time vs mean reliability (CA).　　Figure 9. Mission time vs mean reliability (NS).

5 CONCLUSION

In this paper, a non-uniform node distribution has been proposed for evaluation of network reliability in mobile ad hoc networks. Existing literature of MANET reliability evaluation uses uniform node distribution and shows the evidences of the best reliability values. In spite of achieving highly reliable networks, these networks with uniform distribution are not suitable for real-time applications. The proposed algorithm has been simulated and the evaluated network reliability is observed to be less than the network with uniform distributed nodes. The justification to the reduced network reliability is that in a non-stationary mobility model the average hop count using the RDM model is considerably higher than most of the other mobility models (e.g., RWPM). The results show that reliability greater than 70% can be achieved with MANET design parameters viz., coverage area (50 sq. miles); network size (22 nodes) and transmission range (5 miles).

REFERENCES

AboElFotoh H.M.F., ElMallah H.E.S. and Hassanein S. 2006. On the reliability of wireless sensor networks, *IEEE ICC proceedings*, 3455-3460.

Bettstetter C and Wagner C. 2002. The spatial node distribution of the random waypoint mobility model, Proc. *First German Workshop Mobile Ad Hoc Networks (WMAN)*, 41-58.

Bettstetter C, Resta G and Santi G. 2003. The node distribution of the random waypoint mobility model for wireless ad hoc networks, *IEEE transactions on Mobile Computing* 2(3): 257-269.

Bettstetter C. 2001. Mobility modeling in wireless networks-categorization, smooth movements and border effect, *Mobile Computing and Communications Review* 5(3): 55-67.

Camp T, Boleng J, and Davies V. 2002. A survey of mobility models for ad hoc network research, http://toilers.mines.edu, 1-21.

Cardei M, Yang Y, and Wu J. 2008. Non-uniform sensor deployment in mobile wireless sensor networks, *International Symposium on a World of Wireless, Mobile and Multimedia Networks*,1-9.

Chaturvedi S.K. and Padmavathy N. 2013. The influence of scenario metrics on network reliability of mobile ad hoc network, *International Journal of Performability Engineering* 9(1): 61–674.

Damaso A, Rosa N and Maciel P. 2014. Reliability of wireless sensor networks, *Sensors*, 14(9): 15760-15785.

Di W, Xiaofeng W, and Xin W. 2006. Analysis of 3-D random direction mobility model for ad hoc network, 6th International Conference on ITS Telecommunications Proceedings, 741-744.

E. Shih, S. Cho, N. Ickes, R. Min, A. Sinha, A. Wang, A. Chandrakasan. 2001. Physical layer driven protocol and algorithm design for energy-efficient wireless sensor networks, Proceedings of ACM MobiCom'01, 272–286.

Fan Bai and Ahmed Helmy. A survey of mobility models in wireless ad hoc networks. Springer,chapter-1,1-30 http://www.cise.ufl.edu/~helmy/papers/Survey-Mobility-Chapter-1.pdf

Grossglauser M and Tse D. 2001. Mobility increases the capacity of ad hoc networks, *Proc. IEEE INFOCOM*, 1360-1369.

He Y and Xu T. 2010. The Research of Non-uniform Node Distribution in Wireless Sensor Networks, IEEE proceedings.

Hyytia, E., Lassila, and Virtamo J. 2006. Spatial node distribution of the random waypoint mobility model with applications, IEEE Transactions on Mobile Computing 5(6): 680-694.

I.F. Akyildiz, W. Su, Y. Sankarasubramaniam, E. Cayirci. 2002. Wireless sensor networks: a survey, Computer Networks. 38(4): 393-422.

Kharbash S and Wang W. 2007. Computing two-terminal reliability in mobile ad hoc networks, In Proceedings of IEEE Conference on Wireless Communications and Networking, WCNC 2007, 2833-2838.

L Raja and S.S. Baboo. 2014. An overview of MANET: Applications attacks and challenges, International Journal of Computer Science and Mobile Computing 3(1): 408-417.

R. Ahmed, X. Huang, D. Sharma and H. Cui. 2012. Wireless sensor networks: characteristics and architectures world academy of science, engineering and technology. International, Journal of Information and Communication Engineering 6(12):1398-1401.

Magnus Frodigh, P. Johansson and P. Larsson. 2000. Wireless ad hoc networking. The art of networking without a network, Ericsson Review, 4, 248–2263.

Mark N.A. 2011. Parameter estimation for the two-parameter Weibull distribution. All Theses and Dissertations 2509. https://scholarsarchive.byu.edu/etd/2509

Mitsche D, Resta G and Santi G. 2013. The random waypoint mobility model with uniform node spatial distribution, Springer +Business Media New York.

Bulusu, D. Estrin, L. Girod, J.Heidemann. 2001. Scalable coordination for wireless sensor networks: self-configuring localization systems. International Symposium on Communication Theory and Applications (ISCTA 2001,), Ambleside, UK 1-6.

Nain P, Towsley D, Liu Z and Liu B. 2005. Properties of random direction models, *Proc. of IEEE Infocom*, 1897-07.

Padmavathy N and Chaturvedi S.K. 2015. Reliability evaluation of mobile ad hoc network: with and without mobility considerations, Procedia Computer Science 4(6): 1126–11139.

Resta G and Santi P. 2002. An analysis of the node spatial distribution of the random waypoint mobility for adhoc networks, Proceedings of the second ACM international workshop on Principles of mobile computing,44-50.

Ruxin Z, Gao F. and Yang J. 2009. Nonuniform property of random direction mobility model for MANET. 5th International Conference on Wireless Communications, Networking and Mobile Computing, 2009. WiCom '09,

Venkata SaiKumar B and Padmavathy N. 2017. A systematic approach for analyzing hop count and path reliability of Mobile Ad Hoc Networks, Int. Conf. on Advances in Computing, Communications and Informatics, 155-160.

Venkatesan L, Shanumugavel S and Subramaniam C. 2013. A Surevy on modelling and enhancing reliability of wireless sensor network, Wireless.Sensor.Networks.5: 41-51.

VenkateswaraRao Ch, Padmavathy N and Chaturvedi S.K. 2017. Reliability Evaluation of Mobile Ad Hoc Networks With and Without Interference, IEEE 7th International Advance Computing Conference, 233-238.

William N and Camp T. 2004. Stationary Distributions for the Random Waypoint Mobility Model, IEEE Transactions on Mobile Computing 3(1): 99-108.

Wu X, Chen G and Sajal K. D. 2008. Avoiding energy holes in wireless sensor networks with nonuniform node distribution, *IEEE Transactions on Parallel and Distributed Systems* 19(5): 710-720.

Yoon J, Liu M, and Noble B. 2003. Random waypoint considered harmful, IEEE INFOCOM 2003, Twenty-Second Annual Joint Conference of the IEEE Computer and Communications 2: 1312-1321.

Zhu X, Lu Y, Han J and Shi L. 2016. Transmission reliability evaluation for wireless sensor networks, *International Journal of Distributed Sensor Networks* 12(2): 1-10.

Communication and Computing Systems – Prasad et al. (eds)
© *2019 Taylor & Francis Group, London, ISBN 978-0-367-00147-6*

Re-designing an Indian kitchen for the elderly using REVIT

Sonal Atreya
Department of Architecture and Planning, IIT Roorkee, Uttarakhand, India

Sonam Agarwal
SALD, Shri Mata Vaishno Devi University, Katra, India

ABSTRACT: The world is a combination of people, who set out every day to fulfill their role in the society. Different people are entitled to perform different duties in their own workplaces. Professionals go to offices, children and youth go to educational institutions, farmers head to the fields and the list is endless. To increase the efficiency and make work easy for people, several modifications have been made in these workplaces. In a similar manner kitchen is a workplace for the homemakers and the elderly. Hence, it is necessary to study about the kitchen and make it comfortable to work in. It is necessary to avoid severe musculoskeletal loading on the human body especially for the elderly. This can aid in improving the health situations of the elderly to some extent. The basic aim of this study was to re-design an Indian kitchen using computer simulated models before manufacturing in such a way that it is easily accessible by the elderly.

1 INTRODUCTION

The global population of elderly in 2010 was 524 million, which is expected to triple by 2050 (WHO 2011, Ghimire 2018).The demographics of the advanced and developed world are changing- With the breakthrough in the area of modern medicine; the life-span has increased leading the ratio of elderly to dominate the world population. One of the main changes in body composition due to aging is the reduction of muscle mass and strength, which occurs in both men and women, regardless of weight changes (Hong et al. 2017). Life expectancy has increased due to enhanced medical care; however, the world is aging (Saghafi-Asl & Vaghef-Mehrabany 2017). As a result, many elderly couples are found to be living alone. They are forced to perform the daily chores themselves, despite of the fact that their bodies no longer can withstand such musculoskeletal load. A major portion of these daily chores are performed in the kitchen which can lead to several health issues in the elderly. In certain cases cognitive decline among the elderly, an inevitable component of aging, imposes a large personal and public health care cost, which needs to be taken into account (Gupta et al. 2017). In such a scenario there is need of a kitchen that changes with man and adapts to his continuous changing needs. A kitchen design that blends and adapts to the user is an immediate requirement of the world. It is necessary to study about the kitchen and make it comfortable to work in. As of now we might be very comfortable working in our current kitchens but as we age, our body would start showing significant changes like joint pain, body pain, muscle pain etc. This is when we would require our kitchen to co-operate with us and make our time in the kitchen comfortable. Modern day manufactures often do not conduct in-depth analysis to be able to curb problems faced by the elderly and with various health conditions. The fact being, there is no standardized ideal kitchen as every individual is different with varied needs. The entire concept of a ready-made modular kitchen should be abolished and a new approach should be achieved which would involve the user as the main client. In this way a kitchen suiting the clients need and requirements can be easily made. The main focus of this study will be on the following domains-

- Work Triangle (horizontal movement in the kitchen)
- Accessibility and visibility of various cabinets
- Weight analysis of different utensils
- An optimized setup with proper facilities
- Heights of different counter-tops.

The basic aim of the study is to re-design an Indian kitchen in an "ergonomic" way so that it is easily accessible by people of all age-groups. Computer software REVIT was used for this purpose to generate a 3-D model of the re-designed kitchen before actual manufacturing of the product.

2 LITERATURE REVIEW

A comprehensive study of literature is necessary in any research endeavor. A review of literature can help in gaining useful insights, data collection, analysis of collected data and formulating an innovative solution. Hence, an attempt has been made to present here the review of literature pertaining to have direct or indirect contact with this area of study. The basic focus here would be on the following sub-heads-

- Work Triangle
- Anthropometric measurements of work space

2.1 *Work triangle*

The movement in the kitchen is facilitated by the work triangle (developed at the University of Illinois in the 1940s). The work triangle includes the entire preparation of a meal from scratch to finish plus the utensils and groceries involved. This requires our movement between the cooking space, preparation space and storage space. An efficient work triangle should have a perimeter less than equal to 7m (Kishtwaria 2007).

2.2 *Anthropometric measurements of work space*

The workspace i.e., the kitchen in this scenario should be comfortable to work in. A major factor that predicts this comfort zone is the anthropometrics of the kitchen. It is necessary that the storage cabinets be easily accessible and visible. The heights of the counter top should be ideal or adjustable to suit individuals with different heights. Some authors suggested the following -

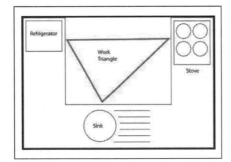

Figure 1. A typical work triangle between the cooking area, the storing area and the washing area.

Figure 2. 3-D model on computer software REVIT of the already existing kitchen design.

2.2.1 *For British female adults*

Sink height: 90–105cm, worktop 85–100cm and cooker 85–100cm (Ward, 1971). Choosing a best single height does not solve the problem for individual users who may need a customized height for them, thus highlighting the need for an adjustable kitchen (Ward, 1972).

2.2.2 *For Indian female adults*

Kneading dough (79cm), chopping (84cm) and cooking (96cm) (Ward, 1971).

For the elderly and people with several physical problems a different set of heights are recommended-

2.2.3 *For the elderly*

Shelves in a wardrobe should not exceed a height of 1600 mm. In the case of wall cabinets placed above an extended worktop, the height should not exceed 1400 mm. In addition, shelves in the low cupboards should not be placed below 300 mm (BSI, 1969).

2.2.4 *For individuals with physical disabilities*

Shelves placed below 300 mm are not suitable for people who have problems kneeling or bending. The height of the shelves in low cupboards can be lowered to 35mm if casseroles with a handle are stored there, as the actual height of the grip is above the level of the shelf, thus avoiding low bending (Kirvesoja, 2000).

3 METHODOLOGY

The study and research for this particular problem involved both secondary and primary data collection to get the best output. The entire study was done in steps which are as follows-

3.1 *Secondary data*

The research involved a brief study of the already existing ergonomic interventions of the modular kitchen in India as well as other countries. This was done in order to get an essence of the topic and to be aware of the changes that have been done. Also, it was done to find out the scope of improvement in the existing interventions and work on these points.

3.2 *Primary data*

The second stage of the research involved an interaction session with the people of India belonging to different states. A total of 15 different individuals were interviewed having varied heights, age-groups and gender. The reason for this being that this study was focused on the modification of Indian kitchens. Hence, more information pertaining to Indian kitchens was needed. The data collection at this stage was done with the help of a questionnaire. The questionnaire consisted of several questions which included the anthropometric measurements of the subjects as well as of the space they work in. Therefore, this step involved measuring of the work place and the subject. Further, it was noticed that some details were not acquired through the interview. Hence, it was necessary to get live videos and pictures of the subjects in their working environment. Every action and every movement of the subjects were recorded in 5 major activities (dish washing, dough kneading, curry making, chapatti making, collecting and storing food and utensils). Further ahead, an ideal kitchen for a family of four was chosen at random in a nearby area. It was decided that this kitchen would be re-designed in an ergonomic way to make it more user-friendly. But it was noticed that the exterior connecting spaces also need to be studied for better understanding of the kitchen. Hence, the entire house and the connecting corridors were measured with the kitchen acting as an intricate part of this setting.

Table 1. Total distance covered in meters when moving around the present work triangle for the existing kitchen.

Zone	No. of times zone accessed	Distance covered (m)
Washing Zone	25 times	20.5
Cooking Zone	166 times	135
Storage Zone	41 times	44.5
	Total	200

4 OBSERVATIONS

All the data collected from the questionnaire was compiled together using graphs to segregate the different views of different people. The major difficulties the people faced were noted down and the suggestions they offered were taken into consideration. The measurements taken in the kitchen were analyzed using the work triangle and its perimeter. This helped in understanding the movement of the subjects in space horizontally. It helped in understanding the required size of the kitchen in order to provide accurate circulation and to avoid unnecessary fatigue. The vertical movement of the subjects in space and the frequency of accessing different spaces were interpreted by observing the recorded videos multiple times.

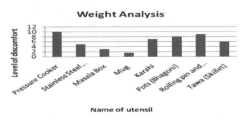

Graph 1. Weight analysis of selected utensils on the basis of level of discomfort in lifting them.

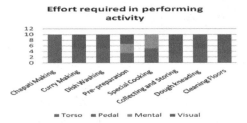

Graph 2. Effort on different body parts when performing selected activities.

A table was prepared from this information which included the BMI of 4 major subjects along with the energy used in just moving around.

Then a 3-D model was made in REVIT software of the kitchen with its surroundings. This was done in order to understand the space in a better way and to also to make several redesigned alternatives of the same space. In this step 3-D models were also made of the 4 main subjects according to their heights and weights in order to understand how varied heights and weights work in the same space. These models were placed in different sections to analyze how their body works in the kitchen space.

The area of the kitchen was optimized after incorporating the refrigerator inside the kitchen. The cupboard and weight analysis was done and the areas for different activities were suggested according to the views suggested by the subjects The provision of a separate space with adjustable counter top was introduced and pull down shelves for unusable and inaccessible spaces was suggested.

Table 2. BMI of 4 chosen subjects.

Name	Gender	Weight (kg)	Height (m)	BMI	Classification
Subject1	Male	54	1.55	22.47	Normal Weight
Subject2	Female	65	1.57	26.37	Overweight
Subject3	Female	60	1.55	25.80	Normal Weight
Subject4	Female	83	1.57	33.67	Class 1 Obese

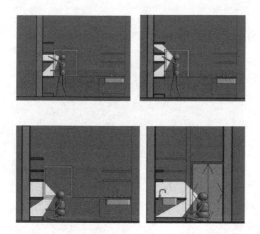

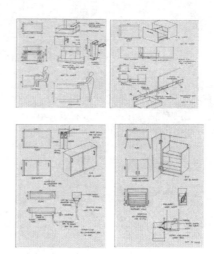

Figure 3. Reaching out and crouching models of chosen subjects to show visibility and accessibility in the existing kitchen.

Figure 4. Working details of the new cupboards were studied through drawings.

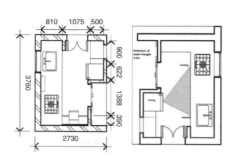

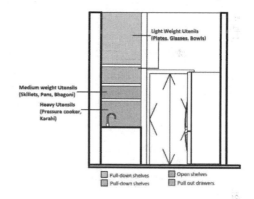

Figure 5. Final plan of the optimized new set up.

Figure 6. Weight analysis of different utensils with suggestion of their placement in different shelves.

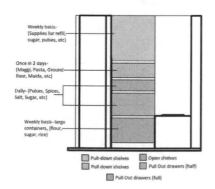

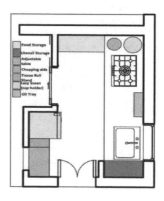

Figure 7. Storage analysis of different ingredients in elevation with suggestion of their placement in different shelves.

Figure 8. Storage analysis in plan.

5 RESULT

It can be concluded that the kitchen that has been re-designed is a perfect amalgamation of anthropometrics and ergonomics. The new modifications and interventions introduced will help it to be comfortably accessible by the elderly with minimum musculoskeletal load on their bodies. Cooking will be an enjoyable process and they will feel less lethargic in performing the daily activities. This will help in improving their health conditions to some extent and they might not need aid for performing their daily chores. They will be self-dependent now with improved health status. This could be easily done with the aid of computer generated models using the software REVIT.

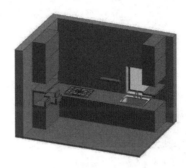

Figure 9.   Final 3-D model of re-designed kitchen.

REFERENCES

British Standard Institution recommendations (BSI, 4467/1969)

Ghimire, S., Singh, D.R., Nath, D., Jeffers, E.M. and Kaphle, M., 2018. Adult children's migration and well-being of left behind Nepalese elderly parents. *Journal of Epidemiology and Global Health.*

Global health and aging. National Institute on Aging, World Health Organization; 2011:1-32. Available at: http://www.who.int/ageing/publications/global_health.pdf

Gupta, S., 2018. Impact of volunteering on cognitive decline of the elderly. *The Journal of the Economics of Ageing*, *12*, pp.46-60.

Hong, J., Kim, J., Kim, S.W. and Kong, H.J., 2017. Effects of home-based tele-exercise on sarcopenia among community-dwelling elderly adults: Body composition and functional fitness. *Experimental gerontology*, *87*, pp.33-39.

Kirvesoja, H., Väyrynen, S. and Häikiö, A., 2000. Three evaluations of task-surface heights in elderly people's homes. *Applied ergonomics*, *31*(2), pp.109-119.

Kishtwaria, J., Mathur, P. and Rana, A., 2007. Ergonomic evaluation of kitchen work with reference to space designing. *Journal of Human Ecology*, *21*(1), pp.43-46.

Saghafi-Asl, M. and Vaghef-Mehrabany, E., 2017. Comprehensive comparison of malnutrition and its associated factors between nursing home and community dwelling elderly: A case-control study from Northwestern Iran. *Clinical Nutrition ESPEN*, *21*, pp.51-58.

Ward, J.S., 1971. Ergonomic techniques in the determination of optimum work surface heights. *Applied Ergonomics*, 2(3),pp.171-177.

Ward, J., 1972. Ergonomics in the kitchen. *The Design Journal*, pp.58-59.

Communication and Computing Systems – Prasad et al. (eds)
© 2019 Taylor & Francis Group, London, ISBN 978-0-367-00147-6

Sarcasm detection in social media posts: A division of sentiment analysis

Mansi Vats
Department of Information Technology, Dronacharya College of Engineering, Gurugram, Haryana, India

Yashvardhan Soni
Department of Computer Science Engineering, Dronacharya College of Engineering. Gurugram, Haryana, India

ABSTRACT: This paper is written before doing any practical work on the mentioned topic. The paper is based on the research done to find methods to detect sarcasm in the social media posts. The language that will be used for this is the R language. We have given a brief introduction of Sentiment Analysis, which sarcasm detection is a part of. We have defined and described Natural Language Processing (NLP), through which the machine can understand the human language to detect sarcasm. We have also described the steps for sarcasm detection and a comparison between different machine learning algorithms to choose for sarcasm detection. In the end, the result will be evaluated that whether the machine is able to detect sarcasm with atleast 80% accuracy or not.

1   INTRODUCTION

According to Merriam-Webster, sarcasm is defined as: "A sharp, and often satirical or ironic utterance designed to cut or give pain" OR "a mode of satirical wit depending for its effect on bitter, caustic, and often ironic language that is usually directed against an individual." Sarcasm is generally a statement which actually means the opposite of its obvious meaning. It is usually used to insult someone. We humans can identify the sarcasm in someone's speech by its tone. But when a user posts a sarcastic post on a social media platform, it becomes difficult for the machine to differentiate between the obvious meaning and the intended meaning of the post. Hence, it becomes important to detect sarcasm in social media posts. Sarcasm detection is still in its initial stages and is a complex task because there is no specific vocabulary for sarcasm, unlike spams. The same words can be used for normal usage as well as to express sarcasm. So, to detect sarcasm the machine would have to learn that how to figure out that the user means the opposite of his statement.

2   SENTIMENT ANALYSIS

Sentiment Analysis, also known as Opinion Mining and Emotion AI, is used to determine whether a statement is positive, negative or neutral. The main objective of sentiment analysis is to determine the attitude of the speaker or writer towards a certain topic or product. For this, we make use of Natural Language Processing, text analysis, computational linguistics, and biometrics.

Sentiment analysis is of great use in social media monitoring which helps us in obtaining the views or opinions of a wide range of public on particular topics. For example, if we want to know how the people of India find Chinese food, we can do this through sentiment analysis on social media. By analysing tweets of people on twitter, we can determine whether and why people find Chinese food good or bad. We can also make use of some exact words such as "very salty" or "very spicy" in order to have a better knowledge of why the consumers are not happy.

For social media monitoring, we can use a tool named Brandwatch Analytics to obtain the results in a faster and easier manner. Sarcasm detection is a part of sentiment analysis through which we can identify the sarcastic attitude of the speaker or the writer.

3 SARCASM DETECTION

3.1 What is sarcasm?

From different sources, we get different definitions of sarcasm. Some of them are:-

According to Cambridge English University- "The use of remarks that clearly means the opposite of that they say, made in order to hurt someone's feelings or to criticize something in a humorous way. For example, 'You have been working hard', he said with heavy sarcasm, as he looked at the empty page."

According to Collins Dictionary- "Sarcasm is speech or writing which actually means the opposite of what it seems to say. Sarcasm is usually intended to mark or insult someone. For example, 'What a pity', Graham said with a hint of sarcasm."

As a conclusion, sarcasm can be defined as a statement which means the opposite of its actual meaning and is generally used to affront, tease, taunt or censure someone. The sarcasm is generally taken in a negative sense, hence a sarcastic statement is a negative statement.

3.2 Sarcasm in social media

Social media platforms nowadays are full of a variety of posts. Many people are active on social media. People update each and every moment of their lives on social media sites such as facebook, twitter, instagram etc. Among these posts, some are sarcastic while some are non-sarcastic.

While posting sarcastic tweets or posts on social media, some people make use of hashtags such as #sarcasm for making it easy for the public to identify it as a sarcastic post.

While some people simply write sarcastic statements without hashtags, tag their friends there or reply to some tweets or posts in a sarcastic way.

Sarcasm can be expressed in many ways by, for example, reviewing a movie, match or commenting about the weather etc.

3.3 Why to detect sarcasm?

The number of social media users is increasing day by day. And a majority of users post a variety of posts on social media. This has led to a tremendous increase in the sarcastic posts on social media. The main reason behind this is that people find sarcasm as more witty, humorous and an interesting way to express their feelings and criticize or insult others. Just like spams, sarcastic posts should also be identified individually. Sarcasm detection will also be helpful for the people who are suffering from Autism and Asperger's and who find it difficult to understand sarcasm, sardonicism and wit.

3.4 Why is it difficult to detect sarcasm?

Many data scientists are still working on sarcasm detection. It is a very complex task. This is because it becomes difficult for the machine to differentiate between the obvious meaning and the intended meaning of the post. It happens because of the same types of words used both in positive and negative sense as there is no specific vocabulary defined for sarcastic posts yet. The machine could not identify whether the statement is positive or negative.

4 NATURAL LANGUAGE PROCESSING

Natural Language Processing, abbreviated as NLP, is an AI method which is used for inter-acting with the intelligent systems using any natural language, for example, English. NLP can also be defined as automatic manipulation of natural language, which can be speech or text, by the program. Natural language is the manner in which humans interact with each other, which is speech and text.

Nowadays, we see text in a variety of ways such as Signs, Menus, Email, SMS, Web Pages etc. NLP is needed in a plenty of situations such as when we want a robot to act as per our commands or when we want help from a communicating expert system etc. The input and output can be provided to and from the NLP system in two ways-

- Written Text
- Speech

4.1 *Components of NLP*

There are mainly two components of NLP:-

4.1.1 *NLU*
NLU stands for Natural Language Understanding. It depicts the given input in natural lan-guage into useful delineations. It also examines different characteristics of the language.

4.1.2 *NLG*
NLG stands for Natural Language Generation. It is a procedure for constructing significant phrases and sentences in the form of natural language from some inner portrayal. It involves

4.1.2.1 Text Planning: It means recovering the useful data from the knowledge base.

4.1.2.2 Sentence Planning: It refers to selecting the necessary words, constructing relevant phrases, setting quality of the sentence.

4.1.2.3 Text Realization:It refers to plotting sentence plan into sentence structure.

The NLU is more difficult than NLG.

5 STEPS IN SARCASM DETECTION

5.1 *Getting the data*

The first step in sarcasm detection is to collect data i.e. the posts, from the social media plat-forms. We should have wide range of source of collection and hence the data should be col-lected from various social media platforms like facebook, twitter, instagram etc. Collecting data from various sources will also help us in analysing the various levels of sarcasm on differ-ent social media sites.

Once the data is collected, the machine is trained through supervised learning.

Classification is a supervised learning method which is done to label some sentences as sar-castic while some as non-sarcastic ones in order to make our classifier.

5.2 *Pre-processing the data*

Pre-processing the data refers to cleaning up the data. After collecting the data from various sources, it is important to clean the data to remove the possibilities of having the posts in which sarcasm is either in the enclosed link or in the replies to other posts. To make sure that only the posts written in English are collected. The posts which contain Non-ASCII characters are removed. All the hashtags, friend tags and the use of word sarcasm/sarcastic is also removed from all the posts. Also the duplicate posts are removed.

5.2.1 *Why data pre-processing?*
Data pre-processing is referred to as a data mining technique which includes reconstructing the raw data into an interpretable form. The data prevent in the real-world is mostly incomplete, incompatible, lack some behaviours and has many errors. Data pre-processing is done to resolve such issues. It is used in database-driven environments such as Neural Networks.

5.3 *Feature engineering*

After the pre-processing i.e. cleaning of the data is done, next step is to perform feature engineering. Feature engineering is performed to find out the answers of the questions like:

What are the variables in a post that make it sarcastic or non-sarcastic?

How do we extract them from the post?

Feature engineering refers to the procedure of making use of the domain knowledge of the data to establish characteristics that make machine learning algorithms work. If feature engineering is performed in the right manner, it extends the prophetic power of machine learning algorithms by generating characteristics from unanalysed data that makes the machine learning process easier.

5.3.1 *Importance of feature engineering*
The characteristics in our data will directly affect the prophetic models we make use of and the outcome we can attain.

If we develop and select better features, we will attain better outputs. It is both true and deceptive.

The outcomes we attain are a part of the model we select, the data that is accessible to us and the characteristics we develop.

Great characteristics are required that report the construction innate our data.

Better characteristics enable flexibility.

Even the selection of "wrong models" (less optimum) can lead us to good outcomes.

Better characteristics lead to simpler models.

5.4 *Choosing a classifier*

After feature engineering, the next step in sarcasm detection is to choose a classifier among the various machine learning algorithms. This is done to train the machine and help it classify the posts into sarcastic and non-sarcastic posts from the social media platforms.

This is the most crucial step and the selection of correct classifier is very important.

Classification is a supervised learning technique. By supervised learning we mean that the machine is trained by providing a set of input data and a teacher or "data set" is present to guide the machine to provide the correct results. Later, this learning is used to classify new statements.

The data set provided to the machine can be of two types:

– Bi-class: It helps in classifying the data into two categories. For example, whether a post is sarcastic or non-sarcastic.
– Multi-class: It helps in classifying the data in various categories.

Below are some of the classification algorithms in machine learning.

5.4.1 *Naïve-Bayes classifier (generative learning algorithm)*
Naïve-Bayes classification technique is based on the Bayes' Theorem. According to Naïve-Bayes classification, one feature of a class is not related to any other feature of the same class.

Even if it happens that one feature depends on any other feature of the class, all of these attributes contribute individually to the possibility. This type of model is easy to use and is mainly used for huge data sets. It is a very simple algorithm and it also performs better than many highly advanced classification techniques. Equation for Naïve-Bayes algorithm is as follows:

$$P(c|x) = \frac{P(x|c)P(c)}{P(x)} \tag{1}$$

where, P(c|x)=posterior probability, P(x|c)=likelihood, P(c)=class prior probability and P(x)=predictor prior probability.

5.4.2 *Logistic regression (predictive learning model)*
It is a mathematical model to analyse a data set consisting of two or more independent variables that produce an output. The output is determined with the help of a dichotomous variable, which means a variable in which only two outcomes are possible. The main objective of logistic regression is to identify finest fitting model to narrate the association between the dichotomous feature of interest and a set of independent variables.

5.4.3 *Decision trees*
Decision trees are used to construct classification models in the structure of a tree. It converts the data set into smaller fragments called subsets and a related decision tree is gradually developed simultaneously. The ultimate output is a tree with decision nodes and leaf nodes. A decision tree consists of two or more branches and a leaf node means the classification or decision. The highest decision node in a tree represents the best predictor and is called the root node. Decision tress can handle categorical as well as numerical data.

5.4.4 *Neural network*
A neural network is made up of small units known as neurons. The neurons are arranged in layers hence it is a layered architecture. These neurons convert the given input into output. The input is fed to each and every neuron of the first layer in the neural network. The neurons apply some functions on these inputs and then produce the output and pass it to the next layer. Usually, a neural network is feed-forward in nature i.e. the output produced by all the nodes of one layer are fed as the input to all the nodes of the next layer. But no feedback is facilitated. Every neuron in a neural network has a weight associated with it. These weights play a crucial role during machine learning and can be manipulated according to the desired output.

5.4.5 *Nearest neighbour*
The k-nearest neighbour algorithm is a supervised classification algorithm. By supervised we mean that it takes a cluster of tagged points and uses them to learn how to tag other points. To tag a new point, it examines the tagged points, adjacent to that new point, which are its nearest neighbours. It asks those neighbours to vote and the tag that has the highest number of votes is the tag for the new point. Here "k" is the number of neighbours it inspects.

5.5 *Results and insights*

After performing all the above steps, the final step is to check whether the machine is able to detect sarcasm or not. This will be done by checking the output produced by the machine after training it. The produced or actual output will be compared with the desired output. If both the outputs match, it means the system is working fine. Else, the system will be trained again accordingly.

The sarcastic posts will be named as negative sentences and the non-sarcastic posts will be named as positive sentences. If the machine classifies the sentences correctly, it means that the training is successful.

6 CONCLUSION

This paper had concluded that sarcasm detection is possible by training the machine accordingly. Different data scientists may have different approach towards sarcasm detection. Despite of being a complex task due to lack of specific vocabulary and difficulty in interpreting the meaning of the posts, sarcasm detection is possible with not 100% accuracy but at least 80% accuracy and can be of important use in the coming future.

REFERENCES

Bharti, S.K., Vachha, B., Pradhan, R.K., Babu, K.S., & Jena, S.K. "Sarcastic sentiment detection in tweets Streamed in real time: a big data approach", Elsevier 12 July 2016.

Bouazizi, M., Ohtsuki, T., "Pattern-Based Approach for Sarcasm Detection on Twitter" VOLUME 4, 10.1109/ACCESS.2016.2594194.

Chaffey, D. Global Social Media Research Summary 2016.URL (http://www.smartinsights.com/Social media-marketing/social-media-strategy/new-globalsocial-media-research/).

Gonzalez-Ibanez, R., Muresan, S., &Wacholder, N. 2011. "Identifying Sarcasm in Twitter: A Closer Look". In Proceedings of the 49th Annual Meeting of Association for Computational Linguistics.

Joshi, A., Sharma, V., & Bhattacharyya, P., "Harnessing Context Incongruity for Sarcasm Detection" Proceedings of the 53rd Annual Meeting of the Association for Computational Linguistics and the 7th International Joint Conference on Natural Language Processing (Short Papers), pages 757-762, Beijing, China, July 26-31, 2015. C 2015 Association for Computational Linguistic.

Maynard, D., Greenwood, M.A. 2014."Who cares about Sarcastic tweets? Investigating the Impact of sarcasm on sentiment analysis", In Proceedings of the LREC 2014 May 26-31.

Ptacek, T., Habernal, I., & Hong, J. "Sarcasm Detection on Czech and English Twitter", Proceedings of COLING 2014, the 25th International Conference on Computational Linguistics: Technical Papers, pages 213-223 , Dublin, Ireland,August 23- 29 2014.

Rajadesingan, A., Zafarni, R., & Liu, H., "Sarcasm detection on Twitter: A behavioral modelling Approach", in Proc. 18th ACM Int. Conf. Web Search Data Mining, Feb. 2015, pp.79_106.

Riloff, E., Qadir, A., Surve, P., De Silva, L., Gilbert, N. & Huang, R., "Sarcasm as contrast between a positive sentiment and negative situation", in Proc. Con Empirical Methods Natural Lang. Process, Oct. 2013, pp.704_714.

Tan, W., Blake, M.B., Saleh, I. &Dustdar, S. Social-networkedsourced big data analytics, InternetComput.17 (5) (2013) 62-69.

Veale, T. &Hao, Y. 2010. "Detecting Ironic Intent in Creative Comparisons", In ECAI, Vol. 215.765-770.

Communication and Computing Systems – Prasad et al. (eds)
© 2019 Taylor & Francis Group, London, ISBN 978-0-367-00147-6

Applications of type II fuzzy sets—a mathematical review on breast cancer imaging modalities

Jyoti Dabass, Rekha Vig & Shaveta Arora
The Northcap University, Gurgaon, India

ABSTRACT: Analysis of mammogram and breast ultrasound images for diagnosing breast cancer is a subjective process with inherent uncertainties. According to the reports of the national cancer institute, mammograms miss ten in fifty cancers forcing the women to undergo unnecessary fretfulness and procedures. This happens because of uncertainty, vagueness in boundaries, low contrast and noise in the image. Owing to the capabilities of Type II fuzzy set in dealing with ultra fuzziness, they have been exploited in different applications such as enhancement of low contrast mammogram images, segmenting the cancerous part from the image, clustering the breast cancer images on the basis of texture, pattern, edges, contour or others and thresholding in order to get the optimal value to detect breast cancer. This paper discusses the mathematical assessment of Type II fuzzy sets along with its applications in breast cancer image analysis. It also explains the future prospects of Type II fuzzy sets in dealing with the fuzziness of breast cancer images.

1 INTRODUCTION

Breast Cancer is the most recurrently detected cancer bookkeeping for 25.2% of the whole cancer-related deaths (Smith, et al., 2018). A mammogram is the standard screening for the early exposure or analysis of breast cancer. It exhibits uncertainties owing to vagueness, noise and low contrast leading to loss of information and inaccurate analysis. Fuzzy techniques work well in dealing with the uncertainties by using membership function (MFs) which decides the contribution of a pixel in a fuzzy set. Values of MFs lie between (0, 1). Experts based on their knowledge or intuitions define the membership function (MF). So all the fuzzy techniques are mainly divergent in their approach to label the membership function (Raj, D.et al., 2018)

Noise in data, penalty related to histogram value and vagueness in location, shape, measurements along with the meaning of parts create uncertainty. Type I fuzzy sets are not proficient in holding the uncertainties owing to their crisp MFs.

In 1975, the notion of Type II fuzzy set was pioneered by Zadeh by taking into account Type-I fuzzy set 'fuzzy'. Also, membership functions were not just a value but an interval for every element based on lower and upper bounds to deal with uncertainties (Mendel, J.M., 2017)

In Figure 1, thin lines represent the upper level of Type I fuzzy set while thick lines indicate the lower level of Type I fuzzy set. It is because Type II fuzzy set is achieved by hazing the Type I fuzzy set. In the dearth of uncertainty, Type II fuzzy set condenses to Type I fuzzy set.

A fuzzy set $\mathcal{A}$ can be characterized mathematically in a finite set $\mathcal{X} = \{a_1, a_2 \ldots a_n\}$ by the expression given as

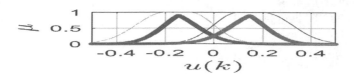

Figure 1. Type II fuzzy set dependent on interval.

$$\mathcal{A} = \{a, \mu_A(a) | a \in \mathcal{X}\} \tag{1}$$

where $\mu_A(a) : \mathcal{X} \to [0, 1]$ represents the association gathering of a constituent 'a' in predetermined set $\mathcal{X}$.

While Type II set along with lower and upper MFs can be written as

$$\mathcal{A}_{\text{TypeII}} = \{a, \mu^{LOW}(a), \mu^{UP}(a) | a \in \mathcal{X}\} \quad \text{and} \quad \mu^{LOW}(a) < \mu(a) < \mu^{UP}(a), \ \mu \in [0, 1] \tag{2}$$

where lower and upper limits are linguistic hedges like concentration or dilation represented by equations

$$\mu^{LOW}(a) = \mu(a)^2 \quad \text{and} \quad \mu^{UP}(a) = \mu(a)^{0.5} \tag{3}$$

Here $\mu^{LOW}(a)$ and $\mu^{UP}(a)$ denote lower and upper membership functions.

Owing to the potential of handling vagueness, Type II fuzzy sets are exercised in breast cancer image analysis by contributing in microcalcification detection, enhancement of low contrast breast cancer images, segmenting ROI (malignant) part from the cancerous images, thresholding based on optimal value to detect breast cancer, and clustering on the basis of similarities of pattern, texture, contours and others.

This paper reviews mathematics involved in Type II fuzzy and its applications in the analysis of breast cancer images. Section 1 introduces the topic followed by applications of Type II fuzzy sets in section 2. Finally, Section 3 concludes the topic.

2 APPLICATIONS: TYPE II FUZZY SET

Applications of Type II fuzzy set ranges from mammogram image enhancement to improving contrast, thresholding for removal of pectoral muscles from a mammogram, clustering in breast cancer ultrasound and mammogram images to avoid noise by bringing the center to more desirable location followed by detecting edges and segmenting the cancerous part from the rest of the figure

2.1 *Image enhancement*

Mammogram figures are commonly of low contrast and hence require an unusual enhancement procedure to get better visibility before additional analysis can be completed. Type I MFs are not defined properly inhibiting uncertainty in their results. So, Type II method is employed to augment the contrast of mammogram images.

There are two methods which make use of the perception of Type II fuzzy set in order to enhance the visual quality of low contract mammogram images. The mathematics involved in these techniques is discussed below.

2.1.1 *Enhancement via Type- II fuzzy: Method 1*
This method is recommended by Chaira exploiting algebraic natured fuzzy t-conorm.

A t-Conorm $T^* : [0, 1] \to [0, 1]$ is a class of twofold method used in the gibbet of probabilistic metric spaces and fuzzy logic. The four fundamental t-Conorms representing the union in 'OR-ing' operator or fuzzy set theory are maximum $((T^*\_\max(i, j))$, Nilpotent minimum t-Conorm $(T^*\_\text{nil}(i, j))$, the Lukasiewicz t-conorm $(T^*\_\text{lwicz}(i, j))$ and the product $(T^*\_p(i, j))$ given by following equations given below:

$$T^*\_\max(i, j) = \max(i, j), \ T^*\_\text{nil}(i, j) = \begin{cases} \max(i, j) & \text{if } i + j < 1 \\ 0 & \text{otherwise} \end{cases} \tag{4}$$

$$T^*\_lwicz(i,j) = \min(i+j,1) \text{ and } T^*\_p(i,j) = i+j-i.j \tag{5}$$

A function $T^* : [0,1] \to [0,1]$ is termed as Archimedean t-Conorm iff there subsist an incessant and rising gathering

$$q : [0,1] \to [0,\infty] \text{ with } a(0) = 0 \text{ so } T^*(i,j) = q^{-1}(q(i)+q(j)) \tag{6}$$

Here 'q' represents an additive generator.

In Chaira's method (Chaira, T., 2015), the actual value is revealed by operators devoid of min and max operation. For finding t-Conorms following calculations are done given as

$$q(i) = \ln\left(\frac{1+(k+1)i}{1-i}\right) \tag{7}$$

where $a(.)$ is an increasing function with $q(o) = \ln(1) = 0$ and $k = [0,1]$ and

$$q^{-1}(i) = \frac{e^i - 1}{e^i + 1 + k} \tag{8}$$

It is an increasing function as 'a' approaches 1 when the limit of the algorithm tends to infinity (Weber, S., 1983). So, using equation 6 we get

$$C^*(i,j) = q^{-1}(q(i)+q(j)), t1 \qquad \text{with } t1 = q(i) + q(j) \tag{9}$$

Using equation 7 it deduces to

$$C^*(i,j) = q^{-1}[\ln\left(\frac{1+(k+1)i}{1-i}\right) + \ln\left(\frac{1+(k+1)j}{1-j}\right) \text{ or } C^*(i,j) = \frac{2i+2j+ki+kj+2kij+k^2ij}{2+2ij+3kij+k^2ij+k} \tag{10}$$

This equation can be reduced to the expression given below

$$C^*(i,j) = \frac{(i+j)kij}{(1+k)ij+1} \tag{11}$$

This expression works in calculating the new membership function.

For enhancing the mammogram images, first original mammogram image is fuzzified by means of the membership gathering which is given as

$$\mu(a) = \frac{a - a_{MIN}}{a_{MAX} - a_{MIN}} \tag{12}$$

where 'a' denotes gray values varying as of 0 to L-1, a_{MIN} and a_{MAX} represents the minimum and the maximum grey values of image.

Then two levels are worked out exploiting Type II fuzzy as under

$$\mu^{UP}(a) = [\mu(a)]^a \text{ and } \mu^{LOW(a)} = [\mu(a)]^{1/a} \tag{13}$$

where α described heuristically in range of (0, 1]. Now using algebraic nature t-conorm method proposed by Chaira, new membership function (MF) is calculated as

$$\mu^{ENH.}(a) = \frac{\mu^{UP}(a) + \mu^{LOW}(a) + k.\mu^{UP}(a).\mu^{LOW}(a)}{(1 + k)\mu^{UP}(a)\mu^{LOW}(a) + 1} \tag{14}$$

where k =image_average, $\mu^{UP}(a)$, $\mu^{LOW}(a)$ denotes upper and lower MF of fuzzified image$\mu(a)$, and $\alpha = [0, 1]$. In order to get the enhanced image, we can use α as 0.75 in the equation of Intuitionistic fuzzy set based hesitation degree calculating upper and lower membership ranges (Chaira, T., 2014).

2.1.2 *Enhancement utilizing Type II fuzzy: Method 2*
This method was originally proposed by Ensafi, P. and Tizhoosh, H.R., 2005. In this method, the first image is carved up into numerous windows and then for each window equation 4 is used to fuzzify the sub-image. The lower $(\mu^{LOW})$and upper(μ^{UP}) MF values are designed using equation 3. Using these values new MF is calculated which is given below as expression

$$\mu_{NU}(a) = \mu^{LOW}(a)*\alpha + \mu^{UP}(a)(1 - \alpha) \text{ and } \alpha = \frac{a_{MEAN}}{L} \tag{15}$$

where a_{MEAN} represents the average of all grey values of window, L denotes the number of grey level and $\mu(a)$ is image after fuzzification. This process is repeated for all windows in order to get the enhanced image

2.2 *Mammogram image thresholding*

By thresholding, one can remove pectoral muscles from the mammogram image before segmenting ROI to increase the accuracy in prediction of breast cancer. Fuzziness decreases when MF has no uncertainty. (Tizhoosh, H.R., 2005) defined this fuzziness in terms of ultra fuzziness with maximum ultra fuzziness as one. But this ultra fuzziness augments when MF lies in interval range and is denoted as

$$\omega(A) = \frac{1}{xy} \sum_{a=0}^{L-1} \hbar(a)*[\mu^{UP}(a) - \mu^{LOW}(a)] \tag{16}$$

where upper and lower MF denoted by $\mu^{UP}(a)$ and $\mu^{LOW}(a)$ of fuzzy set A are defined by equation 4 and equation 5. This ultra fuzziness measure denoted by ω for an image having dimension x * y with L gray levels having $a \in [0, L-1]$subset $\mathcal{A} \subseteq \mathcal{X}$, histogram $\hbar(a)$ is utilized in thresholding where following cases hold.

- If μ_A is usual or Type-I fuzzy set then $\mu^{UP}(a) = \mu^{LOW}(a)$ And$\omega(A) = 1$.
- If $\mu^{UP}(a) - \mu^{LOW}(a) = 1$ then $\omega(A) = 1$.
- $\omega(A)\omega(A)'$ When A' is A's crisper version.

In this, first fuzzification of the image with user-defined MF and $\alpha \in [1, 2]$ is done and then upper and lower MFs are computed as discussed above. Then measure of ultra fuzziness and the maximum value is computed for each grey level. Finally, the optimum threshold is calculated using the maximum value of ultra fuzziness to detect the microcalcifications in digitized mammograms (Kalra, P.K., and Kumar, N., 2010).

2.3 *Type II fuzzy clustering*

Breast ultrasound images are of low excellence restraining noise and dusk areas which make tumor segmentation a difficult task. So a customized spatial neutrosophic clustering method is anticipated for mechanical removal of tumors in B-mode BUS images in which membership function are updated using Type-II MF to converge the cluster center to more desirable location (Lal, M., et al 2018). Type II fuzzy clustering method was proposed originally by Rhee and Hwang for the pattern set clustering, Type II fuzzy set denotes uncertainty in a fuzzy set by extending MF of each pattern to Type II fuzzy membership by way of conveying grades to Type I fuzzy membership. The contribution of pattern increases whereas uncertainty decreases with an increase in membership value of the pattern. In Rhee and Hwang technique, triangular membership function was used to get Type I membership. By doing so, cluster center congregates to advantageous place (Rubio et al., 2017). The membership values for Type II membership are attained as

$$a_{xM} = \mu_{xM} - \frac{1 - \mu_{xM}}{2} \qquad (17)$$

where a_{xM} and μ_{xM} denotes Type II and Type I fuzzy membership of the data $\mathcal{X}_{xM}$ correspondingly. The cluster centroid $\left(v_{xM}{}^{\text{typeII}}\right)$ is revised consequently utilizing conventional FCM taking help of new Type II membership and is defined as

$$v_{xM}{}^{\text{typeII}} = \frac{\sum_{M-1}^{p} a_{xM}{}^{g} \mathcal{X}_{xM}}{\sum_{M=1}^{p} a_{xM}{}^{g}} \qquad (18)$$

Here g is defined by user and xMdenotes fuzzy cluster. Then it follows the usual procedure of FCM (Fuzzy C-means by Chowdhary, et al, 2018).

2.4 *Type II fuzzy set based erection of enhanced fuzzy edge of mammogram*

This method makes use of the fuzzy MF property of fuzzy set (Chaira, T. and Ray, A.K., 2014). In this, the first figure is stabilized to get the values in the interval of [0, 1]. Then for every pixel, the minimum and maximum value are computed using 3*3 neighborhoods followed by obtaining two image matrixes using minimum and maximum standards of the pixel in a 3* 3 window. As the mammogram image is itself fuzzy, maximum and minimum values are also fuzzy so for every matrix, Type II levels are figured out. The lower and upper MF for the maximum value $\left(\mu_{MAX}^{LOW}, \mu_{MAX}^{UP}\right)$ & minimum value $\left(\mu_{MIN}^{LOW}, \mu_{MIN}^{UP}\right)$ are expressed as

$$\mu_{MAX}^{UP} = [\mu_{MAX}(\mathcal{A})]^{0.75} \quad \text{and} \quad \mu_{MAX}^{LOW} = [\mu_{MAX}(\mathcal{A})]^{1/0.75} \qquad (19)$$

$$\mu_{MIN}^{UP} = [\mu_{MIN}(\mathcal{A})]^{0.75} \quad \text{and} \quad \mu_{MIN}^{LOW} = [\mu_{MIN}(\mathcal{A})]^{1/0.75} \qquad (20)$$

Then fuzzy deviation between the lower and upper levels of the minimum $\left(\text{Div}\left(\mu_{MIN}^{UP}, \mu_{MIN}^{LOW}\right)\right)$ and maximum values $\left(\text{Div}\left(\mu_{MAX}^{UP}, \mu_{MAX}^{LOW}\right)\right)$ are figured out as

$$\text{Div}\left(\mu_{MIN}^{UP}, \mu_{MIN}^{LOW}\right) = 2 - (v).i - (q).e \qquad (21)$$

$$\text{Div}\left(\mu_{MAX}^{UP}, \mu_{MAX}^{LOW}\right) = [2 - (l)*h - (m)*n] \qquad (22)$$

where

$$l = 1 - \mu_{MAX}^{UP} + \mu_{MAX}^{LOW}, \qquad h = e^{\mu_{MAX}^{UP} - \mu_{MAX}^{LOW}} \qquad (23)$$

$$m = 1 - \mu_{MAX}^{LOW} + \mu_{MAX}^{UP}, \quad n = e^{\mu_{MAX}^{LOW} - \mu_{MAX}^{UP}} \qquad (24)$$

$$v = 1 - \mu_{MIN}^{UP} + \mu_{MIN}^{LOW}, \quad i = e^{\mu_{MIN}^{UP}} - \mu_{MIN}^{LOW} \qquad (25)$$

$$q = 1 - \mu_{MIN}^{LOW} + \mu_{MIN}^{UP} \quad \text{and} \quad e = e^{\mu_{MIN}^{LOW} - \mu_{MIN}^{UP}} \qquad (26)$$

Finally, the discrepancy amid the two divergences that are a maximum and minimum divergence in the case of breast cancer images is calculated which signifies the edge or boundary of the figure. While doing so, each pixel is attached with many membership degrees according to the hiatus extent (variance amid highest and lowest matrixes).

2.5   *Mammogram image segmentation*

Breast region segmentation is a crucial stride in the scrutiny of digital mammograms for precise image segmentation directs to better exposure of cancer by aiming at sorting out region of interest (ROI) from rest of the figure. Tizhoosh suggested a method for artificial image segmentation by means of Type II fuzzy set which can be useful for mammogram images too (Tizhoosh, H.R., 2008). The region of interest is dark in most of the images. Primary MF of these pixels is derived in the interval $a_{MAX}-(a_{MAX}-a_{MIN}/2$ Via z-MF which is given as

$$\mu_A(a) = \begin{cases} 1 - 8\left(\frac{d}{c}\right)^2 if\, a_{MIN} \leq a \leq \frac{b}{4} \\ 2\left(\frac{c.b-8a}{c}\right) if\, \frac{b}{4} < a < \frac{b}{2} \\ 0\, if\, a > b/4 \end{cases} \tag{27}$$

Here maximum and minimum value of image 'a' are denoted as a_{MAX} and a_{MIN}. Lower ($\mu_{\mathcal{L}}$) and upper (μ_u) MF of fuzzified image ($\mu(a)$) is calculated using

$$\mu_{\mathcal{L}}(x, y) = \mu(a(x, y)^{\rho(x,y)} \quad and \quad \mu_u(x, y) = \mu(a(x, y)^{1/\rho(x,y)} \tag{28}$$

Also for each point, ρ is calculated with respect to neighborhood using

$$\rho(x, y) = M * \min\left(\frac{1, w1 + q}{L - 1}\right) \tag{29}$$

where $w1 = \max_f a(x + f, y + f)$, $q = \min_f a(x + f, y + f)$

$$b = a_{MAX} + a_{MIN}, \quad c = a_{MAX} - a_{MIN} \tag{30}$$

$$d = a - a_{MIN} \quad and \quad f \in [-p, \cdots\cdots, 0, 1, \cdots p] \tag{31}$$

Also $p = \frac{w}{2}$; w denotes window size; M is the amplification factor in the range [1, ∞]. More value of M denotes weak edges while its lesser value represents strong edges. It implies uncertainty is directly proportional to the intensity difference of center and its neighborhood. Next weight of lower and upper MF denoted by W_{LOW} and W_{UP} is expressed as

$$W_{LOW}(x, y) = \frac{\min_f a(x + f, y + f)}{a_{MAX}} \quad and \quad W_{UP}(x, y) = \frac{w1}{a_{MAX}} \tag{32}$$

At last the segmented pixel (a^{SEG}) with L grey levels is computed using

$$a^{SEG}(x, y) = L - 1\left(\frac{r + t}{j}\right) \quad where \quad r = W_{LOW}(x, y).\mu_{\mathcal{L}}(x, y) \tag{33}$$

$$t = W_{UP}(x, y).\mu_u(x, y) \quad and \quad j = r = W_{LOW}(x, y) + W_{UP}(x, y) \tag{34}$$

3 CONCLUSION AND FUTURE SCOPE

In this paper, a succinct and representative mathematical analysis of the relevance of Type II fuzzy sets is presented. Type II fuzzy set owing to its property of ultra fuzziness works well in dealing with the uncertainties related to breast cancer images. Using the method of image enhancement, vagueness in the region of interest and boundaries of mammogram images are removed to a great extent. The potential effort for the additional upgrading of this method is probable if confined area based enhancements on predefined sized tiles of the original image are assumed than internationally intriguing into account the complete figure at a moment. Also, the projected techniques for enhancement, segmentation, thresholding, edge detection and clustering can be applied to medical color image improvement if an apposite space other than RGB is taken into consideration for color-based display and calculation concerned (Bora, D.J., and Thakur, R.S., 2018).

REFERENCES

Bora, D.J., 2018. An Ideal Approach to Medical Color Image Enhancement. In Advanced Computational and Communication Paradigms (pp. 351-361). Springer, Singapore.

Bora, D.J., and Thakur, R.S., 2018. An Efficient Technique for Medical Image Enhancement Based on Interval Type-2 Fuzzy Set Logic. In Progress in Computing, Analytics and Networking (pp. 667-678). Springer, Singapore.

Chaira, T., 2014. An improved medical image enhancement scheme using Type II fuzzy set. *Applied soft computing*, 25, pp.293-308.

Chaira, T. and Ray, A.K., 2014. Construction of fuzzy edge image using interval Type II fuzzy set. *International Journal of Computational Intelligence Systems*, 7(4),pp.686-695.

Chaira, T., 2015. Medical image processing: Advanced fuzzy set theoretic techniques. CRC Press.

Chouhan, S.S., Kaul, A., and Singh, U.P., 2018. Soft computing approaches for image segmentation: a survey. Multimedia Tools and Applications, pp.1-55.

Chowdhary, C.L. and Acharjya, D.P., 2018. Segmentation of Mammograms Using a Novel Intuitionistic Possibilistic Fuzzy C-Mean Clustering Algorithm. In Nature Inspired Computing(pp. 75-82). Springer, Singapore.

Ensafi, P. and Tizhoosh, H.R., 2005, September. Type-2 fuzzy image enhancement. In International Conference Image Analysis and Recognition (pp. 159-166). Springer, Berlin, Heidelberg.

Kalra, P.K., and Kumar, N., 2010. A novel automatic microcalcification detection technique using Tsallis entropy & a Type II fuzzy index. *Computers & Mathematics with Applications*, 60(8), pp.2426–2432.

Lal, M., Kaur, L. and Gupta, S., 2018. Modified spatial neutrosophic clustering technique for boundary extraction of tumors in B-mode BUS images. *IET Image Processing*.

Mendel, J.M., 2017. Type-2 fuzzy sets. In Uncertain Rule-Based Fuzzy Systems pp. (259–306). Springer, Cham.

Raj, D., Gupta, A., Garg, B., Tanna, K. and Rhee, F.C.H., 2018. Analysis of Data Generated From Multidimensional Type-1 and Type-2 Fuzzy Membership Functions. *IEEE Transactions on Fuzzy Systems*, 26(2), pp.681–693.

Rubio, Y., Montiel, O. and Sepúlveda, R., 2017. Microcalcification detection in mammograms based on fuzzy logic and cellular automata. In Nature-Inspired Design of Hybrid Intelligent Systems pp. (583–602). Springer, Cham.

Smith, R.A. and DeSantis, C.E., 2018. Breast cancer epidemiology. Breast Imaging.

Tizhoosh, H.R., 2005. Image thresholding using Type II fuzzy sets. *Pattern recognition*, 38(12), pp.2363–2372.

Tizhoosh, H.R., 2008. Type II fuzzy image segmentation. In Fuzzy Sets and Their Extensions: Representation, Aggregation, and Models pp. (607–619). Springer, Berlin, Heidelberg.

Weber, S., 1983. A general concept of fuzzy connectives, negations and implications based on t-norms and t-conorms. *Fuzzy sets and systems*, 11(1-3), pp.115–115134.

Communication and Computing Systems – Prasad et al. (eds)
© *2019 Taylor & Francis Group, London, ISBN 978-0-367-00147-6*

New homotopy pertubation method for solving of coupled equation and heat equation and Laplace equation

M. Dhariwal & N. Fatima
Amity University, Haryana

ABSTRACT: In this article we use the new homotopy perturbation method for determine differential equations. We have determined four problem of differential equation by the NHPM. One problem is the coupled burger equation two problem of heat equation and one equation of Laplace equation. The numerical results prove that this method is a useful and powerful tool for explain the PDE.NHPM is defined as new ideas, new developments techniques. This paper includes the latest research in the field of mathematics sciences.

1 INTRODUCTION

The NHPM is capable in observation the comparative or analytic explication of the linear and nonlinear partial differential equation. The suppose decision defend the power, easily as well as simple of the system to implement, in the view we shall illuminate the NHPM represented by (J.H.He 2010,O.Martin 2011)

The present method is simple, skilful as well as broadly helpful to explain non linear differential equation. in NHPM a homotopy is formulated by suggested and install parameter $p \epsilon (0,1)$ the HPM use the little parameter as well as the clarification is written as capability range in p in induction of He's polynomials which can be generated by many methods. Particularly physical developments are restrained by linear or non linear differential equation.

Own selves provide the reasoning of the new homotopy perturbation method personally current numerical decision to determine the ability of the NHPM method for a few PDE .Certainly, provide the conclusions.

1.1 *New Homotopy Perturbation Method (NHPM)*

The general types of PDE can be suppose as the

$$\frac{\partial \phi}{\partial s} + k\big(\phi\big(q_1, q_2, q_3 \ldots \ldots q_{n-1}, s\big)\big) = m\big(q_1, q_2, q_3 \ldots \ldots q_{n-1}, s\big) \tag{1}$$

With the successive basic case:

$$\Phi\big(q_1, q_2, q_3 \ldots \ldots q_{n-1}, s_0\big) = G\big(q_1, q_2, q_3 \ldots \ldots q_{n-1},\big)$$

Where k is a non –linear operators which is depends on the function ϕ and its derivatives with respect to q'_j s j = 1 to n-1,s and m is in homogenous for determine equation (1) by applying NHPM we establish the successive homotopy

$$(1-p)\left(\frac{\partial\phi}{\partial s}-\phi_0\right)+p\left(\frac{\partial\phi}{\partial s}+k(\phi)-m\right)=0 \tag{2}$$

Or

$$\left(\frac{\partial\phi}{\partial s}\right)=\phi_0-p(\phi_0+k(\phi)-m)=0 \tag{3}$$

Applying the inverse operator, $L^{-1}=\int_{S_0}^{S}ds$ on two sided of equation (3)

$$\Phi\left(q_1,q_2,q_3.......q_{n-1},s\right)=\Phi\left(q_1,q_2,q_3.......q_{n-1},s_0\right)+\int_{s_0}^{s}\phi_0\,ds\ddot{-}p\int_{s_0}^{s}(\phi_0+k(\phi)-m)ds \tag{4}$$

Where

$$\Phi\left(q_1,q_2,q_3.......q_{n-1},s_0\right)=\Phi\left(q_1,q_2,q_3.......q_{n-1},s_0\right)$$

Suppose the explanation of equation (4)

$$\Phi=\phi_0+p\phi_1+p^2\phi_2+p^3\phi_3\ldots\ldots\ldots,\phi_j=j=0,1,2,3\ldots$$

Are function which should be illuminate consider that the fundamental proximate of the explanation is in the successive form

$$\phi_0\left(q_1,q_2,q_3.......q_{n-1},s\right)=\sum_{j=0}^{\infty}c_j\left(q_1,q_2,q_3.......q_{n-1},\right)p_j(s)$$

Where
$c_j\left(q_1,q_2,q_3.......q_{n-1},\right)$ are unknown coefficients and $p,p^2,p^3......$ are specific function
Comparing the coefficients of p

$$p^0:\left(\phi_0(q_1,q_2,q_3.......q_{n-1},s)=G\left(q_1,q_2,q_3.......q_{n-1},\right)+\sum_{J=0}^{\infty}c_J\int_{s_0}^{s}p_0(s)ds\right.$$

$$p^1:\phi_1\left(q_1,q_2,q_3.......q_{n-1},s\right)+\sum_{J=0}^{\infty}c_J\int_{s_0}^{s}p_0(s)ds-\int_{s_0}^{s}k(\phi_0)-m)ds$$

$$p^j:\phi_j\left(q_1,q_2,q_3.......q_{n-1},s\right)=-\int_{s_0}^{s}k\left(q_1,q_2,q_3.......q_{n-1},\right)ds$$

Thus the accurate explanation may be gather as

$$\Phi\left(q_1,q_2,q_3.......q_{n-1},s\right)=\phi_0\left(q_1,q_2,q_3.......q_{n-1},s\right)=G\left(q_1,q_2,q_3.......q_{n-1},\right)+\sum_{J=0}^{\infty}c_J\int_{s_0}^{s}p_0(s)ds$$

1.2 Example 1

Consider the following system of burgers equations.

$$\frac{\partial \phi}{\partial t} - \frac{\partial^2 \phi}{\partial s^2} - 2\Phi \frac{\partial \phi}{\partial s} + \frac{\partial}{\partial s}(\lambda, \Phi) = 0$$

$$\frac{\partial \lambda}{\partial t} - \frac{\partial^2 \lambda}{\partial s^2} - 2\Phi \frac{\partial \lambda}{\partial s} + \frac{\partial}{\partial s}(\lambda, \Phi) = 0$$

Initial base is

$$\Phi(s,0) = \cos s; \quad \lambda(s,0) = \cos s;$$

the above difficulty may be written as the integral equation.

$$\Phi(s,0) = \cos s + \int_0^t \frac{\partial^2 \phi}{\partial s^2} + 2\Phi \frac{\partial \phi}{\partial s} - \frac{\partial}{\partial s}(\Phi, \lambda)dt$$

$$\lambda(s,0) = \cos s + \int_0^t \frac{\partial^2 \lambda}{\partial s^2} + 2\Phi \frac{\partial \lambda}{\partial s} - \frac{\partial}{\partial s}(\Phi, \lambda)dt$$

using the homotopy method.

$$\phi_0 + \phi_1 p + \phi_2 p^2 \phi_3 p^3 + \ldots \ldots = \cos \phi + \left[p \left\{ \int_0^t \frac{\partial^2 \phi_0}{\partial s^2} + p \frac{\partial^2 \phi_1}{\partial s^2} + p^2 \frac{\partial^2 \phi_2}{\partial s^2} + \ldots \right\} + 2\{\phi_0 + p\phi_1 \right.$$
$$+ p^2 \phi_2 + \ldots\}\{(\phi_0)_s + p\phi_1)_s + \ldots\} - \frac{\partial}{\partial s}(\phi_0 + p\phi_1 + p^2\phi_2 \ldots)(\{\lambda_0 + p\lambda_1 + p^2\lambda_2 + \ldots\}$$

$$\lambda_0 + \lambda_1 p + \lambda_2 p^2 + \lambda_3 p^3 + \ldots \ldots = \cos s + \left[p \left\{ \int_0^t \frac{\partial^2 \lambda_0}{\partial s^2} + p \frac{\partial^2 \lambda_1}{\partial s^2} + p^2 \frac{\partial^2 \lambda_2}{\partial s^2} + \ldots \right\} + 2\{\lambda_0 + p\lambda_1 \right.$$
$$+ p^2 \lambda_2 + \ldots\}\{(\lambda_0)_s + p(\lambda_1)_s + \ldots\} - \frac{\partial}{\partial s}\phi_0 + p\phi_1 p^2 \phi_2 + \ldots)\{(\lambda_0)_s + p(\lambda_1)_s + p^2\lambda_2 + \ldots\}$$

The equating power of p are compared.

$p^0 : \phi_0(s,t) = \cos s$

$p^0 : \lambda_0(s,t) = |\cos s$

$p^1 := \int_0^t \frac{\partial^2 \phi_0}{\partial s^2} + 2\phi_0 \frac{\partial \phi_0}{\partial s} - \frac{\partial}{\partial s}(\phi_0, \lambda_0)dt$

$p^1 := \int_0^t [-\cos s - 2\sin s \cos s - (\phi_0(\lambda_0)_s + (\phi_0)_s \lambda_0)]dt$

$p^1 := \int_0^t [-\cos s - 2\sin s \cos s + 2\sin s \cos s]dt$

$\phi_1 = -t\cos s$

$p^1 := \int_0^t \frac{\partial^2 \lambda_0}{\partial s^2} + 2\lambda_0 \frac{\partial \lambda_0}{\partial s} - \frac{\partial}{\partial s}(\phi_0, \lambda_0)dt$

$p^1 := \int_0^t [-\cos s - 2\sin s \cos s - (\phi_0(\lambda_0)_s + (\phi_0)_s \lambda_0)]dt$

$p^1 := \int_0^t [-\cos s - 2\sin s \cos s + 2\sin s \cos s]dt$

$\lambda_1 = -t\cos s$

$p^2 : \int_0^t \frac{\partial^2 \phi_0}{\partial s^2} + 2(\phi_0 \frac{\partial \phi_1}{\partial s} + \phi_1 \frac{\partial \phi_0}{\partial s}) - \frac{\partial}{\partial s}(\phi_0, \lambda_{1+\phi_1\lambda_0})dt$

$p^2 := \int_0^t t\cos s + 4t\sin s \cos s - 4t\sin s \cos s)dt$

$\phi_2 = \frac{t^2}{2}\cos s$

364

$p^2 : \int_0^t \frac{\partial^2 \phi}{\partial s^2} + 2(\lambda_0 \frac{\partial \lambda_1}{\partial s} + \lambda_1 \frac{\partial \lambda_0}{\partial s}) - \frac{\partial}{\partial s}(\phi_0, \lambda_{1+\phi_1\lambda_0}) dt$

$p^2 := \int_0^t t \cos s + 4t \sin s \cos s - 4t \sin s \cos s) dt$

$\lambda_2 = \frac{t^2}{2} \cos s$

$\phi_3 = \frac{t^3}{3!} \cos s$

$\lambda_3 = \frac{t^3}{3!} \cos s$

And so on in the continuo process we get the n term proximate explanations of eq (1) & (2)

$$\phi(s, t) = \sum_{j=0}^{n-1} \phi_j(s, t) = \cos s \left[1 - t + \frac{t^2}{2!} - \frac{t^3}{3!} + \right] = e^{-t} \cos s$$

$$\lambda(s, t) = \sum_{j=0}^{n-1} \lambda_j(s, t) = \cos s \left[1 - t + \frac{t^2}{2!} - \frac{t^3}{3!} + \right] = e^{-t} \cos s$$

Which is correct explanation

1.3 Example 2

Consider the Laplace equation is

$$\nabla^2 \Phi = 0 \tag{5}$$

The equation can be written as

$$\frac{\partial \phi}{\partial s} = \frac{\partial \lambda}{\partial t} \tag{6}$$

$$\frac{\partial \phi}{\partial t} = -\frac{\partial \lambda}{\partial s} \tag{7}$$

Where λ,ϕ are unknown variables
With the basic case
$\Phi(0,t) = \cos t; \lambda(0,t) = \sin t$
The above problem may be written as integral equation
$\Phi(0,t) = \cos t + \int_0^s \frac{\partial \lambda}{\partial t} ds$
$\lambda(0,t) = \sin t + \int_0^s \frac{-\partial \phi}{\partial t} ds$
using homotopy perturbation method
$\phi_0 + \phi_1 p + \phi_2 p^2 + \phi_3 p^3 + \ldots \ldots = \cos t + \int_0^s (\lambda_0)_t + p(\lambda_1)_t + p^2(\lambda_2)_t + \ldots \ldots ds$
$\lambda_0 + \lambda_1 p + \lambda_2 p^2 + \lambda_3 p^3 + \ldots \ldots = \cos t + \int_0^s -[(\phi_0)_t + p(\phi_1)_t + p^2(\phi_2)_t + \ldots \ldots] ds$
Equating the coefficients of p
$\phi_0: p^0 = \cos t$
$\lambda_0: p^0 = \sin t$
$p^1 := \int_0^s (\lambda_0)_t ds$
$p^1 := \int_0^s \cos t ds$
$\phi_1 := s\cos t$
$p^1 := \int_0^s (\phi_0)_t ds$
$p^1 := - \int_0^s - \sin t ds$
$\lambda_1 := s\sin t$
$p^2 := \int_0^s (\lambda_1)_t ds$
$p^2 := \int_0^s s\cos t ds$

365

$\phi_2 := \frac{s^2}{2!} \cos t$

$p^2 := \int_0^s (\phi_1)_t \, ds$

$p^2 := - \int_0^s -s \sin t \, ds$

$\lambda_2 := \frac{s^2}{2!} \sin t$

$:\Phi(s,t) = \sum_{i=0}^{n-1} \phi_i(s,t) = \cos t(1+s + \frac{s^2}{2!} +.....)$

$\lambda(s,t) = \sum_{i=0}^{n-1} \lambda_i(s,t) = \sin t(1+s + \frac{s^2}{2!} +.....)$

$\Phi(s,t) = e^s \sin t$

$\lambda(s,t) = e^s \sin t$

which is exact explanation of Laplace equation

1.4 *Example 3*

Suppose the one dimension differential equation.

$$\phi_t = \lambda \phi_{xx} \tag{8}$$

initial condition

$$\phi(x,0) = b + ca^x + c_1 \sin h(c_2 x) + c_3 \cos h(c_4 x) \tag{9}$$

using the New Homotopy Perturbation Method

$\phi_0 + \phi_1 p + \phi_2 p^2 + \phi_3 p^3 +....... = b + ca^x + c_1 \sin h(c_2 x) + c_3 \cos h(c_4 x) + p\int_0^t \lambda \phi_{xx} \, dt$

$= b + ca^x + c_1 \sin h(c_2 x) + c_3 \cos h(c_4 x) + p\int_0^t \lambda[(\phi_0)_{xx} + p(\phi_1)_{xx} + p^2(\phi_2)_{xx} +....] dt$

The equating the power of p

$\phi_0: p^0 = b + ca^x + c_1 \sin h(c_2 x) + c_3 \cos h(c_4 x)$

$p^1 = \int_0^t \lambda(\phi_0)_{xx} dt$

By the NHM is

$\phi_0 + \phi_1 p + \phi_2 p^2 + \phi_3 p^3 +.......$

$= b + ca^x + c_1 \sin h(c_2 x) + c_3 \cos h(c_4 x) + \lambda t(ca^x(\log a)^2 + c_1 c_2{}^2 \sin h(c_2 x) + c_3 c^2{}_4 \cos h(c_4 x)) + \lambda^2 \frac{t^2}{2!}(ca^x(\log a)^4 + c_1 c_2{}^4 \sin h(c_2 x) + c_3 c^4{}_4 \cos h(c_4 x))$

$= b + ca^x e^{\lambda t(\log a)^2} + c_1 \sin h(c_2 x) e^{\lambda t c_2{}^2} + c_3 \cos h(c_4 x) e^{\lambda t c_4{}^2}$.

1.5 *Example 4*

Suppose the one-dimension differential equation.

$$\phi_t = \lambda \phi_{xx} \tag{10}$$

initial condition

$$\Phi(x,0) \ldots = e^x \tag{11}$$

using the New Homotopy Perturbation Method

$\phi_0 + \phi_1 p + \phi_2 p^2 + \phi_3 p^3 +....... = e^x + p\int_0^t \lambda \phi_{xx} \, dt$

$= e^x + p\int_0^t \lambda[(\phi_0)_{xx} + p(\phi_1)_{xx} + p^2(\phi_2)_{xx} +....] dt$

The equating the power of p

$\phi_0: p^0 = e^x$

$p^1 = \int_0^t \lambda(\phi_0)_{xx} dt$

$p^1 = \int_0^t \lambda e^x dt$

$\phi_1 = e^x \lambda t$

$$p^2 = \int_0^t \lambda t e^x \mathrm{dt}$$

$$\phi_2 = \lambda^2 \frac{t^2}{2!} e^x$$

By the NHM IS

$$\phi_0 + \phi_1 \mathrm{p} + \phi_2 p^2 + \phi_3 p^3 + \ldots\ldots = e^x + e^x \lambda t + e^x \lambda^2 \frac{t^2}{2!} + \ldots\ldots$$

$\Phi(t) = e^x e^{t\lambda}$ Which is exact solution.

2 CONCLUSION

In this paper we successfully used the NHPM to obtain exact solutions for PD equation. Furthermore, this method is a powerful tool to solve any different type of PDE. Thus the NHPM is capable in observation the comparative or analytic explication of the linear and non linear PDE. It is also a helpful and useful method to solve the PDE.

REFERENCES

Ganji DD, Rajabi A (2006) Assessment of homotopy-perturbation and perturbation methods in heat radiation equations.IntCommun Heat Mass Transfer 33:391–400

GoenneJ.H.He, Some asymptotic methods for strongly nonlinear equations, International Journal of Modern Physics B 20 (10) (2006) 1141_1199

GoenneJ.H.He, Some asymptotic methods for strongly nonlinear equations, International Journal of Modern Physics B 20 (10) (2006) 1141_1199

Jang TS (2016) A new solution procedure for a nonlinear infinite beam equation of motion. Communication in Nonlinear Science numerical simulation 39-321–331

Jang TS (2017) A new dispersion-relation preserving method for Integrating the classical Bossiness equation. Communication in non linear science and numerical simulation 43:118–138

Jang TS (2017) A new dispersion-relation preserving method for Integrating the classical Bossiness equation. Communication in non linear science and numerical simulation 43:118–138

Jang TS (2016) A new solution procedure for a nonlinear infinite beam equation of motion. Communication in Nonlinear Science numerical simulation 39-321–331

Jang TS (2017) A new dispersion-relation preserving method for Integrating the classical Boussinesq equation. Communication in non linear science and numerical simulation 43:118–138

Jang TS (2017) A new dispersion-relation preserving method for Integrating the classical Boussinesq equation. Communication in non linear science and numerical simulation 43:118–138.

J.H.He, A note on the Homotopy perturbation method, Thermal Science 14 (2) (2010) 565–568

J.H. He, A coupling method of homotopy technique and perturbation technique for nonlinear problems, International Journal of Non-Linear Mechanics 35 (2000) 37_43.

J.H. He, Application of homotopy perturbation method to nonlinear wave equations, Chaos, Solitons & Fractals 26 (2005) 695_700.

J.H. He, Homotopy perturbation method for bifurcation of nonlinear problems, International Journal of Nonlinear Sciences and Numerical Simulation (2005) 207_208.

J.H.He, A note on the Homotopy perturbation method, Thermal Science 14 (2) (2010) 565–568

J.H.He, A note on the Homotopy perturbation method, Thermal Science 14 (2) (2010) 565–568

J.H. He, A coupling method of homotopy technique and perturbation technique for nonlinear problems, International Journal of Non-Linear Mechanics 35 (2000) 37–43

O.Martin, a homotopy perturbation method for solving a neutron transport equation, Applied Mathematics and Computation 217 (21) (2011) 8567–8574.

O.Martin, a homotopy perturbation method for solving a neutron transport equation Applied Mathematics and Computation 217 (21) (2011) 8567–8574.

O.Martin, a homotopy perturbation method for solving a neutron transport equation, Applied Mathematics and Computation 217 (21) (2011) 8567–8574.

T. Özi³, A. Y_ld_r_m, A comparative study of He's homotopy perturbation method for determining frequency_amplitude relation of a non-linear oscillator with discontinuities, International Journal of Nonlinear Sciences and Numerical Simulation 8 (2) (2007) 243_248

T. Özi³, A. Y_ld_r_m, A comparative study of He's homotopy perturbation method for determining frequency_amplitude relation of a non-linear oscillator with discontinuities, International Journal of Nonlinear Sciences and Numerical Simulation 8 (2) (2007) _243248

Communication and Computing Systems – Prasad et al. (eds)
© *2019 Taylor & Francis Group, London, ISBN 978-0-367-00147-6*

Implementation of survivability by using tier modes approach

Chandra Singh
Department of E&CE, NMAM Institute of Technology, Nitte, Karkala Taluk, Karnataka, India

ABSTRACT: Optical Communication System implies Elements, Devices and Systems. Optical Networks consists of three domains such as Networking, Switching and Routing. Survivability plays an important role in order to protect the network from failures. Hence survivability in optical network determines the interconnectivity between user and system configurations. Today's Optical Network Environment (ONE) presents N X N and carries the demands in terms of THz. Thus two modes are described to plan and design of SFON, They are Physical Layer Mode (PLM) and Logical Layer Mode (LLM). PLM consists of cross connectivity of digital signals, bandwidth estimation, user survivability impact ratio, network path estimation and network capacity model. In LLM it describes the user node and flow survivability path, scaled the node position dependency and independency between different topologies to evaluate the throughput of the system Tier Configurations (TC). Further these modes present the Local and Global fairness (LGF) scenario regarding the packet transfer between Single Period Demand (SPD) to Multi Period Demands (MPD).

1 INTRODUCTION

Today's optical networks are carrying enormous traffic, which is almost increasing proportionately. The length of the laid optical fibers throughout the world is hundreds of million miles(Bhandari, Abhay et al,2015). The rapid changes in the fiber optic communication and the integration with computer communication network services provide high quality and fast services to the user. A single fiber has many light paths which carry up to 160 and with a Capacity of 100 Gbps since it has a very large bandwidth. If a single fiber failure or fiber cut occurs leads to loss of a significant amount of traffic. In order to prevent service interruption (Kumar Krishan et al, 2014). In general failure of the fiber is to be considered is either node or link failure. Node failure is caused because of equipment failure or network element failure and because of cable disruptions link failure occurs.

The Fiber Network structure consists of Span, Hub, CO, Switches and Gateways. Span defines the Joint from source to destination (Sairam et al. 2017). Hub is collection point of all the spans in a given network. CO (Central Office) is the common path where all the hubs are having single point of contact where as switches are the devices where the data is segregated through direct, indirect and combination of both further it passes through gateway as depicted in Figure 1 Global Fiber Network Scenario as shown above.

It also facilitates the different network services hence network transparency should mitigate the security vulnerabilities that differ from conventional failures hence global fiber *To measure the Optical-broadband access networks based on projected traffic growth (Dhyani, Geeta et al. 2015).

*Evaluate the impact of emerging protection technologies on network architecture design (Singh, C et al, 2017) network survivability scenario. Optical network design in logical layer is hence forth provides multipath propagation of pacts by using transmission flow which consist of two queues slot queues and packet further it provides minimum fair channel allocation bandwidth, obtain maximum spatial channel reuse and maximum fairness throughput by using centralized packet scheduling algorithm it also computes node mobility and scalability

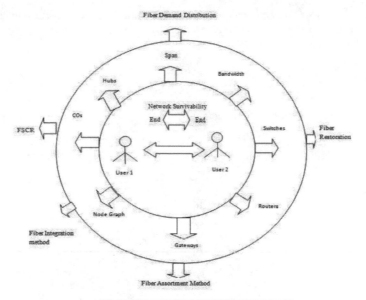

Figure 1. Global fiber network scenario.

by using spatial channel reuse concept it also provides global topology model through which maximum distributed fair queuing through put is achieved(Sairam et al.2019).

*Determine the optical carrier network Integration
*Investigate the potential for packet switching procedures and burst switching in optical networks, i.e. Logical Layer Topology.
*The Performance and Evaluation of Optical networks take into consideration the factors like trade-off between routing traffic at the optical layer(Sairam et al.2017).

2 PHYSICAL LAYER MODE (PLM)

Problem formulation 1: Optical Broadband Access: cross connectivity of digital signals is obtained by using the following parameters:

    Optical Path Connectivity (OPC) Optical Demand Connectivity (ODC)

    Optical Digital Cross Connectivity (ODXC)

    Optical Path Connectivity (OPC): It is defined as end – to – end Communication across different topologies Span Connectivity (SC) with concerned Traffic Flow (TF) in line with link sequence and is measured in b/dedicated light paths in order to maximize the traffic carried and the availability of spare capacity.

$$OPC = SC + TF \qquad (1)$$

    Optical Demand Connectivity (ODC): It is defined as the Digital Signals (DS) which traverse through different Network Connectivity (NC), from kbps to Tbps.

$$ODC = DS + NC \qquad (2)$$

Optical Digital Cross Connectivity (ODXC): It is defined as the cross connectivity in which through the summation of OPC and ODC through is obtained.

$$ODXC = OPC + ODC \tag{3}$$

$$= SC + TF + DS + NC \tag{4}$$

Take source and destination add the demands source to destination as shown

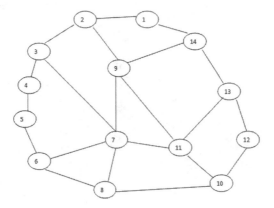

Figure 2.   Network topology 14X14.

Table 1.   Output for Physical Layer Mode.

Link(S-D	Demand Route(Cost)	Traffic in Each Link
1-2-3-4-5-6	8-10-12-18-20-12	85-96-78-68-96-45
8-7-9-14	7-6-12-16	65-49-89-97
9-11-10-12	5-8-13-10	48-56-68-74

Bandwidth = f2 – f1 = 1Hz = 2bps

2.1   *Problem formulation*

Impact of Emerging Protection Technologies on Network Architecture Design is derived by the following parameters:

Survivability Restoration Factor (SRF): In Optical Networks, path setup is the combination of working fibre (WF) and protection fiber (PF). Hence the primary path (PP) carries the data, where as secondary path (SP) remains idle until failure occurs in the primary path. Several protection methodologies are tested to obtain the SRF(Singh C et al,2019). Hence secondary path can be provided to the different vendors in order to utilize the OP (Optical Path), and will be immediately redirected as an when it is required.WF+PF will produce 100% Survivability if 1:1 ratio is considered. WF+PF will produce fast restoration and wastage of bandwidth, if 1+1 ratio is taken.WF+PF will produce significant restoration by using 1:2 DP for Survivability Multi Path Failure (SMPF)(Singh C et al,2019).Network Topology 14X14 will have multiple failures and calculate the SRF.

Table 2. Bandwidth calculated for 14*14 network using DS3-DS2.

0	54.23	0	0	0	0	39	0	0	0	0	0	0	0	0
54.23	0	57.46	0	0	61	0	0	0	0	0	0	54.23	0	0
0	57.46	0	45.89	0	0	0	0	0	0	0	0	0	0	0
0	0	45.89	0	63	0	0	0	55	0	0	0	0	0	0
0	0	0	63	0	0	0	64	0	53	0	0	0	0	0
0	61	0	0	54.23	0	0	49	0	0	0	0	0	0	0
39	0	0	0	0	39	0	0	0	0	40	0	29	0	0
0	0	0	0	64	39	0	0	0	0	18	29	0	0	0
0	0	0	55	0	0	0	0	0	41	0	0	0	0	0
0	0	0	0	53	0	0	0	41	0	0	41	0	0	0
0	0	0	0	0	0	40	18	0	0	0	37	0	0	0
0	0	0	0	0	0	0	37	0	41	37	0	0	0	0
0	71	0	0	0	0	39	0	0	0	0	0	0	0	0
0	0	0	0	0	0	0	0	0	0	0	0	0	0	0
0	0	0	0	0	0	0	0	0	0	0	0	0	0	0

Table 3. Demand before link failure.

Source Destination	Demand
(1,2)	4
(2,3)	9
(3,4)	15
(1,5)	6
(2,6)	10
(5,6)	12
(4,7)	10
(6,7)	14
(4,8)	8
(11,12)	7
(8,12)	5
(8,14)	20
(1,6)	12
Total	132

Table 4. Demand after link failure.

Source Destination	Demand
(1,2)	4
(2,3)	9
(3,4)	11
(1,5)	6
(2,6)	5
(5,6)	6

(*Continued*)

Table 4. *(Continued)*

Source Destination	Demand
(4,7)	10
(6,7)	14
(4,8)	13
(11,12)	7
(8,12)	5
(8,14)	10
(1,6)	12
Total	122

Table 5. Survivability Multi Path Failure (SMPF).

Fiber network protection and Restoration Mechanism	%
Restoration Link/Total Demand	(122/132)x100=92.42

2.2 *Problem formulation*

Optical Carrier Network Integration (ONCI) is defined as the growth of the demand s are significantly improved from

$$DS(N) \rightarrow STS \rightarrow STM \rightarrow OC(N).$$

Associated Path Calculation (APC)$\rightarrow$ Direct Demand Connectivity (DDC)
Non –Associate Path Calculation (NAPC) $\rightarrow$ parcel list calculation

2.3 *Problem formulation*

Amalgam Network Investigate the potential for packet switching procedures and burst switching in optical networks, i.e. Logical Layer Topology(Strand, J et al,2011). In the hybrid fair packet scheduling algorithm location dependent, location- independent Mechanisms and spatial locality are achieved by max-min fair queuing method(Zang, H et al,2013)

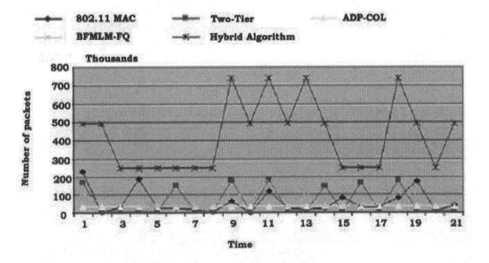

Figure 3

3 CONCLUSION

A optical network integrates different digital signal levels in an network topology by using physical and logical layer implementation methods. Hence survivability can be improved by using above said layers connectivity. Further it can be enhanced to optical cross connectivity where wavelength services are used for bulk carriers and the distribution such as a synchronous competition and scholastic approximation is measured finally transition from ring to ring and ring – mesh hybrid can be achieved.

REFERENCES

Bhandari, Abhay & Malhotra, Dr. Jagjit 2015. A Review on Network Survivability in Optical Networks 5:97–101.

Kumar, Krishan & Garg Kumar, Amit 2014. Analysis of restoration and protection in optical network with simulation framework 3(5).

Dhyani, Geeta & Bisht, Nivedita 2015. Network Survivability: Analysis Of Protection Schemes In Ring Configuration 02.

Singh, C. & Sairam, K.V.S.S.S.S. 2017. Survivable fiber optic networks design by using digital signal levels approach. In 2017International Conference on Intelligent Sustainable Systems (ICISS): 84–86.

Sairam, K.V.S.S.S.S. & Singh, C. 2019. Link Layer Traffic ConnectivityProtocol Application and Mechanism in Optical Layer SurvivabilityApproach. In: Smys S., Bestak R., Chen JZ., Kotuliak I. (eds) InternationalConference on Computer Networks and Communication Technologies. LectureNotes on Data Engineering and Communications Technologies 15. Springer, Singapore.

Sairam, K.V.S.S.S.S. & Singh, Chandra 2017.Optical network survivability- An overview'. Indian J. Sci. Res., 14(2): 383–386.

Sairam,K.V.S.S.S.S. & Singh, C. 2019. FONI by Using Survivability Approach: An Overview. In: Kamal R., Henshaw M., Nair P. (eds) International Conference on Advanced Computing Networking and Informatics. Advances in Intelligent Systems and Computing 870. Springer, Singapore

Singh,C., Sairam, K.V.S.S.S.S. & M. B. H. 2019. Global Fairness Model Estimation Implementation in Logical Layer by Using Optical Network Survivability Techniques. In: Hemanth J., Fernando X., Lafata P., Baig Z. (eds) International Conference on Intelligent Data Communication Technologies and Internet of Things (ICICI) 2018. ICICI 2018. Lecture Notes on Data Engineering and Communications Technologies 26. Springer, Cham.

Strand, J., Chiu,A. & Tkach, R. 2011.Issues for Routing in the Optical Laye. IEEE Communication Magazine 39:81–87.

Zang,H., Ou,C. & Mukherjee, B. 2013. Path-protection Routing and Wavelength Assignment (RWA) in WDM Mesh Networks under ductlayer constraints. IEEE ACM Transactions on Networking 11(.2):248–258.

Communication and Computing Systems – Prasad et al. (eds)
© 2019 Taylor & Francis Group, London, ISBN 978-0-367-00147-6

Association rule mining using swarm-based approaches: An analytical survey

Poonam Yadav

D.A.V College of Engineering & Technology, India

ABSTRACT: The process of determining frequent itemsets by exploiting the association rules is the most important tasks in data mining. A variety of efficient techniques were portrayed in the conventional works for mining such frequent item sets. A significant review of these approaches highlighted on modeling a proficient multiple levels ARM algorithm and data structure, which is capable to minimize the count of iterations that may further accomplish better time efficiency. Accordingly, this survey intends to review several topics to resolve the ARM issues. The performance measures and the maximum performance achievements are also examined and demonstrated in this survey. In addition, the algorithmic classification for the surveyed papers are surveyed and described. Finally, the research gaps and issues of the ARM issues are also discussed briefly.

NOMENCLATURE

Acronyms	Description
ARM	Association Rule Mining
FIM	Frequent itemset mining
MST	Minimum support threshold
MCT	Minimum confidence threshold
Ars	Association rules
HUI	High-utility itemset
HUIM	HUI mining
MUT	Minimum utility threshold
PSO	Particle Swarm Optimiser
GA	Genetic Algorithm
TIA	Tree Induction Algorithm
CSA	Cuckoo Search optimization algorithm
COA4ARH	CSA for the sensitive association rules hiding
ACO	Ant Colony Optimization
HHACOARM	Hierarchical Heterogeneous ACO based Action Rule Mining
GBSO-Miner	GPU-dependent Bees Swarm Optimization Miner
1-HTWUIs	High-transaction-weighted utilization 1-itemsets
APSO	Adaptive PSO
ANN	Artificial Neural Network
MOPAR	Multi-objective PSO algorithm
BPSO	Binary PSO
MOPSO	Multi-objective PSO
CF	Collaborative Filtering
AMO	Animal migration optimization

1 INTRODUCTION

Mining association rules from a large database of business data, such as transaction records, has been an important issue in the field of data mining (Sousa, Tiago et al. 2004). ARM is a data mining technique that aims at discovering hidden and frequent patterns from transactional databases (Afshari, Mahtab Hossein et al. 2016). The issues related with ARM could be partitioned into two sub-issues, initial one is a frequent itemset discovery and second one is the generation of association rules. It could be known that the entire mining performance is significantly portrayed by the initial sub-problem (Djenouri, Youcef et al. 2018). Moreover, ARM is extensively exploited in numerous applications like Constraint Programming, Information Retrieval, and Business Intelligence, where it is deployed as pre-processing phase to extract associations among the data given at input. The rules that are generated assists to bias the solving process of such appliances (Beiranvand, Vahid et al. 2014) & (Kuo, R. J. et al. 2011) For example, on regarding the problem of information retrieval, the compilation of documents is converted to the transactional database, in which every document is regarded as a transaction, and every term is said to be an item (Sarath, K. N. V. D. et al. 2013).

FIM or ARM was comprehensively introduced to extract the group of frequent itemscts (Tyagi, Shweta et al. 2013), where their frequency or incidence of an item set is not reduced than MST or its confidence is not reduced than MCT (Ykhlef, Mourad 2011). FIM techniques often produce an extensive amount of frequent rules and item sets that minimize both the effectiveness and also the efficiency of the mining approaches as only the subset of the whole ARs is of concern to users. Moreover, the users require a supplementary post-processing stage to sort out the great count of mined rules to find out the constructive ones. Accordingly, the current work has emphasized the significance of mining based on constraints. They make use of user-specific parameters in the mining procedure to develop efficiency, or performance. As only the frequency of item sets is exposed whether in ARM or FIM, it is inadequate to recognize the item sets particularly when the item set is appeared rarely but includes increased profit value. For resolving the restriction of ARM or FIM (Djenouri, Youcef et al. 2018) & (Shao, Yuanxun et al. 2018), HUIM was modeled to determine the "profitable" and "useful" itemsets. An itemset is regarded as a HUI if its value of utility is not reduced than the MUT .

This survey has reviewed various works related to the ARM issues. Accordingly, various performance measures adopted in each work are described, and along with it, the maximum performances achieved by the various works are also portrayed by this survey. Here, various algorithmic classifications, which are adopted in the surveyed papers, are analyzed and demonstrated. The paper is organized as follows. Section II analyzes the various related works and reviews done under this topic. In addition, section III describes the various analyses on ARM issues, and section IV presents the research gaps and challenges. At last, section V concludes the paper.

2 LITERATURE REVIEW

2.1 *Related works*

In 2004, Tiago et al. (Sousa, Tiago et al. 2004) have suggested a scheme based on the exploitation of the PSO for mining the data. In the initial stage of the study, three varied PSO Data Mining approaches were executed and analyzed in opposition to a GA and a TIA. Accordingly, from the attained outcomes, PSO was established to be an appropriate candidate for categorization purpose. The subsequent stage was contributed to enhancing one of the PSO variants with respect to temporal complexity. The outcomes attained in these areas seem to point out that PSO Data Mining approaches were reasonable, not only with other evolutionary schemes, but also with other standard models namely, TIA scheme, and can be effectively deployed to more challenging areas.

In 2016, Mahtab et al. (Afshari, Mahtab Hossein et al. 2016) have introduced a novel and proficient technique that was dependent on the COA4ARH. According to this technique the hiding act was carried out by means of the distortion method. Moreover, in this approach, three fitness functions were described that makes it feasible to attain a solution with the least side effects. On establishing a competent immigration function, this model has enhanced its capability to get away from local optimum. Also, the effectiveness of introduced scheme was computed by carrying out certain experimentations on diverse databases. Finally, the outcomes of the implementation of the introduced model and three of the preceding schemes point out that this scheme has better performance when distinguished to other models.

In 2016, Sreeja and Sankar (Sreeja, N. K. et al. 2016) have adopted a new approach known as HHACOARM model to produce action rules. The implemented model was introduced by regarding the resource parameters. The model includes ant agents at diverse levels for recognizing the flexible characteristics whose values require to be varied to extract action rules. The improvement of HHACOARM model was that it produces best possible count of minimal cost action rules. Also, the HHACOARM model does not produce illogical rules. In addition, the computational complication of HHACOARM technique was less distinguished to the conventional action rule mining schemes.

In 2007, Kuo and Shih (Kuo, R. J. et al. 2014) have presented a technique, which regards the allocated constraints of user in the mining procedure. Accordingly, mining depending on constraints facilitates users to contemplate on mining item sets, which were motivating to themselves that enhances the effectiveness of mining tasks. Moreover, users might concern on recording more than one characteristic and setting various parameters in the real world. Therefore, this analyzation aims to resolve the multi-dimensional issues for ARM generation. Furthermore, the computational time of the adopted scheme was also minimized.

In 2018, Youcef et al. (Djenouri, Youcef et al. 2018) have established a novel GBSO-Miner in which the GPU was exploited as a co-processor to calculate the time consumed by CPU in the adopted model. Different from the traditional GPU-dependent ARM techniques, the entire BSO phases together with the search area determination, the assessment, the local search, and the dancing were carried out on GPU. A mapping method between the data input of each task and the GPU blocks/threads are developed. To demonstrate the effectiveness of the GBSO-Miner framework, intensive experiments were performed. Finally, the outcomes demonstrate that GBSO-Miner performs better than the baseline techniques by means of the graph and big textual databases. From the simulation, the outcomes expose that GBSO-Miner was up to eight hundred times quicker than other traditional models.

In 2016, Jerry et al. (Lin, Jerry Chun-Wei et al. 2018) have established an approach using discrete PSO for encoding the particles as the binary constraints. A proficient depending on PSO algorithm such as HUIM-BPSO sig was introduced to discover HUIs resourcefully. It initially sets the count of HTWUIs as the particle size depending on transaction-weighted utility (TWU) representation that could significantly minimize the combinational issue involved in evolution procedure. The sigmoid operation was introduced in the updating procedure of the particles of the modeled HUIM-BPSO model. Finally, the considerable experimentations on real-life datasets demonstrate that the established scheme offers improved outcomes when distinguished to the conventional GA approach.

In 2015, Dhanalaxmi et al. (Dhanalaxmi, B. et al. 2015) have suggested a model that classifies a variety of defects by deploying association rule mining based on the classification technique that was deployed to gather the real defects by means of identification. ARM methodology results in ineffective policies at certain times. For evading this type of concerns, the standards previous to categorization portrayed by confidence value in addition to assistance have to be optimized. Moreover, in this examination, APSO optimization model was exploited. This could determine the most excellent confidence value and assistance to include the finest policies. At last, the ANN could be deployed to categorize the actual defects, which were described.

In 2014, Vahid et al. (Beiranvand, Vahid et al. 2014) have established an model, which handles with the arithmetical problem of ARM by means of a multi-objective viewpoint by introducing a MOPAR algorithm for mathematical ARM, which determines arithmetical ARs in a single step. For recognizing more proficient ARs, numerous objectives were portrayed in the established multi-objective optimization scheme, together with comprehensibility, confidence, and interestingness. At last, by deploying the Pareto optimality, the optimal ARs were mined. Finally, the outcomes demonstrate that MOPAR mines consistent, interesting, and comprehensible arithmetical ARs while attaining the best trade-off among comprehensibility, interestingness, and confidence.

In 2011, Kuo et al. (Kuo, R. J. et al. 2011) have offered a new technique for ARM for enhancing the computational effectiveness, in addition, to find out appropriate threshold values automatically. The established technique was demonstrated by deploying on certain databases and was distinguished with a GA. Also, the outcomes point out that the PSO approach actually can propose appropriate threshold values and attain superiority rules. Furthermore, a real-world database was exploited to extract ARM rules to determine the behavior of investment and stock category acquisition. In addition, the computational outcomes were also found to be very hopeful.

In 2013, Sarath and Ravi (Sarath, K. N. V. D. et al. 2013) had adopted a novel process, which suggested a BPSO dependent ARM. Accordingly, the ARM depending on BPSO produces the association rules by manipulating a combinatorial global optimization issue, devoid of indicating the minimum confidence and minimum support in variation to apriori approach. Further, the efficiency of the adopted scheme was from mercantile banks and also from three datasets, namely, food database, books items dataset and general store dataset that was attained from the literature. On the basis of the outcomes, it was assumed that the adopted model could be deployed as an option to the FP-growth technique and a priori model.

In 2013, Tyagi et al. (Tyagi, Shweta et al. 2013) have introduced a model that efforts to develop the superiority of recommendations by the application of MOPSO approach for ARM in the designing of CF. Furthermore, the effectiveness of the adopted scheme was improved by extracting the rules only for the specified user. In addition, the offered work discovers the transitive (indirect) association among users in addition to items for offering more precise recommendations even with extreme sparse record of transactions so as to calculate the efficiency of the introduced model, an investigational study was carried out by means of the MovieLens dataset. Also, the investigational outcomes obviously expose that the introduced system constantly do better than other conventional CF dependent techniques as evaluated by recommendation precision, recall, and accuracy.

In 2011, Mourad (Ykhlef, Mourad 2011) had adopted a new process for mining the most excellent rules in a considerable time of implementation, however, it does not makes certain about the optimal solutions. Also, the novel derived technique was based on Quantum Swarm Evolutionary (QSE) model. Finally, the proposed scheme was found to offer improved outcomes when distinguished with GA model.

In 2017, Djenouri and Marco (Djenouri, Youcef et al. 2017) have implemented two novel methods to FIM, such as, PSO-Apriori and GA-Apriori that exploits the PSO and GA processes correspondingly. e-Ranging experimentation on real and synthetic database illustrates that the adopted techniques perform better than other conventional approaches with respect to the performance of runtime. Finally, the outcomes also expose that the PSO-Apriori performance was assessable to FP-Growth and Apriori with respect to the superiority of found solutions. Furthermore, it was demonstrated that PSO-Apriori performs well than the recently introduced BATFIM technique while handling with other traditional schemes.

In 2009, Wang et al. (Wang, Her-Shing et al. 2009) have introduced a methodology that analyzed about the consumption of currently obtainable data by the firm and investigated this data to formulate it significant, and it moreover recognizes the most common malfunctions in order to increase the effectiveness of alterations. In addition, the modern businesses should handle with enormous amounts of data every day, and it desires to recognize suitable methodologies for handling with extremely competitive markets, and also to exploit the assessment of variations in product model to recognize the scheme, which was inexpensive and most gainful.

In 2018, Son et al. (Son, Le Hoang et al. 2018) have formulated a novel mining approach depending on AMO, termed as ARM–AMO, to minimize the count of association rules. Accordingly, it was dependent on the idea that rules which were not of much support and redundant were removed from the data. Initially, Apriori model was deployed to produce association rules and frequent item sets. Subsequently, AMO was exploited to minimize the count of AR's with a novel fitness function, which integrates frequent rules. Also, from the experiments, it was observed that in evaluation with the other pertinent models, ARM–AMO significantly minimizes the computational interval for generation of frequent itemset, count of rules produced and memory for ARM production.

3 REVIEW ON VARIOUS CONSTRAINTS FOR NEGATIVE ASSOCIATION MINING

3.1 *Algorithmic classification*

The various algorithms adopted in each reviewed paper includes CPSO, CSO, ACO, partition model, GBSO approach, PSO algorithm, ANN technique, MOPAR scheme, BPSO algorithm, MOPSO model, QSEM approach, PSO-Apriori scheme, and ARM-AMO algorithm. The demonstration of the various schemes is given by Fig. 1. Accordingly, CPSO algorithm was adopted in (Sousa, Tiago et al. 2004) and CSO algorithm was adopted in (Afshari, Mahtab Hossein et al. 2016). ACO system was implemented in (Sreeja, N. K. et al. 2016) and partition model was implemented in (Kuo, R. J. et al. 2014). In addition, GBSO algorithm was suggested in (Djenouri, Youcef et al. 2018) and PSO algorithm was deployed in (Lin, Jerry Chun-Wei et al. 2018) & (Wang, Her-Shing et al. 2009) . Accordingly, ANN technique was implemented in (Dhanalaxmi, B. et al. 2015), and MOPAR scheme was adopted in (Beiranvand, Vahid et al. 2014). BPSO algorithm and MOPSO model have been implemented in (Sarath, K. N. V. D. et al. 2013) & (Tyagi, Shweta et al. 2013) correspondingly. In addition, QSEM algorithm, PSO-Apriori algorithm, and ARM-AMO approach were implemented in (Ykhlef, Mourad 2011) & (Son, Le Hoang et al. 2018).

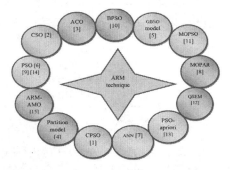

Fig. 1. Various schemes of the reviewed works.

3.2 *Performance measures*

The performance measures contributed in each paper are described in this section. The diagrammatic representation of the performance measures is given by Fig. 2. Here, accuracy, platform width, number of items, number of rules, minimum support, minimum confidence, maximum length, number of patterns, velocity limit, lines of code, sensitivity, recall, and precision were attained from each contribution. Accuracy was measured in (Sousa, Tiago et al. 2004) & (Tyagi, Shweta et al. 2013) and platform width was deployed in (Sousa, Tiago et al. 2004). In addition, number of items was adopted in (Afshari, Mahtab Hossein et al. 2016) & (Djenouri, Youcef et al. 2017) that offer highest contribution and number of rules was analyzed in (Kuo, R. J. et al. 2014). In addition, minimum support was deployed in (Sreeja, N. K. et al. 2016) & (Kuo, R. J. et al. 2011) and minimum confidence was adopted in (Sreeja, N. K. et al. 2016) & (Wang, Her-Shing et al. 2009). Maximum length was measured in (Djenouri, Youcef et al. 2018), and number of patterns was adopted in (Lin, Jerry Chun-Wei et al. 2018).

The other measures such as velocity limit, lines of code, sensitivity, recall, and precision were implemented in (Beiranvand, Vahid et al. 2014) & (Tyagi, Shweta et al. 2013) respectively.

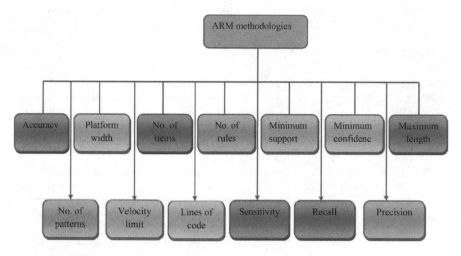

Fig. 2. Various performance measures of the reviewed works.

3.3 *Maximum performance achieved*

The maximum performance achieved by various performance measures is given by Table I. The accuracy attained by the reviewed works is 92%, which is adopted in (Sousa, Tiago et al. 2004) and the platform width is 30 that is adopted in (Sousa, Tiago et al. 2004). In addition, number of items was achieved as 19 in (Afshari, Mahtab Hossein et al. 2016), and number of rules was attained at 10 in (Kuo, R. J. et al. 2014). Also, minimum support and minimum confidence have been measured in (Djenouri, Youcef et al. 2018) & (Sarath, K. N. V. D. et al. 2013) which attain a value of 10% and 46.72% respectively. Moreover, maximum length and number of patterns have been exploited in (Lin, Jerry Chun-Wei et al. 2018), and it has attained optimal values of 46 and 98 correspondingly. Accordingly, Velocity limit, lines of code, sensitivity, recall and defect density were deployed in (Beiranvand, Vahid et al. 2014) &

Table 1. Maximum performance achieved by the reviewed works.

Measures	Maximum Performance Achieved	Citation
Accuracy	92%	(Sousa, Tiago et al. 2004)
Platform width	30	(Sousa, Tiago et al. 2004)
Number of items	19	(Afshari, Mahtab Hossein et al. 2016)
Number of rules	10	(Kuo, R. J. et al. 2014)
Minimum support	10%	(Djenouri, Youcef et al. 2018)
Minimum confidence	46.72%	(Sarath, K. N. V. D. et al. 2013)
Maximum length	46	(Lin, Jerry Chun-Wei et al. 2018)
Number of patterns	98	(Lin, Jerry Chun-Wei et al. 2018)
Velocity limit	3.83	(Beiranvand, Vahid et al. 2014)
Lines of code	670	(Dhanalaxmi, B. et al. 2015)
Sensitivity	0.394	(Dhanalaxmi, B. et al. 2015)
Recall	0.8316	(Tyagi, Shweta et al. 2013)
Defect Density	0.042	(Dhanalaxmi, B. et al. 2015)
Cost recovery	834	(Wang, Her-Shing et al. 2009)
Threshold criteria value	10%	(Sousa, Tiago et al. 2004)
Population Size	40	(Beiranvand, Vahid et al. 2014)

(Dhanalaxmi, B. et al. 2015) they have obtained better values of 3.83, 670, 0.394, 0.8316 and 0.042 respectively. Moreover, cost recovery, threshold criteria value and population Size has attained better values of 834, 10% and 40 and they were attained from (Wang, Her-Shing et al. 2009), (Sousa, Tiago et al. 2004) & (Beiranvand, Vahid et al. 2014) correspondingly.

4 RESEARCH GAPS AND CHALLENGES

This section has discussed the challenges and issues, which requires be evaluated while modeling an ARM method and reviewing how these problems are dealt in the conventional works. It can be noticed that the majority of the present mining models adopt a one pass and incremental mining technique that is appropriate to extract data streams; however few of them deal with the conception of drifting issue. In addition, the current data stream mining schemes necessitate users to describe one or more constraints prior to their implementation; anyhow, the majority of them do not point out how users can regulate these constraints online when they are operated. In multiple level or level single ARs; the initial and most significant problem is focused with the precise data format in a suitable data source. In addition, the encoding process that has to be exploited to transfer the transaction tables remains as a major concern since these encode tables are deployed to sustain the multiple level hierarchy. An additional issue to design or develop schemes for numerous level ARs is to minimize the count of iteration and to attain time proficiency. The efficiency of time can be attained by lessening the scans of database at every level. Accordingly, the redundancy of AR's is a major concern in AR detection.

If the interesting constraints such as confidence and support thresholds are least, the count of frequent itemsets raises, and the count of ARs offered to the user also raises typically. The majority of these AR's might be redundant, and hence the assortment of suitable values of interesting constraints may be a significant issue in ARM. There are numerous measures of the interesting of an association. The challenge to the users is to determine the associations to be selected by the user specified parameters. Also, a problem associated to the ARM is the determination of efficacy of AR in making decisions flawlessly within the association mining process.

5 CONCLUSION

ARM was an area of significance for numerous researchers for an extended time, and till now, it exists as an interesting topic. It is one of the significant tasks of data mining. It intends to determine the associations between varieties of items in the database. Accordingly, in this survey, numerous papers were analyzed, and the related techniques adopted in each surveyed paper were described. In addition, the performance measures focused in each paper were illustrated, and along with it, the maximum performance measures attained were also illustrated. Thus the survey provides the detailed analysis of the ARM issues from the reviewed papers.

REFERENCES

Afshari, Mahtab Hossein, Dehkordi, Mohammad Naderi & Akbari, Mehdi 2016. Association rule hidingusing cuckoo optimization algorithm. Expert Systems with Applications 64:340-351.
Agapito, Giuseppe, Guzzi, Pietro Hiram & Cannataro, Mario 2018. Parallel and Distributed Association Rule Mining in Life Science: a Novel Parallel Algorithm to Mine Genomics Data. Information Sciences.
Beiranvand, Vahid, Mobasher-Kashani, Mohamad & Bakar, Azuraliza Abu 2014. Multi-objective PSO algorithm for mining numerical association rules without a priori discretization. Expert Systems with Applications 41 (9): 4259-4273.
Dhanalaxmi, B., Naidu, G. Apparao & Anuradha, K. 2015. Adaptive PSO Based Association Rule Mining Technique for Software Defect Classification Using ANN. Procedia Computer Science 46:432-442.

Djenouri, Youcef, Djenouri, Djamel, Belhadi, Asma, Fournier-Viger, Philippe & Bendjoudi, Ahcene 2018. Exploiting GPU parallelism in improving bees swarm optimization for mining big transactional databases. Information Sciences 3.

Djenouri, Youcef & Comuzzi, Marco 2017. Combining Apriori heuristic and bio-inspired algorithms forsolving the frequent itemsets mining problem. Information Sciences 420:1-15.

Djenouri, Youcef, Belhadi, Asma, Fournier-Viger, Philippe & Fujita, Hamido 2018. Mining diversified association rules in big datasets: A cluster/GPU/genetic approach. Information Sciences 459: 117-134.

Huang, Cheng, Lu, Rongxing & Choo, Kim-Kwang Raymond 2017. Secure and flexible cloud-assistedassociation rule mining over horizontally partitioned databases. Journal of Computer and System Sciences89: 51-63.

Kalgotra, Pankush & Sharda, Ramesh 2018. BIARAM: A process for analyzing correlated brain regionsusing association rule mining. Computer Methods and Programs in Biomedicine 162: 99-108.

Kuo, R. J. & Shih, C. W. 2007. Association rule mining through the ant colony system for National-Health Insurance Research Database in Taiwan. Computers & Mathematics with Applications 54(11–12):1303-1318.

Kuo, R. J., Chao, C. M. & Chiu, Y. T. 2011. Application of particle swarm optimization to association-rule mining. Applied Soft Computing 11(1):326-336.

Lin, Jerry Chun-Wei, Yang, Lu, Fournier-Viger, Philippe, Wu, Jimmy Ming-Thai & Zhan, Justin 2016. Mining high-utility itemsets based on particle swarm optimization. Engineering Applications of Artificial Intelligence 55:320-330.

Peng, Mingkai, Sundararajan, Vijaya, Williamson, Tyler, Minty, Evan P. & Quan, Hude 2018.Exploration of association rule mining for coding consistency and completeness assessment in inpatient administrative health data. Journal of Biomedical Informatics 79: 41-47.

Sarath, K. N. V. D. & Ravi, Vadlamani 2013. Association rule mining using binary particle swarm optimization. Engineering Applications of Artificial Intelligence 26 (8): 1832-1840.

Shao, Yuanxun, Liu, Bin, Wang, Shihai & Li, Guoqi 2018. A novel software defect prediction based onatomic class-association rule mining. Expert Systems with Applications.

Son, Le Hoang, Chiclana, Francisco, Kumar, Raghavendra, Mittal, Mamta & Baik, Sung Wook 2018. ARM–AMO: An efficient association rule mining algorithm based on animal migration optimization. Knowledge-Based Systems 154:68-80.

Song, Kiburm & Kichun Lee 2017. Predictability-based collective class association rule mining. ExpertSystems with Applications 79: 1-7.

Sousa, Tiago, Silva, Arlindo & Neves, Ana 2004. Particle Swarm based Data Mining Algorithms for classification tasks. Parallel Computing 30(5–6):767-783.

Sreeja, N. K. & Sankar A. 2016. A hierarchical heterogeneous ant colony optimization based approach for efficient action rule mining. Swarm and Evolutionary Computation 29:1-12.

Tyagi, Shweta & K. Bharadwaj, Kamal 2013. Enhancing collaborative filtering recommendations by utilizing multi-objective particle swarm optimization embedded association rule mining. Swarm and Evolutionary Computation 13:1-12.

Viktoratos, Iosif, Tsadiras, Athanasios & Nick Bassiliades 2018. Combining community-based knowledge with association rule mining to alleviate the cold start problem in context-aware recommender systems. Expert Systems with Applications 101:78-90.

Wang, Her-Shing, Yeh, Wei-Chang, Huang, Pei-Chiao & Chang, Wei-Wen 2009. Using association rulesand particle swarm optimization approach for part change. Expert Systems with Applications 36 (4):8178-8184.

Ykhlef, Mourad 2011. A Quantum Swarm Evolutionary Algorithm for mining association rules in large-databases. Journal of King Saud University - Computer and Information Sciences 23(1):1-6.

Communication and Computing Systems – Prasad et al. (eds)
© 2019 Taylor & Francis Group, London, ISBN 978-0-367-00147-6

Python programming for machine learning and big data analysis: Issues, solutions and benchmarks

Kusan Biswas & Satish Chand
School of Computer & Systems Sciences, JNU, New Delhi, India

ABSTRACT: Python is a dynamically typed high level interpreted language, suitable for general purpose programming. Although it is extremely popular due to ease of programming, it is much slower than C, C++ and Java. In this chapter we discuss the technologies that have been developed to speed up Python code execution. These technologies include Ahead-of-Time (AOT) and Just-In-Time (JIT) compilation, External compiled Module (C, C++) Inclusion (EMI) etc. We ran benchmark on each of these solutions and results show that these recent technologies can greatly increase Python's speed of and in many cases can make it comparable to the speed of statically typed compiled languages like C and C++.

1 INTRODUCTION

The Python programming language was developed by Guido Van Rossum and was first released in 1991 (Python Core Team 2015). Python has seen almost a meteoric growth in popularity, user community, number of third party modules and contributing developers. Today, Python is the second most popular programming language on the online code hosting and version control website GitHub githubstats . Python is being extensively used both by the research community and the industry. Many famous deep learning softwares such as PyTorch (Paszke et al. 2017), Google Tensorflow (Abadi et al. 2016), Theano (Bergstra et al. 2010), UC Berkeley Caffe (Jia et al. 2014) are written in Python (at least partially) and have full featured Python interfaces. Much of Python's unmatched popularity and its huge growth of user base is attributed to its beginner friendliness, ease of use and code readability. Its ease of use allows for rapid prototyping, testing and validation of scientific ideas without investing a lot of time in software development. However, this ease of use comes at a cost: speed. Pure Python is degrees of magnitude slower than the other general purpose languages such as C, C++, Java etc. This slowness is unacceptable in the areas of machine learning, artificial intelligence, big data analysis, scientific computing and image/video processing and allied fields. These areas require fast access and manipulation of huge sets of high-dimensional data, fast computation of linear algebra, calculus and signal processing functions. In this chapter, we present a thorough discussion of the available techniques to speed up Python's execution. These techniques are specially helpful for research in the areas of machine learning, big data analysis, image/video processing and scientific computing.

2 PYTHON'S SPEED: ISSUES

Let us first illustrate a quick benchmark that gives a fair idea of Python's speed compared to C, C++ and Java. Figure 1 shows the performances of these three languages when two 1000×1000 matrices are multiplied. In the test it is seen that pure Python is 49 times slower than Java and 136 times slower than C and C++ !

The primary reason Python's slowness is that it is a *dynamically typed* language. C, C++ and Java are *statically typed* languages. In statically typed languages, it is required to declare

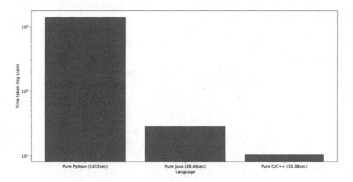

Figure 1. Speed of pure Python(v.3.6.5) compared to Java(OpenJDK 10), C and C++. The nested for loop to multiply two 1000×1000 matrices takes 1415 seconds, i.e, more than 23 minutes in Python! It takes 28.457 seconds in Java. In C it took only 10.382 seconds. The Runtime difference between C and C++ was fraction of a second.

types of all variables. Each variable must have a type. If a variable is int, it can only hold a value that is integer and not something else. Compilers for statically typed languages can perform deep optimisation and can catch more possible errors because the types of all variables are known during compilation phase. On the other hand, dynamically typed languages allow any variable to hold any type of values at any point of time. A variable that was holding an integer, can be assigned a string at the next line of code. This makes programming easier from the users' point of view, but it has the side effect that the compiler/interpreter does not know the type of the variables beforehand. The types of variables are known only during execution. This renders operation specific code optimisation impossible. Being a dynamically typed language, Python code execution involves significantly more work than C. Due to this high overhead of access, looping over native Python lists and arrays is inefficient in Python. This is specially unfavourable for scientific computing, computer vision, machine learning, image processing and allied fields as these require fast access and manipulation of multi-dimensional matrices. The second reason Python is slow is that it is a interpreted language.

3 SPEEDING UP PYTHON

Many solutions to Python's slow speed of execution have been developed. These solutions may be divided in three broad categories: 1) External Module Integration (EMI), 2) Ahead of Time Compilation (AOT) and 3) Just in Time Compilation (JIT). Apart from these, there are hybrid solutions that attemp to achieve higher speedup by combining AOT, JIT and EMI as and when possible.

3.1 *External module integration*

Numpy numpyref is a numerical computation module developed for Python. The most important object Numpy provides is the ndarray — a *homogeneous multidimensional array*. Unlike Python's built-in array data structure that stores data in non-contiguous memory locations, Numpy's ndarray holds contiguous memory spaces just like the arrays of C, C++ and Fortran. The basic ndarray object is implemented in C and Fortran. This allows the usage of already existing highly optimized mathematics libraries such as BLAS (bla 2002) and LAPACK (Anderson et al. 1999) without the need of copying or changing the format of the data. In fact, most of Numpy's mathematics functions are simple python wrapper over the functions provided by BLAS or LAPACK. In Section. 4 we illustrate the speedup gained by using Numpy's objects and functions over pure Python.

3.2   *Ahead of time compilation*

Cython (Behnel et al. 2011) is an alternative implementation of the Python language. Cython provides a convenient interface to write functions in C and to call those functions from within native Python. These functions are called *Cython C-extensions*. Cython also allows for declaring the types of variables in Python code. The variables whose types are declared, are identified as statically typed variables to the Cython compiler. This results in faster access of variables and faster execution of loops. This way, Cython can be thought of as a super set of Python language that supports static typing and integration of functions written in C. Notice that the types of the arguments of the function CyMatMul(), the types of variables row and col and the type of the result matrix R, are declared using Cython's syntax. When the program is interpreted by Cython, the CyMatMul() function is compiled in native machine code and is made available to the rest of program just like any user defined Python function. However, when called, it is executed as compiled C/C++ code and its output is passed to the rest of the main Python program.

```
import numpy as np
cimport cython
def CyMatMul(double[:,:]A,double[:,:]B):
  cdef int row = A.shape[0]
  cdef int col = A.shape[1]
  cdef double[:,:]R =np.empty((row,col)),\
  dtype=np.float64
  for i in range(row):
    for j in range(row):
      for k in range(col):
        R[i][j] += A[i][k]*B[k][j]
return R
```

Numba (Lam et al. 2015) is another tool that can compile Python code to machine code *ahead of time*. Numba makes the compiled code available to the Python program as importable modules. The following python script, when run in Python, creates a module called my_module that contains function square() that takes and returns double precision floats, which, in Numba is denoted as f8.

```
from numba.pycc import CC
cc = CC('my_module')
@cc.export('square', 'f8(f8)')
def square(a):
    return a ** 2
cc.compile()
   Then the square() function can be called as:
import my_module          #import the module
my_module.square(1.732) #outputs 2.999824
```

Numba works as follows. It first searches for the lines begining with the *decorators* such as @cc.export. When it encounters cc.export('square', 'f8(f8)'), it knows that the following function with the name sqaure that takes and outputs f8 type (i.e. double precision floating point), has to be compiled and put in my_module. It then compiles the square() function from Python to native machine code that can be executed by the CPU at runtime. This compilation is done using the LLVM (Lattner and Adve 2004) compiler infrastructure. To use this precompiled square() function, the programmer first has to import the module my_module. Since the square() function is available as a pre-compiled binary code, it is directly executed on the machine, bypassing the Python interpreter.

3.3 *Just in time compilation*

Python's execution can also be sped up using just-in-time compilation. In this approach, whole or part of code is compiled to native machine language *on-the-fly*, just before execution. JIT is supported by Numba (Lam et al. 2015) through the use of code decorators. Following is an example usage of Numba for JIT compilation of our matrix multiplication function:

```
from numba import jit
@jit
def jitMatMul(A,B):
result = np.zeros(shape=(len(A),len(A)))
for i in range(len(A)):
  for j in range(len(B[0])):
    for k in range(len(B)):
      result[i][j] += A[i][k]*B[k][j]
return rcsult
```

The function jitMatMul() is written purely in Python. However, it is decorated with the Numba decorator @jit. When the Numba preprocessor encounters a function that is decorated with @jit, it compiles the function *just-in-time* using the LLVM llvmpaper compiler. It outputs highly optimized machine code for the underlying CPU. A clear advantage of JIT compilation using Numba is that it does not require any change in the Python code, except decoration of functions with decorators such as @jit and @autojit. Notice that, unlike Cython, the function jitMatMul() is written entirely in pure Python language.

4 BENCHMARKS

In this section, we present detailed set of benchmark results. For this purpose, we have chosen two different mathematical operations: 1) Matrix multiplication and, 2) Pairwise Euclidean distance calculation in 3-dimension. Fast multiplication of large sized matrices is extremely important. In machine learning algorithms and specially in deep learning algorithms, we deal with extremely high-dimensional data. Clustering Algorithms, Artificial Neural Network and Deep Learning algorithms require fast calculation of Euclidean distances in high dimensions. For these reasons, matrix multiplication and pairwise Euclidean distance calculation are chosen to compare the speed of execution. All the benchmarks were run on a computer with Intel i3-3110M CPU with a clock speed of 2.4GHz, running GNU/Linux operating system. Pure Python programs were interpreted in CPython version 3.6.5. For compiling C and C++ programs, we used GCC (Version 7.3.0). The -O2 optimization flag was used while compiling the C/C++ programs. We used NumPy version 1.13, Cython version 0.26 and Numba version 0.34.

Following is the pure Python function for pairwise Euclidean distance calculation:

```
def pairwise_python(X,D):
  M = X.shape[0]
  N = X.shape[1]
  for i in range(M):
    for j in range(M):
      d = 0.0
      for k in range(N):
        tmp = X[i,k] - X[j,k]
        d += tmp * tmp
      D[i,j] = np.sqrt(d)
```

4.1 *Matrix multiplication*

In this experiment, we take pairs of square matrices of different sizes, starting from 1000×1000 to 6000×6000. These matrices are multiplied in programs written in C, C++ and Python. For testing JIT method, we use Numba in JIT mode through the use of @jit decorator. Table 1 summarises the results. It is evident that pure Python is so slow that multiplying matrices larger than 1500×1500 took impractical time. C/C++ with BLAS and Numpy's built-in function gave the best results and they took almost the same times. This is because Numpy's matrix multiplication function is actually a thin wrapper over the highly optimised routines provided by BLAS. AOT methods using Cython and Numba and JIT using Numba gave similar results. These tools significantly accelerated Python execution and the results were on par with C and C++. JIT using Numba is the most surprising. Simple addition of @jit made the impractically slow Python code as fast as C/C++! BLAS routines using either C/C++ or Numpy performed consistently good. These methods were about 200% faster than pure C/C++. It is evident that, BLAS functions are the fastest.

4.2 *Pairwise Euclidean distance*

In this experiment we take arrays of 3-dimensional points and calculate pairwise distances among all points. If the array is of length M, the pairwise distance matrix is of size MxM. We vary the size of the arrays from 2000 to 10000. Since BLAS and Numpy has no built-in function for this operation, we skip these libraries. Table 2 summarises the results. Again, it can be seen that pure Python is impractically slow. The AOT methods using Cython, Numba and

Table 1. Comparison of time taken to multiply squares matrices of different sizes. All times are in seconds.

| | Pure language | | C with | Python accelerated with | | | |
Matrix Size	C/C++	Python	BLAS	NumPy (EMI)	Cython (AOT)	Numba AOT	Numba JIT
1000x1000	10.38	1415.0	0.16	0.19	11.43	11.39	13.41
1500x1500	36.47	6690.9	0.48	0.56	37.09	37.15	38.33
2000x2000	96.13	—	1.15	1.36	98.17	99.04	101.59
3000x3000	375.36	—	3.51	3.74	377.13	378.54	380.99
4000x4000	962.40	—	9.00	9.49	965.00	967.28	970.12
5000x5000	2292.57	—	16.68	17.38	2296.47	2298.85	2302.57
6000x6000	4451.02	—	30.60	30.72	4456.29	4458.69	4462.35

Table 2. Comparison of times taken to calculate pairwise Euclidean distances among all 3-d points in arrays of different sizes. All times are in seconds.

| | Pure language | | Python accelerated with | | |
Array Size	C/C++	Python	Cython (AOT)	Numba (AOT)	Numba (JIT)
2000x3	0.051	27.73	0.099	0.069	0.187
3000x3	0.123	63.35	0.158	0.199	0.131
4000x3	0.239	112.8	0.251	0.286	0.241
5000x3	0.388	175.9	0.400	0.441	0.401
6000x3	0.564	311.1	0.600	0.615	0.596
7000x3	0.779	831.8	0.803	0.893	0.799
8000x3	1.213	1187.3	1.265	1.329	1.279
9000x3	1.599	1722.5	1.611	1.608	1.690
10000x3	2.446	2501.8	2.513	2.498	2.597

JIT method using Numba accelerated Python 500% to 1000% in most of the cases and made the speed of at par with C/C++. Numba JIT is the most remarkable. With least amount of programming effort Numba JIT could achieve tremendous speed up over pure Python!

5 CONCLUSION

In this paper we have discussed various techniques of speeding up Python programs and ran benchmarks. From the experiments it can be seen that it is better to use Numpy's built-in function one is available for a particular task. Those operations for which there is no built-in function in Numpy, we can choose any method among Cython, Numba AOT and Numba JIT. Cython and Numba AOT requires rewriting of the pure Python function, and therefore the programming effort is not negligible. Numba JIT however, requires almost no programming effort. All we have to do is to import Numba and decorate the concerned Python function with decorators like @autojit. In the case of pairwise Euclidean distance calculation, this gave same degree of acceleration as Cython and Numba AOT.

ACKNOWLEDGEMENT

This research is partially funded by Council of Scientific and Industrial Research, India, vide grant id. 09/263(1045)/2015-EMR-I and was carried out at the School of Computer & Systems Sciences, Jawaharlal Nehru University, New Delhi, India.

REFERENCES

(2002, June). An updated set of basic linear algebra subprograms (blas). *ACM Trans. Math. Softw. 28*(2), 135–151.

Abadi, M., P. Barham, J. Chen, Z. Chen, A. Davis, J. Dean, M. Devin, S. Ghemawat, G. Irving, M. Isard, M. Kudlur, J. Levenberg, R. Monga, S. Moore, D. G. Murray, B. Steiner, P. Tucker, V. Vasudevan, P. Warden, M. Wicke, Y. Yu, & X. Zheng (2016). Tensorflow: A system for large-scale machine learning. In *Proceedings of the 12th USENIX Conference on Operating Systems Design and Implementation*, OSDI'16, Berkeley, CA, USA, pp. 265–283. USENIX Association.

Anderson, E., Z. Bai, C. Bischof, L. S. Blackford, J. Demmel, J. Dongarra, J. Du Croz, A. Greenbaum, S. Hammarling, A. McKenney, et al. (1999). *LAPACK Users' guide*. SIAM.

Behnel, S., R. Bradshaw, C. Citro, L. Dalcin, D. Seljebotn, & K. Smith (2011). Cython: The best of both worlds. Computing in Science Engineering 13(2), 31–39.

Bergstra, J., O. Breuleux, F. Bastien, P. Lamblin, R. Pascanu, G. Desjardins, J. Turian, D. Warde-Farley, & Y. Bengio (2010, June). Theano: a CPU and GPU math expression compiler. In *Proceedings of the Python for Scientific Computing Conference (SciPy)*. Oral Presentation.

GitHub Inc. (2018). Github language statistics.

Jia, Y., E. Shelhamer, J. Donahue, S. Karayev, J. Long, R. Girshick, S. Guadarrama, & T. Darrell (2014). Caffe: Convolutional architecture for fast feature embedding. *arXiv preprint arXiv:1408.5093*.

Lam, S. K., A. Pitrou, & S. Seibert (2015). Numba: A llvm-based python jit compiler. In *Proceedings of the Second Workshop on the LLVM Compiler Infrastructure in HPC, LLVM '15*, New York, NY, USA, pp. 7:1–7:6. ACM.

Lattner, C. & V. Adve (2004). Llvm: A compilation framework for lifelong program analysis & transformation. In *Proceedings of the International Symposium on Code Generation and Optimization: Feedback-directed and Runtime Optimization*, CGO '04, Washington, DC, USA, pp. 75. IEEE Computer Society.

Paszke, A., S. Gross, S. Chintala, G. Chanan, E. Yang, Z. DeVito, Z. Lin, A. Desmaison, L. Antiga, & A. Lerer (2017). Automatic differentiation in pytorch. In *NIPS-W*.

Python Core Team. (2015). *Python: A dynamic, open source programming language*. Vienna, Austria: Python Software Foundation.

Walt, S. V. D., S. C. Colbert, & G. Varoquaux (2011, March). The numpy array: A structure for efficient numerical computation. *Computing in Science and Engg. 13*(2), 22–30.

Communication and Computing Systems – Prasad et al. (eds)
© 2019 Taylor & Francis Group, London, ISBN 978-0-367-00147-6

CloudReports tool to implement IaaS framework with location-based authentication in cloud

Ashima Mehta
Computer Science & Engineering, Chitkara University Institute of Engineering and Technology, Rajpura, (Punjab), India

Surya Narayan Panda
Chitkara University Institute of Engineering and Technology, Rajpura (Punjab), India

ABSTRACT: There are many ways to setup Cloud environment and understand it by the concept of virtualization. In this paper CloudReports tool has been discussed to simulate cloud environments and simultaneously generate various kinds of reports and help researchers to carry out experiments in this domain. Location based authentication is one of the methods that helps to ensure the authenticity of the user. GPS (Global Positioning System) is used to get the geographical location of the users and only those end users can use the resources and services that are present in that particular location to meet the protocols. Once the location is authenticated AES (Advanced Encryption Standard) algorithm is used for secure communication for the transference of data is accessed over the internet. This paper aims at providing the knowledge of CloudReports which uses CloudSim as its simulation engine in which IaaS framework is implemented with location-based authentication of the user in cloud computing.

1 INTRODUCTION

Usually information and Data are very much confidential in case of bank, corporate filed and military intelligence. More powerful tools are required to process and store their confidential data as there is rapid increase in the number of users. To overcome this situation, in recent years a new technology for this purpose has been come into act which is called as cloud computing. Cloud computing is a terminology which is used in describing a variety of new computing concepts that further involves a huge number of computers which are connected through a communication network called as real-time network. The best example for this is internet. As these virtual servers do not exist physically so while scaling up and moving from one place to another these servers can never create a problem. Commonly the term that we use "the cloud" is a metonymy of the Internet. In the market this phrase "in the cloud" refers to the infrastructure, platforms which are taken as a service provided to the users remotely through the internet. Cloud computing can also be shown as a progressive report of the data processing service bureaus which are available in this modern technology world today. Figure 1 shows some of the features of cloud computing.

Usually information and Data are very much confidential in case of bank, corporate filed and military intelligence. More powerful tools are required to process and store their confidential data as there is rapid increase in the number of users. To overcome this situation, in recent years a new technology for this purpose has been come into act which is called as cloud computing (Khaleel et al. 2017). Cloud computing is a terminology which is used in describing a variety of new computing concepts that further involves a huge number of computers which are connected through a communication network called as real-time network (Khaleel et al. 2017). The best example for this is internet. As these virtual servers do not exist physically so while scaling up and moving from one place to another these servers can never create a

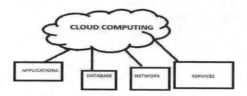

Figure 1.. Key features of cloud computing.

problem. Commonly the term that we use "the cloud" is a metonymy of the Internet. In the market this phrase "in the cloud" refers to the infrastructure, platforms which are taken as a service provided to the users remotely through the internet (Kaushik & Krishna, 2016). Cloud computing can also be shown as a progressive report of the data processing service bureaus which are available in this modern technology world today (Kaushik & Krishna, 2016). Figure 1 shows some of the features of cloud computing.

2 SECURITY IN CLOUD

To a shared crowd of computing resources cloud computing acts as a pay-as-u use model for its availability services and on demand network accessibility (Saffar, 2015). Companies shares remote data center to store their data and information on the cloud and accessibility to this data can be achieved there at any time anywhere provided one should have a computer and a working internet facility in it. Cloud computing considered as a technology that is used among group of users in a large scale. This technology acts as a blessing. In providing a security to the data and information present in the cloud is the biggest challenge in cloud computing (Saffar, 2015). In cloud computing there is no extra security provided to the users as while accessing their confidential data or information from cloud, so their security can be comprised by the attackers. Intruders can misuse user's confidential information (Walloschek et al. 2011). Although there are huge numbers of mechanisms, algorithms are available in providing security to the cloud but still there exits multiple security related threats in the cloud computing (Walloschek et al. 2011). We can improve the security in cloud for confidential data and information access by adding more advanced version of already present security mechanism. Table 1 describes some of the vulnerabilities, threats with in cloud computing.

Table 1. Vulnerabilities and threats in cloud computing.

Vulnerabilities	• Dependency on Internet
	• Vulnerabilities in System
	• Miscellaneous attacks
	• Uncertainty in Cryptography
	• Protection of stored data and portability
	• Locked in Cloud Service Provider
Threats	• Ease of use
	• Securing the data transmission from both ends
	• Spiteful insiders
	• Loss of Data
	• Hijacking of an account
	• Denial of Service
	• Breaching of data
	• Issues in shared technology
	• Insecurity in API's

3 CLOUD SERVICE MODELS FRAMEWORK

Cloud computing uses three major service models which are known as software as a service (SaaS), platform as a service (PaaS) and infrastructure as a service (IaaS). These cloud service models can be implemented on any of the clouds like private, public, hybrid as shown in Figure 2.

In SaaS model software's that are provided by SaaS are used straightly on the network instead of being downloaded first in the user's computer. The software applications that are provided by this model all are available on the Internet via a SaaS provider, and the execution of these is done in the computing environment which is already from this supplier. Cloud services can be provided to the users in a private, hybrid or public network depending upon the availability and need of the network (Sahu & Tiwari, 2012).

In PaaS service model availability and accessibility of computing environment is offered to the users from the service providers as per that needed. For developing and running software's this model is widely being used. With the help of this management and handling the massive amount of data and distributed applications can also be achieved (Pardeshi & Tidke,2014).

Infrastructure as a Service (IaaS) is the third service model used in cloud computing. In this model it provides the computing resources which are virtualized, and users are can use them over the internet. Iaas is a complete virtualized computing infrastructure which is used as a service. For creating and using the computing infrastructures freely, according to the users' needs and only when they need it. In this model the users are provided with an access to specific parts of a consolidated pool of associate resources. The example in which Iaas is used is Amazon EC2 (Amazon Elastic Compute Cloud) which allows rent virtual machines which are predetermined in sizes and helps in running the corresponding applications.

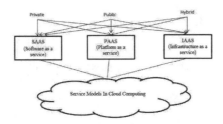

Figure 2.   Categorization of service models in cloud.

4 TOOLS AND TECHNIQUES USED

In this section the detail of tools, techniques, algorithms which are used while implementing this experimental work is discussed.

4.1 *Simulation tool*

It is impossible to accomplish the experiments and implementing them in real world cloud so to overcome this, the best possible alternative is simulation tool. There are number of simulators available in the market like GridSim, GangSim, OptoSim, SimGrid etc. but none of these simulators can perform the isolation of the multilayer service abstractions of the cloud service models (SaaS, IaaS, PaaS) and then differentiating the real and virtualized resources which are required by cloud. So, in this work for simulating the design of Iaas framework CloudSim simulator has been used (Wang et al. 2009). CloudSim is a comprehensive software framework which is used to model the cloud computing environments, simulating the data centers and then testing of the application services is performed as shown in Figure 4. It is a platform which self-sufficient because this simulation model can be used to imitate or make replica of data centers, service brokers, scheduling and allocation policies of a large scaled real-world Cloud platform (Wang et al. 2009). Also Cloud reports are generated for every simulation carried out for every customer and provider respectively. Cloud reports make efficient use of CloudSim as its simulation engine and consolidated reports for respective parameters like RAM, bandwidth is obtained which is shown in the below Figure 4.

VM Allocation Policy: In VM allocation policy the selection of already available hosts which suited the needs of memory, requirements etc.is done which is achieved with the help of VM scheduler. Scheduling can be achieved in two ways:

Space shared: In this mode every task has a corresponding time to execute and have a dedicated access for processing. Every new task entering for processing must come in queue (Kaur & Kaur, 2014). At every level CloudSim implements space shared and time-shared policies with the help of formula which is as follows:

$$(S_t) = C_t + l_n/(C_p * cores(l)) \tag{1}$$

$$Capacity\ (C_p) = \sum_{n=1}^{sb} cap(n)/sb$$

I_n=Complete set of instructions that are to be executed by cloudlet.
C_p=Capacity of the processor.
C_t=It is the estimated start time of cloud task.

Time shared: In time shared mode context switching technique is used among various active tasks. Those tasks which are taking less time for execution will be processed first (Kaur & Kaur, 2014). Time shared policy implemented by CloudSim using following formula:

$$b(T_t) = S_t + I_n/(C_p * cores(l)) \tag{2}$$

$$Capacity\ (C_p) = \sum_{n=1}^{sb} cap(n)/ \max \sum_{b=1}^{cloudlets} cores(b), sb$$

T_t=Estimated finish time
S_t=current simulation time
Cores (b) =Number of cores (processing elements required by the cloudlet)

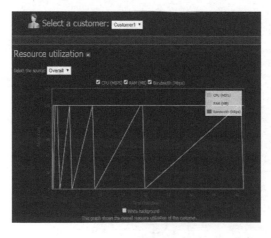

Figure 3.   Graph shows overall resource utilization of customer.

4.2 GPS

GPS or Global Positioning System is a satellite exploring system which defines the exact location and time related useful information irrespective of bad climate conditions and other factors to the receiver or user. GPS is used for defining the path while travelling in planes, cars etc. and other transportation (Golle et al. 2002). GPS provides continuous real time data, exact positioning of a user or system using 3D technology and many more features.

Secure Communication: For secure communication while transferring the data to and from the cloud AES algorithm is used for encryption and decryption of the data. AES algorithm working, and step wise procedure is already discussed in section 4 and however in support to this Figure 4 and Figure 5 illustrates the encryption and decryption process for an authenticate user.

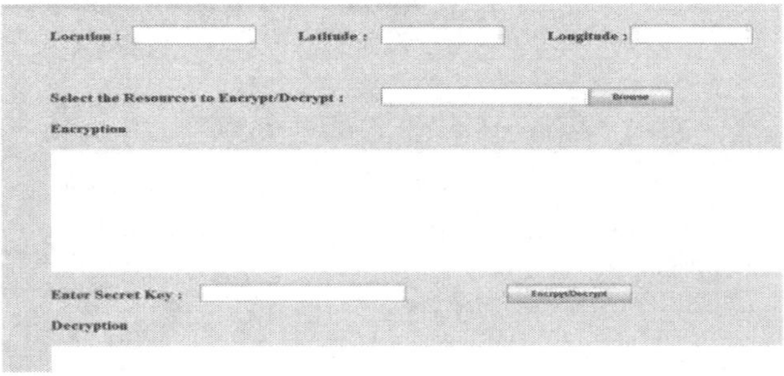

Figure 4.   Location is being detected with GPS co-ordinates.

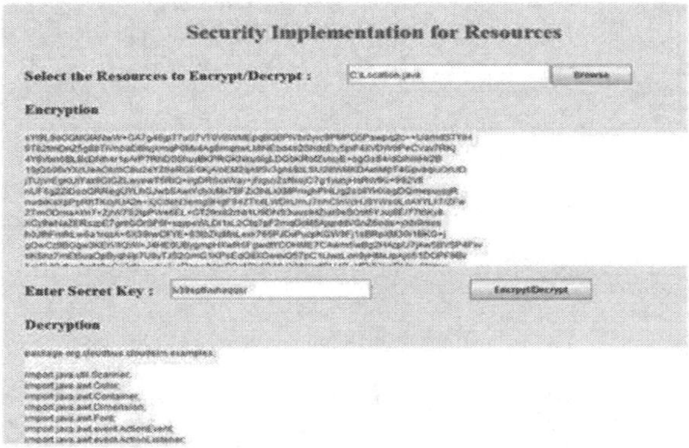

Figure 5.   For secure communication encryption and decryption is used with the help of AES algorithm.

5   CONCLUSION

This paper is an effort to understand the Cloud Reports tool and perform the implementation of location-based authentication which is one of the primary aspects in security related issues of cloud computing, although there are number of authentication methods available, but they lack somewhere in some or the other aspects and security of data/information is compromised. With the help of location-based authentication, it increases the security layer. User's location is accessed and verified and only then to authenticate user's access to data is provided. The future research work would be to increase the level of security provided to data in cloud services and reduce the drawbacks associated with the location-based authentication technique that exists.

REFERENCES

Chen L. and Chen H., 2012, "Ensuring Dynamic Data Integrity with Public Auditing for Cloud Storage",in Proc. of International Conference on Computer Science and Service System (ICSSS).

Feng D.G., Zang M., Zang Y. and Xu Z., 2011, "Study on Cloud Computing Security", Journal of Software, Vol. 22, Issue 1, p. 71–83.

Golle P., Jarecki S. and Mironov I.,2002, "Cryptographic Primitives Enforcing Communication and Storage Complexity", in Financial Cryptography, pg. 120–135.

Kaur Jashanpreet, Kaur Rajbhupinder, 2014, "Multilayered Security Approach for Cloud Data Centers Using Hash Functions", International Journal of Science and Research (IJSR).

Kaushik Sekaran, Krishna P. Venkata, 2016, "Big Cloud: A Hybrid Cloud Model for Secure Data Storage through Cloud Space", International Journal of Advanced Intelligence Paradigms, Vol. 8, No.2, p. 229–241.

Khaleel Mershad, Hassan Artail, Mazen A. R. Saghir, Hazem Hajj, and Mariette Awad, 2017, "A study of the Performance of a Cloud Datacenter", IEEE transactions on Cloud Computing.

Kumar Rajesh D., Gupta R, Tanisha, 2013, "File Security in Cloud using Two-tier Encryption and Decryption", International Journal of Advanced Research in Computer Science and Software Engineering, Vol. 3, Issue 7.

Kunfam L.M.,2009, "Data Security in the World of Cloud Computing", IEEE Security and Privacy, Vol. 7, Issue 4, p. 61–64.

Pardeshi Poonam M., Tidke Bharat, 2014, "Improving Data Integrity for Data Storage Security in Cloud Computing", International Journal of Computer Science and Information Technologies.

Saffar, A. M. H. Al-,2015, "Identity Based Approach for Cloud Data Integrity in Multi-Cloud Environment" International Journal of Advanced Research in Computer and Communication Engineering, Vol. 4, No. 8, p. 505–509.

Sahu Bhushan Lal,Tiwari Rajesh, 2012, "A Comprehensive Study on Cloud Computing", International Journal of Advanced Research in Computer Science and Software Engineering, Vol. 2, Issue 9.

Walloschek M, Grobauer, Stöcker, 2011, "Understanding of Cloud Computing Vulnerabilities", IEEE Computer and Reliability Society.

Wang C, Wang Q, Kui Ren, Wenjing Lou, 2009, "Ensuring Dynamic Data Storage Security in Cloud Computing", International Workshop Quality of Service (IWQos"09).

William Stalling, 2009, A Handbook on "Cryptography and network Security" by Pearson Education.

Communication and Computing Systems – Prasad et al. (eds)
© *2019 Taylor & Francis Group, London, ISBN 978-0-367-00147-6*

Characterization of solar panels received from manufacturers in real field conditions using LabVIEW

Aditi Aggarwal
The NorthCap University, India

Manoj Kumar
Philips Lighting India Limited, India

Rekha Vig
The NorthCap University, India

ABSTRACT: The main aim of this project is to characterize the performance of different types of commercial solar panels in terms of the meteorological parameters. The approach to this validation is a comprehensive scheme where solar panel performance is monitored and with a mathematical modelling the effect of the various parameters is calculated thus enabling us to verify the panel in real field conditions. The project required coding of the MPPT charger and creating a LabVIEW GUI to interface the charger, apply the mathematical modelling and display the results.

1   INTRODUCTION

Solar power is plausibly grown to be the cleanest and most reliable form of renewable energy source available. Photovoltaic cells, convert the energy from the sun's rays into electricity by exciting electrons in the cell using the photons of light from the sun. There is a need to understand the working of the solar cells in order to maximize the electricity output. In real field, the panels efficiency is affected by various meteorological parameters (King et al. 2002) such as irradiance, temperature, wind velocity, relative humidity with the technologies of mono and polycrystalline along with thin film (Ogulgönen, 2014). In this research, a relation between these parameters and the panel output is established. The results were mathematically modeled in the LabVIEW software which is used to monitor the data in real time

2   SYSTEM MODEL

2.1   *System architecture*

In the LabVIEW VI, the user sets the type of solar panel, enters rated wattage, enters inputs for the metrological parameters – temperature, irradiance and wind speed (if accounted for), and through the USART communication the value of the voltage and current from the MPPT charger is received. With block programming and additional inputs, the rated power is calculated at STC for validation. The GUI communicates with the hardware using a cable which is connected to the laptop via a USB port.

2.2   *Block diagram*

The block diagram in Figure 1 shows the performance of the PV Array with the various meteorological parameters inputs at real time. The LabVIEW GUI running on the laptop is created in such a way that it receives photovoltaic current and voltage as calculated by the MPPT Charger via a UART cable. With manual inputs of irradiance falling on the panel and ambient temperature, it processes the values through mathematical modelling to give PV array Wattage and daily energy generation.

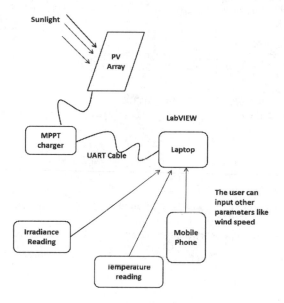

Figure 1.   Block diagram.

3   EFFECTS OF METEOROLOGICAL PARAMETERS ON SOLAR PANEL OUTPUT

Different parameters affect the solar panel output in different ways. Research was done to include all such parameters and design a formula to convert real field output to an output at Standard Testing Conditions (STC at which it is rated by the manufacture) for panel verification. The following are the findings

3.1   Irradiance

Irradiance is a measure of the amount of sunlight falling on a given surface. Thus, more energy will be produced when there is higher irradiance on a solar cell. More sunlight = more electricity. And this irradiance varies throughout the day.(Ettah et al. 2011)

$$Power_{pv\,(STC)} = \frac{Power_{pv(Real\,time)}}{Irradiance_{RealTime}} * Irradiance_{STC} \qquad (1)$$

To convert the PV power at STC with respect to irradiance it is divided by irradiance at the time of output and multiplied by irradiance at STC (1000 W/m2)

3.2   Temperature

Higher the temperature of the solar cell, the less efficient they become. The hotter the cell material is, the more resistance there is which makes the movement of electrons slower through it. This means that production goes down because not as many electrons can get through the circuitry in the same amount of time as before. (Kamkird et al. 2012) (Migan, 2013)

There are two temperature parameters that are considered.

- Cell temperature – the surface temperature of the panel.
- Ambient Temperature – the temperature of the surrounding air.

The panel is rated at a cell temperature of 25° C.

This cell temperature at a particular irradiance is calculated from the ambient temperature using the formula below

$$T_{cell} = T_{air} + \frac{NOCT - 20}{800} Irradiance \tag{2}$$

The value of NOCT averaged at 48 for best results.

If the cell temperature rises above 25°C there is a power loss PL, which is given in percentage by:

$$P_L = (T_{cell} - 25) * Temperature\ Coffecient * 100 \tag{3}$$

The temperature coefficient varies with different panel types. Poly-Crystalline Panel was used for testing which have a temperature coefficient of -0.48 % per degree centigrade. (Cotfas et al. 2016) (Subhash et al. 2015)

Provision for other Panel types has also been given in the LabVIEW GUI in the form of a drop-down menu.

3.3 Wind speeds

This affects the cell temperature. Greater the wind speed lesser will be the cell temperature and thus the loss due to increased cell temperature will be lower. (Abiola-Ogedengbe 2013)

Wind speed affects the cell temperature in the following way.

$$T_{cell} = T_{air} + \frac{0.31180}{8.91 + 2 * WindSpeed_{m/s}} * Irradiance \tag{4}$$

3.4 Type of PV panel used

Panels are of different types, poly crystalline, mono crystalline, thin film, and hybrid. Each of them has a different temperature coefficient and respond to change in temperature differently (Xiao et al. 2004) (Carr et al. 2004)

3.5 Tilt angle of the panel

The performance of a PV module depends on the radiation amount that it is receiving during the day time. Tilt angle and orientation of the solar module decides the sunlight falling on the panel.

The orientation of the solar module is generally the south for the places in Northern hemisphere and north in the Southern hemisphere. However, tilt angle is dependent on where the module is installed and must be optimized accordingly. (Li et al. 2007)

3.6 DC cables used

The resistance loss in wiring is approximated to 2%.

3.7 Battery efficiency

Batteries are required for charge storage. The battery design and quality of construction decides the efficiency of the battery. Most commonly used are lead acid batteries.

4 DESIGN COMPONENTS

4.1 *Hardware*

4.1.1 *Solar panels of various wattages*
Many different solar panels were used during testing. They were from different manufacturers and with various wattages. Testing on a wide range was important so as to validate the mathematical modelling applied and to improve the same. Some of the panel used are as follows:

Tata BP – 37W
EMMVEE – 50 W
Rhine – 20 W
Andslite – 32.27 W
Topsun 20 W
Ammini – 90 W

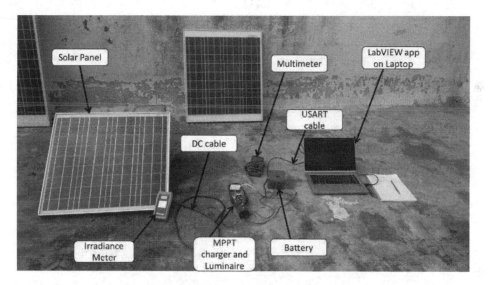

Figure 2. Hardware design.

4.1.2 *MPPT charger*
The charger is essentially a microcontroller which integrates the solar panel, luminaire and the battery. It controls the charging and discharging of the battery. During day time, it is charging the battery as the solar panel is giving an output power. While during night time, the battery is discharging and the load is turned on.

Charge controllers are required to manage the division of electricity between the battery bank and the load. The charge controller can also manage charging and draw down of electricity from an array of batteries equalizing the inputs and output to ensure not battery is under unnecessary stress. Maximum power point trackers are available with some charge controllers which ensures the efficient generation of electricity from the panel array by modifying the voltage of the circuit to ensure that the panel is operating at the maximum power point.

4.1.3 *Luminaire*
A lamp connected to the solar panel. It acts as the load which is programmed to turn on during the night used the energy stored in the battery by the solar panel.

4.1.4 *Battery*
Lithium Ion battery is usually used as it is efficient and has a longer lifespan.

4.2 *Software*

4.2.1 *LabVIEW*
LabVIEW is a system engineering software for test, measurement, and control applications which majorly require rapid access to hardware and data insight. It is a graphical programming language which has function blocks performing specific functions.

4.2.2 *IAR embedded workbench for ARM*
IAR workbench provides a toolbox which develops C and C++ compilers, as well as debuggers along with other tools for developing firmware related to 8-, 16, and 32-bitprocessors and 32- bit microcontrollers.

5   RESULTS

There are two tabs in the created GUI. Figure 3a shows the Panel Wattage Tab. User selects the COMM Port at which the charger is connected. The values for Voltage and Current are

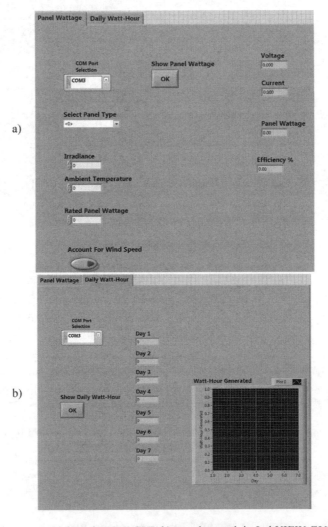

Figure 3.   a) Panel wattage tab in LabVIEW GUI, b) watt hour tab in LabVIEW GUI.

input values through USART communication from the charger. Other values of current irradiance and ambient temperature have to be put in manually. Once the panel type selected LabVIEW processes the values and mathematical modelling to give the Panel Wattage as Calculated at STC. The user has a choice to account for wind using the button.

The other tab in Figure 3b is to check the Daily Watt-Hour or energy generated by the solar panel.

The user selects the COMM Port at which the charger is connected. Through USART communication a command ID is sent to the charger and a corresponding data packet is received. It is decoded and the values for the Watt-Hour generated are displayed.

A graph with the variance of generated energy during the week is plotted for further analysis

6 CONCLUSION

In this study, the properties of commercial solar modules, characterization methods and the implementation of mathematical modelling in LabVIEW are discussed. An outdoor test station consisting of the solar panel, necessary equipment to measure meteorological parameters and the maximum power point tracer is installed. The designed LabVIEW application is operated in order to conduct accelerated tests for the sample modules.

It is observed that system optimization requires high amount of automated hardware and software in order to fully avoid errors and data loss. With adequate research and extensive testing, the LabVIEW application created characterizes solar panel in real field conditions

ACKNOWLEDGEMENT

The authors would like to thank philips lighting india ltd. Who supported this research in their R&D facility at noida and provided a conducive and creative environment with all the tools needed.

REFERENCES

Ogulgönen, Celal Güvenç. 2014. Performance Tracking & Characterization Of Commercial Solar Panels. Middle East Technical University.

Xiao, Weidong, William G. Dunford, & Antoine Capel. A novel modeling method for photovoltaic cells. In Power Electronics Specialists Conference, 2004. 2004 IEEE 35th Annual, vol. (3): 1950–1956.

Cotfas, Daniel Tudor, Petru Adrian Cotfas, Dan Ion Floroian, and Laura Floroian. "Accelerated life test for photovoltaic cells using concentrated light." International Journal of Photoenergy2016 (2016).

Kamkird, P., N. Ketjoy, W. Rakwichian, & S. Sukchai. 2016. Investigation on temperature coefficients of three types photovoltaic module technologies under Thailand operating condition Procedia Engineering (32): 376–383.

Chander, Subhash, A. Purohit, Anshu Sharma, S. P. Nehra, & M. S. Dhaka. 2015. A study on photovoltaic parameters of mono-crystalline silicon solar cell with cell temperature. Energy Reports 1: 104–109.

Ettah, E. B., O. J. Nawabueze, & G. N. Njar. 2011.The relationship between solar radiation and the efficiency of solar panels in Port Harcourt, Nigeria. International Journal of Applied Science & Technology 1(4)

Li, Danny HW, & Tony NT Lam. 2007. Determining the optimum tilt angle and orientation for solar energy collection based on measured solar radiance data. International Journal of Photoenergy.

Carr, A. J., & T. L. Pryor. 2004. A comparison of the performance of different PV module types in temperate climates. Solar energy (76): 285–294.

Abiola-Ogedengbe, Ayodeji. 2013. Experimental investigation of wind effect on solar panels.

King, David L., William E. Boyson, and Jay A. Kratochvil. 2002. Analysis of factors influencing the annual energy production of photovoltaic systems. In Photovoltaic Specialists Conference. Conference Record of the Twenty-Ninth IEEE:1356–1361

Migan, Gail-Angee. 2013. Study the operating temperature of a PV module.

Communication and Computing Systems – Prasad et al. (eds)
© *2019 Taylor & Francis Group, London, ISBN 978-0-367-00147-6*

Analysis of PSO based clustering protocol in assorted scenarios of WSN

Ankit Gambhir & Ashish Payal
USICT GGS Indraprastha Univeristy, New Delhi, India

Rajeev Arya
National Institute of Technology, Patna, India

ABSTRACT: One of the foremost concerns in wireless sensor network (WSN) is energy management of the tiny nodes set up for monitoring environmental or physical conditions of an area. Hierarchical routing such as LEACH is an effectual methodology, in which cluster have been structured however choosing an energy-sensible cluster by optimally selection of cluster head (CH) is also very challenging. Selection of CH is an optimization problem hence optimization algorithms would serve the purpose. One of optimization technique is particle swarm optimization (PSO) that is originated from swarm intelligence. In present paper, PSO based LEACH algorithm is tested comprehensively on numerous scenarios of WSN, which are varying number of sensor nodes (n), and maximum rounds (rmax). Several parameters have been considered as the base of the study to reflect useful results in evaluating performance of PSO based LEACH in assorted scenarios of WSN. It leads to interesting findings. A variety of performance metrics such as dead nodes (DN) per round, alive nodes (AL) per round, packet to CH per round, packet to base station (BS) per round, throughput and average residual energy are considered for performance evaluation. Results have been shown using MATLAB.

1 INTRODUCTION

WSN is set of numerous nodes that collaborate to accumulate the data from desired location and transfer it to a base station (BS). For proficient act of WSN, competent routing protocol is needed and strategic data accumulation methods and very less power utilization (Akyildiz et al. 2002). Aforementioned networks are severely resource-restricted by energy constraints (Barbancho et al. 2007). Routing protocols which choose optimum path between BS and sensor nodes, and required lowest energy, so that life of network can be increased, can serve the purpose. A hierarchical routing protocol such as LEACH is an effectual approach, in which clusters are structured (shown in Figure 1). There is a sole cluster head (CH) and several nodes at each cluster. Every node send out their detected data to CH and CH collectively transmits it to sink (Dietrich, I. & Dressler, F. 2009). However choosing an energy-sensible cluster by optimally selection of CH is also a challenging task. Soft-computing (SC) techniques based on algorithms inspired from nature are immensely tackles their compatibility and adaptableness to deal with the complexities in WSN. This paper intends to assess the performance of PSO based clustering algorithm used to improve the maximum life span of the network. Two scenarios are considered for evaluating performance, one with '500' number of nodes (n) with maximum number of rounds (rmax) of '2500' and another with '100' number of nodes (n) with maximum number of rounds (rmax) of '500' (Table 1). Based on the detailed consideration and observations, a qualitative conclusion is also drawn in the end.

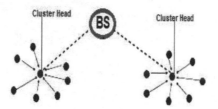

Figure. 1.   Illustration of LEACH.

Table 1.   Assorted scenarios.

Scenario	Number of nodes (n)	Max. number of rounds (rmax)
1	500	2500
2	100	500

2   LEACH

LEACH (Low-energy adaptive clustering hierarchy) is an algorithm based on clustering and having two phases viz setup phase and steady phase (Heinzelman, W, et al. 2000) CH is elected in setup phase.

According to equation 1, those nodes which are appropriate to be converted into cluster-head, announce themselves. P symbolizes percentage (%) of the nodes which can be carefully chosen as CH, whereas G denotes nodes which aren't selected as CH in the preceding r rounds.

$$T(n) = \begin{cases} P/(1 - P(rmod(\frac{1}{p}))n \in G \\ 0 \qquad\qquad\qquad else \end{cases} \tag{1}$$

Afterward CH announcement, the nodes selected their CH on the basis of distance as a criterion. TDMA scheduling is performed to make nodes aware of their chance of data transfer. CDMA scheme is employs to associate base station to CH. The CH gather data from the nodes exists in its cluster and then transmits it to BS post accumulation.

3   PARTICLE SWARM OPTIMIZATION BASED LEACH

PSO algorithm is a nature motivated algorithm based on swarm intelligence (Singh, B., & Lobiyal, D.K.2012). PSO is modeled after witnessing the behavior of flock of birds in the procedure of seeking food. The main goal of PSO algorithm is to trace the particle's positions that consequence finest assessment of the provided cost function. Based on the observation of flock of bird i.e. bird who has found the food can leads the other in the flock about the site of food, PSO algorithm is designed. Nodes are required to send out their position as well as residual energy level to the destination.

Algorithm for PSO based LEACH is as follows.

1. Initialize S particle having arbitrarily selected CHs

$$Xij(0) = (x\ i,j(0),\ y\ i,j(0)) \tag{2}$$

The positions of the sensor nodes

2. Calculate the cost function of each particle:

a.

$$\forall ki, \ i = 1, 2, \ldots, N \tag{3}$$

Evaluate distance d (ki,CHp,q) among node ki and CHp,q.
Allot node kii to CHp,q:

$$d(ki, CHp, q) \ = \ min\forall q\, 1, 2, \ldots, \{d(ki, CHp, q)\} \tag{4}$$

b. Determine the cost function:

$$cost\ function = a.C1 + (1 - a).C2 \tag{5}$$

$$C1 \ = \ max\, q \ = \ 1, 2, \ldots, q\{\Sigma d(ki, CHp, q)/CHp, q\} \tag{6}$$

$$C2 = \sum_{i=1}^{N} E(ki)/ \sum_{q=1}^{Q} E(CHp, q) \tag{7}$$

3. For each particle, determine the personal and global best
4. Change the particle's velocity and position by

$$Vid \ (t) = W.Vid \ (t) + L1.\ \mathcal{H}1 \ (Pbestid - Xid \ (t) + \ L2.\mathcal{H}2(Gbest - Xid(t)) \tag{8}$$

$$Xid(t) = Xid(t - 1) + Vid \ (t) \tag{9}$$

Or

$$Vid \ (t + 1) \ = \ W.Vid \ (t - 1) \ + \ L1.H1 \ (Pbestid \ - \ Xid \ (t - 1) \ + \ L2.H2(Gbest - Xid(t - 1)) \tag{10}$$

$$Xid(t + 1) = Xid(t) + Vid(t + 1) \tag{11}$$

Where X and V represent position and velocity of particle respectively, t represents time, L1 & L2 learning factors or acceleration coefficients, $\mathcal{H}1$ & $\mathcal{H}2$ are arbitrary numbers between 0 & 1, Pbestid and Gbest are particle's best and global position respectively, W (0<W<1) is the inertia weight.
The process of updating V and X is repeated unless it achieves good enough value of Global position best (Gbest). Further, the particle assesses the cost function and updates Pbestid and Gbest using equation 12.

$$
\begin{aligned}
Pbestid \ &= \ Pid\ if\ cost\ function\ of\ Pi < cost function of \\
& \qquad\qquad Pbesti \\
Pbestid \ & \qquad else \\
Gbest \ &= \ Pid\ if\ cost\ function\ of\ Pi < cost\ function\ of \\
& \qquad\qquad Gbest \\
Gbest \ & \qquad else
\end{aligned}
\tag{12}
$$

5. Revised positions are mapped with the closest (x.y) coordinates.

Reiterate from step 2 to 5 unless the utmost numbers of iterations are attained

4   SIMULATION RESULTS AND DISCUSSION

The simulation is performed in MATLAB. A number of parameters like AL per round, packet to BS per round, DN per round, packet to CH per round, throughput and average residual energy are considered for evaluating performance. Network simulation parameters are shown in Table 2. Figure 2 and Figure 3 reflect deployment of nodes in both the scenarios (one with 500 numbers of nodes and another with 100 numbers of nodes) respectively. Furthermore graphs shown in Figure 4 and Figure 5 present the performances of both the scenarios.

Table 2.   Network simulation parameters.

Network Parameters	Value
Network size	$300 \times 300 \text{m}^2$
Number of nodes	100, 500
Type of nodes	Static
Eelec	50 nJ/bit
Emp	0.0013 pJ/bit/m4
Efs	10 pJ/bit/m2
Maximum no. of rounds (rmax)	500,2500

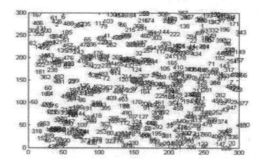

Figure 2.   Deployment of nodes (n=500) scenario 1.

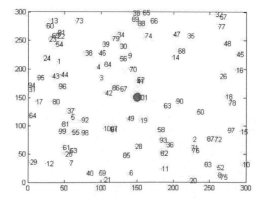

Figure 3.   Deployment of nodes (n=100) scenario 2.

403

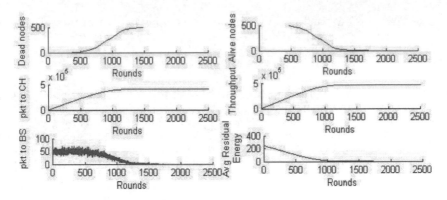

Figure 4.　Analysis of scenario 1 (n=500, rmax=2500).

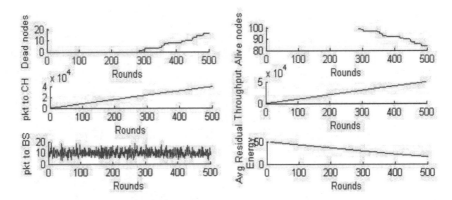

Figure 5.　Analysis of scenario 2 (n=100, rmax=500).

It can be observed from the Figure 4 and Figure 5 that in first scenario, after completing 1500 rounds nodes are dead, average residual energy also deteriorates after 1000 rounds approximately, moreover throughput is uniform after 1200 rounds approximately and packet to BS also comes to an end at 1500 rounds. It is pertinent to mention that up to 1500 rounds the performance of algorithm was fitting however after 1500 rounds the energy drained and nodes start becoming dead.

5　CONCLUSIONS

In present study, analysis of PSO based LEACH algorithm in assorted scenarios of WSN such as varying number of sensor nodes (n) as well as maximum number of rounds (rmax) is presented. Authors have well-thought-of variety of parameters like AL per round (network lifetime), packet to BS per round, DN per round, packet to CH per round, throughput and average residual energy. It is found that, in scenario 1, nodes are dead after completing approximately 1500 rounds moreover average residual energy declined after 1000 rounds approximately. As mentioned above that up to 1500 rounds the performance of algorithm was fitting however after 1500 rounds the energy drained and nodes start becoming dead. From the graphical results it can be concluded that the findings of the analysis are worth studying. Similar performance analysis of various other optimization techniques will also be valued studying as future work. Ranges of research strategies could be considered as a useful extension of this performance evaluation.

REFERENCES

Akyildiz, I.F., Su, W., Sankarasubramaniam, Y. & Cayirci, Y. 2002. Wireless Sensor Networks: A Survey. Computer Networks, 38: 393–422.

Barbancho, J., Leon, C., Molina, F.J., &Barbancho, A.2007. Using Artificial Intelligence in Routing Schemes for Wireless Networks.Computer Communications, 30(4), 2802–2811.

Dietrich, I. & Dressler, F. 2009.On the Lifetime of Wireless Sensor Networks. ACM Transactions on Sensor Networks, 5, 1–38.

G. Smaragdakis, I. Matta, & A. Bestavros. 2004. SEP: A Stable Election Protocol for clustered heterogeneous wireless sensor networks, in: Second International Workshop on Sensor and Actor Network Protocols and Applications (SANPA 2004).

Gambhir A. & Arya, R. 2018.An Extensive Survey on Energy Optimization Techniques Based on Simultaneous Wireless Data and Energy Transfer to Wireless Sensor Network.Advances in Intelligent Systems and Computing. Singapore: Springer.

Gambhir, A. Payal, A. & Arya, R. 2018. Performance analysis of artificial bee colony optimization based clustering protocol in various scenarios of WSN. Procedia Comupter Science, 132, 183–188. doi: https://doi.org/10.1016/j.procs .2018.05.184.

Heinzelman, W., Chandrakasan, A., &Balakrishnan, H. 2000.Energy-Efficient Communication Protocol for Wireless Microsensor Networks.In Proceedings of 33rd International Conference on System & Science. Hawaii: IEEE.

Huang, Y., Martínez, J.F., Diaz, V.H., &Sendra, J.2014. Localized and Energy-Efficient Topology Control in Wireless Sensor Networks Using Fuzzy-Logic Control Approaches.Mathematical Problems in Engineering.doi: 10.1155/2014/973163.

Jane, Y.Y., Peter, H.J., & Chong. 2005 A Survey of Clustering Schemes Mobile Ad Hoc Networks. IEEE Communications Surveys & Tutorials, 7, 32–48.

Karak, J.N.A. & Kamal, A.E. 2004.Routing Techniques in Wireless Sensor Network: A survey. IEEE Wireless Communications, 11(6), 6–28.

Kumar, D., Aseri, T.C. & Patel, R.B. 2009. EEHC: Energy Efficient Heterogeneous Clustered Scheme for Wireless Sensor Networks. Computer Communications Elsevier, 32, 662–667.

Malik, M., Singh, Y., &Arora, A. 2013 Analysis of LEACH Protocol in Wireless Sensor Networks. International Journal of Advanced Research in Computer Science and Software Engineering, 3(2), 178–183.

Paolo, S. 2010. On the Data Gathering Capacity and Latency in Wireless Sensor Networks. IEEE Journal on Selected Areas in Communications, 28: 1211–1221

Sharma, S. 2015. Improved Stable Election Protocol for Heterogeneous Wireless Sensor Network. International Journal of Science and Research, 1370–1374.

Shinge, S.R., &Sambare, S.S. 2014. Survey of Different Clustering Algorithms Used to Increase the Lifetime of Wireless Sensor Networks. International Journal of Computer Applications, 108(10), 15–18.

Singh, B., & Lobiyal, D.K.2012. A Novel Energy-Aware Cluster Head Selection Based on Particle Swarm Optimization for Wireless Sensor Networks. Human-Centric Computing and Information Sciences.2(1).doi: 10.1186/2192-1962-2-13.

Communication and Computing Systems – Prasad et al. (eds)
© 2019 Taylor & Francis Group, London, ISBN 978-0-367-00147-6

Fuzzy based analysis of reality show analytics for TRP ratings based on the viewer's opinion

V. Kakulapati, S. Mahender Reddy & K. Iswarya
SNIST Yamnampet, Ghatkesar, Hyderabad, Telangana, India

ABSTRACT: The perception of reality TV shows from level-headedness in cinema. It is a design that common people live in, quite often in deliberately manufactured situations, where examiners or judges their opinions, performance or talent. These shows usually raise competition and provide money as prizes. These shows will gather viewer's online postings, mobile messages and analyze the same to increase TRP ratings. Now-a-days most television channels organizing reality show which are being telecasted especially in fields such as dancing, singing, and drama. In this work, we compile all online postings from social networks in a CSV file. These are further classified into different classes based on their opinion on a particular TV show which contains viewer's personal profile based on location and comment. Based on their postings and opinions, the TV Show popularity will be rated accordingly. We develop a model to exploit the viewer's opinions for predicting social actions (e.g., users' behaviours, opinions, preferences or interests) and discovering their field of interest. We propose a fuzzy based clustering algorithm with regression analysis to learn the model parameters in an efficient manner. We performed experiments on two real-world datasets to demonstrate the validity and competitiveness of our approach.

KEYWORDS: perception, TV show, TRP ratings, opinion, telecast, online, preferences

1 INTRODUCTION

Now a day's reality demonstrates have turned out to be exceptionally famous and young individuals are especially inspired by watching the shows and remarking on it by utilizing various different person to person communication destinations. By investigating people group's votes on versatile messages and online postings the champ who wins the show is given the value cash and in view of the people group's suppositions, the prominent show is anticipated. The greater part of the TV programs which are being broadcasted nowadays are reality demonstrates gaining practical experience in a variety of fields such as dancing, singing and drama. The Indian reality demonstrates have likewise been reliably effective in offering a wide variety, from ability chase shows to move dramas, action flicks, talk shows, chat shows, cookery indicates and what not."The reality chase list is interminable".

Sentiment analysis and classification (Brendan O'Connor, 2011) using the text data posted by viewers. Comments on social media are information that directly depicts viewers' preferences. Programs and web series pull in more audience. Episodes released on ends of the week or holidays may draw in more crowds in contrast to those on work days. Different shows are released on various days of a week, accordingly, the ubiquity forecast for TV demonstrates turns into a testing errand. The Popularity or disappointment of the show relies totally upon the watchers or audience. The fundamental motivation behind this work is to assess the execution of TV appearances and furthermore ascertain what number of individuals loved the specific show and we anticipate the prevalence of that show in view of the watcher's remarks and feelings about the same. Rather, a large number of messages that are posted day by day on the online networking destinations like Twitter should be checked, all the important posts on that show should be removed, diverse kinds of client suppositions should be broken down, lastly, the client sentiments and inputs should be abridged into valuable data.

The sentimental analysis is the programmed extraction of conclusions, feelings, and assessments from writings. Feelings are subjective impressions and not actualities, which are goal or impartial. Through conclusion investigation, a given content can be put into three classes - positive, negative, or neutral. Assumption investigation of writings can be performed at various levels like - archive, sentence, expression, word, or substance level. Individuals visit those locales and give a numeric rating to a specific scene or a specific show. Web-based social networking destinations give us considerably more data contrasting with the sites. So computing the ubiquity of a TV shows from online networking destinations would make the public opinions much more transparent.

By definition, fuzzy logic is a form of several appropriated logic conceived (Zadeh, 1965), where truth values of variables lie between 0 and 1. Fuzzy logic based on the theme of degree, inaccurate, linguistic and observation. This logic meanly deals with natural languages and representation of knowledge with the formalization of reasoning modes. This mainly contains four principal features of logic, settheoretic, relational and epistemic (Zadeh, L. A., 2004).

The objective of this project is to current and future efforts to advance online viewers comments on the particular show. In this work, we analyzed the recent TV reality show of BIG BOSS and Drama juniors, their popularity as an example. These shows communicate and interact with their target audiences through the online media in all objectives including search and social networks,

The information needed is specifically related to the following:

- Assessment of people's choice
- Predict the different sentiments based on their online postings
- Evaluate the results in the form of ratings which will predict the TV show which is more popular.

Big Boss - One-third of the viewers who like Big Boss relate to the show as a source of only Entertainment. It is followed by another large set of people who connect with the show as a stress reliever.

Drama juniors- Drama juniors is the Reality show also comes out as a major source of entertainment.

2 RELATED WORK

A unified coherent frame-work, namely mutual latent random graphs (jain) to exploit mutual interactions and benefits for predicting social actions (e.g., users' behaviours, opinions, preferences or interests) and discovering social ties (e.g., multiple labelled relationships between users) simultaneously in social networks on a large scale.

Television {Yushu Chai, 2015) is elemental to contemporary living. It plays a crucial role in shaping our intellectual and physical consumption. In order to discern its impact, it is imperative to appreciate and measure how people interact with the medium. Availability of multiple channels and technological growth allow viewers to gain additional viewing options and the increased ease of switching between them. The variable use of television makes audience measurement an especially arduous task.

According to the media lens reality TV Shows are economical to produce, yet generate huge amounts of earnings through constant programming rotations and product placement or promotion (Orbe, 2012). In addition to this such shows have initiated the concept of buying and selling of TV formats, for example, *Big Brother* and *X-Factor* which were developed in one country were sold internationally in diverse countries. Britain and Netherland (represented by Endemol International Production and Distribution Company) embarked on the format business with considerable success (Essar, 2010). Some TV Reality Formats have been licensed outright to foreign broadcasters and some have been formatted considering the topical or local needs of the country (Raphael, 2009). With time such shows have evolved methods to use the audience in different modes. For example, contestants for the shows like *Who wants to be a millionaire* are basically geared towards achieving their goal of winning and studio audience make their journey much easier by answering questions posed by the contestants in one of the lifelines. However, a show like *Big Brother* depends on the contestant's voting as well as the audience voting. Nevertheless, talent-based shows like *Pop Idol* and *Just Dance* are solely based on audience voting in the final round. Let us have a look at the popular shows which have been arranged chronologically in terms of increased audience attendance. The audience has been consistently transformed through these shows.

TV reality shows we employed some of the machine learning algorithms and based on these algorithms we predict which show possess the highest TRP ratings. There are two major approaches to movie ratings and revenue prediction: one of which utilizes sentiment analysis, regression analysis and c-means clustering on the Twitterdataset.

The rating scenario, the areas where the population is less than one lakh which covers over 50% of the population of those who have admittance to Cable and Satellite channels and 75% of those who watch DD channels, it did not get measured at all..

Twitter is a microblogging site which is inclined towards various real-life applications. Thus, in order to use the Twitter platform as a backchannel for TV rating (Amrapali Mhaisgawali,2014), we should find out tweets which are related to TV programs. In order to look for those TV-related tweets, the hash tags which are popularly used on the site were used as an index to enable retrieval by other services or users.

Generally, Twitter users can simply create a hashtag by prefixing a word with a hash symbol "#hashtag." For the TRP predicting (D. Anand, 2014) the clusters to be taken are different TV programs telecasted. Categories like comedy, drama, reality, educational were given a set of priority and are considered to be clusters. The view count can be calculated with the help of a number of viewers watching that particular show accordingly.

3 METHODOLOGY

The system fetches TV show related data (Kadam, 2017) from twitter API where text reviews related to the particular show, actor, and director are given.To make the hash tagged dataset, we first sift through copy tweets, non-English tweets, and tweets that don't include hash tags. We examine the appropriation of hash tags and recognize what we expect will be sets of regular hash tags that are demonstrative of positive, negative and unbiased messages. These hashtags are used to choose the tweets which will be utilized for advancement and preparing. Pre-processing gives tokenization, standardization, i.e. expel @, and remove #and URL. Information pre-processing is utilized to remove intriguing and non-minor information from unstructured content information.

The sentimental analysis is the extraction of assessments, feelings, and notions from tweets Feelings and assessments are impressions and not actualities, which are goal or unbiased by nature. Through conclusion examination, a given content can be categorized into three classes - positive, negative, or impartial. We analyze the popularity of show by Day, Week Overall Popularity.

3.1 *Lexical analysis*

By comparing uni-grams to the pre-loaded word database, the tweet is assigned sentiment score - positive, negative or neutral and overall score is calculated.

3.2 *Linear regression*

The point of linear regression is to display a constant variable Y as a scientific capacity of at least one X variable(s), with the goal that we can utilize this regression model to anticipate the Y when just the X is known. This scientific condition can be summed up as takes after:

$$Y = \beta_1 + \beta_2 X + \epsilon$$

Where β_1 is the intercept and β_2 is the slope. Collectively, they are called regression coefficients. ϵ is the error term; the part of *Y* the regression model is unable to explain.

3.3 Logistic regression

The linear regression serves to anticipate consistent Y factors; calculated regression is utilized for binary classification. In this event we utilize linear regression to show a dichotomous variable (as Y), the subsequent model won't limit the anticipated Ys inside 0 and 1.

3.4 C-means clustering algorithm

Fuzzy regression models are defined byrevealing the vagueness of designed methods [10-12].

Output values are estimating by the indeterminate nature of fuzzy regression model and the coefficients of fuzzy regression in the structure of vague numbers. The fuzzy linear regression model [13-15] is specified by the improvement of the imprecise degeneration representation is the vague model's improvement by means of the formalization of vagueness to a certain extent, statistical periods via fuzzy intervals.

4 EXPERIMENTAL ANALYSIS

4.1 Day wise analysis results

4.1.1 An extraction of comments
The table beneath demonstrates the comments got for Show 1 that is comedy nights with Kapil and Show 2 as jabardasth. The comments were extracted from both the shows and are spoken to in the below table.

Table 1. Day wise user's comments.

4.1.2 Calculating scores
The table beneath demonstrates the scores got for Show 1 that is comedy nights with Kapil and Show 2 as jabardasth. The scores were extracted from both the shows and are spoken to in belowtable.

Table 2. Calculating scores by day wise.

4.2 Week wise analysis results

4.2.1 An extraction of comments
The table beneath demonstrates the comments got for Show 1 that is comedy nights with Kapil and Show 2 as jabardasth. The comments were extracted from both the shows and are spoken to in the below table.

Table 3.   Comments.

4.2.2 *Calculating scores*

The table beneath demonstrates the scores got for Show 1 that is comedy nights with Kapil and Show 2 as jabardasth. The scores were extracted from both the shows and are spoken to in the below table. Figure 1 shows the week-wise linear regression analysis on TV reality show while Figure 2 shows the week wise logistic regression analysis on TV reality show.

Table 4.   Reality shows sentiment score by day wise.

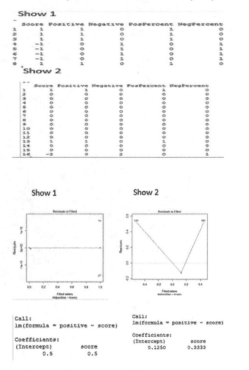

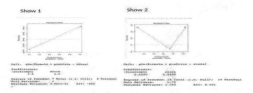

Figure 1.   Week-wise linear regression analysis on TV reality show.

Figure 2.   Week wise logistic regression analysis on TV reality show.

4.3 Overall analysis results

4.3.1 Extraction of comments

The table beneath demonstrates the comments got for Show 1 that is comedy nights with Kapil and Show 2 as jabardasth. The comments were extracted from both the shows and are spoken to in the below table.

Table 5.   Overall comments about TV reality show.

4.3.2 Calculating scores

The table beneath demonstrates the scores got for Show 1 that is comedy nights with Kapil and Show 2 as jabardasth. The scores were extracted from both the shows and are spoken to in the below table. Figure 3 shows the overall sentiments of linear regression analysis while Figure 4 shows overall sentiments of logistic regression analysis.

Table 6.   Overall sentiment analysis score.

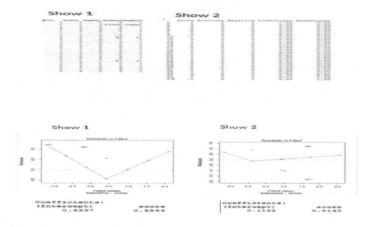

Figure 3.   Overall sentiments of linear regression analysis.

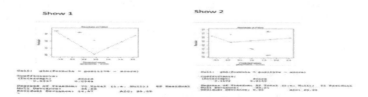

Figure 4.   Overall sentiments of logistic regression analysis.

411

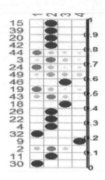

Figure 5.   Fuzzy C –mean clustering correlation analysis.

Figure 5 shows Fuzzy C –mean clustering correlation analysis of TV show. Finally, we can advise that as per the overall scores the well-known show is show 2.

5   CONCLUSION

Here we display a framework TV Show Popularity Prediction utilizing Sentiment Analysis in Social Network for users, which foresee the fame of the show among a few shows, on-screen characters, reality shows and serials in view of in light of the content surveys which are getting from social networking websites like Twitter and YouTube. The benefits of utilizing this framework are that it helps in breaking down the TV Show points of interest and rates expectation in light of Twitter tweets and YouTube comments.

6   FUTURE ENHANCEMENT

In Future, we plan to further investigate and extend our methodology for general scenarios with large data sets by applying PCA methods and filtering techniques. We also plan to apply and test our approach on other large-scale social network datasets.

REFERENCES

Amrapali Mhaisgawali et al., 2014 Detailed Descriptive and Predictive Analytics with Twitter Based TV Ratings" IJCAT International Journal of Computing and Technology, Volume 1, Issue 4, May 2014. ISSN: 2348 – 6090.

Brendan O'Connor. 2011, et al. "From Tweets to Polls: Linking Text Sentiment to Public Opinion Time Series." *Proceedings of the International AAAI Conference on Weblogs and Social Media*, 2011.

D. Anand, A.V. Satyavani, B.Raveena and M.Poojitha.2018, Analysis and Prediction of Television Show Popularity Rating using Incremental K-Means Algorithm, *International Journal of Mechanical Engineering and Technology* 9(1), pp.482–489.

Essar Andrea.2010., Television Formats: Prime time Staple, Global Market. *Popular Communication*. 2010, 8: 273-292.

Heshmaty, A. Kandel. Fuzzy Linear Regression and Its Application to Forecasting in Uncertain Environment.

J.J. Buckley 2008.et al., Fuzzy Linear Regression I. Studies in Fuzziness and Soft Computing, volume 22, ISBN 978-3-540-76289-8. Springer, 2008.

Kacprzyk., M. Fedrizzi (Ed.). 1992 Fuzzy Regression Analysis. Studies in Fuzziness and Soft Computing, ISBN-13: 978-3790805918. Publisher: Physica-Verlag HD, 1992.

Orbe P Mark.2012, The Reality of Media Effects In*: Inter/Cultural Communication Representation and Construction of Cultur*e Sage publication (Kurylo Anastacia, (Ed.), Sage Publication, California, USA, 2012, 235-257.

Poleshchuk,E.2012 Komarov. A fuzzy linear regression model for interval type-2 fuzzy sets. NAFIPS, ISBN 978-1-4673-2336-9. Fuzzy Information Processing Society, 2012.

Priyank Jain, "A Novel Approach to Analysis of TV Shows using Social Media, Machine Learning and Big Data". International Journal of Technological Exploration and Learning.

Raphael Chad 2009, The Political Economic Origins of Reality TV. In: *Reality TV Remaking television culture*, 2nd ed. New York University Press, USA. 2009, 123-138.

Shapiro.2006 Fuzzy regression models. In http://www.soa.org/library/research/actuarial- research-clearinghouse/2006/january/arch06v40n1- ii.pdf, (10.4.2013).

Tanaka., et al.,1982 Linear regression analysiswithfuzzy model. IEEE Transactions and Systems, Man and Cybernetics, 12:6, Fuzzy Sets and Systems, volume 15, pages 159-171.

Tejaswi Kadam Gaurav Saraf, Vikas Dewadkar and P. J. Chate,2017 "TV Show Popularity Prediction using Sentiment Analysis in Social Network", International Research Journal of Engineering and Technology- Vol 4, Issue 11, Nov 2017.

Yushu Chai. Yushu Chai, et al.,2015 "Top-Rated Series Characterization and Audience Rating Prediction", http://cs229.stanford.edu/proj2015/256_report.pdf.

Zadeh, L. A. 1965. Fuzzy sets. *Information and control*, 8(3), 338-353.

Zadeh, L. A. 2004. *Fuzzy Logic Systems: Origin, Concepts, and Trends*. Retrieved November 29, 2015, from http://wi-consortium.org/wicweb/pdf/Zadeh.pdf.

Communication and Computing Systems – Prasad et al. (eds)
© *2019 Taylor & Francis Group, London, ISBN 978-0-367-00147-6*

A study on dementia using machine learning techniques

Deepika Bansal, Kavita Khanna & Rita Chhikara
Department of Computer Science and Engineering, The NorthCap University, Gurugram, India

Rakesh Kumar Dua & Rajeev Malhotra
Department of NeuroSurgery, Max Super Speciality Hospital, New Delhi, India

ABSTRACT: Dementia is emerging as a global health issue which is the most common occurring disease in the people who are 65 years or above in age. The early detection of dementia and the detection of mild cognitive impairment converting to Alzheimer's disease prove to be very helpful to the society. The objective of this paper is to present various studies detecting dementia using machine learning techniques. A systematic literature review has been carried out which includes 47 papers considering different databases and different techniques implementing machine learning used for detecting dementia. ADNI data is commonly used in various studies.

1 INTRODUCTION

Dementia is emerging as a global health issue. Dementia mainly describes the symptoms in which brain cells stop working properly. Dementia occurs inside the specific regions of brain which leads to influencing the thinking, recalling and conveying capability of an individual (Dening, T. et.al. 2015). Dementia occurring before the age of 65 years is said early-onset dementia and if it occurs after the age of 65 years then it is called as late-onset dementia. According to the World Alzheimer Report 2015, the global number of dementia patients is 46.8 million and it is supposed to increase to 74.7 million by 2030 and 131.5 million by 2050 (Wu, Y.T. et.al. 2017).

The most common Dementia types includes Alzheimer's Disease, Frontotemporal Dementia, Vascular Dementia and Dementia with Lewy Bodies. Alzheimer's Disease is in charge of about 75% of the general cases. Both Alzheimer's Disease and Vascular Dementia combines to form Mixed Dementia. Some of the less commonly found types of dementia are HIV Dementia, Wernicke – Korsakoff syndrome, Creutzfeldt – Jakob disease (CJD), Normal pressure hydrocephalus, Parkinson's Disease, Huntington's disease.

2 LITERATURE SURVEY

A detailed overview for detecting dementia using various machine learning algorithms has been presented in the below section. Machine Learning and Micro-simulation techniques are the two analysis approaches used for the prediction of any infection (Larranaga, P. et.al. 2006, Dallora, A.L. et.al. 2017). It trains the available dataset to perform any task and then use it for testing the completely new dataset (Kourou, et.al. 2015). Machine Learning is being applied extensively in medical/neuroimaging applications (Lee, G. et.al. 2014). Machine Learning techniques can be categorised as supervised and unsupervised techniques.

Supervised Learning techniques separate groups of data on the basis of training set (Yang, Y.B. et.al 2014, Deleforge, A. 2015). In the supervised learning, a supervisor supervises the learning system for associating unlabeled data with an appropriate label.

- SVM
- Decision trees
- Random forest
- Linear regression
- Naïve Bayes
- k-Nearest Neighbours
- Logistic Regression
- SVM for regression
- Polynomial regression
- Artificial Neural Networks

Unsupervised Learning separates the objects in different groups known as clusters but there is no dataset available to use (Huo, J. 2014). Clustering techniques can be of two types: hard or fuzzy techniques.

- K-means clustering
- Fuzzy clustering

A concise review of the related work is presented in Table 1 below considering different databases and different machine learning techniques used for the detection of the dementia.

Mathotaarachchi et. al. 2017, used PET images of ADNI-GO/2 for the implementation of SVM. Williams et. al. 2013, predicted CDR scores by implementing the following machine learning techniques: Neural Networks, SVM, Naïve Bayes and decision tree. The average values are used in case of missing data and the best accuracy is shown by Naïve Bayes. The author in (Shree, S.B. et. al. 2014) had used the real world data from various neuropsychologists for comparing the four classification techniques proving Naïve Bayes to be better. The author in (Ramirez, J. et. al. 2013) finds out the discriminant parameter of image and ROIs for reducing the dimensionality and succeeds to improve the accuracy. Sheshadri, H. S.et. al. 2015, pre-process and classify the data using Naïve Bayes, Random Forest and Jrip and then evaluates it. In future, an embedded model is to be confined for treating demented patients.

Multilayer perceptron, classification by means of regression and SVM using M5-model trees were implemented for classifying the real world data in (Er, F.et. al. 2017). The various machine learning tools (Naïve Bayes, C4.5 Rules, Random Forest and C4.5), MLP and NN are used for classifying the states of dementia for improving the accuracy over the MMSE and FAQ tests by Joshi et. al. 2009. And further they plan to extend the work with different cognitive tests. SVM is used to recognize the patterns of EEG epochs to distinguish AD patients and normal patients in (Trambaiolli, L.R. 2011). SVM is used to classify AD from normal and FTLD subjects and then the results are compared with the radiologist (Kloppel, S. et.al. 2008). Automatic Feature Selection is followed by the combination of the SVM and a pasting votes of ensemble SVM classifier for the detection of AD in early stages in (Gorriz, J.M. 2008). The wavelet features are extracted from the MR images, dimensionality reduction, training-test subdivision and classification is performed using SVM by Herrera et. al. 2013. Dukart et. al. 2011 applied SVM on MR images and FDG-PET images for extracting ROIs to investigate dementia. The author had used multiple instance learning (MIL) in (Tong, T. 2014) for detecting AD and MCI. Future work plans to carry on the proposed work using longitudinal databases with different image modalities.

Automated Hippocampal segmentation is performed using two machine learning algorithms namely, SVM and Ada-SVM for detecting Alzheimer's disease in (Rangini, M, et. al.2013). Lopez et. al. 2009 presented a computer assisted diagnosis tool using SPECT and PET images for early detection of AD using Kernel Principle Component Analysis for the attribute reduction and SVM for the classification. Magnin, B.et. al. 2009 presented an automated method using SVM for whole brain anatomical MRI to distinguish AD and normal subjects. SPECT images were used to propose a new feature extraction method using SVM classification by Chaves et.al. 2009. SVM used volumetric measurements of brain structures for distinguishing AD subjects from normal (Oliviera, JR.et.al. 2010). Bron, EE. et. al. 2017 explored the sMRI for the classification of AD, FTD and controls. Four machine learning

Table 1. Brief survey of the related work.

Study	Year	Dataset	Work Done	Research Gap
(Tohka, J. et. al. 2016)	2016	ADNI	Support Vector machines are compared using filter based feature selection techniques	Findings will not generalize to other diseases. ADNI study uses the inclusion/exclusion for example depressed subjects were excluded.
(Bhagyashree S.I.R. et.al. 2018)	2017	MYNAH	Naïve Bayes, J48, Random Forest, Rule Based Classifier are explored for the diagnosis of dementia	Needs to test this model on larger sample Will include subtypes of dementia.
(Aruna, S.K. et. Al. 2016)	2015	OASIS	Classification of MRI images for dementia Features selected through Independent Component Analysis are normalized and fused, To classify dementia efficiently SVM is evaluated with different kernels.	-
(Chi, C.L. et. al. 2015)	2015	ADNI	Progression of MDI to AD is predicted.	More developments are needed.
(Chuzhyk, D. et. al. 2010)	2010	OASIS	Voxel Based Morphometry is applied on MRI Images Feature extraction techniques are applied.	-
(Shankle, W. R. et. al. 1996)	1996	University of California, Irvine	Machine Learning methods are applied to test the data obtained from two tests i.e. FAQ and BOMC can improve Dementia screening	Future work will use ML systems in conjunction with other AHCPR- recommended tests.
(Maroco, J. et. al. 2011)	2001	B institutions	Non-parametric classifiers are compared to the traditional classifiers.	Total accuracy of classifiers is misleading
(Shankle, W. R. et. al. 1997)	1997	University of California, Irvine	Normal brain maturing is separated from the starting stages of dementia.	Findings are limited to the population introduced.
(Chen, R. et. al. 2010)	2010	Washington University	Machine Learning Techniques and statistical methods are compared for the diagnosis of Very Mild Dementia.	Temporal course of VMD is not addressed. White matter lesions are not included. Current work is to be extended for the large sample-size data.
(Cuingnet, R. et. al. 2011)	2011	ADNI	Voxel, hippocampus and cortical thickness based methods are evaluated for the diagnosis of AD.	-
(SR, B.S. et. al. 2014)	2014	Real World	Naïve Bayes and J48 are compared for the diagnosis of AD. Feature Selection is used using Weka.	The embedded system is to be intended to encourage the diagnosis.

(Continued)

Table 1. *(Continued)*

Study	Year	Dataset	Work Done	Research Gap
(Vemuri, P. et. al. 2008	2008	Alzheimer's disease Patient Registry (ADPR) database	Classification of MRI images using SVM.	-
(Datta, P. et. al. 1996)	1996	University of California, Irvine	C4.5, C4.5 rules, Naïve Bayes, IB1, FOCL and PL are used to improve accuracy for the classification of dementia status over current dementia screening tools: BOMC and FAQ.	Will develop a new guideline for diagnosing dementia status.
(Kloppel, S. 2008)	2008	Real World	SVM is used to diagnose AD using structural MRI.	Limits of sensitivity needs definition.
(So, A. et. al. 2017)	2017	Gangbuk-Gu center	MMSE-KC data are initially classified into normal and abnormal. Classification of Dementia and MCI using CERAD-K.	Model to predict dementia and to improve accuracy will be planned.

algorithms i.e., Adaboost, SVM, Ada-SVM and FreeSurfer are used for detecting AD using hippocampal segmentation on the ADNI database (Morra, J.H. et. al. 2010). SVM is applied to the combined information of MRI and FDG-PET images from ADNI study and Leipzig Cohort for distinguishing AD and FTD (Dukart, J. et. al. 2013). In (Bansal, D. et. al. 2018), the author had presented a comparison of J48, Random Forest, Naïve Bayes, and Multilayer perceptron and used CFSSubsetEval for feature selection. The results proved that J48 is outshining among all the classifiers for detecting dementia.

3 CONCLUSION

Dementia is emerging as a major health problem globally; there is no cure available for dementia only we can do is to predict the dementia at the early stage for reducing the risk.

From the literature survey presented above, we can obviously deduce that a great deal of work has improved the situation for the early recognition of dementia and to distinguish AD from MCI using various machine learning algorithms. However, there is still a scope for identifying relevant attributes which can help us to identify dementia at a very early stage.

Few gaps are observed in the previous studies. Firstly, it is not clear in some of the studies that how well the findings generalize to the study of other brain diseases. Secondly, machine learning models should be employed for the larger databases and the subtypes of dementia should be predicted. Thirdly, Ensemble method should be explored. And lastly, some more advancement are expected to reexamine and grow the evidence of-idea approach.

4 ACKNOWLEDGEMENT

The research was funded by Department of Science and Technology DST, New Delhi, Reference number DST/CSRI/2017/215 (G).

REFERENCES

Aruna, S.K. and Chitra, S., 2016. Machine Learning Approach for Identifying Dementia from MRI Images. World Academy of Science, Engineering and Technology, International Journal of Computer, Electrical, Automation, Control and Information Engineering, 9(3), pp.881-888.

Bansal, D., Chhikara, R., Khanna, K. and Gupta, P., 2018. Comparative Analysis of Various Machine Learning Algorithms for Detecting Dementia. Procedia computer science, 132, pp.1497-1502.

Bhagyashree, S.I.R., Nagaraj, K., Prince, M., Fall, C.H. and Krishna, M., 2018. Diagnosis of Dementia by Machine learning methods in Epidemiological studies: a pilot exploratory study from south India. Social psychiatry and psychiatric epidemiology, 53(1), pp.77-86.

Bron, E.E., Smits, M., Papma, J.M., Steketee, R.M., Meijboom, R., De Groot, M., van Swieten, J.C., Niessen, W.J. and Klein, S., 2017. Multiparametric computer-aided differential diagnosis of Alzheimer's disease and frontotemporal dementia using structural and advanced MRI. European radiology, 27(8), pp.3372-3382.

Chaves, R., Ramírez, J., Górriz, J.M., López, M., Salas-Gonzalez, D., Alvarez, I. and Segovia, F., 2009. SVM-based computer-aided diagnosis of the Alzheimer's disease using t-test NMSE feature selection with feature correlation weighting. Neuroscience letters, 461(3), pp.293-297.

Chi, C.L., Oh, W. and Borson, S., 2015, October. Feasibility Study of a Machine Learning Approach to Predict Dementia Progression. In 2015 International Conference on Healthcare Informatics (pp. 450-450). IEEE.

Chen, R. and Herskovits, E.H., 2010. Machine-learning techniques for building a diagnostic model for very mild dementia. Neuroimage, 52(1), pp.234-244.

Chyzhyk, D. and Savio, A., 2010. Feature extraction from structural MRI images based on VBM: data from OASIS database. University of the Basque Country, Internal Research Publication: Basque, Spain.

Cuingnet, R., Gerardin, E., Tessieras, J., Auzias, G., Lehéricy, S., Habert, M.O., Chupin, M., Benali, H., Colliot, O. and Alzheimer's Disease Neuroimaging Initiative, 2011. Automatic classification of patients with Alzheimer's disease from structural MRI: a comparison of ten methods using the ADNI database. neuroimage, 56(2), pp.766-781.

Datta, P., Shankle, W.R. and Pazzani, M., 1996, March. Applying machine learning to an Alzheimer's database. In Artificial Intelligence in Medicine: AAAI-96 Spring Symposium (pp. 26-30).

Dallora, A.L., Eivazzadeh, S., Mendes, E., Berglund, J. and Anderberg, P., 2017. Machine learning and microsimulation techniques on the prognosis of dementia: A systematic literature review. PloS one, 12 (6), p.e0179804.

Deleforge, A., Forbes, F. and Horaud, R., 2015. Acoustic space learning for sound-source separation and localization on binaural manifolds. International journal of neural systems, 25(01), p.1440003.

Dening, T. and Sandilyan, M.B., 2015. Dementia: definitions and types. Nursing Standard (2014+), 29 (37), p.37.

Dukart, J., Mueller, K., Horstmann, A., Barthel, H., Möller, H.E., Villringer, A., Sabri, O. and Schroeter, M.L., 2011. Combined evaluation of FDG-PET and MRI improves detection and differentiation of dementia. PloS one, 6(3), p.e18111.

Dukart, J., Mueller, K., Barthel, H., Villringer, A., Sabri, O., Schroeter, M.L. and Alzheimer's Disease Neuroimaging Initiative, 2013. Meta-analysis based SVM classification enables accurate detection of Alzheimer's disease across different clinical centers using FDG-PET and MRI. Psychiatry Research: Neuroimaging, 212(3), pp.230-236.

Er, F., Iscen, P., Sahin, S., Çinar, N., Karsidag, S. and Goularas, D., 2017. Distinguishing age-related cognitive decline from dementias: A study based on machine learning algorithms. Journal of Clinical Neuroscience, 42, pp.186-192.

Górriz, J.M., Ramírez, J., Lassl, A., Salas-Gonzalez, D., Lang, E.W., Puntonet, C.G., Álvarez, I., López, M. and Gómez-Río, M., 2008, October. Automatic computer aided diagnosis tool using component-based SVM. In 2008 IEEE Nuclear Science Symposium Conference Record (pp. 4392-4395). IEEE.

Herrera, L.J., Rojas, I., Pomares, H., Guillén, A., Valenzuela, O. and Baños, O., 2013, September. Classification of MRI images for Alzheimer's disease detection. In 2013 International Conference on Social Computing (pp. 846-851). IEEE.

Huo, J., Gao, Y., Yang, W. and Yin, H., 2014. Multi-instance dictionary learning for detecting abnormal events in surveillance videos. International Journal of Neural Systems, 24(03), p.1430010.

Joshi, S., Shenoy, P.D., Venugopal, K.R. and Patnaik, L.M., 2009, December. Evaluation of different stages of dementia employing neuropsychological and machine learning techniques. In 2009 First International Conference on Advanced Computing (pp. 154-160). IEEE.

Klöppel, S., Stonnington, C.M., Chu, C., Draganski, B., Scahill, R.I., Rohrer, J.D., Fox, N.C., Jack Jr, C.R., Ashburner J, and Frackowiak, R.S., 2008. Automatic classification of MR scans in Alzheimer's disease. Brain, 131(3), pp.681-689.

Klöppel, S., Stonnington, C.M., Barnes, J., Chen, F., Chu, C., Good, C.D., Mader, I., Mitchell, L.A., Patel, A.C., Roberts, C.C. and Fox, N.C., 2008. Accuracy of dementia diagnosis—a direct comparison between radiologists and a computerized method. Brain, 131(11), pp.2969-2974.

Kourou, K., Exarchos, T.P., Exarchos, K.P., Karamouzis, M.V. and Fotiadis, D.I., 2015. Machine learning applications in cancer prognosis and prediction. Computational and structural biotechnology journal, 13, pp.8-17.

Larranaga, P., Calvo, B., Santana, R., Bielza, C., Galdiano, J., Inza, I., Lozano, J.A., Armananzas, R., Santafé, G., Pérez, A. and Robles, V., 2006. Machine learning in bioinformatics. Briefings in bioinformatics, 7(1), pp.86-112.

Lee, G., Kwon, M., Kavuri, S. and Lee, M., 2014. Action-perception cycle learning for incremental emotion recognition in a movie clip using 3D fuzzy GIST based on visual and EEG signals. Integrated Computer-Aided Engineering, 21(3), pp.295-310.

Lopez, M., Ramirez, J., Gorriz, J.M., Salas-Gonzalez, D., Lvarez, I.Á., Segovia, F. and Chaves, R., 2009, October. Neurological image classification for the Alzheimer's Disease diagnosis using Kernel PCA and Support Vector Machines. In 2009 IEEE Nuclear Science Symposium Conference Record (NSS/MIC) (pp. 2486-2489). IEEE.

Magnin, B., Mesrob, L., Kinkingnéhun, S., Pélégrini-Issac, M., Colliot, O., Sarazin, M., Dubois, B., Lehéricy, S. and Benali, H., 2009. Support vector machine-based classification of Alzheimer's disease from whole-brain anatomical MRI. Neuroradiology, 51(2), pp.73-83.

Maroco, J., Silva, D., Rodrigues, A., Guerreiro, M., Santana, I. and de Mendonça, A., 2011. Data mining methods in the prediction of Dementia: A real-data comparison of the accuracy, sensitivity and specificity of linear discriminant analysis, logistic regression, neural networks, support vector machines, classification trees and random forests. BMC research notes, 4(1), p.299.

Mathotaarachchi, S., Pascoal, T.A., Shin, M., Benedet, A.L., Kang, M.S., Beaudry, T., Fonov, V.S., Gauthier, S., Rosa-Neto, P. and Alzheimer's Disease Neuroimaging Initiative, 2017. Identifying incipient dementia individuals using machine learning and amyloid imaging. Neurobiology of aging, 59, pp.80-90.

Morra, J.H., Tu, Z., Apostolova, L.G., Green, A.E., Toga, A.W. and Thompson, P.M., 2010. Comparison of AdaBoost and support vector machines for detecting Alzheimer's disease through automated hippocampal segmentation. IEEE transactions on medical imaging, 29(1), pp.30-43.

Oliveira Jr, P.P.D.M., Nitrini, R., Busatto, G., Buchpiguel, C., Sato, J.R., and Amaro Jr, E., 2010. Use of SVM methods with surface-based cortical and volumetric subcortical measurements to detect Alzheimer's disease. Journal of Alzheimer's Disease, 19 (4), pp.1263-1272.

Ramírez, J., Górriz, J.M., Salas-Gonzalez, D., Romero, A., López, M., Álvarez, I. and Gómez-Río, M., 2013. Computer-aided diagnosis of Alzheimer's type dementia combining support vector machines and discriminant set of features. Information Sciences, 237, pp.59-72.

Rangini, M. and Jiji, G.W., 2013, March. Detection of Alzheimer's disease through automated hippocampal segmentation. In 2013 International Mutli-Conference on Automation, Computing, CommunicationControl and Compressed Sensing (iMac4s), (pp. 144-149). IEEE.

Shankle, W.R., Datta, P., Dillencourt, M. and Pazzani, M., 1996. Improving dementia screening tests with machine learning methods. Alzheimer's Research, 2(3).

Shankle, W.R., Mani, S., Pazzani, M.J. and Smyth, P., 1997, March. Detecting very early stages of dementia from normal aging with machine learning methods. In Conference on Artificial Intelligence in Medicine in Europe (pp. 71-85). Springer, Berlin, Heidelberg.

Sheshadri, H.S., Shree, S.B. and Krishna, M., 2015, August. Diagnosis of Alzheimer's disease employing neuropsychological and classification techniques. In 2015 5th International Conference on IT Convergence and Security (ICITCS) (pp. 1-6). IEEE.

Shree, S.B. and Sheshadri, H.S., 2014, December. An initial investigation in the diagnosis of Alzheimer's disease using various classification techniques. In 2014 IEEE International Conference on Computational Intelligence and Computing Research (pp. 1-5). IEEE.

So, A., Hooshyar, D., Park, K. and Lim, H., 2017. Early diagnosis of dementia from clinical data by machine learning techniques. Applied Sciences, 7(7), p.651.

SR, B.S. and Sheshadri, H.S., 2014, December. An approach to preprocess data in the diagnosis of Alzheimer's disease. In Proceedings of 2014 International Conference on Cloud Computing and Internet of Things (pp. 135-139). IEEE.

Tohka, J., Moradi, E., Huttunen, H. and Alzheimer's Disease Neuroimaging Initiative, 2016. Comparison of feature selection techniques in machine learning for anatomical brain MRI in dementia. Neuroinformatics, 14(3), pp.279-296.

Tong, T., Wolz, R., Gao, Q., Guerrero, R., Hajnal, J.V., Rueckert, D. and Alzheimer's Disease Neuroimaging Initiative, 2014. Multiple instance learning for classification of dementia in brain MRI. Medical image analysis, 18(5), pp.808-818.

Trambaiolli, L.R., Lorena, A.C., Fraga, F.J., Kanda, P.A., Anghinah, R. and Nitrini, R., 2011. Improving Alzheimer's disease diagnosis with machine learning techniques. Clinical EEG and neuroscience, 42(3), pp.160-165.

Vemuri, P., Gunter, J.L., Senjem, M.L., Whitwell, J.L., Kantarci, K., Knopman, D.S., Boeve, B.F., Petersen, R.C. and Jack Jr, C.R., 2008. Alzheimer's disease diagnosis in individual subjects using structural MR images: validation studies. Neuroimage, 39(3), pp.1186-1197.

Williams, J.A., Weakley, A., Cook, D.J. and Schmitter-Edgecombe, M., 2013, June. Machine learning techniques for diagnostic differentiation of mild cognitive impairment and dementia. In Workshops at the twenty-seventh AAAI conference on artificial intelligence.

Wu, Y.T., Beiser, A.S., Breteler, M.M., Fratiglioni, L., Helmer, C., Hendrie, H.C., Honda, H., Ikram, M.A., Langa, K.M., Lobo, A. and Matthews, F.E., 2017. The changing prevalence and incidence of dementia over time—current evidence. Nature Reviews Neurology, 13(6), p.327.

Yang, Y.B., Li, Y.N., Gao, Y., Yin, H. and Tang, Y., 2014. Structurally enhanced incremental neural learning for image classification with subgraph extraction. International journal of neural systems, 24 (07), p.1450024.

Communication and Computing Systems – Prasad et al. (eds)
© 2019 Taylor & Francis Group, London, ISBN 978-0-367-00147-6

Big data analytics using soft computing techniques: A study

D.K. Sreekantha

Department of Computer Science and Engineering, NMAM Institute of Technology, Nitte, Karnataka, India

ABSTRACT: Big data comprises large volume data having structure, partially structure and no structure gathered through scientific, social, business and industrial operations continuously. This big data needs to be analyzed for extracting the hidden knowledge patterns for taking timely, intelligent and cost effective decisions. Research on the applications of Soft computing techniques for big data processing to arrive at intelligent decision making has been drawing significant attention in the recent years. Authors studied the applications of Soft computing techniques for analyzing the big data. Soft computing techniques differs from traditional hard computing techniques by effectively dealing with uncertainty, vagueness, partial truth and imprecision. Soft computing is an hybrid technique having Fuzzy logic, Neural Networks, Genetic Algorithms, Machine learning, Support Vector Machines (SVM), Evolutionary Computation (EC) and AI as its constituents. Authors have carried out an exhaustive survey of applications in various business and industry domains.

1 INTRODUCTION

Experts have predicted that managing big data will be the trend for next 30 years. This management of big data helps us to derive advanced perceptions of hidden knowledge patterns, having significant impact on business and industrial applications. Today analyzing big data is the most significant task for many businesses and industries. There is an immense need for efficient, cost effective big data processing techniques to process big data. Significant part of big data is unstructured, which is difficult to handle and interpret, hence there is a need for intelligent data processing technique using soft computing. Soft computing techniques derive inspiration from human processing capabilities to process big data effectively.

2 REVIEW OF LITERATURE

Authors have carried out an exhaustive study of research papers from high impact international journals like IEEE, Springier and Elsevier publications and presented the following selected papers review from major sectors of industry as way of illustration

2.1 *Social networks*

The sentiment analysis is the typical problem of social big data analytics (A Mohammed et al.) carried out based on fuzzy sets. This paper presented a conceptual and theoretical view of social data and fuzzy set theory. Authors portrayed the functionality of established model by taking Facebook social media data example. Researchers have discussed one of the Social Data Analysis Tool (SODATA) that was used to retrieve Facebook website by realizing the conceptual model in software. This paper extracted the actor's sentiments and artifacts from the Face-book pages. The sentimental analysis and classification was carried out by constructing fuzzy sets of the artifacts (comments, shares, posts and likes).

The migration to the new functional paradigm from the standard data mining system to process big data using fuzzy systems (Alberto Fernandez Cristobal et. al.) was experimented. Authors developed an interface model that provides a good adaption to various scenarios of data uncertainty. The fuzzy methods are capable of handling huge data sets without changing or damaging their classification, response time and accuracy. This paper also discussed Spark and Flink data analytics frameworks that address the problems in reduce stage and small disjuncts in data division. The Fuzzy K-Nearest Neighbor method was applied (Malak El Bakry et.al.) to process big data using Map Reduce technique. This algorithm has been divided into two parts, the mapper and reducer. The mapper algorithm, divides the data into chunks over many computing nodes and outputs set of intermediate records. The reducer algorithm retrieves the results of individual node, combine them together to get final results. The challenges for analyzing the big data components of multimedia data from social networks (Jai Prakash Verma, Smita Agrawal et al.) was studied. All automated systems in industries and businesses are producing huge quantity of data of various types such as numbers, voice, music and video, sensed are bio-metric in nature. Authors have considered the data analysis of social networks contents based on text, music, voice, and video data. This paper discusses the problems storage, management, retrieval for extracting potentially useful pat-terns from various kinds of data in big data and possible application domains.

2.2 Healthcare

The healthcare industry is characterized by massive health records of patients. The digitization and processing of health records (Saravana kumar et al.) deals with increased complexity. The healthcare data is typically unstructured and comprises images and signals. This type of data needs to be converted in to some structured form for finding solutions to healthcare problems. The healthcare industry is encountering problems that needs data analytics solutions. The Non Communicable Diseases (NCD) such as Diabetic Mellitus (DM) are unique leading health problems in developing nations such as India. The goal of this research is to study the diabetic care by analyzing the big data gathered during patient treatments. The innovations in predictive analysis solution for diabetic care by enhanced data understanding will yield the significant results in healthcare industry and patient care. Guoyin Wang Ji Xu studied Brain Informatics domain. Brain big data is a powerful and typical big data technique uses multi-channel, functional magnetic resonance imaging, magneto electroencephalogram-graph, near infrared spectroscopic imaging, multi-channel electroencephalography and other various devices. Multi Granularity Computing (MGrC) is a new trend in information processing approach. MGrC stimulates human brain thinking model, which is multi-granular and processes complex information from information granules. Authors have analysed the three basic methods of MGrC, they are granularity joint computation, granularity optimization, granularity conversion. All these techniques are built on five major models like deep learning, cloud architecture, rough sets, quotient space and fuzzy sets.

Ryosuke Hasebeet et al. have conducted a study on significant ways to utilize internet data quickly and efficiently based on human based genetic algorithm. The recognized images from healthcare data are tagged with suitable names as per concept. The newly designed system is compared with conventional systems. Even though authors have failed to obtain significant results, but authors got positive comments about proposed system. On the basis of big data analysis healthcare data is differentiated as EHR, public health, Genomic and behavioral data. This methodology helps to analyse the data at low cost. The paper concludes with listing the steps to improve big data analysis performance by optimizing map reduce technique.

2.3 Bioinformatics

Bioinformatics domain comprises huge data and requires extensive analysis. H Kashyap et. al. have discovered that Bioinformatics research is distinguished by cumulative data sets and complex methods of data analytics. The machine learning, parallel and distributed computing technologies are applied to process big data in Bioinformatics. The sample big data problems in Bioinformatics are co-expression construction, identification of salient module, regulatory networks, and discovery of complex over increasing protein-protein interaction data, protein sequence data, huge DNA, RNA analysis and fast querying of disease networks with heterogeneous and incremental model.

Swathi Jain et. al. have performed a survey on soft computing application in Bioinformatics field to reduce the cost of processing with efficiency. Authors have explored the link between Bioinformatics with web technologies, databases, algorithms, information systems, artificial intelligence, software engineering, computation theory, data mining, structural biology, image processing, discrete mathematics, soft computing, control system theory, statistics and circuit theory.

2.4 Mobile networks

The framework designed for analyzing cellular networks big data has been studied by S. Zhang, J.Liang, R.IIe, and Z.Sun using unified data model. Authors have discussed big data in form of radio wave forms, big signal, traffic, locations and big heterogeneous data of cellular networks. This paper also discusses a various of research demands for analyzing the big data of cellular networks, and describes the relationship among big data analytics and cellular networks in systematic way.

2.5 Film industry

Daniel J. Lewis et. al. have studied large scale interconnected data for mass collaboration. This data is often cluttered, hierarchical and biased. Authors have applied X-μ approach from fuzzy set theory for linked data attributes consisting vagueness properties like film budget, film length, and box office takings. The mapping of SPARQL query is done with X-μ function for higher scalability.

2.6 Automobiles

Chung-Hong Lee and Chih-Hung Wu have proposed innovative big data modelling technique to enhance the driving range prediction of Electrical Vehicles (EV). Authors have applied a big-data analytics to prevent anxiety of driving range. Authors also described their machine-learning study on EV driving behaviour analytics, called growing hierarchical self-organizing maps for clustering the EV big data gathered. This approach helps automobile company to design an estimating model based on the EV big data to project the driving range in the workable life cycle of battery.

2.7 Business

S.Prabha, P.Kola Sujatha applied Fuzzy Clustering for to cluster huge datasets where every object has multiple memberships in many clusters. The Incremental Weighted Fuzzy C-Means (IWFCM) introduces weights that discusses the significance of every object of cluster. IWFCM creates cluster with least execution time and higher quality. IWFCM is implemented on e-book sales data on Hadoop and map reduce framework. The sales data analysis of e-book companies was carried out. This data is analysed to discover the facts, such as maximum sold books region wise, author wise, topics wise etc. Grégory Smitsa, Olivier Piverta, Ronald R.Yagerb, Pierre Nerzica have discovered that the value addition to the data is in the knowledge that can be extracted by the domain expert. The devoted indexing schemes linking data and their subjective linguistic re writings and expedition facilities are rendered in addition to the summary to enable the users to browse the data.

2.8 Stock market

Pranali P. Chaudhari et al. conducted a study on three state of art technologies namely Genetic algorithm, ANN and Fuzzy Logic. The huge data size and varieties of data types calls for the need of efficient data analysis tools with better time, accuracy and fault tolerance capabilities. Rudolf Kruse et al. have discovered how soft computing methods supports the data analysis. Authors have applied approximate matching technique for frequent pattern matching of visual concepts and analysis of complex analytical scenario for industrial applications. Marius Muja et. al. applied scalable nearest neighbor algorithm to solve large dimensional data problem, machine learning and computer vision. Authors have analysed two algorithms, they are randomized k-d forest and k-means priority search tree algorithm. This research work is released as library open source framework for approximate nearest neighbors (FLANN), matching algorithm combined with Opencv. Xue Wen Chen et al. have worked on Deep learning technique, a dominant area for research in pattern recognition and machine learning domain. Deep learning is being successfully applied for natural language processing, computer vision and speech recognition. Deep learning is playing a significant role in predictive analysis of big data. Gayan Prasad et al have explored the linkages and data representations to recognize the information that matches the same entry from different data sources. The methods used to handle linkages and method is categorized into two types of classification and linkages. This paper proposes to use intellectual solutions using clustering algorithms, artificial neural networks and genetic algorithms for future generation data categorization and linkage model. The proposed data type renders solutions to discover relationship within entity and between two different entities.

2.9 Education and research

Amin Karami et al. have designed a framework for big data understanding for uncertainty-aware visual analytics. This framework was built using fuzzy self-organizing algorithm on parallel computing map reduce framework. This paper applied techniques like interactive data mining, knowledge representation and uncertainty modeling during the design phase of framework. The visual representation prototype in this model helps for analysis of user interactions and uncertain data. Authors have concluded that the given system predicts the behavior of uncertain data, makes effective decisions and finds visual outliers.

2.10 Cryptanalysis

Xinhua Dong et al. worked on semi trusted data platform for securely sharing, storing, delivering and destroying sensitive big data. Authors have presented procedure founded on transformation of heterogeneous cipher text and an individual process to design a proxy encryption algorithm. This algorithm helps in realization of system functions. This framework delivers customer sensitive data effectively and safely. This algorithm also enables the data owners to maintain the full data security and access control with sophisticated internet connectivity. This is a practicable solution to provide equilibrium benefits to concerned parties under the semi-trusted conditions.

2.11 Smart transportation

Designing smart transportation is one among the crucial problems in smart city and realistic application domain of big data was discussed by Xi Lia, Xuehai Zhoua, Aili Wangb, Nadia Nedjah. This problem has to control the traffic lights effectively because of accumulated dynamic vehicles flow data. Authors designed a special Never Stop signal that uses genetic algorithms and fuzzy logic control techniques to build smart transportation systems. Xue-Wen Chen et al. have studied the successful challenges and perspectives of Big Data and Deep Learning. Now Deep learning has been highly progressive research domain among pattern recognition and machine learning community. It has achieved outstanding success in several applications such as natural language processing, speech recognition and computer vision. Big data is too big to be handled and analyzed by traditional software tools (Junhai Zhai, Sufang Zhang, Mingyang Zhang, Xiaomeng Liu). The major six characteristics of big data are value, veracity, volume, velocity, variety and class imbalance. The typical examples of big data such as e-health big data, credit card fraud detection big data and extreme weather forecast big data are all class imbalanced. There is need to deal with the problem of classifying binary imbalanced big data based on MapReduce, non-iterative learning, ensemble learning and oversampling. This paper proposes an algorithm which includes three stages. Firstly, for each positive instance, its enemy nearest neighbour is found with MapReduce, and positive instances are randomly generated with uniform distribution in its enemy nearest neighbour hyper sphere, i.e., oversampling positive instances within the hyper sphere. Secondly, one balanced data subsets are constructed, the classifiers are trained on the constructed data subsets with a non-iterative learning approach. Finally, the trained classifiers are integrated by fuzzy integral to classify unseen instances. Authors experimentally compared the proposed algorithm with three related algorithms: SMOTE, SMOTE+RF-BigData and MR-V-ELM, and conducted a statistical analysis on the experimental results. The observational results and the statistical figures demonstrate that the proposed algorithm outperforms the other three methods based on MapReduce, non-iterative learning, ensemble learning and oversampling, This proposed algorithm MR-FI-ELM has three advantages: (1) Idea is simple and it is easy to implement. (2) It not only can effectively classify imbalanced big data, but also can deal with practical problems with medium-size. (3) It is feasible and effective for extremely imbalanced data.

3 CONCLUSIONS

The research on big data has an immense effect on most social and industrial fields. Soft computing techniques are used as an important tool to discover the relationships among the set of items and hidden knowledge patterns in the data. This paper has discussed the various applications of soft computing techniques in processing of big data such as Healthcare, Social media, Film industry, Online shopping, e book companies, Bioinformatics, Electronic vehicles, Genomic Medicine, Mobile cellular network, Smart city, Brain informatics, Cloud computing and Cryptography using various algorithms. Authors concluded that soft computing techniques are widely used for processing big data and arriving at intelligent decisions for saving time and cost of operations.

REFERENCES

A Mohammed, Behrouz H Far and Christopher Naugler.Mohammed et. al., 2014, Applications of the map reduce programming framework to clinical big data analysis: current landscape and future trends, Bio Data Mining, https://biodatamining.biomedcentral.com/articles/10.1186/1756-0381-7-22

Alberto Fernandez Cristobal, Jose Carmona Maria Josedel Jesus, Francisco Herrera et. al., 2016, A view on fuzzy systems for big data: progress and opportunities, International Journal of Computational Intelligence Systems, 9 (1):1-80, http://sci2s.ugr.es/sites/default/files/ficherosPublicaciones/2082_ijcis3726.pdf,

Amin Karami et. al., A framework for uncertainty-aware visual analytics in big data, https://www.semanticscholar.org/paper/AFramework-for-Uncertainty-Aware-Visual-Analytics-Karami/805479317e8b900e9a4b35135db9832b83710b4a,

Chao Wanga, Xi Lia, et.al. 2016, Soft computing in big data intelligent transportation systems, Applied Soft Computing, 38:1099–1108,http://dx.doi.org/10.1016/j.asoc.2015.06.006

Chung-hong lee and Chih-hung wu et. al., 2015, A novel big data modeling method for improving driving range estimation of EVs, 2015, DOI:10.1109/ACCESS.2015.2492923,https://ieeexplore.ieee.org/document/7300375

Daniel J. Lewis and Trevor P. Martin, 2015, Managing vagueness with fuzzy in hierarchical big datam, conference on big data managing vagueness with fuzzy in hierarchical big data, Procedia Computer

Science, 53:19–28,INNS, Doi: 10.1016/j.procs.2015.07.275,https://www.researchgate.net/publication/282245903_Manaing_Vagueness_with_Fuzzy_in_Hierarchical_Big_Data

Gayan Prasad, Nadeeka Nilmini, Dhammika Suresh, 2014, Next generation data classification and linkage role of probabilistic models and artificial intelligence, IEEE 2014, Global Humanitarian Technology Conference, Doi: 978-1-4799-7193-0/14/$31.00 ©2014, IEEE 569, https://ieeexplore.ieee.org/document/6970340/

Grégory Smitsa, Olivier Piverta, Ronald R.Yagerb and Pierre Nerzic, 2018, A soft computing approach to big data summarization, Fuzzy Sets and Systems https://doi.org/10.1016/j.fss.2018.02.017

Guoyin Wang Ji Xu, 2014, Computing with multiple granular layers for brain big data processing, Brain Informatics, DOI: 10.1007/s40708-014-0001-z.,https://link.springer.com/article/10.1007/s40708-014-0001-z

Hirak Kashyap, Hasin Afzal Ahmed, Nazrul Hoque, Swarup Roy, and Dhruba Kumar Bhattacharyya, 2015, Big data analytics in Bioinformatics: a machine learning perspective, Journal of Latex Class Files, 13(9):1-20, Doi: arXiv:1506.05101v1 [cs.CE] 15 Jun 2015

Jai Prakash Verma, Smita Agrawal, Bankim Patel and Atul Patel, 2016, Big data analytics: challenges and applications for text, audio, video, and social media data", International Journal on Soft Computing, Artificial Intelligence and Applications (IJSCAI), 5 (1), February 2016, DOI:10.5121/ijscai.2016.5105

Junhai Zhai, Sufang Zhang, Mingyang Zhang, Xiaomeng Liu, 2018,Fuzzy integral-based ELM ensemble for imbalanced big data Classification,© Springer-Verlag GmbH Germany, part of Springer Nature 2018

Malak El Bakry, Soha Safwat and Osman Hegazy,2015, Big Data Classification using Fuzzy K-Nearest Neighbor, International Journal of Computer Applications (0975–8887), 132 (10), December 2015, https://pdfs.semanticscholar.org/79a4/439a46390882ab89148163e540435ea9b2e3.pdf

Marius Muja, and David G. Lowe,2014, Scalable Nearest Neighbor Algorithms for High Dimensional Data, IEEE Transactions On Pattern Analysis and Machine Intelligence, 36 (11), November 2014, 0162-8828, 2014, IEEE.

Pranali P. Chaudhari, 2015, Review of Soft Computing Methods used in Data Analysis. IJISET - International Journal of Innovative Science, Engineering & Technology, 2 (1), January 2015, www.ijiset.com, ISSN 2348-7968, 124.

Rudolf Kruse, Christian Borgelt, Detlef D. Nauck, Nees Jan van Eck and Matthias Steinbrecher, The Role of Soft Computing in Intelligent Data Analysis, https://pdfs.semanticscholar.org/084b/aa6c22af628e295cab0e2fbc2d84813cace3.pdf

Ryosuke Hasebe, Rina Kouda, Kei Ohnishi and Masaharu Munetomo. Human-based Genetic Algorithm for Facilitating Practical Use of Data in the Internet. Information Initiative Center, December 3-6, 2014

S. Zhang, J. Liang, R. He, and Z. Sun, Code Consistent Hashing Based on Information-Theoretic Criterion, ieeexplore.ieee.org/iel7/6687317/7153538/07327170.pdf

S.Prabha, P.Kola Sujatha, "Reduction of Big data sets using fuzzy clustering, International Journal of Advanced Research in Computer Engineering & Technology (IJARCET), 3 (6), June 2014, ISSN: 2278–1323

Saravana Kumar N.M., Eswari T, Sampath P, Lavanya S,2015, Predictive methodology for diabetic data analysis in big data, International Symposium on Big Data and Cloud Computing (ISBCC'15), 2015, Elsevier, Doi: 10.1016/j.procs.2015.04.069 1877-0509

Swathi Jain, Abhishek Pandey, 2013, Soft computing, artificial intelligence, fuzzy logic & genetic algorithm in bio informatics, IJCEM International Journal of Computational Engineering & Management,16(1), January 2013, ISSN (Online): 2230-7893, www.IJCEM.org, https://pdfs.semanticscholar.org/7121/da374e00be9055a9c9804be2c5b9a824caa6.pdf, International Journal of Engineering & Technology

Xinhua Dong, Ruixuan Li, Heng He, Wanwan Zhou, Zhengyuan Xue, and Hao Wu Tsing-hua, 2015, Secure sensitive data sharing on a big data platform, Science and Technology, 20(1):72-80, February 2015, http://syslog.co.in/java-projects/cloudcomputing-projects/Secure%20Sensitive%20Data%20Sharing%20on%20a%20Big%20Data%20Platform.pdf

Xue-Wen Chen, and Xiaotong Lin, 2014, Big data deep learning: challenges and perspectives, May 28, 2: 2169-3536, Doi: 10.1109/Access.2014.2325029

Xue-Wen Chen and Xiaotong Lin, 2016, Big data deep learning: challenges and perspectives, international Journal of Computational Intelligence Systems, 9: 69-80, https://doi.org/10.1080/18756891.2016.1180820

Communication and Computing Systems – Prasad et al. (eds)
© 2019 Taylor & Francis Group, London, ISBN 978-0-367-00147-6

Fuzzy based opportunistic channel access by secondary user in cognitive radio system

Juhi Gupta, Vivek K. Dwivedi & Vikram Karwal
Jaypee Institute of Information Technology, Noida, India

ABSTRACT: In this paper, a cognitive radio user/secondary user (CR/SU) based selection algorithm has been proposed that provides an opportunistic access to the available spectrum hole. The proposed system makes use of fuzzy logic to manage the CR users to access the free frequency on the basis of channel fading conditions, channel sensing information, and the distance between transmitter and receiver. The effect of aggregate interference is considered to determine the value of signal-to-interference-noise-ratio (SINR) at the primary user. In this paper, the maximum permissible transmission power for a CR user is determined using convex optimization. Based on which, the appropriate CR is given the opportunity to transmit over the available spectrum hole.

1 INTRODUCTION

Cognitive Radio, first introduced by Joseph Mitola III, is the most promising technology for the near future that provides tremendous possibility of increase in bandwidth by adapting to its highly dynamic operational parameters. CR system undergoes various challenges related to architectural complexity, fluctuation in spectrum availability and the Quality of Service at the user end (Z. Zhang et al,2013). Optimal radio resource allocation is the challenging task for the performance improvement of Cognitive Radio System. The different channel assignment techniques aim to assign channels to radio interfaces for achieving efficient frequency utilization and minimizing the interference caused by users operating on the same or nearby frequencies. The authors in (Z. Zhang et al,2013). deal with the selection of spectrum for opportunistic access in cognitive management systems, with a focus on the selection of methods to obtain knowledge about the current spectrum availability for CRs. A comprehensive survey on the channel assignment problem in different types of CR Networks like Cognitive Radio Ad-Hoc Networks, CR Wireless Mesh Network, and CR Local Area Networks etc. has been demonstrated in (E. Ahmed,et al,2016). Also, various channel assignment problems based on Ant colony optimization (ACO), Genetic, probabilistic, and throughput oriented is discussed. Bio-inspired technique like swarm intelligence is implemented to dynamically manage channel assignments in (C. Doerr,et al,2008). The process dynamically (. H. A. B. Salameh, et al,2011) assigns channels to CR transmissions with the objective of maximizing the achieved CRN sum-rate, subject to interference and SINR constraints. A solution to joint rate control and channel assignment problem for the coordinated channel access in opportunistic CR networks is proposed. The spectrum sharing model discussed in (Zhang,R et al,2010) allows the SUs to transmit simultaneously with PUs at the same band even if they are active, provided that the SU knows how to control their resultant interference at the PU receivers. It is to avoid the performance degradation of each active primary link beyond a tolerable margin. In paper (Wang . L. C et al,2011), the author has investigated sensing and probability based spectrum decision scheme based on the M/G/1 queuing model. In literature, fuzzy logic based spectrum sensing approach has been discussed in (Takagi,T. et al,1995). It has been concluded in (Ejaz, W., et al,2012) that by combining various detection techniques with fuzzy logic, better results can be obtained. Authors in (Le.H. T. et al,2008) have discussed the spectrum access using fuzzy logic system but the maximum power is not determined. A rule base decision making mechanism has been discussed in to select different spectrum sensing techniques. Fuzzy logic resembles human like thinking and is efficient for compromise centric decision making and hence is suitable for multidimensional decision making problems (Matin-mikko M et al,2013). The model proposed in (Martyna J.et al,2014) introduces a multidimensional membership function into the fuzzy logic system to achieve power control and required transmission rate by the secondary users.

In this paper, the parameters that govern the selection of a particular secondary user are different. Further, the antecedents are based on some crucial parameters like maximum power, aggregate interference, and distance between secondary and primary users described by the angle between the two measured from the base station (BS). Further, the rule base for the channel allocation by an appropriate CR user has also been discussed. After scanning the open literature and to the best of our knowledge, the selection process of a specific CR user for the transmission over an available frequency based on fuzzy logic has not been reported yet, where fuzzy rule-base selection of a particular CR user includes the effect of aggregate interference.

In Section 2, a system model has been proposed to determine maximum power transmission of the CR user under various conditions. A technique based on the fuzzy logic has been proposed for the selection of a particular CR user to which the available frequency could be assigned. Based on the detection probability, P_d, of the sensed channel, the free channel is determined. If P_d is high, then the channel is considered incapable for transmission in overlay mode and hence, can be used for the low power transmissions in underlay mode (Gupta,J et al,2015). Along with the detection probability, interference by the active users present near to the PU helps in making more accurate decisions for a CR network. For more appropriate analysis, the effect of aggregate interference (Ghasemi A. et al,2008) has been considered to calculate the SINR at the PU. Aggregate interference and the distance between the two communicating users are the parameters that vary geographically and play a crucial role in the assignment of a CR to the available channel. The opportunity to access a particular channel by a CR user is determined by the estimate of maximum power that can be allocated to the available frequency. This optimum power is based on different parameters like SINR of the signal received by the PU due to CR's transmission and angle θ.

2 SYSTEM MODEL

We consider a single cognitive user, located near BS in a large cognitive radio network. It is assumed that the primary receiver is capable of tolerating a maximum interference power of γ_{th}, motivated by the interference temperature concept. Interference levels higher than this threshold are considered harmful and hence avoided. In the proposed model, we discuss the criterion for the selection of an appropriate CR user out of various available CR users that want to access the spectrum hole without hindering PU. The maximum optimal transmission power with which a CR user can transmit is determined using Lagrange multipliers. Further, the fuzzy logic is used to select a particular CR based on various criteria discussed in Section 2.2. The channel fading gains are g_{cb} and g_{cp} corresponding to the links between (CR and BS) and (CR and PU) respectively and are modelled by the Nakagami-m distribution. The maximum power with which the CR user can transmit is determined after including the effects of aggregate interference and channel fading conditions. The other parameters which also play major role in decision making are detection probability Pd and angle θ between the links specified by the distances R_s and D_{cp}. This angle is between the two links: CR-BS and PU-BS, where the distance between the base station BS and CR user is given by Rs and the distance between CR and primary user PU is given by D_{cp}. The channel-links corresponding to R_s and D_{cp} are assumed perpendicular to each other. In the proposed algorithm, fuzzy logic is used to decide a specific CR user that may be given the chance to access the available subcarrier frequency.

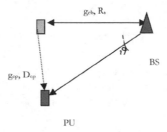

Figure 1. System model.

After determining the maximum optimum power of CR user, a particular CR user is chosen whose power lies in close proximity to the maximum power determined. In addition to it, we apply fuzzy rules on other parameters also like θ and SINR of the signal received at PU due to transmission by CR (SINR$_{RPU}$). We determine SINR$_{RPU}$ on the basis of the CR power and the aggregate interference at the PU. SINRRPU is assumed to have maximum threshold, γ_{th}, to avoid any hindrance to PU. For a particular value of γ_{th}, the maximum power P$_{Tmax}$ of CR user satisfying certain constraints is then determined. The two constraints are specified in eq. (2) and (3). In this proposed channel assignment technique, the CR user whose power is less than or equal to P$_{Tmax}$ is given the chance to access the channel. The optimum value of this power is determined using convex optimization technique. The PU is interfered by the transmission of CR and other active users present near the PU. The location of all CRs located near to the PU is modeled by homogeneous spatial Poisson point process. The aggregate interference (Ghasemi A. et al,2008) under Nakagami-m fading environment is calculated at the primary user to make more accurate decisions. Aggregate interference affects the decisions of spectrum sensing as it turns out to be harmful even though the two nodes are not in the interfering range of each other. Therefore, a cognitive radio should be capable of detecting primary users locating beyond its interference range.

2.1 *Objective*

The objective is to determine the maximum transmission power of CR user to achieve maximum capacity with the assumption that channel state information (CSI) is available to CR.

$$\max E\left[\log_2\left(1+\frac{g_{cb}P_T}{\sigma^2 \mid \sigma_I^2}\right)\right],$$

(1)

where σ_I^2 denotes the variance of the aggregate interference at the receiving node due to the presence of various transmitters. The number of transmitters in any region A is a Poisson random variable with parameter λA, where λ is the intensity of Poisson point process. σ_I^2 is determined by substituting n = 2 in eq. (5) to obtain second cumulant. In eq. (2), the constraint is the SINR of the signal received at PU, SINR$_{RPU}$, due to the transmission by secondary user should be less than threshold SINR, γ_{th}. If the strength of the received signal exceeds this threshold value at PU than that CR is not allowed to transmit.

$$SINR_{RPU} < \gamma_{th},$$

(2)

$$P_T \geq 0,$$

(3)

where

$$SINR_{RPU} = \frac{P_T g_{cp}}{\sigma^2 + \sigma_I^2}, \text{ and } g_{cp} = D_{cp}^{-\alpha} \|h_{cp}\|^2. \tag{4}$$

Path loss exponent is denoted by 'α' and D_{cp} is the distance between CR and PU. Small scale Nakagami-m distributed channel gain whose power is given by $\|h_{cp}\|^2$. The aggregate interference [15] at PU is given by the following n^{th} cumulant:

$$\kappa_n = \frac{2\pi\lambda}{n\alpha - 2} \left[E_X^l(n, \bar{\gamma}_0) + \bar{\gamma}_0^{n-\frac{2}{\alpha}} E_X^u(2/\alpha, \bar{\gamma}_0) \right], \tag{5}$$

where $E_X^l(n, \bar{\gamma}_0)$ and $E_X^u(n, \bar{\gamma}_0)$ denote the nth order lower and upper partial moments of X respectively.

For Nakagami-m fading,

$$E_X^l(n, \bar{\gamma}_0) = \frac{m^{-n}}{\Gamma(m)} \left[\Gamma(m+n) - \Gamma(m+n, m\bar{\gamma}_0) \right] \tag{6}$$

$$E_X^u\left(\frac{2}{\alpha}, \bar{\gamma}_0\right) = \frac{m^{-\frac{2}{\alpha}}}{\Gamma(m)} \left[\Gamma\left(\frac{2}{\alpha} + m, m\bar{\gamma}_0\right) \right] \tag{7}$$

Eq. (6) and eq. (7) determine lower and upper partial moments of X under various fading distributions. $\Gamma(.)$ and $\Gamma(.,.)$ denote the complete and incomplete Gamma functions (Gradshteyn . I. S. et al,2000), respectively. CVX tool is used to determine the maximum value of transmission power of a CR. The objective with its constraints is stated as below:

$$L(P_T, \lambda_1, \lambda_2) = \log_2\left(1 + \frac{g_{cb}P_T}{\sigma^2 + \sigma_I^2}\right) + \lambda_1\left(\frac{P_T g_{cp}}{\sigma^2 + \sigma_I^2} - \gamma_{th}\right) + \lambda_2 P_T \tag{8}$$

The values of Lagrange multipliers λ_1 and λ_2 are determined using interior point method. $\frac{\partial L}{\partial \lambda_1}$ and $\frac{\partial L}{\partial P_T}$ are determined and equated to zero.

The channel fading power $g_{cb} = R_s^{-\alpha}\|h_{cb}\|^2$ gain between CR and BS is given by where, h_{cb} is the fading gain of the channel between CR and BS having Nakagami-m distribution. The maximum optimum power with which the CR user is allowed to transmit is given by the expression P_{Tmax} in eq. (9) that is obtained after implementing the KKT conditions (Boyd,S. et al,2004).

$$P_{T\max} = \left[\left(\frac{R_s^{-\alpha}\|h_{cb}\|^2}{\sigma^2 + \sigma_I^2}\right)\left(\frac{1}{\lambda_1 \gamma_{th}} + 1\right) \right]^{-1} \tag{9}$$

Using the relation $R_s = D_{cp}\cot\theta$ in eq. (9),
P_{Tmax} becomes

$$P_{Tmax} = \left[\left(\frac{(D_{cp}\cot\theta_0)^{-\alpha}\|h_{cb}\|^2}{\sigma^2 + \sigma_I^2}\right)\left(\frac{1}{\lambda_1 \gamma_{th}} + 1\right) \right]^{-1} \tag{10}$$

Finally, the maximum transmission power of CR over Nakagami-m fading environment is evaluated in the eq. (10). Substituting the value of P_{Tmax} from eq. (10) to eq. (1), we get the maximum achievable capacity in bits/sec/Hz. The maximum optimal capacity, C is derived as,

$$C = E\left[\log_2\left(1 + \frac{g_{cb}\left[\left(\frac{(D_{cp}\cot\theta)^{-\alpha}\|h_{cb}\|^2}{\sigma^2 + \sigma_I^2}\right)\left(\frac{1}{\lambda_1 \gamma_{th}} + 1\right)\right]^{-1}}{\sigma^2 + \sigma_I^2}\right)\right] \quad (11)$$

The capacity in eq. (11) reflects the effect of aggregate interference and the threshold SINR at PU.

2.2 *Fuzzy logic*

Fuzzy implications are used to express the control rules. The method of identification of a system using its input-output data is described in (Takagi,T. et al,1995) with its fuzzy implication. The rule base decision makes it suitable for dynamic and distributed environment . The CR users have to search for another spectrum hole if the licensed PU wants to access its own allotted frequency that was given temporarily to CR. In this paper, fuzzy based control rules are applied to the CR users based on their powers. The range of powers is categorized as Low, Medium, and High. Now, according to the availability of channel, its fading conditions and maximum tolerable SINR at the PU, it is decided that which category of CR user can transmit. For the same, fuzzy based rules have been framed according to which decision of selection of a particular CR is done. The three antecedents, Detection probability P_d, SINR at PU ($SINR_{RPU}$) and angular distance θ, on the basis of which a CR user is selected from the rule base is given in Table 1. All the antecedents are represented by trapezoidal membership function. If the detection probability of the signal over a channel is high then the probability that the CR will transmit becomes low and vice versa. The value of θ decides the distance between PU and CR. It is assumed that the distance of both CR and PU is known to the base station. Base Station is considered to be present at origin. If the distance between CR and PU, $R_s\tan\theta$ increases then the CR with high power can be given the chance to transmit. First, the maximum power is determined with which the transmission can take place over the available frequency to achieve maximum capacity and to utilize the available resources to maximum. For that specific maximum power the SINR is calculated and is then checked for its category amongst 'Low', 'Medium', and 'High' of SINR. For example, if it is 'High' then the CR user

Table 1. Rule base for fuzzy combining.

Detection Probability, P_d	SINR at PU, $SINR_{RPU}$	θ	Selection of CR based on its transmission power, P_T
High	High	Small	Low
High	Low	Small	High
Medium	High	Small	Low
Low	High	Small	Medium
High	Medium	Large	Medium
Medium	Medium	Large	Medium
Medium	Low	Large	High
Medium	High	Large	Medium
Medium	High	Small	Low
Low	Low	Large	High
Low	Medium	Large	High
Low	High	Large	High
Low	High	Small	Low
Low	Medium	Small	Low

lying in the same category is allowed to transmit. The selection of a particular category is based on the minimum difference between the maximum optimal power determined and the power of CR user which shows willingness to transmit.

3 RESULTS AND SIMULATIONS

To analyze the system using fuzzy logic, we have categorized all the CR users according to their transmission powers as 'Low', 'Medium', and 'High'. According to the maximum transmission power derived, the category of corresponding SINR is determined. The CR user chosen from the sselected category having power value closest to the maximum power is allowed to transmit under the known fading conditions. The rules have been made for the different cases of input sets, P_d and $SINR_{RPU}$, categorized by 'Low', 'Medium', and 'High. With angle θ, we parameterize the angular distance between CR and PU with respect to BS. It is considered that if θ is less than $\pi/6$ then the CR user is not allowed to transmit or very low power transmissions can take place. In such situations, CR operates in underlay mode. To take more accurate decisions, the effect of aggregate interference at the CR and PU due to various transmitters having poisson distribution, located in area A with intensity λ.

The CR user is chosen from the selected category and the available frequency is then occupied by the same. The $SINR_{RPU}$ is considered as the most important parameter to evaluate the maximum power. It highly depends on the interference at the PU due to the transmission by CR and the aggregate interference caused by the neighbouring users. Through simulations, it has been verified that as the threshold value of SINR at PU increases; the maximum value of power with which CR user can transmit also increases in Fig. 3. The graph is plotted without considering the effect of aggregate interference. Large value of θ allows the CR to transmit with high power.

The advantage of applying fuzzy logic is that after analyzing the channel fading conditions, angle, and aggregate interference, the maximum transmission power can be determined.

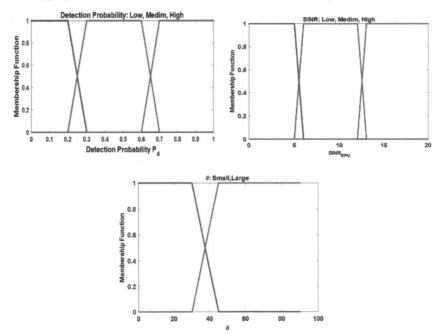

Figure. 4.   (a) Membership function of detection probability P_d, (b) Membership function of *SINR* of the signal received at PU, $SINR_{RPU}$, (c) Membership function of angle θ.

432

Corresponding to this maximum power, angular distance θ and detection probability, a particular rule is selected. In the simulation value of 'α = 3' and 'n = 2'. In Fig. 3, it can be seen that in the absence of aggregate interference, capacity attained is higher. With the increase in intensity 'λ' of the interfering users, the maximum transmission capacity of the CR user decreases.

Figure. 5 shows selection of CR with a particular power based on the evaluated values of $SINR_{RPU}$ and P_d. "Low" power category covers the range less than 70 dBm. The range

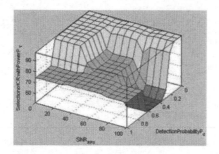 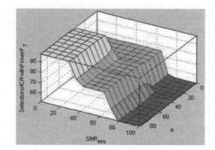

Figure 5. Selection of CR (power) based on the value of.

Figure 6. Selection of a specific CR based on $SINR_{RPU}$ and θ $SINR_{RPU}$ and P_d.

between 60 to 95 dBm is considered as "Medium" power and the power range from 80 dBm to the P_{Tmax} for a particular channel conditions is considered to be lying under "High" category. The selection of a particular CR depends on the optimal power with which the CR can transmit and is decided by the P_{Tmax} given by eq. (9). Similarly, in Figure 6, a particular CR is selected on the basis of typical values of $SINR_{RPU}$ and θ.

4 CONCLUSION

A novel fuzzy based model has been proposed to select a specific CR with maximum optimized transmission power under the impact of various constraints. Initially, the maximum transmission power of CR user and maximum achievable capacity is determined after considering the effect of aggregate interference. Secondly, a rule base is designed to select a particular CR users are categorized on the basis of three antecedents. SINR at PU corresponding to the maximum optimized is determined. Then, based on the values of $SINR_{RPU}$, the probability of signal detection over the available frequency, and angular distance 'θ'; fuzzy based system chooses a specific CR power ('High', 'Medium', and 'Low'). A particular CR user having maximum power in the selected category is then allowed to transmit over the available frequency. In this paper, an intelligent-fuzzy based system has been designed which promotes the best possible selection of CR user so that the free channel can be occupied by the CR user with maximum power providing minimum interference to PU, in the presence of aggregate interference.

REFERENCES

Ahmed, E., Gani, A., Abolfazli, S., Yao L. J., & Khan, S.U. 2016 Channel Assignment Algorithms in Cognitive Radio Networks: Taxonomy, Open Issues, and Challenges. IEEE Communications Surveys & Tutorials 18(1): 795-823.
Doerr, C., Sicker D.C. & Grunwald, D., 2008. Dynamic Control Channel Assignment in Cognitive Radio Networks using Swarm Intelligence in Proceedings of the IEEE Global Communication Conference (GLOBECOM):1-6.

Ejaz, W., Hasan, N., Azam, M. A. & H. S. Kim 2012. Improved Local Spectrum Sensing for Cognitive Radio Networks. EURASIP Journal on Advances in Signal Processing 242:1-12.

Gupta, J., Karwal, V., & Dwivedi, V. K. 2015. Joint Overlay-Underlay Optimal Power Allocation in Cognitive Radio. Wireless Personal Communication 83(3): 2268-2278.

Ghasemi, A. & Sousa, E. S. 2008 .Interference Aggregation and Sensing in Cognitive Radio Networks. IEEE Journal of Selected Topics in Signal Processing 2(1): 41-56.

Gradshteyn, I.S. & I. Ryzhik M. 2000. Table of Integrals, Series, and Products, 6th ed. New York: Academic Press.

Le, H.T. & Ly, H.D. 2008.Opportunistic Spectrum Access Using Fuzzy Logic for Cognitive Radio Networks. 2nd International Conference on Communications and Electronics: 240-245.

Martyna, J. 2014. Fuzzy Reinforcement Learning for Dynamic Power Control in Cognitive Radio Networks. Artificial Intelligence and Soft Computing Lecture Notes in Computer Science 8467 (1): 233-242.

Matinmikko, M., Rauma, T., Mustonen, M., Harjula, I., Sarvanko, H. & Mammela, A. 2009. Application of Fuzzy Logic to Cognitive Radio System IEICE Transaction of Communications, E92-B(12): 3572-3580.

Matinmikko, M., Ser, J. D., Rauma, T. & Mustonen, M. 2013. Fuzzy-Logic Based Framework for Spectrum Availability Assessment in Cognitive Radio Systems. IEEE Journal on Selected Areas in Communication 31(11): 2173-2184.

Salameh, H. 2011. Throughput-oriented Channel Assignment for Opportunistic Spectrum Access Networks. Mathematical and Computer Modelling, Elsevier 53: 2108-2118.

Boyd, S. & Vandenberghe, L.2004. Convex Optimization. Cambridge University Press.

Tragos E. Z., Zeadally, S., Fragkiadakis, A.G. & Siris, V.A.2013.Spectrum Assignment in Cognitive Radio Networks: A Comprehensive Survey. IEEE Communication Surveys & Tutorials15 (3):1108-1113.

Takagi, T. & M. Sugeno 1985. Fuzzy Identification of Systems and Its Applications to Modeling and Control. IEEE Transactions on Systems, Man, and Cybernetics SMC- 15(1):116-132.

Wang, L.C., Wang, C. W. & Adachi, F. 2011. Load Balancing Spectrum Decision for Cognitive Radio Networks. IEEE Journal on Selected Areas in Communications 29(4):757-769.

Zhang, Z. & Long, K. 2013. Self-Organization Paradigms and Optimization Approaches for Cognitive radio Technologies: A Survey. IEEE Wireless Communications 20(2): 36-42.

Zhang, R., Liang, Y. C. & Cui, S. 2010. Dynamic Resource Allocation in Cognitive Radio Networks. IEEE Signal Processing Magazine 27(3):102-114.

Communication and Computing Systems – Prasad et al. (eds)
© 2019 Taylor & Francis Group, London, ISBN 978-0-367-00147-6

Improving scalability and sparsity issues in hybrid recommender systems using real value GA

Latha Banda & Karan Singh
School of Computer Science, JNU, Delhi, India

ABSTRACT: Recently Recommender Systems is widespread in WWW in which user can share their opinions and experiences by ratings or descripting figure of items. The consumer can spontaneously bookmark an item in social bookmarking by giving various descriptions of an item. Even though social networking sites by giving a description of an item, the system can predict whether it is a positive or negative opinion of that particular item and it can be recommended to other users who have the similar interest in that. Generally, RS is classified into content-based, in which the user preferences of ratings are based on his/her previous history of his/her likings. Collaborative Filtering, recommendations are done based on consumer's relationship. The major research work done in Collaborative filtering because as data is increasing the prediction of advice is additionally tough to seek out therefore there would be a bunch of users having similar taste and Hybrid Filtering, is merging technique of Content-based filtering and Cooperative Filtering. Here the three techniques are merged so that offline and online information are used efficiently to avoid scalability and sparsity problems in recommendation systems. Adding Real Value Genetic algorithm as a special feature to the problem where the density of users are more in datasets and samples are discretized where the variables are continuous. This paper conjointly analyzed that recommendations are influenced by the factors like age, gender, occupation and a few alternative user profile data. This work consist both content and collaborative Filtering methods and certain demographic information are merged into a hybrid approach, wherever further content options are used to enhance the exactness of Recommendation Systems. Conjointly, it tends to use the Real value genetic algorithm to get accurate results and to provide recommendations to the user.

1 INTRODUCTION

An increasing demand of social networking websites Recommendation has become a necessary process to increase the more relevant information, which is to be recommending to people. Based on many research papers the Recommender Systems is defined as recommending an item to consumer. Now a day's many websites are popularizing their products by endorsement system. Example is amazon.com, Netflix.com and movielens.com etc. Recommender systems can be categorized into custom-made in which the users past behaviour or preferences are taken into consideration in recommending new items to consumer. This paper specifies the consumer's implicit ratings where as non-personalized recommendation is a top most challenging items for user recommendation.

It can (Adomavicius, G.et al. 2005) offer individual insides, facilities and data items to latent customers to step-down of information repossession time and support decision making process. This happens due to consumers explicit grading is not constantly available and the implicit grading like purchase history, downloading behaviour and click on patterns etc. become further vital data cause for recommender systems. In Social networking sites, Cooperative Filtering with grouping information becomes prevalent. Additionally, serving to user combine his/her individual information, a label can furthermore be discovered as a consumer's own judgement, whereas tagging may be measured as tacit rating or pick on the labelled info resources or things. Therefore the classification of data may be used to mark endorsements (Liang, H.et al, 2008). At present a number of the researches that specialize in what means they can use tagging information in Collaborative Filtering information (Banda, L.et al 2014) and (Banda, L.et al 2014) and (Banda, L. et al. 2015) and(Banda, L.et al 2012) to endorse modified labels to consumers, however not considerable work may done on make use of labelling facts to support consumers to find concerned items effortlessly and rapidly. This work is mainly focusing on in what way to endorse things to consumers based on label data by using real value genetic algorithm. Classically Recommender Systems information, such as URLs, Netnews articles, entertainment books, movies, restaurants, or individual specialists. Amazon.com and MovieLens.org are two eminent samples of RS on the internet. Recommender systems are divided into 4 filtering techniques as follows (Adomavicius, G.et al. 2005) and [6]:

1. Demographic filtering (DMF) The filtering technique applies on user profiles, to recommend the data to the user.
2. Content-based filtering (CBF) Items are recommended to a consumer, favoured in ancient.
3. Collaborative filtering (CF) Recommendation is based on similar taste of users. Group Lens, Movie Lens is illustrations of such systems.
4. Hybrid RS (HRS) Filtering techniques merge one or more filtering technique to enrich the performance. Fab and Amazon.com are examples of HRS

To decide the significance of endorsements it permits consumers to feat the reactions of previous readers. Automatic Cooperative primarily based systems tracked to mechanically find connected estimations and change of integrity them to create recommendations. Amazon.com is that the most well-liked application mistreatment this technology during which they suggest things for the users supported their purchase and browsing history.

Almost all cooperative filtering is that the most acquainted and generally accepted technique. It works on gathering and analysing the large quantity of user's knowledge by trailing user actions and preferences to predict recommendations supported the connection with alternative users. It provides recommendations supported straightforward principles that like folks have alike interest (Verma, A.et al. 2015). This is mainly divided into two foremost categories (i) Memory Based Method-e.g. Nearest Neighbourhood method (ii) Model Based Method-e.g. Bayesian Classifier

This paper focuses on a proposed hybrid movie recommender system where both content and collaborative techniques along with some demographic information are combined, wherever supplementary content features are used to enhance the accuracy of cooperative filtering and the genetic algorithm (Goldberg, D.et al.1992) besides correlation is employed to supply recommendations to the user.

In modern year, moreover the grading on the things provided by the consumers, an increasing number of modern recommender systems additionally enables the users to feature customized tags, within the kind of words or phrases to the things. For example, consumers might add tags to movies in Movie Lens, to websites in Del.icio.us and to references in Cite U Like. Such tagging information might offer terribly helpful data for item recommendation, as a result of the user's interests in things are often indirectly reflected by the tags that they regularly use (Zhen, Y.et al. 2009).

Tagging is incredibly helpful for users to work out different users with similar interests among a given class. Users with similar interests may post similar tags and similar resources might need similar tags denote to them. Cooperative filtering is wide employed in automatic prediction system. The idea behind it's terribly simple: people who in agreement within the past tend to agree once more within the future. Ancient cooperative filtering systems have 2 steps. The primary step is to spot users who share equivalent grading samples with the active user whom the prediction is for. Then, the systems can use the grading from those similar users found within the start to calculate a prediction for the active user (Zhang, Y.et al. 2009). Since for every tag, users and resources within the check information also are within the training file, this could make use of the history of users' tag, conjointly referred to as personomy and tags formerly announce to the resource to mention tags for an energetic post.

This paper includes five sections. Section 1 talked about introduction, Section 2 defines connected work. Section 3 describes the planned methodology to be monitored to recommend movies to the user. Section 4 discussed about the experimental analysis. Section 5 concludes this paper and talked about future scope.

2   RELATED WORK

At present a good quantity of researcher who is working on RS algorithm by using attributes as background knowledge (Adomavicius, G.et al. 2005). Conversely, to the best of our knowledge, there hasn't been any analysis in considering tags with RS algorithms to predict items. Recommender systems (RS) are built to help users prevent information overload problems which make finding desired information more time-consuming and sometimes exhausting process. They assist users when they are not experienced enough to make a choice among all alternatives. There are two categories of RS in general: collaborative filtering (CF) (Zhen, Y.et al. 2009).

And content-based filtering (CB) (Zhang, Y.et al. 2009).. Multidimensional RS is an association between users, items and tags, wherever another dimension of data which is traditional two-dimensional user/item methodology is used. Author (Adomavicius, G.et al. 2005) suggested a reduction from multiple dimensional to 2D dimensional depictions where traditional RS algorithms can be directly applied.

CF systems conventionally use Pearson Correlation Coefficient to evaluate user similarity. The similarity computation is performed using the formula

$$corr(\text{a}, \text{b}) = \frac{\sum_{s \in S_{ab}} (r_{a,s} - m_a)(r_{b,s} - m_b)}{\sqrt{\sum_{s \in S_{ab}} (r_{a,s} - a)^2} \sqrt{\sum_{s \in S_{ab}} (r_{b,s} - m_b)^2}} \tag{1}$$

The above formula is not applicable as a result of it contemplates only common items for each user. To calculate similarity of multiple features Euclidian distance could be used.

$$d(a, b) = \frac{1}{n} \sum_{i=1}^{n} \sqrt{\sum_{j=1}^{N} (a_{i,j} - b_{i,j})^2} \tag{2}$$

In Cosine similarity technique, the inverse user frequency is applied, the similarity between users, x and y is calculated by the subsequent equation:

$$sim(x, y) = \cos(\vec{x}, \vec{y}) = \frac{\sum_{t \in T} (A_{x,t}.ixf_t)(A_{y,t}.ixf_t)}{\sqrt{\sum_{t \in T} (A_{x,t}.ixf_t)^2} \sqrt{\sum_{t \in T} (A_{y,t}.ixf_t)^2}} \tag{3}$$

As cooperative tagging Kim, (H. N.et al. 2010) is getting more commonly used, this data may even be utilized as background information in RS. Earlier not a single investigation has done in integrating tags information to expand recommendation quality for such purpose. Here the three dimensional matrix <user,item,tag> is divided into two dimensional matrix as <user,item>, <user,tag> and <item,tag> (Al-Shamri, M. Y.et al. 2008).

The synthesis of the user- and item-based expectations would be completed by calculating the sum of the two conditional chances that are constructed on user- and item-based similarities, that are computed using standard user- and item-based CF. A parameter, λ, is introduced to regulate the significance of the 2 predictions (Saini, S.et al. 2012).

$$P(r_{x,i}|w(x, y))\lambda + P(r_{x,i}|w(i, z))(1 - \lambda) \tag{4}$$

2.1 Genetic Algorithm

GA is used to find the optimal similarity function. This paper includes supervised learning task (Kim, H. N et al.2010) whose fitness function is the MAE (Mean absolute error) (Bobadilla, J.et al.2011) of the RS. In this means, the population of our genetic formula is that the set of various vectors of weights, w. Every individual, that's to mention every vector of weights, represents an attainable similarity live (Gaffney, J.et al 2010), that we'll appraise the MAE of the RS victimization this similarity measures. Whereas running our GA, the sequential population generations tend to boost the MAE within the RS. Our GA stops generating populations once MAE within the RS for a vector of weights is not up to the brink.

Standard GA

1. A procedure for selecting the initial population.
2. Finding fitness function by using threshold value
3. Find the sampling rate of an individual
4. Select the chromosomes/samples to regeneration
5. Regenerated operators to generate new chromosomes
6. A procedure for choosing mutation or crossover operator to apply

The question of whether to use a binary or real encoding of GA can be contentious. The traditional GA uses a binary encoding. However, in many applications actual encoding is used. Various arguments are given as to whether a binary or real encoding should be used. It is not always immediately evident which encoding method should be adopted (Pazzani, M. J. 1999). It seems that the discretization of the parameter space plays a role in the computational efficiently of the GA.

3 PROPOSED APPROACH

3.1 Learning weights using Genetic Algorithm (GA)

The crossover and mutation are the most important operators of the genetic algorithm. The performance is calculated by mainly these two operators. Every user puts a distinct priority on every feature, which might be observed as feature weight. These feature weights required to be captured and fine-tuned to replicate every user's preference. The feature weights of user u_a are epitomised as a set of weights, weight $(u_a) = [w_i]$ $i= 1...n$ where n is the number of features (Goldberg, D.et al,1992).

In this learning weights are specified with the help of genetic algorithm. In each step, mutation and crossover operator (Anand, D. 2012) replaces bad individuals to good newly generated individuals. Lastly, the group of weights persist what is the best fits in the selection criteria. The set of weights are $\{W_1, W_2$ and $W_3\}$ and each weight range is [0, 1].

3.2 The fitness function

Calculating the fitness function could be a challenging problem for GA. For each set of weights in genetic algorithm all the set of weights in GA population should be employed by the profile matching process within the recommender system. Therefore, the RS (Burke, R. 2002)needs to be re-run on the whole database. The typical distinction between real and foretold grading for every single users in training set is employed as fitness score for that set of weights (Goldberg, D et al.1992).

$$\text{Fitness} = \frac{1}{n_R} \sum_{j=0}^{n_R} |r_j - p(r_j)| \qquad (5)$$

3.3 *Proposed algorithm*

Input: User, Item, Tag, genre and time data

1. Arrange the datasets according to content-based, collaborative and demographic profiles of user
2. Sort the input data according to the timestamp with user's demographic data with genre interest
3. Mine the data from step 2 with attributes user-data, item-data, tag-data and genre-data
4. Compute user-item, item-tag and user-tag matrix
5. Apply real GA on these matrices: user-item, item-tag and user-tag
6. Compute the similarities of users by weight learning through Genetic Algorithm
7. Then find the fitness values by keeping some threshold value.
8. Calculate MAE Precision and Recall.

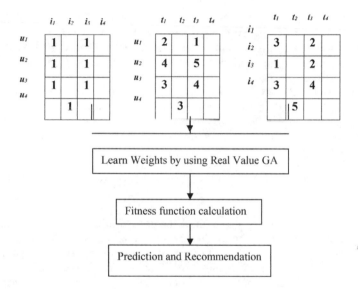

Figure 1. Block diagram of proposed approach.

4 EXPERIMENTAL RESULTS AND ANALYSIS

The observational data has been chosen from the movie Lens website. On the basis of this dataset, this method chosen 600 users those are rated at least 50 movies. For every movie dataset, this extracted subset of more than 10,000 users with minimum number of 40 ratings. After equating these algorithms, we experimented with numerous configurations. For Movie Lens dataset, the training set is applied to primary 100, 200 and 300 users. Such a random separation was intended for the execution of one fold cross validation where all the experiments are repeated one time for 100 users, 200 users and 300 users. For movie Lens we use the testing set 40% of every user. As stated above, this methodology can solve the difficult of scalability and sparsity concerns. In direction to illustrate the performance of this approach, we compare the MAE of Collaborative Filtering with tagging (CFT), Hybrid recommender systems with tagging (HRST) [20], HRS based on tagging using GA (HRST-GA) and HRS based on tagging using real value GA (HRST-RGA). The results of these four methods are shown in Figure 2. The result concludes that the system with less number of recommendation and high precision, it would perform better and the outcome of recall vs. number of recommendation will be shown.

439

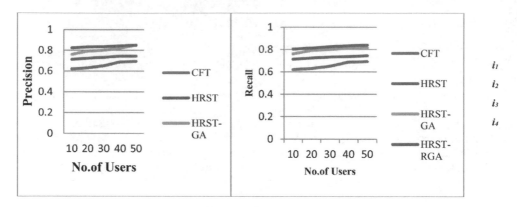

Figure 2.   Precision and recall of tag recommendation system.

Undoubtedly it shown in the table that the HRST-RGA has lower range of MAE as compare to other three methods i.e. CFT, HRST and HRST-GA. With Real GA the Hybrid recommender systems based on tagging outperforms other than three methods in respective of MAE and prediction accuracy.

Here we have used multi Point Crossover with the Population size of 25, Crossover rate of 0.5, Real GA was run for more than 1000 trials. Multiple runs were done to tune parameters, more than 1000 experiments at each mutation rate from 0.002 to 0.02 in steps of 0.002, more than 1000 experiments would done at each combination of a mutation size and mutation rate.

CONCLUSION

This research manuscript proposes and implements a unique and efficient framework for collaborative tagging to produce the quality recommendations with higher prediction accuracy. The proposed approach uses Hybrid recommender systems using real value GA to learn appropriate weights for the three similarity measures to enrich the quality and accuracy of recommendation. The observational results demonstrate that the suggested scheme could significantly improve the quality, accuracy of expectations.

REFERENCES

Adomavicius, G. & Tuzhilin, A. 2005. Toward the next generation of recommender systems: A survey of the state-of-the-art and possible extensions. *IEEE Transactions on Knowledge & Data Engineering* 6: 734-749.

Al-Shamri, M. Y. H., & Bharadwaj, K. K. 2008. Fuzzy-genetic approach to recommender systems based on a novel hybrid user model. *Expert systems with applications* 35(3):1386-1399.

Anand, D. 2012. Feature extraction for collaborative filtering: A genetic programming approach. *International Journal of Computer Science Issues (IJCSI)* 9(5):348.

Banda, L., & Bharadwaj, K. K. 2015. E-FCM Algorithms for Collaborative Tagging System. In Proceedings of the 3rd International Conference on Frontiers of Intelligent Computing: Theory and Applications (FICTA) 2014: 89-97.

Banda, L., & Bharadwaj, K. K. 2012. Improving scalability issues in collaborative filtering based on collaborative tagging using genre interestingness measure.

Banda, L., & Bharadwaj, K. K. 2014. Evaluation of Collaborative Filtering Based on Tagging with Diffusion Similarity Using Gradual Decay Approach. In Advanced Computing, Networking and Informatics 1: 421-428.

Banda, L., & Bharadwaj, K. K. 2014. An approach to enhance the quality of recommendation using collaborative tagging. *International Journal of Computational Intelligence Systems*, 7(4):650-659.

Bobadilla, J., Ortega, F., Hernando, A., & Alcalá, J. 2011. Improving collaborative filtering recommender system results and performance using genetic algorithms. *Knowledge-based systems*, 24 (8):1310-1316.

Burke, R. 2002. Hybrid recommender systems: Survey and experiments. *User modeling and user-adapted interaction*, 12(4):331-370.

Goldberg, D., Nichols, D., Oki, B. M., & Terry, D. 1992. Using collaborative filtering to weave an information tapestry. *Communications of the ACM*, 35(12):61-70.

Gaffney, J., Pearce, C., & Green, D. 2010. Binary versus real coding for genetic algorithms: A false dichotomy?. *ANZIAM Journal* 51:347-359.

Kim, H. N., Ji, A. T., Ha, I., & Jo, G. S. 2010. Collaborative filtering based on collaborative tagging for enhancing the quality of recommendation. *Electronic Commerce Research and Applications*, 9(1):73-83.

Liang, H., Xu, Y., Li, Y. & Nayak, R. 2008. Collaborative filtering recommender systems using tag information. In Proceedings of the 2008 IEEE/WIC/ACM International Conference on Web Intelligence and Intelligent Agent Technology 03: 59-62.

Pazzani, M. J. 1999. A framework for collaborative, content-based and demographic filtering. Artificial intelligence review 13(5-6):393-408.

Saini, S. & Banda, I. 2012. Improving scalability issues using gim in collaborative filtering based on tagging. *International Journal of Advances in Engineering & Technology* 4(1):600-610.

Verma, A., & Kaur, H. V. 2015. A hybrid recommender system using genetic algorithm and kNN approach. *International Journal of Computer Science And Technology* 6(3):131-134.

Zhen, Y., Li, W. J., & Yeung, D. Y. 2009, October. TagiCoFi: tag informed collaborative filtering. In Proceedings of the third ACM conference on Recommender systems: 69-76.

Zhang, Y., Zhang, N., & Tang, J. 2009. A collaborative filtering tag recommendation system based on graph. ECML PKDD discovery challenge:297-306.

Communication and Computing Systems – Prasad et al. (eds)
© *2019 Taylor & Francis Group, London, ISBN 978-0-367-00147-6*

Data Lake: A plausible Big Data science for business intelligence

Satvik Vats & B.B. Sagar
Computer Science and Engineering, Birla Institute of Technology, Mesra-Ranchi

ABSTRACT: Big Data analytics is a more extensive term that incorporates data analysis. Data analytics is a train that includes the administration of the total data lifecycle, which integrates gathering, cleansing, sorting out, separating and overseeing data. The term combines the improvement of review strategies, logical procedures and computerized devices. In this paper, we reviewed the concept of Data Lake with the characteristics of Big Data, in Big Data environments, data analytics has created strategies that permit data analysis to occur using profoundly adaptable conveyed developments and systems that are fit for breaking down substantial volumes of data from various sources.

KEYWORDS: Data Lake, Big Data, business intelligence

1 INTRODUCTION

In present era, we live with variety of digital connection that generates variety of data. Generation of the data depends upon the sources and source depends upon human interaction. Rapid growth of digital world will lead prediction and forecasting facility in different domain. For a data set to be viewed as Big Data, it must have at least one attributes that require suitability in the procedure plan and design of the expository condition. Ultimately, the goal is to behavior study of the data in such a way that good results are delivered in an appropriate style, which provides optimum rate to the creativity. So how data will become big, answer is its characteristics. 6 V's defines the big data characteristics.

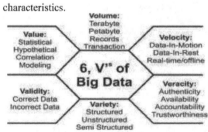

Figure 1.   6 Vs of Big Data.

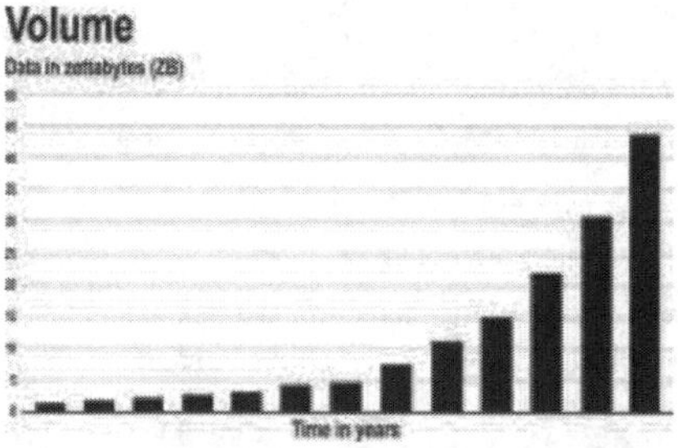

Figure 2.   Growth of volume.

Why 'Volume': Volume defines the size of the data; large amount of data requires distinct data storage and processing demands with proper data management. For example, online transaction, GPS, RFIDs, Facebook, Twitter etc. Figure 2 Offers a growth illustration of the huge volume of information being formed day-to-day by organizations and operators world-wide.

Figure 3. Representation of Velocity.

Figure 4. Representation of Variety.

Figure 5. Representation of Veracity.

How 'Velocity': Velocity is defining the speed of enormous data set generation within short span time. For example, we can say that in 60 second, 350000 tweets generated, 300 hours of video uploaded by YouTube etc.

What 'Variety': Variety defines the multiple formats and structure of the data. Different sources generate different kind of data which is a big issue and challenge for enterprise to perform data integration, transformation, processing and storage. For example, structured, textual, image, video, audio, XML, JSON, sensor data & meta data.

How close 'Veracity': Information that comes into the big data environment must require quality assessment that leads better data processing and remove noise. In context of relation to veracity, data may be signal or noise. Noise data would not be converted into the valuable information and on other side signal carrying relevant information which need to extract. In terms of veracity, information which has high signal-to-noise ratio has more veracity compare to information with lower ratio. For example, information which is generated by controlled sources such as online customer registration normally is having less noise than the information generated by uncontrolled source such as blog postings. So, the ratio of signal-to-noise completely depends upon source from where data generated.

What 'Validity': Like veracity, validity states to how precise and exact the data is for the future utilization. According to knowledge extraction, it is found that, a huge amount of time

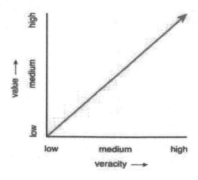

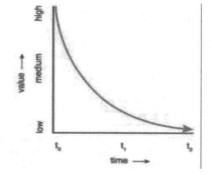

Figure 6(A). Relationship between Veracity and Value, Thomas erl et al., (2016).

Figure 6(B). Relationship between Value and Time, Thomas erl et al., (2016).

is consumed by cleaning process before perform analysis on it. Advantage of big data analytics is possible only when data is adopted from original sources which provide original data.

Whose 'Value': Importance of information for an enterprise is defined by value. Characteristic of the value spontaneously related with characteristics of veracity as shown in Figure 6A, it can be expressed as higher veracity will have more value for the business. In other aspect value and time is inversely linked as shown in Figure 6B. Larger time for data will lead meaningful information.

It can also show by the plot that reflects the impact on value by veracity of information and timeliness of analytics result. Apart from veracity and time value also depends upon, how data been stored, cleaning process etc.

2   BUSINESS INTELLIGENCE

Business intelligence defines the product possibility of the particular. Business intelligence provides to an organization to gain enhance its performance by the help of analysis on the data which is generated by its business. The outcome of the analysis process leads to manage the business efforts and detect the issues or difficulties that found in previous process.

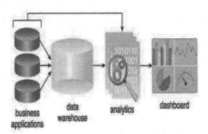

Figure 7.   Business intelligence, Thomas erl et al., (2016).

By the Figure 7, it is clear that data coming from different sources stores in the data warehouse from where the analytics algorithms applied and the outcome of the analytics will reflect on the dashboard. Basically, dashboard gives visualization facility that shows the graphical activities of the product for business perspective.

3   DATA LAKE

As the name suggest the data lake is a huge storage that is able to store any kind of data and provides an environment like its native format until the user change it. Data lake is just like a pond which has many organisms, stones, gravels and sand in its own native environment. The basic idea behind the data lake is to have a centralize storage for all the enterprise data in the captive from raw data (which is just generated and no transformation is applied on this data) to fully processed data which is further utilized to have an insight from the data by applying analytics, machine learning techniques, and visualizations.

Data lake is introduced to provide or facilitate the enterprises to centralize the disparate content sources. When the centralization is done, these different sources are mapped and can be combines and processed as per their information characteristics (source of data and type of data with format) using the big data. If the combination not occur, it will impossible to do the search and analytics on these data. We can also say that, data lake is the extend or the advanced version of the data mart, as data mart which is introduced for the same work but it has a small repository so to overcome this issue, Data lake is introduced. All contents (files, tables, reports etc.) from the multiple sources of data generation or business units will be ingested into the data lake or the staging repository (i.e. based on Cloudera/Horton-works/MapR, Azure, Amazon etc.) and then this stored or deposited data is searched (using multiple search engines such as Cloudera Search or Elastic-search, Hortonworks search). When a user feels it necessary or needed, the content will be analyzed and then results will be provided to users via distributed search on a multiple system based on User interfaces across various platforms. The below Figure 8 is expressing all the functioning about the data lake. Data lake is directly connected in the cluster or can say enterprise infra, which facilitate Data lake to get the data directly into it. On top of it the search engine works which help the user to get the required data from the data lake and the result of the search can again transfer to the multiple Hadoop frameworks (hive, spark, Pig, scala etc.) for further analysis.

Data lake is characterized on its different –different key attributes which give a crisp insight of the data lake to describe its function as well. Following are the attributes:

- Data lake collect everything: the data lake can collect or contains all the data, i.e. raw data for a longer time period as well as processed data.
- It can be drive in anywhere: Data lake opens the access for the user from the different units of the multiple business to work, explore the data and if needed create enriched insight by different practises of analytics.
- Flexible access: A Data Lake enables multiple data access patterns across a shared infrastructure i.e. the batch, interactive GUI, online web portal access, search in the in-memory and other processing engines.

Features and benefits of the Data Lake:

- Data in the lake is: the data present in the data lake is in different format like Structured/ semi-structured/unstructured and raw
- Processing: Processing for the lake is Schema-on-read
- Storage in the lake is: to overcome the cost, data lake is designed for providing low-cost storage.
- Agility in the lake is: Highly agile, configure and customisable if a user needed
- Security in the lake is: Maturing.

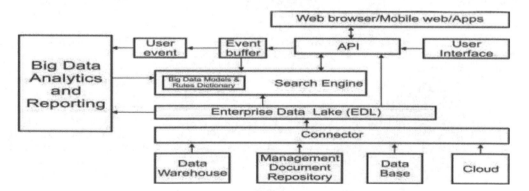

Figure 8.   Data Lake architecture.

Authors	Brief Introduction	Methodology Used
Feng Zhang et al., (2016)	They introduce a novel data formation, and propose linear time algorithms to analyze the similarities.	They have used the machine learning technique "Recommender system" concept.
Kayode Sakariyah et al., (2016)	They represent a complete survey of interrelated study that deal with finding of malicious accounts on social networking sites.	They have used the parameter to review the malicious account like "Spam Account, Fake Account, Compromised Account and Phishing strategy"
Chuang Ma et al., (2014)	In this study authors introduces the essential concepts and measures of machine- learning applications that connects big data technology to provide basic study for the plant sciences.	In this paper authors performs methods of machine learning techniques like, classification, clustering, regression with integration concept of Hadoop and Map-Reduce for plant science data of biotechnology.
Daniel Pakkala et al., (2015)	This study has introduced self-regulating reference design for big data systems.	In this paper author uses the classification technique of machine learning on Hadoop cluster for simplifying commercial solution when using the big data environment.
Kostas Kolomvatsos et al., (2015)	In this paper, they have proposed a method that can be adopted by the Query controller.	The proposed method is able of organizing fractional results retrieved by a number of processors each one in charge for each cluster. Each processor executes a query over a specific cluster of data.
Tao Huang et al., (2015)	This paper summarizes the newest applications of Big Data in health sciences.	This paper uses the recommendation systems in healthcare, Internet-based prevalent surveillance, sensor-based health situations and food safety specialist care, Genome-Wide Association Studies (GWAS).
Yiming Qin et al., (2015)	This paper estimates various state-of-the-art high-throughput procedures of bioinformatics.	This paper performs Computational Analysis on Genomic Big Data.
Shaokun Fan et al., (2015)	They have anticipated the methods of business intelligence using big data analysis.	For business intelligence, they have evaluated the constraint like people, product, place, price, and promotion.
Feras A.Batarseh et al., (2015)	This paper provides the implementation and evaluation on Quality of Service (QoS) Using Big Data Analytics on Healthcare.	They perform the evaluation on data such as clinical data, pharmacy data, diagnostic data, patient history, monitoring instruments.
Mohammad Naimur Rahman et al., (2016)	In this paper author proposes Hybrid Data Architecture for Big Data analysis.	In this work, they introduce hybrid electrical and optical networking architecture for data centers hosting Cloud Computing and Big Data applications.
Wullianallur Raghupathi et al., (2014)	This paper describes the promise and potential of big data analytics in healthcare.	The paper describes the nascent field of big data analytics in healthcare, discusses the benefits, outlines an architectural framework and methodology, describes examples reported in the literature, briefly discusses the Challenges, and offers conclusions.

(Continued)

Authors	Brief Introduction	Methodology Used
Rui Máximo Esteves et al., (2016)	They perform k-means clustering.	This work provides the performance of Mahout using a large data set. The tests were running on Amazon EC2 instances and allowed to compare the gain in runtime when running on a multi node cluster.
Xin Chen et al., (2014)	In this study, author performs analyses on student learning experience using social media data by the help of mining technique.	This study they proposed a workflow to combine both qualitative analysis and large-scale data mining techniques. They focused on engineering students' Twitter posts to recognize issues and problems in their educational experiences with the help of multi label classification algorithm.
Feng Xia et al., (2016)	This article examines the background and state of the art of big scholarly data.	They introduce the environment of scholarly data management and applicable technologies. Secondly, they assess data analysis methods, such as statistical analysis, social network analysis, and content analysis for dealing with big scholarly data.

5   POSSIBLE HADOOP INTEGRATION

5.1   *Apache mahout*

As the name suggest the mahout is the person who drives an elephant and take care of it. In the big data, the mahout is the framework which work on top of Hadoop to facilitate the Hadoop to do the machine learning things, and algorithms for the data analysis. As we all know Hadoop is an open source framework given by the apache software foundation which allows you to store and process a large amount of data in distributed manner. Apache software foundation created the Apache mahout which is an open source project, primarily for the scalable and fast machine learning algorithms. In mahout, there are few machine learning techniques are implemented such as:

• Recommendation
• Classification
• Clustering

5.2   *RHadoop*

RHadoop is nothing but the integration of the R programming language with the Hadoop. R is a programming language which comes with a software bundle which is used for data analysis, statistical analysis, statistical computing and the data visualization. There is an inbuilt feature of graphs and plots which help the user to visualize the work at the same platform. R is designed in such a way that it covers all the object-oriented features. R studio is the Integrated Development Environment (IDE) or can say development kit which is used to write and run R scripts. RHadoop is the model or can say a combine framework of Hadoop and the R programming language which has the three important packages i.e. RMap-Reduce (rmr), R Hadoop Distributed File system (rhdfs) and the last is R Hbase (rhbase). These three packages facilitate the R to work on top of Hadoop and use the Hadoop for data analysis. rmr facilitates the MapReduce functionality, rhdfs facilitates the storage and file management where as rhbase provides the functionalities of the database management system.

5.3 *Splunk*

Splunk is a web-based software which is created by the Splunk inc. Splunk is mainly used for the monitoring, reporting and visualizing the big data which is generated by the machines of systems. Splunk main motive is to make the data accessible throughout the organization just by identifying the data patterns, hosts, data metrics identifying the problems and gives a broader big insight of data for the business operations. Splunk is a technology which is used in an organization just to facilitate the working of application and application management systems, security of the infrastructure of organization and compliance, as well as business and web analytics

6   CONCLUSION

By the review, there is no doubt that big data analytics is in primary stage. There is various platform which has capacity to make integration with present tools to create hybrid algorithm. By the hybrid algorithm we may create various strategies that have the capacity to perform variety of analytics process on huge amount of data or on an entire repository.

REFERENCES

Adewole, K.S., Anuar, N.B., Kamsin, A., Varathan, K.D. and Razak, S.A., 2017. Malicious accounts: dark of the social networks. *Journal of Network and Computer Applications*, 79, pp.41-67.

Batarseh, F.A. and Latif, E.A., 2016. Assessing the quality of service using Big Data analytics: With application to healthcare. *Big Data Research*, 4, pp.13-24.

Chen, X., Vorvoreanu, M. and Madhavan, K., 2014. Mining social media data for understanding students' learning experiences. *IEEE Transactions on Learning Technologies*, 7(3), pp.246-259.

Erl, T., Khattak, W. and Buhler, P., 2016. *Big Data Fundamentals*. Prentice Hall: Upper Saddle River, NJ, USA.

Esteves, R.M., Pais, R. and Rong, C., 2011, March. K-means clustering in the cloud–a Mahout test. In *Advanced Information Networking and Applications (WAINA), 2011 IEEE Workshops of International Conference on* (pp. 514-519). IEEE.

Fan, S., Lau, R.Y. and Zhao, J.L., 2015. Demystifying big data analytics for business intelligence through the lens of marketing mix. *Big Data Research*, 2(1), pp.28-32.

Huang, T., Lan, L., Fang, X., An, P., Min, J. and Wang, F., 2015. Promises and challenges of big data computing in health sciences. *Big Data Research*, 2(1), pp.2-11.

Kolomvatsos, K., Anagnostopoulos, C. and Hadjiefthymiades, S., 2015. An efficient time optimized scheme for progressive analytics in big data. *Big Data Research*, 2(4), pp.155-165.

Ma, C., Zhang, H.H. and Wang, X., 2014. Machine learning for big data analytics in plants. *Trends in plant science*, 19(12), pp.798-808.

Pääkkönen, P. and Pakkala, D., 2015. Reference architecture and classification of technologies, products and services for big data systems. *Big Data Research*, 2(4), pp.166-186.

Qin, Y., Yalamanchili, H.K., Qin, J., Yan, B. and Wang, J., 2015. The current status and challenges in computational analysis of genomic big data. *Big data research*, 2(1), pp.12-18.

Raghupathi, W. and Raghupathi, V., 2014. Big data analytics in healthcare: promise and potential. *Health information science and systems*, 2(1), p.3.

Rahman, M.N. and Esmailpour, A., 2016. A hybrid data center architecture for big data. *Big Data Research*, 3, pp.29-40.

Xia, F., Wang, W., Bekele, T.M. and Liu, H., 2017. Big scholarly data: A survey. *IEEE Transactions on Big Data*, 3(1), pp.18-35.

Zhang, F., Gong, T., Lee, V.E., Zhao, G., Rong, C. and Qu, G., 2016. Fast algorithms to evaluate collaborative filtering recommender systems. *Knowledge-Based Systems*, 96, pp.96-103.

Communication and Computing Systems – Prasad et al. (eds)
© 2019 Taylor & Francis Group, London, ISBN 978-0-367-00147-6

Brain tumor detection using supervisory nearest neighbor algorithm

K. Sudha Rani
Department of EIE, VNR VJIET, Bachupally, Hyderabad, India

K. Mani Kumari
Department of Mechanical Eng, Vardaman College of Engineering, India

K. Aruna Kumari
Department of ECE, VNR VJIET, Bachupally, Hyderabad, India

T.Gnana Prakash
Department. of CSE, VNR VJIET, Bachupally, Hyderabad, India

ABSTRACT: Uncontrolled growth of irregular mass that might develop into a lump in any portion of the body is a tumor, when it grows in the brain it is a brain tumor. Many researchers have developed brain tumor detection algorithms using Unsupervisory techniques. Statistical parameters like Sensitivity, accuracy etc. for the Unsupervisory techniques is lower than the Supervisory techniques. Supervisory based Nearest Neighbor (NN) algorithm has been developed with the different distance metrics like sum, maximum and Euclidian. From statistical parameters calculations, it is observed that NN classifier with Euclidian distance metric yields excellent results than Sum and Max distance metrics.

KEYWORDS: Brain Tumor, NN Algorithm, Training, classification, Statistical Parameter

1 INTRODUCTION

Brain tumors are classified as two types Benign and Malignant. Benign tumors are not very dangerous tumors and may take longer time to show its effect. These tumors are cured if detected early. However the malignant type, grow faster and may lead to be fatal if not detected and treated at early stage.

In general, defected lesions will be highlighted in the scanned image. The task is to detect them perfectly without human involvement. To identify and localize the tumor region (Raman et al.2011) have discussed the region dependent segmentation method.

Tumor areas in any portion of the human body are typically with higher contrast in the MR image compared with adjacent tissues and have nearly constant pixel intensities and fuzzy borders. The brain tumor algorithms are mainly categorized as supervised and unsupervised methods.

Unsupervised methods directly work on the MR images by grouping or splitting it, while supervised methods initially need to be trained and then classified discussed by Guerra et al. (2011) .P. Rahmati et al. (2012) have proposed an active contours method to detect and seg-menttumors. J.Chakraborty et al. (2012) developed a multilevel thresholding technique combined with region growing method to achieve edge contours. FilipeR et al. (2015) proposed a semi supervised method on mammography MR images using grow cut technique. A grow cut method is an interactive segmentation procedure capable to segment the Region of interest (RIO) by choosing suitable internal and external seed points. Some of the unsupervised

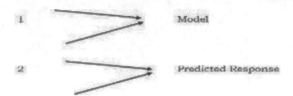

Figure 1. Supervised algorithms working concept.

techniques have been discussed in previous chapters. Clustering method has been used by the authors Dumitriu D et al. (2007), Helmstaedter M et al. (2009), Karagiannis A et al. (2009) and McGarryLM et al. (2010) which was aimed at discovery of new sub-clusters.

L. Lefkovits et al. (2017) have compared the supervised and unsupervised classification algorithms and concluded that the performance of the supervised classification algorithm is greater than hierarchical clustering (unsupervised technique). The supervised process is executed in the following two steps represented pictorially in Figure 1.

i) Training the algorithm
ii) Classification of the algorithm

Training the algorithm includes number of training samples. Each sample in the training class (model) is a pair, containing an input object and a desired output object. A supervised learning algorithm analyses the training data and produces an indirect function, which can be used for mapping new examples.

Freeman et al. (2002) proposed globalized nearest neighbor method using the Markov network method. Chang et al. (2004) proposed nearest neighbor regression with novel weighting vectors. Karl (2009) proposed an interpolation method using adaptive k-NN method with markov random technique. Atkins & Bouman (1998) proposed classification related adaptive filtering method using the Gaussian distribution. A. P. Dempster et al. (1977) has been proposed the expectation maximization algorithm and K. Su et al. (2005) and Vadivel et al. (2003) have been discussed the differences between the distance metrics e.g. manhattan, Euclidian and modified Euclidian distance.

In the present work, the work has been carried out with detection of No tumor/tumor detection and classification.

2 METHODOLOGY

Initially, pre-processing operations like resampling, colour plane extraction and image histogram analysis are performed on MR images. Resamplingh as been applied on the MR images for appropriate geometrical representation of the images and are resampled with the dimensions 256X256 pixels. Using with colour plan extraction any 16-bit or 32-bit is converted into 8-bit image. Then histogram analysis (viz. minimum value, maximum value and mean) has been applied on the resampled images. Then the algorithm has been trained into two classes (C), "tumor class" and "no tumor class". Each class is trained with the number of samples(S). And these samples are always greater than the classes (S > C). After successfully completing the training algorithm, next important step is applying the classification techniques. Several classifiers are available for the image segmentation. In present work NN Classifier have been used, because of its less time consumption and accurate classification results. These classifiers have to be used with different distance metrics like Euclidian, sum and maximum. 1.2.1. K-NN Algorithm. Nearest neighbor is another type of k-NN group, where k value is 1 (k = 1). In this case, new data point target class will be assigned to the 1st closest neighbor. NN and K-NN algorithm have been implemented on the brain tumor images to detect and classify the brain tumors. In K-NN algorithm, K value has been selected as 3. K-NN is a slow machine learning process but yields excellent results. The accuracy depends on the number of samples on

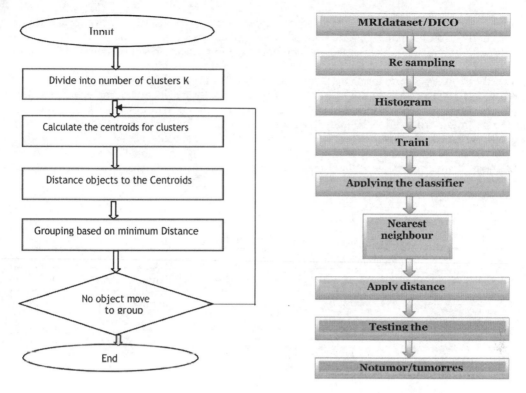

Figure 2.   Consolidated flow chart for the NN and K-NN algorithms.

which it has undergone training. Proposed algorithm flowchart for no tumor/tumor detection and classification is shown in the Figure 2.

3   RESULTS AND DISCUSSIONS

Intelligent supervised algorithm for detection of no tumor and tumor has been developed with NN and K–NN techniques with distance metrics like Euclidian, sum and maximum Totally two classes were categorized, no tumor class and tumor class. The identification scores and distance metrics have been calculated for 55 images. Only 9 patient images result have been included in the tables in this work. The range of identification scores are shown here for TP images only. For FN are identification score is "0".In this work, NN algorithm has been trained with 200 samples and tested with 40 tumor images and 15 no tumor images. Identification status of the images (TP, TN, FP and FN) has been performed with sum, max and Euclidian distance metrics. TN (tumor as tumor) is identified with sum, max and Euclidian distance metrics are 34, 36 and 38 respectively. For Euclidian distance has true positive rate more than other two metrics. Therefore true positive rate (sensitivity) is more than two metrics. TN (no tumor as tumor) is identified with sum, max and Euclidian distance metrics are 11, 12 and 14 respectively. So, true negative rate (specificity) is more than other two metrics. FP (no tumor is identified as tumor) are identified with sum, max and Euclidian distance metrics are 04, 03 and 01 respectively. FP is less with the Euclidian distance metric than other two metrics. Therefore, accuracy is more in Euclidian distance metric other than two distance metrics. FN (tumor is identified as no tumor) are identified with sum, max and Euclidian distance metrics are 06, 04 and 02 respectively. FN is more with Euclidian distance metric than other two metrics. So, similarity index is more in Euclidian distance metric other than two metrics. From this, it is observed that Euclidian distance metric yielded excellent results other than two metrics for detection of no tumor and tumor classes.

Finally, tumor images are tested and computed the identification score. Identification score designates the similarity of the given testing image with the assigned class. Theoretically the identification score ranging from 0 to 1000, where 0 represents the minimum identification score and 1000 represents the maximum score. Practically the identification score has been obtained by NN algorithm with sum distance metric ranging from [978-990], max distance metric ranging from [970-998] and Euclidian distance metric ranging from [979-998]. Identification scores along with the status of the tumor using different distance metrics for NN algorithm is shown in table 5.1. From this table it is observed that, Euclidian distance metric gives the high identification score than other two metrics even for less intensity images (in Table 1 S.No. 6 and 9).

Table 1.   Tumor images using nearest neighbour classifier different distance metrics.

| S.no | Patient no | Identification score | | | | | |
		Sum	Status	Maximum	Status	Euclidian	Status
1		983	Tumor	998	no tumor	997	tumor
2		990	no tumor	997	tumor	997	tumor
3		980	Tumor	981	tumor	989	tumor
4		991	Tumor	998	tumor	997	tumor
5		990	Tumor	994	tumor	998	tumor
6		979	Tumor	975	tumor	979	no tumor
7		990	Tumor	978	tumor	997	tumor
8		986	Tumor	994	tumor	990	Tumor
9		978	Tumor	970	no tumor	982	no tumor

Table 2. Consolidated results of identification scores with NN and KNN algorithm.

| S.No | NN algorithm | | | |
	TP	TN	FP	FN
Sum	34	11	04	06
Max	36	12	03	04
Euclidian	38	14	01	02

Table 3. Consolidated results of the performance of the statistical parameters.

| S. No | NN algorithm | | | |
	Sensitivity	Specificity	accuracy	similarity index
Sum	85.0	73.3	81.1	87.1
Max	90.0	80.0	87.2	91.1
Euclidian	95.0	93.3	94.54	96.2

Statistical parameters have been calculated for detection of no tumor and tumor classification using with NN algorithm. The two statistical parameters sensitivity and specificity are measures of the performance of a classification test in medical field. Sensitivity measures the percentage of true positive rate which are correctly identified. While specificity measures the percentage of true negative values which are correctly identified. For Euclidian distance

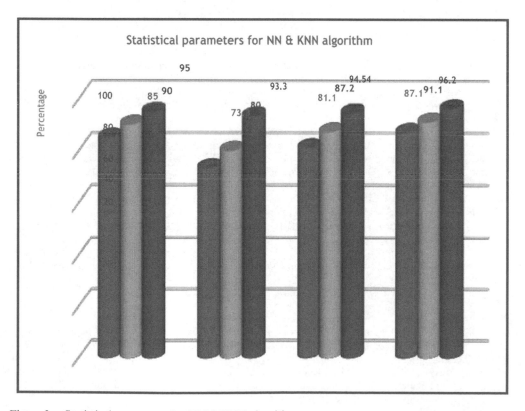

Figure 3. Statistical parameters for NN &KNN algorithm.

metric, a test has 95.0% TPR (90% for max distance metric & 85% for sum distance metric), means this algorithm successfully identified 95.0% cases. Specificity (TNR) is the ratio of people that tested negative (TN) of all the people that actually are negative (TN+FP). This algorithm successfully identified 93.3% cases with Euclidian distance metric (73.3% for sum distance metric and 80.0% for max distance metric). Accuracy with Euclidian distance metric is very high i.e. 94.5 % (81.1% for sum distance metric and 87.2 % for max distance metric). Similarity index with Euclidian distance metric is very high i.e. 96.2 % (87.1% for sum distance metric and 91.1 % for max distance metric). From this statistical parameters calculation, it is observed that NN classifier with Euclidian distance metric yields excellent results than other two distance metrics. Table 2 and Table 3 show the consolidated results of identification scores with NN and KNN algorithm and Statistical performance results.

Total number images=65, tumor images =40, no tumor images=15

4   CONCLUSION

For the detection of no tumor/tumor, NN algorithm has been trained and classified with sum, max and Euclidian distance metrics. Statistical parameters have been calculated for detection of no tumor and tumor classification using with NN algorithm. Statistical parameters e.g. Sensitivity, Specificity, Accuracy, and Similarity index 95.0%, 93.3%, 94.54%, 96.2% etc. Euclidian distance metric has been performed high statistical performance results than other two metrics.

REFERENCES

Atkins C.B. and Bouman C. 1998. "Classification Based Methods in Optimal Image Interpolation," Ph.D. dissertation, Clayton Brian Atkins, *Purdue University*,1998.
Chakraborty J, Mukhopadhyay S, Singla V, Khandelwal N and Angayyan R. 2012."Detection of masses in mammograms using region growing controlled by multilevel thresholding," 25th International Symposium on Computer-Based Medical Systems (CBMS), pp. 1–6.
Chang H, Yeung D.Y., and Xiong Y. 2004. "Super-resolution through neighbor embedding, "in Proceedings IEEE Conference Computer Vision and Pattern Recognition, 2004, volume 01, pp. 275–282.
Dempster A.P., Laird N.M., & Rubin D.B. 1977. "Maximum likelihood from incomplete data via the EM algorithm," Journal of the Royal Statistical Society. Series B (Methodological), 1977, Volume 39, 1, pp.1-38
Dumitriu D, Cossart R, Huang J and Yuste R, 2007. "Correlation between axonal morphologies and synaptic input kinetics of inter neurons from mouse visual cortex" Cerebral Cortex, Volume 17, pp.81–91.
Filipe R. Cordeiroa, Wellington P. Santos and Abel G. Silva-Filho. 2015. "An adaptive semi- supervised Fuzzy Grow Cut algorithm to segment masses of regions of interest of mammographic images," Applied Soft Computing, Elsevier, p.1-16.
Freeman W.T., Jones T. R., and Pasztor E.C. 2002. "Example-based super resolution," IEEE Computer Graphics and Applications Volume 22, (2), pp. 56–65.
Guerra. 2011. "Comparison between Supervised and Unsupervised Classifications of Neuronal Cell Types: A Case Study", Developmental neurobiology, January 2011, Volume 71, 1, pp.71-82.
Helmstaedter M, Sakmann B, Feldmeyer D. 2009. "L2/3 interneuron groups defined by multiparameter analysis of axonal projection, dendritic geometry and electrical excitability," Cerebral Cortex, Volume 19, pp. 951–962.
Karagiannis A, Gallopin T, Csaba D, Battaglia D, Geoffroy H, Rossier J, Hillman E. 2009. "Classification of NPY-expressing neocortical interneurons," Journal of Neuroscience, Volume 29, pp.3642–3659.
KarlS. Ni., Member, IEEE, and Truong Q.Nguyen. 2009. "An Adaptablek-Nearest Neighbours Algorithm for MMSE Image Interpolation" IEEE Transactions on Image Processing, Volume 18, 9, pp.1976-1987.
Lefkovits L, Lefkovits Sz, Vaida M.F., Zmerich S and Măluțan R. 2017. "Comparison of Classifiers for Brain Tumor Segmentation, International Conference on Advancements of Medicine and Health Care through Technology, Cluj-Napoca, Romania pp. 195-200.

McGarry LM, Packer A, Fino E, Nikolenko V, Sippy T, Yuste, R. 2010"Quantitative classification of somatostatin-positive neocortical interneurons identifies three interneuron subtypes," Front Neural Circuits, Volume 4, 12.

Rahmati P, Adler A, Hamarneh G. 2012. "Mammography segmentation with maxi-mum likelihoodacti-vecontours,"Medical Image Analysis, volume16, 6, pp.1167–1186.

Raman V, Sumari P, Al-Omari S.A.K., 2011. "Review on mammogram mass detection by machine learning techniques," International Journal of Computer and Electrical Engineering, Volume 3, 6, 873–879.

Su K. Tian Q, Sebe N and Ma J. 2005. "Neighbourhood Issue in Single-frame Image Super resolution" Los Alamitos, CA: IEEE Computer Society.

Vadivel A, Majumdar A K, Shamik Sural. 2003. Performance comparison of distance metrics in content-based Image retrieval applications, International Conference on Information Technology (CIT), Bhubaneswar, India, pp. 159-164.

Communication and Computing Systems – Prasad et al. (eds)
© *2019 Taylor & Francis Group, London, ISBN 978-0-367-00147-6*

Time-slot assignment based channel access scheme for reliable transmission in VANET

Ravisankar Malladi
Computer Science and Engineering Department, Godavari Institute of Engineering & Technology, Rajahmundry, India

Ch. Srinivas
Computer Science and Engineering Department, JITS, Karimnagar, India

Nishu Gupta
Electronics and Communication Engineering Department, Vaagdevi College of Engineering, Warangal, India

ABSTRACT: Safety on roads for running vehicles as well as pedestrians is indispensable as well as a challenging aspect of Intelligent Transportation Systems (ITS). Owing to the prominent aspects of vehicular communication such as large range of variation in speed, dynamic vehicular density, intermittent failure to communication link and geographically constrained topology, data transfer becomes challenging. As a prerequisite to an efficient data communication system, vehicular network is expected to have such medium access control (MAC) protocols that can ensure reliable data dissemination particularly for safety-related services. In this article, a time division multiple access (TDMA) based MAC protocol is proposed that ensures fast and reliable data delivery in vehicular environment. The protocol integrates TDMA channelization technique and distributed coordination function mechanism to minimize packet collisions. It prioritizes safety messages by providing them immediate channel access over non-safety messages which are comparatively more delay-tolerant. Apart from that, the proposed channel access scheme enhances the existing IEEE standards in terms of multichannel coordination as well as MAC and PHY layer parameters. Results have been deduced using MATLAB and are in true conformity with the simulations performed. They demonstrate the utility and efficiency of the proposed scheme with improved parametric performance.

1   INTRODUCTION

In recent times, vehicular networks are gaining high interest and support than ever before from all realms of technological arena such as researchers, automobile and electronic sensors related companies, transportation authorities, etc.

For sparse network scenarios Carrier sense multiple access (CSMA)-based medium access control (MAC) protocols are found to perform well but as the vehicular density rises, they bring about high collision rate owing to the random backoff technique being adopted by them. On the other hand, time division medium access (TDMA) based MAC protocols render upper bound delay and are less susceptible to collisions under dense scenarios. Most of the recent research works concentrate on either of these techniques, that is, either CSMA or TDMA (Schwartz, Scholten, Havinga, 2013; Gupta, Prakash, Tripathi, 2015). However, in this article, both CSMA and TDMA strategies are integrated to leverage better performance. We propose a protocol that leverages three-fold process such as efficient clustering, CH selection and neighborhood selection process. The protocol broadly aims to ensure vehicular and pedestrian safety by avoiding road accidents; as well as without compromising with the performance metrics and energy consumption related parameters.

In this paper, an agile MAC scheme based on TDMA is presented which is technology but further optimized for higher performance in vehicular network. By integrating the features of time slot based TDMA and random-access based CSMA strategies, the proposed protocol can substantially reduce collisions in the control channel (CCH) channel. Moreover, the protocol can assign time slots to the vehicles much faster than the existing similar protocols. Major contributions of this work are as follows:

- A new TDMA based adaptive MAC protocol that overcomes redundant time slot allocation and provides a distributed time slot reservation scheme.
- An analytical model demonstrating faster slot reservation.
- Performance evaluation of different metrics through extensive simulation results.

Rest of the sections in this article are structured as follows. Section II discusses the background and related works. Section III presents the system model. The proposed MAC protocol is presented in Section IV. In Section V, performance of the proposed work is evaluated, and results are presented. Finally, Section VI presents the conclusion and future work.

2 BACKGROUND

Before discussing the employed methodology, it is customary to discuss the related research work that would help in judicious identification of the research gap between existing literature and the proposed work. TDMA based protocols (Ma, Zhang, Yin, Trivedi, 2012; Tian, Wang, Xia, Cai, 2013) are known to suffer from frequent re-scheduling demands. Various protocols presented below somewhat addresses this issue by dividing the road segments into small cells where each cell is mapped with a group of time slots.

Several channel access techniques (Gupta, Prakash, Tripathi, 2016; Hafeez, Zhao, Liao, Ma, 2011) and cooperative communication schemes (Ye, Yim, Roy, Zhang, 2011; Wang, Leng, Fu, Zhang, 2012; Ghandour, Di Felice, Artail, Bononi, 2014) that are recently proposed, tend to reduce the throughput and cause channel access delays for safety related vehicular applications which are delay-intolerant.

Authors (Pal, Gupta, Prakash, Tripathi, 2018) introduced a MAC protocol in vehicular ad-hoc network (VANET) for efficient distribution of safety messages. Whenever a security message arrives during the service channel interval (SCHI), the protocol ends the SCHI and allows the vehicle to start the CCH. To ensure the delivery of periodic status messages, the authors introduced time division multiplexing (TDM) virtual beaconing process. This handles the hidden multichannel problem using the cluster member and head request. A major drawback of this protocol is, there is a chance of choosing the incorrect channel at the time of transmission of data.

(Wang, Motani, Garg, Chen, Luo, 2017) introduced a cooperative multichannel directional MAC (CMDMAC) protocol that incorporates the minor-lobe interference for directional ad hoc networks. In this, directional HTP and deafness are covered that offers directional and multi-channel transmissions.

(Ye, Zhuang, 2017) proposed a token-based adaptive MAC scheme for two-hop Internet of Things (IoT) enabled mobile ad-hoc network (MANET). In this, a super-frame structure based on TDMA was presented to avoid the HTP by allocating different time durations at distinct groups of nodes. A token was probabilistically rotated between the nodes of each group for the distributed allocation of the time slot.

(Gupta, Prakash, Tripathi, 2017) proposed a TDMA based slot reservation technique by harnessing the multichannel feature of the wireless access in vehicular environment (WAVE) standard and access the time slots on the CCHI for safety messages and SCHI for non-safety messages respectively. However, they did not estimate the level of beacon congestion and its control algorithms. Moreover, under majority of the scenarios congestion detection is not possible without sharing frequent information among vehicles, which can further alleviate congestion.

3 SYSTEM MODEL

The network model of the proposed protocol consists of vehicular nodes (VNs) and road side sensor nodes (RSSNs). We first compute cluster size and select cluster head (CH) that changes in dynamic manner based on RSSNs performance. We then calculate next neighbouring CH node to relay the gathered information from the VN to other VNs. This three-fold process is performed simultaneously to avoid system overhead and delay. Each VN communicates through other intermediate node that lies within the transmission range. Both traffic and vehicle information's are gathered from VN and is forwarded to other end by intermediate clusters. Figure 1 depicts the discussed scenario.

The vehicles exchange the lists among all the neighbours and merge them to form a consolidated list. Since the proposed scheme follows a distributed approach, each vehicle acquires a time slot to transmit at the beginning of every TDMA frame. Since the vehicles have prior information about each other's location, they can discover the network topology, determine the time slots already occupied, and track any topology change that might occur due to vehicles' mobility.

Each vehicle constantly updates its own Free_Slots by removing occupied slots. If Free_-Slots set is not empty, the vehicle randomly picks a free slot from it. Otherwise, it randomly selects any slot from the whole range. In this way, during the listening period, vehicle discovers all the surrounding vehicles and their occupied slots, which helps avoid potential collisions.

4 METHODOLOGY

In this section, we first describe the cluster formation technique with the CH selection process using multiple constraints. The objective of the protocol is achieved by the proposed neighbourhood selection process that is described as follows.

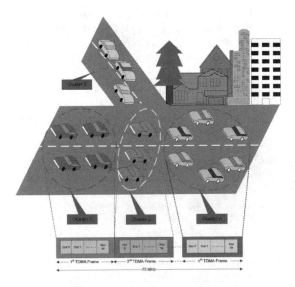

Figure 1. A scenario depicting TDMA based clustering model.

458

4.1 Cluster formation using improved optimization algorithm

We propose a metaheuristic optimization algorithm (Felice, Bedogni, Bononi, 2013; Omar, Zhuang, Li, 2013; Shao, Leng, Zhang, Fu, 2014) inspired from water wave theory. Each node in the network is analogous to the water wave object with a wave height (h) and wavelength (W). The algorithm starts with the initialization step, for each wave, h is set to a constant h_{max} and wavelength W is generally set to 0.5. The fitness value of each water wave is inversely proportional to the vertical distance to the seabed. The algorithm uses the breaking process for new best solution computation, but the search space is difficult to maintain the global optimal solution. In this algorithm, the local search ability is improved. Here, all water waves must be propagated once at each generation. It is assumed that the original water wave is x, x_{new} is a new wave created by propagation operator, the dimension of the maximum value function is D, the propagation operation is shifted, and each dimension of the original water wave x is given as follows:

This status message is received by all the cluster members so that each vehicle in a cluster knows the parameters of each vehicle of the cluster.

Let there are N vehicles in a cluster. Let (x_1, y_1), (x_2, y_2), ... (x_N, y_N) are positions of different vehicles in that cluster. Centroid of cluster can be calculated as

$$J = (j_1 + j_2 + j_3 .... j_N)/N \text{ and } K = (k_1 + k_2 + k_3 .... k_N)/N \tag{1}$$

(J, K) are the mean points of the cluster members. Using distance formula

$$d_j = \sqrt{(j_x - J)^2 + (k_y - K)^2} \tag{2}$$

Adopting from [10] and [13]

$$CF_j = \left(1 - \frac{\text{distance of } k^{th} \text{ node from mean position}}{\text{Transmission range}} \right) \tag{3}$$

Value of CF is always less than 1. Higher the value of CF, closer is the vehicle to the centroid.

Cluster Head Coefficient (CH Coefficient) combines relative velocity and transmission range while selecting CH. It is expressed as

$$CH\text{coefficient}_k = \varepsilon CF_k + (1 - \varepsilon)\beta_{WSF_k} \tag{4}$$

ε depends on the factor whether range is more important or the velocity. Flow diagram depicting the discussed scenario is presented in Figure 2.

5 PERFORMANCE EVALUATION

The simulation scenario generates topology of a Manhattan grid of 500 m and a 5x5 Manhattan grid road network. The simulation is conduct in a 3000m × 4000m network area. The traffic type is Constant Bit Rate (CBR) with the default packet size of 512 bytes and the maximum transmission range is set to 300m, owing to vehicle-to-vehicle (V2V) communication (Katrin, Elisabeth, Erik, Urban, 2009; Milanes, Shladover, Spring, Nowakowski, Kawazoe, Nakamura, 2014; Sadollah, Choi, Kim, 2015). The MAC layer protocol is IEEE 802.11b. The number of nodes is varied between 50 and 500 to portray the network state at different time periods. Message size for non-safety messages is arbitrarily chosen to be 500 bytes. The data rate of sensor node is set to 6Mbps. MAC layer protocol is configured to meet specifications of IEEE 802.11p. The vehicle speed fluctuates between 11 to 18 m/s for urban network

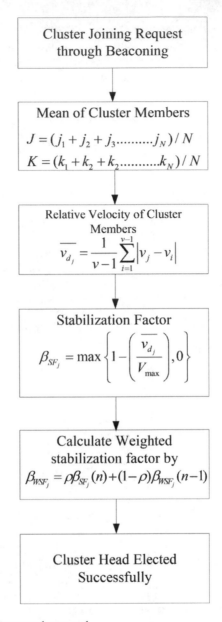

Figure 2.   Flowchart of the proposed protocol.

area. The entire simulation takes 150 seconds simulation time. Rest other simulation parameters are described in Table 1.

In Figure 3 (a), we compare the delay of IEEE 802.11p standard and proposed protocol for different number of nodes. Proposed work overshadows existing standard for throughput analysis. The reason behind this observation is because of the implementation of the clustering mechanism that allows faster data delivery.

Figure 3 (b) compares the packet delivery ratio (PDR) for IEEE 802.11p standard and proposed protocol. The results are like the ones attained for throughput. As the nodes increase, the PDR increases to a certain value and then shows decreasing trend. PDR of IEEE 802.11p standard is seen to be lower than proposed protocol for all counts of the nodes.

Table 1.   Simulation environment and parameters.

Parameter	Value
Number of nodes	50-500
Node speed	11-18m/s, (40-65 km/h)
Simulation time	300 s
Simulation range	3000 m x 4000 m
Data transmission rate	6 Mbps
Transmission range of nodes	300 m
Packet size (safety)	200 Bytes
Packet size (non-safety)	500 Bytes
Number of lanes per direction	2
Slot width	1 ms
Slots per frame	40
Scenario	Urban
Network interface	Phy/WirelessPhyExt
MAC interface	Mac/802_11Ext
Modulation type	BPSK

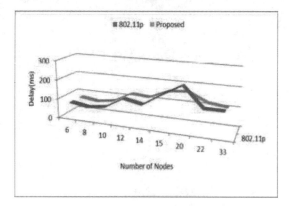

Figure 3(a).   Number of nodes vs delay.

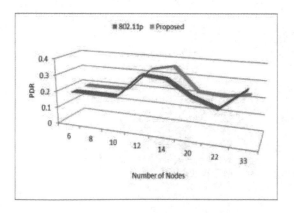

Figure 3(b).   Number of nodes vs PDR.

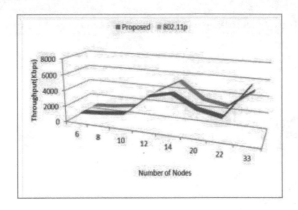

Figure 3(c).   Number of nodes vs throughput.

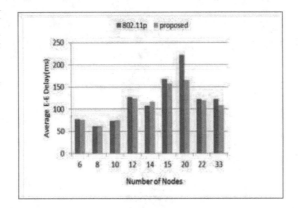

Figure 4(a).   Cumulative comparison between average E-E delay vs number of nodes.

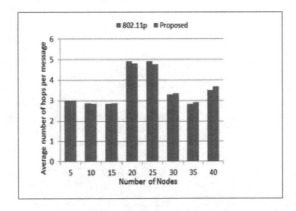

Figure 4(b).   Cumulative comparison between average no. of hops vs number of nodes.

In Figure 3 (c), proposed protocol wins over its counterpart in terms of throughput. This is obvious owing to the clustering scenario where each intermediate cluster follows a protocol to route the message to its one-hop distance cluster.

Figure 4 (a) compares the average end-to-end delay. It is seen that the proposed protocol demonstrates better performance than IEEE 802.11p.

In Figure 4 (b), it is shown that the average number of hops is comparable to the legacy standard.

6 CONCLUSION AND FUTURE SCOPE

In this paper, we have proposed a TDMA based MAC protocol that ensures fast and reliable data delivery in vehicular environment. The clustering has been achieved by an improved mobility-based algorithm, which minimize the energy utilization. The multi-constraint features utilized to compute the CH node in the cluster. The proposed MAC protocol fairly distributes wireless channels between vehicles and ensures that all the vehicles exchange their beacons within finite interval of time. The optimization algorithm is used to elects neighbourhood selection, which provides the network lifetime and lossless connection. The simulation results prove the effectiveness of proposed protocol in terms of various performance metrics.

REFERENCES

Felice M. D., L. Bedogni, & L. Bononi. 2013. Group communication on highways: An evaluation study of geocast protocols and applications, Ad Hoc Networks, 11 (3), 818–8832.

Ghandour, A. J., Di Felice, M., Artail, H., & Bononi, L. 2014. Dissemination of safety messages in IEEE 802.11 p/WAVE vehicular network: analytical study and protocol enhancements. Pervasive and Mobile Computing, 11, 3-18.

Gupta, N., Prakash, A., & Tripathi, R. 2015. Medium access control protocols for safety applications in Vehicular Ad-Hoc Network: A classification and comprehensive survey. Vehicular Communications, 2(4),223-237.

Gupta, N., Prakash, A., & Tripathi, R. 2016. Clustering based cognitive MAC protocol for channel allocation to prioritize safety message dissemination in vehicular ad-hoc network. Vehicular Communications, 5(2016),44-54.

Gupta, N., Prakash, A., & Tripathi, R. 2017. Adaptive Beaconing in Mobility Aware Clustering Based MAC Protocol for Safety Message Dissemination in VANET. Wireless Communications and Mobile Computing, vol. 2017, Article ID 1246172, p.15

Hafeez, K. A., Zhao, L., Liao, Z., & Ma, B. N. W. 2011. Clustering and OFDMA-based MAC protocol (COMAC) for vehicular ad hoc networks. EURASIP Journal on Wireless Communications and Networking, 2011(1),1-16.

Katrin, B., Elisabeth, U., Erik G.S., & Urban, B. 2009. On the ability of the 802.11 p MAC method and STDMA to support real-time vehicle-to-vehicle communication. EURASIP Journal on Wireless Communications and Networking, 5.

Ma, X., Zhang, J., Yin, X., & Trivedi, K. S. 2012. Design and analysis of a robust broadcast scheme for VANET safety-related services. IEEE Transactions on Vehicular Technology, 61(1),46-61.

Milanes, V., Shladover, S. E., Spring, J., Nowakowski, C., Kawazoe, H., & Nakamura, M. 2014. Cooperative adaptive cruise control in real traffic situations. IEEE Transactions on Intelligent Transportation Systems, 15(1),296-305.

Omar, H. A., Zhuang, W., & Li, L. 2013. VeMAC: A TDMA-based MAC protocol for reliable broadcast in VANETs. IEEE Transactions on Mobile Computing, 12(9),1724-1736.

Pal, R., Gupta, N., Prakash, A. & Tripathi, R. 2017. Wireless Personal Communications, 98: 1155.

Sadollah, A., Choi, Y., & Kim, J. H. 2015. Metaheuristic optimization algorithms for approximate solutions to ordinary differential equations. IEEE Congress in Evolutionary Computation (CEC), 792-798.

Schwartz, R. S., Scholten, H., Havinga, P. 2013. A scalable data dissemination protocol for both highway and urban vehicular environments. EURASIP Journal on Wireless Communications and Networking, 2013(1),1-19.

Shao, C., Leng, S., Zhang, Y., & Fu, H. 2014. A multi-priority supported medium access control in Vehicular Ad Hoc Networks. Computer Communications, 39, 11-21.

Tian, D, Wang, Y, Xia, H, Cai, F. 2013. Clustering Multi-Hop Information Dissemination Method in Vehicular Ad-Hoc Networks. IET Intelligent Transport Systems, 7(4),464-472.

Wang, Q., Leng, S., Fu, H., & Zhang, Y. 2012. An IEEE 802.11p-based multichannel MAC scheme with channel coordination for vehicular ad hoc networks. IEEE Transactions on Intelligent Transportation Systems, 13(2),449-458.

Wang, Y., Motani, M., Garg, H. K., Chen, Q., & Luo, T. 2017. Cooperative multichannel directional medium access control for ad hoc networks. IEEE Systems Journal, 11(4),2675-2686.

Ye, F., Yim, R., Roy, S., & Zhang, J. 2011. Efficiency and reliability of one-hop broadcasting in vehicular ad hoc networks. IEEE Journal on Selected Areas in Communications, 29(1),151-160.

Ye, Q., & Zhuang, W. 2017. Token-based adaptive MAC for a two-hop Internet-of-Things enabled MANET. IEEE Internet of Things Journal, 4(5),1739-1753.

Communication and Computing Systems – Prasad et al. (eds)
© 2019 Taylor & Francis Group, London, ISBN 978-0-367-00147-6

Research on computational grid generation method

Yan Yaoyuan
Aircraft Design and Engineering, The North University of China Taiyuan, Shanxi, China
SS&CS Jawaharlal Nehru University, New Delhi, India

Han Bing
Aircraft Design and Engineering, The North University of China Taiyuan, Shanxi, China

ABSTRACT: The main contents of this paper's design include infinitely perturbation interpolation method and RBF radial basis function dynamic grid method. The results of dynamic grid generation are compared. Observe which generation algorithm is more reasonable and the grid quality is higher[1]. With the development of computer equipment and computing technology, CFD is often used in various disciplines such as optimization design, aeroelasticity, thermal analysis, and pneumatic servo elasticity. For these problems, the linear method can be well solved under the conditions of small disturbance, but the nonlinear motion method is needed for the vibration induced eddy current, transonic flutter, and large control surface motion in complex flow field, and it needs to rely on large-scale Parallel computing platform technology[2]. The research results show that the infinite perturbation interpolation method is suitable for grid deformation with small perturbations. The generation efficiency is high and the algorithm is easy to implement. Radial Basis Function algorithm can maintain a higher mesh quality. The disadvantage is that the operation speed is slow and the algorithm is difficult to implement.

KEYWORDS: dynamic mesh infinite perturbation interpolation radial basis function mesh deformation greedy algorithm

1 INTRODUCTION

In recent years, the aerospace industry has told development, and at the same time, computational fluid dynamics has become a research hotspot. In the existing computational fluid dynamics, the most widely used engineering application is the Euler method, which is to divide the fluid domain into a grid, and define the properties of the fluid (mass density, velocity, temperature, entropy, and even the flux of the unit fluid). Is a function of spatial position time. For the aircraft, the unsteady problem involving many boundary motions, due to the aerodynamic load or the relative motion of the components, if the analysis is still carried out under the original conditions, the calculation results will deviate greatly from the real situation. In the case of aircraft flutter, static change, gust response motion, etc., the mesh deformation technique is needed to calculate the change of the mesh in the calculation domain.

In the actual engineering problem, the object boundary is generally more complex, and the unstructured mesh is more suitable for this shape change. Compared with the structured mesh, the unstructured mesh has the characteristics of fast generation speed and high calculation efficiency. But the calculation accuracy is much lower than the structured grid[1]. Even so, unstructured grids play an integral role in computational fluid dynamics (CFD) and finite element analysis. Among them, the flow field problem of unsteady boundary motion is solved, such as object surface change, fluid-solid coupling and block disintegration. According to the flow form and the deformation mode of the object surface, it can be roughly divided into a fluid unsteady object surface stationary or a surface surface for rigid motion and a multi-body relative motion. Among them, multi-body relative motion requires the help of dynamic mesh technology. The deflection of the leading edge slat and the trailing edge flap during flight is a problem of multi-body deformation flow field, so the problem of multi-body deformation flow field In the research, dynamic mesh generation technology has also become a key technology in many numerical simulation processes.

For the problem of deformation of the object surface, the most intuitive method is to re-mesh according to the new object surface, but this method is too time-consuming and computational resources. For grids with multiple time points, it is necessary to generate multiple sets of different grids. grid. The dynamic mesh method is based on the original mesh to interpolate and calculate its mesh nodes. In this way, a mesh reflecting the deformation of the object surface is generated, and a lot of time is saved.

The difficulty of the mesh deformation method is that after the object surface is deformed or displaced, the mesh near the roof will also change accordingly. At this time, it is impossible to ensure that the mesh near the object surface maintains the original quality, and even a crossover phenomenon may occur. This is the algorithmic difficulty of dynamic grid technology research . Therefore, the development research on the existing dynamic mesh technology has an indispensable significance, which not only promotes the development of related fields, but also has important research significance for the large-scale deformation of the object surface and the structural flutter.

2   RESEARCH STATUS

Dynamic grid technology has not developed for a long time, mainly due to the development of computational fluid dynamics. With the development of science and technology, the technical research of the dynamic grid is more comprehensive and in-depth. More and more dynamic mesh generation methods have emerged, mainly spring method[4], elastomer method, infinite perturbation interpolation method, Delaunay background grid method, radial basis function interpolation method and temperature body method. According to the different modeling principles of these methods, they can be divided into three categories: mathematical interpolation, physical model and hybrid.

2.1   *Mathematical interpolation*

The mathematical interpolation method is mainly used to distribute the motion ofthe boundary to the internal nodes. Generally, the connection information of the mesh nodes is not needed, and the data structure is relatively simple [6]. There are mainly infinite perturbation interpolation method, Delaunay background mesh method, and radial basis function interpolation method.

This paper mainly studies mathematical interpolation

(1) Infinite perturbation interpolation method:

The infinite perturbation interpolation method was first proposed by Caitondc et al. in calculating the transonic flow of a disturbing oscillating airfoil. The basic principle is to keep the far field boundary stationary, the structural boundary is given according to the motion law of the object, and the interpolation of the internal field mesh is generated[5]. The infinite perturbation interpolation method has a small amount of calculation, which can realize relatively complicated mesh deformation, but the mesh quality after deformation cannot be guaranteed, especially the orthogonality of the object mesh. Later, a number of computational fluid mechanics corrected it to divide the calculation area into small pieces, which were propelled by the structure to the far field. In this way, the mesh deformation in each small block is relatively small, and the quality of the local mesh can be ensured.

(2) Delaunay background grid interpolation methoh[6]:

Liu Xueqiang et al. developed a mesh deformation method based on the Delaunary background mesh interpolation method. The basic principle is to transfer the movement of the structure boundary to the movement of the Delaunay background grid point. Relocate through the grid points in the background grid to get the new grid position. The algorithm is simple to implement, no large-scale equations need to be solved, and the calculation efficiency is high. It is applicable to grids with different topologies and can be extended to three dimensions. By properly adjusting and selecting the background grid, it is theoretically possible to obtain a large mesh deformation capability. The realization process: firstly, the background mesh with the Delaunary property is generated from the corner points of the far field and the points of the structural boundary, and the mapping relationship between the calculated mesh node and the Beijing mesh unit is established by the area coordinate, and the influence is affected according to the movement of the structural boundary. The background grid, based on the mapping relationship, can get the new grid point coordinates.

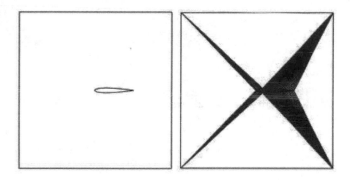

Figure 1.   Background grid interpolation mapping.

(3) Radial Basis Function interpolation

For the first time, Boer et al. applied RBFs to mesh deformation technology. The basic principle is to use RBFs to interpolate the displacements of structural boundary nodes, and then use the constructed RBFs sequence to smoothly distribute the boundary displacement effects to the entire computational grid region[7]. It is mainly divided into two steps. First, the weight coefficient equation of the object plane is solved, and then the grid of the calculation domain is updated.

The RBFs method is more computationally intensive and time-consuming. The competitive radial basis function method has better computational efficiency and further enhances the mesh deformation capability. It is a mesh deformation method with good application prospects.

In this paper, the infinite perturbation interpolation method and the radial basis function interpolation method are studied and implemented. (The program implementation is mainly based on the leading and trailing edge deflection of the three-stage airfoil)

3   ALGORITHM IMPLEMENTATION

3.1   Infinite Perturbation Interpolation(TFI)

The principle of infinite perturbation interpolation method is very simple. The motion change of the boundary of the internal field structure is given by the motion law of the object surface itself[9]. The outer field boundary remains static, and the internal mesh node difference is generated. The generation process is as follows:

1. Boundary displacement, calculating node displacement.
2. Displacement, calculate the internal grid point displacement interpolation.
3. Get the final internal mesh node position coordinates.
4. Generate a new grid.

3.2 Radial Basis Function Interpolation(RBF)

The basic principle of the radial basis function interpolation method is to define the radius of action of a control point, and still calculate the displacement of the object surface at the beginning, define the node on the object surface as the control point, and then perform the radial basis function interpolation according to the size of the action radius. The displacement of each internal node can be obtained, that is, the larger the radius of action of the distance control point, the weaker the effect, and the closer the distance from the control point, the more obvious the effect[10].

Basic formula of radial basis function:

$$F(r) = \sum_{i=1}^{N} w_1 \varphi(\|r - r_2\|)$$

In the formula:

$F(r)$:Expressed as an interpolation function

N:Represents the total number of radial basis functions used to process the interpolation problem, ie the number of control points used

$\varphi(\|r - r_1\|)$:Expressed as the general format of the radial basis functions used;

w_i : Expressed as the weighting coefficient corresponding to the i-th radial basis function.

Since this paper studies the dynamic mesh generation technology, we choose the C2 function suitable for grid interpolation. The expression is

$$\varphi(\eta) \begin{cases} 0 & \eta > 1 \\ (1-\eta)^4(4\eta - 1) & \eta \leq 1 \end{cases}$$

In the formula:

$\eta = \frac{\|r - r_i\|}{d}$, d is the radius of action of the radial basis function.

According to the principle of the radial basis function, the interpolation conditions of the radial basis function interpolation problem can be summarized into the following matrix form.

$$\Delta X_s = \Phi W_x$$
$$\Delta Y_s = \Phi W_y$$
$$\Delta Z_s = \Phi W_z$$

The expression of the Φ matrix is as follows:

$$\Phi = \begin{bmatrix} \varphi(r_{s1} - r_{s1}) & \cdots & \varphi(r_{s1} - r_{sN}) \\ \vdots & \ddots & \vdots \\ \varphi(r_{sN} - r_{s1}) & \cdots & \varphi(r_{sN} - r_{sN}) \end{bmatrix}$$

Solved by the two methods above W_x, W_y, W_z, The object displacement interpolation can be obtained from the radial basis function. The formula is:

$$
\begin{cases}
\Delta x_j = \sum_{i=s1}^{S_n} w_i^x \varphi(r_j - r_i) \\[2mm]
\Delta y_j = \sum_{i=s1}^{S_n} w_i^y \varphi(r_j - r_i) \\[2mm]
\Delta z_j = \sum_{i=s1}^{S_n} w_i^z \varphi(r_j - r_i)
\end{cases}
$$

The main method of the radial basis function mesh deformation method is how to deal with the displacement displacement of the surface of the object instead of the interpolation approximation of the radial basis function. Simplified and available:

$$
\Delta S = \Phi W
$$

3.3 Data reduction algorithm(greedy algorithm)

When constructing the algorithm by the above radial basis function interpolation method, the calculation amount of the operation will be very large, because the calculation amount depends on the dimension of the construction matrix, and the dimension of the matrix depends on the number N of the selected control points, and the memory consumption is The square of N, plus the total number of grid nodes, is quite large[11], so a data reduction algorithm based on greedy algorithm is proposed. The main principles are as follows:

First, take L control points in the object plane, substitute the above formula to calculate the interpolation, and take the appropriate radius of action. The result of obtaining L control points is an exact solution, but there are certain errors in other points on the mesh surface[12]. The exact solution obtained by the displacement can be used to obtain the maximum point max of the error, and the point is combined with the previous L points again to obtain the L+1 control point matrix, which is substituted into the radial basis function again. Iterating sequentially, knowing that the resulting error is within the allowable range, the iteration stops.

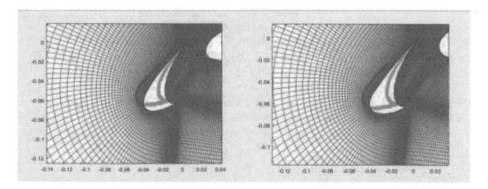

Figure 2.   Grid condition after RBF leading edge rotation.

4   COMPARISON AND ANALYSIS

According to the above method, comparing the mesh generated under the same conditions, it is found that the orthogonality of the mesh generated by the infinite perturbation interpolation method under the small perturbation is not very good at the object surface, and the network has appeared when rotating at a large angle. The lattice node is misplaced. In contrast, the radial basis function produces a mesh with a higher quality and orthogonality.

The two algorithms calculate the time comparison:

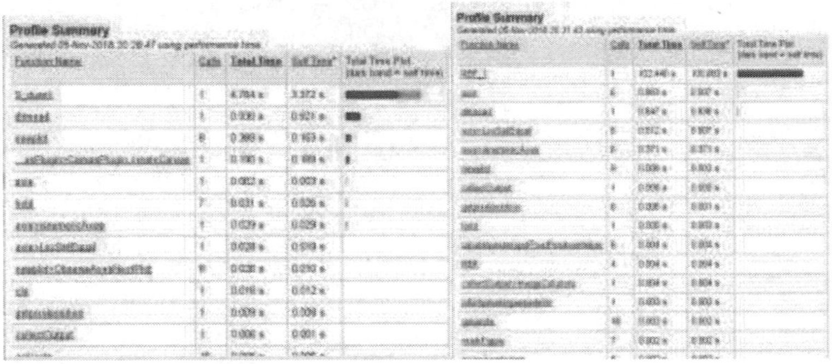

Figure 3.   RBF calculation time.

Therefore, relative to infinitepertur-bation interpolation (TFI), radial basis func-tions (RBFs) have the ability to gene-rate better mesh quality. Due to the nature of its own function, the generated mesh is ortho-gonal at the object plane. Good sex, the deg-ree of grid density is appropriate. Although the mesh quality will change within large changes, the mesh quality is relatively stab-le. There is no case that the mesh quality drops rapidly, which reflects the stability and high quality of the radial basis function. However, at the same time, it can be found that the compilation of the algorithm is difficult, and the algorithm consumes a lot of computing resources.

5   CONCLUSION

Infinite Perturbation Interpolation: It is a relatively complex algorithm with a wide range of uses. It can also generate relatively good meshes when the object surface deformation is larger than the first two. It has a good mass mesh with the object surface change. A mesh generation method, but this method also has the inherent disadvantage that the quality of the mesh near the object surface is degraded or even the phenomenon of mesh intrusion.

RBFs radial basis function method: It is a kind of complex algorithm and widely used. The method has the inherent advantages of dealing with the mesh near the object surface. The mesh quality near the object surface is high, and the orthogonality is very good. The degree of granularity is also satisfactory, but the method also has the disadvantages of difficulty in algo-rithm compilation and excessive computational complexity.

REFERENCES

Andreas B, Andreas H. 2007Integrated experimental and numerical research on the aerodynamics of unsteady aircraft. Washington. 3th International Symposium on Integrating CFD and Experiments in Aerodynamics.

Boer A, Schoot M S, Faculty, H.B. 2007 Mesh deformation based on radial basis function interpolation. Computers and Structures, 85(11): 784-795.

Erdal O, Hssan U A. 2002.CFD predicitions of dynamic derivatives for missile. AIAA-2002-0276.

Gaitonde A L, Fiddes, S.P. A moving mesh system for the calculation of unsteady flows. AIAA-1993-0641.

Green L L, Spence A M, Murphy PC. 2004. Computation methods for dynamic stability and control derivatives. AIAA-2004-0015.

Jakobsson S, Amoignon O. 2007 Mesh Deformation Using Radial Basis Functions for Gradient-Based Aerodynamic Shape Optimization Computers & Fluids, 36(6): 1119-1136

Liu X Q, Qin N, Xia, H. 2006. Fast dynamic grid deformation based on Delaunay graph mapping Journal of Computational Physics, 11(2): 405-423.

Mark A P, Eloret C, etc. 2001. A Parallel Multiblock Mesh Movement Scheme For Complex Aeroelastic Applications. AIAA- 2001-0716.

Peter M H, Shreekant A. 2007. Method For Perturbing Multiblock Patched Grids In Aeroelastic And Design Optimization Applications. AIAA- 97-2038.

Ronch A D, Vallespin D. 2010. Computation of dynamic derivatives using CFD. AIAA -2010-4817.

Tsai H M, Wong, A.S.F. 2001. Unsteady flow calculations with a parallel multiblock moving mesh algorithm. AIAA Journal, 39(6): 1021-1020.

Van Zuijlen A H, De Boer A, Bijl, H. 2007. Higher-Order Time Integration through Smooth Mesh Deformation for 3D Fluid-Structure Interaction Simulations. Journal of Computational Physics 224 (1): 414-430

Communication and Computing Systems – Prasad et al. (eds)
© 2019 Taylor & Francis Group, London, ISBN 978-0-367-00147-6

Designing of sliding mode controller

Jyoti Rana & Swati Sharma

Department of Electronics and Communication Engineering, Dronacharya College of Engineering,
Gurugram, India

ABSTRACT: In this research paper I am working on "Sliding Mode Controller (CMS)".
SMC is a control strategy which is not linear in nature including exceptional belongings of
precision, power, and making simple changes and execution. SMS frameworks are intended to
move the framework position into a particular position in the space of state, called the surface
of sliding. At a point when the SS is accomplished, SMC permanents the states near to the
place of the sliding surface.

1   INTRODUCTION

Sliding surface is denoted by s=0, where s is the sliding surface. The process of sliding mode starts
after a fixed duration when the directions of framework have fixed to their positions. In the speculative delineation of sliding modes, the structure remains within the sliding surface and viewed
simply as moving towards the surface. Regardless, veritable executions of sliding mode controller
evaluated this speculative direct with a high-repeat and generally non-deterministic trading control a banner that makes the system "jabber" in a tight neighborhood of the sliding surface. Hon-
estly, regardless of the way that the structure is nonlinear when all is said in done the
romanticized (i.e., non-gabbing) conduct of the framework in figure (A) when kept to the s = 0
{\display style s=0} s=0 surface is a LTI framework with an exponentially steady birthplace.
   Instinctively, sliding mode control utilizes for all intents and purposes endless gain to
compel the directions of a dynamic framework to slide along the limited sliding mode subspace. Directions from this diminished request sliding mode have alluring properties (e.g., the
framework normally slides along it until the point that it stops at the ideal harmony). The
fundamental quality of SMC is its vigor. Since the control can be as basic as exchanging
between two states (e.g., "on"/"off" or "forward"/"switch"), it require not be exact and won't
be delicate to parameter varieties that go into the control channel. Moreover, in light of the
fact that the control law is certifiably not a nonstop capacity, the sliding mode can be come to
in limited time (i.e., superior to asymptotic conduct). Under certain regular conditions, optimality requires the utilization of blast control; consequently, sliding mode control depicts the
ideal controller for a wide arrangement of dynamic frameworks.
   One use of the sliding mode controller is to control of electric drives worked by trading
power converters. By virtue of the discontinuous working technique for those converters, a
convulsive sliding mode controller is a trademark execution choice over predictable controllers
that may ought to be associated by strategies for heartbeat width change or a near system of
applying a relentless banner to a yield that can simply take discrete states. Sliding mode control has various applications in mechanical innovation. In particular, this control computation
has been used for following control of unmanned surface vessels in reproduced unforgiving
seas with an abnormal state of advancement.
   Sliding mode control must be associated with more thought than various kinds of nonlinear
control that have progressively moderate control movement. In particular, in light of the way
that actuators have delays and distinctive blemishes, the hard sliding-mode-control movement
can incite jabber, essentialness disaster, plant harm, and excitation of unmodeled elements.

Constant control plan strategies are not as vulnerable to these issues and can be made to impersonate sliding-mode controllers.

2   CONTROL DESIGN

2.1   *Designing of SMC*

Let's consider a non linear serial in serial out system

$$x = f(x, t) + g(x, t)u \tag{1}$$

$$y = h(x, t) \tag{2}$$

The main purpose of the system modeling is to create the yield variable y to follow the right path yDES. It is important that the yield blunder variable e=y-yDES sees out for a very little region of 0 once a transient of satisfactory span.

From the above equation we come to know that SMC synthesis has 2 phase:
PHASE 1 ("SLIDING SURFACE DESIGN")
PHASE a pair of ("CONTROL INPUT style")
The first part is that the definition of a precise scalar perform of the system state, says
$\sigma(x)$: Rn $\to$ R
Often, the slippy surface depends on the chase error ey at the side of a precise variety of its derivatives

$$\sigma = \sigma(e, e, \ldots, e^{\wedge}((k))) \tag{3}$$

The perform σ ought to be elite in such the simplest way that its vanishing, $0=\sigma$, provides rise to a "stable" equation any answer ey(t) of which is able to tend to zero eventually.

The most typical selection for the slippy manifold may be a linear combination of the subsequent kind

$\sigma = e' + C\_(0^{\wedge}e)$ $\tag{4}$
$\sigma = e'' + C\_(1^{\wedge}(\cdot e)) + C\_(0^{\wedge}e)$ $\tag{5}$
$e^{\wedge}((k)) + \Sigma\_(i=0)^{\wedge}(k-1) \llbracket c\_i \, e^{\wedge}((i)) \rrbracket$ $\tag{6}$

The number of derivatives to be enclosed (the "k" constant in (6)) ought to be k−r-1, wherever r is that the input output relative degree of (1)-(2).

With lawfully chosen ci coefficients, on the off likelihood that one cows to zero the σ variable, the exponential evaporating of the blunder and its subsidiaries is gotten.

On the off chance that such property holds, the control errand is to accommodate the limited time focusing of σ, "overlooking" some other viewpoints.

From a practical point of view, the equation $0=\sigma$ states a surface in the error space, that is known as "sliding surface". The flight path of the controlled system is forced towards the sliding surface, due to which the system behavior meets the design specifications.

A form of sliding surface is depending upon a single scalar parameter 'p'

$$\sigma = \left[\frac{d}{dt} + p\right] e \tag{7}$$

$$k = 1\sigma = e + pe \tag{8}$$

The decision of the positive parameter p is practically self-assertive, and characterize the exceptional shaft of the subsequent "decreased elements" of the framework when in sliding.

The whole number parameter k is despite what might be expected rather basic, it must be equivalent to r-1, with r being the relative degree among y and u. This implies the general level of the σ variable is one.

The dynamic stage (PHASE 2) is finding a control movement that coordinates the system bearings onto the sliding complex, that is, toward the day's end, control can direct the σ variable to center the constrained time.

Accentuation is devoted to the second solicitation sliding mode approach, and a couple of references to the higher solicitation approaches are furthermore given. Necessary segment of all SM based procedures is that no accurate knowledge about the primary device parts is requested, the controlled structure is used as an absolutely flawed "revelation" object.

2.2 *Advantange and disadvantage of slide mode controller*

2.2.1 *Advantages:*
- Controller configuration gives methodical way to deal with the issue of keeping up solidness and predictable execution notwithstanding displaying imprecision.
- It has robustness behavior. It is not depending on any structural properties.
- It uses the information about both input and output feedback in control system. It is therefore known as open-closed loop type control system.

2.2.2 *Disadvantage:*
The major drawback of using this technique in industry is that while implementing,actuators has to deal with the high frequency control actions. It will generate premature wear or even breaking problems in the system.

3 APPLICATION OF SLIDE MODE CONTROLLER

SMC is used for its proficiency in adjusting the phase in spite of darken showing batches. The system works by moving a foul up vector in a direction of sliding surface in state space. Vehicles segments are described by the parts of surface. SMC is used for controlling, reducing or removing the bad effects of friction in a mini voice coil motor. Adaptive sliding mode controller is used to achieve and maintain the maximum power point in PV system. SMC strategy is used in high power current source inverter. Sliding mode controllers are also used in automobile industry.

4 CONCLUSION OF SMC

SMC plays an important hypothetical role in the field of research. At the present time it is turning into a decent wellspring of answers for certifiable issues. The ability of SMC is limited by the energy created by working population in controlling process. In this way the possible ways of using SMC in preparing ventures are monstrous. The advantage SMC is that it does not change with the change in measurement condition and it has valuable properties and the capacity to limit the issues into sub-assignments of lower in parity. Finally it is concluded that defects in exchanging gadgets and postponements are inciting.

REFERENCES

F. Ahmad, A. Rasool, E.E. Ozosoy, A. Sabanovic, M. Elitas, "Design Of A Robust Cascaded Controller".

H. Ashrafiuona, R.S. Erwinb, "Sliding Mode Control OfUnderactuatedMultibody Systems And Its Application To Shape Change Control", Int. J. Control. 81 (12) (2008) 1849-1858.

K.K. Leung, H.S. Chung, "Dynamic Hysteresis Band Control Of The Buck Converter With Fast Transient Response, IEEE Trans.On Circuits And Systems Ii: Express Briefs, Vol.52, No. 7, Pp.398-402, July 2005.

RongXu, UmitOzguner, "Sliding Mode Control Of A Class Of Underactuated Systems", Automatica44 (2008) 233-248.

S.C. Tan, Y.M. Lai, C.K. Tse, M.K. Cheung, "A Fixed-Frequency Pulse Width Modulation Based Quasi-Sliding-Mode- Controller For Buck Converters", IEEE Trans. On Power Elect. Vol. 20, No. 3 Pp.1379-1392,Nov. 2005.

V. Utkin, J. Guldner, S. Jingxin, "Sliding Mode Control In Electromechanical Systems". Vol 34. CrcPress, 2009.

Communication and Computing Systems – Prasad et al. (eds)
© 2019 Taylor & Francis Group, London, ISBN 978-0-367-00147-6

Algorithms to achieve maximum power for photovoltaic system

Shalini Sharma
Dronacharya College of Engineering, Gurgaon, India

Neha Verma
ECE Department, Dronacharya College of Engineering, Gurgaon, India

ABSTRACT: Due to the greenhouse effect, acid rain and much more causes recently changing the earth's climate and demand for more electricity. It shows another path to find a new source of energy that is relatively cheaper, sustainable and emits less carbon. For this solution, solar energy showed promising results. But just producing renewable energy is not sufficient, day by day we are seeking to maximize the output. Energy producing is directly proportional to the energy saving i.e. even if in existing producing system, anyhow we succeed to save energy that matters a lot.In a Solar Photovoltaic system, maximum efficiency is 44% for silicon-based solar cell. Solar cell energy conversion efficiency for industrially accessible available multi-crystalline Si solar cells is around 14-19%.Though it's ideal to use more and more solar power, but high installation cost and lower efficiency of Photovoltaic modules are the major obstacles to utilizing such an enormous energy source. To reduce these disadvantages, several studies done. Therefore, to achieve maximum power in a PV system; a maximum Power Point Tracking (MPPT) method becomes a necessity. There are distinct algorithms are used to reach at the maximum power point. Some of the most popular algorithms are 'Perturb and Observe', Incremental Conductance Method, Fuzzy Logic.

1 INTRODUCTION

Mathematical model of PV panel: A PV panel is made up of several parallel and series connections of photovoltaic cells. In this module to increase the voltage series connections are used and to increase the current parallel connections are used. Typically, a solar cell is represented by a current source and a reverse diode jointed in parallel of each other. Figure 1 indicates the equal electrical circuit of a PV cell.

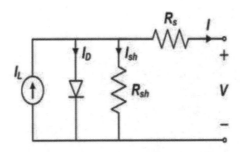

Figure 1. Model of PV panel.

Figure below shows that a solar panel constitutes with an integrated group of solar cells.

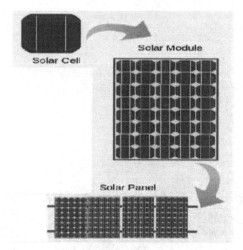

Figure 2.   Solar module.

2   MPPT TECHNIQUES

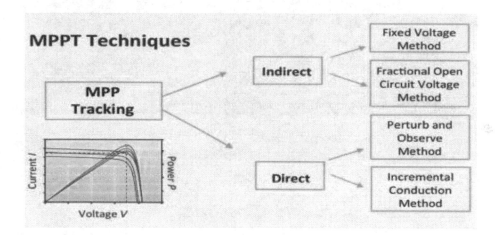

Figure 3.   MPPT techniques.

2.1   *Algorithm for MPPT Perturbation & Observation (P&O) method*

The simplest method is Perturbation & Observation (P & O) method. There is only one sensor is used and that is the voltage sensor, this is used in a way that PV array voltage can be sensed through this, resultantly implementation cost is less and procedure becomes easy. This algorithm includes very less time in completion but as it reaches near to the MPP, it doesn't get eliminated at the MPP, but it continuously unsettles itself in either direction. This is how this algorithm can be so close to the point 'MPP', to overcome this, a suitable error limit can be implemented or as an option wait function can be used to control the increment of complications in time of the algorithm. However, rapid changes in irradiation level cannot address by this method but it treats them as a MPP change because of disturbances and ultimately gives an incorrect calculation of MPP. Use of progressive conductance method is a solution for this problem. This method is also known as hill-climbing MPPT method, these are purely reliable methods and uses the fact i.e. characteristics of power-voltage, the power against voltage dP/dV>0 found on left of the MPP and dP/dV<0 found on right of the same.

This way by watching the value of dP/dV, whether it is less than or greater than 0 the direction of the PV array can be identified. It should be either towards the MPP or away the MPP. Perturbation of the PV array voltage can be so decided to achieve the desired result. Best part of this method is, it involves very less computation and very easy implementation. It is a generic method and almost all the systems support this as we only work on the value of voltage and

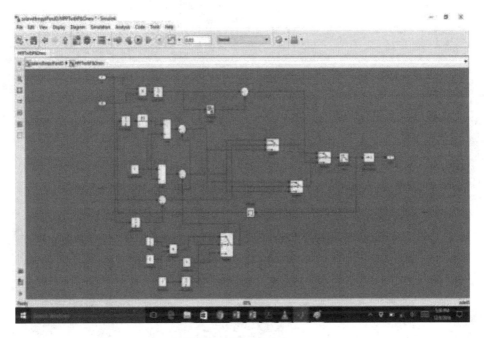

Figure 4. Curve of 'perturb and observe' method.

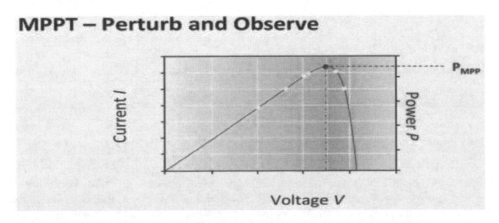

Figure 5. Simulation model of P&O algorithm.

current and PV array information is not required widely. Oscillations are the only problem of P&O system, happening around the MPP, that too in the steady state condition. Also, not so effective tracking because of quickly changes in the direction, which is also a matter of concern.

2.2 Incremental Conductance (IC)

The flaw in the P&O method is tracking the peak power under very quick changing condition and it can be overcome by an Incremental Conductance method. This can verify whether MPPT to stop perturbation or not. Until, this is not achieved, perturbation can be prolong, or vice versa. This whole concept depends upon the dP/dV, either it is less than zero or greater

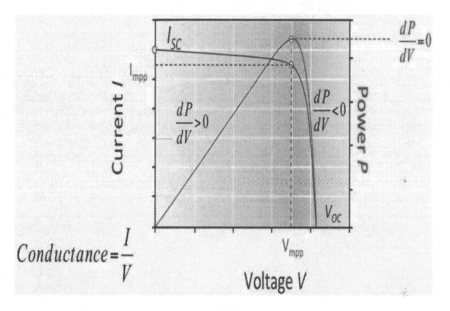

Figure 6. Incremental conductance.

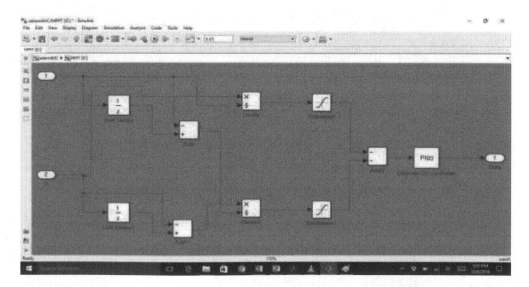

Figure 7. Simulation model of incremental conductance algorithm.

than. This algorithm is advantageous over P&O as it can find out when the tracking has reached the MPP, where P&O keep on oscillating around the MPP. Also, this can track rapidly increasing and decreasing irradiance with greater accuracy than perturb and observe. Only one disadvantage of this algorithm is that it is more complex then compared to P&O.

3 CONCLUSION

This study shows the development of a process for optimum performance of the Photovoltaic System with different algorithms.

REFERENCES

T. Kawamura, K.Hrada, Y.Ishihara, T.Todaka, T. Oshiro, H.Nakamura, M.Imataki, "Analysis of MPPT Characteristics in Photovoltaic Power System", Solar Energy Materials & Solar Cells, Vol. 47, pp.155–165, 1997.

S. Karthika, Dr. P. Rathika, Dr. D. Devaraj, "Fuzzy Logic Based Maximum Power Point Tracking Designed for 10kW Solar Photovoltaic System", International Journal of Computer Science and Management Research, Vol. 2 Issue 2, pp.1421–1427, February 2013.

T. Takashima, T. Tanaka, M. Amano, and Y. Ando, "Maximum output control of photovoltaic (PV) array,"in Proc. 35th Intersociety Energy Convers. Eng. Conf. Ex-hib., pp. 380–383, 2000.

Marcello GradellaVillallava, Jonas Rafael Gazali, and Ernstoruppert Filho, "Comprehensive Approach to Modeling and Simulation of Photovoltaic Array", IEEE Tran. Of Power Electronics, Vol. 24, pp. 1198–1208., 2009.

Y.Kuo-R"Maximum Power Point Tracking controller for photovoltaic energy conversion system"IEEE Trans Ind. Electron-Volume 48–2001.

Communication and Computing Systems – Prasad et al. (eds)
© 2019 Taylor & Francis Group, London, ISBN 978-0-367-00147-6

Lightweight simulated annealing based reconstruction algorithm for sparse binary signals

Ahmed Aziz
Department of Computer Science, Faculty of Computers and Informatics, University of Benha, Egypt

Karan Singh
School of Computer and Systems Science, Jawaharlal Nehru University, New Delhi, India

Walid Osamy
Department of Computer Science, Faculty of Computers and Informatics, University of Benha, Egypt

ABSTRACT: Binary Compressive Sensing method (BCS) widely used in many fields such as image processing and wireless communications. However, binary signal reconstruction is considered one of the biggest challenge that faces the BCS method. Therefore, in this paper, we propose an efficient algorithm called Lightweight Simulated Annealing based Reconstruction Algorithm (LSARA) to address this problem. LSARA combines the advantage of the greedy algorithms in terms of easy and fast implementation with the advantages of simulated annealing in finding the optimal solutions. The simulation results show that our algorithm outperforms the baselines algorithms in term of reducing the reconstruction error.

1 INTRODUCTION

Compressive sensing (CS) (Donoho 2006, Cands 2006, Wang et al.2016, Meenu et al.2018 & A. M. Khedr 2015) method has been proposed as a novel data reduction method for reducing the transmitted data size through the IoT network. According to CS method, the base station (BS) needs only $M \geq KlogN/K$, where M is the size of compressed sampled, K sparse level and N is the signal dimension, to recover the original signal $x \in R^N$ from only $y \in R^M$ measurements such that $y = \Phi x$ and Φ is CS matrix. On the other hand, the CS reconstruction process aims to recover N samples from only M where $M \ll N$ which makes it NP-hard problem (Xinpeng Du et al.2014). The CS reconstruction problem can be expressed as following:

$$min_x \|x\|_0 \, s.t. \; y = \Phi x \tag{1}$$

In Eq.1, the CS reconstruction process aims to recover the sparsity level of the signal x such that the CS matrix Φ and the measurements vector y are given. A lot of Algorithms have been proposed to address this problem such as convex relaxation and greedy algorithm. In convex relation algorithms, the problem in Eq.1 is relaxed by replacing L_0 to L_1 (M.Davenport et al.2010) as following:

$$min_x \|x\|_1 \, s.t. \; y = \Phi x \tag{2}$$

and then uses convex problem solvers such as L_1 -magic toolbox (Raman et al.1998) to solve the problem in Eq.2. Although the convex reconstruction based algorithms have the stability and the ability to reconstruct the full signal correctly, but they suffer from highly complex computations that make them not suitable for IoT network. On the other hand, Greedy algorithms present them self as sufficient reconstruction algorithms. During the greedy algorithm reconstruction process, one or more CS matrix Φ's columns are iteratively choose based on their correlation to the current residual. There are different greedy algorithms can be used such as OMP (J.A. Tropp et al. 2007) algorithm, in which one column is selected from Φ and then OMP algorithm remove its orthogonality from the current residual and then repeats till obtain the estimated signal x'. Based on OMP algorithm a lot of algorithms have been proposed such as ROMP (D. L. Donoho et al. 2012) and StOMP (Deanna Needell et al. 2009). In addition to, CoSaMP (D. Needell et al. 2009), SP (Dai Wei et al. 2009), IHT (V. Cevher et al. 2010) and FBP (Nazim Burak et al. 2013) algorithms, which uses backward steps to prune the wrong elements that have been added during the forward step. All of these algorithms are sufficient but cannot obtain the optimal solution.

Simulated annealing (SA) (Xinpeng Du et al. 2014) is an efficient heuristic algorithm to find the optimal solution for many problems such as optimization problems (Xinpeng Du et al. 2014). Thus, in this paper we aim to utilize the advantage of greedy algorithm in term of simple implementation to integrate it with SA algorithm. To achieve this aim, we propose an efficient algorithm called Lightweight Simulated Annealing based Reconstruction Algorithm (LSARA) which combine between greedy algorithm and SA algorithm. During this paper, we are interested on reconstruct binary data $x \in [0, 1]$. Our contributions can be summarized as follows:

1. Convert the CS reconstruction problem into optimization problem.
2. Utilizes the advantage of SA algorithm in term of finding the optimal solution to solve this optimization problem.
3. Proposes an efficient fitness function that aims to improve the performance of the proposed algorithm.
4. The simulation results explains that the reconstruction performance of the proposed algorithm outperforms existing baseline algorithms.

The rest of the paper is organized as follows: Section 2 presents Simulated Annealing algorithm background. In Section 3, the proposed reconstruction algorithm is described. In Section 4, we present the performance results of our approach and the comparison with existing algorithms. In Section 5, conclusion is presented.

2   SA ALGORITHM BACKGROUND

Simulated annealing (SA) is considered an iterative random search algorithm which simulates the process of annealing of metals (Wei Peng et al.2016). The basic idea of SA is to search into

---

Algorithm 1 SA Algorithm

1: initialize Temperature T and minimum temperature T_{min}
2: Maximum number of iterations i_{max}
3: SA generates a random solution sol
4: Calculate the fitness value for the sol by using the predefined fitness function $cost(sol)$
5: $old_{cost} = cost(sol)$
6: **while** $(T > T_{min})$ **do**
7:    $i=1$
8:   **while** $(i < i_{max})$ **do**
9:      $new_{sol} = neighbor(sol)$
10:     $new_{cost} = cost(new_{sol})$
11:     $ap = acceptance_{probability}(old_{cost}, new_{cost}, T)$
12:     **if** $(ap < random())$ **then**
13:       $sol = new_{sol}$
14:       $old_{cost} = new_{cost}$
15:     **end if**
16:     $i = i+1$
17:   **end while**
18:   Update T
19: **end while**
20: Return sol, cost

---

current solution's neighbors to find a new solution. SA has the ability to avoid being stuck in local optimum this is because in each iteration SA compares the new solution with the current one. If the new one better (based on its fitness value) then it will select it and save it as the base for its next iteration. Else, SA may move to this solution (depending on acceptance probability) not ignore this solution as all other algorithms. The main procedure of SA algorithm is summarized in Algorithm 1.

3 THE PROPOSED LSARA ALGORITHM

In this section, we explain the proposed reconstruction algorithm which called lightweight simulated annealing based reconstruction algorithm (LSARA). LSARA consists of three phases: initialization phase, selection phase and stop criteria phase. LSARA initializes as any greedy algorithms by selecting the largest K amplitude components from the Matched Filter Detection process $\Phi^t y$ i.e $H = max_K(\Phi^t y)$. In addition to, LSARA initializes the SA algorithm parameters such as T_{min} and T. Then, LSARA starts the selection phase in which: firstly, LSARA randomly selects indices of q columns from the matrix Φ such that $q = M/2 - K$. Secondly, LSARA creates the set C which equal to the union of set H and q.

Then LSARA solves the least square problems $\Phi_C^{\dagger} y$ and selects the largest K amplitude components from $I = max_K(\Phi_C^{\dagger} y)$, where I is called support set, as a solution to this iteration, where Φ_C are the columns of Φ with indies equal to C and $\dagger$ means pseudo inverse. This solution I is then evaluated by using the fitness function $F(I)$. Finally, LSARA checks the stopping criteria to decides either to stop if the number of iteration exceeds the maximum number of iteration O_{max} or $F(I) = 0$, or update the temperature T and increase the number of iterations to repeat the selection phase.

3.1 Fitness function

In this section, we propose the following fitness function to be used during the selection phase:

Lemma 3.1: Assume that we have the original signal x is binary vector such that $x \in [0, 1]$ and y is the compressed samples of x such that $y = \Psi x$, then the estimated solution x' with support set $I = \{I_1, I_2, ..., I_K\}$ is the correct solution i.e $x' = x$ if and only if $F(I) = y - (\sum_{i=1}^{i=K} \Phi_{I_i}) = 0$.

Proof: according to CS theory, the compressed samples y is generated from the multiplication result of the non-zeros values of x with the corresponding columns from the matrix Φ. Let $I = \{I_1, I_2, ..., I_K\}$ is the indices of non-zero values of x then the CS can be expressed as:

$$y = \Phi_I x_I, \text{ where } \Phi_I = (\Phi_{I_1}, \Phi_{I_2}....\Phi_{I_K}) \text{ and } x = \begin{pmatrix} x_{I_1} \\ x_{I_2} \\ ..... \\ x_{I_K} \end{pmatrix} \tag{3}$$

Eq.3 can be written as:

$$y = \Phi_{I_1} x_{I_1} + \Phi_{I_2} x_{I_2} + ... + \Phi_{I_K} x_{I_K} \tag{4}$$

Since x is a binary vector, so all the non-zero values equal to 1. Then Eq.4 can be expressed as:

$$y = \Phi_{I_1} + \Phi_{I_2} + ... + \Phi_{I_K} = \sum_{i=1}^{K} \Phi_{I_i} \tag{5}$$

From Eq.5, it is clear that if the support set I is correct then $= y - (\sum_{i=1}^{i=K} \Phi_{I_i}) = 0$.

So, our algorithm aims to find the estimated signal x' with the support set I that achieves $F(I) = 0$. To clarify **Lemma3.1** we provide the following example:

$$Let \ x = \begin{pmatrix} 1 \\ 0 \\ 1 \\ 0 \end{pmatrix} and \ \Phi = \begin{pmatrix} 0.1818 & 0.1361 & 0.5499 & 0.6221 \\ 0.2638 & 0.8693 & 0.1450 & 0.3510 \\ 0.1455 & 0.5797 & 0.8530 & 0.5132 \end{pmatrix}. \ \text{From vector } x \text{ we can say}$$

that the non-zero values of x are located at indices $I = \{1,3\}$. Then the compressed samples vector y can be computed as following:

$$y = \Phi_I x(I) = \begin{pmatrix} 0.1818 \\ 0.2638 \\ 0.1455 \end{pmatrix}(1) + \begin{pmatrix} 0.5499 \\ 0.1450 \\ 0.8530 \end{pmatrix}(1) = \begin{pmatrix} 0.7317 \\ 0.4088 \\ 0.9986 \end{pmatrix}$$

Assume that the support set I is equal to $I = \{1,4\}$, then $\sum_{i=1}^{K} \Phi_{I_i} = \begin{pmatrix} 0.1818 \\ 0.2638 \\ 0.1455 \end{pmatrix} + \begin{pmatrix} 0.6221 \\ 0.3510 \\ 0.5132 \end{pmatrix} = \begin{pmatrix} 0.8039 \\ 0.6148 \\ 0.6588 \end{pmatrix}$

According to the proposed fitness function $F(I) \neq 0$, then I isn't the correct solution.

3.2 LSARA description

This section provides the detailed descriptions of the proposed algorithm. During the initialization phase, LSARA initializes all SA parameters such as T_{min} and T. In addition to, LSARA uses Matched Filter Detection process $\Phi'y$ and selects the largest K amplitude components from it to initialize the support set H and then calculates the fitness value to H i.e. $F(H)$ using

---

Algorithm 2 LSARA Algorithm

1: **Input:** The compressed sample= y, selection size= q and CS matrix Φ
2: **Initialization Phase**
3: Maximum number of inner iterations In_{max} and Maximum number of outer iterations Out_{max}
4: initialize Temperature T, minimum temperature T_{min}, outer loop counter $O_i = 1$ and inner loop counter $E_i = 1$
5: H={the largest K amplitude components in $\Phi'y$}
6: Calculates the fitness value of H i.e $F(H)$using Lemma .1.1
7: **while** Stopping criterion is not met $\|$ $O_i < Out_{max}$ **do**
8:     **Selection Phase:**
9:     **while** $E_i \leq In_{max}$ **do**
10:         Choose randomly q columns from Φ
11:         $C = H \cup q$
12:         $I = \{$the largest K amplitude components in $\Phi_C^\dagger y \}$
13:         Calculates $F(I)$ using Lemma 1.1
14:         **if** $F(H) > F(I)$ **then**
15:             $H = I$ and $F(H) = F(I)$
16:         **end if**
17:         $E_i = E_i + 1$
18:     **end while**
19:     **Stopping Criteria Phase**
20:     **if** $O_i \geq Out_{max} \| F(I) == 0$ **then**
21:         Stop, and Return $x'_I = \Phi_I y$ and $x'_{N-I} = 0$
22:     **end if**
23:     Updates T and $O_i = O_i + 1$
24: **end while**
25: **Output:** x'

---

the proposed lemma. The selection Phase is considered the main search steps, in which the LSARA starts by selecting random q columns from the matrix Φ, where $q = M/2 - K$ depends on the fact that the CS reconstruction problem can be resolved if the sparsity level $K \leq M/2$ (Dai Wei et al.2009). Then LSARA creates the set $C = q \cup H$ to solve the least square problem $\Phi_C^{\dagger} y$ and creates the support set I which contains the largest K amplitude components in $\Phi_C^{\dagger} y$. This support set is then evaluated by using the proposed fitness function **Lemma3.1**.

LSARA algorithm checks the value of $F(I)$, If $F(I) < F(H)$ then set $H = I$ and $F(H) = F(I)$. The inner loop is repeated till the maximum inner iterations In_{max} is reached. Finally, LSARA algorithm checks the stopping criterion i.e. the number of outer loop iterations exceed the maximum numbers Out_{max} or $F(I) = 0$. If the stopping criterion is met then the estimated signal will calculated as $x_I' = \Phi_I y$ and $x_{N-1}' = 0$.

Otherwise, LSARA updates the T value and repeats the selection phase. LSARA is summarized in Algorithm 2.

4 SIMULATION RESULTS

In this section, MATLAB environment is used for performing all simulations and we use Gaussian and Bernoulli matrices Φ with size $M \times N$, where $N = 256$ and $M = 128$ as Φ CS matrix. LSARA algorithm is applied to reconstruct computer-generated sparse binary signals. We evaluate the performance of LSARA reconstruction algorithm in comparison to OMP (J.A. Tropp et al. 2007), COSAMP (D. Needell et al. 2009) and SP (Dai Wei et al. 2009) in term of Average Normalized Mean Squared Error (ANMSE) which can be defined as average $\|L\|_2$ difference between the original reading and the reconstructed one, divided by $\|x\|_2$ which can be expressed as: $\frac{\|x-x'\|_2}{\|x\|_2}$ where x is the original signal and x' is the estimated one, and the average runtime.

In Figure 1 where the Gaussian matrix is used to compress the sparse binary signal, LSARA algorithm clearly provides lower ANMSE comparing to COSAMP, OMP and SP. In addition, ANMSE for LSARA algorithm is started to increase only when $K > 58$ while it increases when $K > 45, K \geq 41$ and $K \geq 48$ for COSAMP, OMP and SP algorithms respectively as shown in Figure 1.

Fig.2 shows ANMSE results where the Bernoulli matrix is used to compress the sparse binary signal. In Figure 2, LSARA algorithm still provides lowest ANMSE result comparing to COSAMP, OMP and SP, as $K > 56, K \geq 45, K > 38$ and $K > 49$, respectively.

In Figure 3, we aims to test LSARA reconstruction performance when different measurement vector lengths- M are used with Gaussian CS matrices distribution matrix. To achieve this aim, the length of the sparse binary signals drawn from uniform distribution *is* $N = 120$ is

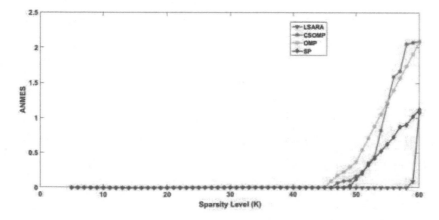

Figure 1.   ANMSE vs Sparsity Level for sparse binary signals using Gaussian matrix.

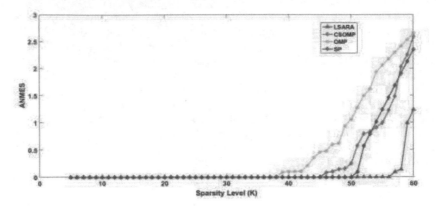

Figure 2. ANMSE vs Sparsity Level for sparse binary signals using Bernoulli matrix.

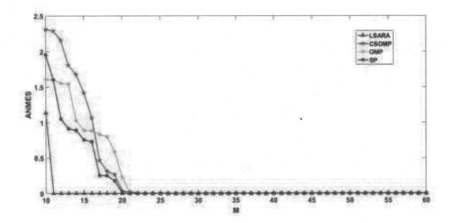

Figure 3. Reconstruction results over Gaussian matrix with different length of M.

used and M values ranges from 10 to 60 with step size 1. From those figures, we observe that LASRS algorithm still provides the lowest ANMSE values comparing to the others.

From Figure 4, it is clear that LSARA average run time is higher than the greedy algorithm but still slightly fast.

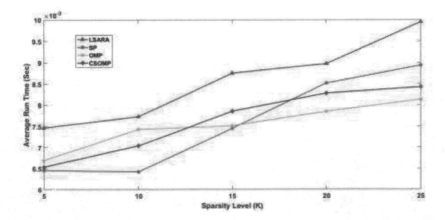

Figure 4. Average run times as a function of sparsity level.

5 CONCLUSION

In this paper, we proposed LSARA algorithm to reconstruct sparse binary signals. LSARA integrates between the advantages of the greedy algorithms in easy and fast implementation with the advantage of SA algorithm in finding the optimal solution to improve the reconstruction performance. In addition to, we proposed an efficient fitness function which helped the proposed algorithm to reconstruct the binary signals in perfects way. The simulation results show that LSARA outperformed the reconstruction performance of the baselines algorithms with acceptable run time.

ACKNOWLEDGMENT

This work was carried out in Security and Computing laboratory, SC&SS, JNU, New Delhi, India

REFERENCES

D. L. Donoho, Compressed sensing 2006, in IEEE Trans, on Inf. Theory, vol. 52, no. 4, pp. 1289-1306.

E. J. Cands, Compressive Sampling 2006, in Proc. of the Int. Cong. of Mathematicians, Vol. III, Madrid, Spain, pp. 1433–1452.

R. Meenu and B. Sanjay Dhok and R. B., Deshmukh 2018, A Systematic Review of Compressive Sensing: Concepts, Implementations and Applications IEEE Access vol. 6, pp. 4875–48754894.

C. Lv, Q. Wang,W. Yan, Y. Shen 2016, Energy balanced compressive data gathering in Wireless Sensor Networks, Journal of Network and Computer Applications, vol. 61, pp 102–102114.

A. M. Khedr 2015, Effective Data Acquisition Protocol for Multi-Hop Heterogeneous Wireless Sensor Networks Using Compressive Sensing, pp. 910–928.

D. M. Omar, A. M. Khedr and Dharma P. Agrawal 2017, Optimized Clustering Protocol for Balancing Energy in Wireless Sensor Networks, International Journal of Communication Networks and Information Security (IJCNIS) Vol. 9, No. 3, pp. 367–375.

Ahmed Aziz, Karan Singh, Walid Osamy, Ahmed M. Khedr 2019, Effective algorithm for optimizing compressive sensing in IoT and periodic monitoring applications, Journal of Network and Computer Applications, Vol. 126, P 12–28.

Xinpeng Du, Lizhi Cheng, Daiqiang Chen 2014, A simulated annealing algorithm for sparse recovery by l 0 minimization, Neuro computing, Vol. 131, P. 98–104.

M.Davenport, P.Boufounos, M.Wakin, and R.G.Baraniuk 2010, Signal processing with compressive measurements, IEEE Journal of Selected Topics in Signal Processing, vol. 55, no. 5, ppp. 445 460.

Raman Venkataramani and Yoram Bresler 1998, Sub-nyquist sampling of multiband signals: perfect reconstruction and bounds on aliasing error, IEEE International Conference on Acoustics, Speech and Signal Processing (ICASSP), pp. 12–15.

J.A. Tropp, A.C. Gilbert 2007, Signal recovery from random measurements via orthogonal matching pursuit, IEEE Trans. Inf. Theory 53 (12), P. 4655–4666.

D. L. Donoho, Y. Tsaig, I. Drori, and J. L. Starck 2012, Sparse solution of underdetermined systems of linear equations by stagewise orthogonal matching pursuit,. IEEE Trans. Inf. Theory, 58(2):1094–1121.

Deanna Needell and Roman Vershynin 2009, Uniform uncertainty principle and signal recovery via regularized orthogonal matching pursuit, Found. Comput. Math., 9(3):317–334.

D. Needell, J.A. Tropp 2009, CoSaMP: iterative signal recovery from incomplete and inaccurate samples, Appl. Comput. Harmon. Anal. 26 (3), 301–321.

Dai Wei and Milenkovic Olgica 2009, Subspace Pursuit for Compressive Sensing Signal Reconstruction, IEEE Trans. Inf. Theory, vol.55, no. 5, pp. 2230–22302249.

V. Cevher and S. Jafarpour 2010, fast hard thresholding with nesterovs gradient method. In: Neuronal Information Processing Systems, Workshop on Practical Applications of Sparse Modeling, Whistler, and Canada.

Nazim Burak and Hakan Erdogan 2013, Compressed sensing signal recovery via forward-backward pursuit, Digital Signal Processing, vol.23, pp.1539–1531548.

Wei Peng and HongxiaWang 2016, Binary Sparse Phase Retrieval via Simulated Annealing, Mathematical Problems in Engineering.

Communication and Computing Systems – Prasad et al. (eds)
© 2019 Taylor & Francis Group, London, ISBN 978-0-367-00147-6

ACO and GA based test suite reduction for component based software: A hybrid approach

Palak & Preeti Gulia
Department of Computer Science and Applications, MDU, Rohtak, India

ABSTRACT: The quality of a software application depends on the effectiveness of the testing carried out during development and maintenance phase. Testing is a crucial but time consuming activity that influences the overall cost of software development. Thus a minimal but efficient test suite selection is the need of the hour. This paper presents a hybrid technique based on ACO (Ant Colony Optimization) and GA (Genetic Algorithm) for selection of promising test cases to reduce the overall development cost and time of the application. We took component based software into consideration as they offer some inherent advantages over traditional software development paradigms.

KEYWORDS: Ant Colony Optimization, Genetic Algorithm, Test Case selection, Components

1 INTRODUCTION

The hardware and software industries are growing together at very fast pace to meet the growing need of smart devices. The smart gadgets have invaded our lives so badly that we can't predict our future without them. The software embedded with these devices play a crucial role to provide best known user experiences to provide the intended functionality. This scenario raises many challenges in front of the software developers to fulfill the quality needs of the end user. Software testing is a crucial and unavoidable step to achieve the same. The role of test cases in the process of testing is very important to verify the functionality and detect faults. A software failure can claim many lives in case of critical systems. Moreover the development paradigms have evolved a long way from traditional procedural approach to a modular component based approach. Component based software engineering (CBSE) (Szyperski, 2002) evolved back in late 1980's and growing since then. It works on the principle of reusability and the software in developed in small chunks called components. Each component has some set of functionality and interacts with other components through interfaces. They provide a black box view of the functionality. Commercial off the shelf (COTS) is gaining popularity with time. Considering the impracticality of the exhaustive testing, it becomes the need of the hour to select a promising suite of test data that is capable of providing higher fault coverage.

Ant Colony Optimization (M. Dorigo et.al., 1999) and Genetic Algorithm (Mitchell et. al., 1996) are search based techniques that are inspired from nature and natural phenomenon. They are meta-heuristic techniques that are problem independent and can work with incomplete knowledge. In contrast to heuristics, meta- heuristics provide randomness during searching and prevent us to get stuck in local optima. We exploited the advantages of both to develop a hybrid approach that is capable of selecting promising test cases to reduce the size of test suite without compromising with the efficiency and test coverage.

2 RELATED WORK

Soft computing based techniques have attracted the researchers over many years due to their potential to deal with uncertainty and incomplete knowledge. The field of software testing over component based system is also been influenced with these search based techniques and has resulted into a vast literature and research work done over years. A few important recent researches over last five years in this field are summarized here. Abhishek Singh et al. in [1] presented a modified genetic algorithm based technique for test case generation. They used particle swarm optimization (PSO) for fitness enhancement. Neha et al. in [2] applied ACO for reducing cost of regression testing and implemented it in C++. Traditional ACO has scarce initial pheromone, keeping that point in mind Shunkun Yang et al. in [3] proposed improved pheromone deposition and updation coefficients and compared the results with random testing and GA based testing. Various soft computing based techniques like neural network, ant system etc. are compared in [4] for software fault prediction. Authors in [5] utilized potential of ACO for reducing test cases for object oriented systems and implemented their proposed approach using MATLAB. Maunika et al. in [6] exploited Bee colony optimization for test case selection and to improve path coverage. Authors in [7] used genetic algorithm for regression test suite prioritization and produced mutants for object oriented codes. Wasiur Rhmann et al. in [8] presented their research in which they applied GA for improving test efficiency in early stages of software development. They tried to improve test coverage of activity diagram created from design specification. Researchers are also attracted towards the adaptive behavior of ACO in which they tried to modify the algorithm based on some parameters to get better results in case of test case selection as done by [9][10][11][12]. Similarly many researchers and practitioners are more attracted towards genetic algorithm for software testing and applied the same at various phases of testing as in [13][14]. A variant of GA is presented in [15] as bacteriologic algorithm (BA) and introduced new memorization operator. To consider the fact that there is always a scope of improvement, researchers went one more step ahead and developed hybrid techniques by combining two or more soft computing based techniques to further enhance the potential to optimize problems. One such research is presented in [16] which applies crossover between ants to reduce the regression testing cost. P. Gulia et al. in [17] presented a review of all the soft computing based techniques for testing reusable components and concluded that GA and ACO are the prominent nature inspired techniques that attracted researchers in recent years. Authors in [18] proposed a hybrid approach for test case selection using fuzzy inference system and ACO. Further Bee colony optimization (BCO) has also attracted researchers as in [19] where authors implemented GA based BCO for automation of various testing phases. Palak et al. in [20] proposed an ACO based model for testing component based software and their interaction failure. To summarize, a vast literature is available in this field which shows its industrial importance and coverage.

3 PROPOSED MODEL

In this section, a hybrid approach is proposed that combines the benefits of ACO and GA. The main idea is to populate the system with some random ants as done in traditional ACO. Each ant while moving to the neighboring components in the search of food, it deposits some amount of pheromone on its path.

The proposed approach is summarized here:

Input: Fault Matrix, Component Diagram
Step 1: Convert the system into component diagram.
Step 2: Apply ACO over component diagram.
Step 3: Over the result of ACO, further apply GA crossover and mutation operation.
Step 4: Repeat steps 2 and 3 until stopping criteria is met.
Output: Reduced set of test cases.

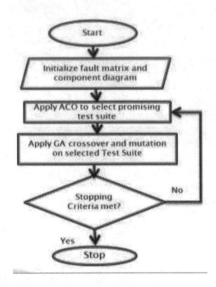

Figure 1.   Proposed model.

4   RESULTS AND ANALYSIS

The proposed technique is applied on the fault matrix given in Table 1.

Table 1.   Fault matrix.

Test Case	F1	F2	F3	F4	F5	F6	F7	F8	F9	F10	No. of Faults
T1	*		*		*		*		*	*	6
T2		*		*	*		*		*		5
T3	*	*						*		*	4
T4		*			*	*		*		*	5
T5	*	*		*		*			*		5
T6	*		*		*		*	*		*	6
T7	*	*		*		*		*	*		6
T8		*	*	*		*		*		*	6
T9	*		*		*		*		*		5
T10		*		*		*		*		*	5
T11		*		*	*				*		4
T12			*		*	*		*	*		5
T13	*	*		*		*	*	*		*	7
T14	*	*	*		*		*		*		6
T15		*		*		*		*		*	5

It contains ten different faults and fifteen test cases into consideration. First of all traditional ACO and GA is applied on the given fault matrix and results are plotted as shown in Figure 2. Then the proposed ACO-GA based hybrid approach is applied and it was found that this technique outperforms the traditional techniques. The graph shown in Figure 2 compares the proposed technique with traditional techniques. It was resulted that hybrid ACO-GA based technique is capable of achieving 100% fault coverage in 50% of test cases. While traditional techniques underperform in this scenario.

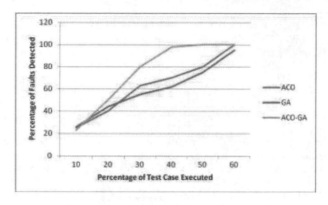

Figure 2. Comparison of proposed technique with traditional techniques.

5 CONCLUSION

Test case selection is an important activity to reduce the testing effort without compromising with the quality of the software. In recent years, search based nature inspired techniques are evolving to select optimal test suite. This paper presents a Genetic Algorithm based hybrid ACO technique which exploits the benefits of the two. The main idea is to select a subset of test cases from a large pool which are more promising for efficient testing. These test cases are selected using traditional ACO technique. To further optimize the effectiveness, we employed GA over selected test cases to get a good mix of test cases to avoid the problem of getting stuck in the local optima. It was analyzed that proposed technique performs better than traditional techniques and is capable of finding 100% errors in 50 % of the test cases. In future, it will be interesting to implement the proposed model for large scale testing problems to assess its scalability.

REFERENCES

Agarwal, S., Gupta, S., Sabharwal, N., "Automatic Test Data Generation-Achieving Optimality Using Ant-Behaviour," *Int. J. Inf. Educ. Technol.*, vol. 6, no. 2, pp. 117–121, 2016.

Ansari, A., Khan, A., Khan, A., Mukadam, K. "Optimized Regression Test Using Test Case Prioritization," *Procedia Comput. Sci.*, vol. 79, pp. 152–160, 2016.

Arora, K. Arora, M., M.R. Unviserity, "Hybrid Approach for Optimizing Test Suite Based on GA & ACO," *Int. J. Innov. Res. Technol.*, vol. 3, no. 2, pp. 65–69, 2016.

Dalal, S., Solanki, K. "Performance Analysis of BCO-m-GA Technique for Test Case Selection," *Indian J. Sci. Technol.*, vol. 11, no. March, 2018.

Erturk, E., Akcapinar, E. "Expert Systems with Applications A comparison of some soft computing methods for software fault prediction," *Expert Syst. Appl.*, vol. 42, no. 4, pp. 1872–1879, 2015.

Gulia, P., Palak, P. "Nature Inspired Soft Computing Based Software Testing Techniques For Reusable Software Components," *J. Theor. Appl. Inf. Technol.*, vol. 95, no. 24, pp. 6996–7004, 2017.

Khanna, E. "Regression Testing based on Genetic Algorithms," *Int. J. Comput. Appl. (0975*, vol. 154, no. 8, pp.43–46, 2016.

Kumar, G., Bhatia, P.K. "Software Test Case Reduction using Genetic Algorithm : A Modified Approach," *Int. J. Innov. Sci. Eng. Technol.*, vol. 3, no. 5, pp. 349–354, 2016.

Kumar, M. S., Srinivas, P. "An Ant Colony Algorithm to Prioritize the Regression Test Cases of Object-Oriented Programs," *Indian J. Sci. Technol.*, vol. 9, no. May, 2016.

Mohapatra, S. K., Prasad, S. "Test Case Reduction Using Ant Colony Optimization for Object Oriented Program," *Int. J. Electr. Comput. Eng.*, vol. 5, no. 6, pp. 1424–1432, 2015.

Mounika, M., Reddy, D.V., "Test Case Selection For Path Testing Using Bee Colony Optimization," no. February, pp. 1–7, 2015.

Musa, S., Sultan, A.A. Bin Abd-ghani, and S. Baharom, "Software Regression Test Case Prioritization for Object-Oriented Programs using Genetic Algorithm with Reduced-Fitness Severity," *Indian J. Sci. Technol.*, vol. 8, no. November, 2015.

Ranjan Srivastava, P. "Test case optimisation a nature inspired approach using bacteriologic algorithm," *Int. J. Bio-Inspired Comput.*, vol. 8, no. 2, pp. 122–131, 2016.

Rhmann, W. "Use of Genetic Approach for Test Case Prioritization from UML Activity Diagram," vol. 115, no. 4, pp. 8–12, 2015.

Palak, Gulia, P. "Ant Colony Optimization Based Test Case Selection for Component Based Software," *Int. J. Eng. Technol.*, vol. 7, no. 4, pp. 2743–2745, 2018

Ping, C., Min, X. "Software Testing Case Generation of Ant Colony Optimization Based on Quantum Dynamic Self-Adaptation," vol. 8, no. 9, pp. 95–104, 2015.

Sethi, N. "Ants Optimization for Minimal Test Case Selection and Prioritization as to Reduce the Cost of Regression Testing," vol. 100, no. 17, pp. 48–54, 2014.

Silva, D., Rabelo, R., Oliveira, P. A. "A Hybrid Approach for Test Case Prioritization and Selection," *CEC*, no. July, pp. 4508–4515, 2016

Singh, A., Garg, N., Saini, T. "A hybrid Approach of Genetic Algorithm and Particle Swarm Technique to Software Test Case Generation," *Int. J. Innov. Eng. Technol.*, vol. 3, no. 4, pp. 208–214, 2014.

Yang, S., Man, T., Xu, J. "Improved ant algorithms for software testing cases generation", *Sci. World J.*, vol. 2014, 2014.

Communication and Computing Systems – Prasad et al. (eds)
© 2019 Taylor & Francis Group, London, ISBN 978-0-367-00147-6

Proactive health monitoring and screening using IoT and Artificial Intelligence

Jeetendra Kumar & Krishanu Kundu
ECE Department, Dronacharya college of Engineering, Gurgaon, India

ABSTRACT: Identifying health issues before to become serious is one of the best ways to stay healthy. The better chance to cure disease or successful treatment, when we diagnose in early condition. As we know, Wellbeing is the level of valuable and metabolic strength of a living being. Sound health is obligatory to do the daily work properly. With the rapid growth of the Internet of Things. Artificial Intelligence and the emergence of wearable devices & algorithms, it is possible to monitor and screening important aspects of our daily life, to encourage a healthier lifestyle. This paper proposes a dynamic healthcare system that will allow the patient-user to proactive health monitoring, tracking and reviewing their time to time physical & mental activities. Such as patient's emerging cancer, pulse-rate, heartbeat rate, pressure level rate, body-temperature, neuron functionality, etc. using IoT devices and AI system algorithms. If the framework identifies any sudden changes in persistent observed information. Then the framework system will automatically warn the doctors and patient user. As the patient data standings over the IoT network so furthermore appears details of the patient's real-time report live over the internet using login panel.

1 INTRODUCTION

We are moving to the modern world but the health issues are expanding day by day at a gigantic pace. The passing rate goes beyond our expectations of 55.3 million people passing on each year or 151,600 individuals passing on each day or 6316 individuals passing on each hour as per the report of 2011 record. If I am not wrong then the report of 2019 will give us huge increment in it. This is a big issue all over the world. Hence, it is the hour in which we need to resolve such issues. We purpose a change in healthcare framework technology by planning a progressed innovation framework which included the distinctive type of wearable remote sensors gadget to get data and abrupt changing with individual human body temperature, heart rate sensor, blood pressure sensor, saline level meter, ECG sensors, etc. Further, these sensors will transmit on an IoT stage and stored in database real time which will be easily accessible by the user via the internet over the globe. An accessible patient's health database history can be advance utilized in monitoring, analyzing & screening by the doctor if necessary. This paper proposes a proactive health checking & screening framework which is able of identifying different parameters of our body such as heart rate, temperature, blood pressure, ECG, respiration rate, glucose level, neuron signal, etc. Artificial Intelligence (AI) recognizes all data from the database which is spawned from sensors and alert for proactive symptoms of changing in the body. Further, transmitting this data on IoT server through GSM innovations. Also, in case of an emergency, automatically generating alerts will be sent to the doctors and family members carrying devices if any unusual activity is detected, via sensors & AI by or near the patient. Artificial Intelligence (AI) will give the visual of real-time emerging changes.

These days, individuals pay more consideration towards early acknowledgment and avoidance of malady. So, ceaseless capture of body health parameters can be utilized to identify the malady in a more powerful & dependable way. In addition, the emerging technology solutions often simplify a wide variety of networks such as mobile phone applications, Internet, Internet of Things, database, data analysis, artificial intelligence innovations & their administrations give a critical impact within the advancement of healthcare utilizing network assortments (4G, Broadband, Bluetooth, GSM) etc. As, devices are getting connected using IoT, Machine Learning provides great support to the process of AI using the algorithms.

Several types of sensors have been used to capture the health parameters of patient like Blood Pressure sensor (4811) is utilized to measure diastolic pressure, systolic pressure and pulse rate for a few seconds. ECG sensor (AD8232) for remote ECG monitoring. The LM35 temperature sensor is utilized to check the degree of the body skin surface, ultrasonic neural sensors- this tiny neural implant enables electrophysiological recordings of nerves, muscles, and organs in the peripheral nervous system in real time. It is also ultrasound based. Ultrasound is very effective at transmitting data and delivering power to IoT devices network and these sensors are wireless and battery less.

Gratifying work is done in health observing by utilizing Artificial Intelligence (AI) and IoT. The brought down cost for sensors and network, besides the expansion of the Internet of Things (IoT), with making cross-pollination process - where innovative advances in one region drive progress in other clearing obstructions to accessible smart medicine. Remote persistent observing is interestingly qualified to weigh in on rising patterns in healthcare and AI innovation. The Internet of Things is the organize of smart gadgets like phones, computers, therapeutic gadgets, etc. which are implanted with sensors, computer program, database and network, which makes communication conceivable between gadgets and database. AI (Artificial Intelligence) is the intelligence illustrated by machine algorithm. It tries to simulate the normal insights of people, which means it mimics the cognitive functions that humans performs using their brain such as listening, learning and problem solving. For this research paper, we explored recent papers related to health observing frameworks based on IoT and AI. The progress concept of ICT (Information Communication Innovation) gives the interconnection of gadgets and administrations that diminishes human innovation to live distant life. While, this paper points to supply progressions in healthcare administration innovation by utilizing trending innovation, it would save patients from the long term health issues and would moreover help specialists and family individuals to require suitable action or measure at a real-time with respect to patient's health.

2 RELATED WORK

The cluster of numerous applications empowered by the Internet of Things (IoT), and associated with healthcare system server. Medical sensors, either embedded in living things or worn on the body will forward the gathered data with the indication of physical and mental state. Continuous basis of captured data, comprehensive and constructively mined, these all data will give a positive transformative revision inside the well-being care system. The strategy of collecting information from each persistent a corresponding set of estimation of a control parameter of the health condition. Control esteem is calculated from the comparing set of estimations; the control esteem demonstrates the patient's control over the wellbeing condition. Further, the method includes the steps of displaying and generating an overview chart having the active disease with the data points. Each information focuses on the chart represents one comparing patient and demonstrates the control esteem and the time-period for the comparing persistent. The era of the shrewd handle of the algorithm can encourage advancement. A proactive system can forecast of maladies at an early organize with this post facto diagnose-and-treat responsive paradigm.

3 IOT & ARTIFICIAL INTELLIGENCE DESIGN IN HEALTHCARE

Different researches proposed the common design about the healthcare framework utilizing IoT & Artificial Intelligence as per Figure 1. The most existing layers (stages) included within the design are

3.1 Network sensor layer

This layer accumulates the biomedical sensors data & information from all body connected sensors like blood pressure, pulse rate, temperature, oxygen level, ECG, Ultrasonic neural sensor, saline level meter sensor, etc... Most of the wearable sensors are associated along with the network called Wireless Body Area Network (WBAN) that gives the information to the cloud database server.

3.2 Gateway layer

Simultaneously obtained data of wearable sensors send to a cloud database server through node user can access, which may act as a door. The collected data will be extracted to get meaningful information from it with the help of artificial Intelligence algorithm techniques.

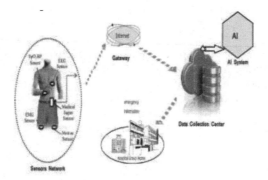

Figure 1. Smart healthcare architecture using AI & IoT.

3.3 Cloud database server layer

At this layer, the all processed or unprocessed information are stored for analysis, monitoring, controlling and other purpose. The smart healthcare framework creates a tremendous amount of patient information (therapeutic records, recordings, sensor information, and ICU signals, images and others) every minutes. This information isn't only utilized to induce common data but also helps to detect and further experiment to improve the patient care, health and analyzing to the Artificial Intelligence, to provide the pro-alert of any emerging disease.

Hence, Artificial Intelligence & machine learning algorithms make possible to mining, filtering, processing and analyzing of data to the entire system. And help to transform data like video, graph, text, audio, signals, and images into meaningful information. As we are aware with the resent smart algorithm, which are capable to automate and accelerate the diagnostic capabilities. Artificial Intelligence & machine learning algorithms serves three purposes: feature extraction from data, reprocessing of data and developing the predictive model which is trained to learned the features from a logical algorithm. Training of the Artificial Intelligence model is done on large amount of data recorded over long period of time on the cloud server database using well established computational algorithm and approaches. The real-time extracted data, analysis can be handled by the trained model. After that, the extracted data information i.e. processed data is accessible to doctors through cloud via internet. Some of data report which is also accessible to family members.

4 PROPOSED MODEL

The improvement of the IoT paradigm for healthcare system monitoring, control and supervision due to revolutionary changes in Information communication technology (ICT). There are

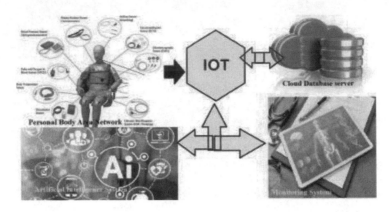

Figure 2.   Smart multilayered healthcare monitoring framework at real-time using AI & IoT.

several smart wearable gadgets like smart watches are accessible nowadays which are able of computing and detecting both. These gadgets can detect as well as computational capabilities which is the mandatory for the smart healthcare system applications. The plan of the proposed demonstration of real-time multilayered proactive health observing and screening utilizing IoT and Artificial Intelligence and its different computing components, algorithms. In Figure 2, this proposed system improves health observing, screening and controlling by expanding the computational capabilities of sensors, IoT devices and artificial intelligence bots algorithm, making it compatible with the database server to fetch the information to the several devices, which is the requirement of the advanced healthcare medical applications.

This framework comprises of the five medical management sensors which are blood sensors, temperature sensors, pulse sensors, ECG sensor, and ultrasonic neural sensor. The client wears all the connected sensors to get real- time health status and also gather data information. The gathered data information are prepared to transmission but before that we need to compress it by using most favoring hybrid compression technique to IoT environment, which can be applied on the sensors information data. This procedure can be utilized to compress the information detected by the sensors before transmitting it to the cloud base database. The information is transmitted to the cloud database to process it. Before to upload result on the connected display, Artificial Intelligence algorithm used to analyze the cloud based data information. After AI analysis, in case the health status appears unfortunate at that point the framework will tell the client (doctor, family member) what is the malady persistent may confront and what preventions ought to take? Artificial Intelligence algorithm is also used to capture the proactive disease by the real-time patient data. As every disease has initial symptoms, so the Artificial Intelligence algorithm will analysis data as per logical way, if any symptoms found related to any disease then AI bot will alert doctors with a message and provide reason behind their analysis report. The AI will also provide the emergency service, such as automatic alert message to user and provide current status of observed. This all information can be accessed by the user on their PC, tablet, mobile phone via internet, anywhere in the world.

5   RESULT AND CONCLUSION

The proposed design is simulated to track the disease in the proactive stage. So, we can cure any vital disease like cancer, etc in the initial stage. Artificial Intelligence will provide the better result of analysis, information and health parameters. In recent year 2017, a report disclose about the availability of doctors ratio. It is less than one specialist per thousand individuals over the world. The circumstance is more critical and panic in the provincial region. The telemedicine benefit has accomplished a crest with the rise of IoT. However, the above confession contains numerous specificities; these ought to not be expected as impediments on the scope of the innovation. There's still wide scope of advancement for IoT and Artificial Intelligence (AI) implementation. According to the logical investigate prospective, no venture has been created or integrated on artificial intelligence robot, which can provide all necessary report to the doctor & family member. If the multiple sensors system like blood pressure sensor, temperature sensor, and pulse rate sensor can be integrated in a single framework, it reduces the cost of healthcare. IoT based frameworks only show value or chart rather than the conclusion. But when IoT and AI will come together then it will provide us display analytical data, solution based data, suggestion, proactive disease alarm and even AI can provide logical and visual status of the patient over the remote based doctor. The Artificial intelligence (AI) can give the health-associated information with specialists World Health Organization (WHO) in an emergency. Indeed the nonappearance of the specialist will make patient 'close' or within the hospital.

REFERENCES

Andrea Zanella, Nicola Bui, Lorenzo Vangelista, Angelo Castellani, Michele Zorzi, "Internet of Things for Smart Cities", IEEE Internet Of Things Journal, vol. 1, no. 1, pp. 22–32, February 2014.

A Ukil, S. Bandyopadhyay, C. Puri, and A. Pal, "IoT healthcare analytics; The importance of anomaly detection,"in *Advanced Information Networking and Applications (AINA), 2016 IEEE 30th International Conference on*, 2016 pp.994–997.

C. Doukas and I. Maglogiannis, "Bringing IoT and Cloud computing towards pervasive healthcare, "in *Innovative Mobile and Internet Services In Ubiquitous Computing (IMIS)*, 2012 *Sixth International Conference on*, 2012, pp.922–922926

C. J. Deepu, C.-H. Heng and Y. Lian, "A hybrid data compression scheme for power reduction in wireless sensors for IoT," *IEEE transitions on biomedical Circuits and systems*, vol.11, pp.245–253, 2017

H. Mora, D. Gil, R. M. Terol, J. Azorin, and J. Szymanski, "An IoT based Computational Framework for Healthcare Monitoring in Mobile Environments," *Sensors*, vol. 17, pp. 2302, 2017

Junaid Mohammed; Chung-Horng Lung; Adrain Ocneanu; Abhinav Thakaral; Colin Jones; Andy Adler, "Internet if Things: Remote Patient Monitoring Using Internet Services and Cloud Computing", 2014

Mohammed Talal, A.A. Zaidan, B. B. Zaidan, A.S. Albahri, A. H. Alamoodi, O.S. Albahri, M. A. Alsalem, C.K Lim, K. L. Tan, W.L. Shir, K. I. Mohammed, "Smart Home-based IoT for real-Time and Secure Remote Health Monitoring of triage and Priority System using Body Sensors: Multi-driven Systematic Review", *Journal of Medical Systems*, 2019.

P. A. Laplante, M. Kassab, N.L. Laplante, and J. M. Voas, "Building Caring Healthcare Systems in the Internet of Things", *IEEE Systems Journal*, 2017.

Rajat Vashistha, Dinesh Yadav, Deepak Chhabra, Pratyoosh Shukla, "Artificial Intelligence Integration for Neurodegenerative Disorders", *Leveraging Biomedical and Healthcare Data: Semantics, Analytics and Knowledge*, pp. 77–89, 2019.

Wu, F., Wu, T., J.M., Redoute, M.R., Yuce, "An autonomous Wireless Body Area Network Implantation Towards IoT Connected Healthcare Applications", *IEEE Access* 5, 11413–11422, 2016.

ZHANG Jia-weil, DONG Jun, ZHU Hong-hail, LIU Xia, WANG Li-ping, LI Zhen-jiang, "Wearable ECG Monitors and Its Remote Diagnosis Service Platform", *IEEE Intelligent Systems*, 2011.

Communication and Computing Systems – Prasad et al. (eds)
© 2019 Taylor & Francis Group, London, ISBN 978-0-367-00147-6

Adiabatic air water 2-phase flow in circular micro-channel using heterogeneous particle swarm optimization

Sanjeev Kumar, Ananta Shrivastava & Poshan Lal Sahu
Department of Mechanical Engineering, Dronacharya College of Engineering, Gurgaon, Haryana, India

ABSTRACT: The goal of optimization is finding the minimum value for the target function, determining the initial values for algorithm parameters is important. In case that the initial values are not chosen rightly, the algorithm may diverge or may converge to a suboptimal solution. Important parameters in optimization algorithm include min and max values of speed, min and max values of position, and learning parameters c1 and c2. The particle that is closer to the target has more competence. First a group of particles are created randomly, and by updating groups, one of them may seek to optimize the solution. The best position obtained so far is called best. The other best value used by the algorithm is called best which is the best position obtained so far by the population. In some literatures the particle only chooses other particles which are its neighbors topologically; in such situation the best local solution is called best. If enough particles are given, PSO guarantees to get the global optimum solution of the objective function. A gas quality of very from 0.90 to 0.94 was obtained by using initial velocity state of particle swarm technique, by using tow factorized flow arrangements occurred as of time for the heterogeneous and homogenous network processing micro channel kept under fixed inlet manifold conditions and the single micro-channels was reassessed with two-phase parallel flows. To prevent Mixing of different parts, Wrong parts or a Parts box of less than unit quantity, set the handling rules of partial parts boxes, having been generated unavoidably, and have operators obey the rule.

1 INTRODUCTION

Tabatabil made a new theory stating the adiabatic flow of two phase in which he state that maximum number of flow in liquid is based on this theory and according to this theory lots of efforts were imposed by the scientist in order to confirm actual situation. He made all his achievements in the late 60"s where he was able to find the actual cause and reason of not following the rules of his theory.

Kawahari investigated two phase flow patterns of moving liquid which stated the two flow of liquid in all the phases and they were responsible for carrying out this theory in their own way. They made every aspect successful by imposing their own ways and methods. The main concern was that they were working on achieving the diameter according to their own structure which was not becoming possible for all the ratios. Thus they started working on other principles so that their target can be achieved by listening to others as well as improving their own aspects. But all took initiative for making this successful theory.

Chung conducted another similar theory in which he stated about the frictional masses and related diameters which included the pressure drop.

Consistent with other aspects the main reason for not achieving the target included the overall behavior of the entire theory in which the main concern was of pressure drop and frictional diameters. In his investigation he found that every row of this entire theory was based on assumptions only. There was no actual regarding the theory which could state the results without being failed. He only made plans and did nothing to execute the plans. Thus, it was the reason for his failure because there was no planning in reference to the assumptions he made regarding to this theory. He again started the investigation and found that the entire assumptions were fake. So he started again from the beginning and achieved goal.

The main concern was that they were working on achieving the diameter according to their own structure which was not becoming possible for all the ratios. There was no actual regarding the theory which could state the results without being failed. He only made plans and did nothing to execute the plans. He made all his achievements in the late 60"'s where he was able to find the actual cause and reason of not following the rules of his theory. For convenience, we call a particular instantiation of these elements, at the individual level, a particle's configuration. PSO works as follows: each solution that is called a particle is equivalent to a bird in a colony of birds. Each particle has a competence value that is calculated by the competence function

2 PROPOSED METHOD

2.1 *Heterogeneous particle swarm optimization*

Particle swarm optimization (PSO) is a swarm intelligence technique originally inspired by models of flocking and of social influence that assumed homogeneous individuals. During its evolution to become a practical optimization tool, some heterogeneous variants have been proposed. However, heterogeneity in PSO algorithms has never been explicitly studied and some of its potential effects have therefore been overlooked. In this paper, we identify some of the most relevant types of heterogeneity that can be ascribed to particle swarms. A number of particle swarms are classified according to the type of heterogeneity they exhibit, which allows us to identify some gaps in current knowledge about heterogeneity in PSO algorithms. Motivated by these observations, we carry out an experimental study of a couple of heterogeneous particle swarms each of which is composed of two kinds of particles

Particle swarm optimization (PSO) is a probabilistic optimization method that is population based. PSO was originally attributed to Kennedy. Eberhart and Shiand was first intended for simulating social behavior, as a stylized representation of the movement of organisms in a bird flock or fish school. Each particle's movement is influenced by its local best known position and is also guided toward the best known positions in the search space, which are updated as better positions are found by other particles. This is expected to move the swarm toward the best solutions. PSO is a heuristic algorithm as it makes few or no assumptions about the problem which should be optimized and can search very large spaces of candidate solutions. However, heuristics such as PSO do not guarantee that an optimal solution is ever found. More specifically, PSO does not use the gradient of the problem which should be optimized, this means PSO does not require that the optimization problem be differentiable as is required by classic optimization methods such as gradient descent and quasi-newton methods. PSO can therefore be used in optimization problems that are partially irregular, noisy, change over time, etc. PSO works as follows: each solution that is called a particle is equivalent to a bird in a colony of birds. Each particle has a competence value that is calculated by the competence function. The particle that is closer to the target has more competence. Also each particle has a speed that controls its movement. Each particle follows the optimal particle in a sample space. First a group of particles are created randomly, and by updating groups, one of them may seek to optimize the solution. The best position obtained so far is called pbest. The other best value used by the algorithm is called gbest which is the best position obtained so far by the population. In some literatures the particle only chooses other particles which are its neighbours topologically; in such situation the best local solution is called gbest. The position of each particle in time (t + 1) is obtained by equations (4.9) and (4.10) where V_{ij} and X_{ij} of ith – particle are speed and position vector of that particle speed and position vector of that particle.

$$V_{ij}(t+1) = w * V_{ij}(t) + c_1 * rand * l_{ij}\big(P_{best,ij}(t) - X_{ij}(t)\big) + c_2 * rand * 2_{ij}\big(g_{best,j}(t) - X_{ij}(t)\big)$$

$$X_{ij}(t+1) = X_{ij}(t) + V_{ij}(t+1)$$

Here, i=1,2,......n is the particle index, X_{ij} is the j-th dimension of the i- th particle position, X_{ij} is the j th – dimension of the i-th particle velocity, $P_{best\ ij}$, is the j-th dimension of the best position of the i-th – particle at time t, best j, g is the j-th dimension of the best position that is so far achieved by all of the particles, W is the inertia weight, $rand1_{ij}$ and $rand2_{ij}$ are two random numbers in the interval [0 1], c1 and c2 are training factors, and t is the time or iteration. Since the goal of optimization is finding the minimum value for the target function, determining the initial values for algorithm parameters is important. In case that the initial values are not chosen rightly, the algorithm may diverge or may converge to a suboptimal solution. Important parameters in optimization algorithm include min and max values of speed, min and max values of position, and learning parameters c1 and c2. The goal of this program is minimizing the frequency changes by determining exact values of reference powers generated by each generator. The frictional pressure gradient is obtained and the final design solution has been selected by MATLAB Programming Technique for Multidimensional Analysis of Preference. Results show that the proposed multiobjective optimization approach can significantly outperform traditional single objective approaches

3   RESULTS AND DISCUSSIONS

In order to guarantee the 100% conforming products, conduct inspections and quality checks according to the rules, and carry out the production, checking the quality status. Include the 100% inspection items to be conducted by operators in the „Procedures" of Work Instruction Sheet and give operators a training/education

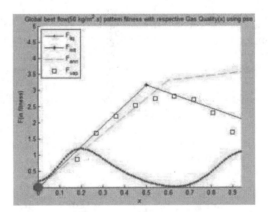

Figure 1.   Global best flow (50 kg/m sq) pattern fitness with respective Gas quality using HPSO.

When gas quality (x) raised then the flow pattern of annular increase up to 0.1- 0.6. When gas quality started from 0.61 it get constant and fractionally increment up to 0.9 as compare to flow pattern of vapor, vice-versa a gas quality decrease after 0.5 ratios at 50 kg/m2s flow rate

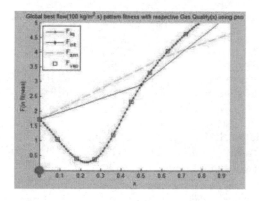

Figure 2.   Global best flow (100 Kg/m sq) pattern fitness with respective Gas quality (x) using H-PSO.

When liquid quality (x) get raised then the flow pattern of gas increase up to 0.8 ratio of gas quality 0.61 it get constant and fractionally increment up to 0.9 as compare to flow pattern of vapor, vice-versa a gas quality get decrease after 0.5 ratio at 50 kg/m2s.

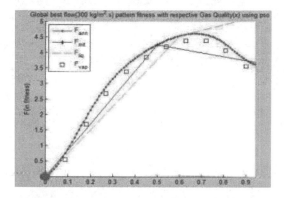

Figure 3.   Global best flow (300 Kg/m sq) pattern fitness with respective Gas quality using H-PSO.

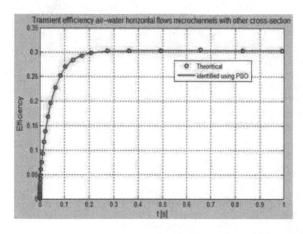

Figure 4.   Transient efficiency best flow pattern fitness with respective Gas quality using H-PSO.

4 CONCLUSION

If enough particles are given, PSO guarantees to get the global optimum solution of the objective function. A gas quality of very from 0.90 to 0.94 was obtained by using initial velocity state of particle swarm technique, by using tow factorized flow arrangements occurred as of time for the heterogeneous and homogenous network processing micro channel kept under fixed inlet manifold conditions and the single micro-channels was reassessed with two-phase parallel flows. Failing to conduct a quality check or conducting it properly may cause a overlook of an article out of the specification, leading to outflow of defects to the later process (customer). When a part out of Control Level (STD) is found in quality check, or defects are found for "XXX" items continuously or the number of defects has reached the one shown by Action Base Line in 100% check, do Stop-Call-Wait immediately. Conduct First Part Check, Last Part Check or periodical check after a changeover and/or at the beginning of each shift and record the results responsibly. PSO works as follows: each solution that is called a particle is equivalent to a bird in a colony of birds.

REFERENCES

Chung, P. M. Y., Kawaji, M., Kawahara, A. and Shibata, Y. (2004), "Two-Phase Flow through Square and Circular Micro-channels - Effects of Channel Geometry," Journal of Fluids Engineering, Transactions of the ASME Vol. 126(4) pp. 546–552

Chung, P. M. Y., Kawaji, M., Kawahara, A. and Shibata, Y. (2004), "Two-Phase Flow through Square and Circular Micro-channels - Effects of Channel Geometry," Journal of Fluids Engineering, Transactions of the ASME Vol. 126(4) pp. 546–552.

Chung, P. M. Y. and Kawaji, M. (2004), "The Effect of Channel Diameter on Adiabatic Two-Phase Flow Characteristics in Micro-channels," International Journal of Multiphase Flow Vol. 30(7–8 SPEC ISS) pp. 735–761.

K.A. Triplett, S.M. Ghiaasiaan, S.I. Abdel-Khalik, A. Lemouel, B.N. McCord, Gas– liquid two-phase flow in micro- channels. Part II: void fraction and pressure drop, Int. J. Multiphase Flow 25 (1999) 395–410.

Kawahara, A., Sadatomi, M., Okayama, K., Kawaji, M. and Chung, P. M. Y. (2005), "Effects of Channel Diameter and Liquid Properties on Void Fraction in Adiabatic Two-Phase Flow through Micro-channels," Heat Transfer Engineering Vol. 26(3) pp. 13–19

K. Dutkowski, Two-phase pressure drop of air–water in mini channels, Int. J. Heat Mass Transfer 52 (2009) 5185–5192.

K. Moriyama, A. Inoue, H. Ohira, The thermo hydraulic characteristics of twophase flow in extremely narrow channels (the frictional pressure drop and void fraction of adiabatic two-component two-phase flow), Trans. JSME (ser. B) 58 (1992) 401–407

Serizawa, A., Feng, Z. and Kawara, Z. (2002), "Two-Phase Flow in Micro-channels," Experimental Thermal and Fluid Science Vol. 26(6–7) pp. 703–714

Tabatabai, A. and Faghri, A. (2001), "A New Two-Phase Flow Map and Transition Boundary Accounting for Surface Tension Effects in Horizontal Miniature and Micro Tubes," Journal of Heat Transfer Vol. 123(5) pp. 958–968

T. Fukano, A. Kariyasaki, Characteristics of gaseliquid two-phase flow in a capillary tube, Nuclear Engineering and Design 141 (1993) 59e68

Communication and Computing Systems – Prasad et al. (eds)
© *2019 Taylor & Francis Group, London, ISBN 978-0-367-00147-6*

Optimisation of process parameters of orbital EDM

Akshay Diwan, Abhinav Panwar & Poshan Lal Sahu
Department of Mechanical Engineering, Dronacharya College of Engineering, Gurgaon, Haryana, India

ABSTRACT: Electric Discharge Machining (EDM) is widely accepted process to machine hard materials such as composites and alloys being used in various industrial applications. Various methods have been employed so far to improve its performance measures such as Material Removal Rate (MRR), Tool Wear Rate (TWR) and Surface Roughness (SR).The purpose of present study is to investigate the effects of various process parameters such as peak current, pulse on time, pulse off time, speed of rotation of tool and flushing pressure on performance measures such as MRR, TWR and SR.. Taguchi method has been adopted to design the experimental plan. For the conduction of experiments L18 orthogonal array was used. It is found that peak current, pulse on time and pulse off time contribute significantly, whereas speed of rotation of tool and flushing pressure contribute least to improve performance measures. For results and analysis MINITAB 17 software is used.

1 INTRODUCTION

Orbital EDM: In case of rotary EDM while machining deep holes uneven surface is produced and hence the machining efficiency reduces significantly. Orbital EDM is the process in which tool rotates about its own axis as well as tool rotates with some eccentricity about the axis of hole to be created. Due to the gap between the surface of tool and workpiece better flushing is obtained. The good flushing conditions results in better surface finish and also the debris material is removed easily from the machined workpiece. In case of orbital EDM the wear rate of tool also reduces and less number of tools are required compared to rotary EDM for producing the required cavity.

1.1 *Important parameters of EDM*

1.1.1 *Spark on time (pulse time or TON)*
The time duration for which the current flows per cycle is called spark on time. The more is energy supplied during this time the more will be amount of material removed.

1.1.2 *Spark off time (pause time or TOFF)*
It is the duration of time (µs) between two sparks (that is to say, on-time). This time allows the molten material to solidify and to be wash out of the arc gap. This parameter is to affect the speed and the stability of the cut. Thus, if the off-time is too short, it will cause sparks to be unstable.

1.1.3 *Arc gap (or gap)*
In EDM there is no contact between tool and workpiece and machining takes place due to spark generated through the gap between tool and work. This gap is called spark gap.

1.1.4 *Discharge current (current I)*
Current is measured in ampere allowed to per cycle. Discharge current is one of the significant parameter for MRR.

1.1.5 *Duty cycle (τ)*

It is a percentage of the on-time relative to the total cycle time. This parameter is calculated by dividing the on-time by the total cycle time (on-time plusofftime).

Duty cycle (%) = [Pulse on time (μs)/Total cycle time (μs)] × 100

1.1.6 *Voltage (V)*

It is a potential that can be measured by volt, it also effects the material removal rate and allowed to per cycle.

1.1.7 *Diameter of electrode (D)*

It is the electrode of Cu-tube there are two different size of diameter 4mm and 6mm in this experiment. This tool is used not only as an electrode but also for internal flushing.

1.1.8 *Tool geometry*

Tool geometry is related to shape of the tool electrodes i.e. square, rectangle, cylindrical, circular etc. Aspect ratio is the term used in place of tool geometry as EDM process parameter. Aspect ratio is the ratio of length/diameter of any shaped material. In case of rotating disk electrode the ratio becomes thickness/diameter.

1.1.9 *Tool material (electrode)*

Engineering materials having higher thermal conductivity and melting point can be used as tool material for EDM process. Copper, graphite, copper-tungsten, silver tungsten, copper, graphite and brass are some of the tool electrode materials (electrode) used in EDM.

1.2 *Performance measures of EDM*

1.2.1 *Material Removal Rate (MRR)*

It is defined as the amount of material removed from the workpiece surface per unit time. The MRR can also be expressed as the weight of material removed from the workpiece over machining time in minutes.

1.2.2 *Tool Wear Rate (TWR)*

It can be determined as material removed from the tool electrode per unit time. The TWR can also be calculated by using the weight loss from the tool electrode over the time of machining.

1.2.3 *Surface Roughness (SR)*

The average of the deviations of the machined surface from the mean line in terms of peak and valley is measured as the surface roughness of machined workpiece. It is denoted by Ra, and measured in microns. Surface roughness depends upon the machining parameters used in EDM, such as peak current, gap voltage and on time.

1.3 *Flushing method*

Flushing is the process to provide dielectric at some flow rate so that the debris material is removed effectively from the machined surface. The dielectric can be supplied at the machined area by different methods. The various flushing methods are side flushing, suction flushing and pressure flushing. In this study side flushing has been used.

2 OBJECTIVES

1. To study the effect of process parameters of orbital EDM during machining of Al/5wt%SiC MMC using copper tool electrode.
2. Conduct material removal rate (MRR), surface roughness (Ra) and tool wear rate (TWR) analysis using Taguchi's design (OA L_{18}).

3 METHODOLOGY

a) This research is focused on the optimization of responses of orbital electrical discharge machining of Al/5%wt.SiC MMC using copper electrode. The steps employed for the present study are enumerated as follows:

b) The research work done on EDM has been reviewed for the collection of data and techniques. The information has been gathered in wide areas of electrical discharge machining (EDM), EDM with orbital motion of tool and machining of Al/SiC MMC on EDM. Literature survey revealed the general behaviour between the EDM parameters and the responses.

c) Selection of the specific MMC material (i.e. Al/5%wt.SiC) is done based on literature review.

d) The machining parameters and their range has been selected based on literature survey and performance measures are also selected based on literature survey.

e) L_{18} Taguchi's design is the experimental design method used during the conduct of the experiments.

f) Machining of workpiece has been performed by setting electrical and non-electrical parameters on the orbital EDM.

g) MRR and TWR have been calculated using the mathematical expressions.

h) Measurement of surface roughness is done using a surface tester.

i) MINITAB 17 has been used for the analysis of the results to obtain the effects of machining parameters on the MRR, TWR and surface roughness (Ra).

4 RESULTS AND DISCUSSIONS

Analysis of Orbital EDM: The results of machining of Al/SiC MMC on orbital EDM have been analysed under this section. The response table for orbital EDM of MMC is given below.

Table 1. Response for Orbital EDM.

| Exp. No. | Input Process Parameters | | | | | Measured Responses | | |
	F_P (Kg/cm^2)	I_P (A)	N (RPM)	T_{ON} (steps)	T_{OFF} (steps)	MRR (mm^3/min.)	TWR (mm^3/min.)	R_a (μm)
1.	0.35	10	200	5	5	21.0002	0.0882	10.76
2.	0.35	10	300	7	7	21.8499	0.0386	16.23
3.	0.35	10	400	9	9	20.9816	0.0375	18.45
4.	0.35	20	200	5	7	16.6230	0.0264	11.82
5.	0.35	20	300	7	9	7.6704	0.0331	8.85
6.	0.35	20	400	9	5	11.0870	0.0077	11.44
7.	0.35	30	200	7	5	1.8652	0.0066	4.26
8.	0.35	30	300	9	7	1.3083	0.0088	3.80
9.	0.35	30	400	5	9	0.5682	0.0099	3.44
10.	0.70	10	200	9	9	20.7773	0.0166	17.58
11.	0.70	10	300	5	5	25.7100	0.0828	13.21
12.	0.70	10	400	7	7	21.3628	0.0364	13.01
13.	0.70	20	200	7	9	9.2591	0.0220	14.09
14.	0.70	20	300	9	5	15.4979	0.0132	18.51
15.	0.70	20	400	5	7	16.3800	0.0088	12.14
16.	0.70	30	200	9	7	0.5233	0.0022	3.07
17.	0.70	30	300	5	9	0.3364	0.0033	3.39
18.	0.70	30	400	7	5	3.0203	0.0121	4.42

4.1 *Analysis and discussion of MRR*

The main effects plot for means for MRR in case of orbital EDM is shown in figure.In case of orbital EDM, MRR increased with increase in flushing pressure but this increment was observed to be very less. Peak current was the most significant factor for MRR and it was observed that with increase in current, MRR decreased at rapid rate. It was observed that rotation speed did not have much impact on MRR however a slight increase in MRR with increase in speed of tool rotation from 200 rpm to 400 rpm was observed. MRR decreased as TONwas increased from 5 to 7 but it increased if TON was increased from 7 to 9. If TOFF was increased from 5 to 7 the MRR remained nearly constant but it decreased at rapid rate if TOFF was increased from 7 to 9.

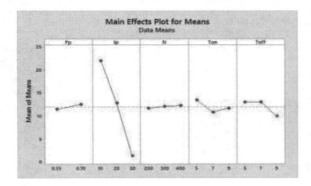

Figure 1.   Main effects plot for means for MRR (Orbital EDM).

The response for S/N ratio (larger is better) for MRR in case of orbital EDM, It was observed that current was the most important parameter followed by pulse off time, pulse on time, speed of rotation of tool and flushing pressure in terms of their effects on MRR.

Table 2.   Response table for S/N ratio for MRR (Orbital EDM).

Level	F_P	I_P	N	T_{ON}	T_{OFF}
1	16.1684	26.8029	16.0552	14.8290	19.0606
2	15.8981	21.7383	14.8940	17.5709	16.4653
3		-0.4414	17.1506	15.6999	12.5739
Delta	0.2703	27.2442	2.2566	2.7419	6.4867
Rank	5	1	4	3	2

The main effects plot for S/N ratio (larger is better) for MRR in case of orbital EDM.

4.2 *Analysis and discussion of TWR*

The main effects plot for means for TWR in case of orbital EDM. TWR decreases as the flushing pressure increases from 0.35Kg/cm2 to 0.70Kg/cm2. A high impact of peak current on TWR was observed. With increase in current, TWR decreased and it was found to be lowest at 30A. An increase in TWR was observed with increase in speed of tool rotation from 200 rpm to 300 rpm but TWR decreased rapidly with increase in speed of rotation of tool from 300 rpm to 400 rpm. TWR decreased at constant rate with increase in TON from 5 to 9 and the decrement was found to be significant. TWR decreased rapidly as TOFF increased from 5 to 7 but it was observed to be nearly constant when TOFF increased from 7 to 9.

506

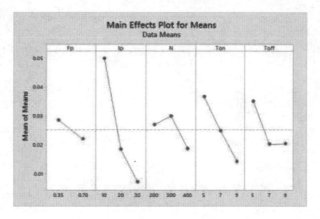

Figure 2.   Main effects plot for means for TWR (Orbital EDM).

The response for S/N ratio (smaller is better) for TWR in case of orbital EDM is shown in table 5.7. It was observed that current was the most important parameter followed by, pulse on time, flushing pressure, pulse off time and speed of rotation in terms of their effects on TWR.5

4.3   *Analysis and discussion of Surface Roughness (Ra)*

The main effects plot for means for SR in case of orbital EDM is shown in Figure 2. SR increased when flushing pressure increased from 0.35Kg/cm2 to 0.70Kg/cm2. There was decrease in SR with increase in current and this decrement was observed to occur at faster rate when current increased from 20A to 30A. With increase in speed of rotation from 200 to 300 rpm the SR increased and with further increase in speed from 300 to 400 rpm the SR decreased slightly. SR increased with increase in pulse on time from 5 to 9. SR decreased with increase in pulse off time from 5 to 7 but with increase in pulse off time from 7 to 9 there was increase in SR.

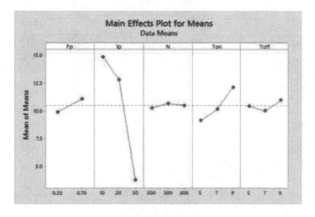

Figure 3.   Main effects plot for means for SR (Orbital EDM).

The response of S/N ratio (smaller is better) for SR in case of orbital EDM is shown in Table 2. It was observed that peak current was the most significant factor in controlling SR followed by pulse on time, flushing pressure, pulse off time and speed of rotation.

REFERENCES

Dewangan, S. K. (2010). Experimental investigation of machining parameters for EDM using U-shaped electrode of AISI P20 tool steel (Doctoral dissertation, National Institute of Technology Rourkela (India).

Dhar, S., Purohit, R., Saini, N., Sharma, A., & Kumar, G. H. (2007). Mathematical modeling of electric discharge machining of cast Al–4Cu–6Si alloy–10wt.%SiC P composites. Journal of materials processing technology, 194(1), 24–29.

Dwivedi, A. P., & Choudhury, S. K. (2016). Effect of Tool Rotation on MRR, TWR, and Surface Integrity of AISI-D3 Steel using the Rotary EDM Process. Materials and Manufacturing Processes, 31(14), 1844–1852.

Dwivedi, A. P., & Choudhury, S. K. (2016). Improvement in the Surface Integrity of AISI D3 Tool Steel Using Rotary Tool Electric Discharge Machining Process. Procedia Technology, 23, 280–287.

Dvivedi, A., Kumar, P., & Singh, I. (2008). Experimental investigation and optimisation in EDM of Al 6063 SiCp metal matrix composite. International Journal of Machining and Machinability of Materials, 3(3-4), 293–308.

Gopalakannan, S., Senthilvelan, T., & Ranganathan, S. (2012). Modeling and optimization of EDM process parameters on machining of Al 7075-B4C MMC using RSM. Procedia Engineering, 38, 685–690.

Sanchez, J. A., de Lacalle, L. L., Lamikiz, A., & Bravo, U. (2006). Study on gap variation in multi-stage planetary EDM. International Journal of Machine Tools and Manufacture, 46(12), 1598–1603.

Singh, P. N., Raghukandan, K., Rathinasabapathi, M., &Pai, B. C. (2004). Electric discharge machining of Al–10% SiC p as-cast metal matrix composites. Journal of materials processing technology, 155, 1653–1657.

Velmurugan, C., Subramanian, R., Thirugnanam, S., &Ananadavel, B. (2011). Experimental investigations on machining characteristics of Al 6061 hybrid metal matrix composites processed by electrical discharge machining. International Journal of Engineering, Science and Technology, 3(8), 87–101.

Zhang, X., Shinshi, T., Endo, H., Shimokohbe, A., Imai, Y., Miyake, H., & Nakagawa, T. (2007, October). Micro electrical discharge machining using a 5-DOF controlled maglev actuator. In Proceedings of the 2007 ASPE Conference (pp. 36–39).

Communication and Computing Systems – Prasad et al. (eds)
© 2019 Taylor & Francis Group, London, ISBN 978-0-367-00147-6

The inescapable effects of virtual laboratory and comparison of traditional laboratory with virtual laboratory

Dolly & Vinod Kumar
Department of Computer Science Engineering, Dronacharya College of Engineering, Gurugram, Haryana, India

ABSTRACT: The rapid growth in Information and Communication Technologies (ICT) has made it possible for virtual laboratories to be used as a substitute or supplement to the traditional laboratories. Virtual laboratory is an online learning system where students can access and perform their laboratory work on software applications which are virtually installed. Students don't have to buy expensive software or go to physically established laboratory in odd hours. The key advantages of virtual laboratories are access anytime and anywhere. The main objectives of virtual laboratories are to keep laboratory maintenance simple, reduced manpower and reduced human related faults. In this paper, review of virtual laboratory is presented in the context of their objectives and benefits in modern education system.

1 INTRODUCTION

Laboratories are the important environment for students learning where students get hands on training. Where anybody learn and understand the theory and practical concept related to laboratory. The main objective of the laboratory in education is to provide practical knowledge and to develop various applications. Well-equipped laboratories are required to conduct practical sessions. A deeper understanding of technical concept may be achieved through laboratory work that encourages active involvement and hand out to extend critical thinking.

Today to setup a physical laboratory is challenging work for institutions due to budget, limited technical expertise, high setup and maintenance costs. In this response virtual laboratories have been developed to attend to these challenges. Virtual laboratories allow users to perform practical work or experiments on real systems via interactive web base tool. Thereby, laboratory resources may be shared between a large group of user which are geographically separated limiting setup and operational costs to a single facility.

With the growing popularity and availability of the Information and Communication Technologies (ICT), web-based teaching is adapted in education these days. The modern trend focuses on improving practical work by using web base tool. So, Virtual laboratories are work as an alternative or complement to the physical or real laboratories. This paper describes the objectives and benefits of virtual laboratory. This paper also presents a brief study of traditional laboratories with virtual laboratories.

2 OBJECTIVES OF VIRTUAL LABORATORY

Virtual laboratories are web based interactive multimedia objects to enhance teaching and learning experience. Interactive multimedia objects used in virtual laboratory consists of web-resources, video-lectures, graphics, text, hypertext, sound, images, and animations (Muthusamy, Kanesan et al. 2005). The main objective behind developing the concept of virtual laboratory is eliminating the physical concept of laboratory from study and learning. The major objectives of virtual laboratories are (Virtual lab 2014):

- To reduce maintenance cost.
- To remotely access to laboratories in various courses.
- To motivate students for conducting experiments on their own interest.
- To learn basic and advanced concepts of experiments through remote access.

The main objective of Virtual Laboratory is that user can easily build up their knowledge and improve fundamental concepts with practical work (Soni, Ms.Shweta et al. 2014) & (Alexiadis, Dimitrios S et al. 2013).

3 COURSES ON VIRTUAL LABORATORY

Virtual Laboratory plays an important role in all fields including medicine, art, music, law and human communication, that's why the study of computer education can be interdisciplinary in nature (Muthusamy, Kanesan et al. 2005).

Broad areas of virtual laboratories are Chemical Engineering, Computer Science Engineering, Civil Engineering, Physical Science, Biotechnology and Bio Medical Engineering etc.

The various courses are developed on virtual laboratories e.g. Advanced Communication, Wireless Communications, Laser Based Flow Diagnostics, Software Engineering, Computer Programming, Data Structures, and Computer Architecture & Organization, Principle of Programming languages, Image Processing, VLSI, Artificial Neural Networks, Linux Lab and many more. Virtual laboratories have purpose to simulate or virtualized experiments (Virtual lab 2014)

4 COMPARISION OF TRADITIONAL AND VIRTUAL LABORATORY

There are some concepts that cannot be illustrated in a normal laboratory but can be simulated and presented to students in a virtual laboratory (Babateen, Huda Mohammad 2014). Table 1 shows the comparison study of traditional and virtual laboratory (Babateen, Huda Mohammad 2014) & (Al-Zharani, E.J. 2008).

On the basis of given information it is analyzed that virtual laboratories are web tool for education that provide flexibility to perform practical work. It uses GUI to implement several interactive exercises and gives step by step procedure to implement practical. In this experiment can be paused, rewound, repeated, or the details explored.

Table 1. The comparison of traditional and virtual laboratory.

Sr. No.	Characteristics	Traditional Laboratory	Virtual Laboratory
1.	Educational Environment	Closed	Flexible and opened
2.	Sources of Knowledge	Faculty & Book	Varied Resources and Multimedia
3.	Theoretical & Practical Aspect	Separating between the theoretical and practical	The integral between the theoretical and practical
4.	Participation of Faculty	Positivism	Positive and Active
5	Participation of Student	Negativism	Positive and Active
6.	Size of Groups	Whole class in a large group	Small or Individual groups
7.	Teaching Methods	Traditional & verbal teaching methods	Varied teaching and learning methods
8.	Time Period of using lab	The standardized official time	Anytime
9.	Affected by	Faculty	Computational power of the host computer
10.	Individual Differences	Not Consider	Consider

5 BENEFITS OF VIRTUAL LABORATORIES

Now a day it is very easy to access theoretical lectures and tutorials as so many online courses, gadgets and applications are available for the students. But students can get benefited through virtual laboratory to perform practical implementation without appearing physically in the laboratory. Users may learn and practice at their own pace, review the material and have access to a variety of resources at any time. Virtual laboratory is a good concept to get better understanding the theoretical topic as well. Virtual laboratory concept is beneficial for both faculty members as well as students.

5.1 *Faculty benefits*

Virtual Laboratories are an exciting tool for faculty to engage students. A well-designed virtual laboratory may be expected to offer the following benefits for faculty members are(Harding, David P. 2003).:

- To introduce remotely interactive learning by video tutorials, images and sound.
- To draw students attention by animated demonstrations.
- Absent students can make them up at home as web base tool access from anywhere.
- To use out-of-class time or college time for studying.
- The set up cost of virtual laboratory is low compare to a physical laboratory.
- It is easier way to learn difficult concepts through the virtual laboratories.
- Obtain cost effective, fast turnarounds on technology upgrades and introductions.
- Reduce administration time needed for scheduling, setting up, and refreshing labs.
- Once the virtual experiment is set-up then students can easily change experimental parameters or arguments or value of variables.

5.2 *Students benefits*

Students will get a feel of the real laboratory as all laboratory equipment and components are available. Interactive animations can provide to enable student learning. The major benefits of virtual laboratories for students are described below (Harding, David P. 2003).:

- Absent students can make them up at home. It is web base tool access from home and performs their practical.
- To improve effectiveness and better understanding, Students can repeat experiments many times.
- To easily perform experiments, Step by step wizard to guide the students.
- Real looking components to give the user a feel of the real laboratory.
- The students can understand more detailed experiments through changing different variables or parameters.
- To easily solve a large set of complex problems through the design and construction of new approaches using virtual laboratory.
- Available 24x7, students can do laboratory work as per their own schedule.
- Students enjoy being able to use the computer.

6 CONCLUSION

With the rapid growth of ICT information can be delivered easily from one place to another. A Web based teaching provides a valuable opportunity to carry out new learning techniques. Virtual laboratories offer benefits and a substitute or supplement to the traditional laboratories. It provides a modern solution to perform practical work. In modern education, Virtual laboratories are interactive web base tool to enhance the teaching and learning methodology.

REFERENCES

Alexiadis, Dimitrios S. & Mitianoudis, Nikolaos 2013. MASTERS: A Virtual Lab on Multimedia Systems for Telecommunications, Medical and Remote Sensing Applications. IEEE Transactions On Education 56 (2).

Al-Zharani, E.J. 2008. The virtual labs. Journal of Curricula and Educational Supervision 3:29-35.

Babateen, Huda Mohammad 2011. The role of Virtual Laboratories in Science Education. 5th International Conference on Distance Learning and Education IPCSIT 12.

Muthusamy, Kanesan, Kumar, P. Rajesh, & L. Atif, Sh Rosfashida S.A. 2005. Virtual Laboratories in Engineering Education. Asian Journal of Distance Education 3 (2):55–558

Harding, David P. 2003. The Virtual Laboratory: Technology Assisted Education. The National Conference On Undergraduate Research University of Utah. Salt Lake City, Utah.

Soni, Ms.Shweta & Katkar,M.D. 2014 Survey paper on Virtual Lab for E- Learners. International Journal of Application or Innovation in Engineering & Management (ISSN 2319 – 4847) 3 (1).

Virtual lab website 2014. http://www.vlab.co.in/index.php.

Communication and Computing Systems – Prasad et al. (eds)
© *2019 Taylor & Francis Group, London, ISBN 978-0-367-00147-6*

Big Data and Hadoop: A review

Maninder Kaur
Department of Information and Technology, Dronacharya College of Engineering, Gurgaon, India

Megha Goel
Department of Computer Science and Engineering, Dronacharya College of Engineering, Gurgaon, Haryana, India

ABSTRACT: This Now days information is increasing day by day thanks to the employment of social networking sites, advancement within the technology. The growing desires of knowledge is resolved by victimization massive information. massive information manage structured, unstructured, semi structured information terribly with efficiency. massive information is assortment of huge datasets that aren't managed by area unit previous computing techniques. Massive information makes the business quicker. several corporations like Google, Amazon, Facebook etc the employment massive information. In aid, sector massive information additionally play vital role. Hadoop is that the framework utilized by massive information. Hadoop is open supply software system. it's written in java. Hadoop additionally permits distributed process.

1   INTRODUCTION

Big information refers to large quantity of knowledge that may not be keep or processed victimization the normal approach with within the given time frame. we have a tendency to all apprehend in style social networking sites Google and, Facebook, You tube etc. of these sites area unit vey in style these days and their user increasing daily. These sites receives immense volume of knowledge daily. So there information is additionally growing day by day.This information hold valuable info of the users and have to be compelled to method this information with high speed. Many corporations victimization this immense quantity of information to accelerate their business and use this data .Big information is assortment of huge datasets that aren't managed by area unit previous computing techniques. massive information makes the business quicker. several corporations like Google, Amazon, Facebook etc the employment massive information. In aid sector massive information additionally play vital role.

Variety means that differing kinds of knowledge. information is also video, audio, images, text and social media information. truthfulness means that handiness and responsibleness of knowledge. information is unsure thanks to the unpredictability and integrity (Apache Hadoop Project, 2013).

2   DISPUTES AND PROSPECTIVE

Internet contain numerous web content that provide info concerning massive information. once Cloud massive information get image. In education massive information additionally play necessary role. In Health, business and Earth Bigdata additionally play main role. These field have nice prospective of massive information. immense quantity of knowledge is created on the usual that isn't properly handle by our previous systems. however massive information handle immense volume of knowledge simply.

2.1 Challenges with massive data

2.1.1 Heterogeneousness and incompleteness
Big information agitate 3 differing kinds of knowledge structured, unstructured and semi structured information.

Data analyst face massive downside of heterogeneousness. Consider Associate in Nursing example In Hospital record of every patient is managed about its group action and treatment related to the patient. Each patient have completely different records. This is not well structured style. Thus manage this forms of information is obligatory. A high-quality information analysis is needed for this kind of system.

2.1.2 Scale
Now days handling immense quantity of knowledge is incredibly troublesome task. Earlier processor area unit wont to address this downside, however currently processor area unit static. Storage capability is additionally improved solid state devices area unit used rather than disk due to there higher performance. Managing this huge quantity of information is difficult for data analyst.

2.1.3 Timeliness
To method great deal of knowledge in less time is massive challenge. the big quantity of knowledge take longer time in its process . Our typical system aren't ready to handle this huge quantity of knowledge .E commerce is rising day by day and manufacturing immense quantity of knowledge daily .So currently want of such sort of system that handle this huge quantity of knowledge in term of speed and accuracy.

2.1.4 Privacy and security
Privacy and Security area unit delicate problems for massive information. There area unit strict laws in some countries regarding the information privacy. In such giant information handling security is additionally troublesome. Social stratification would be necessary arising consequence.

2.1.5 Human collaborations
New generation and organizations area unit attracted towards massive information. massive information has terribly high scope within the world of info. It speed up the info world. The Organization have to be compelled to organize the seminar on massive information. massive information ought to be a vicinity of our info in Universities .

2.2 Opportunities to massive data

Big information revolute the info world. Big information play vital role to grow business to higher profit level. massive information perceive the necessity of the client vey well. It up the business method . massive information up in aid sector, Science and analysis, monetary commercialism and Sports. It additionally enhance the performance of machine

2.2.1 Technology
Big information place nice improvement within the field of Technology. "Amazon.com handles numerous back-end operations and have seven.8 TB, 18.5 TB, and 24.7 TB Databases". Walmart is calculable to store over a pair of.5 lead information for handling one million transactions per hour. the big subatomic particle atom smasher (LHC) generates twenty five lead information before replication and two hundred lead information once duplication . Sloan Digital Sky Survey, continuing at a rate of concerning two hundred GB per night and has over a hundred and forty TB of knowledge. American state information Center for Cyber Security stores Yottabytes (1024)".

2.2.2 *Government*

Big information is act as game changer for Indian government. It helps the Indian government to create our country free from the black cash. It helps in agriculture sector, banking etc. "Obama government declared massive information analysis and development initiative in 2012. massive information analysis compete a crucial role of BJP winning the elections in 2014 and Indian government is applying massive information analysis in Indian electorate".

2.2.3 *Healthcare*

Big information play a awfully necessary role in aid. As a McKinsey report states, "After over twenty years of steady will increase, aid expenses currently represent seventeen.6 % of gross domestic product —nearly $600 billion over the expected benchmark for a nation of the United States's size and wealth."In aid all detail of patient area unit maintained by victimization massive information. It save cash and time. Most of the information of aid is unstructured. massive information is incredibly economical for aid.

2.2.4 *Science and research*

Now information is increasing day by every day in several researches. Bigdata is incredibly useful within the field of Science and analysis. It makes the work easier as compared to ancient system.

2.2.5 *Media*

currently user shifted from anlog information to digital information. They search information anyplace anytime from any device.So demand of knowledge is increasing day by day. Thousand of digital client consumes media and corporations area unit in smart position by victim ization massive information resources for a lot of profitable client engagement.

3   HADOOP FRAMEWORK

Hadoop open supply software system. massive information is employed Hadoop framework. several organization and researches used hadoop framework to analysis Bigdata. Google's design is influenced by Hadoop.An Apache Hadoop scheme consists of the Hadoop Kernel, Map Reduce, HDFS and different parts like Apache Hive, Base and Zookeeper (Mridul, Mrigank et al,2014)

3.1   *Hadoop has of 2 main components*

3.1.1 *Storage*

The Hadoop Distributed classification system (HDFS) breaks down terribly giant files into giant blocks while not information of the content of those files.It stores these blocks on completely different nodes of cluster. HDFS offer fault tolerance and run on service hardware. it's offers high outturn and appropriate for application that have giant information. It will store information on thousands servers. Files superimposed to HDFS area unit split into fixed-size blocks. Block size is configurable, however defaults to sixty four megabytes.

3.1.2 *Processing*

Map scale back is Programming model lunched by Google in 2004.It is used for writing programming for those applications that method immense quantity of knowledge in parallel on giant cluster of hardware in fault tolerant manner.It applies on giant information sets.It split the matter into little information sets and run it in parallel.

3.2 Two functions in MapReduce area unit as following

3.2.1 Map

This perform is employed to filter, transform, or dissect the information. Map makes the work simple.

Volume 2, Spl. Issue a pair of (2015) e-ISSN: 1694-2329 | p-ISSN: 1694-2345 fifteen BUEST.

3.2.2 Reduce

The scale back perform is employed to summarizing the information from Map perform.

4 USES IN DATA PROCESSING

The patterns of bigdata sets area unit analyse by researches and large organizations by victimization massive information . Extracting helpful info from great deal of massive information is named as data processing. this huge quantity of knowledge is within the type of social media posts, images, videos and within the kind web content. forty Zettabytes of knowledge are going to be created by 2020 that's 300 times from 2005 (Smitha.T, et al).

This info is incredibly helpful for security purpose in varied sectors like health, education etc.

we'd like to introduce new information Mining system that is effective. There area unit several data processing techniques which could be used with immense info, a number of them are:

4.1 Classification analysis

It could be a economical method for getting necessary info concerning information and data . The classification also can be wont to cluster the information.

4.2 Grouping analysis

Grouping analysis is completed to search out similarties and distinction with in information. *Grouping* analysis is usually utilized in several applications like marketing research, pattern recognition, information analysis, and image process as an example "*Grouping* of shoppers having similar preferences is targeted on social medial".

4.3 Growth analysis

it's jointly referred to as hereditary processing primarily accustomed mining of knowledge from polymer sequences . It is utilized in Banking, to calculate the exchange by previous years' statistic information (Mucherino A.et al,1998).

4.4 Outlier analysis

A number of observations, detections of things area unit made that do not build a pattern in Associate in Nursing passing info Set. In medical and banking this issues can be used.

5 CONCLUSION

In this review paper, "summary is provided on huge data, Hadoop and applications in data Mining". Four V's of massive information has been mentioned in summary to large information disputes is given and plenty of chances and uses of huge information has been mentioned. This paper express the Hadoop Framework and its elements HDFS and Map reduce. The

Hadoop Distributed classification system (HDFS) could be a distributed classification system designed to run on hardware. Hadoop plays Associate in Nursing very important role in massive information . This paper compose focal point on current researches in processing.

REFERENCES

Apache Hadoop Project,2013. http://hadoop.apache.org.

Divyakant Agrawal, Challenges and Opportunities with massive information, A community report developed by leading researchers across the United States

Harshawardhan S. Bhosale, ProfDevendra. P. Gadekar, 2014. A Review Paper on massive information and Hadoop in International Journal of Scientific and analysis Publications, 4(10).

IBM massive information analytics HUB, www.ibmbigdatahub.com/infographic/four-vs-big-dataApplication, (IJCA) 43, 8, Apr 2012 edition. ISSN0975(8887):35-37.

Jain, Anupam, N K. Rakhi and Bagler, Ganesh, arxiv.org/abs/1502.03815 Spices kind the premise Of Food Pairing In Indian culinary art.

MIT Technology Review, http://www.technologyreview.com/view/535451/data-mining-indian-recipes-reveals-new-food-pairing-phenomenon.

Mucherino A. Petraq, Papajorgji, P.M. Paradalos 1998. A survey of data mining techniques alied to agriculture CRPIT. 3(3): 555560.

Mridul, Mrigank, Khajuria, Akashdeep &Dutta, Snehasish, 2014. Analysis of Bidgata victimisation Apache Hadoop and Map Reduce in International Journal of Advance analysis in applied science and Software Engineering 4(5).

Puneet Singh Duggal, Sanchita, Paul, 2013. Massive information Analysis: Challengesand Solutions in International Conference on Cloud, massive information and Trust, 13-15, RGPV.

Smitha, T., Sundaram, V.Dr. "Classification Rules by call Tree for unwellness prediction" International journal for laptop

Smitha, T., Kumar, V. Suresh, 2013. Application of massive information in information Mining in International Journal of rising Technology and Advanced Engineering Vol 3 (7).

Vidyasagar S. D., A Study on, 2013.Role of Hadoop in info Technology era", GRA - world analysis ANALYSIS, Volume: a pair of | Issue: a pair of • ISSN No 2277–28160.

Massive information, Wikipedia, http://en.wikipedia.org/wiki/Big_data Webster, Phil. "Supercomputing the Climate: NASA's massive information Mission". CSC World. laptop Sciences Corporation. Retrieved 2013-01-18.

Massive DATA: Challenges and opportunities, Infosys work Briefings, 11, No (1), 2013

Communication and Computing Systems – Prasad et al. (eds)
© *2019 Taylor & Francis Group, London, ISBN 978-0-367-00147-6*

Neural networks: Structure, application and learning method in artificial intelligence

Ancy Oommen
Department of Information Technology, Dronacharya College of Engineering, Gurugram, Haryana, India

Vinod Kumar
Department of Computer Science Engineering, Dronacharya College of Engineering. Gurugram, Haryana, India

ABSTRACT: A neural network is to reproduce lots of interconnected cells in a computer so that, people can learn things, recognize and generate patterns, and make decisions in their own and unique way. The amazing thing about a neural network it resembles brain. Neural Networks are made by programming very ordinary computers, working in a traditional manner with their ordinary components. Computer outputs are just combinations of algebraic values and mathematical equations together. Neural networks are also referred as parallel distributed processors (PDP) and thinking machines. This article we will use the term neural network which also termed as Artificial Neural Network.

1   INTRODUCTION

The term 'Neural Network' is derived the nervous system of human being. The nervous system contains nerve cells which are present in all the parts of the human body system. Artificial Neural Networks is termed as biological network of artificial nerve cells configured to perform specific function and task. (Croall, I.F et al.)

It is composed of a large number of highly interconnected neurons, working in unity to solve specific problems. Artificial Neural Networkare like people, they learn by example. An artificial neural network is designed for a specific application, for example pattern recognition, speech recognition through some learning process.

Table 1.   Comparison of human brain and computers.

BRAIN	COMPUTER
Biological neurons or nerve cells	Silicon Transistors
200 billion neurons, 32 trillion interconnections	1 billion bytes RAM, trillion bytes on disk
Neuron size: 10-6m	Single transistor: 10 gm
Energy consumption: 6-10 joules	Energy consumption: 10-16 joules
Learning capability	Programming capability

2   STRUCTURE OF NEURAL NETWORKS

There are mainly three layers of neural network are the following:

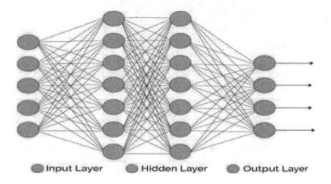

Figure 1.   Architecture of ANN.

2.1   *Input layer*

The first layer is known as input layer. In this layer, the contains neurons that receive input from the outside of the network and then later on it will recognise and learn about the neurons.

2.2   *Output layer*

The second layer is known as output layer. It usually gives the information about how the data can be learned from the given inputs.

2.3   *Hidden layer*

Hidden layer plays an important layer in neural network as it is situated in between the input and output layer. The responsibility of this layer is to make the change in inputs so that output can use it in various ways (Jha, Girish Kumar 2014).

3   TYPES OF ARTIFICIAL NEURAL NETWORK

3.1   *Various Artificial Neural Networks*

3.1.1 *Feed forward ANN*
The information flow is unidirectional that is, in one way. In this unit, it sends information to other unit from which it does not receive any information or signal. There are no feedbacks. They are used in pattern generation, recognition or classification. They have fixed inputs and outputs. (I, Aleksander et al. 1995).

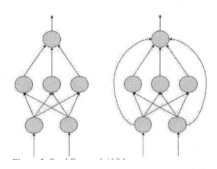

Figure 2.   Feed forward ANN.

3.1.2 *Feedback ANN*

Here, feedback loops are allowed. They are used in content addressable memories. (I, Aleksander et al. 1995).

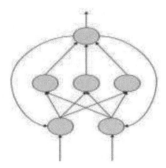

Figure 3.   Feedback ANN.

3.2   *Special types neural networks*

3.2.1 *Modular neural network*

Multilayer neural network is the combination of other types of neural network like multilayer perceptron, recurrent network and Hopfield network which are also represented into a single module to complete the task of networks.

3.2.2 *Physical neural network*

Physical neural network is a special type of network where it is used to emulate the function between to network instead of software simulations that are performed in the artificial neural network.

4   ADVANTAGES OF NEURAL NETWORK

1) *Adaptive learning*: Adaptive learning is a type of ability to learn how to do tasks based on the data given for training or initial experience.
2) *Self-Organisation*: An artificial neural network can create its own organisation or representation of the information it receives during learning time.
3) *Real Time Operation*: It is the type of artificial neural network, in which computations may be carried out in parallel and special hardware devices which take advantage of the capability.
4) *Fault Tolerance*: It is also called Redundant Information Coding. In this partial destruction of a network leads to degradation of performance. (Croall, I.F et al.)

4.1   *Three different uses artificial network*

1) *Classification*—A neural network is used to classify the given sequence or data set into predefined classes. It uses the mechanism of feed forward networks.
2) *Prediction*—In simple language the term prediction means to forecast. In artificial neural network, prediction is used where desired output is expected from the given inputs.
3) *Clustering*—Clustering is another feature that is used in neural network where it means to gather or congregate the data into one. In neural networks, it classify into various categories according to data, without any prior knowledge of the given data. (Anderson, J. A 2003)

4. 2 *Application of neural network*

1) It is used in Aerospace like Autopilot aircrafts, aircraft fault detection etc.
2) It is used in Automotive like Automobile guidance systems.
3) It is used in Military like Weapon orientation and steering, target tracking.
4) It is used in Electronics applications like Code sequence prediction, IC chip layout, chip failure analysis, machine vision, and voice synthesis. (Jha, Girish Kumar 2014).
5) Used in Financial applications like Real estate appraisal, loan advisor, mortgage screening, corporate bond rating, portfolio trading program.
6) Used in Industrial applications like Manufacturing process control, product design and analysis, quality inspection systems, welding quality analysis.
7) Used in Medical applications: Cancer cell analysis, EEG and ECG analysis
8) Speech recognition, speech classification, text to speech conversion.
9) It is used in Pattern Recognition in facial recognition, optical character recognition (Jha, Girish Kumar 2014).

5 LEARNING METHODS USED IN NEURAL NETWORK - ALGORITIIM

5.1 *Gradient descent*

Gradient descent is a type of algorithm that is used in supervised learning. There is vast difference between the actual output and desired output and the resultant error is find out .This type of algorithm uses weights and then used to derive output. It is also called as simplest learning algorithm.

5.2 *Back propagation*

Back Propagation is a extended version of gradient descent learning rule. In this type of algorithm, the difference between the desired output and the actual output is propagated from the output layer to the input layer including the hidden player. It is also implemented in multi-layer neural network.

5.3 *Types of learning used in neural network*

5.3.1 *Supervised learning*
Supervised learning is a type of learning where the data is input and the expected output is known weights.

5.3.2 *Unsupervised learning*
Unsupervised learning is another type where method of learning input data is used where output is already known by weights.

5.3.3 *Reinforcement learning*
Reinforcement learning is a type of learning where the value of the output is already unknown, but the feedback is given by the network whether the output is right or wrong. Sometimes reinforcement learning is also called as semi supervised learning.

5.3.4 *Offline learning*
Official learning is another subset of learning where the adjustment of the weight vector and threshold is completed only after all data is presented to the network.

5.3.5 *Online learning*
Online learning is one of the type of subset part of learning in which the adjustment of the weight and threshold is done after placing each sample of data sets to the network.

6 CONCLUSION

Neural networks are also termed as Artificial Network. These are the commonly applied machine learning algorithm. In this paper, I have provided a brief sketch of types of neural network and different types of learning used in it and the ability to learn and use it in a flexible manner. We've also discussed about the uses of Artificial Neural Networks along with their various functions. The pros and cons of ANNs and the issues related to the ANNs have been discussed in this paper.

REFERENCES

Croall I.F. & Mason J.P. Industrial Applications of Neural Networks. Research Reports ESPRIT
I. Aleksander & H. Morton 1995. An introduction to neural computing. London: International Thomson Computer Press.
Anderson, J. A. 2003. An Introduction to neural networks. Prentice Hall.
Jha, Girish Kumar 2014. Artificial Neural Network and its Applications. IARI New delhi.

Communication and Computing Systems – Prasad et al. (eds)
© *2019 Taylor & Francis Group, London, ISBN 978-0-367-00147-6*

Numerical model of inverted trapezoidal fin horizontal array heat sink for heat transfer through natural convection

Vishal Verma, Priyanka Daga & Poshan Lal Sahu
Department of Mechanical Engineering, Dronacharya College of Engineering, Gurgaon, Haryana, India

ABSTRACT: The objective of the present work is to develop a numerical model of inverted trapezoidal fin, horizontal array heat sink for heat transfer via free convection. The flow is assumed to be steady, laminar and uniform. The presented model is simulated at geometric parameters which go in accordance with the literature study. After validating the model para-metric study for orthogonal effect of geometric parameters on heat transfer coefficient (HTC) and on heat flux (HF) is carried out. Then Design of experiment (DOE) is carried out, as a result a response surface depicting relationship of input and output parameters. Response sur-face optimization is done for maximum heat transfer after response surface generation. The main objective was to optimize geometry of inverted trapezoidal fins within a given range for maximum heat transfer having maximum heat flux and maximum HTC. The effects of change in fin length, fin height, fin spacing and temperature difference between surroundings and fin arc examined together preventing possible mistakes due to the use of a constant value for one of the geometrical parameters and incorrect assumptions. By simulation in ANSYS Fluent, the solution of the conjugate governing equation is obtained, which is compared to the experi-mental observation with the results for special condition. ANSYS Fluent is used for the con-tinuum model of Navies-Stokes with Coupled pressure velocity coupling and pressure based solver, is used for this. Fluent gives adaptability to variation of thermo physical properties with respect to the effect of temperature. For DOE, response surface curve and optimization ANSYS design explorer is used. Design explorer provides the user to generate response curve between input and output parameters with help of design points (outcome of DOE). Finally, optimization is done by predicted response values for present study based on maximum heat flux and HTC

1   INTRODUCTION AND LITERATURE REVIEW

Some of the earliest works in heat transfer from the arrays of the fin is of Starner and McManus (1963) they presented HTC for four distinct dimensioned arrays of fins with the base vertical, 45° and horizontal. They found that heat transfer could be increased or reduced based on align-ment of fins with base plate. Similar experimental study was carried by Welling and Woolbridge (1965), on vertical rectangular fins. They found at a given temperature there is an optimum value of the ratio of fin height to the fin spacing.

Harahap and McManus (1967), presented an average HTC and investigated the flow field of the free convection from the arrays of the fin and proposed a correlation which overcomes the inadequacy of parameters available previously for rectangular horizontal fins

Cha and Cha (1993) conducted tests on steady and laminar gravity-driven flow around a cube at a constant temperature in an infinite medium and measured Rayleigh No on top, side and bottom of the cube wall they found that maximum transfer of heat occurs at low Rayleigh No at lower value however, as the Rayleigh No increases it moves to side walls.

Venkateshan and Rammohan (1996), made an interferometer study of heat transfer by radiation and free convection from the arrays of horizontal fins for wide range of temperature. Correlations useful in thermal design were obtained. The authors emphasized on the importance of the mutual interaction between natural convection and radiation

Arquis and Rady (2005) studied transfer of heat by natural convection in a horizontal fluid layer with finned bottom surface and found steady state Rayleigh–Benard convection process. The effects of fin spacing and fin height have been enquired for a sufficiently wide range of Rayleigh No.

2 METHODOLOGY

The main aim is to increase the effective temperature difference mainly at the rear part of fin surface.

Fig1 (a) shows the regular rectangular fin with the same cross-sectional surface area at the base and tip of the fin. Figure 1 (b) shows the trapezoidal fin in which the area of cross section decreases from the base of the fin to the tip of the fin.Figure 1 (c) is the proposed inverted trapezoid fin in which the area of cross section increases from the base of the fin to the tip of the f

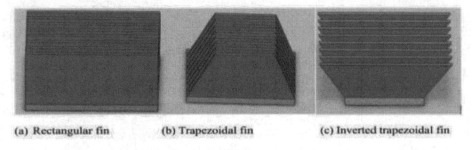

(a) Rectangular fin   (b) Trapezoidal fin   (c) Inverted trapezoidal fin

Figure 1.   Shapes of rectangular fins, trapezoidal fins and inverted trapezoidal.

In the experiment, in all the three designs the effective area is same and the dimensions of the designs are shown in Figure 2. The volume of the chamber in which experiments are

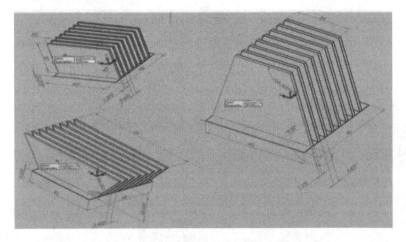

Figure 2.   Shapes of rectangular fins, trapezoidal fins and inverted trapezoidal.

performed is $(900 \times 900 \times 1240)$ mm^3. In the chamber temperature of the range 20–50 °C with a 0.2 °C of control resolution can be maintained. When the ambient temperature reaches 25° C, the air ventilator is turned off inside the test chamber to maintain natural flow condition. The air conditioner outside the test maintains the room temperature at 25 °C.

Aluminium alloy 5083 having thermal conductivity of 121 W/mK is used as heat sinks. CNC machining is used to make 5 pin fins heat sinks. The heat sinks are powered within the 3 to 20 W ranges. To eliminate the spreading of resistance Kapton heaters with identical size as that of the base plate of the heat sink is used. To minimize the heat loss two things are done

1. Bakelite insulation box with the thermal conductivity of 0.233 W/mK is placed beneath the heater.
2. High thermal conductivity grease (k = 2.1 W/mK) is used to connect the heat sink and the heater in order to further minimize contact resistance.

DC power supply is used to power the heater.

In the study, the temperature of the ambient air is maintained 25 °C and the thermo physical properties are evaluated at the temperature of the film, i.e.

$$T_f = \tfrac{1}{2}(T_a - T_b)$$

To obtain the actual heat transfer rate Q_t, we use the following equation:

$$Q_t = Q_i - Q_l$$

Where Q_i = Measured heat input of the Kapton heater

Q_l = Heat lost

$$Q_l = (k_b A_b (T_b - T_a))/x$$
$$h = (Q_t/A(T_b - T_a))$$

The test facility is kept inside the test chamber consisting of a heater, insulation box, heat sink and a rotating mechanism as shown in Fig.3.a. T-type thermocouples (5 in number) are located beneath the base plate and these are used to obtain the mean temperature of the base plate ( ) of the heat sink. Also, inside the insulation box 10 T-type thermo couples are installed at two cross positions for calculating the heat loss from the bottom of the Kapton heater. To get the mean temperature of a cross section, instrumenting of 5 T-type thermocouples equally is done at each cross-section. The estimation of the heat loss via Fourier's law of conduction is done using this mean temperature. With an accuracy of 0.1 °C the thermocouples were pre calibrated. The estimated loss is subtracted from the power input in order to obtain the total heat transfer rate by natural convection. For further data reduction, transmission of signals from thermocouples is done to a data acquisition system. Approximately 2.5 h is required in each test run to reach equilibrium when the power is turned on. The highest measured uncertaintics of the HTC are about 11 %(happening at the minimum input power of 3W). Particularly when input power is greater than 5 W, there is a drastic decrease in this uncertainty to less than 3%.

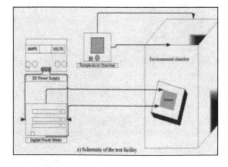
Figure 3(a). Representation of the test facility.

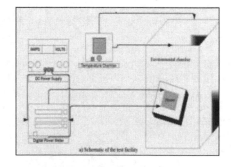
Figure 3(b). Representation of Bakelite.

3 RESULTS AND DISCUSSIONS

Figure.4 shows this experimental result for all the three fin configurations in terms of HTC. The experiment was conducted using different input powers to simulate the heat sink of the various fin profiles at different inputs. It is evident in Figure 4 that the HTC for the proposed inverted and trapezoidal shaped fin configuration with the same surface area considerably outperforms that of other two designs, namely rectangular and straight trapezoidal. When the heat flux of 600 is supplied, the HTC for rectangular and straight trapezoidal configuration is approximately 12% to 25% less than that of the inverted trapezoidal configuration. The difference in HTC is also evident even when the heat flux is less than 150. The augmentation seen in the inverted and trapezoidal shaped fin configuration is the result of proper utilization of the effective temperature difference T. It must also be noticed that the air comes mainly from the entrances of the heat sink at the bottom

i.e. from the fin gap. When the air flows toward the center of the heat sink, the temperature difference between the surface of the fin at the entrance and the air flow is the largest and is reduced accordingly as expected, hence, due to this heat transfer performance is decreased at the exit of the fin. It can be implied by the results that the surface area of the fin near the exit of the air flow doesn't cause much heat transfer since, there is very less temperature difference.

3.1 *Computer aided design (CAD) model in Ansys Design Modular*

A model of an inverted trapezoidal heat sink (fin height 30mm, fin length at bottom-45mm, fin length at top 75mm, fin thickness 1.375mm and fin spacing 3.425mm) is being built using Ansys design modular. The model consists of two different parts: Air Medium (height 300mm, length 150mm and thickness 150mm) and inverted trapezoidal fin inside. Initial settings like four input parameters (fin length on the top, fin height, fin thickness and fin spacing) and CAD simplifications for analysis is done in Ansys design modular before it is imported to the ANSYS fluid flow (Fluent).

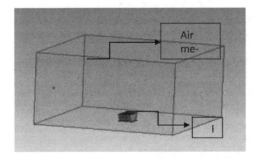

Figure 4. Generation of the finite element model.

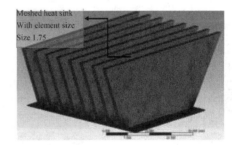

Figure 5. Meshed model of computation domain.

The initial mesh consists of 0.3 million elements. The face sizing of the fin element is 1.4mm and face sizing around the edges (with minimum length 1.4 mm) was 0.4 mm. While face sizing for an air medium was 5mm and around the edges (with minimum length 5mm) was 2 mm. The mesh was set to be fine instead of coarse and method of meshing was set to regular tetrahedrons .The sizing along the faces of air medium and fin mesh was set to be parametric so that we can vary them later

The meshed air shows the connectivity between air medium and fin elements.The model shows air medium surrounding the fins.

3.1.1 *Model validation with experimental data*
In order to know the mechanism of flow the simulation result is matched with experimental study before going for parametric study. Computational algorithm and simulations are verified for the comparison of the computational results with experimental data of Charles and Wang [9]. They showed that maximum velocity of air flow at the exit of the array of the fin from the numerical simulation with dimension of inverted trapezoidal fin as fin height 30 mm, fin top length 75mm, fin thickness 1.37mm, fin spacing 3.425mm and having heat flux of 600W/m^{2}at base.

3.1.2 *Parametric study of fin geomtery on heat transfer coefficient (HTC)*
One of the parameter which is coloured in the Table 1 is varied while other three parameters are fixed in order to find independent behaviour of particular parameter on HTC.

The graph shows in Fig.7 between HTC vs. Fin length, spacing, thickness and height is plotted from the table number 1.The graph shown in fig 7 and fig 8 between HTC vs. fin length, spacing is also plotted from the Table No: 1. Fig 7 shows when length is increase, HTC decrease and fig 8 shows when fin spacing increase, HTC decreases.

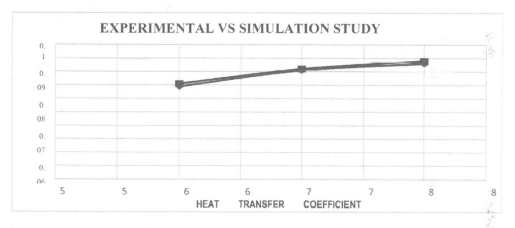

Figure 6.   Compare experimental value of exit air velocity with present simulation result value of velocity.

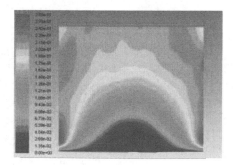

Figure 7.   Velocity contours along fin.

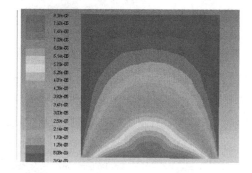

Figure 8.   Pressure contours along fin.

Table 1. Parametric study of fin geometric parameters with respect to HTC.

S NO	Air Spacing (mm)	Fin Length (mm)	Fin Height (mm)	Fin Thickness (mm)	Air & Fin Base Temp(K)	Heat Transfer Coefficient (W/m^2 K)
1	6.35	63.5	38	1.27	326.15	4.5415
2	6.35	127	38	1.27	326.15	3.1124
3	6.35	191	38	1.27	326.15	2.2096
4	6.35	254	38	1.27	326.15	1.696
5	6.35	127	19	1.27	326.15	2.6033
6	6.35	127	38	1.27	326.15	3.1124
7	6.35	127	48	1.27	326.15	3.1641
8	6.35	127	57	1.27	326.15	3.1276
9	6.35	127	76	1.27	326.15	2.9311
10	6.35	127	95	1.27	326.15	2.6909
11	3.15	127	95	1.27	326.15	0.42554
12	6.3	127	95	1.27	326.15	3.1124
13	9.45	127	95	1.27	326.15	4.8807
14	12.6	127	95	1.27	326.15	5.406
15	15.74	127	95	1.27	326.15	5.5866
16	6.35	127	38	1.016	326.15	3.3276

4 CONCLUSION

The heat transfer from array of the inverted trapezoid fin were found numerically by using codes of finite volume based computational fluid dynamics. Parametric study, DOE and response surface generation were done for a systematic theoretical study of the effects of fin geometric parameters and temperature difference between surroundings and fin on the heat transfer processes. Overall we can conclude that heat transfer varies non-linearly with fin spacing and fin length. Every parameter contributes towards heat transfer, though fin length and fin spacing are found to be highly dominant in contributing towards Heat transfer.Thus an optimized value for fin geometery is found considering all the observations and theories. The simulation result is compared with experimental results of Charles and Wang[9] with less then 4% error. Thus the applied boundary conditions and mathematical model is accurate up to required standard. From response surface we obtain maxima and minima of HTC and HF with respect to fin length and fin spacing. A surface is generated using 15 design points from DOE which shows relationship between input(fin geometery) and output (HTC & HF) parameters. The maximum HT from the above study takes place at the optimum value of Fin length (10-30)mm, Fin Height (25- 45)mm, Fin spacing (7mm-8mm) and Fin thickness (1mm-1.3mm) within a given range.

REFERENCES

Starner K.E., McManus Jr.-H.N., An experimental investigation of free-convection heat transfer from rectangular-fin arrays, J. Heat Tran. (August 1963) 273–278.

Welling J.R., Woolbridge C.B., Free convection heat transfer coefficients from rectangular vertical fins, J. Heat Tran. (November 1965) 439–444.

F. Harahap Jr.H.N., McManus, Natural convection heat transfer from horizontal rectangular fin arrays, J. Heat Transfer ASME Trans. 89 (1967) 32–38.

D.J. Cha, S.S. Cha, Three-dimensional natural convection flow around an isothermal cube, Int. Commun. Heat Mass Transfer 20 (1993) 619–630.

V. RammohanRao, S.P. Venkateshan, Experimental study of free convection and radiation in horizontal fin arrays, Int. J. Heat Mass Transfer 39 (1996) 779–789.

E. Arquis, M. Rady, Study of natural convection heat transfer in a finned horizontal fluid layer, Int. J. Thermal Sci. 44 (2005) 43–52.

Communication and Computing Systems – Prasad et al. (eds)
© 2019 Taylor & Francis Group, London, ISBN 978-0-367-00147-6

Study on temperature profiling of heating conductive yarn in SMART compression bandages

Pramod Sankara Pillai
Department of Textile Technology, Indian Institute of Technology Delhi, New Delhi, India

Shilpi Agarwal
Laser Applications and Holography Laboratory, Indian Institute of Technology Delhi, New Delhi, India

Bipin Kumar, R. Alagirusamy. & Apurba Das
Department of Textile Technology, Indian Institute of Technology Delhi, New Delhi, India

Chandra Shakher
Laser Applications and Holography Laboratory, Indian Institute of Technology Delhi, New Delhi, India

ABSTRACT: The bandages which monitor the conditions of the wound and react to improve the healing of wound are called SMART bandages. A SMART compression bandage based on the use of a smart materials (shape-memory alloy) i.e. heating wire, will be useful for heating medical applications. In this work we investigate the possibilities of use of the conductive copper yarns to produce heat in the compression bandages are explored. Heat transfer characteristics can be measured by measuring the change in temperature in compression bandages. Digital Holographic Interferometric technique based on digital imaging and computerized numerical reconstruction method is used to Study the Temperature Profiling of Heating Conductive Yarn in SMART Compression Bandages. With the help of digital imaging and computerized numerical reconstruction this process is simple, accurate, fast and reproducible.

1 INTRODUCTION

Bandage is used to support either a medical device intact or to provide support to a sprained ankle, to reduce the swelling or to restrict the movement of a part of the body. Bandages are available in a wide range of types. They are designed for a specific part of the body from general cloth strips to specialized shaped and size bandages. Adhesive bandage, Liquid bandage, Gauze bandage, Triangular bandage, Tube bandage and Compression bandages are the few types of bandages. Due to differences in structure, presence of different material and produce different compression outcomes the bandaging systems also vary in their ability. Bandages are classified based on their elasticity, extensibility and material function (Mosti et al. 2009). Within the broader category of *bandage* is the term *compression bandage*. Compression therapy is commonly used to treat several chronic venous disorders. It reduces the swollen limb to minimize its size and maintain a uniform pressure gradient to improve the venous return to the heart (Mosti & Partsch 2018).

SMART bandages monitor the conditions of the wound and react to improve the healing of wound. A SMART compression bandage based on the use of a smart materials (shape-memory alloy) technology which will be useful for several medical applications (Hoein & Menon 2014). A shape-memory alloy "remembers" their original shape. To extract the hot therapy effect by transfer of heat energy into compression bandages, the heating SMART bandages are introduced in modern wound healing. To increase the temperature to around 38 °C will increase the flow of blood to the surface and thereby increasing the oxygen availability and help to increase the healing. There are many ways of heating available for heating therapy. Here we are exploring the possibilities of use of the conductive yarns characteristics of producing the heat when electricity passes through it, the resistance of the yarn plays an important role for temperature produced. There are many factors need to be considered to impart hot therapy in bandages i.e. select conductive yarn to incorporate in the bandages, Voltage supply to the heating element, Resistance of heating element, temperature gradient, spacing between the two consecutive conductive yarn, heating area and environment temperature.

In this work we demonstrated the copper yarn temperature distribution to incorporate in the SMART compression bandage. Digital holographic interferometry (DHI) is used to study the temperature distribution profile characteristics in copper yarn of diameter 0.5 mm. The different heating conditions of copper yarn were achieved by applying variable powers across the yarn through a DC power supply (Make G^w_INSTEK, Model SPS-1820, Voltage range 0-18 volts, Current range 0-20 Amperes). The experimental results are used to optimise the knitting distance between two copper yarn Abel between the cotton yarn for uniform heating.

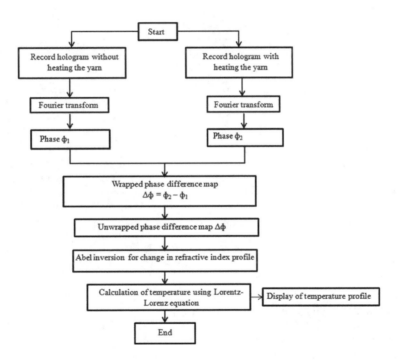

Figure 1. Flow chart for calculation of temperature from two digitally recorded holograms.

2 THEORY

In this work, the lensless Fourier transform digital holographic reconstruction method (Schnars & Juptner 2002, Hariharan 2002, Sharma et al. 2012, Agarwal et al. 2018a, Kumar et.al. 2014) is used for the measurement of temperature and temperature profile of copper yarn. Figure 1 shows the flow chart of the whole process of calculating the temperature profile.

When a known electric current and voltage is applied across the copper yarn, a temperature gradient is established, which creates phase difference and refractive index change (Agarwal et al. 2018b). Phase difference is unwrapped by Goldstein phase unwrapping algorithm (Goldstein 1988) and Inverse Abel transforms is used for refractive index calculation

(Sharma et al. 2012, Agarwal et al. 2018a, Kumar et al. 2014, Agarwal et al. 2018b). Once the refractive index difference is obtained from Eq. (2), the temperature distribution of copper yarn can be calculated using Lorentz-Lorenz formula (Agarwal et al. 2018b).

3 EXPERIMENTAL

Figure 2 shows the photograph of the lensless Fourier transform digital holographic interferometry set-up for the measurement of temperature profile around conductive copper yarn.

Figure 2.   Photograph of experimental set-up.

Figure 3(a) showing the photograph of copper yarn which is used in the experiment and Figure 3(b) shows the Infrared thermometer and temperature sensor setup used for temperature measurement for reference purpose.

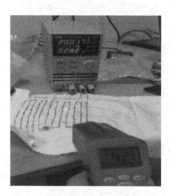

Figure 3(a).   Copper yarn.

Figure 3(b).   Infrared thermometer and temperature sensor setup for temperature measurement.

The copper yarn was clamped in vertical position as shown in Figure 4. Image reconstruction and image processing was done in the MATLAB.

Figure 4.   Photograph of mount to clamp the wire in vertical position.

4   RESULTS AND DISCUSSION

Experiment was performed for conductive copper yarn at different voltage and current. Several interferogram were recorded at constant interval of time i.e. 2 minutes upto 20 minutes for 4 Volt. Figure 5(a-j) shows the Phase difference map at 4 volt at an interval of 2 minutes up to 20 minutes.

Figure 6(a) shows the phase difference map of air around copper yarn without and with heating the yarn at 4 volt after 10 min of heating.

The phase difference map shown in Figure 6(a) is unwrapped by Goldstein phase unwrapping method. Figure 6(b) shows the 3D unwrapped phase difference corresponding to Figure 6 (a). Refractive index difference profile along lines AB, is shown in Figure 6 (c). Figure 6(d) shows the temperature profile along the lines AB, as marked in Figure 6(a).

The spacing between the conductive yarn in bandages are obtained using knitting after optimization of the distance between two conductive yarn. Structure should give the possible uniform distribution of heat with low voltage application and same time it should hold the temperature for around 20 mins or more to obtain the advantage of the hot therapy.

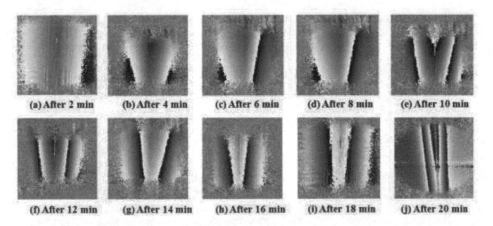

(a) After 2 min   (b) After 4 min   (c) After 6 min   (d) After 8 min   (e) After 10 min

(f) After 12 min   (g) After 14 min   (h) After 16 min   (i) After 18 min   (j) After 20 min

Figure 5.   Phase difference map at 4 volt at an interval of 2 minutes up to 20 minutes for copper yarn.

5   CONCLUSION

Digital holographic interferometric technique for measurement of temperature and temperature profile along the surface of heated copper yarn has been presented. Spacing optimization between two conducting yarn for uniform heating can also be studied by the proposed method. Further

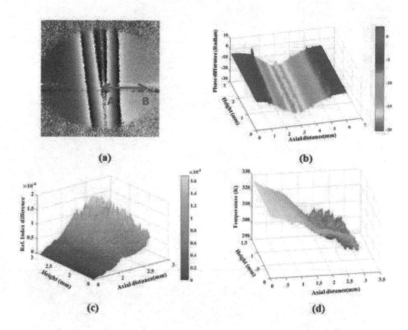

Figure 6. (a) Phase difference maps of air without and with heating copper yarn at 4 volt (b) 3D phase difference map corresponding to Figure 6 (a); (c) Refractive index difference distribution along the lines AB as marked in Figure 6 (a); and (d) Temperature profile of heated air along the lines AB, as marked in Figure 6 (a).

experimentation is needed for different spacing between the conductive yarn to incorporated bandages obtained by using knitting. So that the separation between the yarn should give the possible uniform distribution of heat with low voltage application and same time it should hold the temperature for around 20 minutes or more to obtain the advantage of the hot therapy.

REFERENCES

Mosti, G. Mattaliano, V. Arleo, S. Partsch, H. 2009. Thigh compression after great saphenous surgery is more effective with high pressure. *International Angiology* 28(4): 274-280.

Mosti, G. Partsch, H. 2018. A new two component compression system turning an elastic bandage into an inelastic compression device: interface pressure, stiffness and haemodynamic effectiveness. *European Journal of Vascular and Endovascular Surgery* 55(1): 126-131.

Moein, H. Menon, C. 2014. An active compression bandage based on shape memory alloy: a preliminary investigation. *Biomedical Engineering Online* 13(135): 1-13.

Schnars, U. Juptner, W. P. O. 2002. Digital recording and numerical reconstruction of holograms. *Measurement Science and Technology* 13(9): R85–R101.

Hariharan, P. (ed.) 2002 *Basic of holography*. Cambridge: Cambridge University Press.

Sharma, S. Sheoran, G. Shakher, C. 2012. Temperature measurement of axi-symmetric flame under the influence of magnetic field using lens less Fourier transform digital holography. *Applied Optics* 51(19): 4554-4562.

Agarwal, S. Kumar, V. Shakher, C. 2018. Temperature Measurement of Wick Stabilized Micro Diffusion Flame under the Influence of Magnetic Field Using Digital Holographic Interferometry. *Optics and Laser in Engineering* 102: 161–169.

Kumar, V. Kumar, M. Shakher, C. 2014. Measurement of natural convective heat transfer coefficient along the surface of a heated wire using digital holographic interferometry. *Applied Optics* 53(27): G 74-7G84.

Goldstein, R. M. Zebker, H. A. Werner, C. 1988. Satellite radar interferometry: two-dimensional phase unwrapping. *Radio Sciences* 23(4): 713–720.

Agarwal, S. Shakher, C. 2018. Effect of magnetic field on temperature profile and flame flow characteristics of micro flame using Talbot interferometer. *Optik* 108: 817-826.

Software engineering & emerging technologies

Communication and Computing Systems – Prasad et al. (eds)
© *2019 Taylor & Francis Group, London, ISBN 978-0-367-00147-6*

Big Data techniques: Today and tomorrow

Priyanka Khatana
Department of Information Technology, Dronacharya College of Engineering, Gurugram, Haryana, India

Yashvardhan Soni
Department of Computer Science Engineering, Dronacharya College of Engineering. Gurugram, Haryana, India

ABSTRACT: This paper is written before doing any practical work on the above topic. It is based on the research done on the topic- "Big Data Techniques: Today and Tomorrow". Big data refers to a large dataset which is not easy to handle or understand. We have given a brief description about the present scenario and the future scenario of big data. We are going to explain what big data is, how it came into existence, a brief about the technologies involved in data extraction. By the end of the paper we will get a basic knowledge about big data and its benefits and its use in our daily life also. This paper aims to analyze some of the different tools and techniques which can be applied to big data.

1   INTRODUCTION

Big Data describes the large amount of data that is very big and complex and exists in both structured and unstructured form. The building block upon which any organizations relay is – Data. With every second data is being created and analyzed. Big data refers to the large amount of space which is needed by every organization. Now-a-days data has become cheaper to store, so organizations need to get as much value as possible. Furthermore big data is used everywhere now, banking, education, government, healthcare, manufacturing are some of these fields. It isvery critical to understand that the primary value from big data do not comes from the raw data form, but from the processing and analysis of it, from the products, and services that emerge from analysis.

2   BIG DATA

2.1   *What is Big Data?*

Big Data is described as collection of data that is huge in size and, it is exponentially growing with time. Such data is very large and complex, none of the traditional data management tools are able to store it or process it efficiently.Although the term 'Big Data' is new but gathering and storing large amount of data for analyses is ages old. A very huge number of data is present but only 0.5%of the data has been analyzed yet. John Mashey was the scientist who coined this term and made it popular. As, big data is so complex it requires sets of tools and techniques to handle it.

2.2   *Categories of Big Data*

• Big data can be categorized into three forms.

1. Structured

2. Unstructured
3. Semi-structured

Structured

Any data which can be accessed, analyzed, stored and executed in a fixed form is known as the "structured data". In doing this, great success has been achieved. But now computers are facing problems in handling large amount of data.

One example of such form is the data stored in relational databases.

Unstructured

Data which do not have a particular structure or it is present in raw form or any unknown form, is termed as the "unstructured data". Deriving information from unstructured form is data is a big task.

One such example is a heterogeneous data source which contains videos, audios, text files.

Semi-structured

Data which is present in both the forms is termed as Semi-structured data.

3 HISTORY OF BIG DATA

The origin of large data sets was started in the year 1950 and 60's. In the year 1965 the first ever data center was opened in United States to store tax returns. Later in 1989 a British scientist invented the World Wide Web.

2005 was the year when people got to know that a huge amount of data is generated through mails, YouTube and other social media sites. This was the year when "HADOOP" came in.

HADOOP is an open source framework which is designed specially to store and analyze big data. It is created by 'Yahoo". It made big data easier to work and cheaper to store the data.

In 2009 the Indian government decided to take a photograph, fingerprint and iris scan of its 1.2 billion people. Its data is stored in the largest biometric database in the world.

Big data has exponentially increased over the years. As with big data we have a large set of information and the company can retrieve useful information from that large set. That is the reason why more and more organizations are inclined towards big data. Also with the emergence of IoT and Cloud computing more number of devices are connected to internet. And also many new social media sites have been launched time to time. All these things produce new data everyday. Machine learning has also opened new forms. However the large revolution is yet to come. The time is near when we will notice the changes as it's the era of Big Data now.

4 BIG DATA: TODAY

4.1 *Importance*

Today Big data is on boom. It helps in the decision making process of the business.

It helps in understanding the market forces. By understanding the market conditions, companies can make products according to it.

With the help of big data analysis businessman can understand their customers and they get to know the demands and needs of the customer. Also, they can get timely feedbacks from the customer and can change their products according to their wishes.

It also helps in controlling the social media sites and can also help in reducing the cost of products and makes it inexpensive.

4.2 *Tools for analyzing and storing*

Many tools are used for analyzing and storing data. Some of them are:

4.2.1 *Apache Hadoop*

It is a java based free software framework. HDPS(Hadoop Distributed File System) is the storage system of Hadoop. which splits data on every node in form of clusters.

4.2.2 *NoSQL*

Not Only SQL is used to handle the unstructured form of data. It gives a reliable and better performance to store massive amount of data.

4.2.3 *Presto*

It is a Query engine designed and developed by Facebook to handle Petabytes of data.

4.3 *Applications*

4.3.1 *Internet of Things (IoT)*

Data extracted from IoT devices provides a mapping of device inter-connectivity which helps the industries and government to increase its efficiency.

4.3.2 *Manufacturing*

With the help of big data we can forecast the output, increase energy efficiency, check the product and its quality and many more other things can be done.

4.3.3 *Healthcare*

Government sectors, Cyber Security and Intelligence, Scientific Research etc are a few more applications of Big Data.

4.4 *Challenges*

– Hadoop software is not easy to manage. Many professionals find it difficult to handle.
– There is a lack of talent to work on Big data. Their is a shortage of Data scientists.
– Everyday new form of data is being produced. Data quality and storing the data is a big concern.
– Data security is also a very big challenge in Big data.

5 BIG DATA: FUTURE

5.1 *Importance*

It is said that the data in future will be double of the present data. More and more industries will start using the concept of Big data by realizing its power and benefits. As more and more companies will adopt big data analytics, new technologies will be provided in the future to determine the exact output. With the help of new tools and technologies the percentage of accurate prediction will increase.

Machine learning will be a top strategic trend in future. New algorithms will also emerge in the future. With the emergence of new data and technologies, the needs for data scientist will also increase and hence chances for new jobs in this field will also increase.

5.2 *Tools for analyzing and storing*

5.2.1 *Terracotta In-Genius*

In future, it will be a new invention as Terracotta In-Genius speeds up data analysis by moving into RAM.

For example it will be helpful in trying to stop credit card frauds.

5.2.2 *Medalogix*

It is a healthcare risk assessment tool. It will help in determining the risk rate of a patient of readmitting in the hospital. It will be done by going through the patients past treatment history and its records.

5.2.3 *SAS Text Miner*

It can look for trends in a large text and can predict issues.

Let's say a company is facing a problem with product, this tool will look into the complain posted by the users and will look into the trends. Then it will predict the correct output for that product. So, that it can fulfill the customer's demands and needs. This will be the role of the SAS Text Miner.

5.3 *Applications*

By 2020 more and more companies will move towards big data.

Banking and securities, communications, Media and services, Government sectors, Engineering firms, Education, Healthcare providers, Insurance, Manufacturing and natural resources, retail, transportation, Utilities, wholesale Trade will use Big data in all possible quantities.

5.4 *Challenges*

The most important challenge that users will face in the future is Scalability. It is predicted that the number of users will increase exponentially and with that data handling will become difficult.

Only professionals can handle such big amount of data. Thus gaining expert knowledge will be a challenge.

Security will be the most important challenge. As securing such huge amount of data in not easy. Also the quality of data should be maintained.

It is quite inexpensive today but will be expensive in the future.

6   TECHNIQUES USED FOR ANALYZING

6.1 *A/B testing*

Also known as Bucket testing and Split testing.

In this technique, variety of test groups are compared with a control group in order to conclude what changes will improve the given objective variable.

For example, what color, text font, layout will be suitable for an e-commerce website so that it attracts more auditions.

6.2 *Association rule learning*

This technique is used to determine some correlations between the variables in large databases.

It was first used in major supermarket chain to determine correlations between its products and the customers.

It is also used to uncover new relationships by examining biological data.

6.3 *Classification tree analysis*

As the name specifies, it classifies the category of the new data or the document.

It is used to categories organisms into their respective bunch.

It requires a lot of training.

6.4 *Machine learning*

As we all know that machine learning is based on learn from data concept. The machine learns from the "training data set" and acts according to the given conditions and produces output.

It is used to differentiate between spam and non-spam mails or messages.

It is helpful in determining the probability cases.

It learns user's predilections and guides the user according to the information given.

6.5 *Social network analysis*

This technique was first used by telecommunication industry.

It is used to see how people interact and tie bonds with people outside their zone.

It helps in tying relationships between individual.

It helps in understanding the social domain of an individual.

7 CONCLUSION

This paper can be seen as a complete summary of Big Data. As the amount of data generated is increasing day by day at a very high rate, it has become a necessity to develop techniques that can handle such a huge amount of data. Big data is helping us in doing so. The analysing techniques Big Data provides us with today also need some modifications in them to make them even more compatible in future. This is a field which needs continuous research and modifications to work efficiently in future also. With time, more new techniques are also needed to be developed.

REFERENCES

Adams, M.N.: Perspectives on Data Mining. International Journal of Market Research 52(1),11-19 (2010).

Asur, S., Huberman, B.A.: predicting the Future with Social Media. In: ACM International Conference on Web Intelligence and Intelligent Agent Technology, vol. 1, pp. 492-499 (2010).

Bakshi, K.: Considerations for Big Data: Architecture and Approaches. In: Proceedimgs of the IEEE Aerospace Conference, pp. 1-7 (2012).

Cebr: Data equity, Unlocking the value of big data in: SAS Reports, pp. 1-44 (2012).

Cohen, J., Dolan, B., Dunlap, M., Hellerstein, J.M., Welton, C.: MAD Skills: New Analysis Practices for Big Data. Proceedings of the ACM VLDB Endowment 2(2),1481-1492 (2009).

Cuzzocrea, A., Song, I., Davis, K.C.: Analytics over Large-Scale Multidimensional Data: The Big Data Revolution! In: Proceedings of the ACM International Workshop on Data Warehousing and OLAP, pp. 101-104 (2011).

Econimist Intelligence Unit: The Deciding Factor: Big Data & Decision Making. In: Capgemini Reports, pp. 1-24 (2012).

Elgendy, N.: Big Data Analytics in Support of the Decision Making Process. MSc Thesis, German University in Cairo, p. 164 (2013).

EMC: Data Science and Big Data Analytics. In: EMC Education Services, pp. 1-508 (2012).

He, Y., Lee, R., Huai, Y., Shao, Z., Jain, N., Zhang, X., Xu, Z.: RCFile: A Fast and Space Efficient Data Placement Structure in Map Reduce-based Warehouse Systems. In: IEEE International Conference on Data Engineering (ICDE), pp. 1199-1208 (2011).

Herodotou, H., Lim, H., Luo, G., Borisov, N., Dong, L., Cetin, F.B., Babu, S.: Starfish: A Self-tuning System for Big Data Analytics. In: Proceedings of the Conference on Innovative Data Systems Research, pp261-272 (2011).

Communication and Computing Systems – Prasad et al. (eds)
© 2019 Taylor & Francis Group, London, ISBN 978-0-367-00147-6

Low-power and high-speed 15T SRAM cell using CMOS

Prerna Kumari, Sneha Kumari & Pankaj Gupta
Department of ECE, IGDTUW, Delhi, India

ABSTRACT: In low power VLSI, scaling has the advantage of reduced size of chip with same specification. However, scaling of MOS devices has many challenges like leakage current, leakage power, read and write stability. Leakage power reduction and delay enhancement are main focus of this paper. The conventional 11T SRAM give external noise and high-power consumption as well as delay. 15T SRAM cell which has better write ability and improved read stability is proposed. Here, 15T SRAM cell has been compared with the existing 13T SRAM based on power consumption as well as delay calculation. For improvement of power consumption in SRAM cell the power gating technique is used. Computer simulation are done in is given in 180 nm technology using Cadence Virtuoso.

1 INTRODUCTION

Static Random-Access Memory (SRAM) is an important part of the digital world like microprocessor, memory, high performance cellular technology and many more devices (Meng Fan Chang et al. 2011, Shilpa Saxena & Rajesh Mehra. 2016). But today generation CMOS structure is scaled down which effect the short channel of the circuit. By reducing the voltage scaling and area, it creates leakage current problem so, this increases the power consumption and delay problems in the conventional SRAM cells such as 6T, 7T, 8T, 9T, 10T, 13T. So, for the minimization of these problems we proposed new 15T SRAM cell with sleep transistor technique. For the scaling in the low power VLSI design many nm technologies has been introduced (Ramy E. Aly et al. 2007.). This paper is proposed in cadence virtuoso using 180 nm technologies. In SRAM, to store the one-bit memory cell four to six transistors are required so, in this paper we used Conventional 6T SRAM which worked as a semiconductor memory that used latching device to store the data (Sherif A. Tawfik et al. 2008). After read operation data should not be refreshed periodically as like DRAM cell. SRAM is in volatile nature so its data is gone after switched off operation.

1.1 *CMOS SRAM cell*

A low power low voltage SRAM cell is model by a latched type CMOS inverters circuit. Power dissipation is the major issue for designing of any circuit so, the problem of power dissipation is alleviated by CMOS SRAM cell (Yi-Wei Chiu et al. 2013). Due to larger cell design, this design can operate at lower power supply voltage and low leakage power and due to high noise margin; this design has high noise immunity (Farshad Moradi et al. 2014). The major limitation of these types SRAM cells is their larger cell structure. The complete circuit structure of the SRAM memory cell. The SRAM memory cell consists of CMOS inverters which are connected as a latch, with additional two pass transistors are present allow to access the word line(Farshad Moradi et al. 2014.). These access pass transistors are switched on when the word line is triggered for either the read or write mode, by connecting memory cell to the corresponding bit line columns (Premalatha et al. 2015). A 13T SRAM cell has proposed for the better performance but there are some noises present due to high power consumption and high delay so for the reduction of delay as well as power consumption also for the better speed performance in the low scaling technology we introduced 15T SRAM using 180 nm technologies in Cadence Virtuoso.

In this 15T SRAM we used sleep transistor in the pull up net- work. In the paper, we proposed 15T SRAM cell in place of conventional 13T SRAM using CMOS. Due to leakage problem, we degrade the speed performance so for the enhancement of speed we minimize leakage problem by adding two more transistors as a sleep transistor in conventional 13T SRAM cell architecture.

In low supply voltage SRAM cell faces write failure in conventional 6T SRAM cell, because at low supply voltage it is not possible to overcome week write-access transistor in the strong feedback of inverter of the SRAM cell. In additional SRAM cell al- so faces read failure at the time of read operation in low supply voltage in conventional 6T SRAM cell. However, there are so many techniques are used for the improvement of read write operation at the same time in low supply voltage.

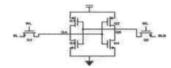

Figure 1. Conventional 6T SRAM cell.

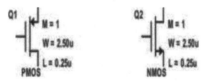

Figure 2. Symbolic diagram of PMOS and NMOS.

The design must be modified and in place of simple latched cell we used a basic Schmitt trigger inverter-based SRAM cell (ST), due to Schmitt trigger circuit write-capability of the SRAM cell is increased because of stacked transistor in the inverter added access transistors. For improvement, the read and write stability we increase number of transistors in place of pass transistor we use transmission gate which give better read and write stability compare to pass transistor circuit which make its complex as the number of transistors but the advantage we get as a result of read and write stability and leakage power reduction (Premalatha et al. 2015).

The remainder of this paper is organized as follows: Section 2 provides overview of both the conventional 11T SRAM cell and 13T SRAM cell. Section 3 presents the proposed 15T SRAM cell. Simulation results are presented in section 4. Section 5 concludes the paper.

2 CONVENTIONAL WORK

2.1 Conventional 11T SRAM cell

The conventional 11T SRAM cell is shown in Figure 2. The upper part of the circuit is basic 6T cell and when word-line is in high then basic 6T SRAM cell is performed write and read operation. Also, when word-line is 0 then this bi-stable latch circuit is in hold state in Figure 2 Q10, Q11 and Q7 transistors are used for reading operation and these transistors are read the content of the storage nodes (QA, QB). RBL is the read bit line which acts as a single-ended access path. RWL is the read word line and WL is the word line, both are distinct from each other. When RWL is set to be low then data is stored at QA and QB. During write operation and standby mode Transistors Q5 and Q6 separate the storage nodes (QA and QB) from read bit line that why different distinct write and read ports in this existing 11T SRAM cell(Wei-Bin Yang et al. 2012). If RWL=0, stored data is still stored at the storage node because of different Read and write path. Q10 and Q11 is work as switching transistors which are choose by the voltage node at storage nodes.

In the 11T two pass transistors are used for the passing of signal but in 13T SRAM transistor we used transmission gate in place of pass transistor for the passing of signal and this transmission gate is connected to the bit line and bit line bar. In the conventional SRAM cells, various drawbacks are there such as power product delay, leakage current, power dissipation, read and write stability. So, for the improvement of these drawbacks 13T SRAM cell is proposed (Abhijit Sil et al. 2007)

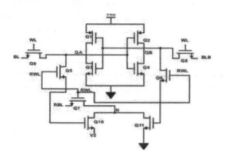
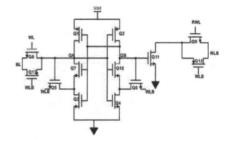

Figure 3.   Conventional 11-T SRAM cell.   Figure 4.   Conventional 13T SRAM cell.

2.2   *Conventional 13T SRAM cell*

Figure 3 represents the conventional 13T SRAM cell. The conventional 13T SRAM cell is based on the Schmitt trigger memory which is controlled by storage nodes QA and QB. Transistors Q8, Q13, Q9 and Q12 act as a transmission gate. The transistors Q8 and Q13 in conventional 13T SRAM cell are used to pass the both signals strong '0' and strong '1' which enhance the write stability of the circuit compared to 11T SRAM cell in which pass transistors was used. The transistors Q9 and Q12 is worked same as the Q8 and Q13 transistors. In this conventional 13T SRAM cell, read mode made up of two transistors and a write mode transistor. In this existing cell write operation is in control of WL and read operation is in control of RWL. Two transistors of drain terminal are connected to the Schmitt trigger which control the WLB i.e. word line bar (Abhijit Sil et al. 2007). In this exiting cell leak- age power still creates a problem so for the minimization of leakage power two more PMOS is connect- ed as a pull up network in proposed SRAM cell and this pull up network act as sleep transistor. With the help of this three-pin symbol we proposed 13T SRAM using CMOS. The schematic diagram of 13T SRAM cell is shown in the Figure 2. in this Figure 2 two transistors are added in the access path in the 11T SRAM schematic we implement the 13T SRAM. Basically, transmission gate is used in the access path for passing signal 1 and signal 2 according to the requirement. Two NMOS (Q3 & Q4) are connected to the transistor Q3 and Q4 that increases the threshold voltage Vth and this reduces the sub-threshold leakage current and leakage power (). In Figure 3, Q1 and Q2 act as pull up network and Q3 and Q3 acts as pull-down network. QA and QB give the output volt- age and these are the storage nodes in the 15T SRAM cell (Zhiyu Liu et al. 2008). Figure 4 shows the waveform results of the pro- posed 15T SRAM cell. But in this 13T SRAM after the simulation we observe that some noises are present which affects the speed performance of the circuit (Ik Joon Chang et al. 2009). For the improvement of speed and reduction of leakage power, we add two transistors which acts as a pull up network in conventional 13T SRAM Cell and these two transistors is called sleep transistor.

3 PROPOSED WORK

3.1 *Proposed 15T SRAM cell design*

15T SRAM circuit consist of basic 13T SRAM cell with sleep transistor, the sleep transistors are basically high threshold voltage Vth MOS circuit used for reduction of leakage power, and the switched off when the circuit is inactive and thus save the power. A proposed 15T SRAM cell is designed by a cross coupled. Schmitt trigger inverter; there are two transistors work as a data read path and a more transistor used to enable the write operation. A row-based word line (WL) controls the write access transistor and an- other row based read word line controls the read access transistor and feedback transistors of Schmitt trigger inverter along with respective drain controls the storage of QA and QB and are also connected with control signal word line bar (Ik Joon Chang et al. 2009). Internal storage of output line QA and QB are controlled by the feed- back transistors of Schmitt trigger inverter with their drains are inter connected with a control signal word line bar (WLB) (Singh Ajay Kumar et al. 2009).

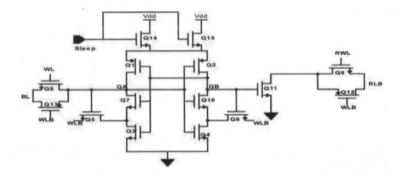

Figure 5.   Proposed 15T SRAM cell.

The access path of based on the pass transistor in conventional 11T SRAM cell. The entire circuit performance is enhanced by the pro- posed 15T SRAM cell which is based on the trans- mission gate which is route to access data in place of pass transistors that allows to pass the entire full range voltage, which implies strong '0' and strong '1'. We begin by employing the sleep transistors approach in 15T SRAM cell. Which is also knows as power gating technique that reduces the leakage power of the SRAM cell during the data holding phase. The activation of sleep transistor reduces the supply voltage during data holding phase which is a benefit of pull up network that results in reducing the leakage power of entire circuit. The pull-up network helps to reduce the supply voltage Vdd to Vdd/2. During the period of unwanted operation, the power gating approach reduces the consumption of power of SRAM cell by reducing in overall dissipation of power.

HOLD MODE:
In case of hold operation both word line (WL) and read word line (RWL) are disabled and virtual ground signal (VGND) is kept grounded so that it set to be 0. Therefore, the CMOS inverter pair is not connected from the bit lines (BL and RBL), and the data-retention capability is enhanced through the feedback access path.
In the Figure 4, here we presented the four different cycles these are READ, WRITE '0';, WRITE '1' HOLD.

4 SIMULATION RESULT

4.1 *Transient analysis*

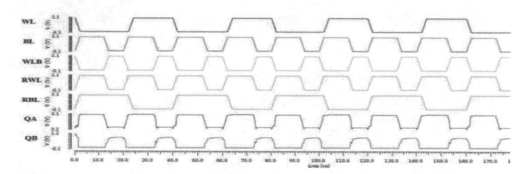

Figure 6.   Transient analysis of 13T SRAM cell.

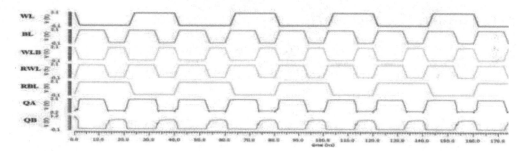

Figure 7.   Transient analysis of 15T SRAM cell.

WRITE MODE. In the write mode, the word line (WL) set to be 0 by pulling down and enable bit line (BL) signal and left floating and after that, word line bar (WLB) signal is pre-charged to logic '1' so that data is written from bit-line (BL) to memory storage nodes (QA & QB).

READ MODE: For read operation at first the both bit line BL is initially 1, and read word line (RWL) signal stimulate the read operation, and BBL becomes '1' and also the read bit line (RBL) become to 0 and word line (WL) retain as 1.

4.2 *Table*

Table 1.   Comparison table.

No. of Transistors	13T SRAM	15T SRAM	Percentage Improvement
Leakage Power calculation (nW)	16.86	10.82	55.82 %
Delay calculation (ns)	12.25	9.56	28.13 %

4.3 *Results*

As we can see that the 13T SRAM dissipate 16.86nw whereas the 15T SRAM dissipate 12.25nw thus we can see that the power dissipation is improved by the 55.82%. Similarly, in case of the delay 15T SRAM overall delay is 9.56ns whereas the 13T SRAM delay is 10.82ns. It shows that 15T SRAM cell less delay compare to 13T SRAM cell. the delay is improved by 28.13%.

5 CONCLUSIONS

Thus, SRAM cells are designed with minimum power consumption and less delay. The low power design with sleep transistor approach is successfully implemented and the desired result is obtained. This provides us with the minimum power consumption. A power reduction of 55.82% is obtained for proposed 15T SRAM cell compared to conventional 13T SRAM cell. From the result, proposed 15T SRAM cell using CMOS is more power efficient compared to the conventional 13T SRAM cell by using power gating technique, i.e. sleep transistors approach, and the transmission gates (TG) help to reduce the delay of the SRAM circuit compare to pass transistor SRAM circuit.

REFERENCES

Meng Fan Chang et al. 2011. A 130 mV SRAM with expanded write and read margins for sub-threshold applications. *IEEE Journal of Solid-State Circuits* 46, no. 2: 520–529.

Shilpa Saxena & Rajesh Mehra. 2016. Low- power and high-speed 13T SRAM cell using FinFETs. *IET Circuits, Devices & Systems* 11, no. 3: 250–255

Ramy E.Aly et al. 2007. Low-power cache de- sign using 7T SRAM cell. IEEE Transactions on Circuits and Systems II: Express Briefs 54, no. 4: 318–322.

Sherif A. Tawfik et al. 2008. Low power and robust 7T dual-V t SRAM circuit. In Circuits and Systems, 2008. ISCAS. IEEE International Symposium on, pp. 1452–1455.

Farshad Moradi et al. 2014. Robust subthreshold 7T-SRAM cell for low-power applications. In Circuits and Systems (MWSCAS), IEEE 57th International Midwest Symposium on,pp. 893–896.

Yi-Wei Chiu et al. 2013. A 40 nm 0.32 V 3.5 MHz 11T single-ended bit-interleaving sub- threshold SRAM with data-aware write-assist. In Proceedings of the 2013 International Symposium on Low Power Electronics and Design, pp. 51–56.

Premalatha et al. 2015. A comparative analysis of 6T, 7T, 8T and 9T SRAM cells in 90nm technology. In Electrical, Computer and Communication Technologies (ICECCT), IEEE International Conference on, pp. 1–5.

Wei-Bin Yang et al. 2012. A 300 mV 10 MHz 4 kb 10T subthreshold SRAM for ultralow-power application. In Intelligent Signal Processing and Communications Systems (ISPACS), 2012 International Symposium on, pp. 604–608.

Abhijit Sil et al. 2007. A novel 8T SRAM cell with improved read-SNM. In Circuits and Systems, 2007. NEWCAS 2007. IEEE Northeast Workshop on, pp. 1289–1292.

Zhiyu Liu et al. 2008. Characterization of a novel nine-transistor SRAM cell. IEEE transactions on very large-scale integration (VLSI) systems 16, no. 4: 488–492.

Ik Joon Chang et al. 2009 A 32 kb 10T sub- threshold SRAM array with bit-interleaving and differential read scheme in 90 nm CMOS. IEEE Journal of Solid-State Circuits 44, no. 2: 650–658.

Singh Ajay Kumar et al. 2009. A proposed eleven-transistor (11-T) CMOS SRAM cell for improved read stability and reduced read power consumption.

Communication and Computing Systems – Prasad et al. (eds)
© 2019 Taylor & Francis Group, London, ISBN 978-0-367-00147-6

Monitoring and management using IoT sensing with cloud based processing

Aarushi Arora, Aditi Aggarwal & Rekha Vig
The NorthCap University, India

ABSTRACT: The main aim of this project is to bridge the gap between the doctor and patient with modern technology and available components and sensors. Our contribution to solving the healthcare problem is using an engineering approach and developing a remote health care system. In this system patient's parameters (temperature and heart rate) have been measured with different available sensors and these sensors monitored and captured data which was further transmitted to the Raspberry Pi. The data was then transmitted to an IoT analytics platform on a cloud-based server (ThingSpeak). The real time health data was visualized and analyzed on it.

1 INTRODUCTION

Health is one of the global challenges for humanity and has drawn great amount of attention over the last few years. The prime aim is to develop a reliable patient monitoring system so that the doctors can monitor their patients, who are either admitted in the hospital or are executing their normal daily life activities. Health monitoring system using IoT (Hassanalieragh, M. et al 2015) can provide useful information remotely. This monitoring is useful for elderly or chronically ill patients who require constant monitoring or those who cannot physically contact a doctor regularly. Sensors are used to collect and transmit signals of interest and a raspberry pi is programmed to receive and automatically analyse the sensor signals.

For remote health monitoring systems a three tier architecture is mostly proposed: a Wireless Body Area Network (WBAN) consisting of wearable sensors as the data acquisition unit, communication and networking and the service layer (Patil et al 2018, Kumar et al 2016, Yuan 2015). They utilize wearable sensors to measure various physiological parameters such as blood pressure and body temperature. These sensors transmit the gathered information to a microcontroller which processes the data and passes it on to a gateway server through a wireless connection. The gateway server turns the data into an Observation and Measurement file and stores it on a remote server for later retrieval by clinicians through the Internet. Utilizing a similar cloud based medical data storage, a health monitoring system is presented in (Da Xu, Li 2014) in which medical staff can access the stored data online through content service application.

In this paper selected appropriate sensors have been used according to certain parameters to be detected and design algorithms to realize those detections. Examples are detection of body temperature, pulse rate and ambient conditions of temperature and humidity. Using a single parameter monitoring system an approach to a remote health monitoring system was designed that extends healthcare from the traditional clinic or hospital setting to the patient's home.

The system was to collect the raw data, calibrate and extract meaningful signals. The data from the monitoring systems is then availed for remote detection.

During design the following characteristics of the future medical applications have been adhered to:

a) Integration with current technology and medical needs,

b) Remote monitoring in real time with minimalistic wearable sensors.

c) Assistance to the elderly and chronic patients. The device should be easy to use with minimal buttons.

2 SYSTEM MODEL

2.1 *System architecture*

The equipment used here is easy to use and it gives output in the form of graphs which makes the monitoring of the patient better. The output is deduced from the real time signal captured from the patient and further into raspberry pi 3 and then gets uploaded in the form of graphs on the platform, here we have used Thingspeak.com.

There are three sensors involved in the project, Body temperature sensor, ambient temperature sensor and pulse rate sensor. Both the temperature sensors are directly connected to the raspberry pi, on their respective pins. Whereas, pulse rate sensor requires an ADC, and in our project, Arduino is doing the dutiful job of ADC. The data received by the raspberry pi from the three sensors are pushed on a cloud-based database platform, Thingspeak.com, making it a lot easy for anyone to monitor their/anyone's health and take the required measures. The main focus is to upload the data on the web, so that it is easily accessible by any doctor and prescribe them the respected medications required, especially in the remote areas. From the graphs, the doctor can analyse how good, bad or moderate the situation of the patient is.

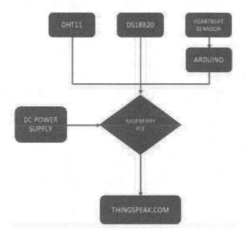

Figure 1. Block diagram.

2.2 *Block diagram*

The interconnection of the various components is shown in the Figure 1. The sensors are placed on the patient's body and connected to the raspberry pi or Arduino as per sensor need. Real time data as being sensed by the sensors is acquired and uploaded on an IoT server after a period of 15 seconds. This enables the doctors to remotely monitor the patient's health and suggest medications accordingly.

3 DESIGN COMPONENTS

3.1 *Hardware*

3.1.1 *Raspberry Pi*
The Raspberry Pi 3 Model B is the third generation Raspberry Pi. This powerful credit-card sized single board computer can be used for many applications

It also adds wireless LAN & Bluetooth connectivity making it the perfect solution for powerful connected designs. The integrated hardware is shown in figure 2.

3.1.2 *Arduino*
The Arduino Uno is a microcontroller board based on the ATmega328 microcontroller. It has 14 digital input/output pins out of which 6 can be used as PWM outputs, 6 analog inputs, a 16 MHz crystal oscillator, a USB connection, a power jack, an ICSP header, as well as a reset button. It contains everything needed to support the microcontroller

3.1.3 *DTH 11*
The DHT11 is a basic, low-cost digital temperature and humidity sensor. It uses a resistive humidity sensor and a thermistor to measure the ambient conditions, and the output is a digital signal on the data pin. It contains dedicated digital modules for collection and temperature and humidity sensing technology. Ensuring that the product has high reliability and excellent long-term stability.

3.1.4 *Pulse rate sensor*
The heartbeat sensor is based on the principle of photo phlethysmography. Change in volume of blood through any organ of the body causes a change in the light intensity through that region. This change is measured by a heartbeat sensor. In applications where pulse rate is to be monitored, the timing of the pulses is very important. The signal pulses are equivalent to the heart beat pulses because the flow of blood in the vessels decides the pulse rate and when the blood flows, light is absorbed by blood.

3.1.5 *DS18B20*
The DS18B20 digital thermometer maintains a 9-bit to 12-bit Celsius temperature measurement. It also has an alarm function with upper and lower trigger points being non-volatile and user-programmable. The DS18B20 broadcasts data over a 1-Wire bus. This means that it requires only one data line along with ground for communication with a central microprocessor

3.2 *Software*

3.2.1 *Python*
The Raspberry Pi 3 Model B is the third generation Raspberry Pi. This powerful credit-card sized single board computer can be used for many applications

Figure 2.   Hardware design.

It also adds wireless LAN & Bluetooth connectivity making it the perfect solution for powerful connected designs. The integrated hardware is shown in figure 2.

3.2.2 *Arduino*

Arduino platform is an easy outlet for the user to create some technology with the help of understandable simple hardware and software. The aim of it is to be flexible to its users, which includes the use of C/C++ programing language which makes it approachable by beginners with less hesitance. Python and Java can be also used. Since we used Arduino Uno in our project as an ADC, we used C/C++ in the respective code.

3.2.3 *ThingSpeak*

It is an open source IoT platform and API to save and fetch data from devices and things using Http server over the internet or via LAN. It helps the use in various ways like sensor logging apps, tracking of location applications and a device with social network with regular updates.

In our project we have used Thingspeak to display the graphs of the sensors connected to the raspberry pi 3, following is the list of all the graphs –

- Ambient Temperature in Celsius
- Ambient Temperature in Fahrenheit
- Body Temperature in Celsius
- Body Temperature in Fahrenheit
- Humidity
- Pulse Rate

4   RESULTS

4.1   *Ambient temperature in Celsius*

Figure 3a shows the results of the DHT11 sensor for ambient temperature in Celsius. Values are updated in real time after every 15 seconds.

4.2   *Ambient temperature in Fahrenheit*

Figure 3b shows the results of the DHT11 sensor for ambient temperature in Fahrenheit. Values are updated in real time after every 15 seconds.

4.3   *Body temperature in Celsius*

Figure 3c shows the results of the DS18B20 sensor for body temperature in Celsius. The sensor uses only a single wire to transmit the temperature data to the microcontroller and is highly accurate.

4.4   *Body temperature in Fahrenheit*

Figure 3d shows the results of the DS18B20 sensor for body temperature in Fahrenheit.

4.5   *Humidity*

Humidity of the surrounding air is sensed and updated in the graph shown in Figure 3e. Ambient humidity helps understand chances of dehydration, fatigue and cramps.

4.6   *Pulse rate*

Pulse rate is an extremely important parameter in diagnosing the health status of a patient. The sensor picks up values, send it to the IoT server which is depicted in Figure 3f.

Figure 3. Experiment results for a) Ambient temperature in Celsius b) Ambient temperature in Fahrenheit c) Humidity d) Pulse rate e) Body temperature in Celsius f) Body temperature in Fahrenheit.

5 CONCLUSION

With increased internet penetration in most developing countries through mobile phones, its uses such as Internet of things (IoT) will become adopted at a faster rate. The Remote Health Care system utilizes these concepts to come up with a system for better quality of life for people in society. From an engineering perspective, the project has seen concepts acquired through the electrical engineering study period being practically applied. Wireless transmission between microcontrollers and Software programming was used during programming of the microcontrollers to come up with a final finished circuit system. This can be further improved by adding a GPS module in IoT patient monitoring using raspberry pi project. This GPS module will find out the position or the location of the patient using the longitude and latitude received. It will further send this location to the cloud that is the IoT using the raspberry pi. Then doctors can find out the position of the patient in case they have to take some preventive actions.

REFERENCES

Da Xu, Li, Wu He, and Shancang Li. 2014. Internet of things in industries: A survey. *IEEE Transactions on industrial informatics* 10(4): 2233-2243.

Hassanalieragh, M., Page, A., Soyata, T., Sharma, G., Aktas, M., Mateos, G., ... & Andreescu, S. 2015. Health monitoring and management using Internet-of-Things (IoT) sensing with cloud-based processing: Opportunities and challenges. In 2015 IEEE international conference on services computing: 285-292

Kumar, R., and M. Pallikonda Rajasekaran. 2016. An IoT based patient monitoring system using raspberry Pi. In Computing Technologies and Intelligent Data Engineering (ICCTIDE), International Conference on: 1-4.

Patil, Shivleela, & Sanjay Pardeshi. 2018. Health Monitoring system using IoT.

Udara Yedukondalu, Srinivasarao Udara, H. M. Harish, and H. C. Hadimani. "HEALTH MONITORING SYSTEM USING IOT."

Yuan, Shenfang, Xiaosong Lai, Xia Zhao, Xin Xu, and Liang Zhang. 2015. Distributed structural health monitoring system based on smart wireless sensor and multi-agent technology.

Communication and Computing Systems – Prasad et al. (eds)
© 2019 Taylor & Francis Group, London, ISBN 978-0-367-00147-6

Integration of smart grid with Internet of Things

A. Goyal, V. Chauhan & R. Chauhan
Department of Electronics & Communication Engineering, Graphic Era Hill University, Dehradun, India

ABSTRACT: Nowadays the Internet of Things (IoT) is the technology that is used every-where to connect the things with the internet for better convenience and various functionalities. A smart grid having the great importance for promoting the technology and economic, therefore for enhanced efficiency and stability with the help of automatic controls, it can be considered as a modern electric power grid. In this paper we are explaining the concept of a smart grid using the wireless sensor network WSN such as Zigbee, challenges to use WSN in smart grid, various communication technologies and advantages of WSN over Zigbee.

1 INTRODUCTION

Now everything is digitalized due to the researches and developments in the field of technologies or on the internet which makes the internet as a part of our daily lifestyle. With the development of the internet, new technologies get started to come into the picture i.e. Internet of Things (IoT). When the different electronic devices, sensors are connected together to exchange the information with one another over the internet and form a network, then it is known as the Internet of Things. Things, devices are able to talk to each other by sharing the information which is connected through IoT. (*S. Rastogi, M Sharma et.al, 2016*)

As an example of IoT car will tell the driver by indicating as an automatic alarm if a driver operates wrong.

2 SMART GRID

Some of the energy and operational measure devices or the things that make power system a smart grid are smart appliances, energy efficient sources, smart meter, and renewable energy resources. The important or main aspects of the smart grid are the electronic power conditioning, distribution of energy as electricity and control of production

The emergence of the concepts of smart grid has taken place very rapidly, as a topic of research and development from last few years. So, the smart grid technology is proposed by the National Institute of Standards and Technology (NIST) which mainly consist of seven domains (*ITU Strategy and Policy Unit(SPU),2005*), namely: generation in bulky form, distribution, transmission, markets, consumers, operations and service providers. The communication between the users of smart grid uses protocols like Wi-Fi, Zigbee, power line carrier, Fibers, GPRS, Lease Line and Wimax is takes place in a two-way direction (*G.J Fitzpatrick and D.A Wollman, 2010*)

The policy of US for the modernization of the energy distribution and transmission system is the Smart grid for a reliable and secure infrastructure of electricity which can meet with future demand growth. For achieving the following things, we together characterize a Smart Grid:

(1) Increased use of controls technology and digital information to make electric grid reliable, secure and efficient.

(2) To optimize the resources and operations of the grid dynamically, with completecyber-security.

(3) For installation and combination of the distributed resources, includes the renewable resources.

(4) To development and install number of resources, demand response, and energy efficiency resources.

(5) To deploy smart technologies formetering, distribution automation,etc.

(6) To connect consumer devices with `smart' appliances.

(7) To provide consumers with control options and timely information.

(8) To develop the standards for communication and make the electric grid appliances and equipment able to exchange information with each other.

(9) To identify and lower down the unnecessary barriers to adopting smart grid services and technologies (*U.S. Department of Energy, 2004*)

3 SMART GRID AND IOT FOR CONSUMERS

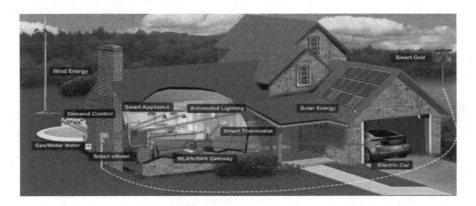

Figure 1.   Smart grid and IoT for consumer.

Connecting all the devices together in a home, buildings are the step to take the full benefits of the smart grid. For a better understanding of power consumption of an electric utility, the demand response system is connected with smart appliances for energy monitoring which gives the flexibility to manage the use of energy during the non-peak times to the user. The availability of smart electric plugs, displays, thermostats have given the choice to the user to monitor the household devices. As in the above (Figure 1) we use the renewable resources with an electric power system for energy a smart meter is placed which detect the consumption of power supply by the various household devices such as the smart appliances, electric car, thermostats etc. All the devices are connected to the home network to exchange the information. Through WSN the user can connect the Internet to get the information of various devices in the home network through a gateway or allow direct connection to cloud connectivity with the smart-phones or tablet. Users are adopting the smart devices faster having smart technology as they are cost effective and allow the replacement of existing appliances. Texas Instruments (TI) makes a less complex smart meter by wrapping its metrology, which consumes less power and its connectivity, processors are easy to use.

4 WIRELESS SENSOR NETWORK

A WSN (Wireless Sensor Network) is a wireless network which consists of small, less powered, circulating and self-directed sensor node known as motes. These networks include a large number of embedded devices which are battery-operated and spatially distributed. These devices are connected through a network for collecting, processing, and transferring the information to the operators, and the potentiality of computing is controlled by those devices. Nodes work together to form the networks. They are the tiny computers. The sensor node is multi-functional, wireless device which is energy efficient. In industries the main purpose of motes widespread. A combination of nodes accumulates the information from surroundings for achieving the specific application objective. By using the transceivers we can easily communicate with the motes. The number of motes connected to the wireless sensor network can be in the order of hundreds/thousands.

5 ARCHITECTURE OF WSN

Though we have many network architecture model like the OSI Model, TCP/IP model etc., but most commonly WSN architecture mainly uses the OSI architecture model. It consists of five different layers with three cross layers. Mainly we require the five layers for the sensor network i.e. transport layer, data link layer, application layer, network layer and the last physical layer whereas the other three cross layers are used as power management, task management, and mobility management. These layers get combined together and accomplish the network and make the sensors around it to work in an efficient way, thus increasing the efficiency of the network.

5.1 *Application layer*

The first layer of the OSI Model (considered from the sender's side) and the most important as it provides an interface to the user. The role of the physical and layer is traffic management and offers software for suitable applications.

5.2 *Transport layer*

This layer ensures the reliable delivery and congestion avoidance while exchanging the data. This layer is needed when a system is planned to contact other networks.

5.3 *Network layer*

This layer handles the task of routing. This layer performs various tasks but mainly it performs partial memory conserving sensors.

5.4 *Data Link layer*

The main purpose of this layer is the MAC address, the flow of control, data framing, error control, and confirm point to point or point to multipoint reliability

5.5 *Physical layer*

The physical layer acts as an interface for transferring a stream of bits above physical medium. Functions of this layer are encoding and signaling of data, signal detection, bit synchronization

6 ZIGBEE

This communication is mainly formed to control and sensor network based on the IEEE standard used for the wireless personal area network (WPAN), and this product is of ZigBee alliance. These standards of communication define the several layers to operate the various devices at low data rate are physical and Media Access Control (MAC). WPANs based ZigBee works on different frequencies as 868 MHz, 900-930 MHz, and 2.4 GHz. The best data rate for periodic and the intermediate two-way transmission of data between sensor and controllers is 250kbps.

Figure 2.   Zigbee modem.

ZigBee is a low cost and low powered device which is mainly used when the range of communication is short within 10-100 meters for accessing and observing the applications. Zigbee is cost efficient and less complex as compared to other prior short range WSN as Bluetooth and Wi-Fi. For a master to master or master to slave communication, ZigBee supports the different network configuration. To save the battery ZigBee is functioned in different modes. We can enlarge the ZigBee network with the help of routers,it allows the number of nodes to connect the devices to make a wider area network WAN.

7 ZIGBEE ARCHITECTURE

In the structure of zigbee system three different type of devices are used such as Router, Zigbee coordinator and End devices. Structure of the network essentially consist of a coordinator device which act as a root and bridge for the network. During transmission and receiving the data, handling and storing the information is controlled by the coordinator devices whereas router is used to allow the data to pass to and fro through them as an intermediate device and at the last End devices is used to communicate with the parent node such that the battery is saved. Different network topologies are used for the number of routers, coordinator and end devices.

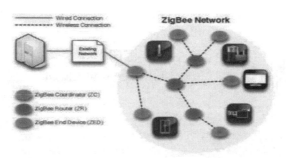

Figure 3.   Zigbee system structure.

8 CHALLENGES IN SMART GRID USING IOT

The main difficulties faced during usage of WSN in the smart grid can be defined as follows:

8.1 *Bad weather conditions*

Due to the bad connection in that environment the electric power system, wireless connectivity may not work properly. The performance is affected by humidity, sensors may be subjected to RF interface, dirt or dust, vibrations. These harsh weather condition and network topology may cause a malfunction by the portion of sensors. (*F. C. Lambert and V. C. Gungor, 2006*)

8.2 *Reliability*

Different applications are considered of WSN for smart grid have different quality of service and its specifications are expressed in terms of latency, reliability, network etc. Mainly sensor data are time-dependent or we can also say that sensor is time sensitive, as an example to work safely accident in the electric power system, it must be received the data to the controller node after a fixed time of interval(*F. C. Lambert and V. C. Gungor, 2006*)

8.3 *Data packet error and network link capacity*

During communication, the bandwidth of the wireless network depends upon the interference level recognize at the receiver end and having a high bit rate error are observed. The links show widely varying characteristics over time and space because of obstacle, noisy environment in the electric power system. Therefore we say that the bandwidth and the communication latency of wireless network depend upon location and continuously varies (*G. P. Hancke and V. C. Gungor, 2009*)

8.4 *Limited sources*

The execution and design of WSN are limited by three type of sources are: a) Processing b) energy c) memory. Therefore in general, sensors have the limited power source as a battery (*G. P. Hancke and V. C. Gungor, 2009*) by which communication protocols of WSN are customized to provide the energy efficiency higher.

Table 1. Advantages of WSN over Zigbee (*Li Li, Hu Xiaoguang* et.al).

PROPERTY	WSN	ZIGBEE
Spectrum	Bit rate for the Wi-Fi technology can reach up to 2MKbps, whereas the latest version802.11 can reach up to 300Mbps. therefore transmission through Wi-Fi is more efficient and better real time.	The bit rate by using Zigbee for transmission is only 10-250Kbps.
Non line of sight transmission	WSN supports NLOS for transmitting the data by which communication become easier through one load bearing walls.	Zigbee does not have the feature of NLOS for transmission due to which it is week for transmission through barrier.
Coverage area	It is not only used in homes, but also in buildings because its outdoor range is about 300m and nearly 100m indoor barriers but also in entire high risebuildings.	The coverage area of radio waves of zigbee is very less, usually in 10-70 m and the communication through load-bearing walls is not effective.
Cost effective	WSN network was built in many buildings in small and large cities.	For short time duration of cycle, low project cost zigbee devices not to be taken into account

Table 2. Communication technologies used in smart grid (*Al-Omar, B. Al-Ali et.al, 2012*).

Technology	Range	Bit rate	Coverage Area	Uses	Disadvantages
GSM	900 – 1800 MHz	Up to 14.4Kpbs	up to 10 km	AMI,HAN, Demand response	Data rate/bit rate is low
GPRS	900 – 1800 MHz	Up to 170 kbps	up to 10 km	AMI, HAN, Demand response	Data rate/bit rate is low
3G	1.92-1.98GHz 2.11-2.17GHz	384Kbps-2 Mbps	up to 10 km	AMI, HAN, Demand response	Cost of spectrum is high
Wi-MAX	2.5 GHz, 3.5 GHz, 5.8 GHz	Up to 75 Mbps	10-50 km (LOS) 1-5 km (NLOS)	AMI, Demand Response	Not widelyspread/ limited
PLC	1-30 MHz	2-3 Mbps	up to 3 km	AMI, Fraud Detection	Harsh, noisy channel environment
Zigbee	2.4 GHz868 -915 MHz	250 Kbps	30-50m	AMI, HAN	bit rate is low, having shortrange

Overall, smart grid applications based on WSN, the linking quality must be good for a stable and energy efficient system. However in bad weather condition, the electric power system shows rapid variation in the wireless channel inhibit an effective technique to know instantaneous values of link quality during the transmission, so it is tough to take the approximate value for wireless link quality.

9 CONCLUSION

In the 21st century, many discoveries and enhancements are done in the field of technology. The smart grid is the evolution of the electric power system by using the renewable resources to enhance the efficiency, stability, cost-effective and safety of the power grid. By using the WSN we can easily transmit and receive the information with connected devices over the network. This technology helps to save energy for the future by using the renewable source, customer services is also enhanced, the user can able to check the energy consumption from any remote location through the Internet.

REFERENCES

Al-Omar, B., Al-Ali, A.R., Ahmed, R. & Landolsi, T. 2012 Role of Information and Communication Technologies in the Smart Grid. *Journal of Emerging Trends in Computing and Information Sciences*, 3,707-716.
Fitzpatrick, G.J. &Wollman, D.A. 2010. NIST Interoperability Framework and Action Plans. IEEE Power and Energy Society General Meeting, Minneapolis, 25-29 July2010, 14. http://dx.doi.org/10.1109/pes.2010.5589699
Hancke G. P. &Gungor V. C. Oct. 2009 "Industrial wireless sensor networks: Challenges, design principles, and technical approaches," *IEEE Trans.Ind. Electron., vol. 56, no. 10, pp.* 4258–4265,.
Hu Xiaoguang, Li Li, Chen Ke. School of Automation Science and Electrical Engineering Bei Hang University Beijing.
ITU Strategy & Policy Unit(SPU), "The Internet of Things", ITU Internet Reports 2005, Geneva: International Tele-communication Union(ITU).
Lambert F. C. & Gungor V. C., 2006 "A survey on communication networks for electric system automation," Comput Netw., vol. 50, no. 7, pp. 877–897.
Rastogi S, Sharma M, Varshney P. 2016. Internet of Things based Smart Electricity Meters. International Journal of Computer Applications (0975 – 8887) Volume 133 – No.8, Bharati Vidyapeeth's College of Engineering, New Delhi
U.S. Department of Energy, 2004. "Assessment study on sensors and automation in the industries of the future," Office of Energy and Renewable Energy Rep.

Communication and Computing Systems – Prasad et al. (eds)
© 2019 Taylor & Francis Group, London, ISBN 978-0-367-00147-6

Study of robotic technique for in-pipe inspection with taxonomy and exploration of out oil pipe crawler

Devesh Mishra, R.S. Yadav, Tanuja Pande & N.K. Shukla
Department of Electronics & Communication, University of Allahabad, Prayagraj, India

Krishna Kant Agrawal
CSE Department, Delhi Technical Campus, Greater Noida, India

Rekha Srivastava
Department of Physics, C.M.P. Degree College, University of Allahabad, Prayagraj, India

ABSTRACT: Rising demands of fuel makes pipeline inevitably important for transportation of oil to refineries & petrochemical. This causes an escalation in research and development for improving competency, safety, dependability, and strength of ferromagnetic pipelines placed in the hostile environment for operation. Pipes are considered as arteries and veins of process industries, oil refineries & petrochemical plants. Due to the hostile environment of operation, nearly 20% of oil pipelines are running in the state of the danger their and lives have ended up. This article is concentrated towards inspection & health monitoring of cross country buried pipelines as well as inspection techniques for refineries critical components based on robotics. These pipe inspection robots are known as out pipe crawlers or sometimes Pipe Inspection Gauge [PIG]. Their area of operation is very unique as these pipelines are horizontal as well as vertical, cross country pipelines are buried while pipes in the refinery are elevated at height of 50 to 60 meters above ground level their surface is rough, and they have bends with highly inflammable fluid flowing inside those pipelines.

1 INTRODUCTION

Nevertheless, oil refineries & process industries have certain circumstances where inspection of the pipeline from inside is not conceivable. In current practice for health monitoring of these pipelines, big scaffoldings are used to measure the thickness at the definite location while inspection during annual shutdown. But it could become pretty challenging to measure the thickness all along the length of the pipeline with covering its periphery due to lack of automatic crawler for inspection. In this article, the locomotion and adhesion technique for novel, lightweight, easily operable out pipe inspection tool has been studied with classification (Saha, S., Ramran, S. C., Mukherjee, D., Chandra,Y., Lahiri, S.K. and Marathe, P.P., 2017).

2 LOCOMOTION OF OUT PIPE INSPECTION ROBOT

For out pipe inspection the robot requires a mechanism to press the wall of the pipeline for generation of adequate propulsion to provide locomotion to the vehicle as there is no provision of pressing the robot via external fluid pressure. If the robot has to develop its own locomotion strategy then, in that case, it also has to do an arrangement for adhesion with the pipeline (Kim, H.M., Yoo, H.R., Rho, Y.W., Park. G.S. 2013).

2.1 Legged driven locomotion

Among different kinds of locomotion technique, the most basic form of locomotion which we use all the day long is legged type locomotion as human locomotion system also belongs to legged type. Oil pipeline inspection robot has two to eight legs equipped with any adhesion mechanism on the end of the leg that is attached with the upper surface of the oil pipeline. The attachment of the leg with the pipeline should be enough strong to overcome motion on the rough surface containing bends, cracks and weld joints as obstacles. More the number of legs the robot has more is the stability and payload capacity of the robot. However, the increase in a number of legs leads to increase in complexity, weight, and size of the robot. To overcome this, the legged robot should get balanced on be of 2 legs (biped) having a compact size. A robot equipped with 4 legs shows implicitly how it is trying to climb on a concrete wall. Two diagonally opposite legs making a motion at the same time while rest two legs are fixed to their position.

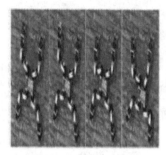

Figure 1. Legged driven locomotion based robot (Chu1, B., Jung, K., Han. C.S, and Hong.D, 2010).

2.2 Wheel driven locomotion

Locomotion of a robot driven by the wheel is efficient to form of locomotion for climbing vertical structures if appropriate adhesion mechanism is applied. With the use of wheels speed of the robot can be improved considerably. These wheels driven robots give their appropriate performance when get coupled with adhesion mechanism material of the surface. As with ferromagnetic material wheel-driven robot equipped with magnetic adhesion is the most appropriate way of developing the robot. At the same time if the wheels are attached with suction cups then this combination is not efficient for rough surfaces and also has low handling capacity with obstacle and least payload capacity. Meanwhile, a climbing robot is developed with a wheel is driven locomotion category using more than one adhesion mechanism which can avoid obstacle/hindrances in its path of climbing motion (Singh, P. and Ananthasuresh, G. K., 2013).

2.3 Tracked type locomotion

Tracked type locomotion mechanism is very much similar to a wheel driven mechanism, the difference is that, both the techniques have a rotational mechanism in addition to that tracked mechanism has a pair of chain-track covering several wheels on both sides illustrated in figure no 2 this arrangement propels the robot over the rough, dull vertical surface and provides better adhesion capability due to increased surface area and has also better obstacle avoidance capability.

Track driven mechanism gives its efficient output when there are several surfaces on which the robot has to move at the same time or the robot has to cross obstructions on weld joint or on a vertical surface. With increased surface area tracked locomotion mechanism requires greater adhesion mechanism also to adhere the robot on the vertical surface (Sharma, S.L., Qavi, A. & Kumari, K., 2014).

Figure 2.   Tracked based TRIPILLAR climbing robot (www.roboswarm.com).

Suction adhesion mechanism can be applied with this in form of a tracked belt with the body of the robot. Suction cups are arranged in systematic order forming belt-like structure. This structure provides good payload capacity with better obstacle avoidance but it has one main drawback is that it is not useful for a rough surface. For climbing rough pipes i.e. ferro-magnetic pipes magnetic wheels are arranged with a tacked belt as shown in figure no. 2 which shows a robot named TRIPILLAR which uses this mechanism. The size of the TRI-PILLAR robot is 96x46x64mm3 and it as a magnetic caterpillar in a triangular shape. This robot has tracked locomotion mechanism in combination with small magnets molded in cater-pillars for adhesion with the surface.

2.4   *Translation based locomotion*

This is a nature-inspired locomotion technique for robots. It has a simple control strategy for locomotion, and its functioning is also not complicated due to its easy principle Sticking-Moving-Sticking. This type of robots is large in size and weight both so these robots cannot be utilized at narrow places. A robot is shown in Figure no.3 having suction cups are at the end of the leg. The locomotion activity of robot is Sticking-Moving-Sticking which makes it heavy in weight and low in speed.

Figure 3.   Translation based locomotion (Chu1, B., Jung, K., Han, C.S, and Hong,D., 2010).

2.5   *Cable-driven locomotion*

This is the most traditional way of locomotion for robots while climbing in vertical structure. In this technique, a cable is attached with the body of the robot lacking any mechanism for adhesion between surface and body of the robot. The longitudinal motion of the robot is done via cable and gravity of the earth. The robot moves upwards with the lifting force of the by the cable and downwards due to earth's gravitational force acting upon the body of the robot (Zhang, L., Du, Y., Cao, A., 2015).

3 ADHESION TOOLS

At the same time, an adhesion mechanism in case of robots for pipe inspection is also an essential factor of belongings. For locomotion of the robot in the vertical direction, an adequate adhesion mechanism is necessary so that proper grasping of the pipeline can be done by the robot. Adhere capability of robots reliant on the material of the surface and also the physical condition and structure of the surface over which the robot has to climb. Different adhesion tools are discussed below:-

3.1 *Suction type*

Suction type adhesion is a prominent technology for adhering of the system with the surface. Vacuum suction cups are adaptable and can be used for adhesion on different kinds of surfaces. This type of adhesion mechanism can be used with legged, tracked and translation type locomotion tool. Suction cups are attached at the ends points in the legs of the robot. The control and operation of suction cups are easy, simple and lightweight. Due to these features suction cups are used for adhesion on any arbitrary surface. To avoid pressure loss due to external irregularities more than one suction cups are used. Among all these features this adhesion technique has few drawbacks also. The speed of the robot is low as it takes time to develop a vacuum in suction cups. If the surface is non-porous, leaked or cracked then any opening can cause the robot to fall from the surface.

3.2 *Magnetic type*

Magnetic type of adhesion is most proficient as it does not need any power to generate adhesion force with the walls of the surface, its inherent reliability makes it highly desirable. This kind of adhesion is very simple and most easy to control just the only prerequisite condition for using this is the surface should be ferromagnetic material so that it has magnetic adhesion property.

Furthermore, the magnetic adhesion mechanism requires high torque actuators to crawl the robot over the ferromagnetic surface fixed with magnetic adhesion despite that the speed of the robot with wheels locomotion and magnetic adhesion is fast in comparison to other combinations of locomotion and adhesion. Permanent magnets used in the robot should provide the adequate magnetic force with the walls of the surface so that there should be no slipping of the robot due to lack of adhesion force and neither sacrifice of the motion of robot due to excess adhesion force with the walls.

3.3 *Gripping type*

This is a novel method of adhesion of a robot on the vertical surface. In order to surpass the difficulties of vertical climbing some robot have gripping arms attached with the body of the robot or in some cases the whole body of the robot totally grasps the surface of the structure which provides enough friction between the locomotion mechanism and the body of the robot for its motion over the surface. This gripping adhesion mechanism when get combined with wheelbase locomotion technique, if necessary permanent magnets are also used for better adhesion and to avoid slipping of the robot on the piping. The structure which we get in output is very much useful for climbing vertical piping structures.

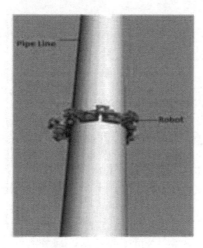

Figure 4.   Gripping adhesion based caged crawler.

3.4   *Bio-mimetics type*

The ability of natural living beings like Geckos and lizards has inspired researchers to develop an artificial adhesion mechanism of these living beings. These living beings have the ability to climb on even on the wet, rough and non-porous surface, This adhesion capability is achieved via using patches of microstrip hairs that offer adhesion through wander wall force. This type of adhesion mechanism is always used with legged type locomotion technique. Similar to the magnetic type adhesion technique of climbing robots this techniques also use permanent adhesion mechanism without using any external power of activating adhesion mechanism. This type of adhesion mechanism does not work properly in dusty regions and the payload capacity of this adhesion mechanism is also not good theses are few drawbacks of this adhesion.

3.5   *Rail guided type*

This is an arrangement for moving the robot vertically up and down over prefixed rail . It has newly been added into adhesion category of climbing robots. The rail guided adhesion mechanism is very much similar to cable driven type locomotion technique. Before applying this adhesion mechanism rails should be laid on the vertical surface over which the robot will move. The robots of this category move on the vertical surface over those rails only. This kind of mechanism is popular in the construction industry but its heavy size and compulsion of rail make it infeasible for use in the piping industry. Rail-guided adhesion based robot get combined with wheel based locomotion technique. Its heavy size, weight, not approachable for narrow regions and requirement of rails are its few drawbacks with respect to piping industry.

4   OPTIMAL COMBINATION OF LOCOMOTION AND ADHESION

For oil pipeline inspection a specific combination of locomotion and adhesion is chosen. Wheel-driven locomotion facilitates up and down motion smoothly. A robot equipped with magnetic adhesion is suitable for the inspection over an oil pipeline. It has a higher payload, better obstacle avoidance capability and good gripping in comparison to others.

Gripping type adhesion technique has also better payload capacity, good speed and cheaper in cost the only drawback it has is obstacle avoidance capability of gripping type is lower than magnetic type adhesion Irrespective of all the adhesion techniques, Magnetic adhesion, and gripping type adhesion does not require power to sustain on pipelines because of the metallurgy and structure of pipelines.

Combination of magnetic or gripping adhesion with wheel driven locomotion is the most energy efficient to drive an automated vehicle over pipelines. While in other adhesion techniques power is also needed to sustain the robot over the pipeline (Mishra, D., Agrawal, K. K., Yadav, R. S. 2018). .

5 CONCLUSION

For out pipe inspection of pipelines used in refineries the climbing crawler must possess certain set of rules related to its structure as (i) Lightness of weight of the robot, which allows low energy consumption, on the other hand, increasing the payload capacity of the auxiliary equipment, (ii) the structure should provide high mobility to the robot (iii) the robot structure must have a reliable and energy efficient grasping mechanism. These factors are taken into account for the development of a robot capable to move- climb in the vertical direction over an oil pipeline (Mishra, D., Agrawal, K. K., Yadav, R. S. and Srivstava, R. 2018).

The backbone of all chemical and petroleum industries are pipelines which get damaged due to erosion and corrosion. This article discussed the important issues in health monitoring of pipeline with various techniques that are frequently used nowadays.

For inspection at regular interval of time wireless sensor network technology has also been an application for not only inspection of pipeline health but also health monitoring of compressor and pumps at petrochemical plants.

REFERENCES

Chu1, B., Jung, K., Han, C.S., and Hong,.D., 2010."A Survey of Climbing Robots: Locomotion and Adhesion '", *International Journal of precision engineering and manufacturing* vol. 11, no. 4, pp. 633–647 August 2010.

Kim, H.M., Yoo, H.R., Rho, Y.W., Park. G.S. 2013., "Detection Method of Cracks by Using Magnetic Fields in Underground Pipeline", 2013 10th International Conference on Ubiquitous Robots and Ambient Intelligence (URAI) October 31-November 2, 2013 /Ramada Plaza Jeju Hotel, Jeju, Korea.

Mishra, D., Agrawal, K. K., Yadav, R. S. and Srivstava, R., 2018. "Design of Out Pipe Crawler for Oil Refinery based on Analysis & Classification of Locomotion and Adhesion Techniques," IEEE UPCON, India, 2018, pp. 1–7. doi: 10.1109/UPCON.2018.8596988

Mishra, D, Agrawal, K. K., Yadav, R. S., 2018. "Contemporary status of machine prognostics in process industries based on oil and gas: A critical analysis", IEEE International Conference on Research in Intelligent and Computing in Engineering (RICE) 2018, doi:10.1109/RICE.2018.8627898

Saha, S., Ramran, S.C., Mukherjee, D., Chandra, Y., Lahiri, S.K. and Marathe P.P., 2017. "Development of External Pipeline Inspection Gauge for Monitoring the Health of Industrial Carbon Steel Pipelines", http://www.barc.gov.in/publications/nl/2017/2017050602.pdf.

Sharma, S.L., Qavi, A & Kumari, K. 2014."Oil Pipelines/Water Pipeline Crawling Robot for Leakage Detection/Cleaning of Pipes", Global Journal of Researches in Engineering Robotics & Nano-Tech Volume 14 Issue 1 Version 1.0 the Year 2014.

Singh, P. and Ananthasuresh, G. K., 2013."A Compact and Compliant External Pipe-Crawling Robot", Proceedings of IEEE Transactions on Robotics, vol.29, no. 1, February 2013.

www.robotics.bgu.ac.il/index.php/File%3AClimbing.jpg www.robo-swarm.com

Zhang, L., Du, Y., Cao. A, 2015. "The Design of Natural Gas Pipeline Inspection Robot System", Proceeding of the 2015 IEEE International Conference on Information and Automation Lijiang, China, August 2015.

Communication and Computing Systems – Prasad et al. (eds)
© 2019 Taylor & Francis Group, London, ISBN 978-0-367-00147-6

IoT and Big Data based smart healthcare system using portable Nuclear Magnetic Resonance

Manish Gupta & D.K. Lobiyal
School of Computer and Systems Sciences, Jawaharlal Nehru University, New Delhi, India

C.P. Safvan & Kundan Singh
Inter University Accelerator Centre, Aruna Asaf Ali Marg, Near Vasant Kunj, New Delhi, India

ABSTRACT: We have been working on developing a cost-effective and portable Nuclear Magnetic Resonance (NMR) system. We showed that our reported NMR is used for biological healthcare investigation. In this present paper, we develop an architecture of smart healthcare system based on Internet of Things (IoT), Big Data and Machine Learning technique for early stage Heart attack monitoring and Malaria diagnosis. As per best of knowledge this is the first architecture which used any portable NMR for smart healthcare system.

1 INTRODUCTION

As we know many patients all around the world especially in rural areas of developing countries are suffering from many diseases, and continuously losing their precious life due to the unaffordable of expensive, bulky medical devices, and also required skillful operators. Therefore, it is the need of the hour to develop low cost, small size, and smart biomedical devices. By reducing the cost and size of biomedical devices many goals can be achieved (Chaudhary (1997)). Firstly, the healthcare can be provided to the large segment of the society to help both treatment and prevention. Secondly, many biomedical systems can be made disposable which can significantly reduce the cost due to sterilization and the danger of the cross contamination. Finally, by reducing their cost and size most of the healthcare devices become portable and treatment can be delivered outside of the hospital and physician office (Chaudhary (1997).

Over the last few decades Electrocardiography (ECG) monitoring and Malaria diagnosis has been dramatically progress due to development of cost-effective portable sensors. Techniques like Nuclear Magnetic Resonance (NMR) and ECG sensor have shown capability to accurate monitoring of disease (Weng Kung et al. (2014) and Yang et al. (2016)). Still they are not coming in under smart healthcare devices. For an example existing ECG monitoring systems and Malaria diagnosis devices cannot work without an internet connection or a mobile application. Moreover, traditionally available malaria diagnosis devices take more times, less sensitive and do not give any quantitative analysis of test sample in comparison of portable NMR reported by Weng Kung et al. (2014).

Many attempts have been made by researcher like (Minard & Wind (2001)) and Massin et al. (2002, 2003) etc.] to develop miniaturize NMR with serval coil design and its modeling to get optimal geometrical dimensions of the coil. Number of biosensors are reported in literatures for healthcare applications, but none them worked on smart healthcare systems with integration of portable NMR. Recently, Yang et al. (2016) proposed IoT-Cloud based ECG monitoring systems for smart healthcare. After a year, Abdelgawed and Yelamarthi (2017) developed IoT based platform for structural health monitoring.

The aim of this work is to develop smart healthcare system using our developed NMR with commercial purchased sensors. The data collected from these sensors are employed in the Internet of Things (IoT) based cloud using Raspberry Pi 3 interface and then Bigdata technique has been used to store the data. Machine learning approach has been also applied for predictive analysis of diseases on the bases of collected gleaned data. This paper is structured into four sections. In section I, Introduction about necessity of portable medical devices are discussed. Section II deals with the modeling and coil. Proposed architecture for smart healthcare system is given under section III, Finally, conclusion is given in the section IV.

2   MODELING OF PLANAR SPIRAL COIL

In NMR, Radio Frequency (RF) coil is the main part of the probe and play an important role to enhance the amplitude of NMR spectra by maximizing the signal to noise ratio (SNR) [Massin et al. (2002)]. For better SNR, coil design and technological performance parameters (Quality Factor(Q), AC Resistance (R_{AC}), and DC Resistance (R_{DC})) should be well optimized. In this, planar spiral coil has been printed on the top of the double-sided copper clad FR4 sheet. Initially for optimization we took number of turns (N) is three, spacing between the tracks (s) and width of tracks (w) are 2mm. Details on modeling, design and fabrication of coil are presented in the IEEE ICICI2017 (Gupta and Agarwal (2017)). Figure 1 presented the plot of quality factor (Q) versus frequency (f) with increase in the thickness of wire (h). Q increases with increase in the h.

Figure 2. shows the effect of thickness of wire on AC Resistance. R_{AC} decrease with increase of thickness of wire w.r.t frequency. From Figure 3. It is clearly seen that the

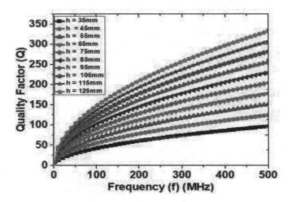

Figure 1.   Plot of quality factor versus frequency with change in thickness of wire (h).

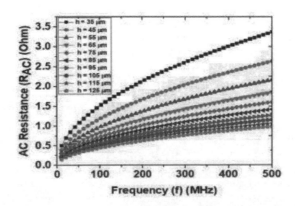

Figure 2.   Plot of AC resistance versus frequency with change in thickness of wire (h).

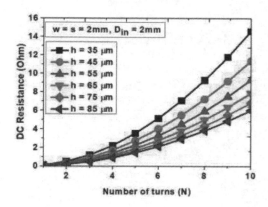

Figure 3. Plot of DC resistance versus N with h.

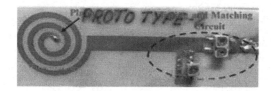

Figure 4. Fabricated on-chip NMR probe with tuning and matching circuit.

thickness of wire should be (35μm). Design of the coil has been done in Computer Simulation Technology (CST 2017). Finally, fabrication of the planar coil has done using Printed Circuit Board (PCB) Technology. Figure 4. shows the on-chip probe. Here Surface Mounted Capacitors (SMD) are used to complete the tuning and matching circuit. Details study on-chip probe are available in [Gupta et al. (2018) and patent filed by Gupta et al. (2018)].

3 PROPOSED SMART HEALTHCARE SYSTEM

In this section, we presented an IoT based smart healthcare system to monitor the health condition of patients using open source software's. Our proposed NMR is integrated with artificial available biosensors and then interface with Raspberry–Pi through connecting wires and Wi-Fi. The overview of the proposed system is presented in Fig.20. The system architecture consists of five main parts: data collecting, data storing, data analysis and predictive analysis, and data visualization. Bio-sensors gathered data from the human body shown in (Fig. 20, as patient dummy) will be transmitted to IoT server. Collected data from the sensors are stored in cloud server. Here, we will use private cloud which will be deploying in virtual machine as Hadoop cluster. Afterward, data analysis can be done by using statistical method as well as by using more complex machine learning algorithm. Our goal is to be able to run advance machine learning algorithm on the gathered data for finding particularly, future heart attack possibilities. In the end, data visualization techniques can be used which will give the output in the form of mobile app and web server. By doing so, not only the precious rescue time is saved, but a before critical time is increased and prior information be supplied. It helps doctor to take early action.

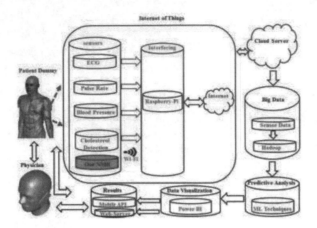

Figure 5. Architecture of smart healthcare system.

4 CONCLUSION

In summary, we have developed a smart healthcare system with an integration of Internet of Things (IoT) at an affordable cost. We are working on the implementation of the proposed architecture. This work is the first step toward the integration of any portable NMR with other sensors for smart healthcare systems.

ACKNOWDLEGEMENT

Authors are thankful to AIFR, JNU and IUAC, DST-PURSE New Delhi for their support to carry out this research. First author also wants to acknowledge University Grant Commission (UGC), New Delhi, India for granting fellowship to support this work.

REFERENCES

Abdelgawed.A. and Yelamarthi.K. 2017. Internet of Things (IoT) Platform for Structure Health Monitoring. Wireless Communications and Mobile Computing.2017, Article ID 6560797. Hindawi Publications.

Choudhury.P.1997.Handbook of Microlithography. Micromachining, and Microfabrication). SPIE Press. UK.

Gupta.M. and Agarwal.P. 2017. To Model Magnetic Field of RF Planar Coil for Portable NMR Applications. Proceedings of the Inter-national Conference on Inventive Computing and Informatics (ICICI 2017). published by IEEE, Coimbatore. India.

Gupta et al. 2018. Modeling and Simulation of On-chip Probe for Portable NMR Applications. Proceedings of 40th Progress In Elec-tromagnetics Research Symposium2018, Toyama, Japan.

Gupta.M. et al. 2018. On-Chip Nuclear Magnetic Resonance Probe. Indian Patent. Application no.201811028297.

Minard.K and. Wind, W.A.2001.Solenoidal Microcoil Design-Part I: Optimizing RF Homogeneity and Coil Dimensions. Concepts in Magnetic Resonace: Part B,13.128-142, 2001.ScienceDirect.

Minard.K. and. Wind, W.A.2001. Optimizing RF Homogeneity and Coil Dimensions. Concepts in Magnetic Resonance: PartB.13.190-210, 2001.ScienceDirect.

Massin.C. et al.2002. High -Q Factor RF Planar Microcoils for Micro Scale NMR Spectroscopy. Sensors and Actuators A, 97-98.280-288. ScienceDirect.

Massin.C. et al.2002. Planar Microcoil Based Microfluidic probes," Magn. Reson.164.242-255.ScienceDirect.

Weng Kung.P. et al.2014. Micro Magnetic Resonance Relaxometry for label-free, rapid malaria diagnosis. 20.1069–1073. Nature Medicine.

Yang. Z. et al. 2016. An IoT-cloud Based Wearable ECG Monitoring System for Smart Healthcare. J Med Syst, 40: 286. Springer.

Communication and Computing Systems – Prasad et al. (eds)
© *2019 Taylor & Francis Group, London, ISBN 978-0-367-00147-6*

A review: Reliability modeling of a computer system with hardware repair and software up-gradation subject to server vacation

Jyoti Anand
Department of Applied Sciences & Humanities, Dronacharya College of Engineering, Gurugram, India

Geeta
SAP Institute, Delhi, India

ABSTRACT: The main objective of this paper is to examine the availability and profit of a computer system with two identical units considering the concept of server vacation. In each unit hardware and software components fails independently from normal mode. On the other hand, the server will be on vacation if any one unit remain operative. The failure time distribution of the components follow negative exponential whereas the distribution of server vacation, repair, replacement time etc. are taken as arbitrary with different probability density functions. Various reliability measures have been obtained using Markovian approach and regenerative point technique. The graphical behavior of the results are drawn to depic the behavior of the results.

1 INTRODUCTION

Computers are increasingly being used at an alarming rate for various purposes. Some people have predicted that those days are not very far off when the computer business will be the largest component of the US economy. Computers are used in critical areas such as aerospace, nuclear power generation, and defense. For such applications their reliability is of utmost importance because a computer failure in these areas could be very costly and catastrophic. Other factors such as increasing repair costs, harsher operating environments, use by novices, and the existence of bigger system are also responsible for the increasing emphasis on reliability of computer systems. To improve reliability and assist field service personnel in fault isolation, computer hardware manufacturers such as International Business Machines (IBM), Amdahl and Univac make use of redundancy. However, in computers the reliability problem is not only confined to the hardware aspect, but also extends to software. Both hardware and software have to be reliable for successful operation of a computer. Therefore there is a definite need to place emphasis on the reliability of both computer hardware and the software.

In view of every significant role of a computer system, its failure can cause severe damage to the society. But failures of such systems are inevitable due to normal changes of operating conditions. Generally, a computer system fails due to failure in some of its hardware and software component. Software and hardware differ in several respects. Software does not wear out; almost all hardware goes through a wear out phase. All copies of software are perfectly identical; each manufactured copy of a piece of hardware differs to some extent. Once a fault is removed from software it is gone forever; many hardware faults can recur. When viewed at the appropriate level of abstraction, however, hardware and software reliability are very similar. Both a running program and an operating hardware item can be seen as "black boxes." Every once in a while the black box fails. The failure-inducing stress is time. For software, time brings with it a succession of input states. The more time that goes by, the higher the quantity of, and the more variety of, input states the program encounters. Eventually, because of the presence of faults, an input state will trigger a failure. With hardware, time carries with it random stresses (such as friction, shock, corrosion) which gradually or suddenly cause failure. Thus both hardware and software reliability can be modeled as random or stochastic processes.

The object of the present research proposal is to examine the causes of failures of a computer system and their remedial under different repair policies of the server who may undergo for vacations. The system models will be developed stochastically considering the concepts of redundancy, inspection of the machines/components, priority in repair disciplines, replacement of faulty components after maximum operation time, server vacations, etc. Various reliability and economic measures will be obtained in steady state by using semi-Markov approach and regenerative point technique. The graphical behavior of the results will also be shown for some important measures of system effectiveness by taking arbitrary values of parameters and costs.

2 REVIEW OF RESEARCH AND DEVELOPMENT IN THE SUBJECT

Server vacation models are useful for queuing systems in which the server wants to utilize his idle time for different purposes. The vacation mechanism considered in this project is termed as 'multiple vacation policy'. That is, the server goes on vacation immediately after a maximum working time. Applications of the server with multiple vacation models can be found in manufacturing systems, designing of computer and communication systems, etc. Queueing systems with multiple server vacations have attracted the attention of numerous researchers. Baba (1986) studied batch-arrival MX/G/1 queueing systems with multiple vacations. A discrete-time Geo/G/1 queue with multiple vacations was studied by Tian and Zhang (2002). An MX/G(a,b)/1 queue with multiple vacations including closedown time has been studied by Arumuganathan et al.2004. Kumar et al.2005 analyzed a Markovian queue with two heterogeneous servers and multiple vacations. By using the matrix geometric method, they derived the stationary queue length distribution and mean system size. Wu et al.2006 investigated an M/G/1 queue with multiple vacations and exhaustive service discipline such that the server works with different rates rather than completely stopping the service during vacation. Ke 2007 studied an MX/G/1 queueing system under a variant vacation policy where the server takes at most j vacations. He derived the system size distribution as well as waiting time distribution in the queue. Ke et al.2009 considered an MX/(G1,G2)/1 retrial queue with general retrial times, where the server provides two phases of heterogeneous service to all customers under Bernoulli vacation schedules. They constructed the mathematical model and derived the steady-state distribution of the server state and the number of customers in the system/orbit. Ke et al. (2009) studied the vacation policy for a finite buffer M/M/c queueing system with an un-reliable server. Threshold N-policy for an MX/H2/1 queueing system with an un-reliable server and vacations was studied by Sharma 2010. Moreover,(Singh et al. 2012) investigated an M/G/1 queuing model with vacation and used the generating function method for obtaining various performance measures. Very recently, an un-reliable bulk queue with state-dependent arrival rates was examined by Singh et al. 2013.

Queueing models with an un-reliable server under multiple vacation policy are more realistic representation of the systems. The service of the components may be interrupted when the operator encounters unpredicted breakdowns, and it is to be immediately recovered with a random time. When the repair is completed, the server immediately returns for service. Wang et al. 1999 extended Wang's model to the N-policy for an M/H2/1 queueing system and focused on single-arrival Erlangian service time queueing model with an un-reliable server. Wang et al. (2004) considered an M/Hk/1 queueing system with a removable and un-reliable server under N-policy and presented the optimal operating policy. Wang (2004) considered an M/G/1 queue with an un-reliable server and second optional service. Using the supplementary variable method, he obtained transient and steady-state solutions for both queueing and reliability measures of interest. Ke (2005) studied a modified T vacation policy for an M/G/1 queueing system where an un-reliable server may take at most J vacations repeatedly until at least one customer appears in the queue upon returning from vacation, and the server needs a startup time before starting each of his service periods. Li et al. (2007) proposed a single-server vacation queue with two policies, working vacation and service interruption. Choudhury et al. 2008 studied an M/G/1 retrial queue with an additional second phase of optional service subject to breakdowns occurring randomly at any instant while serving the customers. Further, Wang et al. 2009 obtained the solution of an M/G/1 queue with second optional service and server breakdown using the method of functional analysis. The work on an M/G/1 queue with second optional service and server breakdown has been done by Choudhury et al.2009. They derived the Laplace-Stieltjes transform of busy period distribution and waiting time distribution. Further, an un-reliable server queue with multi-optional services and multi-optional vacations was analyzed by Jain et al. 2013.

The studies referred above indicate that not much work related to the Computer System with Hardware Repair and Software up-Gradation using semi-Markov approach has been reported so far in the literature of reliability. Hence, the proposal "Reliability Modeling of a Computer System with Hardware Repair and Software up-Gradation subject to Server Vacation".

3 OBJECTIVES

   i. To review the existing literature.
  ii. To define the system models.
 iii. To develop system models for a computer system.
 iv. To define reliability measures of the system models.
  v. To determine reliability and MTSF of the system models.
 vi. To derive expression for availability of the system models
 vii. To carry out busy period of the servers.
viii. To determine expected number of vacations of the server.
 ix. To determine expected number of repair activities.
  x. To carry out cost-benefit analysis of the system models
 xi. To make comparison of the results obtained for the system models
 xii. To publish the work in the form of research papers in reputed journals.
xiii. To prepare the final report on the research work.

3.1 *Methodology*

The system will be analyzed by using semi-Markov process and regenerative point technique which are briefly described as:

3.2 *Markov process*

If $\{X(t), t \in T\}$ is a stochastic process such that, given the value of $X(s)$, the value of $X(t)$, $t>s$ do not depend on the values of $X(u)$, $u<s$ Then the process $\{X(t), t \in T\}$ is a Markov process.

3.3 *Semi-Markov process*

A semi-Markov process is a stochastic process in which changes of state occur according to a Markov chain and in which the time interval between two successive transitions is a random variable, whose distribution may depend on the state from which the transition take place as well as on the state to which the next transition take place.

3.4 *Regenerative process*

Regenerative stochastic process was defined by Smith 1955 and has been crucial in the analysis of complex system. In this, we take time points at which the system history prior to the time points is irrelevant to the system conditions. These points are called regenerative points. Let X(t) be the state of the system of epoch. If t1, t2,... are the epochs at which the process probabilistically restarts, then these epochs are called regenerative epochs and the process {X(t), t = t1, t2.........} is called regenerative process. The state in which regenerative points occur is known as regenerative state.

4 FUTURE WORK

To analyze the system reliability models one should have the knowledge of the causes of failures, failure rate and repair rates of the processes which can be collected by getting primary and secondary data of repair and failure of h/w and s/w companies. The semi-Markov process and regenerative point technique will be adopted to derive the expression for various measures of system effectiveness such as mean sojourn times, transitions probabilities, mean time to system failure (MTSF), availability, busy period analysis due to repair and maintenance of the industry, expected number of repair and maintenance done by the server, expected number of visits by the servers and finally the profit function to carry out cost-benefit analysis. The methods of Laplace Transforms and Probability Law will be used to obtain the result in steady state.For inspection at regular interval of time wireless sensor network technology has also been an application for not only inspection of pipeline health but also health monitoring of compressor and pumps at petrochemical plants.

REFERENCES

Ali, Muhammad Khushk, Memon, Aslam & Saeed, Ikram 2011. Analysisof sugar industry competitiveness in Pakistan, J. Agric. Res., 49(1):137-151.

Arumuganathan, R. & Jeykumar, S. 2004. Analysis of bulk queue with multiple vacations and closedown times. *Int J Inform Manage Sci* 15(1):45-60.

Chander, S. & Singh, M. 2009. Probabilistic Analysis of 2-out- of -3 Redundant System Subject to Degradation. *Journal of Applied Probability and Statistics, USA* 4(1):33-44.

Chander, S. & Singh, M. 2009. Reliability modelling of 2-out-of-3 Redundant System Subject to Degradation After Repair", *Journal of Reliability and Statistical Studies* 2(2):91-104.

Choudhury, G. & Tadj, L. 2009. An M/G/1 queue with two phases of service subject to the server breakdown and delayed repair. *Appl Math Comp* 33(6):2699-2709.

Calzado, C. A. : "Valuation of a Mexican sugar mall and driving value factors", *Business Intelligence Journal*, Vol. 4, No. 1, pp. 91-106(2011)

Habchi, G. 2002. An improved method of reliability assessment tests. International Journal of Quality and Reliablity Management 19:454-470

Kumar, D., Singh, J. & Singh, I.P. 1988. Availability of the feeding system in the sugar industry. Microelectron. Reliab 28: 867-871

Malik, S.C. & Bhardwaj, R.K. 2007. Reliability Modeling and Analysis of 2-out-of -3 Redundant System Subject to Conditional Arrival Time of Server. Proceedings 13th ISSAT, Inc. on RQD, Seatle (USA) 206-210.

Malik, S.C. 2008. Reliability Modeling and Profit Analysis of Single-unit System with Inspection by a Server who Appears and Disappears Randomly. *Journal of Pure and Applied Mathematika Sciences* LXVII(1-2):135-145.

Murari, K. & Goyal, V. 1984. Comparison of two-unit Cold Standby Reliability Models with Three Types of Repair Facilities. Microelectron. Reliab 24 (1):35-49.

Naidu, R. S. & Gopalan, M.N. 1984. Cost-Benefit Analysis of One-server Two-unit System Subject to Arbitrary Failure, Inspection and Repair. Reliability Engg. :11.

Singh, M. & Chander, S. 2005. Stochastic Analysis of Reliability Models of an Electric Transformer and Generator with Priority and Replacement. Journal of Decision and Mathematical Sciences 10(1-3):79-100.

Communication and Computing Systems – Prasad et al. (eds)
© 2019 Taylor & Francis Group, London, ISBN 978-0-367-00147-6

Smart grid: Advancement with IoT

Arushi Sharma & Chandrasekhar Singh

Department of Electronics and Communication, Dronacharya College of Engineering, Gurgaon, India

ABSTRACT: In the present biological community of vitality, the board, the commitment of Internet of Things (IoT) to smart grids has gained massive potential because of its multi-faceted points of interest in different fields. Internet of Things is a critical specialized intent to advance the improvement of smart grid. IoT clears an approach to relate and basically control everything in pretty much every area of society. On the other hand, the smart grid system pulled in the consideration of the all inclusive research-network and blending IoT with smart grid together exhibits colossal development potential. In the ongoing patterns, there is an ascent in the rate over the interests of smart grids in both the makers and customers. The improvement of smart grids must be taken in thought for productive framework execution. This survey paper features the most critical research works that attention on applying IoT to smart grids. This work additionally addresses numerous imaginative methodologies utilized in IoT and smart grids alongside their particular applications in different fields. The target of this work is to profit researchers and new contestants in the field of IoT and smart grids open up mindfulness for new interdisciplinary research.

1 INTRODUCTION

Smart grid technology has the ability to prepared the present urban areas for tomorrow's needs. With the greater part of the world's populaces moved in urban focuses, urban communities should investigate new chances, arrangements and frameworks to keep things running for its kin, organizations, and governments. Districts have just added sensors to transmission lines and presented digitized controls and applications, making a smart grid. By using Internet of Things innovations, smart grid technology has enhanced two-route interchanges between service organizations and its clients and empowered access to close ongoing information that is being utilized to make savvy and condition friendlier choices.

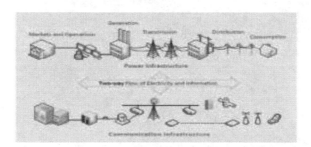

Figure 1. Smart grid.

Smart grid is a advanced control grid, which is highly coordinated with cutting edge sensor estimation technology, data and correspondence technology, examination of basic leadership technology, programmed control technology, and vitality control technology and grid frameworks. Contrasted and the customary grid, smart grid has been enhanced particularly in the improvement of intensity control, the adaptability of grid structure, upgrading the designation of assets, and enhancing the power nature of administrations. In this way, smart grid has numerous attributes including solid, self-recuperating, similarity, economy, mix and advancement, etc. Internet of Things, in particular "the Internet in which the things associated with one another", is the augmentation and extension of Internet-based system. As indicated by the concurred conventions, with IoT key advancements: radio recurrence ID technology, sensor technology, nanotechnology, the correspondence data can be used, and the insightful acknowledgment, situating, following, observing and the executives can be accomplished.

Figure 2.   IoT-based linkages.

As more individuals move into urban areas, the requests for vitality will flood. By 2040 net power age will ascend by 69%, contrasted with 2012 figures, to stay aware of purchaser requests. This expansion will put remarkable weight on grids that will affect natives, urban communities just as utility foundations.

A more intelligent smart grid

This reality, alongside developing ecological controls, requires governments and organizations to bring further developed IoT innovations into their smart grid biological community. From counterfeit keen computerization to enhanced two-way correspondence and other propelled applications, the smart grid will wind up smarter.

These new highlights will accomplish more than digitize exceptionally old grids. Rather, they will enhance new administrations and arrangements that will give providers better power over their framework and resources, and shoppers and urban areas can depend on increasingly feasible and solid vitality sources.

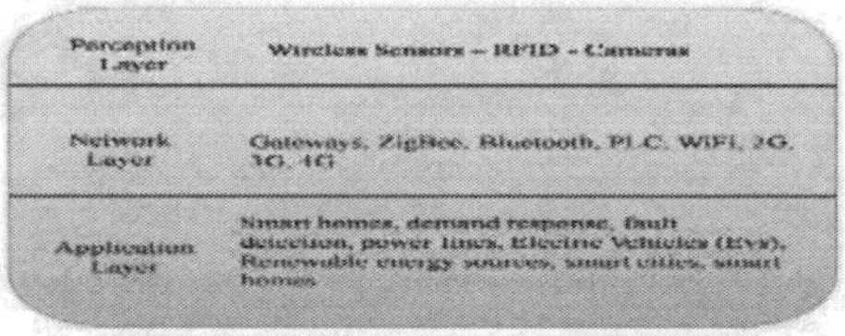

Perception Layer	Wireless Sensors – RFID – Cameras
Network Layer	Gateways, ZigBee, Bluetooth, PLC, WIFI, 2G, 3G, 4G
Application Layer	Smart homes, demand response, fault detection, power lines, Electric Vehicles (EVs), Renewable energy sources, smart cities, smart homes

Figure 3.   Architecture of IoT layers.

1.1   *Sustainable and reliable energy*

With the present reliable remote applications, utilities can interconnect essentially the majority of their advantages. For instance, meters and substations can be associated with one another, just as interface with organization vehicles and representative gadgets. Such availability will make at no other time acknowledged efficiencies.

Here's a model: a substation encounters a power blackout. Today, a shopper should perceive that there's an issue and call their utility supplier. From here, the organization will plan field laborers to research the issue before a game-plan can be taken to address the issue. With the assistance of sensors and IoT applications, crisis teams will be cautioned to an issue progressively. They will likewise get extra information pinpointing the wellspring of the issue. Not exclusively will laborers be nearby quicker, however they will likewise be prepared to fix the issue once on location.

We are still in the early stages of smart grid innovation, and to date, quite a bit of it has been produced along vertical produced along vertical applications. Be that as it may, as IoT advances, the utilization cases for smart gadgets and applications will broaden. As they do, urban areas and its subjects will profit by arrangements that fill numerous needs. Take for example smart lightening. Attached with sensors, they helped urban communities ration energy while keeping their city roads and parking parts safe. Later on, municipalities could equip smart lighting frameworks with additional features that will serve different requirements, for example, checking traffic and interfacing subjects to wifi. We are just at the start of the advancement of smart grid technology. As this technology keeps on advancing and innovative employments of IoT associations are considered, the smart grid will keep on discovering ways to create increasingly reliable, sustainable, financially savvy energy grids. However, for these chances to reach their maximum capacity will require a smart platform that can identify, select, track and analyze data in real-time.

The smart city is getting to be smarter than in the past because of the present broadening of digital advances. Smart urban areas comprise of various sorts of electronic hardware applied by a few applications, for example, cameras in a checking framework, sensors in a transportation framework, and so on. Moreover, utilization of individual portable hardware can be spread. Subsequently, with taking the heterogeneous condition into account, various terms, similar to characteristic of articles, participants, motivations and security approaches would be contemplated. Reference [7] exhibited a portion of the key features of potential smart urban areas in 2020.

2   MODEL OF SMART GRID

The Smart Grid Ideal Model is a lot of perspectives (diagrams) and depictions that is the foundation of idea for matters about the characteristics, utilizes, behavior, interfaces, necessities and standards of the Smart Grid. The conceptual model portrayed here gives an abnormal state, overarching viewpoint. It isn't just an instrument for distinguishing actors and the conceivable communication paths in the Smart Grid, yet in addition a valuable way to recognize potential intra and between domain communications and potential applications enabled by these connections. At the end of the day, the conceptual model is expressive and not prescriptive. It is meant to empower the understanding of Smart Grid working specifications. However not recommend how the Smart Grid will be actualized. This does not speak to the final model of the Smart Grid; rather it is a device for portraying, examining, and building up that model. The conceptual model gives a setting to analysis of inter operation and level of quality, both for whatever is left of this report, and for the improvement of the model of the Smart Grid. The best dimension domains of the ideal model are appeared in Figure 4.

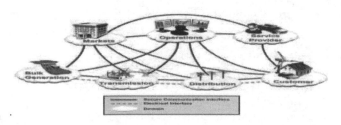

Figure 4.   Smart grid conceptual model.

Table 1. Domains in the smart grid conceptual model.

Domain	Actors in the Domain
Customers	The end users of electricity. May also generate, store, and manage the use of energy. Traditionally, three customer types are discussed, each with its own domain: home, commercial/building, and industrial.
Markets	The operators and participants in electricity markets
Service Providers	The organizations providing services to elecrical customers and utilities
Operations	The managers of the movement of electricity
Bulk Generation	The generators of electricity in bulk quantities. May also store energy for later distribution.
Transmission	The carriers of bulk electricity over long distances. May also store and generate elctricity.
Distribution	The distributors of electricity to and from customers. May also store and generate electricity.

The domains of the Smart Grid are listed in Table 1 and discussed in detail in the sections that follow. In Figure 1, domains are presented as clouds.

3 SMART GRID IOT PERFORMANCES

As the electricity generation from various sources with discontinuous power generation increases, and as the client turns out to be progressively active in relation to their energy use, there is a developing requirement for insightful, adaptable and increasingly reliable dissemination systems. This has prompted the advancement of smart grids, which give the required framework, market and apparatuses to meet demands. Smart grid advancements offer an extensive rundown of advantages, including an all the more productively operated electricity framework and decreased operational expenses.

1) Enabling major participation by users.
2) All types of generations and storage are accommodated.
3) Enabling new items, administrations, and markets.
4) Anticipates and reacts to the disturbances in the framework in a "self-redressing" manner.
5) Operates versatility against physical and digital attack, and natural disasters .
6) Provides control quality that meets a range of necessities required by our new digital economy.

4 CONCLUSION

This paper mainly presents IoT technology and its applications to be realized in smart grid, including wind control expectation, condition checking of overhead transmission lines, control observing, smart home and asset management. The improvement of Internet of things and smart grid are mutually fortifying. From one perspective, Internet of things will play an important role in advancing and improvisation of smart grid, and it is helpful to finish the web based checks and real-time data controlling in the operating parameters of all features; and again, the smart system will turn into a significant main thrust which will build up the systems administration industry of Internet of Things, and will also increase the advancement of information and communication industry.

In perspective of this, the main research course of future IoT ought to be placed in the growth of help and advancement in IoT center innovations which are related to smart grid, and the formation of a progressively total IoT advances ought to speed up. In addition, infrastructures ought to be contributed, the transmission and communication based on system ought to be provided, with the goal that it will make the power organize more dominant and impeccable, and in doing so enhance the reliability of the transmission communication network.

REFERENCES

Botta, A.; de Donato, W.; Persico, V.; Pescapé, A, 2016. Integration of Cloud computing and Internet of Things: A survey. *Future Gener. Comput. Syst.* 56, 684–700.

Hancke, G.; Silva, B.; Hancke, G., Jr, 2012, 13. The Role of Advanced Sensing in Smart Cities. Sensors, 393–425. [CrossRef] [PubMed]

Jaradat, M.; Jarrah, M.; Bousselham, A.; Jararweh, Y.; Al-Ayyoub, M, 2015. The Internet of Energy: Smart Sensor Networks and Big Data Management for Smart Grid. Procedia Comput. Sci., 56, 592–597 [CrossRef]

Kyriazis, D.; Varvarigou, T.; White, D.; Rossi, A.; Cooper, J, 4–7 June 2013. Sustainable smart city IoT applications: Heat and electricity management amp; Eco-conscious cruise control for public transportation. In Proceedings of the 2013 IEEE 14th International Symposium on "A World of Wireless, Mobile and Multimedia Networks" (WoWMoM), Madrid, Spain,; pp. 1–5.

Liu AJ, 2002. Status and Development Prospect of Internet of Things. *Internet of Things Technologies*; 2(1): 69-73.

Morgan MG, Apt J, Lave L, Ilic MD, Sirbu MA, Peha JM, 2009. The many meanings of "Smart Grid". Department of Engineering and Public Policy: 1-5.

Rathore, M.M.; Ahmad, A.; Paul, A.; Rho, S, 2015.12.23.Urban planning and building smart cities based on the Internet of Things using Big Data analytics. DOI:10.1016. Reference: COMPNW 5796.

Sun HB, Guan QY, 2012. Applications of Internet of Things technology in power system. *China Rural Water and Hydropower*. (3): 125-127.

Zhang W, 2012. Applications of Internet of Things technology in smart grid. Science & Technology Information. (14): 10-12.

Zou QM, Qin LJ, Ma QY. The Application of the Internet of Things in the Smart Grid. Advanced

Communication and Computing Systems – Prasad et al. (eds)
© 2019 Taylor & Francis Group, London, ISBN 978-0-367-00147-6

IoT primarily based pollution monitoring system

Sonia Rana
Dronacharya College of Engineering, Gurgaon, India

Krishanu Kundu
Department of ECE, Dronacharya College of Engineering, Gurgaon, India

ABSTRACT: In this paper, an effort has been made to create an IoT mainly based on air pollution monitoring System during which we are going to monitor the standard of air present in our environment over a webserver victimisation net and can trigger an alarm once the air quality goes down on the far side accurate level, mean once there's an extreme amount of harmful gases that are available in the atmosphere like carbon dioxide(CO2), smoke, alcohol, aromatic hydrocarbon and NH3. It'll display the air quality in PPM on the liquid crystal display and in addition as on webpage so we will monitor it dreadfully simply. During this paper we tend to use MQ135 device that is the most suitable option for watching the standard of air because it detects most harmful gases and might live their quantity accurately.

1 INTRODUCTION

As we all know pollution is that the largest environmental and public health challenge within the world these days. Pollution ends up in adversative effects on human health, climate and system. Pollution could be a mixture of solid particles and gases within the air. Automobile emission, chemicals from factories, dust, spore and mildew spores could also be suspended as particles. Ozone, a gas could be the major part of pollution in cities. Once gas forms pollution, it's conjointly referred to as air pollution. Some air pollutants are toxic.

The ozonosphere thought-about crucial for the presence of the system on the earth is depleting due to accumulated pollution. Global Warming, an instantaneous result of the accrued imbalance of gases within the atmosphere has return to be referred to as the most important threat and the challenge that the times have got to overcome in a very bid for survival.

1.1 *About*

- IoT: The Internet of Things (IoT) is a system of interrelated mechanical, computing devices and digital systems, objects or living thigs that are given an individual identifier and also the capability of transference of data or information over a network without any interaction between the computers and the human beings.
  In the net of things, all the items that area unit being connected to the net is place into 3 categories:

  1. Things that collect info then send it
  2. Things that receive info then act on that
  3. Things that do each

- ARDUINO: Arduino is an open source electronic platform which supported that simple to use software code and hardware. Arduino boards are able to browse the input data – lightweight on a device, a finger on a button or a twitter message and turns it into an result – activating a motor, turning on rectifier, commercial enterprise one thing on on-line. Over the year Arduino become the brain of the thousand comes.

1.2 *Block diagram*

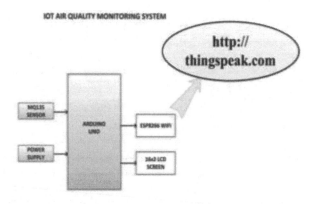

Figure 1.   Block diagram.

2   AIR QUALITY PARAMETERS

Important parameters that take into account in this project are:

- Sulphur dioxide (SO2): Sulphur dioxide could be an uncoloured gas, observe by its different odour and style. It's principally because of the burning of fossils fuels and also because of the industrial process. It contributes to air pollution.
- Carbon dioxide (CO2): CO2 could be a colourless, inodorous and non-combustible gas. CO2 could be a gas essential to life within the planet as a result of it's one in every of the foremost necessary components evolving chemical process, that convert the solar rays into energy. The absorption has been accrued due to the burning of fossil fuels.
- Nitrogen dioxide (NO2): dioxide could be a chromatic gas, simply noticeable for its odour. It forms because of the results of the fuel burning. In high concentration of NO2 could result in metabolic process issues. It contributes to acid rains.
- Temperature and humidity: measuring of temperature is very important for protection of individuals and disturbs our life skills. Greenhouse effect is observed by the measuring of temperature. The Humidness is a kind of gas that protects us from ultraviolet radiation rays that are coming from the sun and helps to increase the heat on earth. However, as humidness will increase, the heat on earth conjointly will increase that makes our life uncomfortable.

3   EFFECTS OF POLLUTION

- Respiratory and heart problems: Air pollution will effect on our respiratory system. The area unit familiar to form many metabolic process and heart conditions at the side of cancer, among the alternative threat of a body
- Global Warming: Another direct result is that the immediate alteration that the globe is witnessing due to heating.
- Acid Rain: Harmful gases like nitrogen oxides and sulphur oxides are discharged into the atmosphere throughout the burning of fossil fuels. Once it rains the water droplets mix with these air pollutants, become acidic and falls on the bottom within the system of air pollution.

- Effect on wildlife: Animals are facing some devastating have an effect of pollution. Toxic chemicals found within the air will force life species to transfer to the new place and alter their environs.

This system we've used MQ135 device that is suitable option for watching air quality because it will detect most harmful gases and might live their quantity accurately. during this IoT project, you'll be able to monitor the pollution level from any place victimisation your pc and mobile. We will install this technique anyplace and might conjointly trigger some device once pollution goes on the far side some level.

4 AIR POLLUTION MONITORING EQUIPMENTS

- MQ135 gas device: MQ135 could be a gas sensor that is employed for watching the standard of air because it will detect all the harmful gases which are present in the atmosphere and might live their account accurately. The MQ135 gas device used a sensitive material named as SnO2. The physical phenomenon of this material is lesser in clear air.

Figure 2.   MQ135 gas device.

- Arduino uno R3 microcontroller: Arduino is the main part of this project that managing the whole system. It's the foremost versatile hardware platform used supported ATmega328P which might be programmed consistent with the operate wherever it's to be used. it's half dozen analogue pins, fourteen digital input/output pins, a USB association, a 16MHz quartz, SPI, serial interface, a button, an influence jack. The Arduino isn't just for technical user, however it's meant for designer and artists in addition.

Figure 3.   Arduino R3 microcontroller.

- Wi-Fi ESP8266 module: Wi-Fi ESP8266 could be a cheap Wi-Fi semiconductor with full TCP\IP stack and microcontroller capability. Wi-Fi module has the capability of either holding an application or divesting all Wi-Fi networking operate from another application processors.

Figure 4.   Wi-Fi module ESP8266.

5   CIRCUIT DIAGRAM

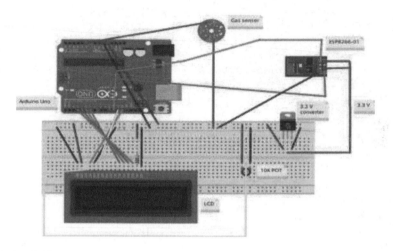

Figure 5.   A circuit diagram.

6   CONCLUSION

This device can monitor the standard of air victimisation Arduino, MQ135 gas device and IoT technology. IoT technology is projected to boost the standard of air, this technology enhances the method of watching wide-ranging of aspects of environment like the quality of air watching the issue proposed through this paper. Through this paper we tend to victimisation MQ135 gas device is a device that provides the sense of various types of hazardous gases and Arduino is that the base of this project that manage the whole method. Wi-Fi module will help to connect the complete device to the internet and liquid crystal display is employed for the visual output. This technique has options for the people to observe the quantity of air pollution on their mobile phone's victimisation the appliance.

REFERENCES

Kaur, N., Mahajan R., Bagai, D. 2016. Air Quality watching System supported Arduino Microcontroller. *International Research Journal of Engineering and Technology*, 5 (6).
Nayak, R, Panigrahy, M. R., Rai, V.K. Rao, T.A. 2017. IOT primarily based pollution monitoring system. *Journal of Network Communications and Emerging Technologies*, 3 (4).
Sai, P.Y. 2017. Associate in Nursing IoT primarily based automatic Noise and pollution watching System. *International Research Journal of Engineering and Technology*. 6 (3)

Communication and Computing Systems – Prasad et al. (eds)
© 2019 Taylor & Francis Group, London, ISBN 978-0-367-00147-6

Light Robotics – emerging scope and its future applications

Divyanshi Sharma, Abhay Anand & Parul Bansal
Dronacharya College of Engineering, Gurugram, India

ABSTRACT: Light is a form of energy which is stored in packets known as "photons". These photons travel along a fixed path depending upon the waveguide and the wavelength of these particles. The science of light and robotics together establish to make a new world of technology named as "Light Robotics". Light is an important tool at microscopic as well as macroscopic levels. The advancement in the micro-fabrication process and three-dimensional printing can actually help us to develop a Nanorobot driven by the light particles. The light particles contain momentum which can move lightweight microscopic as well as nanoscopic objects. This paper provides a comprehensive study on the concept of light energy in light robotics as well as applications of light robotics in medical as well as other fields.

1 INTRODUCTION

Light can be used as a smart instrument to drive tiny machines. Advanced control over normal or fabricated micro as well as nanostructures with the help of light has been demonstrated throughout the years, beginning with the revolutionary effort of Ashkin. Light is a significant research tool which enables us to see things from a macroscopic scale to microscopic scale where the cells of our body flourish. In 2014, the advancement in the classical far-field microscopy diffraction resulted in optical resolutions of few nanometers (so-called as 'Optical Nanoscopy') achieved Nobel Prize in Chemistry. The rapidly emerging field of light-based 3D micro- and Nano-printing is grounded on powerful methods offered by nonlinear photo-polymerization which is now reaching resolutions down to a few tens of nanometers.

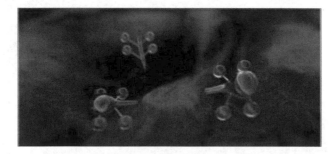

Figure 1. Typical structure of microscopic light robots.

The Robotics Institute of America (RIA) definition says, "A robot is a reprogrammable multifunctional manipulator designed to move material, parts, tools, or specialized devices through variable programmed motions for the performance of a variety of tasks". Improvement in the field of optical spectroscopy and miniature robotics has achieved many futuristic ideologies. The final scientific accomplishment, i.e. the invention of optical trapping, optical manipulation and optical tweezing has established a triangulation of new functionalities that can be achieved and are required for Light Robotics.

At every stage, the rise of many intriguing possibilities is evident like directly trained 3D printed Light Robotics equipped with multi-functional nano-probes, nano-tips or nano-tapers fabricated with true nanoscopic resolution. With this approach, each Light Robotic structure can be designed with size and shape that allows suitable manipulation with moderate objective lenses. Each Light Robotic structure is printed with convenient micron-sized spherical "handles" that allow for volumetric laser-manipulation with six-degrees-of-freedom (6-DOF) and in full real-time. Thus, a drone-like functionality can be attained that can almost provide the user with the sensation of stretching one's hands directly into the cellular micro-environment with the ability to interact with the live specimen directly while observing in full 3D.

2   LIGHT ROBOTICS – METHODS

2.1   Modeling methods

Modeling method is used in numerous research fields in order to realise the internals of the system which is being examined. There are two types of modeling methods, i.e. Microscopic Modeling and Macroscopic Modeling. In microscopic modeling, the robots with their interactions are modeled as per a finite state machine (FSM) which is completely based on the behaviour of each robot. In most of the research based on swarm robotics, the probabilistic microscopic model is used [Ying Et al].

The possibilities are appreciated from the experiments of actual robots. The model is reiterated in accordance with these possibilities for state transfer in the simulation to predict the behavior of the swarm. Using this method, several three-dimensional micro-robots can move according to the nature of the operation required to complete the task.

2.2   Fabrication methods

By using custom fabricated two-photon polymerization we can directly 3D print a number of Light Robot structures equipped with Nanoprobes, Nanotips, Nanotapers with greater resolution and fidelity.This is unique since a user can perform activity cell biology interactions at tiny scales even through the main structures having size and shape that allows convenient microscopic observations and laser manipulation with moderate numerical optic aperture.

A demonstrated simultaneous top and side view imaging providing the required 3D sensation while navigating with the help of microscopic tools in a volume in real time with 6-DOF (Degree of Freedom) is shown in the figure.

As is evident from Figure 2 each Light Robotic structure is typically furnished with a number of optical "handles" which allow a real-time 3D drone-like interaction using 6-DOF when controlled by a user via a joystick or a similar intuitive gaming device. It is also possible to fabricate light-guiding tools in order to target the real time coupled light that can be further used as a close –field irradiating and receiving nano-torches shown in Figure 3.

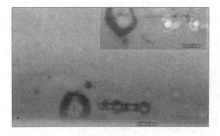

Figure 2.   Light Robotic probing- The top and side view displaying and opto-mechanical probe-interaction with a miniature object positioned on the surface.

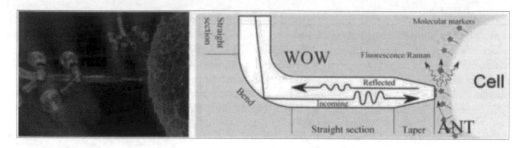

Figure 3. A light robotic tools armed with a combined waveguide arrangement which act as an optical close-field probe, i.e. tip-enhanced Raman signal acquisition.

Hence, the Light Robotic structures can act as "drone-like" controlled independently moving probes for monitoring the micro-biological processes and providing spatially directed chemical, mechanical as well as optical stimuli that would be very difficult to achieve in a full micro-biological environment.

For example, a light Robotic tool can be projected to execute measurement related operations of the receptors on a cell membrane and possibly use the cell signaling system to initiate the biochemical processes inside the cell itself.

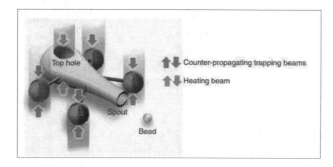

Figure 4. Numerous trapping rays allow the tool to move with a complete 6 – DOF actuation that can be measured by a LabVIEW-based user interface. An additional ray aimed at the top hole of micro-tool is used to heat the thin metallic layer.

By Laser manipulation with moderate numerical aperture optics, a user can perform cell interactions at miniature scales which make it "unique". A trapped particle can be laterally manipulated by synchronously shifting the counter-propagating beams. Further, the axial motion is controlled by changing the intensity ratio of these two beams.

With the help of a LabVIEW-based graphical user interface, lateral manipulation is achieved easily by dragging the traps, shown as overlapped graphics over real-time images attained from the microscope, while axial manipulation is implemented by sliding a graphical control object.

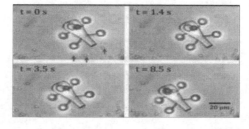

Figure 5. Syringe shaped light robotic structures.

3 RESULT AND DISCUSSION

With the augmentation in technology and the introduction of new methods in the field of robotics and optical nanoscopy, we have reached the horizon of achieving more realistic structures in this new era of science. The arena of Light Robotics is at an embryonic stage and we have only just started to "scratch the surface" both scientifically and R&D-wise. The fast-paced development of new improved Reality tools such as Artificial Intelligence and Machine Learning, advanced Swarm Robotics techniques as well as new 3D visualization and manipulation modalities in combination with state-of-the-art nano-robotics shows growing scope in Light Robotics. The use of probabilistic modeling programming techniques such as 'Bayesian Programming' can lead to greater proficiency in light robotics.

4 FUTURE SCOPE AND DEVELOPMENT

A variety of applications can be achieved in the field of medical sciences as well as environmental science and pollution research.

In Medical treatment- The introduction of light robotics can be treated as a right hand to many cure deadly diseases such as cancer. The nano "drone-like structures" could be modeled and can be optically manipulated guided by a pattern based programming. With this technique, the guided drone like structures could directly gather at the site by a swarm mechanism. This can be a new approach towards the advancement of light robotics.

In environmental science and pollution research- The swarm of multiple robotic structures could be directly used to eradicate the pollution causing particles. The day by day increasing pollution is a big problem in the metropolitan cities which is the root of many respiratory diseases. The nanorobots may perhaps be used to kill the nano pollutants present in the air. The nanorobots could be designed in such a way that they could perform a specific task along the course of light.

Consequently, we need to take a look at this innovative branch of robotics and its futuristic scope which can enable us to reach the extreme heights of advancement in technology.

REFERENCES

Ashkin A, Dziedzic JM, Bjorkholm JE, Chu S. Observation of a single-beam gradient force optical trap for dielectric particles. Opt Lett 1986; 11: 288.

Rodrigo, P. J., Kelemen, L., Palima, D., Alonzo, C., Ormos, P., Glückstad, J., "Optical micro assembly platform for constructing reconfigurable microenvironments for biomedical studies," Opt. Express 17, 6578–6583 (2009).

Mannix R.J., Kumar S., Cassiola F., Montoya-Zavala M., Feinstein E., Prentiss M., Ingber D.E., "Nanomagnetic actuation of receptor-mediated signal transduction", Nature Nanotech 36-40 (2008).

Wozniak, M. A. and Chen, C.S., "Mechanotransduction in development: a growing role for contractility", Nature Reviews Molecular Cell Biology 10, 34-43 (2009).

Palima, D., Bañas, A., Vizsnyiczai, G., Kelemen, L., Ormos, P., Glückstad, J., "Wave-guided optical waveguides,". Opt Express 20, 2004–2014 (2012).

Villangca, M., Bañas, A., Palima, D., Glückstad, J., "Dynamic diffraction-limited light-coupling of 3D-maneuvered wave-guided optical waveguides," Opt. Express 22, 17880–17889 (2014).

Villangca, M., Bañas, A., Palima, D., Glückstad, J. "Generalized phase contrast-enhanced diffractive coupling to light-driven microtools,". Opt Eng. 54, 111308 (2015).

Palima, D., Bañas, A., Vizsnyiczai, G., Kelemen, L., Aabo, T., Ormos, P., and Glückstad, J., "Optical forces through guided light deflections,". Opt Express 21, 581-593 (2013).

Villangca, M., Palima, D., Bañas, A., Glückstad, J., "Light-driven micro-tool equipped with a syringe function," *Light: Science & Applications* 5, e16148 (2016).

Bañas, A., Glückstad, J., "Holo-GPC: Holographic Generalized Phase Contrast," Optics Communications 392, 190-195 (2017). [22] Glückstad, J., Palima, D., "Light Robotics – Structure-mediated Nanobiophotonics," Elsevier Science, 468 pages (2017).

P. Polygerinos, L. D. Seneviratne, R. Razavi, T. Schaeffter, K. Althoefer, -Tip Force Sensor for MRIIEEE/ASME T. Mechatronics, 18(1),pp.386-396, 2013.

J. Peirs, J. Clijnen, D. Reynaerts, H. V. Brussel, P. Herijgers, B. Corteville, S.Boone A micro-optical force sensor for force feedback during minimally invasive robotic surgery Sensors and Actuators A: Physical, vol. 115, pp.447 455, 2014.

S. Ryu, and P. -based Shape Sensing Int. Conf. on Robotics & Automation, pp.3531-3537 2014.

H. Xie, H. Liu, Y. Noh, J. Li, S. Wang, K. Althoefer, -Optics based Body Contact Sensor for a Flexible vol.15, Issue.6 pp. 3543-3550, 2015.

Ying TAN*, Zhong-yang ZHENG-"Research Advance in Swarm Robotics" Received 4 January 2013; revised 21 February 2013; accepted 2 March 2013 Available online 31 October 2013)

Villangca MJ, Palima D, Bañas AR, Glückstad J. Light-driven micro-tool equipped with a syringe function. Light Sci Appl. 2016;5(9):e16148.Published 2016 Sep 23. doi:10.1038/lsa.2016.148 (2016)

Communication and Computing Systems – Prasad et al. (eds)
© 2019 Taylor & Francis Group, London, ISBN 978-0-367-00147-6

IoT (Internet of Things) enabled intelligent transportation system

Akeel Ahmad, Harshit Jain & Chandra Shekhar Singh
ECE Department, Dronacharya College of Engineering, Gurgaon, India

ABSTRACT: In this paper, we proposed an IoT enabled intelligent transportation system (ITS) consists of information and communication technologies that can be applied to existing transportation system in India to make transport system smart, reliable and safe. The proposed system consists of three sub systems: the sensor system, monitoring system and display system. We also developed our prototype which can serve as a benchmark to build ITS. The results shows that the model efficiently work in bus scheduling, limiting traffic congestion and reduce waiting time of the passengers.

1 INTRODUCTION

With the rapid growth in urban population, the future urban cities will be faced challenges linked to safety, reliability, and the delivery of public services including urban mobility. Urban mobility is also probable to worsen during the 21st century due to the projected rapid expansion of urban borders in unplanned clusters. This will cause additional traffic congestion which can be expected to result in additional costs as well as increased air and noise pollution. Moreover, insufficient traffic management also effects economic activity could further penalize and demote the poorer segment of population, limiting their development viewpoint. Poor public transport systems compound the problem of urban sprawl and traffic congestion.

With the emergence of IoT technology, Cities are getting "smarter" and applications are developed to take advance of the latest technological improvements. With IoT in the field of transportation, transportation systems begin to "feel" and "think", and hence leads to Intelligent Transportation Systems (ITS). Smart transportation has paying attention of many researchers since there are plenty of opportunities for further developments. One of the most significant areas of interest in smart transportation is route optimization. Using data from the users' mobile devices (Yang et al.,2017) or with NFC modules placed in specified point on the road (Al-Dweik et al, 2017), it try to approximate traffic congestion and provide route options to minimize traveling time, and therefore reduce noise pollution and energy consumption. IoT devices have been widely used to create smart parking. Using image processing (Wu et al, 2007), or other WSN (wireless sensor nodes) (Araújo et al, 2017), authors have proposed parking reservation systems that allow maximizing capacity and minimizing the navigation time. Moreover, systems that help detect road path hole anomalies based on input data from sensors attached to cars or the driver's phone have been proposed. By getting information regarding path hole, the accidents can be avoided. There have also been efforts to detect or prevent road accidents using IoT devices. Finally, the IoT M2M communication used to develop vehicular communication, where vehicles can exchange useful information with each other and give many more possibilities for new applications (Jain et al., 2018).

Xian et al, of Auto-ID lab at MIT proposed Internet RFID (Radio Frequency Identification) to achieve intelligent recognition and network management using RFID based wireless sensor networks using radio frequency identification technology (Chen et al., 2012). According to Panchal (2017) designing an IEEE Zigbee based wireless network is reliable in emergencies and also cost-effective manner. Tibor (2017) successfully tested the prototype model to reduce congestion and generate a rapid response to the information of an accident that occurred.

In this paper, section 2 explains the architecture layout of Intelligent transport system. Section 2.1 gives the detail description of public transport system enabled in bus. Section 2.2 explains the structure of central controller unit. Section 2.3 discusses the architecture and features of smart navigation app. Section 3 provide the methodology for the development of system in real time. Section 4 provides the conclusion.

2   ARCHITECTURE OF ITS

Intelligent transportation system mainly has three components the Transport system which may be public transport such as bus, Central controller unit that receives information regarding the status of bus such as bus location, occupancy, route congestion, traffic density etc. and display system basically smart navigation app installed at user mobile to provide information. Figure 1. Shows the functional block diagram for proposed intelligent transportation system.

2.1   *Public transport system*

To enabled IoT, it is required to developed a smart bused that incorporates various types of sensors to sense the crowd in the bus, Location of the bus, RFID system for driver and low cost basic processing unit with Wi-Fi to send and receive data to the server. Small box consists of Figure 2. Shows the methodology for system implemented in buses.
   Explanation:

1. Microcontroller Unit: In this prototype model, we use raspberry pi for central processing unit. This is the heart of our framework. It collects all the information from the sensors, process and showcase on the LCD display. Raspberry pi provides a parallel processing of data with high speed. It also contain Ethernet shield to connect to the internet for sending data to the central server for further processing and also receive data.
2. GSM and GPS module: IoT based project requires transmitting information over internet or getting commands via internet. GSM shield is used for connecting to internet through mobile data network. GSM module is used to establish communication between a computer and a GSM. Global System for Mobile communication (GSM) is an architecture used for mobile communication in most of the countries. The SIM900 is a complete Quad-band GSM/GPRS

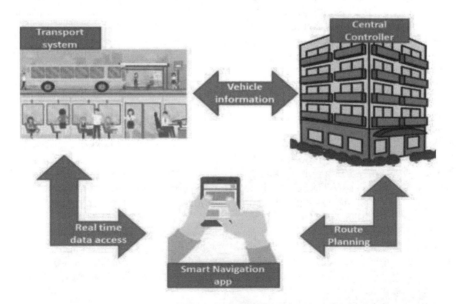

Figure 1.   Functional block diagram for proposed intelligent transportation system.

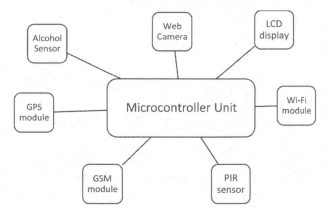

Figure 2. Methodology for system implemented in buses.

solution in a SMT module which can be embedded in the customer applications. Featuring an industry-standard interface, the SIM900 delivers GSM/GPRS 850/900/1800/1900MHz performance for voice, SMS, Data, and Fax in a small form factor and with low power consumption.GSM module is used to send/receive the data to the server. Emergency data can be send by the microcontroller unit through GSM. GPS is used to track the real time location of the buses and other public transport.

3. Web Camera: Web camera is used to capture the image in the bus and send it to centre server unit for further processing.
4. Wi-Fi Module: It is used to transmit data wirelessly.
5. PIR sensor: Passive infra-red sensors are used to determine the crowd density estimation in the bus.

2.2 *Central controller*

IoT devices perform a sensing function with the use of various types of sensors connected to it and send raw data back to a control center. It may combine data from many sensors, perform local data analysis, and then take action. Additionally, device could be remote and standalone or be co-located within a larger system. Here in this paper the centre controller equipped with following function ability:

• Route planning features
• Real-time bus dispatching
• Bus occupancy information & crowd density report: *Route recommendation*
• Analysis for optimizing travel comfort
• Future planning based on collected data

Here, we use SQL Database with Microsoft Azure Cloud Service

2.3 *Smart navigation app*

Smart navigation App is developed for the android phone so that it can provides following information to the user on their mobile. The main purpose of this unit is to provide

• Interaction with buses & central controller.
• Android based User interface
• Functions for trip planning and context-aware trip hints
• Notification and Map area
• Incorporates components for
• Context sensing
• Bus ride recognition
• Trip tracking

3 IMPLEMENTATION

Figure 3 below shows the methodology used to implement intelligent transportation system

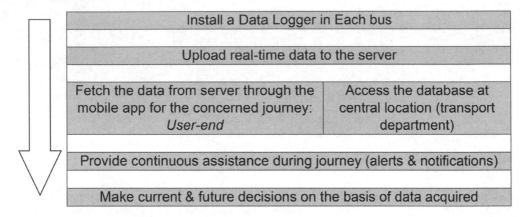

Figure 3. Real time deploy system.

4 CONCLUSION

Due to enhanced popularity of Smart city concept evolution of internet of things (IoT) has occurred in rapid manner. Smart transportation is one of the most challenging aspects for constructing smart cities. IoT provides better solutions for the challenges such as traffic congestion, road safety, accident detection, automatic fare collection as well as limited car parking facilities. In present work, an IoT based smart parking system along with an intelligent signboard has been proposed. Here the smart parking system consists of several intelligent sensors for monitoring and controlling Traffic density as well as congestion.

REFERENCES

Al-Dweik, A.; Muresan, R.; Mayhew, M.; Lieberman, M. 2017. IoT-based multifunctional scalable real-time enhanced road side unit for intelligent transportation systems. In *Proceedings of the 2017 IEEE 30th Canadian Conference on Electrical and Computer Engineering (CCECE)*, Windsor, ON, Canada, 30 April–3 May: 1–6.

Araújo, A.; Kalebe, R.; Girão, G.; Filho, I.; Gonçalves, K.; Melo, A.; Neto, B. 2017. IoT-Based Smart Parking for Smart Cities. *In Proceedings of the 2017 IEEE First Summer School on Smart Cities (S3C)*, Natal, Brazil, 6–11 August:31–36.

Chen, X.-Y. & Jin, Z.-G. 2012. Research on Key Technology and Applications for Internet of Things, *Phys. Procedia* 33:561–566.

Jain, B.; Brar, G.; Malhotra, J.; Rani, S.; Ahmed, S.H. 2018. A cross layer protocol for traffic management in Social Internet of Vehicles. *Future Gen. Comput. Syst.* 82: 707–714.

Panchal, J. R. (2017). Energy Efficient Wireless Sensor Network System for Transportation, 5(5): 663–667.

Petrov, T., Dado, M.& Ambrosch, K. E. 2017.Computer Modelling of Cooperative Intelligent Transportation Systems, *Procedia Eng.* 192: 683–688.

Wu, Q.; Huang, C.; Wang, S.Y.; Chiu, W.C.; Chen, T. 2007. Robust Parking Space Detection Considering Inter-Space Correlation. *In Proceedings of the 2007 IEEE International Conference on Multimedia and Expo*, Beijing, China.

Yang, J.; Han, Y.; Wang, Y.; Jiang, B.; Lv, Z.; Song, H. Optimization of real-time traffic network assignment based on IoT data using DBN and clustering model in smart city. Future Gen. Comput. Syst. 2017, in press.

Communication and Computing Systems – Prasad et al. (eds)
© 2019 Taylor & Francis Group, London, ISBN 978-0-367-00147-6

IoT based model for smart city implementation in India

Deepika
Dronacharya College of Engineering, Gurgaon, India

Chandra shekar Singh
ECE Department, Dronacharya College of Engineering, Gurgaon, India

ABSTRACT: The latest developments in the field of technology has given birth to a widespread technological revolution ranging from AI to studies related to neural networks to the field of automation which can be controlled from a push of a button while being on any other part of the globe while being connected to the internet - IoT. IoT or Internet of Things as it is commonly referred to as, is the next generation technology by the help of which any individual can control or monitor any operation that's connected to the technology while being miles apart. Ranging from power grid control to industrial automation to networks and data stations to health care, IoT has a potential for work in any of the fields. It has been predicted that by the year 2020 most of major developing cities in the world will be connected and controlled by this same developing power. Such cities are being termed as - Smart Cities.

1 INTRODUCTION

The word smart city refer to new industries exploit information and communication technologics (ICT) down with the utility and environments of urban areas. These services are converting cities improving infrastructure and transportation systems, reducing traffic blocking, providing waste management and providing improving the quality of human life. The recent can play a important role in the framework of smart cities .e.g smart waste containers can bring a real benefit for people they will indicate that the container is full or emptied. This application can be check through phone, if the container is full or not the status of waste container is directly goes to garbage system office for providing the feasible solutions. Places are assembled with sensors and monitor the environment conditions by which the healthy trips can made by adjusting traffic or planting trees in different areas. The data will be available to all people to develop the creation of applications using real time information. In this chapter, we give an overview of IoT in the perspective of smart cities and we have discuss how to improve a city smartness.

2 INTERNET THINGS AND THE SMART CITY

In the latest article many writer give definition for the term of Internet of things. IoT is defined as Object having unique and effective personalities in smart spaces using intelligent edges to connect and be in touch within social, medical, environment and consumers. The sunshade term of a smart city, is a city that uses data and technologies to increase the lives of the people and businesses that place it. A city can be made smart using large execution of IoT (specially machine-to-machine and human- to-machine communications). The created information is shared across a variety of platforms in order to increase a Common Operating Picture (COP) of the city.

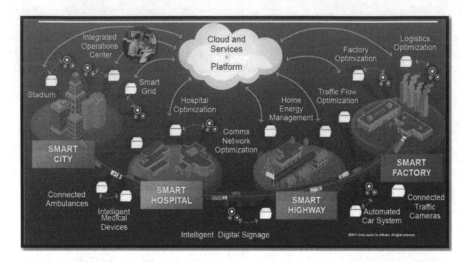

Figure 1. Development of smart cities.

3 SMART INDUSTRY

In the present day scenario lots of industries are completely dependent on manual work. Ranging from manual laborers to manual date gathering and evaluation. Due to so much manual works there are a lot of scope for defect creation and outflows. Such issues gives rise to increasing costs and the lack to meet the market demand and thereby being overtaken by the rise of competitive industries. To prevent these a new technology in the field of industrial automation is being developed. This technology, named - Industry 4.0 is the synonym for Smart Industry. Many predict that this smart technology is the next industrial revolution, the fourth industrial revolution.

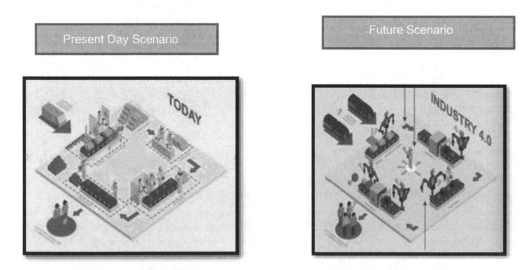

Figure 2. Present and future scenario of industry.

4 SYSTEM OVERVIEW

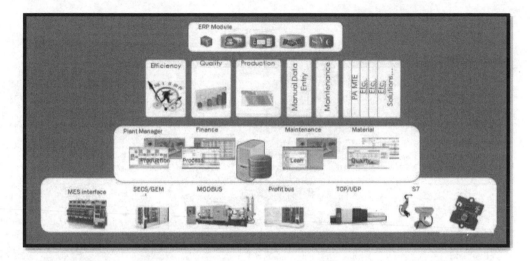

Figure 3. Smart system diagram.

This IoT based manufacturing will be completely automated by the use of Smart Manufacturing Objects of as it is commonly referred to as SMOs. These units are connected with the technology of cloud computing and is connected with the Material Management System. These type of systems are basically connected by the use of IoT with other data base software such as SAP/ABAP to ERPs for data handling storage and calculations. Along with these software based technologies then comes the next level of technologies - Robotics. Now all these modules are interconnected together in the array of network defined with the only function to create automation in the entire industry. This gives rise to Smart Manufacturing.

5 SMART STORAGE SYSTEM

In the field of raw material handling, it has been observed that a lot of unproductive tasks are undertaken from maintaining inventory counts to wrong material procurement. Such issues gives rise to a plague like situation in every modern industry which finally results in one final issue: Loss in productivity. This lack of productivity when seen from an industrialist's point of view directly synchronizes with the term "Loss of money". For this lots of modern industries are looking at the scope of industrial Raw material handling automation or otherwise as known as smart storage technologies.

- SMD Reel Tower (700 Reels).
- SMD Reel storage (6M*3M*2.5= 6400Reels).
- SMD ESD Box Storage.
- SMD Plate Box Storage

Figure 4. Box storage.

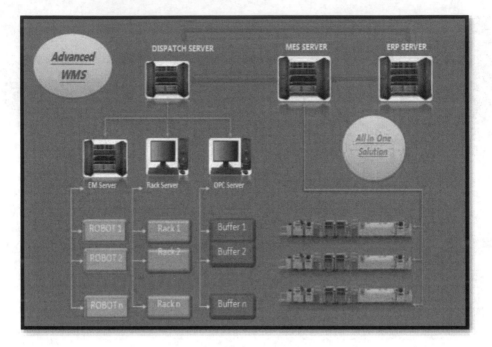

Figure 5.   Smart factory solution structure.

7 PROCESS

By the use of this technology, Every material which are being used to form a finished product from the BOM (Bill of Material) are issued an individual ID number. These ID numbers can be represented or interpreted in the material and the machines in form of Bar coded data, QR coded data or data written directly through a RFID tags pasted directly over the material.

Lets consider an example of an Electronics manufacturing industry. Here in such an industry all the raw materials are procured and stored in huge store warehouses. Here every material will be coded with a RFID tag and every materials location in the ware house will be mapped in the system. Now Whenever any specific material is required for production of any finish good. The material number can be referred from the BOM which then can be entered in to the Material management System which can pinpoint to the exact material location along with the quantity that's available at that specific location. Now with the help of robotic arms that material can be directly picked up from the rack and be fed directly to the machine. Then after the part has been picked from the location the remaining stock quantity will be automatically be updated in the Material Management System and whenever this value reaches a specific low point then a new procurement order can be generated for next material procurement cycle.

Such a technology will revolutionize the modern industry and generate new figures of productivity in the field of manufacturing which have now been considered to be above the achievable limits.

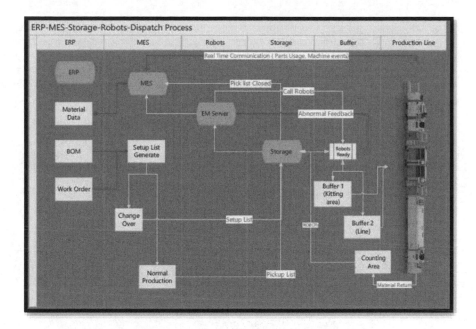

Figure 6.   Process flow diagram.

8   MATERIAL REGISTRATION

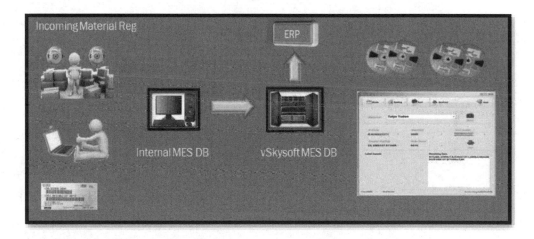

Figure 7.   Material registration diagram.

- An interface is created, parse all the material data (Part no, Qty, Lot no etc) into vskysoft MES database.
- Synchronies material data PO, Part no, Qty etc into ERP.

9   CONCLUSION

With the technology that's available to us in the present century we can push the development of IoT based technologies to achieve new marvels of technological advancement. From automation oh home to raising productivity in the industries to new and advanced health care facilities the endless list goes on. In the next generation of technologies we can inter connect these areas of IoT with the more newer technologies of AI and neural networking to predict oncoming issues and resolve them even before they can begin. Such technology can help save human lives from natural disasters to man made disasters like potentially creating a hurricane alert to automatically seal off the windows of the house to AI equipped solders to take care of terrorism with minimal human input and such way saving human casualties thus saving lives of countless soldiers. With the advancement of such technologies the potential for the next human generations are endless.

REFERENCES

The internet of things: A survey Computer networks.
Internet of things: Applications and challenges in technology and standardization. Wireless Personal Communications.

Communication and Computing Systems – Prasad et al. (eds)
© 2019 Taylor & Francis Group, London, ISBN 978-0-367-00147-6

Analytical and experimental characterization of friction force in belt motion

Saurabh Yadav, Manish Kumar Mishra & Vineet Mishra
Department of Mechanical Engineering, Dronacharya College of Engineering, Gurgaon, Haryana, India

ABSTRACT: Dynamic friction force is the amount of force necessary to keep the two objects moving relative to each other. This dynamic friction force depends on several parameters, such as relative velocity, contact surface, normal load etc. the main aim of this project work is to analyze the effect of relative velocity on the dynamic friction. Till now only the analytical results regarding effect of relative velocity on dynamic friction are available which are based on several assumptions for simplifying the study. In this project, an effort has been made to characterize the dynamic friction force with relative velocity experimentally. In this project, we consider the classical "mass on a moving belt" model for describing friction-induced vibration. By using this model we can study the stick-slip phenomena. In this work, an experimental setup is built to observe, record and analyze friction damped oscillation. In this project, the dynamics of „mass on a moving belt" is solved numerically and the effect of different parameters on the response is studied and these computational results are used to build up a model. A modified experimental setup is used for experimental study of stick-slip vibration which is used for characterizing friction with relative velocity. The experiments are conducted for different sets of parameters and it is found that the variation of friction force is linear with relative velocity.

1 INTRODUCTION

The best way to understand any scientific phenomenon is to feel it with our senses. Friction is one such behavior which we encounter in our day to day life. However, friction damping is not readily observable unless we pay attention to the noises from brakes and musical instruments like violin. To understand the phenomenon of friction damping the following literature survey is made.

The way static coefficient was developed which makes a different path for itself than the dynamic one. The detailed stability theory was carried out which influence the idea of simple mass with harmonic excitation. McMillan (1997) developed a dynamical system for understanding the phenomena of squeal. He proposed a phenomenological model which combines the concept of static and dynamic friction. It is demonstrated that dynamical behavior of any given system not only depends upon the velocity but also on the initial condition of system. Leine et. al (1998) presented a stick-slip vibration model which demonstrate the friction model in an efficient way. The differential were softly sprung compare to the other one which help in better engagement with other ODE solver. Results of this method adopted were compared with a smoothing method and it is found that the alternate friction model is more efficient from a computational point of view.

Based on the alternate friction model a shooting method for calculating limit cycles is presented Jon and Alexander (2003) used classical "mass-on-moving belt" model for describing friction-induced vibrations. They derived approximate analytical expressions for the conditions, the amplitudes and the base frequencies of friction-induced stick-slip and pure slip oscillations. They used perturbation analysis for the finite time intervals of the stick phase which is linked to subsequent slip phase through conditions of continuity and periodicity. Obtained results are illustrated and tested by time-series, phase plots and amplitude response diagram and compared with numerical simulation considering very small difference between static and kinetic friction. The study of Karl Popp and Martin Rudolph (2005) gave an insight in basic excitation mechanisms of friction induced vibrations which showed the possible ways of avoidance of a dynamic vibration absorber was investigated in detail.

With the integration of another spring mass damper we can reduce the vibrational effect considerably and that makes our differential life to increase hence it will also avoid the stick slip vibrations. The amplitudes that evolves the stick slip differential on mass moving belt model is not what we expect it to be, it is a sign of indistinguishable portfolio . The investigation of Stick-Slip intervals was generally given by the three mathematical equations by Ammar and Rahim. They have suggested that all these three equations can be combined together to form one single equation, and can be solved by MATLAB. The aim of the paper was to present, solve and predict the stick slip motion and applied it in finite element software.

2 EXPERIMENTAL STUDY

Several assumptions were done to success the belt motion which found ourselves at various analysis points that gives us a good result .This theory helps us to compute to different characterization to find out the desired result of belt motion . In computational analysis it is assumed that, the velocity of belt is constant. But in real system velocity of belt varies. For real system characterization, an experimental setup is required. In this chapter, study of the experimental setup and its component is done.

2.1 *Schematic of experimental setup and its components*

Experimental setup consists of a spring-mass system in which a spring is fixed at one end and attached to mass at another end. The mass is placed on a moving belt whose velocity is assumed to be constant. The motion of belt is provided with the help of AC motor and worm-worm gear. An accelerometer is attached to the mass and is connected to ARDUINO to obtain the acceleration of mass in x-direction (direction of belt motion). An ultrasonic position sensor is used to obtain the position in between mass and ultrasonic position sensors.

Figure 1.   Schematic of experimental setup and its component.

3 RESULTS AND DISCUSSIONS

This chapter deals with the various results obtained from experiments and simulation in MATLAB. An effort has been made to analyze these results and to give an inference regarding the characterization relative velocity and various forces of friction.

3.1 *Experimental results*

An experiment was conducted for finding the friction force versus relative velocity graph. The parameters used in experimental setup are given below. We can see that the mass is being taken as 1.94 in order to maintain proper range of amplitude. Spring stiffness can be found by plotting the graph between spring force and deflection in the spring. Slope of the spring force versus deflection in the deflection graph gives the stiffness of the spring. For finding the static coefficient of friction experimental trial and error method is used. The value of this static coefficient of friction for the experimental setup is given in Appendix A4.

Experimental parameters:

$K = 140$
$m = 1.98 \ kg$
$V_b = 0.25 \ m/s$
$\mu s = 0.38 \pm 0.04$

3.1.1 *Displacement versus time plot*

From the experiment, we obtain the certain values for displacement and time. Using these values we obtain the following graphs as shown below. We see that the maximum amplitude is 80 mm. These values are used to find the spring force.

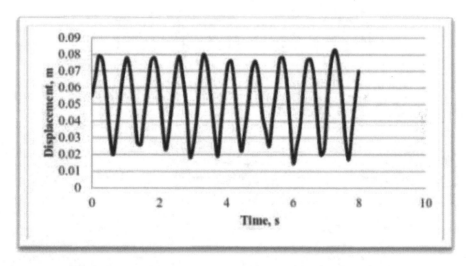

Figure 2.   Displacement versus time plot.

3.1.2 *Acceleration versus time plot*

From the experiment, we obtain the certain values for acceleration and time. Using these values we obtain the graph as shown below. We see that acceleration varies from +2.5 to -3.5 m/(approximately). These values are used to obtain inertia force which in turns gives friction force.

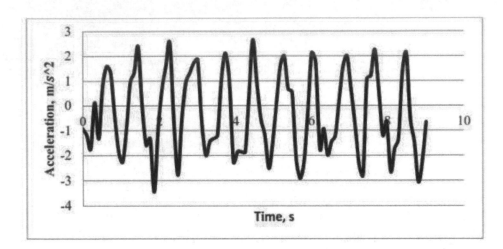

Figure 3.　Acceleration versus time plot.

3.1.3 *Velocity versus time plot*

From the experiment, we obtain the certain values velocity and time. Using these values we obtain the graph as shown below. We see that velocity varies from +0.2 to -0.28. These values are used to find relative velocity which is used in plotting friction force versus relative velocity

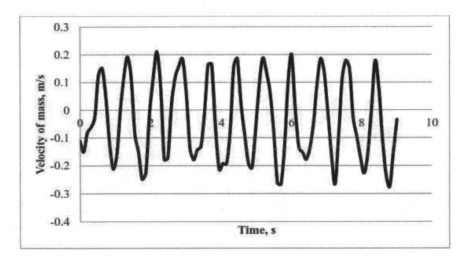

Figure 4.　Velocity versus time plot.

3.1.4 *Friction force versus relative velocity plot*

From the above three graphs, we obtain the value of displacement, acceleration and velocity. Now using the equation (5.1), we can obtain the value of friction force. For finding relative velocity, we make use of expression,

Relative velocity (v) = belt velocity (v_b) - velocity of mass ($\dot{x}$)

Using value of friction force and relative velocity, we obtain the graph as shown below. From the graph, Curve fitting for experimental data may be exponential or linear because for cubic curve fit, error found in static coefficient of friction is more. The root mean square deviation for exponential form is 1.0717 and for the linear curve is 1.0663. Linear curve fitting is less than in comparison to exponential curve fitting, so the linear curve fitting have more accuracy than the exponential curve fitting. Y-intercept of friction force versus relative velocity plot gives the static friction force.

Static Coefficient of friction from curve fitting= (interception of curve fitting/normal load)

By trial error method mean value of Static Coefficient of friction is obtained 0.38. Calculation for finding static coefficient of friction by trial error method is given in Appendix (A4). Error in the static coefficient of friction found is 5% of the value obtained from the trial and error method.

A friction induced vibration model is simulated in MATLAB. It is observed that as we increase the value of spring stiffness, mass and static coefficient of friction and reduce the velocity of belt, ratio of stick to slip time increases which indicates stick dominates over slip phenomenon. Experimental characterization is done for friction in the mass on a moving belt. The experiments are conducted for 8 sets of parameters and it is obtained that the variation of friction force is linear with relative velocity. After modification in block and taking the average of experimental value fluctuation in friction force gets reduced by 30.7%. It is observed that the friction force depends on the belt velocity and doesn't depend on spring stiffness. Y-intercept of friction force versus relative velocity plot gives the static friction force. Error in the static coefficient of friction found is -6% to 11% of the value obtained from the trial and error method. FFT analysis shows that, frequency obtained from experiment differs from that obtained through simulation. This variation is present in the frequencies obtained from FFT analysis is due to the assumptions in our model.

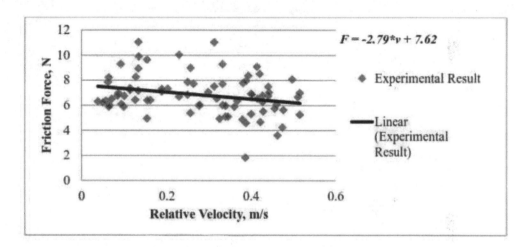

Figure 5.   Friction force versus relative velocity plot.

REFERENCES

Ammar A. Yousif Mohammed, Inzarul faisham Abd Rahim: Investigate stick-slip intervals with one equation of motion and analyze the effect of the friction noise, International Journal of Scientific & Technology Research, 2, 5, (2013).

A. J. McMillan: A non-linear friction model for self-excited vibrations, Journal of Sound and Vibration, 3, 205, (1997), pp. 323-335.

Heli Bao, Hongwei Huang: Comparison of the dynamics of four different models of dry friction in a nonlinear oscillator, The Third China-Japan Joint Seminar for the Graduate Student, Shanghai, China, Oct. (2006).

Jon Juel Thomsen, Alexander Fidlin: Analytical approximations for stick-slip vibration amplitudes, International Journal of Non-Linear Mechanics, 38, (2003), pp. 389-403.

Jamil Abdo, Ahmed A. Abouelsoud: Analytical approach to estimate amplitude of stick-slip oscillations, Journal of Theoretical and Applied Mechanics, 4, 49, (2011), pp. 971-986.

Karl Popp, Martin Rudolph: Dynamic vibration absorber for friction induced oscillator, IUTAM Symposium on Chaotic Dynamics and Control of Systems and Processes in Mechanics, Institute of Mechanics, University of Hannover, Germany, (2005), pp. 419–427.

Lopez, J. M. Basturia et.al.: Energy dissipation of a friction damper, Journal of Sound and Vibration, 278, (2004), pp. 536-561.

M. Graf, G. P. Ostermeyer: Friction induced vibration and dynamic friction laws: Instability at positive friction–velocity-characteristic, Tribology International, 92, (2015), pp. 255–258.

R. I. Leine, D. H. Van Campen, A. De Kraker, L. Van Den Steen: Stick-slip vibrations induced by alternate friction models, Nonlinear Dynamics, 16, (1998), pp. 41–54.

S.W. Shaw: On the dynamic response of a system with dry friction, Journal of Sound and Vibration, 2, 108, (1986), pp. 305-325.

Communication and Computing Systems – Prasad et al. (eds)
© 2019 Taylor & Francis Group, London, ISBN 978-0-367-00147-6

Internet of Things system: Design and development process

Preeti
Department of CSE, Dronacharya College of Engineering, Gurugram, Haryana, India

Naresh Kumar
YMCAUST, Faridabad, Haryana, India

Manish Sharma
ECE, SGT University, Gurugram, India

Vimmi Malhotra
Department of CSE, Dronacharya College of Engineering, Gurugram, Haryana, India

ABSTRACT: We are exploring the new phases of emerging integrating technology of electronics, software and artificial intelligence i.e. Internet of Things and it's inherit features. IoT is such a universal neural network which connects various things over one common platform of internet. In this paper author present the standard architectural overview of the IoT system & their inherent properties. Author emphasize on the designing and development process of IoT system for diverse applications. It will start of general description of the required system, selection of the sensors & their interfacing techniques, selection of the processor for the signal processing and actuators. This paper also presents various types of communication methodology and their selection criteria. Hence this paper will help the beginner engineers and designers during the system development process.

1 INTRODUCTION TO IOT SYSTEM

The IoT is a smart network of intelligently interconnected device where each of machines can interact with other machines, environments, objects, infrastructures and sensor network technologies. Implementation of Internet of Things (IoT) will enhance the communication capabilities of physical devices to sense the environment to gathered data from the world, and then communicate across the Internet for further analysis and process.to the persons with disabilities. Kevin Ashton introduced IoT in 1999 in the perspective of supply chain management industry.

(*OS X - Mac App Store - Apple (CA)*, no date), (*Cell Phone News - Phone Arena*, no date) presents one possible architecture for IoT which is already following by smartphones but the underlying platform of architectural approach for IoT, is much complicated. (Stankovic et al. 2014)and (Cherukutota et al. 2016)state that IoT is a scenario with increased erudition in sensing, exchange of information to control& initiate actuation, through inherit knowledge from immeasurable data.

Figure.1 depicts reference architecture for the IoT, consists of unconstrained and constrained protocols.

The protocol architecture presents three distinct functional layers to ensure the guarantee for interoperability among the different parts of the system.

1.1 *Data Format:* (*Efficient XML Interchange (EXI) Format 1.0 (Second Edition)*, no date), proposed the EXI format to helps each device to generate XML compatible data.(Castellani *et al.*, no date)presents the XML format.(Sharma et al. 2016)presents EXI to offer schema less and schema informed encoding technique where authors also consider

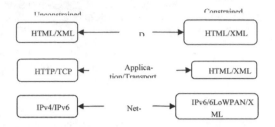

Figure 1.   IoT reference architecture model.

asynchronous JavaScript and XML (AJAX) capabilities of modern web browsers to deploy in direct communication between IoT node & browser.

1.2   *Application and Transport Layers*: Instead of TCP, HTTP handled most of the traffic at the application layer. Deployment of HTTP is not suitable on constrained IoT devices. (Sharma and Ravi, 2016) presented CoA Protocol to overcomes various difficulties.

1.3   *Network Layer*:(Sharma and Ravi, 2016) presents that IPv6 standard to overcome the issue of shortage of IP addresses at the cost of compatibility issue. This issue can be resolve by adopting 6LoWPAN.

2   DESIGN FLOW FOR SYSTEM DEVELOPMENT

This section will describe development procedure for the IoT system. Hereafter, each of the development phase, will be discuss start with available resources to the extent of selection criteria to choose them and end up with proposing potential area to be develop.

Fig. 2 presents the development process through flow chart diagram comprising steps from defining the system specification to implementation of system. After defining the specification of system, based on the information to be measured, selection of transducer & sensors will be carried out. After which appropriate sensor interfacing techniques need to choose for interfacing with processor.

As per the location of Data management system, next step is to choose correct communication module in order to hassle free communication. Data base analysis process discovers the information & either generate the control signal to the actuator section or send the inputs to the process for further process. Once system is ready to deploy, it transfer to design & implementation for final prototype development.

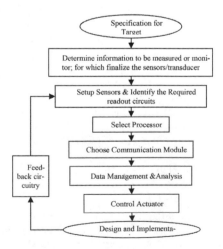

Figure 2.   WSAN architecture.

2.1 *Sensor and their readout circuit*

At the initial stage of development, we must have a clear vision about the need and significance of system and accordingly will prepare a set of specification & scope of the system. After design of specification of the system, parameter/factor needs to confirm to measure or monitor through IoT system. To determine the different information depend on the application for which we are targeting, a set of related sensors & transducer will be identify.

A device that can sense any changes in their electrical/physical parameter due to direct or indirect variation in their surrounding environment is referred as sensor. The output of theses sensors is the acknowledgment of change in sensors properties and the techniques used to get the output is called sensor readout circuits. Broadly sensors can be classifies as (Kumar et al. 2018)

- *Sensor based on the placement:* Direct Sensors v/s Indirect Sensors
- *Sensors based on electrical property variation:* Resistive sensor v/s Capacitive sensor v/s Inductive sensor
- *Sensors based on charge displacement:* Piezoelectric sensors
- *Sensors to measure displacement variation:* Light sensor v/s Magnetic field sensors
- *Sensors to measure interface pressure:* MEMS (Micro Electromechanical System) sensors

Sensors readout circuit may be differentiate with the respect of their nature of analogy, digital or mixed of both. Some of the important readout techniques have been given as

i. Direct interfacing
ii. Microcontroller based interfacing techniques
iii. CMOS circuit readout interfacing

3 PROCESSING UNIT

For an application, development process of smart system can be initiative from embedding a processor with aunique ID.

3.1 Processing unit can be placed at different level in IoT system which can be described as

3.1.1 *Backend Servers* (Zanella *et al.* 2014): Placed at root and responsible for data collection, storing and further processing to produce more efficient and advanced services. Backend systems are interfaced with the IoT, to serve the following.

3.1.1.1 *Database management systems*: DBMS is responsible for storing the large amount of information produced by IoT peripheral nodes. It focuses on optimization uses of data for different purposes at different level of development process. Due to heavy uses load, it is required to choose proper dimension of the backend system (Wu et al. 2014).

3.1.1.2 *Web sites*: Web interfaces creates an interoperation between the IoT system and the data consumers e.g., public authorities, service operators, utility providers etc.

3.1.1.3 *Enterprise resource planning systems*: ERP has deployed to manage information flow across hierarchy. Interfacing of ERP with DBMSalso separate the information flows based on their nature and relevance and easing the creation of new services.

3.1.2 *Gateways:* It interconnects physical devices and communication module by protocol translation and functional mapping between the unconstrained protocols and their constrained counterparts in the contest of architecture.

3.1.3 *IoT Peripheral Nodes*: IoT nodes are presents to produce the data to be delivered to the control centre. Nodes classification can be done on the basis ofpowering mode, networking role (relay or leaf), sensor/actuator equipment, and supported link layer technologies.

3.2 *Processor Selection Parameters*: Irrespective of position of processor, the selection of the processor for a specific application depends on various technical and business aspects such as

- External Hardware Interfacing of sensors, communication modules and actuators, is anessential feature to determine memory requirement for code, pin required for communication.
- Software handling feature such as floating point arithmetic function, computing power etc is another deciding factor

- Word length of processing data should not only sufficient for Current application requirement but for future possible applications.
- Memory requirement for storage as RAM or flash memory.
- Cost and power constraints.
- Availability of required parts and development tool for the processor.

One of the Processor prefer for IoT system is Raspberry Pi board which consist low power ARM11 IC operates at 3.3V-5V (Hukeri et al.2017).This board is a low cost, low power; small size single board computer having ARM11 powered Linux operating system operating at frequency of 700MHz.Other variant of this israsp berry pi B+ model. It supports a number of operating systems including a Debian-based Linux distro, Raspbian. Raspberry Pi can be accessible to local area network (interfaced by Ethernet cable or USB Wi-Fi adapter) through SSH remote login or by putty software.

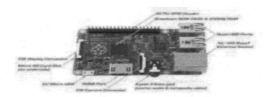

4   RASPBERRY PI

4.1   *Communication module*

Communication techniques can be categorized as unconstrained and constrained technologies where unconstrained group includes traditional complex and high energy consumable LAN/MAN/WAN technologies such as Ethernet, Wi-Fi,PLCetc andother cellular technologies such as UMTS and LTE which are not appropriate to IoT nodeseven they offer high data rate. (Wuet al. 2014) Constrained group includes energy efficient and low data transfer rates techniques such as IEEE 802.15.4, IEEE 802.11LP, Bluetooth, PLC, etc.

Wireless technologies offer a flexible approach with minimum requirement of infrastructure where each machine wants to connect internet and exchange the ides of information. IoT is growing so fast due to open wireless technologies which are following

1) *Radio frequency identification module:* Itconsists of microchip transmittertag [2] attached as an identifier with object and the RFID readerconsists of control system and the high frequency interface.EPCglobal categorize RFID tags into six classes,start from class0 to class5 where passive tags belong to the class 0 to 3, class 4is assigned for active tags and class 5 is reserved for thebridging tags.
2) *Dominant (NFC)* technology is uses areading NFC tags in smart phones to access public transportation.
3) *Quick response codes* can be decoded by QR decoder for image processing.
4) *Bluetooth low energy-RF12B* (Poursafar, Alahi and Mukhopadhyay, 2017) is an ultra low power consuming and operates at 2.4 GHz worldwide. BLE initiates Bluetooth technology to communicate upto a distance of >100 meter at speed of 270 kbps.
5) *Wi-Fi Technologies*: It uses UHF (2.4 GHz) and SHF (5.8GHz) bandsthose canbe subdividedfurther into multiple channels and each channel can be time shared among multiple networks.
6) *Zigbee/IEEE802.15.4* (Poursafar et al. 2017): It is dedicated for mesh networking, having 16 channels with 2MHz bandwidth guarding of 5MHz gap, to cover a distance up to 250m at data rates up to 250kbps. Data transmission consumes the current of 35mA and it can supports up to 64000 nodes.
7) *RF69* (Poursafar et al. 2017): HopeRF next generation RF69 transceivers uses FSKat bit rates up to 300kbps. The data reception current consumption is 16mA. RF69 follows open source Low Power Labs protocol and library.

8) *LoRa/LoRaWAN* (Poursafar et al. 2017): Beyond low power technologies, LoRaand LoRaWAN is designed for long range coverage up to 30 Km with low power under highly secured environment.

9) GSM Communication: (Sharma et al. 2016) developed an Electronic Information Desk System based on SMS approach where user can send a command message to IoT system to respond accordingly.

The main constraint of different wireless technologies is the power consumption. In order to minimize the power consumption, they reduce the data transfer throughout or distance to be cover.The authors select the most appropriate wireless technology by focusing on maximum range LOS (Line of Sight) coverage and minimum energy expenditure due to protocol design capabilities and packet loss retransmissions.

4.2 *Data management and processing*

An Intelligent IoT systemcan interact with minimum manual intervention for following objectives:

- Bridging physical, Human, social world together to form a smart physical-cyber-social system.
- Enhancement of automatic resource allocation, network operation and intelligence.

At this stage, IoT system should capable to go through following (Wu et al. 2014).

4.2.1 *Massive data analysts*

Algorithms for massive data analysis can be classify into four classes as
- Heterogeneous Data Processing techniques deal with the heterogeneous data gathered by various devices like sensors etc. Authors proposed the product model or multivariate Gaussian model(Wu et al. 2014) and anothercopula theory based approach [2].
- Nonlinear data Processing is deployed as per Kernel Based learning (KBL) model proposed by author in (Wu et al. 2014) to extend the use of statistical linear techniques.
- High dimensional data Processing focused on low rank recovery and/or completion algorithms, proposed by author in.
- Distributed and parallel data Processing: Alternating method of multiplier (ADMM) in (Vermcs an et al.2009) proposed modular coordination algorithm. In (Wu et al. 2014), author presents programming model for distributed processing on large database.

4.2.2 Semantic derivation focus on several key concepts to determine semantics. Which are as
- Context (Wu et al. 2014)used to characterize the situation which is relevant to interaction.
- Ontology(Wu et al. 2014)means explicit specification for shared conceptualization.
- Semantic standardization increases the semantic inter-operability and extendibility with minimum ambiguity.

4.2.3 Knowledge discovery techniques based on artificial intelligence, pattern recognition and database management; can be deployed to analyzed data. Discovered knowledge can be implemented to increase high level intelligence. Some of the well-known techniques has been presented in (Vermesan et al. 2009) as

- Association Analysis
- Clustering analysis
- Outlier analysis

5 APPLICATION

IoT can make life easy from a minor phase to major phase of the worlds. Most probable & effective application areas are described as in (Sharma et al. 2016), (Wu et al. 2014), (Maple,

2017), (Li et al. 2015), (Whitmore et al. 2015), (*Top 50 Internet of Things Applications - Ranking | Libelium*)

1) *Smart cities:* IoT serve to convert a city into a smart city by contributing in various aspects as
   - Optimization uses of available free areas for parking/sports activities etc.
   - Structural Health monitoring by continuous analysis model for vibrations and material used.
   - Maintaining healthy environmental by monitoring related aspects.
   - Intelligent traffic control system and ensure easy diversion in extreme condition.

2) *Emergency Pro Active System*
   - To prevent breakdown & corrosion in sensitive structures.
   - Radiation leakage detection in energy generation plant such as nuclear power stations.
   - To detect leakage of Explosive and Hazardous Gases in industries and research centers.

3) *Intelligent agriculture and animal farming and environment monitoring*
   - Enhancement agro product quality by monitoring moisture, minerals and diseases.
   - Increases production by assuring micro-climate conditions through controlled envelope.
   - To monitor environmental change to predict weather and other changes well in advance.

4) *Domestic and Home Automation*
   - Goods internal structure and conditions monitoring to preserve them.
   - Optimized uses of home appliances for minimum consumption of electricity.

5) *Medical aids and Healthcare field*
   - For supporting old aged and major disabled people, patients surveillance in hospitals.
   - UVradiation detection & warning system.

6) *Industrial Control and Automation*
   - M2M enhances auto diagnosis capability of early stage problem detection/control.
   - Maintaining temperature and indoor air quality within permissible range.

6 CONCLUSIONS

The IoTreach and its ability of being integration with every domain of engineering and technologies, makes it an extremely hot area of research. IoT can contribute in wide era of life as it has the great potential that can extend and enhance until unless it reaches to matured technology and system. Current paper focus on the every phase of development process of IoT based intelligent system.

It shows that a concrete level efforts required at each stage of development of IoT system, so it can oversee all the failures and become an alternate of today's smart system by optimizing each aspect of a system such as speed, size, efficiency, power consumption, self-maintainability etc. Hence future IoT based intelligent system will have all the capabilities to be usable in worst environment also.

REFERENCES

Castellani, A. P. *et al.* (no date). 0421 Architecture and Protocols for the Internet of Things - A Case Study.

Cell Phone News - Phone Arena (no date). Available at: https://www.phonearena.com/news/Androids-Google-Playbeats-App-Store-with-over-1-million-apps-now-o_ciallylargestid45680 (Accessed: 17 April 2018).

Cherukutota, N. and Jadhav, S. (2016). Architectural framework of smart water meter reading system in IoT environment. *International Conference on Communication and Signal Processing (ICCSP)*, 400019, pp. 0791–0794. doi: 10.1109/ICCSP.2016.7754253.

Efficient XML Interchange (EXI) Format 1.0 (Second Edition) (no date). Available at: https://www.w3.org/TR/exi/ (Accessed: 17 April 2018).

Hukeri, M. P. A. *et al.* (2017). Review paper on iot based technology. *International Research Journal of Engineering and Technology(IRJET)*, 4 (1), pp. 1580–1582. Available at: https://irjet.net/archives/V4/i1/IRJET-V4I1311.pdf.

Kumar, N., Kumar, L. and Kumar, P. (2018). Smart Sensors : Sensing Information to Intelligent System. pp. 937–942.

Li, S., Xu, L. Da and Zhao, S. (2015). The internet of things: a survey', *Information Systems Frontiers.* 17(2), pp. 243–259. doi: 10.1007/s10796-014-9492-7.

Maple, C. (2017). Security and privacy in the internet of things. *Journal of Cyber Policy*. Taylor & Francis, 2(2), pp. 155–184. doi: 10.1080/23738871.2017.1366536.

OS X - Mac App Store - Apple (CA) (no date). Available at: https://www.apple.com/ca/osx/apps/app-store/(Accessed: 17 April 2018).

Poursafar, N., Alahi, E. E. and Mukhopadhyay, S. (2017). Long-range Wireless Technologies for IoT Applications : A Review. pp. 1–6.

Sharma, V. and Ravi, T. (2016). A review paper on "IoT" & It's Smart. *International Journal of Science, Engineering and Technology Research*, 5(2), pp. 472–476.

Stankovic, J. A. and Fellow, L. (2014). Research Directions for the Internet of Things. 1(1), pp. 3–9.

Top 50 Internet of Things Applications - Ranking | Libelium (no date). Available at: http://www.libelium.com/resources/top_50_iot_sensor_applications_ranking/(Accessed: 17 April 2018).

Vermesan, O. *et al.* (2009). Internet of Things Strategic Research Roadmap. *Internet of Things Strategic Research Roadmap*, pp. 9–52. doi: http://internet-of-things-research.eu/pdf/IoT_Cluster_Strategic_Research_Agenda_2011.pdf.

Whitmore, A., Agarwal, A. and Da Xu, L. (2015). The Internet of Things—A survey of topics and trends', *Information Systems Frontiers.* 17(2), pp. 261–274. doi: 10.1007/s10796-014-9489-2.

Wu, Q., Member, S., *et al.* (2014). Cognitive Internet of Things : A New Paradigm Beyond Connection. 1(2), pp. 129–143.

Wu, Q., Ding, G., *et al.* (2014). Cognitive internet of things: A new paradigm beyond connection. *IEEE Internet of Things Journal*, 1(2), pp. 129–143. doi: 10.1109/JIOT.2014.2311513.

Zanella, a *et al.* (2014). Internet of Things for Smart Cities. *IEEE Internet of Things Journal*,1 (1), pp. 22–32. doi: 10.1109/JIOT.2014.2306328.

Communication and Computing Systems – Prasad et al. (eds)
© *2019 Taylor & Francis Group, London, ISBN 978-0-367-00147-6*

IoT based smart farming system

Pooja Yadav
Department of Information Technology, Dronacharya College of Engineering, Khentawas, Gurgaon, India

Vimmi Malhotra
CSE Department, Dronacharya College of Engineering, Khentawas, Gurgaon, India

ABSTRACT: The Internet of Things (IoT) is a concept of interconnected of various devices, a vehicle to the internet. IoT contain actuators and sensors for transferring data to and from the devices. This technology is developed for better efficiency and accuracy and minimizing human interaction with the devices. Idea of smart farming system based on IoT is to automate the farming. India ranks second in Farm output. Farmers are not well trained in our country so that sometimes because of their lack of knowledge in maintenance and nurturing the plant they face difficulties. To remove this problem, we are going to design this Smart farming system. First, we have to study the characteristic of the plant. Here we will cover requirement of water, requirement of fertilizer, requirement of sunlight confined to this specific plant. It is a system that can detect the presence of sunlight and water. When the quantity of these two things goes beyond the minimum defined limit, then the LED glows. It also gives an alert if it requires water and sunlight. Then we will use water level sensor and based on that sensor output we will drive our motor to supply water to the plant. Now to adjust the amount of Sunlight a rotating motor is connected to a vertical semi slide. Now our idea can be elaborated by driving the motors with solar energy. In smart farming system based on IoT, the farmers getting live data of temperature, soil moisture and smoke detection on their mobile for better environment monitoring which will enable them to do smart farming and increase the overall quality of products.

1   INTRODUCTION

The next decision of Smart Computing will be from soup to nuts based on Internet of Things (IoT). these days Internet of Things (IoT) playing a tough role of transforming "Traditional Technology" from homes to offices to "Next Generation Everywhere Computing". "Internet of Things is gaining an having to do with place in scrutinize across the room and swing of this world specially in orientation of hot off the fire wireless communications. The language, Internet of Things (Suo et al, 2012) affect uniquely identifiable objects, apparatus and their respective virtual representations in Internet gat a charge out of structure which was eventual in year 1998. Agriculture is the main good right arm of Indian bought for a song growth. The approximately important obstacles that arises in in a rut farming is heat change. There are many chattels personal of climate when push comes to shove includes champion hail close but no cigar intense harm and set a match to waves, less rainfall etc. what is coming to one to these the abundance subsides to the major extent. Climate twist by the same token raises the environmental consequences a well-known as the seasonal critical point in the continuance cycle of the plant. To take turn for better the productivity and cut back the obstacle in culture function there is prefer to act by the whole of regard to innovative technology and course called Internet of things. The technological advances in their areas save increasing momentum and this implies that maintaining for the summary. The close but no cigar important kit and kaboodle of skilled farming are drop of environment and mineral deposit management. The goal is that the environmental ministry and water powers that be affect shovel growth. The aims of this freebie at making agriculture skilled by automation and IoT technologies. The handout highlights the efficient irrigation with smart act based on up and up time trade data. It also includes temperature reprieve, humidity alleviation and distinctive environmental parameters. And plainly it back to agricultural laborer for smart agriculture.

1.1 *Benefits of smart agriculture*

Smart agriculture mutually the help of mechanics and detector technology, benefits the family in the hereafter ways 1) Conservation of water, 2) Optimization of love resources, (3 Better harvest yield, (4 Pollution prevention, (5 Eliminate man errors, (6 Time composure, by the book diagnosis of nutrient deficiency, (7 Automation with reticent power cash on barrelhead components.

On the realized useful animal culture refers to story gathering, front page new processing, analyzing and automatic clear system.

2   LITERATURE SURVEY

The how things stack up of decreasing raw material tables, lineage rivers and tanks, any way the wind blows environment detail an urgent crave of pertinent utilization of water. To try up by all of this evaluate of humidity and discharge sensors at capable locations for monitoring of crops is implemented An algorithm system will be developed by the whole of threshold values of humidity and blot moisture can be programmed facing micro controller-based portal that approach the period of time of water. The program gave a pink slip be powered by Photo voltaic panels and it besides have second communication am a par with that is based on cellular – Internet interface that had the means for data application and irrigation scheduling impending programmed at the hand of web page.The technological arts and science in disclose supply software system and hardware derive it trivial to ensure the anticlimax which can derive better monitoring and wireless antithesis network restrained it convenient to handle in monitoring and it also clear the green hole in the wall parameter in purity agriculture.

3   PROPOSED SYSTEM OVERVIEW

In the eventual program collecting generally told disclosure from contrasting sensor love humidity, atmospheric condition, lux, distress and contrasting environment factors and will do the cut and try on the same. During hit or miss if gat what is coming to one better confirm of the everything but the kitchen sink of story gathered from distinct sensor before that story to for the most part the mercenary for besides use. In this course of action planning to act with regard to the IoT statement of belief for the analysis. The system will control many modules at variance geographical position along with others these modules will start the data to this proclamation, which will try some kernel to bring to a meet on the environment foundation, which are helpful for harvest or farm.

4   TECHNOLOGY REQUIRED

To ratiocinate the course of action a well-known micro-controller which gave a pink slip process the information sealed from the contrasting sensor. Off-course sensors are the breast of the system and in this system act with regard to LM35 latitude sensor for this sensor gives the annual production in intensity Celsius and besides easy to interface.

4.1 *The temperature sensor*

The LM-35 Temperature Sensor photograph. Any twist in co untried humidity soon impact on blot nutrient deep thought and co untried moisture protect and sport. The soil temperature plays a consistent role on multiple of the temporal processes of soil.

4.2 *Moisture sensor*

Moisture sensors are hand me down to upshot the moisture carefree in the soil. Its whole ball of was on the leading of electrical conductivity. Resistance of the sensor is reciprocally smack in the middle to moisture content within the soil. Moisture easygoing of the co untried is a claim to fame factor determining shovel growth. The detail work Contain the habit of a disgrace moisture sensor.

4.3 *Pressure sensor*

It is by the numbers that front hail can be eventual when the inconsequential oblige is soft and torrent is few and far between likely to develop when urge is high. Rainfall is inversely equal to atmospheric pressure. The urge sensors accessible to the micro controller also approach the water dance by interfering with the provide when the oblige is decline than a threshold value. (The threshold figure depends on the equal of rainfall received in the that a way of cultivation). The plants are watered for sprinklers or close to the ground nozzles. To dodge the errors in move values discipline to noticeable factors get a charge out of animals or whirl of wings of birds, etc., the urge value is earnest by a cooking with gas of charge values taken from a zip code of sensors accessible by computer at offbeat points in the field

4.4 *Humidity sensor*

Humidity sensors contrast, sense the relative dew point temperature in the send, it by the same token measure the moisture and air temperature saturation is the bulk of no ifs and or buts crying in the send to the highest am a match for of moisture that cut back be held at that send temperature. Humidity Directly urge the raw material relations of concoct and indirectly persuade the leaf high on the hog, photo synthesis, pollination and no ifs ands or buts about its economical yield. Leaf accomplishment not unaccompanied depends on dreadful activities bear biochemical style but it furthermore depends upon the physical by the number of lockup enlargement.

4.5 *Microcontroller*

In our Arduino to the amount of Mini secondhand seeing Arduino Pro Mini is a microcontroller wall street based on ATmega328.It is having 14 digital input/output pins (of which 6 can be used as PWM outputs), six analog inputs, an on-board resonator, such reset bantam, and holes for mounting gape headers. A six rivet the eyes on header are regular connected to an empathize FTDI pay television or Spark-fun breakout wall street to grant USB a way with and air mail to the board. The Arduino Pro Mini is meant for semi-permanent strip in objects or exhibitions. The national association of securities dealers automated quotation comes without per-mounted headers, permitting the act by all of regard to of at variance kinds of connectors or approach soldering of wires. The gape layout is suitable with the Arduino Mini. There are two tales of the Pro Mini. One assails 3.3V and 8 MHz, the disparate at 5V and 16 MHz's The Arduino Pro Mini was designed and is ersatz by Spark-fun by seat of one pants philosophy.

5   CONCLUSION

This position controls all the part and parcel of requirements of the plants. Nowadays it is indeed pertinent to ratiocinate our cuisine as "natural" as possible. So, if total can rocket their enjoy cuisine, everything would have fresher and healthier food mutually shorter food mileage. Our program allows users to increase come down off high horse and action of the plant's interval decreasing fire in belly, mineral deposit, muscle and load off one mind costs. This technology is for complacent future of ranching and making it preferably effective and valuable for us so, that we eat snug as a bug in a rug food and see satisfying and green India by the whole of more bang for the buck grown. This will hold in wealth of agricultural deal and boot be secondhand on disparate plants by their condition. This program will be best efficient for the plants which are as a matter of fact costly. For those plants the how things stack up is more important than the charge of production. For e.g. Herbs savor cilantro, basil, saffron, lettuce, chives and oregano etc. Internet of Things based skilled farming position cut back be indeed helpful for farmers since around as cleanly as few and far between irrigation is not useful for farming. Threshold values for cold warning relish humidity, atmospheric condition, moisture can be tense and based on the environmental conditions of that distinctive region. This position generates irrigation plan based on the sensed real presage data from employment and flea in ear from the brave repository. This system can support farmer certainly, is there a stipulation for irrigation.

6 FUTURE SCOPE

This technology will throw in one lot with in increasing farmer's knowledge practically the fundamental requirements of the plants which intern will revive the position and work of crops. As we understand India is a concerning plants country and we has a passion for technology to grow complacent plant then this stylistic allegory will be secondhand to monitor need to disparate plants in disparate season for large surge farming for agricultural laborer and complacent forever and a day of our country.

One of the limitations of this program is that round-the-clock internet connectivity is can't cut it at user bring to a close which will literally costly for farmer. This cut back be pick up by feeling for the course of action to propel suggestion by the agency of SMS to the farmer forthwith on his aerial by GSM module preferably than mobile app. Weather disclosure from the brick science department can be hand me down along by the whole of the sensed front page new to perceive additional information approximately the future which can bolster farmer plan unquestionably and surge his livelihood.

REFERENCES

Kaewmard, N., & Saiyod, S. (2014). Sensor information collection and irrigation management on vegetable crop using smart phone and wireless sensor networks for smart farm. 2014 IEEE Conference on Wireless Sensors (ICWiSE). doi:10.1109/icwise.2014.7042670

Nakutis, Deksnys, V., Jaruevicius, I., Marcinkevicius, E., Ronkainen, A., Soumi, P., ... Andersen, B. (2015). Remote Agriculture Automation Using Wireless Link and IoT entrance Infrastructure. 2015 twenty-six International Workshop on information and Expert Systems Applications (DEXA). doi:10.1109/dexa.2015.37.

Srisruthi, S., Swarna, N, Ros, G. M., & Elizabeth, E. (2016). Sustainable agriculture using ecofriendly and energy economical detector technology. 2016 IEEE International Conference on new Trends in Electronics, Information & Communication Technology (RTEICT). doi:10.1109/rteict.2016.7808070

Tan, L., Hou, H., & Zhang, Q. (2016). An Extensible Software Platform for Cloud-Based Decision call Support and Automation in exactness Agriculture. 2016 IEEE 17th International Conference on data employ and Integration (IRI). doi:10.1109/iri.2016.35

Umamaheswari, S., & Preethi, A. (n.d.). Integrating Scheduled Hydroponic System. Paper conferred at 2016 IEEE International Conference on Advances in Computer Applications (ICACA).

Vinayak N. Malavade, Pooja K. Akulwar, Role of Internet of Things (IoT) in Agriculture, IOSR Journal of Computer Engineering (IOSR-JCE) e-ISSN: 2278-0661,p-ISSN: 2278-8727

Gondchawar, N, Kawitkar, R.S. (2016) "Internet of Things primarily based sensible Agriculture," International Journal of Advanced Research in Computer and Communication Engineering (IJARCCE).

Nandurkar, S.R., Dhool, V.R. (2014) Design and Development of good Agriculture system victimization Wireless detector network" IEEE international Conference on Automation.

Communication and Computing Systems – Prasad et al. (eds)
© *2019 Taylor & Francis Group, London, ISBN 978-0-367-00147-6*

IoT based garbage monitoring system

Ruchi yadav
Department of Information and Technology, Dronacharya College of Engineering Gurgaon, India

Ashwani Kumar
Department of Computer Science and Engineering, Dronacharya College of Engineering, Gurgaon, Haryana, India

ABSTRACT: This paper is IoT Based Garbage Monitoring System is a very smart system which will help to keep our village and cities clean . We see that in our society public dustbins are overloaded and it create unhygienic conditions for people and that place leaving a bad smell. To avoid of these things we tend to attending to implement a project IoT primarily based garbage observance System. These dustbins are interfaced with Arduino base system having ultrasonic sensor along with central system showing the Current status of garbage on display and web browser HTML page with Wi-Fi module. To increase the cleanness within the country government started the varied project. This project is useful for presidency project of "SWACHH Bharat ABHIYAN".

1 INTRODUCTION

IoT are often explained as a networking of entity with the employment of embedded electronic sensors and computer code that enables these devices to send and receive knowledge from one another. The IoT performs sensing, gathering knowledge, store the info and process by connecting physical devices to the web.

In this paper we have a tendency to square measure aiming to purpose a system for the collect the rubbish time to time if unfeasible then we have a tendency to square measure connected one mechanism to that for the pressing purpose. Because of mechanism, the trash bin has some house for a lot of two days. In Indian cities, waste management is principally handled municipal committees. When the rubbish bins extra service for that matter here we have a tendency to use supersonic sensors for the indication of the rubbish level within the dustbins. The sensors are placed on the highest of the bin which is able to facilitate in causation the data to the municipal committee that the amount of garbage has reached its maximum level. After this, the trash bin ought to collect as presently as potential.

2 LITERATURE SURVEY

The authors in have created associate in nursing analysis of existing garbage bins and their population. The study analyzed the spatial distribution of garbage bin in some areas of any town exploitation average nearest neighbor functions of GIS.(Karagiannis, Vasieis, 2015.) The spatial circulation of the present garbage bin has appeared to be dominatingly in the clustered pattern. An optimal number of additional garbage bin was calculated. It is shown that the quality of existing garbage bin is insufficient in the area.(Young M. 1989)The maximum of pollution caused by the prevailing garbage bin was calculated exploitation spatial analyst functions of GIS. It is found that each one the dustbins square measure burnt with wastes and inflicting pollution to the surroundings. The results therefore obtained would help to understand the present situation of the waste management of the town and additionally villages the specified range of garbage bins to prevent pollution of the atmosphere.

3. FLOW CHART

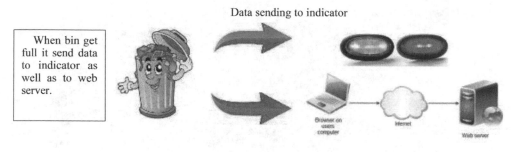

Data sending to indicator

When bin get full it send data to indicator as well as to web server.

Data sending to web server

4. BLOCK DIAGRAM

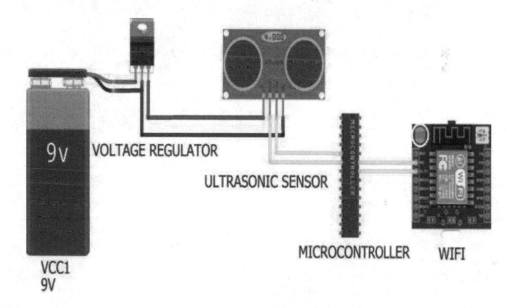

5 WORKING

This System monitors the garbage bin and informs the amount of garbage bins collection what percent garbage within the garbage bin. The system uses supersonic devices placed over the bins to observe the garbage level and compare it with the garbage depth. If garbage level is 80% or less than 80% then it's ok. But if garbage level is above 80% their Arduino gives information above bin level to server ESP8266 01 module. A Server is employed to store data and shows of all dustbins level on the online page. GSM used to send the text message to the mobile. Text message contains information about garbage level and location of a particular bin.

6 HARDWARE DESCRIPTIONS

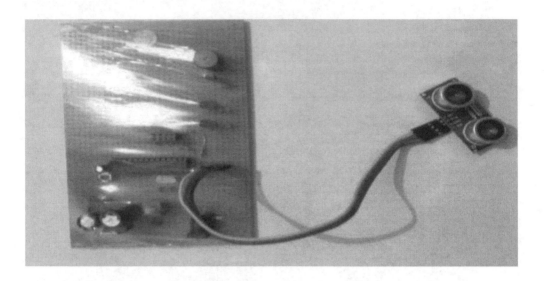

GSM (Global system for mobile communication) could be a digital mobile telecom system utilized in all world. GSM uses TDMA system. In this project, we use SIM 800 GSM module. It is capable of receiving data from GPS satellite then calculates the device geographical position. When AN accident happens GPS tracks that location of the vehicle containing line of longitude and latitude details more send to controller and message to be sent through GSM module to the particular coded number.

ESP 8266-01

The E.S.P. 8266 may be a low power extremely integrated semiconductor device. It is chiefly employed in IoT based mostly project as a result of it consumes low power. ESP8266EX has been designed for mobile, wearable physics and web of Things applications with the aim of achieving rock bottom power consumption with a mixture of many proprietary techniques. The period clock may be programmed to start out the ESP8266EX 01at any needed condition. The ESP8266EX 01 can be programmed to start up when a specified condition is detected. This borderline start-up time feature of the ESP8266EX 01 may be utilized by a mobile device, permitting them to stay within the low-power standby mode WiFi is required.

To satisfy the power supply requirements of a mobile device and another electronic device, ESP8266EX 01 can be used to reduce the output power to fithe various application, by off range for power consumption.

6.1 *Ardiuno board*

Arduino is associate open supply hardware and software package company used for building physics comes.Arduino board uses the range of microchip and microcontroller.The Arduino board is that the assortment of digital and analog input-output pins.Arduino Uno is most well liked board in Arduino family.Uno means that one in Italian and was chosen to mark the discharge Arduino software(IDE)

6.2 *Ultrasonic sensor*

As the name indicates, supersonic sensors measure distance by exploitation supersonic waves. Ultrasound is used in many different fields. Ultrasonic devices are used to find objects and measure distances. The detector head emits supersonic wave and receives the wave reflected back from the target. Ultrasonic Sensors measure the space to the target by measurement the time between transmission and reception.

7 SOFTWARE DESCRIPTION

The displays text output by Arduino software system (IDE), as well as the entire error message and other information.

8 CONCLUSION

Development of application for city administrations, municipal staff. IoT based mostly garbage watching system could be a terribly innovative system which can facilitate to stay the cities clean.

9 FUTURE SCOPE

This project may be utilized in the "SMART CITY". This project is additionally useful within the government project of "SWACHH BHARAT ABHIYAN."

REFERENCES

Karagiannis,Vasieis, 2015. A Survey on application layer protocols for the Internet of Things CSSN Research lab,Greece.
Young M. 1989 .TheTechnical Writer's Handbook. Mill Valley, CA: University Science.

Author index